THE
EMERGING
EKKLESIA
Acts Thru Jude

Reflections by
Russell Bloodworth, Jr.

ISBN: 978-1-54395-904-8

*To all of my Grandchildren, both those present
(Tully, Jack, William, Claire, Christopher, Parker,
Emmy, Ellen, Jonathan, Teddy) and those to come.*

Pops loves you very much!

TABLE OF CONTENTS

Preface..xvii

Introduction...1
    Not a Chronological Record 2
    Rough Chronology of New Testament Writings *(AD)* 4
    Tips on How to Read This Book...4

Five Themes 5
    I. The Kingdom..5
    II. The Covenant...7
    III. The Promise of the Holy Spirit 10
    IV. God as Father – The Family of God 14
    An Intimate Connection..16
    V. Restoration of All Things 16
    Summary...17

Preface to the Acts of the Apostles 18
    The Immediate Context 20
    The Broader Context 23
    Conclusion...23

Acts of the Apostles 24
    Acts 1 24
    Acts 2 29
    The Initial Harvest..37
    Nuances to Verses 38 and 39...38
    The Result..40
    Acts 3 42
    The Anwer to the Question, "Who Healed this Man?" 44
    Invitation: Repent and Return 45
    Acts 4 48
    The Cornerstone..50
    The Response of the Jewish Leaders 52
    The Response of the Believers 52
    Acts 5 55
    The First Sour Note...55

Regular Public Gatherings Lead to More Trouble..57
Jailed and Released..58
Acts 6 59
Growing Pains and Further Trouble with the Sanhedrin..........................59
Stephen on Trial...61
Acts 7 62
Stephen's Speech...62
Acts 8 64
Scattering After the Stoning of Stephen..65
Samaria...65
Simon the Magician and Receiving the Holy Spirit....................................67
Philip, an Angel and the Ethiopian..71
Acts 9 73
The Damascus Road...73
Healings and Raising the Dead...74
Acts 10..75
Cornelius and Gentile Believers!...75
Out of Normal Sequence..77
Acts 11..77
Acts 12..79
Acts 13..81
Barnabas and Paul's 1st Missionary Journey..81
Apostles, Prophets and Teachers..81
Acts 14..84
Appointing..85
Acts 15..88
Controversy...88
The Jerusalem Council...88
Acts 16..92
Paul's Second Missionary Journey..92
Timothy on Board...92
Luke On Board...94
Macedonia...95
Acts 17..98
Acts 18..101
Paul's Third Missionary Journey..105
Acts 19..106

Ephesus and the Lacking Disciples 106

Acts 20.. 110

Acts 21.. 116

Rocketing to Jerusalem 116

Acts 22.. 118

Acts 23.. 120

Acts 24.. 122

Acts 25.. 123

Acts 26.. 126

Jesus's Words on the Damascus Road Recalled by Paul: 126

Acts 27.. 129

Acts 28.. 132

Romans... 136

Romans 1 136

Beloved of God and Saints 139

Romans 2 140

Romans 3 142

Romans 4 145

Romans 5 148

Romans 6 150

Romans 7 153

Romans 8 154

Romans 9 158

Romans 10... 160

Romans 11... 162

Romans 12... 164

Romans 13... 167

Romans 14... 169

Romans 15... 170

Romans 16... 174

1ˢᵗ Corinthians.. 177

1ˢᵗ Corinthians 1.. 177

1ˢᵗ Corinthians 2.. 181

The New Covenant Promise: 182

1ˢᵗ Corinthians 3.. 183

1ˢᵗ Corinthians 4.. 187

1st Corinthians 5...189

   Immorality Rebuked 189

1st Corinthians 6...191

1st Corinthians 7...195

1st Corinthians 8...200

   Dream of the Two Wine Glasses 201

1st Corinthians 9...203

1st Corinthians 10...205

1st Corinthians 11...209

   Signs of Submissiveness 209

   The Issue of Headcovering..212

1st Corinthians 12...215

   Gifts of the Spirit..215

   Ministries 218

   Gifts of People 222

1st Corinthians 13...223

1st Corinthians 14...225

   Pursuing the Gift of Prophecy..225

   The Gift of Tongues..225

1st Corinthians 15...231

   Kerygma and Resurrection 231

   Creedal Development 234

1st Corinthians 16...237

2nd Corinthians...241

2nd Corinthians 1...241

   Focused on Their Joy..245

2nd Corinthians 2...246

2nd Corinthians 3...248

2nd Corinthians 4...251

2nd Corinthians 5...254

2nd Corinthians 6...257

2nd Corinthians 7...260

2nd Corinthians 8...263

2nd Corinthians 9...266

2nd Corinthians 10...268

2nd Corinthians 11...271

2nd Corinthians 12...273

2nd Corinthians 13 277
    Built Up and Complete 278

Galatians 283
Galatians 1 283
Galatians 2 287
Galatians 3 291
Galatians 4 295
Galatians 5 297
    Acts of the Flesh 300
    Fruits of the Spirit 301
Galatians 6 302

Ephesians 305
Ephesians 1 305
Ephesians 2 309
    His Grand Amour 310
    A Holy Temple in the Lord 312
Ephesians 3 314
    The Great Mystery 314
    God's Great Purpose 315
Ephesians 4 319
    Oneness, the Reality of Unity 320
    People Gifts 321
    The Body 323
Ephesians 5 325
    A Prescription for Life 325
    Authority 328
Ephesians 6 330
    Honor 331
    Spiritual Warfare 333

Philippians 338
Philippians 1 338
Philippians 2 343
Philippians 3 349
Philippians 4 352

Colossians 356
Colossians 1 356

Colossians 2 362

Colossians 3 366

Colossians 4 369

1ˢᵗ Thessalonians 372

1ˢᵗ Thessalonians 1 372

1ˢᵗ Thessalonians 2 375

1ˢᵗ Thessalonians 3 377

1ˢᵗ Thessalonians 4 379

1ˢᵗ Thessalonians 5 383

2ⁿᵈ Thessalonians 390

2ⁿᵈ Thessalonians 1 390

2ⁿᵈ Thessalonians 2 394

What Has to Happen (Verses 3-5) 395

What Is Happening Now (Verses 6-7) 395

What Will Happen at the End (Verses 8-10) 395

What Is Happening Now (Verses 11-12) 396

2ⁿᵈ Thessalonians 3 398

1ˢᵗ Timothy 402

1ˢᵗ Timothy 1 402

A Vibrant, Living Relationship 404

1ˢᵗ Timothy 2 407

1ˢᵗ Timothy 3 410

Church Leadership 410

Deacons and Deaconesses 415

1ˢᵗ Timothy 4 417

1ˢᵗ Timothy 5 421

1ˢᵗ Timothy 6 426

2ⁿᵈ Timothy 431

2ⁿᵈ Timothy 1 431

2ⁿᵈ Timothy 2 436

2ⁿᵈ Timothy 3 442

2ⁿᵈ Timothy 4 447

Titus 451

Titus 1 451

The Mission 455

Men Off Track...458

The Question of Elders and Bishops...459

Titus 2..460

Titus 3..463

The Importance of Baptisms..464

Good Deeds..465

Personal Instructions..466

Philemon..467

Hebrews...471

Hebrews 1...471

Better Than Angels...471

How God Speaks..472

Who is Jesus?...473

Hebrews 2...474

Lest We Drift Away..474

Better than Angels. Made Perfect through Sufferings...................476

Hebrews 3...478

Jesus, Apostle and High Priest...478

The Peril of Unbelief and the Deceitfulness of Sin.......................480

An Annual Atonement...483

Hebrews 4...484

Hebrews 5...488

Jesus: High Priest Forever...488

Hebrews 6...489

Hebrews 7...495

The Power to Bless..495

The Need to Change..497

Hebrews 8...499

Hebrews 9...504

The Making of a Better Covenant..504

One Important Closing Observation to Chapter 9........................509

Hebrews 10...510

The Shadow..510

Hebrews 11...516

Faith, Confidence and Trust...516

A City With Foundations..519

Hebrews 12...520

The Race! 520

Hebrews 13 525

James 533

James 1 533

   Old Camel Knees 533

   Pillar 534

   Early Book 535

   Digging In 535

   Temptation 537

   Pure Religion 539

James 2 540

   Partiality 540

   The Law 543

   Faith and Works 544

James 3 545

   The Tongue 546

   Godly Wisdom Versus Dark Wisdom 548

James 4 549

   Lust and Envy 549

   Resist the Devil 551

   Who Are You to Judge Your Brother? 552

   Lord Willing 552

James 5 553

   Weep and Howl 553

   The Lord's Return 555

   Oaths 555

1st Peter 559

1st Peter 1 559

1st Peter 2 564

   As Newborn Babes 564

   As Living Stones 564

   A Royal Priesthood – The People of God 567

   A Holy Nation 567

   Honor Authority 568

   Christ Is Our Example 569

1st Peter 3 570

Wives and Husbands..570

Suffering for Right and not Wrong...573

The Good News of the Gospel 573

1st Peter 4 574

Therefore 575

The Time for Fervent Love 576

Your Special Gift 577

Tough Times Coming...578

1st Peter 5 579

Elders 579

Humility...581

Satan Tricks 581

Perfect, Confirm, Strength and Establish 582

Stand Firm 582

2nd Peter...583

2nd Peter 1..583

Everything Pertaining to Life and Godliness....................................583

A Step Ladder to the Nature of God...585

Eyewitness and the Prophetic...588

2nd Peter 2..589

The Rise of False Prophets 589

Heresy...591

Underlying Motivations...591

Expulsion 592

To Whom Do You Listen?..593

2nd Peter 3..594

End of the Age...594

1st John 598

1st John 1..598

1st John 2..602

Paraklētos...602

Propitiation 602

Truth Man..603

Enmity and Darkness...604

Lust, Lust, Pride..604

Luster in God's Will..605

Antichrists 606

The Anointing 606

1st John 3 608

1st John 4 612

Testing the Spirits 612

1 John 5 616

What Does It Mean to Believe? 616

Three Stamps 617

Life Bubbling Up 617

Conclusion 618

2nd John 621

3rd John 627

Gaius 627

The Child Walking in the Truth 627

Loving to be First is a No 628

Do Not Imitate What is Evil 630

Jude 631

Kept 632

Contend for the Faith 633

Bibliography 641

Index 646

Preface

"You are no longer strangers and aliens, but you are fellow citizens with the saints, and are of God's household, having been built on the foundation of the apostles and prophets, Christ Jesus Himself being the corner stone, in whom the whole building, being fitted together, is growing into a holy temple in the Lord, in whom you also are being built together into a dwelling of God in the Spirit." (Ephesians 2:19-22).

The wonder of the early *Ekklesia* (a Greek word in Scripture often translated as *"Church"*) has been with me most of my life. Coming from a Christian stream that was always interested in the earliest foundations, I have been mining New Testament texts since the age of twelve or thirteen – over 60 years.

My initial goal in compiling this excursion into the early Church was two-fold. First, on a personal basis, I wanted to more deeply dive into the truth and drama of the Church's early beginnings. Second, I wanted to share my thoughts and observations that had built up over my lifetime. Sixty years is a long time to study something consistently, and I thought sharing insights that had come over such a long filter of time might be helpful to others.

I re-visited what had captured my heart in the 1960s. The Church was launched on the foundation of Jesus's sacrifice - His suffering, crucifixion and resurrection. He was and is very much God's gift to us. In truth, the reign of God was dawning for so many - activated when Jesus poured out God's Spirit onto mankind 50 days after His resurrection.

The Church was founded in the midst of simultaneous suffering, demonstrations of power and the immeasurable benevolence of God. It was founded in blood - divine blood - and through Jesus's own words and the underlying nature of covenant; it expressed the beginning of a New and Everlasting Covenant between God and mankind. There is much to cover as we dive into the various letters before us.

Suffice it to say, I owe significant thanks to others that I was able to stick with this work. First, to Bob Phillips whose invitation to a chapter-a-day Bible study sparked my effort. Second to my initial readers: my wife Fran, David and Judy Vaughan, Tina Bowie, daughter Faith and a young man named Bill Hart (well, he's 77). Then to numerous proofreaders – Christie Mullins, Fran, daughter Elizabeth and son Christopher. And to Steve Happ who suffered through numerous questions regarding format issues. His help was brilliant.

But I also owe my historic mentors a debt of immeasurable magnitude: Terry Smith and those who have gone before him – including the Apostles John, Peter and Paul, Yves Congar, Abraham Malherbe, Watchman Nee, Henri Nouwen, Bob Mumford, Derek Prince, John Paul II and John XXIII – as well as my brothers and sisters with whom I have walked these forty years: Steve and Tina Bowie, David and Judy Vaughan, Steve and Fran Happ, Chuck Walker, David and Catherine

Mullins, Barry and Kim Watson and the more recent additions like Barry's son, Matt and his wife, Erica, and my friend, Joel Jassu. Also, to a string of spiritual mentors that include Dr. Carroll Stone, Bob Frahm, and Brother Joel McGraw, whose prayers have supported me for decades, and my lifelong friends - the Toms, the Lewises and the Nixes. Special thanks to Dr. Richard Oster who put up with many technical questions and encouraged me to include an index. Finally, for my good brother Kit Mays, who bears significant responsibility for encouraging my earlier book, *Visions, Dreams and Encounters* as well as this effort. To all - a hearty, "Thank you!"

There are a good number of excellent books that shed deep insight into various aspects of the 149 chapters before us. Please review the Bibliography section at the back of the book for specific suggestions for further study.

Introduction

"Every soul had become Jerusalem, a Temple of God, a living stone in a spiritual sanctuary."

(The Mystery of the Temple, Yves Congar, p. 79).

Have you ever tried to imagine what life was like in the emerging Church right after the crucifixion? Do you suppose it came complete with all of its beliefs developed, its practices perfected, and its doctrines grasped and understood? I don't think so.

As a deeper understanding of God's intentions developed, persecution continued. Jesus Himself had been handed over to the Roman authorities - stripped, mocked, tried and crucified. The days that followed were filled with confusion, turmoil, danger and despair. Revelation of the character and nature of the community of God's people that formed after the crucifixion came slowly - in the midst of persecution – as lives were turned upside down.

If one reads the 149 chapters that begin with Chapter 1 of the "Acts of the Apostles" and end with the short letter of Jude, one will see a morphing outline of the Church as it responds to the Spirit of Truth that Jesus had promised. Truth does not morph, but believers and their communities shift this way and that as each one is touched by the Grace and Love of God.

Each person who responded to the call of God did his or her best to follow the lead of the Spirit that was so amply poured out on the day of Pentecost. There were mistakes, but grace abounded in spite of them.

When we immerse ourselves in these 149 chapters, it is as if we are helicoptered into a variety of places and times that basically cover an approximate fifty-year period after Jesus's resurrection. Our geographic range will span most of the Roman Empire, ethnically and geographically, from Italy on the West to Syria on the East.

The journey we launch is a chapter-by-chapter excursion filled with adventure, conflict, sacrifice, discovery, awe and encounter with a living God. We will also meet many ordinary people doing extraordinary things.

Not a Chronological Record

The books of the New Testament in most of our Bibles are only partially arranged chronologically. The first four books that we call "Gospels" present the basic story of Jesus of Nazareth - His birth, His ministry, His death and resurrection. Three are mostly parallel, and the fourth, written by the Apostle John, includes extended intimate moments with Jesus that the other three authors did not include.

Acts itself is organized chronologically, but once we pass the book of Acts, the collection of letters is jumbled from a chronological point of view. The Book of Revelation is likely the proper end as are the letters of Jude, Peter and the "little Johns." But other than that general symmetry, Paul's letters are not chronologically arranged in most of our printed Bibles.

The fact that one must jump around to keep track of the sequence has caused some publishers to rearrange Paul's letters to make them better fit with their chronology. I have not made that adjustment. In other words, we will use the more standard ordering: Romans will follow Acts, then First Corinthians, then Second Corinthians and so forth until we end with Jude's short letter.

The word the King James Bible translated as *"Church"* is the word *ekklesia* in Greek, which simply means a "called forth congregation or assembly." In the Bible, *ekklesia* most often refers to the covenant community called forth in assembly. When the Hebrew "Old Covenant" Bible was translated into Greek prior to Jesus's birth, the word was sometimes used for the *"congregation"* of Israel (see Deuteronomy 23:1) and the *"congregation"* of the *LORD* when it was in the wilderness (Deuteronomy 31:30). The Hebrew word that *ekklesia* translated was the word, *"qahal,"* which also means assembly or congregation. In many ways, the word "church" has taken on other meanings in Western society, and though I will use the word interchangeably with *Ekklesia*, it will be good to remember the underlying word meaning when you come across the word "church," that is, a congregation or assembly of those who have been called – and in particular, called as the Covenant People of God.

In general, Biblical quotes are taken primarily from the Lockman Foundation's New American Standard Bible® (NASB), Copyright © 1960, 1962, 1963, 1968, 1971, 1972, 1973, 1975, 1977, 1995 by The Lockman Foundation and used by permission. (www.Lockman.org).

Additionally, to keep track, included below is a *rough guess* of the *chronological* order of all the New Testament books and some general dates. This will be a guide worth bookmarking as we move through the various chapters.

Rough Chronology of New Testament Writings *(AD)*

James mid-40s

1 Thessalonians *50-51*

2 Thessalonians *50-51*

Galatians *55*

1 Corinthians *55*

2 Corinthians *56*

Romans *57*

Mark late 50s-early 60s

Matthew late 50s-early 60s

Philemon *61-62*

Colossians *61-62*

Ephesians *61-62*

Luke *61-62*

Acts 61-early 70s

Philippians *62*

1 Timothy *63-64*

Titus *63-64*

1 Peter *63-64*

2 Peter *65*

2 Timothy *65*

Hebrews *68*

Jude late 60s-early 70s

John late 80s-early 90s

1 John late 80s-early 90s

2 John late 80s-early 90s

3 John late 80s-early 90s

Revelation late 80s-early 90s

Tips on How to Read This Book

How to read this book? Ideally, read it parallel to its related chapter in the Bible: Acts 1 with my reflection on the same day or the following day. Be sure to sit with each chapter of the Bible for a period of time. New insights will pop up if you pray for insight. I would recommend no more than a new Bible chapter every other day. That would allow you to finish in ten months.

Reading all the way through at a set pace will provide its own profit. Perhaps you can choose a partner who can read along with you – not physically, but on your timetable. That brings the opportunity for rich sharing and a nudge to keep up your chosen pace. And perhaps you will consider writing your own reflections as you go along. My prayer is that God will mightily bless your journey with the Early Church!

Five Themes

Be on the lookout for five themes as you read. The first is the issue of Kingdom. The second is the concept of Covenant. The third is the Promise of the Holy Spirit, the fourth is God as Father and the fifth is Restoration.

I. The Kingdom

The very first verse in Acts sums up the focus of Jesus's earthly ministry: the announcement of the Kingdom – the Government of God. We find this consistent summation throughout the New Testament writings:

"Now after John had been taken into custody, Jesus came into Galilee, preaching the gospel [good news] *of God, and saying, 'The time is fulfilled, and **the kingdom of God is at hand**; repent and believe in the gospel.'"* (Mark 1:14).

*"But when they believed Philip **preaching the good news about the kingdom of God** and the name of Jesus Christ, they were being baptized, men and women alike."* (Acts 8:12).

*"And he [Paul] stayed two full years in his own rented quarters and was welcoming all who came to him, **preaching the kingdom of God** and teaching concerning the Lord Jesus Christ with all openness, unhindered."* (Acts 28:30-31).

Jesus was ushering in and preaching the Kingdom (Government) of God. He knew that it was dawning in a new way as He ministered to Israel. Thirty years ago, during worship in late January of 1988, one of my spiritual brothers, Steve Bowie, saw a vision of a medieval kingdom and its King in royal regalia. Outside of the walls of the Kingdom, the countryside was desolate. Peasants born outside of the Kingdom were at the mercy of the world. Steve saw the King extend an invitation to those beyond the walls to come and enjoy being part of his household. In the King's household, there was peace and security, joy and celebration – hope. Outside his household, there was only war and strife, thievery and destruction – hopelessness. Those who chose to remain outside the walls had nothing but what they could scrounge. They clearly had made a decision to be subject only to themselves or an ungodly master.

The colors were vivid in the King's palace, but totally washed out - grey and lifeless - outside of the palace. The peasants had no idea that there was little color where they lived, because they had never gone near the King's palace. It is far easier for someone from the palace to see the difference than it is for someone outside. As the King's domain extended, Steve could see the colors returning to the countryside. Steve's "seeing" followed Jesus's many parables about the Kingdom.

Jesus's parables and Steve's vision spotlight the great difference between being within and under the Government of God or beyond it. It certainly describes my personal experience. Most travelers are struck when they go into a foreign country with the impact of corrupt government - just how dark and impoverished things are. Jesus's call contained a message prophesied centuries earlier, but whose fruit was now at hand: God was establishing a change in His connection to the human race. *His* government, made perfect in every way, is available in reality to ALL. It is like my friend's vision from 1988.

"Your faithful...make known, O Lord, the glorious splendor of your Kingdom." (Psalm 145:10-12).

As young Christians, we sang, *"The Kingdom of God is not meat nor drink, but Righteousness, Peace and Joy in the Holy Spirit."* (Romans 14:17). God's government is expressed in and through His Spirit and in and through His Son. After Jesus's resurrection, He was able to proclaim, *"All authority has been given to Me in heaven and on earth."* (Matthew 28:18). Authority is a Kingdom attribute. When we come across the term, *"the Lord Jesus"* in our texts, the descriptor, *"Lord,"* is the Greek word, *"Kyrios,"* which refers to Jesus's governmental function. It is not used accidentally. He *is* in charge.

II. The Covenant

Though Luke does not mention it in Chapter 1 of Acts, a New Covenant had just been *"cut."* I say "cut" because it is the root meaning of the English word, "covenant." We have to go back to the earliest times to retrieve the Hebrew word that in most of our Bibles is translated "covenant," the Hebrew word, *"beriyth."*

Beriyth means *cutting*, and its first occurrence is in Genesis 6:18 where God promises Noah, *"I will establish My covenant with you; and you shall enter the ark—you and your sons and your wife, and your sons' wives with you."* The literal translation would be *"I will confirm My cutting with you."* It seems a strange thing for the God of the Universe to say, but the Hebrew word references the ancient practice of binding two wills into one.

As a young boy exposed to western movies, my mind was impressed with the concept of being a "blood brother." The exact episodes escape me, but it was more than once that I watched the nine-inch black and white screen portray an Indian and a White Man becoming "blood brothers" by cutting their arms and letting their blood mingle. I can remember doing this in reality once as a child when two of us pricked our fingers and pressed them together. It is a wonder we didn't transmit some terrible disease. But trust me, it was a serious action. In Noah's time, it was a life and death matter.

In the Hebrew mind four thousand years ago, the concept of cutting and covenant were directly related to the shedding of blood as a sign of the utter seriousness of binding two wills into one. That basically is the meaning of "covenant" – binding two wills into one. God Himself demonstrated the ancient practice to Abraham in Genesis. God's covenantal binding was extremely clear:

"I will establish My covenant [cutting] between Me and you and your descendants after you throughout their generations for an everlasting covenant, to be God to you and to your descendants after you." (Genesis 17:7).

We read about the ritual that God Himself acted out in Genesis 15 when God appeared to Abraham:

"'I am the Lord who brought you out of Ur of the Chaldeans, to give you this land to possess it.' He [Abraham] said, 'O Lord God, how may I know that I will possess it?' So He said to him, 'Bring Me a three year old heifer, and a three year old female goat, and a three year old ram, and a turtledove, and a young pigeon.' Then he brought all these to Him and **cut** *them in two, and laid each half opposite the other; but he did not cut the birds. The birds of prey came down upon the carcasses, and Abram drove them away."* (Genesis 15:7-11).

"Then God appeared during the night in smoke and fire and sealed the covenant being made, It came about when the sun had set, that it was very dark, and behold, there appeared a smoking oven and a flaming torch which passed between these pieces. On that day the Lord made a covenant with Abram...." (Genesis 15:17-18).

Cutting the animals and passing between them said that it was a life and death matter to bind wills. What God said He would do, He would do. He "owned" His word that He was speaking to Abraham. As God figuratively walked between the pieces of dead flesh, He was saying, "May it be so for Me if I fail to keep My word." God was using a human practice of making a binding, life-backed-up agreement to emphasize to Abraham that God's words could be totally trusted. God's binding of His will was like a rock – solid as could be. A New Era began relationally between the two – God and Abraham. The Covenant that began with Noah was being extended and amplified to Abraham and his descendants. It was *"cut"* in blood.

Why is this important? Because, with Jesus's death, God was using the most precious life imaginable to "cut" a New Covenant. And, just like the previous covenants of old, there would be a sign. For Noah, the sign was the rainbow. For Abraham, the sign was circumcision (see Genesis 17:11). For us, in one sense the sign is Jesus's death on a cross - His cutting. But in another sense, the sign is the Promise of the Holy Spirit's pouring out - a "seal" of *"having also believed - you were sealed in Him with the Holy Spirit of Promise, who is given as a pledge of our inheritance...."* (Ephesians 1:13-14). A third sign is water baptism – an action that repeats in a symbolic way the death experience of Jesus. And finally, there is the "Lord's Supper" that Christians take in memory of Jesus's death. All four speak to the "cutting" and thus to Covenant.

Before the histories recorded in Acts commence, this amazing event – this final "cutting" - had just occurred, and everything that followed rests on the New Covenant that God had "cut" in the flesh of His Son.

The second important point is that the Covenant exemplifies a marvelous characteristic of God – His *Chesed*. This key word in the Hebrew Scriptures (בְּרִית) is roughly translated, "A stubborn determination to remain faithful in a relationship no matter what!" Sometimes symbolized by salt or a salt block in the field, it is sticky and does not easily erode. God is sticky. He is full of *Chesed,* and this characteristic undergirds the growth of the community of followers after Jesus's ascension to the Father. As He is faithful, so they are called to be faithful to both God and one another.

So, be on the lookout for expressions of Covenant!

III. The Promise of the Holy Spirit

The first thing highlighted was the advent of the Kingdom of God. The second was the cutting: The Covenant is "cut" in Jesus's very life. The third spotlight is on the great *"Promise"* – the pouring out of the Holy Spirit. We must look at this Promise to better understand how monumental all of this is. The Promise is tied directly to Kingdom and Covenant. It doesn't take long in the first chapter of Acts to encounter "the Promise."

*"He had, by the Holy Spirit, given orders to the apostles whom He had chosen…. Gathering them together, He commanded them not to leave Jerusalem, but to wait for what the Father had **promised, 'Which,'** He said, 'you heard of from Me; for John baptized with water, but you will be baptized with the Holy Spirit not many days from now…. you will receive power when the Holy Spirit has come upon you; and you*

shall be My witnesses both in Jerusalem, and in all Judea and Samaria, and even to the remotest part of the earth.'" (Acts 1:2,4-5,8).

This was a predicted paradigm change if there ever was one. Immediately after the crucifixion, the disciples had been confused, filled with sadness at their loss and terrified of the Sanhedrin. Now, joy fills their hearts as they anticipate the broad *"pouring out"* of the Holy Spirit promised by both the ancient prophets as well as Jesus. Yet, there remained trepidation about the Sanhedrin. We see the disciples return to Jerusalem to wait until this special "Promise" is poured out just as the Prophets Jeremiah and Joel had predicted some 600 years earlier:

> *"Thus you will know that I am in the midst of Israel,*
> *And that I am the Lord your God,*
> *And there is no other;*
> *And My people will never be put to shame.*
> *It will come about after this*
> *That I will pour out My Spirit on all mankind;*
> *And your sons and daughters will prophesy,*
> *Your old men will dream dreams,*
> *Your young men will see visions.*
> *Even on the male and female servants*
> *I will pour out My Spirit in those days."* (Joel 2:27-29).

*"'Behold, days are coming,' declares the Lord, 'when **I will make a new covenant** with the house of Israel and with the house of Judah, not like the covenant which I made with their fathers in the day I took them by the hand to bring them out of the land of Egypt, My covenant which they broke, although I was a husband to them,' declares the Lord. 'But this is the covenant which I will make with the house of Israel after those days,' declares the Lord, '**I will put My law within them and on their heart I will write it; and I will be their God, and they shall be My people.** They will not teach again, each man his neighbor and each man his brother,*

saying, "Know the Lord," for they will all know Me, from the least of them to the greatest of them,' declares the Lord, 'for I will forgive their iniquity, and their sin I will remember no more.'" (Jeremiah 31:31-34).

In one sense, Chapters 23 and 24 of Luke plus Chapter 1 of Acts are like a hinge between two great realities – between two great covenants. We need to remember that there were earlier bindings of God's will with Noah, Abraham and the children of Israel.

Jesus's band of close friends and followers are being transformed into a greatly enhanced covenant community – a people bound together by the blood of a New and Better Covenant. **And the required activating power and energy will be through the action of God's indwelling Spirit.** What we call "Spirit" refers to the Hebrew word, *"Ruach"* which means *"breath"* or *"wind."* It signifies in the most electrifying way life – an activating force that brings the fullness, power and character of God full front and center.

Jesus had spoken extensively on this "promise" to the Twelve at the preceding Passover. The Apostle John, seated that evening beside Jesus, recorded Jesus's words carefully:

"But now I am going to the one who sent me, and not one of you asks me, 'Where are you going?' But because I told you this, grief has filled your hearts. **But I tell you the truth, it is better for you that I go. For if I do not go, the Advocate [Paraclete] will not come to you. But if I go, I will send him to you.** *And when he comes, he will convict the world in regard to sin and righteousness and condemnation: sin, because they do not believe in me; righteousness, because I am going to the Father and you will no longer see me; condemnation, because the ruler of this world has been condemned.*

"I have much more to tell you, but you cannot bear it now. But **when He comes, the Spirit of truth [pneuma alētheia], He will guide you to all**

truth. He will not speak on his own, but He will speak what He hears, and will declare to you the things that are coming. He will glorify me, because He will take from what is mine and declare it to you. Everything that the Father has is mine; for this reason I told you that He will take from what is mine and declare it to you." (John 16:5-15).

There are many other references, but one from the Apostle Paul stands out because it really presents a remarkable synopsis of what God is doing:

*"Blessed be the God and Father of our Lord Jesus Christ, who has blessed us with every spiritual blessing in the heavenly places in Christ, just as He chose us in Him before the foundation of the world, that we would be holy and blameless before Him. In love He predestined us to adoption as sons through Jesus Christ to Himself, according to the kind intention of His will, to the praise of the glory of His grace, which He freely bestowed on us in the Beloved. In Him we have redemption through His blood, the forgiveness of our trespasses, according to the riches of His grace which He lavished on us. In all wisdom and insight, He made known to us the mystery of His will, according to His kind intention which He purposed in Him with a view to an administration suitable to the fullness of the times, that is, the summing up of all things in Christ, things in the heavens and things on the earth. In Him also we have obtained an inheritance, having been predestined according to His purpose who works all things after the counsel of His will, to the end that we who were the first to hope in Christ would be to the praise of His glory. In Him, **you also, after listening to the message of truth, the gospel of your salvation—having also believed, you were sealed in Him with the Holy Spirit of promise,** who is given as a pledge of our inheritance, with a view to the redemption of God's own possession, to the praise of His glory."* (Ephesians 1:3-14).

IV. God as Father – The Family of God

A seed that appeared lifeless had been buried. Water and warmth have stirred the DNA inside the seed, and life is sending forth a tendril from the seed. The ground shifts minutely as the tendril rises toward the warmth and breaks out. In a sense, it is *called* forth. So it is with the *Ekklesia*; it is called forth from the shed blood of Jesus. In Acts, we see the shoot breaking forth from the seed. We will dive more deeply into that reality in the book of Hebrews.

But these "called-out" ones, this assembly of those who have been called and have responded to the call, are being formed as part of the Family of God - both here on the earth and eventually in the heavenlies. It is because of this that we call each other brother and sister, aunt and uncle in the *Ekklesia*. In the Spirit, we are family and not just any family. We are adopted into God's family. Jesus, the Son of God, is now our elder brother. This dynamic expresses itself in numerous ways. Most of all, we call the God of the Universe, "Father."

In two of his letters, Paul emphasized the special familial tie that we have to the Godhead. Paul testified that the Spirit that we receive as born-again believers is the spirit of adoption as sons and daughters. We cry, *"Abba, Father."* The word *Abba* comes straight from the Hebrew/Chaldean language and perhaps is better translated *"Papa"* as it reflects a most tender and intimate view of a father.

"For you have not received a spirit of slavery leading to fear again, but you have received a spirit of adoption as sons by which we cry out, 'Abba! Father!'" (Romans 8:15).

"Because you are sons, God has sent forth the Spirit of His Son into our hearts, crying, 'Abba! Father!'" (Galatians 4:5).

To underscore how remarkable our family connection is to God, note that Jesus uses the very same phrase in the Garden of Gethsemane immediately before his trial and crucifixion when he cries out *"Abba! Father!"* (Mark 14:36). Being brought into the Household of God, into the Family of God, as an adopted child highlights both the intimacy God seeks as well as the high calling He extends to us.

Paul reflects, *"For all who are being led by the Spirit of God, these are sons of God. For you have not received a spirit of slavery leading to fear again, but you have received a spirit of adoption as sons by which we cry out, 'Abba! Father!' The Spirit Himself testifies with our spirit that we are children of God...."* (Romans 8:14-16).

The ancient image of a temple is another closely associated line of revelation – a place for God to dwell. In the New Covenant, followers form a temple, both corporately and individually, in which God dwells – the House of God. This is another way of expressing the remarkable impact of being a "child of God." Paul asks, *"Do you not understand that **you** are God's temple, and that God's spirit has His dwelling in you?"* (Corinthians 3:16). And later, we will see God's corporate intention to build us together into a holy and spiritual temple, i.e., a dwelling place for God's spirit:

"And coming to Him as to a living stone which has been rejected by men, but is choice and precious in the sight of God, you also, as living stones, are being built up as a spiritual house for a holy priesthood, to offer up spiritual sacrifices acceptable to God through Jesus Christ." (1 Peter 2:4-5).

Peter addresses yet another aspect of God's special call to the Family of God – to serve as a *"royal"* priesthood. The term "royal" reminds us that the service will be a Kingdom service. The word "priesthood" reminds us that as the Family of God, we will be representing our Father and the Spirit to all of creation.

*"But you are a chosen race, a **royal** priesthood, a holy nation, a people for God's own possession, so that you may proclaim the excellencies of Him who has called you out of darkness into His marvelous light; for you once were not a people, but now you are the people of God; you had not received mercy, but now you have received mercy."* (1 Peter 2:9-10).

An Intimate Connection

Reflect on the intimacy Jesus's death has wrought. In a real sense, His followers are now identified as being part of His body. Paul, in his letter to the Ephesian church, makes this very clear:

"Speaking the truth in love, we are to grow up in all aspects into Him who is the head, even Christ, from whom the whole body, being fitted and held together by what every joint supplies, according to the proper working of each individual part, causes the growth of the body for the building up of itself in love." (Ephesians 4:16).

Paul highlights that we find ourselves *in* the very Body of Christ, hidden *in* Him, yet - through the sovereign connections between believers and the energetic working of the Spirit - that "Body" grows in love.

Let's sum up these different ways of seeing God's intention for us relationally from the preceding short passages:

- Family
- Temple
- Priesthood
- Body

V. Restoration of All Things

The final theme to watch for is Restoration. At the very beginning of the Book of Acts, we find the disciples, *"asking Him, saying, 'Lord, is it* *at this time You are **restoring** the kingdom to Israel?' He said to them, 'It is not for you to know times or epochs which the Father has fixed by His own authority; but you will receive power when the Holy Spirit has come upon you; and you shall be My witnesses both in Jerusalem, and in all Judea and Samaria, and even to the remotest part of the earth.'"* (Acts 1:6-8).

In a sense, the issue of Kingdom contains the theme of Restoration, but my focus here is on the completion of God's intention - when all things will be fully restored. We will find that the Early Church was focused both on "now" and "that which is to come." The apostle Peter, in his second speech recorded in Acts, had a final restoration in mind when he shared,

*"Therefore repent and return, so that your sins may be wiped away, in order that times of refreshing may come from the presence of the Lord; and that He may send Jesus, the Christ appointed for you, whom heaven must receive until **the period of restoration of all things** about which God spoke by the mouth of His holy prophets from ancient time."* (Acts 3:19-21). Jesus spoke at long length on the coming Age. Be on the lookout!

Summary

As we move into the 149 chapters from Acts through Jude, we will want to keep these five contextual points in mind. Be alert for them as you read each chapter: *The Kingdom - The Covenant - The Promise - God as Father - The Restoration.* Each is expressed in what God did and is doing so momentously in the gift of His Son.

Preface to the Acts of the Apostles

"...Luke has made clear the nature and mission of the church. The church in her nature reflects Jesus and the pattern of His life. The church in her nature reflects Jesus and the preaching of his message. Between the ascension and return of Jesus, the kingdom of God is realized in the church on earth, where God's will is done as in heaven." (Gerald Stevens, *Acts: A New Vision of the People of God*, Chapter 2, 2016).

"The first account I composed, Theophilus, about all that Jesus began to do and teach, until the day when He was taken up to heaven, after He had by the Holy Spirit given orders to the apostles whom He had chosen. To these He also presented Himself alive after His suffering, by many convincing proofs, appearing to them over a period of forty days and speaking of the things concerning the kingdom of God. Gathering them together, He commanded them not to leave Jerusalem, but to wait for what the Father had promised, 'Which,' He said, 'you heard of from Me; for John baptized with water, but you will be baptized with the Holy Spirit not many days from now.'" (Acts 1:1-5).

The very first paragraph of Acts keys us to multiple facts, not the least of which is that we are reading the second half of a longer document. The first half we know as the Gospel of Luke, which contains a similar salutation to the *"excellent"* Theophilus. *(See Luke 1:3).* Luke, a Christian worker long associated with the Apostle Paul, appears to have written this carefully drawn history of the early Church perhaps around 61 or 62 AD. Some believe it could have been written even after the fall of Jerusalem in 70 AD though the author is oddly silent on that event if the date is after the city's destruction. Acts itself covers approximately thirty years of history.

We know for sure that the book was written after Paul's two-year imprisonment in Caesarea and Paul's transfer to Rome because Luke records detailed accounts of both. Dating is simplified for this time period because Luke notes that the two Roman Governors who served during Paul's imprisonment in Caesarea were Antonius Felix and Porcius Festus. The latter was governor from approximately 59 to 62 AD. Luke was in Judea during this timeframe and likely used the time to do extensive research for his history.

So, who is Luke? Paul calls him a physician in his letter to Colossae – "one who heals" in the Greek – as well as the "beloved." From Luke's own account in Acts 16, it appears he joined Paul's growing ministry team by the time Paul got to Troas on his second missionary journey (around 50 AD).

Are we sure Luke wrote the Gospel of Luke as well as Acts? Both Irenaeus (c. 180 AD) and Tertullian (c. 208 AD) affirmed Luke's authorship, but our best biographical sketch came early in the fourth century from Eusebius, Bishop of Caesarea:

"But Luke, who was of Antiochian parentage and a physician by profession, and who was especially intimate with Paul as well as acquainted

with the rest of the apostles, has left us, in two inspired books, proofs of that spiritual healing art which he learned from them. One of these books is the Gospel, which he testifies that he wrote as those who were from the beginning eye-witnesses and ministers of the word delivered unto him, all of whom, as he says, he followed accurately from the first. The other book is the Acts of the Apostles, which he composed not from the accounts of others, but from what he had seen himself. And they say that Paul meant to refer to Luke's gospel whenever, as if speaking of some gospel of his own, he used the words, 'according to my Gospel.'" (*Church History of Eusebius*, c. 324 AD, Book III, Chapter IV:6,7).*

I interpret Eusebius's reference to Antioch to be Antioch-in-Syria, though I may be incorrect. The latter is where the Apostle Paul lived and ministered for several years. Antioch-in-Pisidia was basically in the middle of what the Romans then called *"Asia"* and what we think of today as modern-day Turkey. Paul visited this "Antioch" on his first three missionary journeys, and Luke may have been converted there.

Regardless, Luke was one of the most skilled writers in the Greek language of his day and of remarkable intellect. Assuming that the early Church fathers were right about his authorship, he personally wrote over a quarter of our "New Testament."

One thing for sure, he was an amazing historian for his time and place. Taking his Gospel and Acts together, Luke identifies accurately over 30 countries, 54 cities, 9 islands and numerous historical figures with their appropriate titles. Most of us would have a hard time duplicating that feat today. Luke was meticulous in his facts and writing.

The Immediate Context

Immediately prior to the events recorded in the Book of Acts, Jesus had been wounded, judged and crucified. On the third day, He had risen as Lord and appeared to a rag-tag group of friends and followers. We know that both fear and love gripped these followers. Out of love, several of the women had gone to Jesus's tomb before the sun had risen and discovered that His body was missing. Fear certainly gripped them - perhaps partially because an angel had told them that Jesus had been raised from the dead. They also may have been terrified of falling into the hands of the Sanhedrin.

"They went out and fled from the tomb, for trembling and astonishment had gripped them; and they said nothing to anyone, for they were afraid." (Mark 16:8).

Jesus appears behind Mary Magdalene as she is weeping. Her sadness and sense of loss turn to joy. He sends her back to the disciples (Matthew 28:9) along with the other Mary, telling them to go to Galilee where He will meet them.

Later in the day, Jesus joins two of his disciples who are on their way to Emmaus pondering the recent wrenching days and the report they had just received from Mary Magdalene and the other women. The two disciples then eat with Jesus, recognize Him in the breaking of the bread, and hurry immediately back to Jerusalem. (Luke 24:13-30).

By the time they reach the assembled disciples, Jesus separately has appeared to Peter. (Luke 24:34).

Jesus miraculously then appears to those assembled that evening. The disciples had been gripped with fear that the Sanhedrin, too, might seize them, but now their emotions mingle with joy as they grasp the astonishing reality that Jesus truly had risen from the dead:

"So when it was evening on that day, the first day of the week, and when the doors were shut where the disciples were, for fear of the Jews, Jesus came and stood in their midst and said to them, 'Peace be with you.'

And when He had said this, He showed them both His hands and His side. The disciples then rejoiced when they saw the Lord. So Jesus said to them again, 'Peace be with you; as the Father has sent Me, I also send you.' And when He had said this, He breathed on them and said to them, 'Receive the Holy Spirit. If you forgive the sins of any, their sins have been forgiven them; if you retain the sins of any, they have been retained.'" (John 20:19-23).

It appears that Jesus's initial concern was to relieve the terrible anxiety the disciples were experiencing. His appearance brought them both peace and new focus – *"as the Father has sent Me, I also send you."* Finally, late that Sunday, Jesus breathed on them that they would receive the Spirit of God. Their world was in major flux!

There is no record of Jesus appearing again until the following Sunday. Jesus appears where they had gathered a week earlier. Thomas, one of Jesus's original Twelve, had not been with them. This time, he is present. All week, he had doubted the reports from the other disciples. Jesus tells him to *"Reach here with your finger and see My hands; and reach here your hand and put it into My side; and do not be unbelieving, but believing."* (John 20:27). Thomas does so, and finally believes.

After this, some of the disciples travel northwest a trek of 60 miles to the Sea of Galilee where Jesus has promised to appear again. Since several had made their living as fishermen, Jesus finds seven of them fishing off the shore of the Sea, and unbeknownst to them, Jesus has prepared a breakfast of roasted fish accompanied by bread. The seven (including Peter, Thomas, Nathanael, James and John) had fished most of the night but caught nothing. It is only when Jesus calls to them, *"Friends!"* from the shore and tells them to cast their net to the boat's right side that they are able to catch a full haul.

It is at this point that Jesus re-commissions Peter – the disciple who had denied Him three times immediately before the crucifixion.

The Broader Context

It is amazingly important to catch what is happening. This is a hinge point – a bit like Jesus's crucifixion, but without the pain. Brought to fulfillment by the pain. A new Age is dawning, and it has such importance for us today for we are in that Age.

Conclusion

Remember, as we move into the Acts of the Apostles, we will want to keep these five contextual points in mind. Be alert for them as you read each chapter: *The Kingdom - The Covenant - The Promise - God as Father - Restoration*. Each is expressed in what God did so momentously and is doing in the gift of His Son.

Acts of the Apostles

"To many people this book, both its content and its author, is so little known that they are not even aware it exists. I have therefore taken this narrative for my subject.... For indeed it will profit us no less than the Gospels themselves, so replete is it with Christian wisdom and sound doctrine, especially in what is said concerning the Holy Spirit. Let us then not pass it by but examine it closely. For here we can see the predictions Christ utters in the Gospels actually come to pass." (John Chrysostom, *Homilies on the Acts of the Apostles*, Homily 1, c. 400 AD).

Acts 1

The narrative after Jesus's crucifixion in Luke's Gospel is picked up in Acts 1. For forty days, Jesus appears to many of His disciples while giving particular instructions to his 11 remaining apostles *("special envoys")*. First, Jesus has been with them in Jerusalem and then in Galilee. Immediately prior to His great ascension into Heaven on the fortieth day, Jesus directed the Eleven to return to Jerusalem to wait for the great Promise: the pouring out of the Holy Spirit of God. All of this was in the context of His earthly ministry where He had been focused on announcing one key thing: the Kingdom (Government) of God.

Verse 4 gives us a greater understanding of the great gift that the disciples are expecting. Jesus uses a term that they know well – the term *"baptism."* (Note: His actual word was likely in Aramaic and translated for Greek readers in the ancient texts). The Greek word has been so important to the Church that it has come down 2,000 years to us almost intact - the word in the Greek is *baptizô*. Jesus further references John the Baptist's prophetic declaration: *"Gathering them together, He commanded them not to leave Jerusalem, but to wait for what the Father had promised, 'Which,' He said, 'you heard of from Me; for John baptized with water, but you will be baptized with the Holy Spirit not many days from now.'"* (Acts 1:4-5).

Matthew records John's prophecy in detail: *"I baptize you with water for repentance, but He who is coming after me is mightier than I, and I am not fit to remove His sandals; He will baptize you with the Holy Spirit and fire."* (Matthew 3:11).

Think about what Jesus and John the Baptist predicted. The disciples are to receive something God promised multiple times (through the ancient prophets, through John the Baptist and through Jesus Himself) and that promise is a baptism in the Holy Spirit and fire. Baptism in the Greek means to submerge, immerse, and surround with water in such a way that a thing (or a person) is fully enveloped and cleansed. It differs from the Greek word for dip *(baptô)* in that baptism can represent a continuing condition.

A reference by a Greek physician named Nicander (who lived about two centuries before Jesus) provides further color on the word *baptizô*. Nicander recorded a recipe for making pickles from turnip roots using both the word for dip *(baptô)* and the word for immerse *(baptizô)*. First, you dip *(baptô)* the vegetable into boiling water and then you immerse *(baptizô)* the vegetable into a solution. The first action is temporary while the second is continuing, i.e., the roots stay in the solution producing a permanent change.

So, what have we learned? The Promise is the Spirit of God that will be given and poured out in such a way that the recipient will be washed, surrounded, immersed and submerged - by and into the Spirit of God – the Spirit of Truth Jesus that predicted (see John 16:5-15). If *we* are so baptized, we will be like Nicander's pickle: permanently changed!

Now, let's think about the big picture and the five big themes we outlined earlier: The Kingdom, The Covenant, The Promise, God as Father and the Restoration of All Things. Jesus has died and His flesh has been cut. This means that God has inaugurated the prophesied New Covenant. This Covenant ushers in an entirely new era for mankind, one in which deep forgiveness is available as well as the potential of being an actual child of God, part of God's heavenly household, with God's promised stamp clearly embossed.

But, in one sense, we are in an in-between time. There is a throne in Heaven not yet occupied. During the forty-day period, Jesus is still very much on the earth. But, after His ascension, He will sit down at the Father's right hand as both King and Lord. This will be the time for Him *then* to pour forth His and the Father's Spirit in a powerful way upon those who respond to God's call. But first, He must ascend to do so, and Luke records His ascension a third of the way through Chapter 1.

The ascension account occurs immediately after Jesus had told them that they were to receive power when the Spirit of God *"comes upon you."* Then, they would witness to what had occurred - in Jerusalem, Judea, Samaria and even the most remote parts of the earth.

Having said these things, Jesus rose from the mountaintop and a cloud enveloped Him. Two men in white (I assume angels) appear as this is happening, and their report tells us two key things. First, Jesus is transitioning from earth to Heaven. The vacant seat in the Throne Room of Heaven is about to be filled. Second, Jesus will return from Heaven just as the disciples have seem Him ascend.

Jesus had spoken of His return at great length in the Gospels. Matthew recorded many of His parables that speak directly to His coming, but Jesus's own words were adequately descriptive and in line with what the two men in white declared:

"But immediately after the tribulation of those days the sun will be darkened, and the moon will not give its light, and the stars will fall from the sky, and the powers of the heavens will be shaken. And then the sign of the Son of Man will appear in the sky, and then all the tribes of the earth will mourn, and they will see the Son of Man coming on the clouds of the sky with power and great glory. And He will send forth His angels with a great trumpet and they will gather together His elect from the four winds, from one end of the sky to the other." (Matthew 24:29-31).

Jesus had given specific warnings just a few weeks before His crucifixion of the struggles the disciples would encounter immediately before His eventual return so what the two men reported must have been bitter-sweet, recalling Jesus's earlier words:

"But before all these things, they will lay their hands on you and will persecute you, delivering you to the synagogues and prisons, bringing you before kings and governors for My name's sake. It will lead to an opportunity for your testimony. So make up your minds not to prepare beforehand to defend yourselves; for I will give you utterance and wisdom which none of your opponents will be able to resist or refute. But you will be betrayed even by parents and brothers and relatives and friends, and they will put some of you to death, and you will be hated by all because

of My name. Yet not a hair of your head will perish. By your endurance you will gain your lives." (Luke 21:12-19).

The disciples returned to Jerusalem after Jesus's ascension, sober but filled with anticipation. None of them knew exactly what was happening. They gathered perhaps in the same "upper room" where they had celebrated their last meal with Jesus before His crucifixion. The Eleven were present along with Jesus's mother, "brothers," and the women who had followed Jesus faithfully during the last days of His earthy ministry. We can already detect the work of the Holy Spirit, because Luke records that they were of *"one mind"* and *"continually devoting themselves to prayer"* as they waited for the Promise. Being of *"one mind"* with eleven people is a miracle in itself!

During these intervening days, the assembled group had increased to nearly 120 people. Peter was moved to share from Psalm 109:8: *"Let his days be few; and let another take his office,"* in reference to Judas's previous position a one of the Twelve key men Jesus had chosen. Judas's tragic death leaves a slot that needs to be filled.

The process the disciples used to fill Judas's slot casts an important spotlight on the difference between having the power of the Holy Spirit fully functioning within the Covenant Community and not having it. How do they make the decision? They basically "draw straws." Matthias is chosen by this method. This will be the LAST time any such method is recorded to determine God's will in a matter. Once the promised Holy Spirit has been poured out, there will be no future mention of casting lots to make any community decision. Prayer, the written word of God and the leading of the Holy Spirit will be more than sufficient!

Chapter 1 is a key chapter. Like the 23rd and 24th chapters of Luke's Gospel, Chapter 1 contains one of the key steps that must be taken to fully activate God's intention to usher in an entirely new era: Jesus must ascend to the Father. Jesus has prepared His disciples for His ascent, and He has ascended! The chair in Heaven has been filled. The enthroned Jesus is ready to take the next key step as we move to Chapter 2.

Acts 2

"How shall we picture the kingdom of God, or by what parable shall we present it? It is like a mustard seed, which, when sown upon the soil, though it is smaller than all the seeds that are upon the soil, yet when it is sown, it grows up and becomes larger than all the garden plants and forms large branches; so that the birds of the air can nest under its shade." (Mark 4:30-32).

Prepare to witness (along with all those assembled in Jerusalem) the first visible signs that a powerful new plant is emerging in the Earth – God's *Ekklesia*. Jesus has died; He has been buried; the power of God has quickened Him in the tomb, and a life force is emanating. That life force is the Spirit of God that was promised. It will soon become manifest as the enabling power behind a new covenant community – the "Church" as the King James translators would have it.

Jesus's parable recorded in the 4th chapter of Mark reminds us that those who hear the call of God after the resurrection and respond form together a true kingdom where God in all of His dimension is fully on the Throne. Jesus said after the resurrection, *"All authority has been given to Me in heaven and on earth. Go therefore…."* (Matthew 28:19). He is *"the blessed and only Sovereign, the King of kings and Lord of lords,"* (1st Timothy 6:15). The Throne Room of Heaven already was filled as the Day of Pentecost came fifty days after Passover!

No doubt, the day of Pentecost was not accidental. The God of the Universe had established the feast day of *Shavuot* during the time of the children of Israel's exodus from Egypt. *"You shall observe the Feast of the Harvest of the first fruits of your labors from what you sow in the field."* (Exodus 23:16). Its timing related to Passover, and reflected the initial bringing in of the first harvest of the calendar year: from the sixteenth of the month of Nisan (the second day of the Passover), seven complete weeks (forty-nine days) were counted and the feast was held on the fiftieth day. The word we use comes almost directly from the original Greek, *pentēkostē,* which means fiftieth.

The day of Pentecost also had a long history of being connected to the giving of the Law on Sinai – thought to be fifty days after the Israelite exodus from Egypt began. A new Law was commencing – the Law of the Spirit and the first fruits of a new harvest were to be harvested. Let's see what happens!

Jerusalem was filled with Jews who had come from afar for the great Feast. Evening temperatures likely had gotten into the 50s, but the morning dawned with clear skies and temperatures rising into the 70s. Rainfall had been dropping each month since January until the dry season had arrived. Wheat planted in the fields four months earlier was just beginning to reach the time for an early harvest.

The Twelve Apostles gathered that Pentecost morning in a house, perhaps the same house of the Last Supper. It was probably about 9 am, roughly the third hour from sunrise. The Jewish people calculated the anticipated hours of daylight and divided by 12. There is significant controversy about the date, but May 24th, 33 AD around 9 AM seems most probable to me. Regardless, suddenly,

"from Heaven noises came like a violent rushing wind, and it filled the whole house where they were sitting. And there appeared to them tongues

as of fire distributing themselves, and they rested on each one of them. And they were all filled with the Holy Spirit and began to speak with other tongues, as the Spirit was giving them utterance." (Acts 2:2-4).

Luke is describing exactly what the Prophets prophesied. Apparently the *"violent rushing wind"* made sufficient noise to draw bystanders – plus it appears the apostles were speaking simultaneously in various languages concerning *"the mighty deeds of God."* It is possible they were singing psalms of praise about God. We just don't know for sure. The clamor made by the different languages and the remarkable way the Apostles were acting made many in the increasing crowd think the Apostles were drunk.

I have to assume that at some point the Apostles may have gone up and out onto the flat roof of the housetop. Otherwise, it is hard to picture how a large Jewish crowd (which apparently eventually numbered over 3,000 souls) possibly could have gathered inside a Jerusalem home of that era to hear the voices of the Apostles. The crowd represented an amazing cross section of the eastern world of the Mediterranean: Parthians, Medes, Eliamites and Mesopotamia (today's Iraq and Iran), Judea and Cappadocia (today's Israel and eastern Turkey), Pontus (northeastern Turkey), Asia (western Turkey), Phryia and Pamphylia (middle Turkey), Egypt, Libya and Cyrene (northwest Libya), Rome, Cretans from the island of Crete and finally Arabs.

The whole scene is electric. Fire, a mighty wind, noise, unknown languages. The disciples had heard Jesus speak of the Holy Spirit as *"The wind [that] blows where it wishes, and you hear the sound of it, but do not know where it comes from and where it is going; so is everyone who is born of the Spirit."* (John 3:8). The Hebrew language does not differentiate between wind, breath and spirit. The word, *ruach*, in Hebrew can mean each. The *Ruach Adonai* (the Spirit of God) was not a new, unexplored concept for a Jew. Any Jew off the street would have believed that all of the Prophets manifested some "anointing" of the *Ruach Adonai / Ruach Elohiym* (the Spirit of God). They were clothed (enveloped) with it. And this would have included Moses, the 70 elders during the Exodus (see Numbers 11:24), King Saul and King David. The latter had oil "poured out" on them, and the Spirit clearly fell on Saul as recorded in 1st Samuel 19:23-24: *"the Spirit of God* [Ruach Elohiym] *came upon him also, so that he went along prophesying continually until he came to Naioth in Ramah..., and he too prophesied before Samuel and.... Therefore they say, 'Is Saul also among the prophets?'"*

There are occurrences, but they were relatively rare. The ordinary person until Pentecost had little or no personal experience with God's Spirit aside from stories. But they had hope. God had used wind to illustrate the vitality and connection between wind, breath and the Spirit of God through the Prophet Ezekiel's words some 600 years before Jesus's appearance. God gave the ordinary person hope of a dimensional change through Ezekiel's encounter:

"Then He [God] *said to me, "Prophesy to the breath, prophesy, son of man, and say to the breath, 'Thus says the Lord God, "Come from the four winds, O breath, and breathe on these slain, that they come to life."' So I prophesied as He commanded me, and the breath came into them, and they came to life and stood on their feet, an exceedingly great army. Then He said to me, 'Son of man, these bones are the whole house of Israel; behold, they say, "Our bones are dried up and our hope has perished. We are completely cut off." Therefore prophesy and say to them, "Thus says the Lord God, 'Behold, I will open your graves and cause you to come up out of your graves, My people; and I will bring you into the land of Israel. Then you will know that I am the Lord, when I have opened your graves and caused you to come up out of your graves, My people. **I will put My Spirit within you and you will come to life,** and I will place you on your own land. Then you will know that I, the Lord, have spoken and done it,'" declares the Lord."* (Ezekiel 37:9–14).

So, when Peter stood up and in a loud voice began to address the gathering, the crowd had plenty of context and background on to understand how momentous Peter's concluding remarks would be. Here is the beginning of Peter's famous speech:

"Men of Judea and all you who live in Jerusalem, let this be known to you and give heed to my words. For these men are not drunk, as you suppose, for it is only the third hour of the day; but this is what was spoken of through the prophet Joel:

> *"'And it shall be in the last days,' God says,*
> *'That I will pour forth of My Spirit on all mankind;*
> *And your sons and your daughters shall prophesy,*
> *And your young men shall see visions,*
> *And your old men shall dream dreams;*
> *Even on My bondslaves, both men and women,*
> *I will in those days pour forth of My Spirit*
> *And they shall prophesy.*
> *And I will grant wonders in the sky above*
> *And signs on the earth below,*
> *Blood, and fire, and vapor of smoke.*
> *The sun will be turned into darkness*
> *And the moon into blood,*
> *Before the great and glorious day of the Lord shall come.*
> *And it shall be that everyone who calls on the name*
> *of the Lord will be saved.'"* (Acts 2:14-21).

Many wonder whether we are in Joel's prophesied "Last Days," but it seems obvious to me that we have been in the Last Days for over 2,000 years from Peter's reckoning. It was time for the Spirit to be *"poured forth on all mankind,"* and you would know this was the time because of the signs. Peter pulled from a prophecy that the Prophet Joel had prophesied. There would be celestial signs like both the Blood Moon and the eclipse during Jesus's crucifixion as well as a clear sign that the Spirit was intimately communicating to a host of people:

> *"your sons and your daughters shall prophesy,*
> *And your young men shall see visions,*
> *And your old men shall dream dreams;*
> *Even on My bondslaves, both men and women,*
> *I will in those days pour forth of My Spirit*
> *And they shall prophesy....*
> *And it shall be that everyone who calls on the*
> *name of the Lord will be saved."*
> (Acts 2:17-18, 21).

Those assembled were seeing with their own eyes signs of the Spirit's activity: the Apostles appeared to be on fire, they were prophesying, and from that time forth sons and daughters, young men and old men, God's servants - both men and women - would prophesy, have visions and dream God dreams. An intimacy with the Creator was being proclaimed that was available that very day to all that were assembled and willing to become fully given over to God. A bond-slave in the Prophet Joel's time was someone who could walk away from slavery but chose instead to fully submit to his or her Master for life.

These are not just words to contemplate; they are a call to action. My modest book, *Visions, Dreams & Encounters*, records only a number of the visions, dreams and God-encounters that our tiny fellowship received over a forty-year period. The Promise of the Spirit is not academic; it is real, vibrant and available to all who become a *"bond-slave"* of God. The gifts of the Spirit help change our direction and our lives.

God's intention goes much further than outward manifestations of signs and wonders, important though they may be. Through His very Spirit, God wants to transmit His divine character. We see His character clearly outlined when He appears before Moses as recorded in Exodus 34:6ff. We will return to this often in our journey through the 149 chapters. It is worth quoting here and dwelling on - because, in a very real way, God is all about transmitting these seven aspects of His DNA to us:

"The Lord, the Lord God,
compassionate and gracious, slow to anger,
and abounding in lovingkindness [steadfast covenantal love –
chesed] *and truth; Who keeps lovingkindness for thousands,*
Who forgives iniquity, transgression and sin;
yet He will by no means leave the guilty unpunished....."

One of the challenges of reading is that one tends to move from one word to another rather than stop and contemplate each word. Take a moment and think about God. Every time I stop and contemplate, I get goose bumps. Amazing.

Back to Peter's speech. In the middle of his speech, he unpacks the most recent events. There is both good and bad news. Jesus was fully present with them, doing miracles, wonders and signs, yet God knew that the people would end up rejecting Jesus, and through their action, Jesus was nailed to a cross and put to death. But God raised Him from the dead, and Peter and his comrades saw Him alive. At this point, Peter inserts a word that we always want to be on the look for – the word *"Therefore,"* because we always want to know what reason the "therefore" is there!

"Therefore, having been exalted to the right hand of God, and having received from the Father the Promise of the Holy Spirit, He has poured forth this which you both see and hear." (Acts 2:33).

And in verse 36, we hit another *"Therefore:"*

"Therefore, let all the house of Israel know for certain that God has made Him both Lord and Christ—this Jesus whom you crucified." (Acts 2:36).

What declarations! God has made the crucified one both Lord *AND* Christ. The word "Christ" comes directly from the Greek word *"Christós"* which in the Hebrew is the word, *"mashiach,"* a word we translate in English as Messiah. Both words mean *"anointed"* or *"the anointed one."* In the history of Israel, priests "anointed" people whom God was setting aside for a special task. This was signified physically by pouring extremely fine oil on the head of the appointed one. It was anticipated that, simultaneously, this act would be accompanied by a special spiritual grace from God – a dose (for lack of a better word) of God's Spirit. This special gifting might manifest itself with special talent or the ability to know what God wanted to be spoken at any point in time. We know that King Saul prophesied immediately after his anointing. (1ˢᵗ Samuel 10:6). Moses himself anointed the first Hebrew Priests: *"Then he poured some of the anointing oil on Aaron's head and anointed him, to consecrate him."* (Leviticus 8:12). This confirms an additional dimension to the act of anointing: it *consecrated* (set apart) the person for a special service to God.

The Jewish people had been looking for a promised *Mashiach* (Anointed One) for centuries. Moses had shared that God would raise up one like him in the future: *"I will raise up a prophet from among their countrymen like you, and I will put My words in his mouth, and he shall speak to them all that I command him."* (Deuteronomy 18:18). Another example was a forward-looking prophecy from the Prophet Malachi who lived over 400 years before Jesus: *"Behold, I am going to send My messenger, and he will clear the way before Me. And the Lord, whom you seek, will suddenly come to His temple; and the messenger of the covenant, in whom you delight, behold, He is coming, says the Lord of hosts. But who can endure the day of His coming? And who can stand when He appears? For He is like a refiner's fire and like fullers' soap. He will sit as a smelter and purifier of silver...."* (Malachi 3:1-3).

This *"Anointed One"* would be sent for the special task of *delivering* and *purifying* the Jewish people. In English, we render this *"a promised Messiah."* Remember the word, Messiah, comes directly from the Hebrew word, *Mashiach.* Therefore, when Peter declared Jesus both Lord and *Messiah*, the *Anointed One* of God, Peter was announcing electrifying things - epoch shaking things. All that was happening on Pentecost confirmed the arrival of a dimensionally new epoch.

The Initial Harvest

*"Now when they heard this, they were pierced to the heart, and said to Peter and the rest of the apostles, 'Brethren, what shall we do?' Peter said to them, 'Repent, and each of you be baptized in the name of Jesus Christ for the forgiveness of your sins; and you will receive the gift of the Holy Spirit. For the **promise** is for you and your children and for all who are far off, as many as the Lord our God will call to Himself.' And with many other words he solemnly testified and kept on exhorting them, saying, 'Be saved from this perverse generation!' So then, those who had received his word were baptized; and that day there were added about three thousand souls."* (Acts 2:37-41).

How appropriate that the first harvest of souls under the New Covenant occurred on the Feast of the Harvest of the First Fruits!

Imagine the logistics of baptizing 3,000 people *"in the name of Jesus"* in the hot, rainless month of May. There were pools where this could have occurred - the Gihon Spring led to the Pool of Siloam in the ancient city of Jerusalem. Even today, Jewish men on occasion will use it for a ritual *mikvah* (*immersion*). But, 3,000 is an astounding number.

Nuances to Verses 38 and 39

Luke's account of this critical portion of Peter's speech captures the very earliest Christian answer of what one is to do when faced with Jesus's call to repentance and new life. It certainly was not very complicated: *"Repent, and each of you be baptized in the name of Jesus Christ for the forgiveness of your sins; and you will receive the gift of the Holy Spirit. For the promise is for you and your children and for all who are far off, as many as the Lord our God will call to Himself."* (Acts 2:38-39).

At first glance, what could be more simple? It appears there are three parts to Peter's answer:

- Repent
- Be Baptized
- Receive the gift of the Holy Spirit

A more lingering look reveals at least eight nuances as well as the harsh reality that human beings have an amazing egotistical stubbornness that makes what looks easy actually very hard. First, let's look at the nuances.

"Repent" in the Greek is the word *metanoeō*. In the New Testament Scriptures, it signifies a deep sorrow for one's past as well as a *radical* change in direction so that God is the central focus of one's life. Men and women resist God's call because they want to remain in control of their lives. Before we repent, we carry about the great sin of Satan who was unwilling to let God be God. Rather, *he* wanted to be God. True repentance requires a softening that God might break through into one's heart. Verse 37 shows that those listening were already **"pierced to the heart."** Let us all allow God to pierce our hearts that deep change may come!

Being baptized is also resisted worldwide as it is an outward sign of both the need for forgiveness and submission to God's will. Many will resist out of pride. Naaman, a captain in the army of the King of Syria, refused out of pride to heed the Prophet Elisha's call to wash seven times in the Jordan that his leprosy might be cured.

And Peter is calling for those that repent to be baptized *"in the name of Jesus Christ"* (remember "Christ" simply means the "Anointed One"). *"In the name of Jesus Christ"* means that one is doing more than mere submersion in water. Peter is calling people to be **fully identified with Jesus**. The preposition used is the Greek word *"epi"* which could be translated *"on."* Here, Peter emphasizes the substance of the immersion: Jesus Himself. As the Scriptures unfold through Acts and the letters, we will dive deeper into this sacrament. More on that later!

Baptism also has a purpose Peter wants to emphasize: forgiveness. One of the key elements that drives repentance is one's sense of guilt for sins committed and a desperate need for forgiveness. Peter presents baptism as a physical act that deals with the spiritual reality of impurity in the one being baptized. The ability - nay - the desire for God to forgive comes with His turf, that is, God's nature *is* to forgive. The result of baptism (forgiveness **and** cleansing) is brought about by the costly sacrifice God has just made (Jesus's crucifixion) and reflects that wonderful DNA of God Himself as we see in Exodus 34:6-7.

"You will receive." This is important. There are three actions on our part in responding to Peter's direction: repenting, being baptized, and receiving. Receiving is an action that *we* must do so that the Promise of the Holy Spirit will be activated in our lives. Jesus has a key role here on his side: He *"pours out"* on us what the Father has given Him, i.e., the Holy Spirit. But we have an action as well: *receiving*.

Years ago, I realized that being sent a present at Christmas time had little impact if the present actually wasn't received, opened and used. The same is true of the Gift of the Holy Spirit. This point seems lost on many who emphasize the first two actions for which we are responsible but neglect the third - the receiving. There are many presents left unopened and unused under God's tree.

Another nuance is that Luke and Peter make very clear that the Promise of the Holy Spirit is not just for those assembled that day in Jerusalem and certainly not just for the Apostles. "For **the promise is for you and your children and for all who are far off**, *as many as the Lord our God will call to Himself*." (Acts 2:39). The Promise is for *YOU*; the promise is for us!

"And with many other words he solemnly testified and kept on exhorting them, saying, 'Be saved from this perverse generation!" So then, those who had received his word were baptized; and that day there were added about three thousand souls." (Acts 2:40-41).

Finally, it is worth noting that Peter was proclaiming a message we often hear today – even within our households: *"Be saved from this perverse generation."* The Greek word used for *"saved"* means to be rescued from the danger of destruction, and surely the society we are in today qualifies as particularly dangerous and perverse. So, Peter's message certainly was a "salvation" message. He wasn't just speaking platitudes; he was like a man in a movie theatre that had caught on fire, and he was exhorting the audience to *"be saved"* from the danger. Three thousand souls responded to the call. Note that they *RECEIVED* Peter's words. We must actually receive what we are given by God; we need to open the package!

The Result

"They were continually devoting themselves to the apostles' teaching and to fellowship, to the breaking of bread and to prayer. Everyone kept feeling a sense of awe; and many wonders and signs were taking place

through the apostles. And all those who had believed were together and had all things in common; and they began selling their property and possessions and were sharing them with all, as anyone might have need. Day by day continuing with one mind in the temple, and breaking bread from house to house, they were taking their meals together with gladness and sincerity of heart, praising God and having favor with all the people. And the Lord was adding to their number day by day those who were being saved." (Acts 2:42-47).

Luke wraps up a most extraordinary chapter with the initial results of what happen that Pentecost day in verses 42 through 47. His summary of the impact should be a good outline of any normal Christian community:

- Teaching
- Fellowship
- "Breaking of Bread" (in reference to the Last Supper remembrance)
- Prayer
- Signs and Wonders
- All things in common
- Sharing as need occurred
- Of one mind
- Meeting daily with one another
- Eating together in each other's homes
- Exhibiting gladness and sincerity of heart

I would encourage you to slowly review these aspects of the Christian community and consider your own experience. Bottom-line, the established culture of your community predicts what you normally are willing to embrace. It takes a big dose of the Holy Spirit to truly activate authentic communal life in God. It is less a question of what others should do; it is more a question of what *you* are doing and what *you* can do. It is a question of whether *you* are willing to receive, unwrap and activate the many personal gifts that God has already bestowed on you. I am assuming you have - *"in sincerity of heart"* - already truly repented and been baptized. But you also must unwrap! When you do so and allow God to truly activate you on the inside, then He will use *you* to help change the culture if it does not line up with this glorious outline!

Acts 3

Chapter 2 gave us a glimpse into the fellowship life of the emerging congregation of Holy Spirit clothed people. We saw a simple outline of how the Spirit's presence manifested itself in community. Luke shifts in Chapter 3 to give us an early record of how the message of Jesus and the Kingdom of God was being transmitted publicly.

The setting is instructive. We join two of the key believers (Peter and John) after they have climbed up to the temple mount for prayer around 3 PM.

Peter and John are functioning like the rest of their Jewish brethren. The immense changes in their internal worlds and the epoch changing events of Pentecost have not changed their Jewishness. They are still in transition with regard to their identity as well as their understanding.

Near the temple gate called Beautiful, they walk alongside a lame man who was being carried to his normal position to beg for alms. The man catches their attention by asking for money – perhaps with eyes downcast. At this point, things go very differently from what would have occurred in the past.

Three things happen. First, Peter and John fix their eyes on the man and direct him to look in their eyes. It is at this point that the man actually engages with them, thinking he is about to get some money. But Peter responds with a wonderful reply,

"I do not possess silver and gold, but what I do have I give to you: In the name of Jesus Christ the Nazarene—walk!" (Acts 3:6).

I must confess; I prefer the Kings James translation I learned as a child: *"Silver and gold have I none; but such as I have give I thee: In the name of Jesus Christ of Nazareth rise up and walk."*

Taking the man's hand, Peter raises him. As he does, the lame legs strengthen and he *"leaps up."* Fantastic! The man is intermittingly leaping as he walks along with Peter and John toward the temple, and at the same time, he is praising God. The commotion draws a large crowd as they reached Solomon's Portico, a long double colonnade on the Eastern side of the Court of The Gentiles immediately outside of the temple itself.

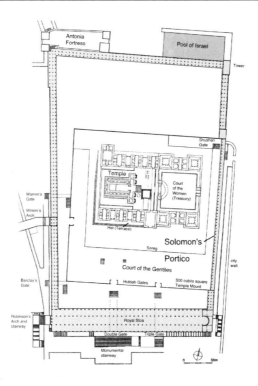

Temple Mount. *Copyright Ritmeyer Archaeological Design*

Depending on the exact location along the quarter of a mile portico to which the crowd rushed, Peter had before him a court that could contain a large number of people. The southern court was perhaps 400 feet wide and 800 feet deep. It is there that he addressed those assembled with an explanation and an invitation.

The Anwer to the Question, "Who Healed this Man?"

"Men of Israel, why are you amazed at this, or why do you gaze at us, as if by our own power or piety we had made him walk? The God of Abraham, Isaac and Jacob, the God of our fathers, has glorified His servant Jesus, the one whom you delivered and disowned in the presence of Pilate, when he had decided to release Him. But you disowned the Holy

and Righteous One and asked for a murderer to be granted to you, but put to death the Prince of life, the one whom God raised from the dead, a fact to which we are witnesses. And on the basis of faith in His name, **it is the name of Jesus which has strengthened this man whom you see and know; and the faith which comes through Him has given him this perfect health in the presence of you all.***"* (Acts 3:12-16).

The man had been healed by the *"Prince of Life"* or at least by action in the name of Jesus who is the Prince of Life. That action was grounded in the faith that came through Jesus. Imagine, the one who has healed the lame man was the one they had *"put to death."* Consider the wonder of this proclamation to those assembled! Undoubtedly, some had heard of the Pentecost event, but this was confirmation that the Spirit of God was functioning through Jesus's emissaries.

"Prince of Life" is a translation of the Greek word *"archēgos"* which means *author* or *captain*. This is the only time in Scripture that the phrase occurs. It is early in the history of the church, but Peter, clearly acting under the inspiration of the Spirit (Luke devotes an entire chapter to this event), recognizes that true life comes from and is under the direction of the One who was just slain. That makes this phrase and the content behind it all the more amazing.

Invitation: Repent and Return

"And now, brethren, I know that you acted in ignorance, just as your rulers did also. But the things which God announced beforehand by the mouth of all the prophets, that His Christ would suffer, He has thus fulfilled. **Therefore repent and return, so that your sins may be wiped away, in order that times of refreshing may come from the presence of the Lord; and that He may send Jesus, the Christ appointed for you, whom heaven must receive until the period of restoration of all things** *about which God spoke by the mouth of His holy prophets from*

ancient time. Moses said, 'The Lord God will raise up for you a prophet like me from your brethren; to Him you shall give heed to everything He says to you. And it will be that every soul that does not heed that prophet shall be utterly destroyed from among the people.' And likewise, all the prophets who have spoken, from Samuel and his successors onward, also announced these days. It is you who are the sons of the prophets and of the covenant which God made with your fathers, saying to Abraham, 'And in your seed all the families of the earth shall be blessed.' For you first, **God raised up His Servant and sent Him to bless you by turning every one of you from your wicked ways.**" (Acts 3:17-26).

The second part of Peter's speech begins with, "*I know you acted in ignorance.*" I can't help but connect Peter's kindness in saying this to what Jesus said at His crucifixion and the forgiveness he extended to Peter who had denied Him three times. The Spirit of Jesus was working on Peter. Peter clarifies that Jesus is the one prophesied by the Prophets, but that is just to back up Peter's strong admonition that they "***repent and return****, so that your sins may be wiped away, in order that times of refreshing may come from the presence of the Lord; and that He may send Jesus,* **the Christ appointed for you***, whom heaven must receive until the period of restoration of all things....*"

Repent and return ("*from their wicked ways,*" verse 26) are the two actions he commands. Peter is speaking boldly with authority, and the authority backing him up is five-fold: the authority of God, the authority of Jesus, the authority of the Holy Spirit, the authority of the Prophets and the authority of Scripture. As on Pentecost, the results he promises to a Jew are staggering: the presence of the Lord will be with those that repent and return and Peter is preaching a Lord who will bring refreshing as opposed to punishment. Plus, their positive response will hasten Jesus's return where all things will be restored. (Acts 3:21).

We should ask, "Exactly what will be restored?" Peter's answer is, *"All things"* - the things spoken by the Prophets of old. The Greek word translated *"restoration"* is the word *apokatástasis* that can also mean, "reestablish." Times when everything would be put together in an entirely new way. Jesus Himself had said, *"Heaven and earth will pass away, but My words will not pass away."* (Matthew 24:35).

Origin, a Christian teaching doctrinal foundations about 200 years later in Alexandria and Caesarea, gave his thoughts about the restoration: *"The consummation of all things is the destruction of evil.... Many things are said obscurely in the prophecies of the total destruction of evil and the restoration to righteousness of every soul, but it will be enough for our present discussion to quote the following passage from Zephaniah: '...For my determination is to gather the nations, that I may assemble the kings, to pour upon them my indignation.... For then I will bring about a transformation of pure language among the people, that they may all call upon the name of the Lord, to serve Him with one consent.'"* (Origen *"Against Celsus,"* 8.72).

We also see a bit of the mystery of God's restoration revealed by Paul in his letter to the Ephesians: *"He made known to us the mystery of His will, according to His kind intention which He purposed in Him with a view to an administration suitable to the fullness of the times, that is, the summing up of all things in Christ, things in the heavens and things on the earth."* (Ephesians 1:9-10).

Whether Peter knew many specifics of the restoration at this point, I do not know. But He did know Jesus was coming again and that his brothers and sisters, the Jewish community, needed to be ready for His return.

My final emphasis is Peter's clear understanding that the Jewish people were *"the sons of the prophets and of the covenant which God made with your fathers, saying to Abraham, 'And in your seed all the families of the earth shall be blessed.'* We have been amazingly blessed by those God chose to bless, of course Jesus stands out at the top, but I am thankful we live in a time when deep friendships can occur between Gentiles and God's ancient people. May the Spirit that was on Peter be upon us all!

Acts 4

Luke's record of the healing of the lame man continues into Chapter 4. Peter and John addressed the crowd at Solomon's Portico until late in the day.

The captain of the temple guard, priests and some of the Sadducee sect joined the crowd and eventually confronted them when they heard Peter and John glorifying Jesus's resurrection from the dead. The Sadducees were a powerful Jewish priestly sect that took responsibility for many functional needs of the temple. They did not believe in life after death.

We know a good bit about the Sadducees, not only from the Gospels but also from the 1st century Jewish historian, Josephus, who recorded that *"the doctrine of the Sadducees is this: that souls die with the bodies; nor do they regard the observation of anything besides what the law enjoins them...."* (Josephus, *Antiquities of the Jews,* 18.16.4). *"They take away fate, and say there is no such thing, and that the events of human affairs are not at its disposal; but they suppose that all our actions are in our own power, so that we are ourselves the causes of what is good."* (Josephus, AJ, 13.173). No doubt, the Sadducees were aggravated for multiple reasons with Peter and John, but particularly for Peter's testimony that it was possible to live after death.

The resulting encounter was violent: *"And they laid hands on them and put them in jail until the next day, for it was already evening."* (Acts 4:3). Jesus had predicted this sort of conflict would occur early in His ministry: *"But beware of men, for they will hand you over to the courts and scourge you in their synagogues; and you will even be brought before governors and kings for My sake, as a testimony to them and to the Gentiles. But when they hand you over, do not worry about how or what you are to say; for it will be given you in that hour what you are to say. For it is not you who speak, but it is the Spirit of your Father who speaks in you."* (Matthew 10:17-20). Luke says, *"the Holy Spirit will teach you in that very hour what you ought to say."* (Luke 12:11-12).

The next morning, Peter and John were pulled out of a cell and placed in the middle of some of Jerusalem's highest-ranking religious leaders including Annas, the high priest, and other members of the priestly caste. *"By what power, or in what name, have you done this?"* they demanded. At this point, it should be no surprise that Peter boldly answered them through the power and direction of the Holy Spirit:

"Let it be known to all of you and to all the people of Israel, that by the name of Jesus Christ the Nazarene, whom you crucified, whom God raised from the dead—by this name this man stands here before you in good health. He is the stone which was rejected by you, the builders, but which became the chief corner stone. And there is salvation in no one else; for there is no other name under heaven that has been given among men by which we must be saved." (Acts 4:10-12).

Peter takes absolutely no credit for the healing. What he did was done *"in the name of"* Jesus. This is a precise way of saying that Jesus did the healing through the agency of an emissary. It also means that the Spirit of God in Peter, because of Jesus's Spirit being upon him, moved with healing power. *"In the name of"* spotlights an important fact that the whole event rests on the issue of authority. When an emissary of a

King arrives at a foreign court, that emissary comes "in the name of the King." When the policeman pulls your car over, the policeman does so "in the name of" the Mayor of the city. The authority of an emissary comes from the one he or she represents. Peter was operating as emissary with the spiritual tools given him by receiving *"The Promise."* Jesus was on the throne in heaven; all authority in heaven and on earth was His. (See Matthew 28:18). The lame man's healing was another sign that the Kingdom of Heaven was touching the earth in the presence of its emissaries! That was not just for Peter's time. It is for us as well.

The Cornerstone

Only a few months earlier, the priests and elders at the temple had accosted Jesus. After sharing two parables, Jesus repeated a portion of a Psalm verbatim (see Matthew 21:42-44):

> *"The stone which the builders rejected*
> *Has become the chief corner stone.*
> *This is the Lord's doing;*
> *It is marvelous in our eyes."*
> (Psalm 118:22-23).

Peter refers back to Jesus's imagery, and his point is important in seeing the relational aspects of the Kingdom and Jesus's key role in it. Though the Jewish leaders have rejected Jesus, God has made Him the chief cornerstone in a whole new building that is rising.

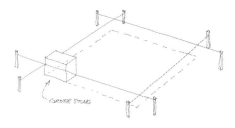

CORNER STONE

A cornerstone's placement determines everything about the emerging building. There are three other important and related texts that spotlight how important the cornerstone is.

First, the prophecy from Isaiah:

*"Thus says the Lord God, 'Behold, I am laying in Zion a stone, a tested stone, A costly **cornerstone** for the foundation, firmly placed. He who believes in it will not be disturbed.'"* (Isaiah 28:16-17).

Paul picks up the same theme in his letter to the Ephesians: *"So then you are no longer strangers and aliens, but you are fellow citizens with the saints, and are of God's household, having been built on the foundation of the apostles and prophets, Christ Jesus Himself being the **cornerstone**, in whom the whole building, being fitted together, is growing into a holy temple in the Lord, in whom you also are being built together into a dwelling of God in the Spirit."* (Ephesians 2:19-22). We will return to this when we get to Ephesians.

And finally, Peter himself, recalling his earlier address that we now are studying, included the same section from Psalms in his own epistle:

"And coming to Him as to a living stone which has been rejected by men, but is choice and precious in the sight of God, you also, as living stones, are being built up as a spiritual house for a holy priesthood, to offer up spiritual sacrifices acceptable to God through Jesus Christ. For this is contained in Scripture:

> *"'Behold, I lay in Zion a choice stone, a precious **cornerstone**,*
> *and he who believes in Him will not be disappointed.'*
> *This precious value, then, is for you who believe;*
> *but for those who disbelieve,*
> *'The stone which the builders rejected,*
> *This became the very **cornerstone**,'"* (1 Peter 2:4-7).

The Response of the Jewish Leaders

The middle of Chapter 4 is devoted to the response that came from the religious leaders. Their response appears politically motivated. They are worried about the populace since the healing is undeniable and that it will be associated with the death of Jesus. They may not have felt the situation as dire as the timing of Jesus's trial since both the feasts of Passover and Pentecost are over, and Jerusalem is not teeming with people.

Regardless, the leaders command Peter and John no longer to speak or teach *"in the name of Jesus."* What is remarkable and certainly further sign of the Spirit's enablement is that Peter and John have a reply that has affected 2,000 years of Christian behavior toward laws against proclamation: *"Whether it is right in the sight of God to give heed to you rather than to God, you be the judge; for we cannot stop speaking about what we have seen and heard."* (Acts 4:19-20). Bottom-line, we must always heed God rather than men, even when it may be very costly.

The Response of the Believers

No doubt, the community of believers was stunned that Peter and John had been released – particularly after they heard how the two men had responded to the prohibition. I have always loved the community's response and how Luke focused on another sign of the Holy Spirit's activity – unity of mind.

"And when they heard this, they lifted their voices to God with one accord and said, 'O Lord, it is You who made the heaven and the earth and the sea, and all that is in them, who by the Holy Spirit, through the mouth of our father David Your servant, said,

"Why did the Gentiles rage, and the peoples devise futile things?

'The kings of the earth took their stand, and the rulers were gathered together against the Lord and against His Christ." (Psalm 2:1).

"'For truly in this city there were gathered together against Your holy servant Jesus, whom You anointed, both Herod and Pontius Pilate, along with the Gentiles and the peoples of Israel, to do whatever Your hand and Your purpose predestined to occur. And now, Lord, take note of their threats, and grant that Your bond-servants may speak Your word with all confidence, while You extend Your hand to heal, and signs and wonders take place through the name of Your holy servant Jesus.' And when they had prayed, the place where they had gathered together was shaken, and they were all filled with the Holy Spirit and began to speak the word of God with boldness." (Acts 4:24-31).

I am often reminded of this remarkable event when we share a responsive reading during worship. To be so much of one mind that all pray in the Spirit orally and simultaneously the very same words is a miracle. They are praying very much in the Spirit for boldness and that God will continue to heal and demonstrate signs and wonders while touching the earth through the name of Jesus. In other words, they are praying that they will be fully activated and authorized emissaries, bringing the veritable finger of God to what they touch. As communities of believers, may we also pray in the Spirit for the very same thing!

The chapter ends with another sign that this growing band of believers is walking together in the Spirit. In addition to unity of heart and soul, there were none needy amongst them. This truly is a sign of God's grace functioning in a most fluid way. These early believers supplied whatever was needed. Whatever they had, they held in trust for God, using it for the benefit of others as required – even to the extent of selling property and land. We will see some restrictions on this approach as we get further into Acts as well as Paul's letters, but the main thrust should hold true in every community under the authority and guidance of the Spirit of God.

We also encounter here the first clear definition of role within the emerging *Ekklesia*. Where were the funds that were gathered for those in need deposited? At the feet of the Apostles. This term, *"at the Apostles' feet"* occurs twice. I recall running across a somewhat similar phrase forty years ago from the First Apology of Justin Martyr writing around 155 AD:

"And those who are well to do, and willing, give what each thinks fit, and what is collected is deposited with the president [of the community] who succors the orphans and widows, and those who, through sickness or any other cause, are in want, and those who are in bonds, and the strangers sojourning amongst us, and in a word take care of all who are in need." (1st Apology of Justin, LXVII).

I also am reminded of the Aristides' remark some 25 years earlier: *"They love one another, and from widows they do not turn away their esteem; and they deliver the orphan from him who treats him harshly. And he who has, gives to him who has not, without boasting. And when they see a stranger, they take him in to their homes and rejoice over him as a very brother; for they do not call them brethren after the flesh, but brethren after the Spirit and in God. And whenever one of their poor passes from the world, each one of them according to his ability gives heed to him and carefully sees to his burial. And if they hear that one of their number is imprisoned or afflicted on account of the name of their Messiah, all of them anxiously minister to his necessity, and if it is possible to redeem him they set him free. And if there is among them any that is poor and needy, and if they have no spare food, they fast two or three days in order to supply to the needy their lack of food."* ("The Apology of Aristides," XV, from the Syriac manuscript, c. 130 AD).

And then around 180 AD, Irenaeus wrote an important series of books against heresy and related how things continued to be handled in the *Ekklesia*:

"instead of the law enjoining the giving of tithes, [He told us] *to share* (Matthew 19:21) *all our possessions with the poor; and not to love our neighbors only, but even our enemies; and not merely to be liberal givers and bestowers, but even that we should present a gratuitous gift to those who take away our goods. For to him that takes away your coat, He says, give to him your cloak also; and from him that takes away your goods, ask them not again; and as you would that men should do unto you, do unto them* (Luke 6:29-31): *so that we may not grieve as those who are unwilling to be defrauded, but may rejoice as those who have given willingly, and as rather conferring a favour upon our neighbors than yielding to necessity."* (Irenaeus, Against Heresies, Book IV, Chpt. 13, c. 180 AD).

The Kingdom of God - I don't believe the Holy Spirit knows another approach!

Acts 5

The First Sour Note

If healing a man lame for over forty years wasn't enough, the story of Ananias and Sapphira makes abundantly clear that this new emerging community was an amazing place – *"refreshing,"* as Peter said, but also terrifying. I am reminded of the Israelites' experience during their forty-year trek to the Promised Land. And what happened to Uzzah when he touched the Ark of the Covenant during the time of David. These encounters recall C.S. Lewis's words spoken through Mr. Beaver concerning Aslan, the great lion who represents God in *The Lion, the*

Witch and the Wardrobe: "'Aslan is a lion - the Lion, the great Lion.' 'Ooh' said Susan. 'I'd thought he was a man. Is he - quite safe? I shall feel rather nervous about meeting a lion'... 'Safe?' said Mr Beaver,... 'Who said anything about safe? 'Course he isn't safe. But he's good. He's the King, I tell you.'" (C.S. Lewis; *The Lion, the Witch and the Wardrobe*).

At the end of Chapter 4, Barnabus had sold a piece of land and laid the proceeds at the feet of the apostles. Now, in Chapter 5, we find another couple in the little community of Jesus followers appearing to duplicate that action – though, in fact, they lied about the amount, and because the Spirit of God was present and active in Peter, they had lied not only to Peter and the community but to God's Spirit as well. Additionally, Peter apparently had received a "Word of Knowledge" from God as the lies were occurring. Nothing is hidden from God.

This is the first sour note recorded by Luke after Pentecost *within* the community of believers, and it recalls several of Jesus's parables about tares mixed amongst the wheat in the field. But here, like the story of Achan in Joshua 7, God removes the tare. No doubt, the hoped for outcome had been recorded at the time of Moses: *"Then all Israel will hear and be afraid, and will never again do such a wicked thing among you."* (Deuteronomy 13:11). Here, *"Israel"* had become the new community of believers. Luke records, *"And great fear came over the whole church, and over all who heard of these things."* (Acts 5:11).

As a side note, this is the first time the word *ekklesia* - here translated *"church"* - occurs in Luke's writings, including his Gospel. I suppose that initially the phrase could have been translated *"and great fear came over the whole group that had assembled,"* but clearly the emphasis is on the entire community of believers.

Now we have the small band associated not only with people being raised from the dead and dramatic healings but also with death.

"At the hands of the apostles many signs and wonders were taking place among the people; and they were all with one accord in Solomon's portico. But none of the rest dared to associate with them; however, the people held them in high esteem." (Acts 5:12-13).

Regular Public Gatherings Lead to More Trouble

It appears the disciples were gathering on a regular basis in Solomon's portico, that is, inside the Temple precinct but outside of the Temple itself. They were in clear view of the Temple guards as well as many who came daily to pray and offer sacrifices. The impact of the believers hit both men and women:

*"**multitudes** of men and women, were constantly added to their number, to such an extent that they even carried the sick out into the streets and laid them on cots and pallets, so that when Peter came by at least his shadow might fall on any one of them. Also the people from the cities in the vicinity of Jerusalem were coming together, bringing people who were sick or afflicted with unclean spirits, and they were all being healed."* (Acts 5:14-16).

The picture we see reminds us of Jesus's own ministry, but there is a difference. Jesus is at the right hand of the Father in the heavenlies but also very much present through the indwelling power of the Spirit that is filling the newly baptized believers. Followers of the Messiah (the Anointed One) had become a "messianic" (anointed) community. My imagination is stretched to imagine how fast this was occurring.

Not surprisingly, the reaction from the established religious leaders of Israel was swift. Again they throw the apostles (it is not clear whether the most prominent or whether all of them) into jail, but during the night, they are released through the actions of an angel. The angel tells them specifically to *"Go, stand and speak to the people in the Temple the whole message of this Life."* (Acts 5:20).

Jailed and Released

The apostles appear the next morning as instructed by the angel *in* the Temple and began to teach. Whether *"in the Temple"* means actually inside the Temple itself or back at Solomon's Portico is not entirely clear. Meanwhile, the Sanhedrin (Luke calls it *"the Senate of the sons of Israel"*) has assembled to interrogate the apostles and discovers the apostles mysteriously had been released during the night. Having taught against the Sanhedrin's clear instruction, Peter and the apostles are brought before the Sanhedrin. Peter answers them with his famous reply, "We must obey God rather than men." Peter succinctly sums up in two sentences the core of the Gospel message they have been sent to proclaim:

"The God of our fathers raised up Jesus, whom you had put to death by hanging Him on a cross. He is the one whom God exalted to His right hand as a Prince and a Savior, to grant repentance to Israel, and forgiveness of sins. And we are witnesses of these things; and so is the Holy Spirit, whom God has given to those who obey Him." (Acts 5:30-31).

The respected teacher Gamaliel, a Pharisee member of the Sanhedrin, directed that the apostles be put outside, and after they had been removed, he advised his fellow Council members to leave the apostles alone since, in all likelihood, the movement would die out if left to itself. And if it did not, God might indeed be behind the movement, and they would find themselves fighting God Himself.

The Council followed Gamaliel's lead, but still had them flogged. Additionally, they were ordered to not speak again "in the name of

Jesus." The amazing result is that the apostles went away rejoicing that they had been counted worthy to suffer because of Jesus's very name.

Chapter 5 ends with this remarkable report: *"And every day, in the temple and from house to house, they kept right on teaching and preaching Jesus as the Christ."* (Acts 5:42).

There are three things I note in this ending sentence. First, they were meeting, teaching and preaching *"every day."* And they were doing it in public (*"in the temple"*) as well as *"house to house."* And the message concentrated on presenting Jesus as the "Anointed One" – that is, the promised Messiah who was to be empowered by God. Certainly, that is a good meeting pattern for today's *Ekklesia*.

Acts 6

Growing Pains and Further Trouble with the Sanhedrin

The *Ekklesia* in Jerusalem was expanding rapidly. From the very beginning, men and women were coming to faith who were from other regions. Chapter 6 describes in some detail the logistical problem of daily serving food to the widows that needed support. It is difficult to tell from the text whether this food was exclusively going to widows and other needy (think orphans and the infirm), but regardless, there was some favoritism being shown to those who were from Judea. Each year, three large festivals brought Jewish people from far away places. We have a list of how diverse the crowd was for Peter's Pentecost message: *"Parthians and Medes and Elamites, and residents of Mesopotamia, Judea and Cappadocia, Pontus and Asia, Phrygia and Pamphylia, Egypt and the districts of Libya around Cyrene, and visitors from Rome, both Jews and proselytes, Cretans and Arabs"* to name a few.

(Acts 2:9-11). Most of these people spoke Greek. They were Jewish but of the Diaspora. Their native tongue was Greek, and therefore they were called Hellenists. In the daily distribution, *"Hellenist"* widows who had become followers of Jesus were being neglected.

The distribution problem was presented to the twelve apostles, but the apostles didn't want to get pulled aside from prayer and proclaiming the Gospel message to *"serve tables."* Rather, they wanted the Hellenists to collaborate in selecting seven good men to help, men well-respected and full of the Spirit of God, men who had evidenced wisdom in their dealings. The text says simply that the community *"chose"* the seven men, but no description is given about how they were chosen. Certainly, there is no mention of lots being cast. I imagine that they called the whole community (or at least the Hellenists) to prayer and fasting about this significant step. The question to put to God would have been, at minimum, "Who is wise, trustworthy and filled with the Spirit for this special task?"

When we look at the names of those chosen, we see that they all have Greek names: *"Stephen, a man full of faith and of the Holy Spirit, and Philip, Prochorus, Nicanor, Timon, Parmenas and Nicolas, a proselyte from Antioch."* (Acts 6:6). Their task, *"to serve tables,"* in Greek is the word, diakoneō, which means *"to be a servant, to serve, to wait upon."* It is the word from which the English speaking church gets the term "Deacon." Spiritually, it meant someone filled with the Spirit and set apart for a special service. This is the beginning of another office/role in the church community in addition to that of apostle.

This need for solid, logistical help for the growing church community is met by selecting "spirit-filled" people. Logistical needs spawned men and women who were appointed for a special and specific service. We will return to this need as we advance.

Meanwhile, the church was *"increasing greatly."* Even a good number of priests joined the growing community.

One of the Seven was a man full of the Spirit - of faith, grace and power. The word *"power"* in Greek is the word *"dynamis"* from which we get our word, dynamite. The word is frequently used in the New Testament to describe the mighty works of God and Jesus. Jesus associated faith in God with the ability to perform mighty works, and Stephen had both. In a real sense, the gifts of faith and power are directly tied together. Seeing the two gifts at work was and is electrifying.

Stephen on Trial

No doubt, those in Jerusalem seeing these *"great wonders and signs"* paid close attention to Stephen's preaching, but his words and actions inspired both jealousy and concern amongst established Jewish communities like the Synagogue of the Freedmen where Jews from Cyrene and Egypt frequented. His eloquence and wisdom caused them to secretly report him to the Jewish authorities. Stephen was charged with blasphemy - attacking Moses, God, the Temple and portions of the Law. The Sanhedrin assembled to hear the case against him.

Imaginary View of the Sanhedrin

The Sanhedrin in Jerusalem was the "Great Sanhedrin," composed of 71 Elders. It functioned on a national basis like the combined Supreme Court and Senate of the United States. The concept traces all the way back to the time of Moses when the Israelites were instructed to establish Judges and Officers (or Scribes) in all their communities. (Deuteronomy 16:18). Brought before the assembled Judges, accusations were made, but simultaneously a supernatural peace and confidence came over Stephen, and his face shown like that of an angel.

Acts 7

Stephen's Speech

Luke devotes nearly ten percent of his history of the early church to the story of Stephen - his initial selection as a *diakoneō*, his demonstration of power and wisdom as many are healed and mighty works effected and then his long speech before the Sanhedrin. Acts 8 will give us the aftermath.

The speech as recorded is most remarkable. Stephen recalled in perfect order and attribution some of the early history of God's Chosen People – beginning by recounting in great deal the life of Abraham as well as Moses and ending with Solomon and the Prophets. In the process, Stephen was careful to make clear six points. First, God has been involved with the Jewish people intimately and directly the entire time. Second, the promises given to Abraham and Moses did not come to pass in their lifetimes. Third, the people consistently missed and resisted what God was doing and whom He was sending. Fourth, their resistance caused God to remove them geographically from the Promised Land. Fifth, Stephen addressed the issue of the Temple – one of the very things that had caused him to be accused:

"However, the Most High does not dwell in houses
made by human hands; as the prophet says:
'Heaven is My throne,
And earth is the footstool of My feet;
What kind of house will you build for Me?' says the Lord,
'Or what place is there for My repose?
'Was it not My hand which made all these things?'"
(Acts 7:48-50).

Finally, Stephen told them clearly that they were off track: their hearts had hardened, and they were unwilling to listen to the voice of the Holy Spirit. He asked, *"Which one of the prophets did your fathers not persecute...you who received the law as ordained by angels and did not keep it?"* (Acts 7:52-53).

This set the Sanhedrin on fire, but simultaneously Stephen, *"full of the Holy Spirit, gazed intently into heaven and saw the glory of God and Jesus standing at the right hand of God; and he said 'behold, I see the heavens opened and the Son of Man standing at the right hand of God.'"* At this, they drove him out the city gates and stoned him. A young man named Saul stood by, guarding their robes, which they undoubtedly had put aside because of the heat of the day and the effort expended in throwing heavy stones. Stephen cried out to Jesus, calling him Kyrios (Lord) and asking Him to *"receive my spirit."* Falling to his knees, his final words echoed those of Jesus on the cross: *"Lord, lay not this sin to their charge."* And he died there from the stoning even though Luke emphasizes Stephen's future resurrection by using the phrase, *"he fell asleep."*

Two short reflections on this entire presentation: Throughout Luke's recording, Luke is emphasizing the movement and direction of God's Spirit. Stephen is chock-full of God's Spirit. He speaks the truth boldly and with great confidence. At the same time, he submits to a horrible death by stoning and, miracle of miracles, he petitions Jesus to not hold this heinous sin against the Elders. God's Spirit is boldly revealed throughout the story.

Acts 8

Stephen's witness before the Sanhedrin kicks off a serious persecution of the *ekklesia* in Jerusalem. The only parallel I can think of is the Nazis rounding up Jewish families in Germany or Spanish "Christians" rounding up Jewish families during the Inquisition. This man, Saul, who stood by guarding the robes of the perpetrators, appears to have been one of the ringleaders, *"**ravaging** the church, entering house after house, and dragging off men and women"* to put them in prison. Ravaging, entering house after house, dragging off men and women…. Horrific.

This may be the first time in Luke's writings that he formally means "the church" when he uses the word *ekklesia* though it could be argued that Luke meant it in a similar way in Acts 2:47. The translating challenge is that *ekklesia* can also mean simply *"assembly"* or *"those called to assemble and those who came."* Here it seems clear that Luke (or the early church community) was searching for a way of describing all the believers. If there was at this time in Jerusalem a great persecution *"against the* ekklesia," (referring to all the believers who had to number more than 3,000), it is highly unlikely that Luke is referencing an actual assembly. I believe he means the whole community. We will come back to this question later, but our modern-day use of the term *"church,"* needs vetting in light of what we see in Acts. More on that later.

Scattering After the Stoning of Stephen

Persecution pushes movement. The large multitude of new followers of Jesus scatters beyond Jerusalem. Those scattered bring their witness of the recent happenings in Jerusalem and their New Life in the Spirit with them, *"proclaiming the word."* It is worth getting in touch with this phrase. In the Greek, it is *"euaggelizō logos."* We get the word "evangelize" from the first word. This word comes from two Greek roots which mean simply *"good"* and *"tidings,"* so *"good tidings"* or *"good news."* *Logos* is a heavy content Greek word that normally means "declaration," "message" or "speech." When you put it altogether, you get those scattered *"declaring good news."*

Clearly, what the *"scattered"* had seen in Jerusalem was so life impacting that, in spite of severe persecution and the deaths of both Jesus and Stephen, those forced abroad felt they had some wonderful news to share. Think of that for a moment. Death and persecution on one side; a change in one's view of life so remarkable that only the words, "good news" are adequate to describe it on the other. The news had broken beyond the bounds of Jerusalem. A new chapter was being written.

Samaria

In the scattering, Philip, one of Hellenists recently chosen as *diakoneō*, went *"down"* to the City of Samaria. Luke says *"down"* because one had to descend from the heights of Jerusalem, head north and traverse 30 miles of terrain to reach Samaria. Nine centuries earlier, when Asa was king of Judah, the Israelite King Omri had purchased the "hill of Samaria" in the region north of Jerusalem and constructed a residence and city there. His son and successor was the infamous King Ahab.

The city had a checkered history. Besieged many times, it was nearly destroyed in 109 BC. Politically, Samaria had split from Judah and

Simeon, the two southern tribes of Israel and formed the Northern Kingdom along with the other nine tribes. Spiritually, the inhabitants built a competing temple to Solomon's and worshipped on nearby Mount Gerizim. The Samaritans were looked down upon by Judean Jews.

When Philip *"began proclaiming Christ to them,"* he was going beyond the boundaries just as Jesus had during His ministry. Philip's focus was simply Jesus. In the Greek, he *"heralded the Anointed."* The Anointed Jesus embodied the broader message of the Kingdom of God. Practically, when faced with those with Kingdom of God authority, the kingdom of Darkness had to submit: *"Many who had unclean spirits, they were coming out of them shouting with a loud voice; and many who had been paralyzed and lame were healed. So, there was much rejoicing in that city."* (Acts 8:7-8).

We need to remember one intriguing fact: Jesus, prior to His crucifixion and prior to the pouring out of the Holy Spirit, had given Kingdom authority to seventy disciples who were sent out in twos. (Luke 10:1-19). The demons were subject to the "Seventy." Having authority means that one is backed up by a higher level of power. In the case of Jesus and his envoys, they were backed up by the very power of God. So, in a real sense, the fact that unclean spirits were coming out of deeply troubled people was a sign not only of mercy and power, it was a sign of Kingdom authority. Philip had the faith and courage to represent both Jesus and God the Father. His faith knew who Jesus was and who he was in Him. One reason the early Church grew so rapidly was that the witnesses to God's power had become certain of who was in charge. We can ask ourselves, "What would happen if *our* faith increased?"

Undoubtedly, Jesus was rejoicing from Heaven as He watched Philip. This was Jesus's response when the Seventy returned and gave their report as recorded in Luke 10:21. Luke records Jesus *"agalliaō pneuma,"* that is, He *"rejoiced exceedingly in spirit."* The word *agalliaō ("exceedingly rejoice")* occurs only a few times in the New Testament. Seeing the Kingdom piercing the darkness as Philip cast out unclean spirits no doubt made Him exceedingly glad. The populace of Samaria rejoiced as well.

Simon the Magician and Receiving the Holy Spirit

"Now when the apostles in Jerusalem heard that Samaria had received the word of God, they sent them Peter and John, who came down and prayed for them that they might receive the Holy Spirit. For He had not yet fallen upon any of them; they had simply been baptized in the name of the Lord Jesus. Then they began laying their hands on them, and they were receiving the Holy Spirit. Now when Simon saw that the Spirit was bestowed through the laying on of the apostles' hands, he offered them money, saying, 'Give this authority to me as well, so that everyone on whom I lay my hands may receive the Holy Spirit.' But Peter said to him, 'May your silver perish with you, because you thought you could obtain the gift of God with money! You have no part or portion in this matter, for your heart is not right before God. Therefore, repent of this wickedness of yours, and pray the Lord that, if possible, the intention of your heart may be forgiven you. For I see that you are in the gall of bitterness and in the bondage of iniquity.'" (Acts 8:14-23).

Luke's report in verses 14-23 is important. As he moves through his history, Luke is carefully recounting the various ways the Early Church participated in baptism and the bestowal of the Spirit of God upon new believers. This is one of those accounts. This is the first time that we learn that the Spirit of God always did not fall upon the repentant after baptism. Samaritan Jews apparently had believed in Philip's message, repented of their sins that they might be cleansed from previous wrongdoing, been baptized (immersed) in water but did not receive the Spirit.

Had Philip's message been deficient (perhaps his hearers came only for forgiveness but not to enter into the Kingdom where God's authority would supersede their own)? Was there something about the baptism itself (the quality of the water or the words spoken by the baptizer) deficient? It appears that Philip didn't know what was wrong.

Whatever the problem, when news of the difficulty reached Jerusalem, Peter and John immediately made the thirty-mile journey to Samaria and discerned that there was at least one thing that had not occurred: *"Hands"* had not been *"laid"* on them. But there is also a hint that the baptizer saying that he was representing Jesus ("in the name of the Lord Jesus") may not have been sufficient. We know for certain that Peter and John did in fact *"lay hands on them"* and they were *"receiving the Holy Spirit."* (Acts 8:17). All of these phrases are important because they describe mysteries that were not fully understood at the time and shed light on the nature of how the Holy Spirit came to rest on new believers.

We can note that there were multiple actions on the part of the baptized. We know from Acts 2 that the short-hand norm was for the believers to:

1. **Believe** in Jesus's atoning and Lordship sacrifice.
2. **Repent** of your sins.
3. **Be baptized** in water by someone representing Jesus.
4. **Receive** the Holy Spirit.

A believer had to do his or her part at each step.

God the Father, Jesus and the Holy Spirit had their part to play as well – in a sense, their responsibility:

1. Jesus had to **die** for our sins.

2. God had to **exalt** Jesus to His right hand and give Him authority to **pour out** His Spirit.

3. Jesus had, through the agency of a representative, to **baptize** the believer in both water and the Spirit.

4. The Holy Spirit had to **fill**, pour upon, and surround the believer.

It would appear that in a normal transformation, all of these things would be done. What hasn't been mentioned until Acts 8 was the *"laying on of hands."* What does it mean? The "laying on of hands" is a remarkable sign of representation and transmission. First, the baptizer very much IS *representing* Jesus. When he lays hands on a believer, it is as if Jesus Himself is touching the person being baptized or healed. And through the intimate contact of flesh on flesh, the acceptance and the transmission of the Spirit is occurring. We could speculate that some of the Spirit on the baptizer is actually transferring itself to the believer.

In a very interesting encounter recorded in the Book of Numbers, God told Moses that He would, *"come down and speak with you there, and I will take of the Spirit who is upon you, and will put Him [or it] upon them; and they shall bear the burden of the people with you, so that you will not bear it all alone."* (Numbers 11:17). The *"them"* in this verse refers to the Seventy Elders chosen to help shepherd the rebellious flock of Israel. But our focus is on the transmission of the Spirit. Most interestingly, we see the outcome in Numbers 11:25, *"Then the Lord came down in the cloud and spoke to him; and He took of the Spirit who was upon him and placed Him upon the seventy elders. And when the Spirit rested upon them, they prophesied."* Hands were not laid upon them so far as we know, but the concept is similar. And we see an immediate sign that the Spirit was upon them: The Seventy *"prophesied."*

Exactly, how God transmits His Spirit is still a mystery to me, and of course it was a mystery in some degree to our forefathers. In follow-up verses in the 11th Chapter of Numbers, we see that the Spirit that was put on the Seventy was not Moses's spirit but God's Spirit: *"But two men had remained in the camp; the name of one was Eldad and the name of the other Medad. And the Spirit rested upon them (now they were among those who had been registered, but had not gone out to the tent), and they prophesied in the camp. So, a young man ran and told Moses and said, "Eldad and Medad are prophesying in the camp." Then Joshua the son of Nun, the attendant of Moses from his youth, said, "Moses, my lord, restrain them." But Moses said to him, "Are you jealous for my sake? Would that all the Lord's people were prophets, that the Lord would put **His** Spirit upon them!"* (Numbers 11:26-29).

We see the *"Laying on of Hands"* throughout the annals of ancient Israel. Touching was paramount to blessing and transmission. From at least Jacob onwards, fathers passed on blessings to their children through the laying on of hands. Jacob blessed his two grandsons, Ephraim and Manasseh by putting his hands on their heads.

In consecrating priests for service, hands were laid upon the Levites by the community, and the Levites in turn laid each of their hands up the head of a bull – one for a sin offering (their sins were symbolically bring transferred to the bull) and one for representing their whole giving over to the Lord. *"So you shall present the Levites before the tent of meeting. You shall also assemble the whole congregation of the sons of Israel, and present the Levites before the Lord; and the sons of Israel shall **lay their hands** on the Levite. Aaron then shall present the Levites before the Lord as a wave offering from the sons of Israel, that they may qualify to perform the service of the Lord. Now the Levites shall **lay their hands** on the heads of the bulls; then offer the one for a sin offering and the other for a burnt offering to the Lord, to make atonement for the Levites."* (Numbers 8:9-12).

For commissioning to a special service or office, hands were laid by one in authority. When Moses commissioned Joshua to take his place, we read, *"Then he **laid his hands** on him and commissioned him, just as the LORD had spoken through Moses."* Numbers 27:23.

Whether the Holy Spirit directly prompted John and Peter to lay hands on those who had already been baptized we do not know, but we do know that once they had laid hands on the Samaritan converts, they *"were receiving the Holy Spirit."*

Simon the Magician wanted the same authority that the apostles were demonstrating and offered to buy it. As in the case of Ananias and Sapphira, Peter once again appears to have received a Word of Knowledge. We will think on this more deeply as we move along. In the case of Simon, Peter has a clear insight into Simon's internal world. Peter replied, *"Your heart is not right before God. Therefore, repent of this wickedness of yours, and pray the Lord that, if possible, the intention of your heart may be forgiven you. For I see that you are in the gall of bitterness and in the bondage of iniquity."* (Acts 8:21-23).

Philip, an Angel and the Ethiopian

"...an angel of the Lord spoke to Philip saying, 'Get up and go south to the road that descends from Jerusalem to Gaza.'.... So, he got up and went; and there was an Ethiopian eunuch, a court official of Candace, queen of the Ethiopians, who was in charge of all her treasure; and he had come to Jerusalem to worship, and he was returning and sitting in his chariot, and was reading the prophet Isaiah. Then the Spirit said to Philip, 'Go up and join this chariot.' Philip ran up and heard him reading Isaiah the prophet, and said, "Do you understand what you are reading?' And he said, 'Well, how could I, unless someone guides me?'" (Acts 8:26-31).

God send Philip on a very specific mission along a road in the desert. In the process, the Gospel message goes out to a key figure in a country that adjoins Egypt west of the Nile. Philip was sent to engage one man, an Ethiopian eunuch. There is much in the story to catch. For one, eunuchs were excluded from the *Ekklesia* of the Lord by Jewish law: *"No man who is emasculated or has his male organ cut off shall enter the assembly of the Lord."* Yet, the Lord has sent Philip to this very man – a man of a different race, a different country and a man excluded from the assembly. We will see a similar breaking beyond the boundaries of Jewish norms in Chapter 10. And all of this for one man.

As my friend, Kit Mays, often says, "God is very efficient." And most loving. Like a parent, He cares about each one as much as He cares about the family. And God is a great strategic thinker. He can pick just the right person for us to meet. God picked this one Ethiopian for a special encounter and issued an assignment to Philip to go help him. We may not be transported, but God can give us a nudge or prompting in our spirit to send us on our way. The least nudge is so important to follow.

We also see in this account a stretching of the community's understanding of just how far reaching is Jesus's sacrifice. He is making those who cannot enter, fully able to enter. Fantastic. And, we learn a tad more about baptism and connecting to the Godhead.

The eunuch gains understanding of a key passage in the Book of Isaiah as Philip *"preaches Jesus,"* and apparently Philip's discourse included how to come into a vibrant relationship with the Godhead by baptism. It is a great scene. They come upon what must have been a small body of water. The Eunuch exclaims, *"Look! Water! What prevents me from being baptized?"*

Philip responds, *"'If you believe with all your heart, you may.' And he answered and said, 'I believe that Jesus Christ is the Son of God.'"* At that, the two get out of the chariot and go down into the water, and Philip baptizes him, no doubt laying hands on him that he would receive the Spirit. Then, most dramatically, the Spirit of the Lord snatched Philip away, and the Eunuch went on his way *"rejoicing."* We learn one of the questions normally asked as one is about to be baptized: *"Do you believe with all your heart that Jesus Christ is the Son of God?"* And we note that like those at Pentecost and in Samaria, there are clear signs that the Spirit has been given and received. Here, the Eunuch rejoices.

The final sentence of the chapter tells us that Philip finds himself in Azotus, one of the five principle cities of the Philistine people, and that he preaches the Gospel to all the cities in the vicinity until he comes to Caesarea on the Mediterranean coast, about thirty miles northwest of Samaria and thirty miles southwest of Nazareth.

Acts 9

What a remarkable chapter from our friend Luke. I know he had to be excited to tell the story of Paul's conversion since he discipled under Paul. And he waited all the way until Chapter 9 to mention it. Had we been writing, we might have put that up front to introduce the overall story through our own eyes since Luke's whole walk in the Spirit probably began with his introduction to Paul. Instead, Luke patiently waited until Paul's encounter with Jesus appeared chronologically. Luke is a good writer!

The Damascus Road

Paul's encounter with Jesus is similar to Moses's encounter with God at the burning bush. But instead of immediate commissioning, Paul has to depend on the very people he has been persecuting. Blinded, he has to be led by hand to the home of a man called Judas who is living in Damascus but is from Paul's hometown of Tarsus. And then wait. While praying there, Paul receives a vision of a man named Ananias coming to **"lay hands on"** that he might see.

Across town, Jesus also calls a Jesus disciple named Ananias in a vision much as God called the Prophet Samuel. Ananias replies, *"Yes, Lord,"* and is told to go *"lay hands on"* Paul. Then we have a back and forth between Jesus and Ananias as Ananias pushes back because of the harm Paul has inflicted on disciples in Jerusalem. Jesus gives him an emphatic command, *"Go!"* Jesus explains that Paul will be called to stand before Gentiles and Kings to proclaim the name of Jesus.

Healings and Raising the Dead

The *"laying on of hands"* was not just for the receipt of the Holy Spirit as an indwelling gift, but also for Saul to regain his sight. Since we have the healing/raising from the dead of Tabitha by Peter later in the chapter as well as the healing of Aeneas, we might have anticipated that Peter would have *"laid hands on"* them as well, but the text does not mention it. A Jewish man would not want to touch a dead person because it would have made him ritually unclean, so perhaps Peter would not have touched Tabitha. In the case of the paralyzed Aeneas, Peter could have laid hands on him, but Luke didn't record it. In Samaria, we saw that the laying on of hands had something to do with the transmission of the Holy Spirit. We also saw the laying on of hands in the investiture (the empowerment and equipping) of the Seven Hellenists for their ministerial role. Now we see that Saul is filled with the Spirit as well as healed of blindness through the laying on of hands. Encounters, visions, healing, empowering and Holy Spirit baptizing. The Spirit of God seems to be working overtime through the laying on of hands.

Luke takes great pains to show that the sequence involved in the receipt of the Spirit varies. That may be happening in verses 17 – 19 of Chapter 9, although it is not absolutely certain. Ananias lays hand on Saul and Saul's eyes open. It is not clear whether the Holy Spirit then falls upon Paul or not. But his next step is baptism. It is possible that the Holy Spirit did not fall upon him immediately when the laying on of hands occurred. It appears that the normal pattern would be for the Holy Spirit to come *DURING* baptism or immediately upon rising from the water (see Jesus's own baptism as the NORMAL pattern), but we have already seen that pattern broken in Samaria, i.e., disciples are baptized and then days later had hands laid on them for receipt of the Holy Spirit - apparently because they had not been baptized in the Name of the Holy Spirit but only in Jesus's name. The early church was finding its way. There was no "Discipleship for Dummies" handbook to use as the New Testament had not yet been written. In a way, Luke *IS* writing a pattern book for disciples as he moves through Acts.

Acts 10

Cornelius and Gentile Believers!

A huge turning point occurs as the Gospel spreads to the Gentiles. Here, Luke spotlights a new sequence of the gifting of the Holy Spirit as God breaks beyond religious boundaries. It also is a chapter chock-full of the supernatural: angel, trance and vision.

Peter would not have wanted to go to Cornelius (the centurion) and probably would have refused had it not been for the *"trance."* The word for trance in the Greek is *ekstasis*. We get the word *"ecstasy"* from that Greek word, and it describes what happens when a man *"by some sudden emotion is transported as it were out of himself, so that in this rapt condition, although he is awake, his mind is so drawn off from all surrounding objects and wholly fixed on things divine that he sees nothing but the forms and images lying within."* (Thayer and Smith, *"Ekstasis," The NAS New Testament Greek Lexicon,* 1999).

While Peter was praying, we have God throwing him into a trance, and Peter seeing clearly (though it took three times) that some things that he thought were unclean, were not. I am paying attention that the "Spirit of God" is speaking to Peter clearly as he contemplates the vision. A different Greek word, *horama,* is used for the vision or dream portion of Peter's encounter.

The fact that it took three times for Peter to be able to receive God's revelation is a great example of both the patience of God as well as how deeply engrained was Peter's childhood belief system. The Father of the Universe was dynamiting a crevice deep into Peter's belief system and gently adjusting Peter's internal beliefs. The fact that both a trance and a dream had to be used highlights one of the values of both visions and dreams. From God, they are a gentle mercy and an important help.

Obediently, Peter goes to Cornelius's house, and sums up Jesus's earthly ministry in four sentences: *"The word which He sent to the sons of Israel, preaching peace through Jesus Christ (He is Lord of all)— you yourselves know the thing which took place throughout all Judea, starting from Galilee, after the baptism which John proclaimed. You know of Jesus of Nazareth, how God anointed Him with the Holy Spirit and with power, and how He went about doing good and healing all who were oppressed by the devil, for God was with Him. We are witnesses of all the things He did both in the land of the Jews and in Jerusalem. They also put Him to death by hanging Him on a cross. God raised Him up on the third day and granted that He become visible...."* (Acts 10:36-40).

Peter then gave the invitation, *"through His name everyone who believes in Him receives forgiveness of sins,"* and suddenly, *"while Peter was still speaking these words, the Holy Spirit fell upon all those who were listening to the message."* (Acts 10:44).

Out of Normal Sequence

Here, the Holy Spirit was poured out *before* baptism, not after and during. And, no hands had been laid on them. It was "the gift of the Holy Spirit" - just like what had happened at Pentecost where they were speaking in "*glossa*," in "tongues." Amazed at this and almost pleading, Peter asks himself and those with him, *"Surely no one can refuse the water for these to be baptized who have received the Holy Spirit just as we did, can he?"* (Acts 10:47). *"And he ordered them to be baptized in the name of Jesus Christ."* (Acts 10:48).

The Twelve and those with them on the day of Pentecost had the same experience: the gift of the Holy Spirit fell upon them. A few years earlier they most likely had been baptized in John's baptism, but the Holy Spirit fell on them at Pentecost without being re-baptized into the name of Jesus and the Holy Spirit. Peter probably would have had a really hard time baptizing Cornelius if the normal sequence had not been altered unilaterally by God. We will see him defend his actions in Acts 11 when he returns to Jerusalem and clearly identifies what happened to Cornelius and his household as having been *"baptised with the Holy Spirit"* and having received the *"gift of the Holy Spirit."*

Acts 11

In Chapter 11, we get a repeat of the critical proof that the Gentiles were being brought into the Kingdom of God. It does seem amazing to me that Peter missed God's intent while Jesus ministered on earth, but clearly he did. This meant that this encounter with Cornelius was a huge thing for both Peter and the rest of the Jewish band of early believers. Hard, since the Gentiles were really viewed the way we would probably view Muslims or even worse, dogs. Peter repeats what Luke has already recorded in Acts 10:

"as I began to speak, the Holy Spirit fell upon them just as He did upon us at the beginning. And I remembered the word of the Lord, how He used to say, 'John baptized with water, but you will be baptized with the Holy Spirit.' Therefore, if God gave to them the same gift as He gave to us also after believing in the Lord Jesus Christ, who was I that I could stand in God's way?" (Acts 11:15-17).

Peter clearly connects what happened to Cornelius with the Baptism of the Holy Spirit that John the Baptist had prophesied *JESUS* would bring. It is abundantly clear that Jesus *Himself* is the one doing the baptizing as no one touches Cornelius and his household, nor are they being immersed in water. It is a God encounter, and Peter remembers that the very same manifestations happened to them on Pentecost. His retelling emphasizes that the Baptism in the Holy Spirit is a GIFT; it is not earned - something important to grasp.

Then we have Barnabas going up to Antioch to minister to the new believers. I am struck with Luke's description of Barnabas:

"for he was a good man, and full of the Holy Spirit and of faith. And considerable numbers were brought to the Lord." (Acts 11:24).

The word translated *"full"* in verse 24 is the Greek word, *plērēs*. The word means: *"full, i.e., filled up (as opposed to empty), full, i.e., complete, lacking nothing, perfect. It is used in various ways which include the condition of hollow vessels which have been filled, of surfaces covered in every part, and of the soul which is thoroughly permeated."* (Composite taken from Thayer's Greek Lexicon, Electronic Database).

This underscores the condition that God wants for every believer: a fully transformed nature. God wants us to be "filled" with the Holy Spirit so that we are thoroughly permeated, filled completely, lacking nothing of God, perfect in every way. A remarkable call and a remarkable transformation!

Finally, we catch a view of the activity of the Holy Spirit with a brother named Agabus who has the gift of Prophecy. He moves trans-locally (leaving Jerusalem to go to Antioch) to deliver a "warning" prophecy. His prophecy is not doctrinal but a foretelling of coming climate difficulty. When we run into a gift of the Holy Spirit, ask, "What is the nature and function of this gift in this particular setting?"

The passage allows us to place a date on the time that Barnabas was in Antioch as the text discloses that the predicted famine would occur during the reign of the Emperor Claudius. Claudius reigned from 41 to 54 AD, but scholars place the famine around 47 or 48 AD – about 15 years after Jesus's resurrection. This means the events in Acts 11 are earlier. We also see an early example of the Body of Christ mobilized to help on a trans-local basis.

Acts 12

The story of Peter in prison challenges us to gather together in times of crisis to pray. We already have seen this pattern in the church community after Jesus ascended. In Acts 8:14, we had Peter and John praying together for the believers in Samaria to receive the Holy Spirit. In Acts 6:4, the text says part of the function of the apostles was to devote themselves to prayer though we don't know for sure how this was done. In Acts 4:23-24, we have one of the most powerful moments of corporate prayer (which almost had to have been orchestrated by the Holy Spirit) where they "*of one accord*" lifted up their voices to God. This occurred after Peter's powerful testimony was delivered to the Jews earlier in Chapter 4. In Acts 3:1, we have Peter and John going up to the temple at the hour of prayer. I feel sure they went in to pray, but this seems a very different gathering for prayer than the type that occurred in Acts 4. In Acts 2:42, after Peter's amazing speech and the visitation of the Holy Spirit and the baptism of 3000 souls, it says the disciples *"continued steadfastly in prayer"* though we don't know exactly in what form. Finally, at the very beginning of Acts and prior to the pouring out of the Holy Spirit, we have Acts 1:14: *"they continued with one accord in prayer."*

My point is simply this - the early church community gathered in groups to pray - particularly when there was a crisis, and no doubt prayed separately as well. We often have set this aside (crisis-initiated corporate prayer times) partially because there was the danger of interfering with people's plans, but in retrospect, I believe we erred when we did so.

I remember when a newborn in our community was dangerously ill from a toxic baby formula, and our community not only came together for prayer but also corporately fasted. We felt that God intervened and, for certain, we saw the child survive and thrive. We have had several "called to prayer and fasting" times over the last forty years, not the least of which were for several of my grandchildren. Still, I think we have not taken enough advantage of corporate prayer.

There is a pattern in me that wants to avoid bothering people - a fear-based pattern. My faith and love are in tension with my underlying fear of disappointing or bothering others. These instances of corporate prayer call us to set aside our fears.

Acts 13

Barnabas and Paul's 1st Missionary Journey

It is probably 47 or 48 AD, approximately 15 years after Jesus's resurrection. From the very first verse of Chapter 13, we see men in the church at Antioch who had such clear giftings that they were called by those giftings – in this case, prophets and teachers. These two giftings immediately call to mind one of the earliest Christian documents that is not a part of scripture – an ancient document called the *Didache*. Certainly, it sheds a great deal of light on practices in the communities that the author addressed. The author covers the "how to" – how to baptize, how to observe the Lord's Supper, how to pray, how to live.

Apostles, Prophets and Teachers

The *Didache* goes on at some length concerning the apostles when they come into town, as well as how to relate to the teachers and prophets. All these men were functioning in particular spiritual vocations. But like a few evangelists, some were taking advantage of their supposed rights, and the Didache warns that they should not be hosted more than three days - *"If he remains three days, he is a false prophet...."* There were clear restrictions:

"11:4 Let every apostle who cometh unto you be received as the Lord.
11:5 He will remain one day, and if it be necessary, a second; but if he remain three days, he is a false prophet.
11:6 And let the apostle when departing take nothing but bread until he arrive at his resting-place; but if he ask for money, he is a false prophet.
11:7 And ye shall not tempt or dispute with any prophet who speaketh in the spirit; for every sin shall be forgiven, but this sin shall not be forgiven.

11:8 But not every one who speaketh in the spirit is a prophet, but he is so who hath the disposition of the Lord; by their dispositions they therefore shall be known, the false prophet and the prophet.

11:9 And every prophet who ordereth in the spirit that a table shall be laid, shall not eat of it himself, but if he do otherwise, he is a false prophet;

11:10 and every prophet who teacheth the truth, if he do not what he teacheth is a false prophet;

11:11 and every prophet who is approved and true, and ministering in the visible mystery of the Church, but who teacheth not others to do the things that he doth himself, shall not be judged of you, for with God lieth his judgment, for in this manner also did the ancient prophets.

11:12 But whoever shall say in the spirit, Give me money, or things of that kind, listen not to him; but if he tell you concerning others that are in need that ye should give unto them, let no one judge him." (Didache 11:4-12).

The author goes on to say that when you have prophets and teachers living as part of the community, they should be supported.

"13:1 But every true prophet who is willing to dwell among you is worthy of his meat,

13:2 likewise a true teacher is himself worthy of his meat, even as is a labourer.

13:3 Thou shalt, therefore, take the firstfruits of every produce of the wine-press and threshing-floor, of oxen and sheep, and shalt give it to the prophets, for they are your chief priests;

13:4 but if ye have not a prophet, give it unto the poor.

13:5 If thou makest a feast, take and give the firstfruits according to the commandment;

13:6 in like manner when thou openest a jar of wine or of oil, take the firstfruits and give it to the prophets;

13:7 take also the firstfruits of money, of clothes, and of every posses-sion, as it shall seem good unto thee, and give it according to the com-mandment." (Didache 13:1-7).

The Didache helps us see how Antioch might have viewed and treated *their* "prophets and teachers." But Luke's own record shows a more central focus: the activity of the Holy Spirit having nearly full sway in directing the community and individuals in the community.

"Now there were at Antioch, in the church that was there, prophets and teachers: Barnabas, and Simeon who was called Niger, and Lucius of Cyrene, and Manaen who had been brought up with Herod the tetrarch, and Saul. While they were ministering to the Lord and fasting, the Holy Spirit said, 'Set apart for Me Barnabas and Saul for the work to which I have called them.' Then, when they had fasted and prayed and laid their hands on them, they sent them away. So, being sent out by the Holy Spirit, they went down to Seleucia and from there they sailed to Cyprus." (Acts 13:1-4).

The picture I see is that those with similar gifts involving the mouth (prophecy and teaching) in the Antioch community were gathering as a group to worship God while at the same time fasting. In the midst of worship, one of the prophets delivers a directive Word to the group: *"set apart for me Barnabas and Saul for the work to which I have called them."* Then, other gifted brothers commission the two men by more fasting and prayer. Only when complete did they *"lay hands on them."* Getting a Word from God, fasting, praying, laying on hands to impart special grace as well as commission - we see the Holy Spirit on the move! A great example for us today.

Acts 14

Paul and Barnabus' determination to complete the mission on which God had sent them is remarkable. They faced serious opposition and danger. But the effects were salutary. Some received their words and became disciples! They had traversed perhaps 400 miles by the time they had arrived at the small village of Derbe where they finally turned around.

First Missionary Journey

Looking back years later, Paul writes to Timothy, his son in the faith, about the sad reality that many of the converts *"in Asia"* made during this time had deserted him. I think he refers in 2 Timothy 1:15 to a rift that Paul had encountered amongst the believers. He was attacked perhaps on doctrinal grounds. He doesn't amplify, and I feel sure over-states the magnitude *("everyone in the province of Asia has deserted me)."* Yet it is very sad when we think about his labors for those *"in Asia"* - brothers deserting brothers.

In Chapter 14:23, we see for the first time the recognition and appointment of certain older believers to leadership and governance in the emerging communities. This will occur in many of the clusters of believers that Paul and Barnabas will visit. Here, Luke calls these clusters of believers *"ekklesia"* in the Greek. Remember this is the word from which we get our word *"Church"* – an assembly with the underlying sense of those called out.

"Paul and Barnabas appointed elders (presbyteros) *for them in each church* (ekklesia) *and, with prayer and fasting, committed them to the Lord, in whom they had put their trust."* (Acts 14:23)

This recalls governing councils similar to the Jewish Sanhedrin in Jerusalem. In Luke 22:88, the Greek word *presbyterion* is used to refer to the Jewish Sanhedrin. Paul uses the same word in his first letter to Timothy: *"Do not neglect the spiritual gift within you, which was bestowed on you through prophetic utterance with the laying on of hands by the presbytery (presbyterion)."* (1 Timothy 4:14). The early communities were structured to some degree by trans-local brothers who themselves had been *"ordained."* The word *"ordained"* means simply *"one on whom hands have been laid."* Paul had been appointed and ordained to at least three functions himself.

We know from Church history that the word *presbyteros* later morphed into the Catholic word for *"priest."* But that is another story.

Appointing

Be alert to "appointing" as we read - how church communities are structured and how positions are filled. We want to pay particular attention because the structure of the early church slowly morphed into what might be called the historical Catholic structure. In Acts 14, we are at the very beginning of the morphing process, moving from a band of like-minded brothers and sisters loosely organized to a more formally structured community.

There are several Greek words that involve early church leadership. In no order, the first is *presbyteros,* which we see here in verse 23. This is the word we normally translate as *"Elder."* Then there is the Greek word *poimen* which was used for Jesus and which we translate as *"Shepherd"* and will meet functionally in Acts 20. There is the Greek word *episcopos* which we translate as *"Bishop"* and also will encounter in Acts 20 and in Titus 1:5-7 where the term for Elder and Bishop appear interchangeable. We also have the Greek words for evangelist, prophet and teacher. All of the ministries/offices had some directive role in the early church community. But here at the very beginning, we see Paul focused initially on the elders.

"For this reason I left you in Crete, that you would set in order what remains and appoint elders [presbyteros] in every city as I directed you, namely, if any man is above reproach, the husband of one wife, having children who believe, not accused of dissipation or rebellion. For the overseer [episcopos] must be above reproach as God's steward, not self-willed, not quick-tempered, not addicted to wine, not pugnacious, not fond of sordid gain," (Titus 1:5-7)

Since we know how fallible and human we all are – even after receiving the Spirit of God, we can reasonably wonder if inserting men into the community as protectors and guides was and is a mistake. It requires a lot of faith in God and the Spirit of God to imagine that men could be helpful in government. Think of John's declaration in 1st John 2, verse 20 and verse 27 where he says to the individual believer, *"You have an anointing from the Holy One, and you know all.... As for you, the anointing which you received from Him abides in you, and* **you have no need for anyone to teach you, but as His anointing teaches you about** *all things, and is true and is not a lie, and just as it has taught you, you abide in him."* So why would the individual need any outside help?

The problem is clearly stated in 1st John: *"These things I have written to you concerning those who are trying to deceive you."* One reason for these special offices (prophet, teacher, shepherd, elder, bishop) is because the Enemy is on the prowl. The primary function of a shepherd is to be sure the sheep are being fed wholesome food, to stand watch for wolves, and to bind up the wounded. Some oversight is clearly needed even though at the deepest level we must depend on the Holy Spirit to lead us into truth. Though each believer has the anointing of the Holy Spirit, there is always the danger of personal deception. There are other reasons, but those three are paramount.

Verse 23 of Chapter 14 again reveals some of the normal *appointing* process. We already have noticed how frequently investiture involves the laying on of hands. There is a long history of that sign being sacramental – sacramental in the sense that something is happening at a spiritual level that coincides with an outward and specific human act. We see this with Baptism. We see it in the Torah scriptures when the priest or high priest "lays hands" on the bull or the ox. There is both identification with the thing laid hands upon as well as a representation of God Himself in the form of the one laying on hands. It very much is as if Jesus is standing there, laying on *His* hands. By the absolute grace of God, the transmission of gifting that flows from the Godhead is, in fact, flowing. My hope is that anyone receiving baptism or the laying on of hands will grasp fully that reality.

Thus, in verse 23, we meet again the laying on of hands, prayer and fasting. Remember how the brothers acted when they sent out Barnabas and Paul in Acts 13:3? *"Then, when they had **fasted and prayed and laid their hands on them**, they sent them away."* So, being sent out by the Holy Spirit…

In Paul's letter to Timothy, we will find:

"Do not lay hands upon anyone too hastily...." (1ˢᵗ Timothy 5:22). *"... I remind you to kindle afresh the gift of God which is in you through the laying on of my hands, for God has not given us a spirit of timidity, but of power and love and discipline."* (2ⁿᵈ Timothy 1:6).

Acts 15

Controversy

A pivotal chapter, Chapter 15 gives a view of how the Holy Spirit works in the church community in the midst of controversy. We find "rubber meeting the road" expansion into Gentile territory and a further picture of governance and submission to authority. Over the years, I have referred back to Acts 15 many times for practical examples and direction.

The church is in full swing up in Antioch, filled with Gentiles as well as Jews, and the new Gentile converts are not being circumcised. Jewish brothers come up to teach the new converts and tell them they must be circumcised if they want to truly be saved. Barnabas and Paul appear to have gone ballistic at this direction, and the community sends them (along with a few others) down to Jerusalem to the *"apostles and elders"* to thrash out the question.

The Jerusalem Council

In Jerusalem, we see the *presbyteros* in Jerusalem serving along with the apostles as a governing council. There is not one person to go see (Peter, for example), but a group of people. On arrival, the whole church community as well as the apostles and elders receive them, and

Barnabas and Paul give their report to all - telling the amazing things occurring amongst the Gentiles.

The apostles and elders pull aside to consider the question of the new Gentile converts.

A great brouhaha then occurs with plenty of disputing. I am always impressed that discussion was allowed – there was an openness to what the Holy Spirit might say through any of these men who had been "appointed" to an office of leadership and invested presumably with the Holy Spirit gifting necessary for their office.

AFTER all the disputing, Peter arises and reminds those assembled of his experience with Cornelius. In the case of Cornelius and his household, the clear sign of acceptability to God through the Holy Spirit had fallen on them without circumcision, and they had received it just as the apostles and the 3,000 had received it on Pentecost. Why now would an additional yoke be appropriate? The reformer, Luther, no doubt was pleased with Peter's closing words, *"but we believe that through the grace of the Lord Jesus Christ we shall be saved, even as they."*

After Peter had finished speaking, those assembled let Paul and Barnabas weigh in on what had happened with the Gentiles.

We see James rise and sum up his view, bringing scripture forward, and saying it is his *"krino"* in the Greek, his *"judgment"* to bind on the Gentiles three things only: pollution from idols, no fornication and no food strangled and filled with blood. (See similarities to God's covenant with Noah in Genesis 9:4). It is because of this *"judgment"* and the sequence of events that many scholars view James as serving basically as the *episcopos (bishop)* of the Jerusalem church. A solo *episcopos* pattern will be evident in townships and provinces by the end of the first century.

This "James" is not James the son of Zebedee. Instead, he was a close relative of Jesus. He could have been a brother of the Lord or a cousin. Regarding his position in the Jerusalem church, toward the end of the 2nd century Clement of Alexandria recorded that, *"They say that Peter and James (the Great) and John the Apostle, after the ascension of our savior, as if also preferred by our Lord, strove not after honor, but chose James the Just as bishop of Jerusalem."*

I mention all of that because this is the first time we see in detail the early structure of the Jerusalem church and its initial sway and jurisdiction over other churches in other towns. It was a big deal for one community to put restrictions on another community of believers - in this case on the Gentile brothers in Antioch - but James felt that was the answer. This spotlights the early importance of the Jersualem church community which at the time contained many of the apostles. Yet clearly, as Luke so carefully records, other churches were growing in stature. By the end of the century or during the first forty years thereafter, we will see the church at Rome weighing in on issues of concern in Corinth.

"Then the apostles and elders, with the whole church, decided to choose some of their own men and send them to Antioch with Paul and Barnabas. They chose Judas and Silas, men who were leaders among the believers." (Acts 15:22). They sent them with a letter outlining the restrictions.

To me, the most important verse is verse 28, which is directly from the letter: *"It **seemed** good to the Holy Spirit and to us not to burden you with anything beyond the following...." "It **seemed** good to the Holy Spirit."* I have always been impressed with the great care that proof was given or certainty expressed when articulating what the Spirit of God was saying. *"It seemed good."* This is a humble way of stating their conclusion. Today, we must be careful not to fall into presumption. Men and women need to be ever so humble in their certainty of what both the Word says and what they feel the Spirit is saying. If this early Council was careful, so must we be.

There are one or two more things of interest to me as the chapter wraps up. In verse 32, we see that the two men chosen to take the letter have the gift of prophecy and deployed their gifting in Antioch, *"encouraging and strengthening the believers."* In verse 35, we see that the teaching and proclaiming function in Antioch was not a one- or two-man affair. Many taught and preached the word of the Lord. As it should be today.

We also see a subtle shift in the order between Barnabas and Paul. Up to and midway in Chapter 15, Luke orders the two with Barnabas first. After the Council and after verse 22, Paul comes first. Then we have the sad disagreement between the two men at the very end. After they split, Barnabas goes back to see the Cyrus believers while Paul takes Silas with him to Syria and Cilicia, *"strengthening the churches."*

I can say unequivocally that God did not want Barnabas and Paul to be at odds with one another. The Spirit of God is the Spirit of Unity – not division. Paul will address this problem head on in his letter to the Corinthian church. Different perspectives and disagreements will occur for a variety of reasons, and we must keep our hearts pure toward one another and be freed from the trap of entangling our identities with our relationships

In summary, Chapter 15 is one remarkable chapter.

Acts 16

Paul's Second Missionary Journey

Perhaps the book of Acts of the Apostles should be renamed, "Acts of the Holy Spirit," because throughout we have the continuous thread of the Holy Spirit showing up and manifesting God's presence in all sorts of ways. The recorded manifestations, visions, dreams and inner promptings do not appear to be isolated, but rather in the midst of the life of the emerging church and at the edges of the amazing proclamation that Jesus has come - there is a new life available to all who will respond to the evangelistic call.

In his book, *Acts, A New Vision of the People of God*, Professor Stevens reminds us that the language Luke employs to describe this "second" mission is quite different from the first. There is no recorded prophetic word from the Holy Spirit sending out a mission team. Rather, Paul appears to have simply gotten the idea. And then we have a disagreement about who will go. In the first mission, the people chosen to be deployed were specifically named through the operation of the Holy Spirit. But for the second, *Paul* "decides" not to take John Mark and ends up separating from Barnabas. Further, as they journey, Paul and Silas are like billiard balls from a destination point of view. They try to go one way, and the Spirit of God blocks them. They try to go another way and are blocked. Is Paul being willful, or is Luke simply recording that God is giving Paul more opportunity to try his wings?

Timothy on Board

Paul and Silas initially make their way cross country (as opposed to by sea on Paul's first journey), visiting many of the villages in which Paul and Barnabas had originally proclaimed the good news. Young brother

Timothy shows up in the narrative for the first time in Lystra. It really surprised me that Paul circumcised Timothy whose father was Greek. But Paul wanted to have Timothy accompany him. The circumcision shows how much Paul wanted to reach his fellow Jews as he removed any impediment in his entourage.

I've never been to Asia Minor nor Greece, but I have tried to get a sense of the terrain and vegetation as Paul and Silas journeyed north east through modern day Turkey. Amazingly, the Romans had constructed a good number of roads made of large stones sitting on two layers of subsurface stones throughout the region. Mile markers were set in place showing the distance to the next town. Most likely, Paul and Silas walked these roads as they traveresd their initial course. The following photo taken by Professor Stevens is of a section of a Roman road between Perga and Antioch-in-Pisidia. It gives a good feel of both the terrain and context one finds.

Courtesy of Gerald L. Stevens

Three things strike me as Paul revisits these cities. Rather than go to entirely new locations where he had not been stoned and beaten, he returns to the very places he had been hostilely received in order to strengthen the small bands of believers left behind and to give them more teaching about life, taking care to transmit the Jerusalem Council's edicts.

Second, the Holy Spirit *is* actively directing this journey. The text does not say whether this is by prophetic word, dream, vision or internal prompting, but the phrase, *"forbidden by the Holy Spirit to speak the word in Asia"* had to be more than an internal inclination. I assume it more likely that a clear prophetic word was given as they journeyed. We should note that God is entirely able to give us rather minute direction about what we do and where we are to go if only we are willing to listen.

In Troas, Paul has a vision of a man in Macedonia beckoning him. This is a double encouragement. It is always an encouragement to have God speak to us through a vision or dream, but this also suggests that some people were praying for help in Macedonia, and God heard their plea and used a vision as an effective way of rousing Paul to go even further from home, into a significantly different culture. Macedonia was on the other side of the Aegean Sea. Of course, Paul and Silas took this as a serious call and left *"immediately."* I've spent a good bit of time trying to grasp the linguistic meaning of vision and dream in the Greek. They are different, but closely related. Normally, the word we translate *"vision"* comes when one is awake. The mind is "seeing" something, but the person is awake. In a dream, we are asleep, and the screen of our mind "sees" during our sleep. Either way, God is breaking in. Often, God uses break-ins like this when there is emotional resistance to what God wants to reveal to us.

Luke On Board

As an aside, we also notice that the text changes the group's description in verse 10 from "they" to "we." Dr. Luke is now physically present with the group and will be reporting as an eyewitness. They immediately head from Troas to Macedonia by boat, landing near the inland town of Philippi.

Macedonia

Philippi was fairly prosperous because there was gold being mined nearby. The *Via Egnatia* also ran through Philippi, which meant it was on an important crossroads. Three different countries had governed the area over the preceding four centuries. 500 years earlier, settlers from the northern most of all the Aegean islands had settled there, calling their settlement Krenides, which means "the Springs" because water sources in the region were abundant. Philip II (father of Alexander the Great) of Macedon, the kingdom southwest of Krenides, took jurisdiction during his reign about 358 BC and brought in Macedonians to help protect the gold mines. The Greeks ruled for two hundred years, and then the Romans took over in 168 BC. The result: a very syncretic and mixed culture.

On their first Sabbath in town, Paul and Silas sought out where Jews might have been assembling for prayer. They looked specifically for a river or creek outside of town. Josephus in his *Jewish Antiquities* tells us that there was a policy in some Roman jurisdictions that *"as many men and women of the Jews as are willing so to do, may celebrate their Sabbaths, and perform their holy offices, according to Jewish laws; and may make their* proseuchae *[place of prayer] at the sea-side, according to the customs of their forefathers; and if any one, whether he be a magistrate or private person, hindereth them from so doing, he shall be liable to a fine, to be applied to the uses of the city."* (Josephus, AJ, Book 14, Chpt. 10, sect. 256).

You might wonder what running water and the Sabbath might have to do with one another. *Tashlich* may be the reason. *Tashlich* in Hebrew means "to cast," that is, to cast away one's sins *via* an ancient Jewish custom which is hinted at in Nehemiah 8:1. The process of "shaking off" dirt from one's clothes into a river is particularly associated with acts of repentance during Rosh Hashanah and Yom Kippur, but normally not done on the Sabbath.

There may have been so few Jews in the town that there was not a physical synagogue, though the term *proseuchae* can refer to both a place to gather or to a physical house of prayer. Like today, back then it might have taken ten men to have a *"minyan,"* a grouping sufficient for some Jewish religious activities. It is unclear how many Jews were in Philippi, but it had to be a small group since Luke only records women being present at the river.

Paul takes the opportunity to address the Jewish women gathered. A woman who specialized in purple dye named Lydia was deeply moved: *"the Lord opened her heart to respond to the things spoken by Paul."* Baptism surely must have been a part of what he shared, because she was baptized along with her household. This is very similar to the story of Cornelius and his household.

River Ganites outside Philippi

Days later and faced with a curious form of harassment by a slave girl possessed by an evil spirit, Paul casts out the demonic spirit of divination with a forceful verbal command: *"I command you in the name of Jesus Christ to come out of her."* What an encouragement to deal straight up with spiritual problems rather than psychology! It is the authority of Jesus at work here and the power of the Holy Spirit. Paul simply serves as an instrument.

We see a parallel in the later jail scene with Peter's experience earlier. Both times, people were praying when deliverance came. But we also see the intimate, sweet experience of prayer interspersed with hymns of praise. It is not incidental that the modifier is "praise." Paul and Silas were locked up in a crummy prison; they might have been singing songs of lament. But no, they were singing songs of praise to God.

In verse 30, we have the same question that the crowd on Pentecost asked, *"What must be done ... to be saved?"* Paul gives a very simple answer: *"Believe on the Lord Jesus, and you will be saved, you and your household."* We could go off here on the interesting parallel between Cornelius and Lydia: the power of the head of the household and the head's belief. Infant baptism will eventually emerge partially from that thought.

Once released, Paul and Silas went to the *"brothers,"* clearly including the ladies, and *"encouraged them."* This, too, is the work of the Holy Spirit in the midst of community. Encouragement comes in many ways including what we say and how we treat each other.

Acts 17

As Paul and his band moved into Greece in the preceding chapter, I have thought a good bit about Uganda and our community's mission there. Greece would have been a further cultural shift for Paul. The people would have been significantly different, and he no doubt felt like he had been dropped down on a different planet when contrasted with Judea. I notice significant cultural differences just going down into the state of Mississippi a hundred miles.

Note that Luke's descriptor of the group changes once again back to *"they"* from *"we."* It is possible that Dr. Luke stayed behind in Philippi while the rest of the group pressed on to the large Greek city of Thessalonica which lay on the seacoast about 100 miles southwest of Philippi. Unlike Philippi, we are certain that Thessalonica had a synagogue, perhaps the first the travelers had encountered since arriving in Greece.

As had been his pattern that is recalled in Romans 1:16, *"to the Jew first, and also to the Greek,"* Paul went first to the synagogue where his deep Jewish learning under the renowned Jewish scholar, Gamaliel, allowed Paul to both share and teach. He worked carefully out of the scriptures, showing how the Messiah was prophesied to suffer, die, and rise from the dead, and that Jesus was He.

Once again Paul and Silas meet internal opposition when what they had shared was believed by a good number of Jews. When you have people whose identity has been challenged (their associates are going over to Paul and Barnabas), we see how dangerous envy can be in a religious community. In this case, those riled actually pay some *"lewd fellows of the baser sort"* to help create a disturbance. This allows those enflamed with envy to bring a charge of sedition against Paul and Silas before the city fathers.

At first glance, you may be dismayed with what happened next. Since the authorities cannot find the missionary band, Paul and Silas' supporter, a Greek named Jason, who apparently had been housing the trio, agrees to put up bond and pledges to send Paul and Silas away. This has been the pattern up until now: when dangerous difficulty arises, Paul will move on – though we know from our Bibles that he will stay in touch by mail. So perhaps Jason's "pledge" was not a betrayal of trust.

The new believers send the band by night to a much smaller settlement 30 miles southwest of Thessalonica and about 22 miles west of the Aegean Sea. Surprisingly, this small town also has a synagogue. Scholars have speculated that the Jews, who were persecuted in almost every country, were generally few in number in Greece and might have avoided the larger cities and have chosen smaller villages in which to band together. We certainly saw that pattern in Poland before WWII where many small villages had significant Jewish populations. For whatever reason, small Berea was large enough to have a synagogue. Further, Luke contrasts the Jewish community there to the Thessalonica community: the Jew of Berea were *"more noble,"* more open to new information and well skilled in the scriptures where they could search *daily* whether what the missionaries were teaching jived with scripture.

Luke was impressed with what he heard about the Bereans and their stance as a community. I've always wanted to be like a Berean – well acquainted with the Word of God, familiar with the entire text, able to search out whether what I are hearing and doing aligns with the will of God. The text indicates many were won over in Berea, and here not just the women, but also a good number of men and Gentiles. I love the Bereans. But regardless of how great their attitude was, the Thessalonians sent Jews down to foment trouble. Paul leaves for Athens *"with all speed,"* but I think it is significant that both Silas and Timothy are left behind in Berea to deepen the work there.

It is not clear who went with Paul from Berea, if anyone. He most likely boarded a boat on the coast. Athens, too, was near the sea, but almost 200 miles south of Berea - near the southernmost tip of Greece.

It may have been easier to find a god in Athens than a man. The city had long been the glory of the Mediterranean, but it was full of idolatry. If you ever visit the remarkable replica of the original Parthenon in Nashville, TN and enter into the enormous inner room enclosed by the colonnade, you will see a replica of the goddess Athena's statue. The heavy sense of the occult lingers even in the replica. That is what Paul found when he entered this city that had at least a quarter of a million people. Perhaps that is why Paul, once in Athens, sends for Silas and Timothy to come quickly.

Of course, in spite of the occult odor, I am struck by the architectural wonder of the city when Paul arrived. It must have been breathtaking, but Luke makes no mention of that whatsoever. However, the way the Greeks built their cities and their democratic culture *was* important to Paul because the physical pattern of their cities allowed him to openly address the overwhelmingly Gentile population in the Agora, a large, open market and civic space where people gathered freely, and anyone could speak.

Like the Romans who later copied them, the Greeks built carefully symmetrical buildings. But unlike the Romans, the Greeks worried little about the relationship of buildings one to another. The result was a hodge-podge. There were random open spaces between many of the buildings, and commercial and retail activities often occurred in the residual areas.

Paul continues his practice of going to the Jews first, but I suspect he was in the large Agora soon after arriving. There, he found an entirely different audience from the Jews - a people who believed in gods but not the true God. This meant Paul had to shift his approach, and Luke gives us a near complete recall of his preaching in Athens in Chapter 17. It moves me – particularly verses 26 through 28: *"and He made from one man every nation of mankind to live on the face of the earth, having determined their appointed times and the boundaries of their habitation, that they would seek God, if perhaps they might grope for Him and find Him, though He is not far from each one of us.* **For in Him we live and move and having our being,** *as even some of your own poets have said, "For we also are His children."*

Acts 18

In Chapter 18, *"Paul left Athens and went to Corinth."* Corinth was due west about 50 miles – a strenuous two day journey. No doubt, he hugged the coast, passing over the location of a future canal which woud tie the two separated bodies of water together. In Paul's day, shipments were actually rolled on carts from one body of water to the other.

In Corinth, Paul meets two friends that remain dear to him the rest of his relatively short life: Aquila and Priscilla. Aquila is definitely a Jew, and it is likely that Priscilla is as well. Verses 2 and 12 give us an ability to calculate roughly the dates Paul was in Corinth. Claudius, of course, had been Emperor when Aquila had to leave Rome because Claudius had forced every Jew to be expulsed by emperial edict. Plus, during Paul's 18 months in Corinth, he was brought before Gallio, the procon-sul of Achaia (Greece). Claudius' reign and Gallio's term tighten the date to around 50 or 51 A.D. – approximately 17 or 18 years after Jesus's resurrection. Paul at this point is perhaps forty-five years of age.

Indicative of the frequent ethnic and religious aversion to the Chosen People, the Jews had now been expelled from Rome three times. The first time was over 130 years before Jesus's birth. In 59 BC, Cicero criticized the Jews for being too influential in public assembles and referred to them as a race *"born to be slaves."* In 39 BC, anti-Jewish riots erupted in Alexandria and countless Jews were killed. Lastly, they were expelled again from Rome only 30 years before Claudius' expels them again. Jewish stereotyping is nothing new, and we see that in Gallio's response to the Jews when they bring charges against Paul.

This heavy anti-Semitism surely affected Paul's reception everywhere that he journeyed. For the Jews, they were hypersensitive to anything that might provoke persecution. For the Gentiles, the Jews simply were held in outright contempt. This animosity and hypersensitivity makes Paul's boldness all the more remarkable.

Aquila originally was from Pontus in what is now eastern Turkey. Earlier, Pontus had been a Greek Colony. Surprisingly, it was just east of Bithynia, a place that the Holy Spirit had prevented Paul from entering. Aquila had moved a very long way from his homeland all the way to Rome, almost undoubtedly via the sea. Then, persecution in Rome drove him to Corinth. He was trained in tent making, and tent making was a good business in Corinth because many goods were shipped to Corinth and then taken overland to Cenchreae (which Paul had just visited). The shippers apparently used tent material in various ways.

Initially, Paul works to support himself as a tentmaker and again teaches in of one of the local synagogues on Saturdays. I am assuming that there were multiple synagogues in Corinth because, like Athens, it was a big city. But unlike an Athens steeped in Greek philosophy, Corinth was an international trade port and shipping center. Like similar trade centers related to the sea, it was a wicked city for lack of a better word. I am reminded of Marseilles in France that still retains a similar character and reputation. Those working on the ships were from all over the Mediterranean and totally transient. One found a polyglot of languages and cultures. And we can assume the influence of Rome was stronger in Corinth than the other cities Paul had visited.

In verse 5, Silas and Timothy arrive. Because of Acts 17:16, I had assumed that they would have come down from Berea to meet Paul in Athens and would have accompanied him on to Cenchreae and Corinth, but apparently, they stayed for a season in Berea. Their arrival allows Paul to completely devote himself to ministry. It is likely that Timothy and/or Silas worked to support Paul's activities in Corinth.

In verse 6, it would appear that Paul had shifted his ministry focus to the Gentiles, but only two verses later we see that Crispus, leader of the synagogue, has become a believer along with a Gentile neighbor who lived beside the synagogue. Many were believing.

Then we have the Lord coming to Paul in a "night vision" – a night vision that, in fact, may have been a dream. The message reminds me of God speaking to Joshua as they begin to enter the Promised Land. This message that Corinth will be an important community of believers causes Paul to settle there for 18 months. Corinth's strategic location – somewhat in the center of the Empire and also on all the converging trade routes is a wonderful spot to sow the seed of the Gospel because the message can go great distances quickly.

During Paul's 18 month sojourn, some of the Jews accuse him before the Proconsul, Gallio. We see a good bit of anti-Jewish sentiment in the way these Jews are received by the Proconsul. I always have the feeling that the Romans viewed the Jews as dogs. Certainly, Gallio treated the Jew, Sosthenes, poorly.

The latter part of the chapter takes Paul back to Antioch by sea via Ephesus and Caesarea. Aquila and Priscilla accompany him as far as Ephesus. *"When they* [the Ephesians] *asked him to spend more time with them, he declined. But as he left, he promised, "I will come back if it is God's will."* (Acts 18:20-21).

Paul's response is noteworthy. His mantra has become, "Do what God wants you to do." After heading out on his own several times and having the Spirit of God thwart his actions, he very much wants his only guide to be the will of God. Many of us want the same, but wanting and possessing are different things. We hope to do the will of God, but fallable as we are, we cannot always be certain our willfulness is not in charge. Paul sets sail from Ephesus to Caesarea, then on to Jersualem and eventually back to Antioch.

Paul's Third Missionary Journey

Before we know it, Paul is off once again on what we call his third missionary journey. Thinking about the time line, it appears he has done all of this extensive traveling in a span of nine years from the years 47 AD to 56 AD Some sources have him pushing off on his first journey in the year 47 AD, spending 48 AD on his first journey, attending the Jerusalem Council in 49 AD and departing on the second missionary journey late in that same year. The *Blue Letter Bible* commentary assumes that he takes over a year to get up to Troas on the second journey, then he stays in Greece all of 51 and 52 AD - putting him back in Antioch to leave on his third journey in 53 AD. On this last missionary journey, he will be gone three years. At this point, he would be approximately 48 years of age – heading off on a journey of over 3,300 miles!

I can't help thinking about my friend, Steve Happ, the Uganda mission and all of Steve's constant travel activity. And our friend, Medad Birungi, who seems to be always on the road. It is easy to discount the challenges if you are not the one traveling. Particularly on foot or in a modestly equipped sailing vessel.

The chapter ends with a new character introduced - Apollos, a Jew from Alexandria, one of the most important cities in the Roman Empire. He has come to Ephesus and is *"mighty in the scriptures."* I love that. May it be so for all of us! He knew something about Jesus but apparently had not been discipled in depth. My guess is that he had not encountered the Holy Spirit in a direct and demonstrative way.

Pricilla and Aquila take him aside privately to teach him, rather than issue some type of public reproof. God's nature of graciousness shines forth in their approach.

Acts 19

Ephesus and the Lacking Disciples

An important chapter for me for over forty years because Acts 19 gives us additional nuances about the spiritual doorway one enters as a disciple. Paul has made his way back to Ephesus and encounters disciples of some sort. It is a bit hard to tell whether they know about Jesus or not, but they are clearly disciples from Paul's point of view. My guess is that they are Jewish disciples – Jews in training. Perhaps they are disciples originally taught by Apollos when he was earlier in Ephesus (see Chapter 18), preaching but not knowing of the fullness of God's plan. They are familiar with John the Baptist's ministry even though over twenty years have passed since John's death. They are trying to be faithful to God and have repented of their sins and been baptized in water.

Paul must not have sensed the energizing activity and aroma of God's Spirit working within them and asks point blank, *"Have you received the Holy Spirit since you believed?"* The fact that Paul says, *"since you believed"* raises the question, "In what did they believe?" Jesus? Perhaps they have heard that Jesus was a good man who also ministered during the time of John. The next verse (19:4) suggests that they should have believed on Jesus since John pointed to Him. But Paul's focus here is on the Spirit of God - the Promise that Jesus ushered into the world.

Paul's 3rd Missionary Journey

Verses 5 and 6 bring us to the pivotal point. Paul baptizes them once again in water, but this time he baptizes (immerses) them in or into *"the name of Jesus."* (Note that this is the same "formula" used in Acts 8:16 with the same result). What does this mean: *"the name of Jesus?"* There are two possibilities that I can see. He either means that he, as the baptizer, is baptizing them as if Jesus Himself was baptizing them (in other words, Paul stands as Jesus's representative, and is, as an anointed believer, Jesus's hands on earth). But it could also mean that he is baptizing these disciples "into" Jesus's identity. We know from Paul's letter to the Romans that Paul clearly identified baptism with the death, burial and resurrection of Jesus. In this case, Paul is affecting an outward act that places them "into" Jesus in a spiritual way.

But, there is a problem. When they come up from the water, Paul does not see any manifestation of the Holy Spirit. No tongues, no praise, nothing to indicate that they have *"received power from on high,"* (Jesus's words to His disciples in Acts 1). It certainly appears from Acts 19:6 that Paul lays hands on them AFTER the baptism in water and undoubtedly prayed that they might receive the Holy Spirit. This action causes these disciples to *"speak in tongues as well as prophesy."*

Hilary of Poitiers, a marvelous bishop of the fourth century, wrote the first fully extant Latin commentary on the Gospel of Matthew approximately 25 years after the Council of Nicaea. While commenting on verse 13 of Matthew, Chapter 19, which deals with Jesus *"placing His hands on them* [little children] *and praying for them,"* Hilary is reminded of the Gift of the Holy Spirit. He writes, *"Now the gift and the offering of the Holy Spirit through the laying-on of hands and prayer are bestowed on the pagans because the works of the Law are ended."* (*On Matthew*, Hilary of Poitiers, The Fathers of the Church, p. 202). His words summarize Paul's sequence, undoubtedly by then part of the baptismal sacrament, where the *"gift of the Holy Spirit"* is given through the laying on of hands and prayer.

Verse (19:6) is a critical verse to the folks we call Pentecostal because it stands as proof that there are TWO baptisms, the *"baptism in water"* and the *"baptism in the Holy Spirit."* In Hebrews 6:1-2, we will encounter the writer outlining the foundational doctrines of the Christian faith which include six foundation stones: the essential need for *"repentance from dead works and faith toward God, of the doctrine of baptisms* (note plural) *and the laying on of hands and the resurrection of the dead and of eternal judgment."* Of course, John promised the dual baptism as we saw in Luke 3:16.

Throughout his account, Luke is focusing on these foundation elements: how critical they are and how they function at the beginning of a believer's life. They are "normal" to the beginning of a Christian's walk, yet today, I fear many people who believe in Jesus have not really received the indwelling Spirit so anticipated by the early believers. Just as Phillip and Paul struggled with this initiation zone as they tried to implement a sequence of events that gave each new believer what he or she needed, we see how hard this was to get right. Some would say God is in the details; I would say I still don't fully understand what is ALWAYS and absolutely required. We have seen that God is sovereign, compassionate and not bound by human law.

My conclusion is that we should do everything for the new believer that could possibly help them be fully released into God's arms. The early Church soon developed required preparatory teaching so that initiates would have a deep understanding of what was ahead of them once they were "baptized." Paul certainly wanted to do his part. And, of course, we should as well.

One of the results of these two experiences (Samaria and Ephesus) is that "normal" procedure at baptism involved baptizing people "into the name of the Father, and the Son and the Holy Spirit." The baptizer also "lays hands on" the one being baptized and prays. In ancient liturgy, the one being baptized also is anointed with oil, which clearly represents the Holy Spirit. Everything possible is done to avoid the Ephesus disciples' problem. One wants a full transmission and experience of God's Spirit at the very beginning. And, there is no harm in asking that hands be laid on a disciple with prayer after baptism if the internal energy and outward manifestation has not been present in the believer's life.

I will restrict myself to only three other comments. First, Paul was there in Ephesus at least two years. His later letter to the Ephesians is in truly exalted language to a people he intimately trained and loved deeply.

Second, Luke uses a very ancient term for the Christian faith in this chapter: *"the Way."* (See verse 9). In Greek, the word is *"Hodos,"* and it could be that today people would call us *Hodosians* as opposed to Christians if this terminology had stuck. *Hodos* refers to a traveler's way - the road on which he journeys. It is frequently used in the New

Testament (100 times) and most often refers to the road or path one is taking. Luke repeats the words of Isaiah in Luke 3:4: *"Make ready the Way of the Lord, make His paths straight."*

I assume the term, if it were a formal term, would be used as a shorthand for that very thing: the Way of the Lord. If you were a believer, you were walking in the Way of the Lord. You would be, in a sense, a member of the Way. That's the way I would like to walk. Let us be members of the *Hodos*!

Third, we have the remarkable energy of the Lord being manifested through handkerchiefs. This testifies to the amazing power of God, but I have to confess all I can think about is the TV evangelists pushing handkerchiefs for profit. Faith in God IS a remarkable and powerful thing just as Jesus point out. (See Luke 17:6).

Acts 20

"...he was hurrying to be in Jerusalem, if possible, on the day of Pentecost.

"From Miletus he sent to Ephesus and called to him the elders of the church. And when they had come to him, he said to them,

"'You yourselves know, from the first day that I set foot in Asia, how I was with you the whole time, serving the Lord with all humility and with tears and with trials which came upon me through the plots of the Jews; how I did not shrink from declaring to you anything that was profitable, and teaching you publicly and from house to house, solemnly testifying to both Jews and Greeks of repentance toward God and faith in our Lord Jesus Christ. And now, behold, bound by the Spirit, I am on my way to Jerusalem, not knowing what will happen to me there, except that the Holy Spirit solemnly testifies to me in every city, saying that bonds and afflictions await me. But I do not consider my life of any account as

dear to myself, so that I may finish my course and the ministry which I received from the Lord Jesus, to testify solemnly of the gospel of the grace of God.

"'And now, behold, I know that all of you, among whom I went about preaching the kingdom, will no longer see my face. Therefore, I testify to you this day that I am innocent of the blood of all men. For I did not shrink from declaring to you the whole purpose of God. Be on guard for yourselves and for all the flock, among which the Holy Spirit has made you overseers, to shepherd the church of God which He purchased with His own blood. I know that after my departure savage wolves will come in among you, not sparing the flock; and from among your own selves men will arise, speaking perverse things, to draw away the disciples after them. Therefore be on the alert, remembering that night and day for a period of three years I did not cease to admonish each one with tears. And now I commend you to God and to the word of His grace, which is able to build you up and to give you the inheritance among all those who are sanctified. I have coveted no one's silver or gold or clothes. You yourselves know that these hands ministered to my own needs and to the men who were with me. In everything I showed you that by working hard in this manner you must help the weak and remember the words of the Lord Jesus, that He Himself said, 'It is more blessed to give than to receive.'"

"When he had said these things, he knelt down and prayed with them all. And they began to weep aloud and embraced Paul, and repeatedly kissed him, grieving especially over the word which he had spoken, that they would not see his face again. And they were accompanying him to the ship." (Acts 20:16-38).

This is an extraordinary wrap up of Paul's life to this point.

Paul had retraced much of his earlier journey, and his missionary band has grown extensively. But something happened to him in the Spirit.

He felt *"bound by the Spirit"* to go to Jerusalem to arrive by Pentecost. You can sense his urgency in verse 22. This could be a sign of Paul's obstinacy (see Gerald L. Stevens' book on Acts), but he says is going no matter what because the Spirit of God has convicted him to do so. To me, this is a great example of both obedience and confidence, no matter what hardships may befall him.

Really, it appears Paul will do anything for God and for the people to whom God has sent him. He is "all out" for God. I can see how dear he would be to the Ephesians and others in that vicinity and vice versa. He has worked with his hands to support himself and those with him so that he might minister to those in the region. He is a true gift.

Verse 20: He was straight out with them, i.e., he told them what was what. In other words, he was bold (didn't shrink back), and told them what he thought God wanted them to hear. This actually is marvelous to me because I know I suffer from the opposite as do many others: often paralyzed by the fear of hurting someone's feelings or being rejected, I hold back things I believe are true and helpful from those close to me as well as far off. It takes a complete sellout to be as bold as Paul. I hope to be more straightforward, and I hope others will be with me.

Verse 21: Paul sums up his gospel in one sentence: Repentance toward God and faith in the Lord Jesus, the Anointed One.

Verse 23: In Macedonia, the Holy Spirit has been speaking to him every step of the way that things will be difficult. Reading between the lines, this means practically one of two things: either Paul has been dreaming in every city that trouble is ahead, or a brother or sister in every city has had a "Word of Knowledge" or a "Prophecy" that trouble is ahead and shared it with Paul. Given the language, I think the latter.

Verse 25: An even tighter summary of his gospel which coincides with summaries of Jesus's message as He went about Judea: *"preaching the Kingdom,"* the Kingdom of God.

Verses 28-31: *"Be on guard for yourselves and for all the flock, among which the Holy Spirit has made you overseers, to shepherd the church of God which He purchased with His own blood. I know that after my departure savage wolves will come in among you, not sparing the flock; and from among your own selves men will arise, speaking perverse things, to draw away the disciples after them. Therefore be on the alert, remembering that night and day for a period of three years I did not cease to admonish each one with tears."*

These are very important verses for me. They give us functional insight into a group within the church who serve as elders. We saw the Greek word *presbyteros* (elder) earlier and talked about it. Here Paul outlines the function of an elder while expanding on two other key protective functions within the church communities: shepherds and bishops (overseers). All three words show up describing the task of the *presbyteros* as outlined below:

1. Be on guard for themselves as well as the entire flock under their charge. Watch out for spiritual danger to yourself and those with whom you walk.

2. Shepherd those called out to God (i.e., shepherd the church). This implies leading, caring and protecting).

3. You can be sure trouble will arise internal to the church communities – some even from the ranks of the elders: wolves will arise who want to destroy and consume the members of the Body. They will speak things totally wrong and perverse, and their intent will be to draw people away to themselves rather than to God. I can say from excruciating experience that this has happened several times in my

own experience, and it is absolutely amazing how difficult the situations can be.

4. Be on the alert. The *presbyteros* must really be on guard. Paul begins with that thought in verse 28 and ends with it in verse 31.

Verses 33-34: Paul worked with his hands and asked no one for help. Quite an example to challenge our activities today.

Verses 36-38: Extremely tender verses that show the essence of what God builds: extremely tight and tender relationships oozing love. It is hard to find words to express the tenderness of his farewell.

"Be on guard for yourselves and for all the flock, among which the Holy Spirit has made you overseers, to shepherd the church of God which He purchased with His own blood." (Acts 20:28).

Remember, Paul is addressing the *presbyteros* but using two additional modifiers to describe their function. Earlier, we have seen Luke shed light on some of the key directive roles in churches. Initially, he started out emphasizing the role of apostle. Then, we saw the prophets and teachers functioning in Antioch. Next, Paul establishes *"elders"* in the churches. We saw the emphasis on apostles and elders at the Jerusalem Council. Throughout, we see Paul's function as apostle moving trans-locally to first establish believers, and after believers are established, we see him helping form functioning church communities.

In Acts 20, after three missionary journeys spanning eleven years, we see him call the *"elders"* from the churches (plural) down to Miletus to give this special talk. Then, we come upon verse 28. I am laboring with this because of several reflections.

First, there are three specific functions mentioned here with these "elders:" *being wise old men* (elders), *shepherding* and *overseeing*. These are characteristics that may overlap, but if you think about it, you will see that they are distinctively different.

Now I want to pull in Ephesians 4:11: *"And He gave some as apostles, and some as prophets, and some as evangelists, and some as pastors and teachers,"*

This is from Paul's glorious letter to his beloved Ephesians, the very group from which he has called elders down to Melitus. In Paul's letter, he talks about certain gifts given by God to build up the Church. We see in the Ephesians' passage men and women being given as gifts to the church plus their general functions: apostles, prophets, evangelists, shepherds and teachers. This list has often been called the fivefold ministry because there are five terms in the Greek. Interestingly, *presbyteros* is not amongst them and neither is *episkopos (overseer)*, With Paul's great emphasis on setting elders in place in every city, you could rightly wonder why.

I probably am not qualified to answer that question, but I do want to emphasize that the Church is in transition and Luke is recording as accurately as he can what is happening. If we fast-forward 75 years, we will see further change. Paul, Peter and John will address some of the change in the internal world of the Church doctrinally in their letters. In other words, they will try to bring forward both God's fundamental intention and direction in the Church, the Body of our Lord Jesus.

We want our brains on alert.

Acts 21

Rocketing to Jerusalem

Paul is headed like a rocket toward Jerusalem in Acts 21, and no one can stop him. But there are sweet moments along the way, ending in a similar fashion to his departure from Miletus. After they had stayed in the port of Tyre a full week, we read:

"When our days there were ended, we left and started on our journey, while they all, with wives and children, escorted us until we were out of the city. After kneeling down on the beach and praying, we said farewell to one another." (Acts 21:5)

These tender moments are made all the more special by the natural response of kneeling and praying together. The brothers and sisters entrusted both Paul and his band to the Grace of God. What is it that keeps us in America in the early part of this new century from getting on our knees more frequently? Certainly, this is a terrific example for today.

Chapter 21 is full of prophetic overtones; the prophets in the various communities continue the same refrain: *"Trouble awaits you in Jerusalem."* Paul remarkably ignores what seems to be a part of the refrain: *"Don't go."* I think this emphasizes one of two things: either Paul feels his personal revelation to go to Jerusalem cancels out what others feel the Spirit is saying – that is, that he must be obedient to what he himself has received in the Spirit, regardless of what others are saying, or he realizes that he is dealing with human beings who frequently mix their emotions with their interpretation of what the Spirit of God may be saying to them. Either way, Paul's reaction is important. Difficulty does not deter him. My friend, Dr. Gerald Stevens, feels this could be another occurrence of Paul's willfulness: even when the Holy Spirit is active, we find apostolic resistance. But, my thought is that Paul may be in the same position Jesus was in on HIS way to Jerusalem. Going, in spite of the certain outcome.

Chapter 21 also contains Paul's remarkable visit to Philip, our Chapter 8 evangelist who was one of the original seven Deacons in the Jerusalem church - a man who has experienced first-hand amazing manifestations of the Spirit of God. We learn that he has four prophetically gifted daughters. That is a LOT of prophetic gifting in one household. Like Anna in the temple at Jesus's dedication, women are in the list of the five ministries.

Finally, we have an amazing demonstration of the modern-day prophet in the mid-first century. The prophet Agabus appears to have been from Antioch. He had been functioning in a prophetic trans-local role in the universal Church for some time. We met him back in Chapter 11 when Agabus predicted famine. He reminds me so much of Jeremiah as God calls Jeremiah to do physical things to express what God is saying. (See Jeremiah 13 for an example). Agabus binds himself in front of Paul to foretell what will happen in Jerusalem. It is very dramatic.

In Acts 21:18, we return to the theme of how the churches are structured and how they are changing. This time, we see Paul coming to *"James and the elders."* James is clearly functioning in the role of what we would call the modern day bishop, that is as the overseer of the Jerusalem church. Of course, we saw this to some degree at the Jerusalem Council in Chapter 15. And I have to assume that the Holy Spirit is actually morphing how things operate. There may be two reasons. First, it could be God's intention in all places and all times. Second, it may simply be because of who is present and what giftings they have individually received from God. Think about that.

The next part is interesting. *"They"* tell Paul how excited they are about his ministry. They warn, however, that there are now thousands of Jewish believers in the city and they fear rumors about what Paul has been doing abroad will cause disruption unless he can clearly show himself to be a Jew and take advantage of the Jewish ritual of purification along with four others who need it.

This is remarkable request. It reminds me of having Timothy circumcised *after* having worked through the acceptance of Gentiles and Peter's vision on the rooftop. The *"they"* appears to be James and the elders. Most amazing to me, Paul does exactly as they suggest. I cannot believe that he doesn't have deep questions about what they ask him to do, but his deep devotion to peace (which is, in fact, a deep devotion to God's very character) causes him to submit. Paul had to shave his head, and the ritual itself took seven days. But in spite of it, the Jews are in a total uproar. Paul is nearly killed, but he persuades the Roman soldiers to intervene, and we leave Chapter 21 with Paul about to address his detractors.

Acts 22

Such an aversion to Gentiles and what an obsession with identity! For me, that sums up what we see in the "devout" Jews of Jerusalem. Paul's testifies in a simple, straightforward manner about his strict training in Judaism as a young man, his life-changing "God Encounter" and his resulting mission to the Gentiles. I thought that surely the devout ones who served God would be able to receive Paul's story, but no, once he mentions the evil word, "Gentiles," the crowd goes crazy.

This calls to mind two quotes from Richard Rohr's book, *Things Hidden – Scripture as Spirituality*:

"Our unconverted and natural egocentricity uses religion for the purposes of gaining self-respect. If you want to hate somebody, want to be vicious or vengeful or cruel or vindictive, I can tell you a way to do it without feeling an ounce of guilt: Do it for religious reasons!"

"Our 'belonging system,' instead of any good news for the world, is not. In any kind of 'exclusive election,' the 'chosen' do not see their experience as a gift for others, but merely a gift for themselves. We end up with a very smug and self-satisfied religion."

Surely, Rohr's observations fit the remarkable violent outburst of the *"pious ones"* in Acts 22 who are ready to tear Paul limb from limb for simply suggesting that Gentiles could be a target of God's affection. It should be readily apparent that these "Covenant People" know little of the Old Testament scripture where God's heart for the Gentiles is clearly revealed through the prophets. (For example, see Hosea 2:23). But rather than hearing with both ears, they hear only the part about themselves and their own chosen group.

Emphasizing group identity as the most essential thing remains a dangerous trap for thousands of Christian denominations and their splinter groups that walk the earth today. We might think we would never act like the Jerusalem Jews so intent on racial and doctrinal purity, but there are plenty of tragic examples in recent history to prove otherwise.

When we focus too much on concrete behaviors and beliefs – this is "right," this is "wrong," "I am right, you are wrong," we suggest that we have God figured out. This posture endangers everyone - including us.

We end Chapter 22 with this remarkable observation from St. Symeon, the "New" Theologian from around the year 1000:

"What is this awesome mystery that is taking place within me? I can find no words to express it; my poor hand is unable to capture it in describing the praise and glory that belong to the One who is above all praise, who transcends every word.... My intellect sees what has happened, but cannot explain it. It can see, and wishes to explain, but can find no word that will suffice, for what it sees is invisible and entirely formless, simple, completely uncompounded, unbounded in its awesome greatness. What I have seen is totality recapitulated as one - received not in essence but by participation. Just as if you lit a flame from a flame, it is the whole flame you receive."

Our Jewish brothers in Jerusalem were locked in total certainty that they had God figured out and also were entirely dependent on having their identity maintained as it had previously developed. There was no place for "unknowing" and uncertainty. Symeon's reflection recalls that being near God brings us to mystery and wonder and what earlier believers have called the great *Cloud of Unknowing*. It is hard to get sucked into Group Think when we are in the cloud of mystery, particularly when the very essence of God is compassion, kindness and love.

Acts 23

People in groups, heavily attached to their group identity, can be extremely dangerous when their identity is threatened. When our identity is threatened, all of us are dangerous. The fervently religious Jews, wrapped in their different denominational mindsets (Pharisees, Saducees, etc), have their very Law challenged in so many ways by Paul's simple allegiance to God that they show themselves capable of murder in Chapter 23.

The initial scene is chaotic. The Roman commander had arranged the meeting that begins in verse one. But, the language is a bit confusing. It appears that Paul is not within the temple area, but that may not be the case. It certainly doesn't seem like the meeting is before the Sanhedrin Council of 70 men. It seems to be an even larger meeting where many, if not most, of the Jewish Council are present but along with many others. This may be why Paul does not recognize the Chief Priest by his position in the room, and makes the mistake of rebuking the Chief Priest when he orders Paul struck for simply saying that Paul had lived all of his life *"with a perfectly good conscience before God."* That really offended the Chief Priest!

Things quickly deteriorated, and Paul saw that he needed to shift his thrust or face being torn limb from limb. He pivots and focuses on Pharisaical doctrine to introduce the heavily disputed question of life after death. The crowd is in an uproar. The Pharisees and Saducees shift their attention momentarily to each other. Seeing the crowd getting out of control and in fear for Paul's life, the commander has him taken away and safeguarded in the barracks overnight.

During the night, Jesus appears to Paul. I have to imagine that Paul was very shaken at this point and comforted to have Jesus personally affirm that Paul is on track - doing exactly what God wanted him to do. When we are uncertain of whether we have been doing what God wanted us to do, we are miserable, internally fearful and confused.

We don't know whether the Lord came to Paul in a vision or a dream, but His message is clear: *"Just as you have solemnly witnessed to my cause in Jerusalem, you must also witness in Rome."* Paul is on track and eventually will go to Rome.

The scene shifts again the next day. We learn through Paul's nephew that there was a serious conspiracy afoot to murder Paul before the Council. More than forty men had taken a solemn oath to kill him when he was brought forth. Learning of this from the nephew, the commander gets in high gear. Since he will be in serious trouble if a Roman citizen is murdered on his watch, he packs Paul off to Caesarea to see the governor, Felix, under an enormous guard, sending a hand-written letter from which we learn the commander's name: Claudius Lysias. Literally hundreds of men are being used to move Paul at no expense all the way to Rome. God is working, using all sorts of people to accomplish His purposes!

Acts 24

The amount of detail in the account of Paul's arrival in Jerusalem and his hearings before the Jews and Romans is quite extraordinary. Luke was with him in Jerusalem (Acts 21:17) and provides such a detailed account that I have to assume he was journaling during these traumatic events. The text does not say that he traveled with Paul to Caesarea, but he must have done so because the attention to detail before Governor Felix continues in Chapter 24.

Interestingly, the lawyer, Tertullus, associates Paul and the Christians with a Jewish sect - one that Tertullus calls the Nazarenes. There were many different Jewish sects in Jerusalem, just as they are today. The fact that Paul was still seen as a Jew within a Jewish group is part of the affront that the Jews felt. Tertullus blames the Roman commander, Lysias, of preventing the Jews from completing their judgment of Paul in Jerusalem.

Paul's defense is terrific. He beautifully argues for his release and stays on the main point - that he did nothing in Jerusalem to deserve censure. He only had been in the city a week, and *"neither in the synagogue, nor the city itself did they find* [him] *caring on a discussion with anyone or causing a riot."* He had brought alms and offerings to the nation. Paul blames the Jews from Asia who had come down to Jerusalem, but who had not appeared to bring any accusation. He ends by focusing on the statement that had caused the Jewish outburst in Jerusalem: *"For the resurrection of the dead I am on trial before you today."*

During Paul's defense, he references the accusation that he is simply a member of a Jewish sect by using the term we have seen Luke use earlier for the bands of believers: they are members of *"the Way."*

Since Lysias is not present, Felix adjourns the session. In the interim, Felix and his Jewish wife, Drusilla, meet privately with Paul. We find a summary of what Paul was able to share in that setting: *righteousness, self-control and the judgment to come.* The line of Paul's presentation must have focused on the issue of human willfulness and the resultant separation from God who is entirely righteous. Felix's reaction is deep fear suggesting that Paul painted a vivid picture of Hell.

But Felix also is hoping for a bribe. Amazingly, he continues to call Paul in for discussions over what must have been a two-year period (see verse 26-27).

A long length of time passed for Paul in Caesarea. If I am reading the text properly, Luke basically skips over the two years of imprisonment and picks back up at the beginning of Chapter 25.

Acts 25

Mt. Carmel is approximately 1,700 feet high above the Mediterranean and lies between Caesarea and the village of Nazareth. Nazareth, of course, is where Jesus grew up. Mt. Carmel is the same mountain on which Elijah offered sacrifice to the Lord and challenged 450 prophets of Baal to do likewise. The geography of Jerusalem, Caesarea and Nazareth is brought forward in the drama of Paul at Caesarea. The lawyer representing the Sanhedrin brought up the *"Sect of the Nazarenes"* in Chapter 24, so the location of Nazareth might have some bearing to the use of the term during Paul's initial hearing.

Look carefully at the map of this portion of ancient Israel:

The Roman Guard Rushes Paul to Caesarea

All of these towns have been in the Acts story to this point. On Paul's recent arrival from his third missionary journey, his boat docked at Tyre and he stayed there seven days (Acts 21:4). Then Paul went on to Caesarea - staying *"many days,"* and then *"up"* to Jerusalem (Acts 21:15). Eventually, Paul is bound in Jerusalem and taken back *"down"* to Caesarea, which is where we find him in Chapter 25.

All of these "ups" and "downs" require us to throw out our 21st Century map awareness. "Up" today normally means North on a map, and "down" on a map means South. But Luke is reflecting altitude. Since Jerusalem is nestled in the Judean Mountain range that runs north and south just west of the Jordan River and the Dead Sea (please look at the map again to get this straight) at a height above sea level of nearly 2,500 feet, going down to Caesarea meant descending 2,500 feet vertically while traversing about 60 miles – no small feat. The reverse is also true, going *up* from Caesarea, one had to *climb* that 2,500 vertical change – no small feat. And Nazareth, though relatively close to Caesarea, was separated from it by the mountain range that begins at Mount Carmel (elevation 1,700 plus or minus). So to get to Nazareth from Caesarea, one had to traverse 25 miles of barren land while crossing a formidable mountain range – again not easy.

We have no idea exactly how Paul went up and back down in the four preceding chapters, but regardless, it wasn't a piece of cake.

We know from early historical documents that the Ebionites and probably the "Nazarenes" followed the way of Jesus within the bounds of their Jewishness. They were never described as terrorists; rather, they functioned as Jesus "believers" in only a shallow sense. The Ebionites held Paul to be a heretic because of Paul's open attitude toward the Gentiles as well as his teaching that Gentiles did not have to observe anything more than the Jersualem Council's "minimum." (See Acts 15:28*ff*).

In Acts 25, Paul's time in Caesarea draws to a close. He has been there under some restrictions for two entire years - unable to travel but entirely able to think thoughtfully about what has happened to him during the twenty-five years or so since his conversion. It is approximately 59 A.D. If Paul was born around 5 A.D., he would be 54 years old. If he became a believer on the road to Damascus at age 29, he has been a follower of the *"Way"* for twenty-five years.

During his imprisonment, Paul could reflect on the wonder of God's action in both his life and all of creation. At least four of our New Testament books were written by Paul from prison: Ephesians, Colossians, Philippians and Philemon. He was imprisoned several times (Clement of Rome, *circa* 90 AD, says seven times; see Clement's 1st Epistle to the Corinthians, Chapter 5). These confinements included prisons in Ephesus, Caesarea, and eventually Rome. In the latter two cities, Paul had ample time to both write and think. There is no question that his constriction in Caesarea could have been a source for some of his writing. Certainly, it affected his entire view of God's call, his mission and his life history.

Acts 26

Chapter 26 contains a detailed record of what actually was said during the interrogation of Paul by King Agrippa so Luke may have been present and making notes. There are three voices recorded; Agrippa's, Paul's and Jesus's. In many Bibles, Jesus's comments will be in red so you won't miss that important words from Jesus are included. In Jesus's comments as well as Paul's, we see the kernel of the Gospel and the intent of God the Father. So it is well worth pausing and letting the essence of God's intention soak into our souls:

Jesus's Words on the Damascus Road Recalled by Paul:

*"But rise and stand on your feet; for I have appeared to you for this purpose, to make you a minister and a witness both of the things which you have seen and of the things which I will yet reveal to you. I will deliver you from the Jewish people, as well as from the Gentiles, to whom I now send you, **to open their eyes, in order to turn them from darkness to light, and from the power of Satan to God, that they may receive forgiveness of sins and an inheritance among those who are sanctified by faith in Me.**"* (Acts 26:16-18, NKJV).

Let's break this down. First, Jesus has knocked Paul off his horse for a reason: to make him a minister (servant) and a witness, pulling him out of his own people and sending him to the Gentiles. But for what reason?

1. To *open* the eyes of both the Jews and the Gentiles.

2. To *take them out* of darkness and *put them in* light.

3. To *deliver* them from the power of Satan.

4. To *put them under* God's government (Kingdom).

5. SO THAT they may *receive* forgiveness of sins.

6. SO THAT they may *receive* an inheritance with all the saints.

Then we have Paul in two verses summing up *his* whole mission:

"to this day I stand, witnessing both to small and great, saying no other things than those which the prophets and Moses said would come— that the **Christ would suffer, that He would be the first to rise from the dead, and would proclaim light to the Jewish people and to the Gentiles."** (Acts 26:22-23). Note the emphasis on bringing **light** in both passages.

Unpacking this further, Paul...

1. Is witnessing to everybody.

2. Saying only what the Scriptures (Moses *and* the Prophets) had predicted.

3. Saying that the Anointed One of God would come (remember "Christ" simply means the Anointed One) and suffer (be crucified).

4. Saying that the Anointed One would rise from the dead.

5. Proclaiming that light had come to both Jew and Gentile.

I try to be alert to these tight "summary kernels." In our walk, it is sometimes easy to get confused about what is essential. We see Paul in Ephesians unpacking the mystery of God, the kernel, in different words. John 3:16 does this in one sentence. In 1st Corinthians 15, Paul again summarizes his activity, delivering what may be the earliest recording of his message:

"Moreover, brethren, I declare to you the gospel which I preached to you, which also you received and in which you stand, by which also you are saved, if you hold fast that word which I preached to you—unless you believed in vain. For I delivered to you first of all that which I also received: that Christ died for our sins according to the Scriptures, and that He was buried, and that He rose again the third day according to the Scriptures, and that He was seen by Cephas, then by the twelve. After that He was seen by over five hundred brethren at once, of whom the greater part remain to the present, but some have fallen asleep. After that He was seen by James, then by all the apostles. Then last of all He was seen by me also, as by one born out of due time." (1st Corinthians 15:1-8, NKJV).

While reading Scripture, be a detective – always on the lookout for the proclamation, for the essence, for what theologians call the *Kerygma*. *Kerygma* (from the Greek *keryssein*, "*to proclaim*," and *keryx*, "*herald*") refers to the initial and essential proclamation of the gospel message. The word appears nine times in the New Testament: once in Matthew (12:41), once in Mark (16:20), once in Luke (11:32), and six times in the letters of Paul (Rom. 16:25; 1st Cor. 1:21, 2:4, 15:14; 2nd Tim. 4:17; and Titus 1:3). To put it simply, the *kerygma* is the very heart of the gospel, the core message of the Christian faith that all believers are call to proclaim.

Kerygma is distinct from *didache*, another Greek term that refers to teaching, instruction, or doctrine. While *kerygma* means the initial gospel proclamation designed to introduce a person to Christ and to appeal for conversion, *didache* concerns the fuller and more extensive doctrinal and moral teaching and instruction in the Faith that a person receives once he has accepted the *kerygma* and has been baptized.

It is easy to get lost in the minutia of our faith and sometimes miss the *kerygma*, the unequivocal proclamation of the person of Jesus Christ, His saving grace, His teaching, His life, His promises and our promised inheritance in Him.

Acts 27

Chapters 27 and 28 would make an absolutely thrilling movie. Undoubtedly, Luke is along for the great voyage from Caesarea to Rome via MANY stops. Reading Chapter 27 feels a bit like looking at Steve Happ's itinerary to Uganda, only MUCH more complicated. Many ships going many places. It occurs to me God was very good to use Roman Empire funds to pay for this trip for Paul. It would have been exorbitant otherwise.

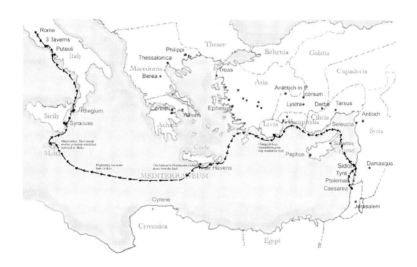

Paul's Voyage to Rome

Luke does appear to be on board along with the friendly centurion, Julius, as well as other prisoners. They sail by many places Paul had visited, including Cyrus and Pamphylia and Asia, but my attention is on the general quality of the voyage. It seems a total nightmare. On the sea, when one cannot sail into the wind and has to turn backward and is driven by the wind, watch out! It is SO dangerous. This happens several times.

Imagine 276 people on a boat like this.

Important Holy Spirit encounters occur for Paul and those traveling with him. Some occurred during times of fasting. We see the *"sailing was now dangerous because the Fast was already over"* in verse 9. The fast referred to is most likely the Fast of the Day of Atonement which occurred each year in September or October. Like our hurricane season in the Gulf of Mexico, autumn was a treacherous time for crossing the Mediterranean. Paul appears to have fasted on that day for sure. Regardless, in one way or another, the Holy Spirit gives Paul an overview of what is ahead.

Though Paul appears to be well received in general by his Centurion guardian, Julius resists Paul's sense that all will be lost (verse 10). Paul ends up being right on two counts (the ship and its cargo *will* be lost), but wrong about everyone losing their lives. Instead of turning back, the majority, including the pilot and the ship's owner, vote to proceed. This ends in the loss of boat and cargo as Paul had predicted.

Two thoughts: majority vote is not helpful if one has a clear word from God, and second, assuming that one thing God shows you necessarily leads to another (loss of all the men), can be a mistake.

Stop for a moment and think about what the ship was experiencing in verse 18 - "*being violently storm-tossed.*" The passengers eventually end up having to lighten the ship. Think of that ship; think about what that must have been like; think about how in the world they lightened the boat without losing one of the 276 people in the process.

Three days of storm, and they threw off even the tackle which basically meant disaster. Paul at this point was fasting again. The scripture says, in verse 21, "*after long abstinence from food.*" Paul stands in the midst of them and tells them what an angel the night before had told him. The angel said, "*don't be afraid.*" Because God wants Paul in Rome, all on board will be saved. However, the angel also has told him they must first run aground on an island.

A week passes, and they near Malta. Terrified, some try to jump overboard. Paul warns them that if any leave, they will all perish. He urges them to begin to eat again because it appears many also have been fasting.

The centurion intervenes when some of the soldiers, fearing their own deaths if the prisoners were deemed to have escaped, were planning to kill the prisoners. Luke shows that this kindness is really directed at Paul. We end Chapter 27 as they arrive on land. Many swam; many relied on broken parts of the ship for flotation, but all arrived safe and sound.

What an ordeal.

Acts 28

We've come to the last chapter of Acts. It is hard to guess what happened to this chapter. There is the normal amount of significant detail through verse 30, and then, suddenly, we are left with one sentence to wrap up the next two years of Paul's life and eventual death. It seems very doubtful that this wrap-up verse was written by Luke. Rather, I suspect it was added by a believer who had Luke's scrolls up to verse 30, is missing perhaps another roll, and adds the concluding verse to finish out the account without inserting any false gloss. When you think of the detail of the journey from Caesarea to Rome in Chapters 27 and 28, and then consider the one verse summary of two years in the most important city in the known world at the time, it really doesn't make sense. I wish I knew what happened!

We can see God's providential hand on Paul throughout Chapter 28 - from the welcome they receive from the islanders on Malta, his deliverance from the snake, his healing ministry (first to Publius's father and then to many on Malta), and finally, having two years in Rome in a private home, being able to entertain and speak to many from his makeshift headquarters all while a prisoner - it is quite remarkable.

Adjoining Malta proper, there is a small island, entirely rock and beach, less than a hundred yards off shore and 1.5 miles in length. Tradition holds that the 276 survivors landed there.

For an architectural context of Paul's Malta visit, Publius's villa was likely extensive, with internal loggias and beautiful Roman inspired tile mosaics on the floors. The photograph following is of a reconstruction of a similar villa's courtyard, which would have been entirely open to the sun. The remarkable mosaic and geometric floor and a portion of some of the columns were found in excavations on Malta.

"*The father of Publius lay sick of a fever and dysentery. Paul went in to him and prayed, and he laid his hands on him and healed him.*" (Acts 28:8). This is the healing sequence that all early Christians employed: they would go to the sick person, pray, lay hands on the person and find him healed. The only thing missing in the account is oil – we find James's admonition in James 5:14 for the elders of the church to come, pray and also anoint the person with oil. Without doubt, the oil represented an outward sign that the Spirit of God would do the actual healing.

I find it remarkable that a "sect" so infamous to the Jews had made such headway in Italy - Paul finds "brethren" in Puteoli and word is passed over to followers in Rome that Paul is in route. The scene is very moving beginning in verse 13:

"*From there we circled round and reached Rhegium. And after one day the south wind blew; and the next day we came to Puteoli, where we found brethren, and were invited to stay with them seven days. And so we went toward Rome. And from there, when the brethren heard about us, they came to meet us as far as Appii Forum and Three Inns. When Paul saw them, he thanked God and took courage." (Acts 28:13-15, NKJV).*

Paul must have been moved at his reception for Luke to write "*he thanked God and took courage.*"

Once in Rome, Paul continued his practice of addressing the Jews first and then the Gentiles. Luke again summarizes the message Paul delivered to the Jewish leaders, the *kerygma:*

*"So when they had appointed him a day, many came to him at his lodging, to whom he explained and solemnly **testified of the kingdom of God, persuading them concerning Jesus from both the Law of Moses and the Prophets**, from morning till evening. And some were persuaded by the things which were spoken, and some disbelieved." (Acts 28:23-24).*

Paul's response as the Jewish leaders depart is from Isaiah:

"Go to this people and say,
'You will keep on hearing, but will not understand;
And you will keep on seeing, but will not perceive;
For the heart of this people has become dull,
And with their ears they scarcely hear,
And they have closed their eyes;
Otherwise they might see with their eyes,
And hear with their ears,
And understand with their heart and return,
And I would heal them.'
Therefore let it be known to you
that this salvation of God
has been sent to the Gentiles;
they will also listen."
(Isaiah 6:9-10).

It is certainly worth sitting with Paul's response. We all, in one way or another, are like the leaders Paul and Isaiah addressed – hearing, but not understanding - with hearts that have become dull, scarcely grasping God's intention for our lives. But Paul's words contain great promise *if* we can hear and allow our hearts to understand: God *will* heal us! Truly, this is a great, monumental promise.

Finally, we come to a most remarkable abbreviation of Paul's two years in Rome – the ending sentence of the entire Book of Acts:

"Then Paul dwelt two whole years in his own rented house, and received all who came to him, preaching the kingdom of God and teaching the things which concern the Lord Jesus Christ with all confidence, no one forbidding him." (Acts 28:30-31)

We will have to wait for more light to be shed as we read some of the Pastoral letters thought to have been written by Paul *from* Rome. But now we move on to the "Book" of Romans, a letter written *to* Rome by Paul from elsewhere!

Romans

Romans 1

"I was saying these things and weeping in the most bitter contrition of my heart, when, lo, I heard the voice as of a boy or girl, I know not which, coming from a neighboring house, chanting, and oft repeating, 'Take up and read; take up and read.' Immediately my countenance was changed, and I began most earnestly to consider whether it was usual for children in any kind of game to sing such words; nor could I remember ever to have heard the like. So, restraining the torrent of my tears, I rose up, interpreting it no other way than as a command to me from Heaven to open the book, and to read the first chapter I should light upon. For I had heard of Antony, that, accidentally coming in while the gospel was being read, he received the admonition as if what was read were addressed to him, 'Go and sell that you have, and give to the poor, and you shall have treasure in heaven; and come and follow me.' And by such oracle was he immediately converted unto You. So quickly I returned to the place where Alypius was sitting; for there had I put down the volume of the Apostles, when I rose thence. I grasped, opened, and in silence read that paragraph on which my eyes first fell — 'Not in rioting and drunkenness, not in chambering and wantonness, not in strife and envying; but put *on the Lord Jesus Christ, and make not provision for the flesh, to fulfill the lusts thereof.'* (Romans 13:13-14). *No further would I read, nor did I need; for instantly, as the sentence ended — by a light, as it were, of security infused into my heart — all the gloom of doubt vanished away."* (Confessions, Augustine of Hippo, Chpt. 12:29).

Paul's letter to the Roman church spoke directly to Augustine's heart nearly 330 years after Paul wrote it. The letter moved Augustine to a life of faith and certainty. May it do so to us!

Probably written from the city of Corinth around 56 to 58 AD during his third missionary journey, Romans is an extensive outline of Paul's personal faith. Some scholars think it is Paul's sixth "Pastoral" letter, having written already Galatians, 1st and 2nd Thessalonians (six years earlier from Corinth), as well as 1st and 2nd Corinthians. Paul will soon depart for Jerusalem with gifts for the church there, so we can be fairly sure of the dates.

"Now, however, I am on my way to Jerusalem in the service of the Lord's people there. For Macedonia and Achaia were pleased to make a contribution for the poor among the Lord's people in Jerusalem." (Romans 15:25-26).

Paul had never been to Rome at this point, but obviously a group of believers had emerged there. They could have come from the beginnings of the church at Pentecost or even from some of Paul's converts in Greece and Macedonia. Regardless, Paul hopes to physically see the believers in Rome one day:

"But now that there is no more place for me to work in these regions, and since I have been longing for many years to visit you, I plan to do so when I go to Spain. I hope to see you while passing through and to have you assist me on my journey there, after I have enjoyed your company for a while." (Romans 15:23-24).

Unlike Paul's other letters, Romans does not focus on many specific issues within the Roman church with the exception of the relationship between Jewish and Gentile believers. His whole theme is summarized in verses 16 and 17 of Chapter 1:

"For I am not ashamed of the gospel, because it is the power of God that brings salvation to everyone who believes: first to the Jew, then to the Gentile. For in the gospel the righteousness of God is revealed—a righteousness that is by faith from first to last, just as it is written: 'The righteous will live by faith.'" (Romans 1:16-17).

The Good News reveals the righteousness of God that is summed up by faith. These verses were critical in Martin Luther's development. In fact, Luther lectured on Romans for the entire year of 1515 AD, and later wrote an extensive preface to his later translation of Romans which began:

"This epistle is in truth the chief part of the New Testament and the purest Gospel. It would be quite proper for a Christian, not only to know it by heart word for word, but also to study it daily, for it is the soul's daily bread. It can never be read or meditated too much and too well. The more thoroughly it is treated, the more precious it becomes, and the better it tastes." (Luther's Preface to Romans).

Since one of the key texts for Luther's view of Grace was found in the first chapter, it is worth thinking hard on the issue of grace and faith as we move through the book. Several centuries later than Luther, John Wesley heard Luke's preface being read, and apparently something in Luther's words moved Wesley to faith.

There are several sections in Chapter 1 that have always intrigued me. The initial salutation reveals that Paul very much considers himself a *"bond-slave"* of Jesus, the Anointed One of God. A bond-slave is a slave who has been set free but then willing binds himself to his Master after his release. In the very first sentence, Paul wraps up his identity in Christ: a bond-slave, called as an apostle and set apart for bearing the good news of God's nature and action to mankind in keeping with the prophetic words spoken of the messiah – this Jesus who was declared the Son of God by being raised from the dead – our Lord. Then Paul identifies those he writes – listen to this: *"all who are beloved of God in Rome, called **saints**."*

Beloved of God and Saints

This is an amazing understanding of who believers in God are – beloved of God and considered to be saints. What a wonderful way to see other people, particularly the people of God. Can we say the same?

Another impacting section deals with the native awareness of who God actually is. Paul writes, *"that which is known about God is evident within them; for God made it evident to them. For since the creation of the world His invisible attributes, His eternal power and divine nature, have been clearly seen, being understood through what has been made...."* (Romans 1:19-20).

When I was a young boy, I wondered about those who had not been chosen by God – unlike Abraham and the Israelites. How would they be able to know that there even was a God much less that He was full of kindness and compassion? Paul shares that we are all endowed (think of the Declaration of Independence) with an innate ability to grasp and perceive God. Yet that independence that Adam and Eve displayed almost always leads us to our own downfall.

The first book of the Bible recalls the sad result of mankind run amuck: *"Then the Lord saw that the wickedness of man was great on the earth, and that every intent of the thoughts of his heart was only evil continually."* (Genesis 6:5). The Hebrew word *"ra"* translated *"wickedness"* comes from a root word that means *"to spoil (literally, by breaking to pieces); figuratively, to make (or be) good for nothing, i.e., bad (physically, socially or morally); break (down, in pieces))."* (From Strong's definition H7489). In other words, corrupt in the sense of decaying flesh.

But the wonder of God, so visible on a star lighted night or when peering into a microscope, *IS* visible. His ways ARE wonderful if only we will take the time to truly gaze at His creation.

Paul does not mince words regarding the results on a mankind gone astray. He uses the term, *"degrading passions"* – passions that cause a progressive corruption in the person and in society. God is not causing this corruption; He lets the consequences stand which is simply a corruption that leads to death – spiritually and physically.

Paul cares enough about men and women to speak straight – hoping that many will heed the call to embrace God's love and God's ways. In Western culture today, we find ourselves in situation where that which leads to corruption and disintegration is exalted and that which leads to life and true happiness is disdained. May God help us!

Romans 2

"You can recognize the riches of God's kindness if you consider how many evils men do every day on earth. Almost everyone has fallen away and become worthless, traveling down the wide and broad way of perdition, ignoring the narrow road that leads to eternal life. Yet God lets His sun shine daily on all of them and sends them rain, however much they may blaspheme Him.... Therefore, if anyone despises God's kindness and forbearance and patience, he does not know that he is being encouraged by these things to repent." (Origen's Commentary on Romans).

In one respect, the backdrop for the whole book of Romans is summed up toward the end of Paul's letter to the Romans: *"Therefore receive one another, just as Christ also received us, to the glory of God."* (Chapter 15:7). As Paul's view of the immensity of God's grace has developed over his lifetime and his encounters with God have increased, Paul's "good news" has naturally focused on the issue of God's choice and God's grace.

Paul is a Jew. All of his early training was based on one clear generational reality: Paul's forefathers *had* been chosen by God for a special relationship. It is a bit like being Prince William of England. Because of his ancestry, he has been chosen to be the future King of England. He might abdicate as his great uncle did, but otherwise, he is in the line of inheritance, and his behavior while on earth must always reflect it. 99.999 percent of all other people in the United Kingdom are NOT. They may act differently, but he may not.

Paul's understanding of his innate *"chosenness"* as a young man before he encountered Jesus on the Damascus Road was like Prince William's. He saw his life entirely through this narrow "chosen" lens. But now, over the last thirty years, his lens has been marvelously expanded. Gentiles are included as well. God's favor also rests on Gentiles. This view is what got Paul in hot water everywhere he ministered.

Most of Paul's ministry was focused on bringing the "kernel" of the message to both Jew and Gentile, and always in the same pattern: "to the Jew first and then to the Gentile." Already, we have seen in Acts how much trouble this caused the early church communities. It was so difficult for the Jewish contingent to receive the news. The news, so to speak, was TOO good, too broad. It was so broad that for many Jewish believers, that portion of the Good News was Bad News.

Undoubtedly, this was the situation in Rome, and if you keep that thought in mind, I think we will find that Paul's approach and his language throughout the letter work to help both groups, Jew and Gentile, to "receive one another." What Paul wants at the end of the day is that the Jewish and Gentile believers in Rome "receive one another, just as Christ received us."

We experience the same problem today even in the Church. We have an internal struggle: what to think about and how to receive believers who are followers of Christ but with a cultural and religious identity different from ours. Protestants, Orthodox and Catholics on the surface appear as if they are from different planets, and their speech, beliefs, religious attire, music, daily readings and cultural habits can drive us up the wall when we are forced into contact.

That might be a good backdrop to remember as we read each chapter of Paul's letter to the Roman "church."

Romans 3

By Chapter 3, we are deep into Paul's exposition of the value of believing faith compared to works. So far, Paul has argued four main points.

(1) Mankind has gone terribly astray. Those that are not Jewish had rejected the clear evidence that there is a wonderful and creative God. Most had turned to idols, and having rejected the living God, men and women have engaged in the most heinous sins. (Chapter 1).

(2) In spite of the fact that the Jews had been chosen by God for special blessing and had received written revelation about how to live righteously, the descendants of Abraham and Israel largely ignored the revelation. They, also, had given themselves over to the flesh. (Chapter 2).

(3) Going off track affects everyone – the entire human race. No one can stand before God and boast of perfection. One stain ruins the cloth, and the knowledge of knowing how something should be (the Law) does not remove the stain. (Romans 3:1-20).

(4) God's response to this problem is the gift of His sinless Son, who freely offered Himself as a substitute for mankind – for those willing to receive Him. (Romans 3:21-30).

Paul starts off Chapter 3 dealing with one of the biggest controversies amongst the Christians in Rome – what about circumcision? It is a "work," something we do, but not to be justified. It is an outward sign of what should be our heartfelt devotion to God. Verse 20 sums up the human dilemma: even though a male is circumcised, *"by the works of the Law, no flesh will be justified in His sight."*

In Verse 21, Paul explains that God's deep righteousness extends beyond what we do. God's righteousness is something beyond, *"witnessed by the Law itself and the Prophets."* That righteousness is the unbelievable kindness and grace that constitutes the very nature of God who choses, because of His "rightness," to forgive those who are not able to walk perfectly.

I am blown away by Paul's insight. God is more right than a human judge who simply ascertains that an infraction of a rule has occurred. God shows Himself more righteous because He is willing to find a way to forgive us legitimately. A debt is owed to the Mosaic Law, and God pays it. Paul doesn't actually spell that out clearly in Chapter 3, but it is implied. God's nature and ability to forgive trumps what people are due. His summary in Chapter 3 of this point is another *Kerygma*, another kernel, another summation of the Good News in Paul language:

"the righteousness of God through faith in Jesus Christ for all those who believe; for there is no distinction; for all have sinned and fall short of the

glory of God, being justified as a gift by His grace through the redemption which is in Christ Jesus; whom God displayed publicly as a propitiation in His blood through faith." (Romans 3:22-25)

All that is required is to believe that what God's messengers proclaim is true, i.e., that all have sinned and fallen short, but are *"being justified as a GIFT by His grace through the redemption that is in Christ Jesus."* He adds that everything turns on Jesus's shedding of blood – *propitiation* in His blood, which one activates on a personal level by simply believing. The word *"propitiation"* carries the basic idea of appeasement or satisfaction. The word reflects a two-part act that involves both appeasing the wrath of an offended person and being reconciled to him. Neither by Circumcision nor Torah rituals or anything else – by simply believing. Later in Romans, Paul will tie in Baptism.

There is a "Law" at work, but it is the Law of Faith, the belief and trust in Jesus as the Anointed One of God and His saving death and resurrection. (Verse 22). Obedience to that "Law" leads us into an entirely new realm where Jesus is King. He is the crucified King who has risen and who is in charge of this new Kingdom. *"Do we then nullify the Law through faith? May it never be! On the contrary, we establish the Law."* (Verse 31).

There is no boasting to be done except in the gracious kindness of God. I am particularly impressed with his argument that he will make in Chapter 4. We are not due salvation by what we have done (see Romans 4:4). Rather, we are due salvation by what God has done. It is to His glory, not to ours.

Paul observes: *"Where then is boasting? It is excluded. By what kind of law? Of works? No, but by a law of faith. For we maintain that a man is justified by faith apart from works of the Law. Or is God the God of Jews only? Is He not the God of Gentiles also? Yes, of Gentiles also, since indeed God who will justify the circumcised by faith and the uncircum-cised through faith is One."* (Romans 3:27-30).

This is important. Paul's response is straightforward: the real issue is faith - a faith that involves a complete trust. His argument is critical to the position that Gentiles need not observe certain key "laws" like physical circumcision if their heart is right. Verses 22-25 make it very clear that we are *"justified as a gift by His grace through the redemption which is in Christ Jesus."* I think we can safely say this is a kernel of our Good News: our *Kerygma*.

Romans 4

In Chapter 4, Paul deals directly with expounding the kernel of the Gospel he began in the preceding chapter. Let's look at that one more time:

"the righteousness of God through faith in Jesus Christ for all those who believe; for there is no distinction; for all have sinned and fall short of the glory of God, being justified as a gift by His grace through the redemption which is in Christ Jesus; whom God displayed publicly as a propitiation in His blood through faith." (Romans 3:22-25).

He focuses on whether covenantal signs are necessary for all believers. He starts with the Father of the Jews, Abraham. God chose Abraham, but Paul is quick to say in the first four verses that the choice was God's - it was not caused by something Abraham did - it was caused because Abraham *"believed God:"*

"What then shall we say that Abraham, our forefather according to the flesh, has found? For if Abraham was justified by works, he has some-thing to boast about, but not before God. For what does the Scripture say? 'Abraham believed God, and it was credited to him as righteousness.' Now

to the one who works, his wage is not credited as a favor, but as what is due." (Romans 4:1-4).

When Paul says, *"believed,"* he is not just saying that Abraham thought God existed. Paul is addressing the fact that Abraham took God for who He was and trusted God in a way that measured up to who He was.

That last sentence bears emphasis: "Abraham took God for who He was and trusted God in a way that measured up to who God was in all reality." Paul's (and God's) focus on belief was relational and about Abraham's heart. Jesus says our unconscious behavior simply expresses our internal heart.

Verse 3 of Romans is nearly an exact quotation from Genesis 15:6:

"Then he believed in the Lord; and He reckoned it to him as righteousness."

The passage is significant because it spells out the basis of Abraham's justification before God. It was his internal belief in the Lord and the Lord's promise, not an external action. Abraham was deemed righteous because of his faith, not because he was circumcised. (Rom 4:9–10).

Deuteronomy 30:6 reveals what God is truly focused on: the heart. *"Moreover the Lord your God will circumcise your heart and the heart of your descendants, to love the Lord your God with all your heart and with all your soul, so that you may live."*

Paul can prove that Abraham had done nothing religiously to merit God's choice – a choice based on a righteousness that was imputed to Abraham because of the way Abraham related to God, felt about God, trusted God. He does this by simply answering the question: When God chose Abraham and imputed righteousness to him, was Abraham circumcised?

The answer is NO! Abraham would not be circumcised until Chapter 17 of Genesis. Further, Abraham was 99 years old at the time that he was circumcised.

> *"Now when Abram was ninety-nine years old, the*
> *Lord appeared to Abram and said to him,*
> *"I am God Almighty;*
> *Walk before Me, and be blameless.*
> *I will establish My covenant between Me and you,*
> *And I will multiply you exceedingly."* (Genesis 17:1-2).

It is from this powerful thought of when Abraham was deemed righteous that much of Paul's revelation rests. But the following text is also worth reading carefully as it spotlights the tension with the Jewish position that circumcision must be required.

"...God said further to Abraham, 'Now as for you, you shall keep My covenant, you and your descendants after you throughout their generations. This is My covenant, which you shall keep, between Me and you and your descendants after you: every male among you shall be circumcised. And you shall be circumcised in the flesh of your foreskin, and it shall be the sign of the covenant between Me and you. And every male among you who is eight days old shall be circumcised throughout your generations, a servant who is born in the house or who is bought with money from any foreigner, who is not of your descendants. A servant who is born in your house or who is bought with your money shall surely be circumcised; thus shall My covenant be in your flesh for an everlasting covenant. But an uncircumcised male who is not circumcised in the flesh of his foreskin, that person shall be cut off from his people; he has broken My covenant.'" (Genesis 17:9-14).

The responsibility for circumcision falls on blood descendants and even their slaves! It doesn't fall on the Gentiles. So, Paul's reasoning certainly releases the Gentiles from obligation for outward religious signs like circumcision, but many Jewish believers would be highly stressed if they thought it was unnecessary for their own children.

What I am sure of is that Paul, no matter the answer a Jew would have, was certain that the *main* issue was the heart, the internal world of belief – not just a cognitive function but a relational certainty about the wonder of God's nature. If I had to express what I think Abraham had in his heart, it would be a belief that the God of all creation was wonderful, magnificent and entirely trustworthy. Over several millennia, we would come to learn that God was gracious beyond imagination. That really is the Gospel.

Romans 5

One of my early Bible teachers, Derek Prince, once said that there were at least 5 experiential results of being reckoned righteous by our faith and trust in God and Jesus's atoning sacrifice, and the five come in the first five verses of Chapter 5. Since they come in Chapter FIVE, and there are FIVE experiential results, it makes the chapter a bit easier to remember.

Bob Mumford, another Biblical teacher in my early days, would note with Derek that the whole chapter begins with the focus word, *"Therefore."* There are a lot of "therefores" in Romans, and two in Chapter 5 (verses 1 and 12). So, as my teachers advised me long ago, let's see what the "Therefore" is there for!

What are the five experiential results of faith in who God is, what God has done and what God will do in the future? I am talking about a firm belief that God is who He says He is, that He has drawn close to you and brought you in and intends only your very best. So, let's count them.

Number One, we have **PEACE**. *Shalom* in Hebrew is closely connected to the word for completeness. Without enmity or strife toward God nor to ourselves.

Number Two, our faith causes us to be brought into GRACE. Another translation of the Greek word is **FAVOR**. We now have access to the grace of God; we are favored because of God's love which becomes real and experiential because of our faith. If we did not have this relational faith, we would not be in a position to walk in an innumerable number of grace gifts that come from our relationship. In a sense, our ability to believe ushers in the amazing experiential, continuous flow of favor gifts.

Number Three, our faith causes us to experience **EXULTATION** in the **HOPE of GLORY**. This, too, is experiential. We experience an amazing joy for which there is probably no higher descriptor that the word *"exult."* We exult because we have hope in the wonder and majesty of God which we can now see through faith. Once one experiences the personal exultation in the hope of God's glory, he or she understands how totally amazing it is that God is who He is and that we have been brought near by the blood of Jesus.

Number Four, our faith causes us to **EXULT** in our **TRIBULATIONS**. O my, this doesn't seem very positive at first glance. It is a result of our faith, because Jesus predicted that while on this earth we would face trials. But our faith causes us to exult in the tribulations that we experience, knowing that they bring about perseverance, proven character and deepen our hope in God.

Finally, **Number Five**, our faith has put us into a position to receive the **LOVE** of God because it has been poured out into our hearts by the indescribable **gift of the Spirit of God**. We experience God's love, and our love for God and others deepens.

One more thought. We have another "kernel" summation of the Gospel in Chapter 5:

"while we were still helpless, at the right time Christ died for the ungodly.... But God demonstrates His own love toward us, in that while we were yet sinners, Christ died for us. Much more then, having now been justified by His blood, we shall be saved from the wrath of God through Him. For if while we were enemies we were reconciled to God through the death of His Son, much more, having been reconciled, we shall be saved by His life." (Romans 5:6,8-10).

Helpless

Christ died for us (the ungodly)

Justified us by His blood

Saved us from God's wrath

Reconciled us to God through Jesus's death

Saved us by His life (His resurrection)

Romans 6

"And Your godly ones shall bless You.
They shall speak of the glory of Your Kingdom
And talk of Your power;
To make known to the sons of men Your mighty acts
And the glory of the majesty of Your Kingdom.
Your kingdom is an everlasting Kingdom,
And Your dominion endures throughout all generations."
(Psalm 145:10-13).

Reading Romans 6, I think about the multiple words and "seeings" that Steve Bowie brought to our community in the early days. What triggered my memory was the word *"slavery"* and the words *"slaves to sin,"* and *"death no longer has mastery."* In one sense, Paul is describing the Kingdom of Darkness. Jesus came preaching the Kingdom of God, and we know that after His resurrection, God has made him both King and Lord over that Kingdom. It is the total antithesis of the Kingdom of Darkness.

Another word for Kingdom is Dominion. Dominion conveys a geographic dimension to the issue of authority, one of the key underlying implications of either word. Watchman Nee rightly observed that Authority is the greatest question in the Universe. To whom do you submit? Whose direction will you follow?

A slave has only one option: death or submission. But think of what this means when an entire culture is under the Dominion of Darkness, the Dominion of Death, the Dominion of Sin. All three are characteristics of any dominion in opposition to God's Dominion. God's Kingdom is the exact opposite of Satan's. God's Kingdom is one of Light, Life and Righteousness.

As I mentioned in the Introduction, during worship in late January of 1988, Steve Bowie saw a vision of a medieval kingdom and its King in royal regalia. It is worth repeating in case you skipped the Introduction. Outside of the King's fortress, the countryside was desolate. Peasants born outside of the kingdom were at the mercy of the world. Steve saw the King extended an invitation to all of the peasants outside to come and enjoy being part of his household.

In the King's household, there was peace and security, joy and celebration – hope. Outside his household, there was only war and strife, thievery and destruction – hopelessness. Steve saw that those who chose to remain outside the walls had nothing but what they could scrounge. They clearly had decided to be subject only to themselves.

During worship on the next Sunday, Steve received further insight: "When I saw the previous vision, I realize now the colors were vivid in the King's palace, but totally washed out, grey and lifeless outside of the palace. The peasants had no idea that where they lived, there was little color because they had never gone near the King's palace. It is far easier for someone from the palace to see the difference than it is for someone outside." As the King's domain extends, Steve could see the colors returning to the countryside.

"They shall speak of the glory of Your Kingdom!"
(Psalm 145:11).

May we leave every vestige of the Kingdom of Darkness and rest in the richness of God's glorious Kingdom!

Romans 7

"...there are those who yield to their weaknesses
and they will have troubles and sorrows unending."
(Psalms 16:4, Passion translation).

"Or do you not know, brethren (for I am speaking to those who know
the law), that the law has jurisdiction over a person as long as he lives?"
(Romans 7:1).

There are other laws that exist in the world. One of these is the Law of
the Torah, the rules and regulations as transcribed by Moses. A better
"law" is at work in the freedom granted by the Kingdom of God – the
Law of the Spirit which, in fact, is the Law of Love. Derek Prince once
said that the most powerful thing in the universe is Love. At first, that
seems impossible because we often think of Love as soft, but the most
inevitable thing in life on earth is death. Yet God's Love conquers death.
The Law of rules and ordinances is not strong enough to conquer death
or unrighteousness. The Law in the Torah reduces bad consequences
and in that sense is good. But all it can do is reveal wrong actions and
reduce tragic life outcomes by improving our choices. The Law of Love
empowers us and translates us into *vessels* of righteousness. The Law of
Love is the only Law needed in the Kingdom of God.

Verses 3 and 4 amplify this thought:

"if while her husband is living, she is joined to another man, she shall
be called an adulteress; but if her husband dies, she is free from the law,
so that she is not an adulteress though she is joined to another man.
Therefore, my brethren, you also were made to die to the Law through
the body of Christ, so that you might be joined to another, to Him who
was raised from the dead, in order that we might bear fruit for God."
(Romans 7:3-4).

At first glance, my interpretation may not be evident, but what Paul is saying is that by the death of one Authority (her husband has died), a wife is free to come under an entirely new authority, a new dominion. Choosing God as our new husband, translates us into an entirely different dominion with a new "rule" of behavior. It is no longer the Torah; it is the Law of Love. What allows this translation is the death of the old Adam and the beginning on an entire new race under the new Adam: Jesus.

Verse 6 continues the thought:

"…now we have been released from the Law, having died to that by which we were bound, so that we serve in newness of the Spirit and not in oldness of the letter." (Romans 7:6).

We were under one Law, but now we are under an entirely new Law, the Law of Kingdom of God and His Spirit, the Law of Love. The Apostle John says the Spirit of God is Love. (1st John 4:8).

Paul finishes out the chapter assuring everyone that there is nothing wrong with the Torah – it is appropriate and helpful in reducing the impact of dealing with the Kingdom of Darkness in which resistant mankind finds itself, but it is unable to make anyone righteous. It simply cannot. What is does do is reveal how much we stand in need of God's Grace.

Romans 8

Romans 8 is one important chapter. Not that it is more important than all the rest, but it does hold a very important place for me in understanding what God is doing with us – what he intends for us to be. In some ways, Ephesians Chapters 1-3 parallel Romans to this point and offer a very tight summation of God's intention. Think about whether or not that is true, and also do you find it helpful as you read the following from Paul's letter to the Ephesians:

"In love He predestined us to adoption as sons through Jesus Christ to Himself, according to the kind intention of His will, to the praise of the glory of His grace, which He freely bestowed on us in the Beloved. In Him we have redemption through His blood, the forgiveness of our trespasses, according to the riches of His grace that He lavished on us. In all wisdom and insight He made known to us **the mystery of His will, according to His kind intention which He purposed in Him with a view to an administration suitable to the fullness of the times, that is, the summing up of all things in Christ, things in the heavens and things on the earth.** *In Him also we have obtained an inheritance,"* (Ephesians 1:4-11).

"And you were dead in your trespasses and sins, in which you formerly walked according to the course of this world, according to the prince of the power of the air, of the spirit that is now working in the sons of disobedience. Among them we too all formerly lived in the lusts of our flesh, indulging the desires of the flesh and of the mind, and were by nature children of wrath, even as the rest. But God, being rich in mercy, because of His great love with which He loved us, **even when we were dead in our transgressions, made us alive together with Christ (by grace you have been saved), and raised us up with Him, and seated us with Him in the heavenly places in Christ Jesus** *so that in the ages to come He might show the surpassing riches of His grace in kindness toward us in Christ Jesus. For* **by grace you have been saved through faith; and that not of yourselves, it is the gift of God***; not as a result of works, so that no one may boast."* (Ephesians 2:1-9).

"For this reason I bow my knees before the Father, from whom every family in heaven and on earth derives its name, that He would grant you, according to the riches of His glory, to be strengthened with power

through His Spirit in the inner man, so that Christ may dwell in your
hearts through faith; and that you, being rooted and grounded in love,
may be able to comprehend with all the saints what is the breadth and
length and height and depth, and to know the love of Christ which sur-
passes knowledge, that you may be filled up to all the fullness of God."
(Ephesians 3:14-19).

Really, it is difficult to not be overcome with the sweep of Paul's revelation and insight. Romans 8 answers the question, "What *IS* the Law
in the new life we live?" He has said clearly in the preceding chapters
of Romans that it is NOT the Torah. Rather, it is the Law of Love, or
as he articulates it in Chapter 8 beginning with a great "Therefore:"
"Therefore, there is now NO condemnation for those who are in Christ
*Jesus. For **the law of the Spirit of life in Christ Jesus** has set you free*
from the law of sin and of death." (Romans 8:1-2).

The Law of the Spirit of Life which we find in Jesus is to be our only law.
It is a law made evident within us when we walk in the Spirit. Jeremiah
prophesied this very accurately:

> *"This is the covenant I will make with the people of Israel*
> *after that time," declares the Lord.*
> *"I will put my law in their minds*
> *and write it on their hearts.*
> *I will be their God,*
> *and they will be my people.*
> *No longer will they teach their neighbor,*
> *or say to one another, 'Know the Lord,'*
> *because they will all know me,*
> *from the least of them to the greatest,"*
> *declares the Lord.*
> *"For I will forgive their wickedness*
> *and will remember their sins no more."*

(Jeremiah 31:33-34).

As we discussed previously, Jesus told the disciples in Chapter 1 of Acts to wait in Jerusalem until the Father sent them **the gift He promised** - *"as I told you before. John baptized with water, but in a few days, you will be baptized with the Holy Spirit."* The atoning sacrifice of Jesus and the gift of the Holy Spirit, that is full immersion into the very nature and Spirit of God, is what the disciples needed to walk and function in as the Kingdom of God dawned. In the second chapter of Acts, Peter affirmed the same thing as he tied the events of the day with the Spirit was being poured out in accordance with the Prophet Joel's vision (Joel 2: 28-32).

The apostle John affirms the incredible dimensional change which is brought about by the Spirit of God being poured out in 1st John 2:20: *"But you have an anointing from the Holy One, and you know all things."* It is the anointing that is focused on in Romans 8. Without God's Spirit, we actually are left to the letter of the Torah. Therefore, it is absolutely critical that we receive the gift of the Holy Spirit. Further, it is critical that we distinguish how incredibly different it is to walk by and in the Spirit as opposed to by and in what *WE* think is right in our own reasoning.

I am not suggesting that we do not use the gift of the incredible mind that God has given us each one of us. God has given us the written word against which we test both by the Spirit and by our rational minds whether that which we think is God's love is, in fact, His will and not a subterfuge of the Enemy.

We are called to *"not walk according to the flesh but according to the Spirit. For those who are according to the flesh set their minds on the things of the flesh, but those who are according to the Spirit, the things of the Spirit. For the mind set on the flesh is death, but the mind set on the*

Spirit is life and peace, because the mind set on the flesh is hostile toward God; for it does not subject itself to the law of God, for it is not even able to do so, and those who are in the flesh cannot please God. However, you are not in the flesh but in the Spirit, if indeed the Spirit of God dwells in you." (Romans 8:4-9).

If we set our minds of the flesh, we reap death. If we set our minds on the Spirit of God, we reap life.

Knowing my own long history of struggling to keep my mind on the Spirit and my personal daily battle to let God's divine love guide my every action as well as my long term goals, I take immense comfort in verses 12-17 of Romans 8: *"if you are living according to the flesh, you must die; but if by the Spirit you are putting to death the deeds of the body, you will live. For all who are being led by the Spirit of God, these are sons of God. For you have not received a spirit of slavery leading to fear again, but you have received a spirit of adoption as sons by which we cry out, 'Abba! Father!' The Spirit Himself testifies with our spirit that we are children of God, and if children, heirs also, heirs of God and fellow heirs with Christ, if indeed we suffer with Him so that we may also be glorified with Him."*

My comfort comes from the hope that by the Spirit I will put to death the deeds of the body, and by His Spirit I have great hope of accomplishment – not by my strength, which is nothing, but by the kindness of His grace. And I have no question that my spirit cries out with agony, *"Abba, Father!"*

Romans 9

"To whom... of whom... from whom." Paul's deep awareness of the special place held by the Jewish people is fully on display in Chapter 9. Look at the three prepositional phrases in verses 4 and 5: *To whom are*

the gifts, promises and actions of God, *of whom* are the patriarchs and *from whom* the Anointed One came. The Jewish people have been so special to God to end up in anyway estranged.

Like Paul's case that circumcision is of no effect unless it is a circumcision of the heart, Paul argues that not all who appear to be Jewish are children of promise. God's covenant with Abraham is the true beginning of the chosen children, and not all of his seed is included but only the line that came from Abraham and Sarah. Abraham's other children are not included in this very special covenantal relationship.

Covenants are two-sided. The blessings of a "bound will" between two parties are many. I am also struck with how many generations of the seed of Abraham came through Sarah. Many remained faithful to the covenant God made long ago with the great Patriarch. I think of my own relationship to a widow that flowed from my special relationship with her deceased husband. It is not just my *obligation* to her that moves me; she is caught up in the *love* that her husband and I shared as great friends. I am *for her* no matter what, but for the relationship to work after her husband's death, my friend's widow must extend trust that I will be faithful to her. Otherwise, the blessings of covenant will not flow.

The Jewish people are like that widow. God is faithful in a special way to them because of the great relationship He enjoyed with their father, Abraham. Like my relationship with my deceased friend's two daughters, God is there for them as well – amazingly, throughout their generations. God bound himself to Abraham and Sarah's miraculous offspring: for all generations, but those generations have to trust the relationship and honor their side of the covenant. Those who did so were able to receive the promises that flowed generationally.

...ॐe 13, Paul brings forward an observation that conflicts with my certainty of how far covenantal binding goes. Jacob and Esau are both children of the seed of Abraham through Sarah. There was something in Esau that caused God to withhold His blessing. Surely, that withdrawal of covenantal blessing must have been triggered by Esau's attitude. I can only cipher this by imputing a relational mistrust on Esau's side so great that the Bible records that God *hated* Esau. Paul rightly emphasizes that God CAN chose to whom He will extend blessings. God is attentive and faithful to all, but His covenant blessings still flow according to His mercy and His choice. As Paul says of the Jews in verse 32, one could say of Esau: *"he did not seek God by faith but by works and stumbled."* Something was amiss.

With the immeasurable gift of God's son, God has chosen to bring into His special covenantal relationship Gentiles. We have the picture of a potter working on the potter's wheel. He has been making pots from one batch of clay and bowls from another batch. Now, the potter intermixes the batches to make very special vessels that come from an intermingled batch that includes both Jew and Gentile. Paul asks, "Isn't the potter is free to chose what to make as He proceeds in His work and what batch to draw from?" We live in a time where he has chosen to shift, so to speak, what He is making. Now He makes New Covenant vessels, and we are included by the Grace of God.

Romans 10

When our underlying belief is that we are "not good enough," our unconscious world seeks in innumerable ways to fix the problem. We earnestly try to be good enough, but Paul is reminding us and the Jewish people that we are doomed to failure. We can never get good enough through our own efforts. For me personally, this has been a constant battle. My "little boy," my unconscious world, feels "not good enough." But God definitively says, "You are good enough when your identity is merged with Me - with My Son's identity."

Since Paul is still in struggle for the Jewish people, he pulls a key verse from Deuteronomy 30:14: *"But the word is very nigh unto thee, in thy mouth, and in thy heart, that thou mayest do it."* And what is His word for you and for me? Another kernel, another *Kerygma*:

"...if you confess with your mouth the Lord Jesus and believe in your heart that God has raised Him from the dead, you will be saved." (Romans 10:9).

This would be a great memory verse for the week. We can rush right over this promise and miss entirely that it is speaking to our inner hearts. Have I confessed with my mouth that Jesus is my Lord, and have I believed in my heart that Father raised Him from the dead? The answer IS yes! I have. So here I have a simple but powerful rebuttal to the Evil One who wants every day to trip me up with the lie that I am "not good enough." In Jesus, I am good enough. Romans 10:9 nails it!

Paul gives us another, even shorter, kernel in verse 13:

"For whosoever shall call upon the name of the Lord shall be saved!"

Do I call on the name of the Lord to be saved? Yes. Nailed again. And again, Paul pulls from the Old Testament scriptures, from Joel 2:32 where Joel writes, *"whosoever shall call on the name of Lord shall be delivered."*

Paul finishes out the chapter with observations about the importance – even necessity, of proclaiming the Good News. Asking the simple question, "How can the Jewish people possibly believe in Jesus if they have not heard Him truly proclaimed," Paul again pulls from the Old Testament to affirm the sweetness of those who share the *"gospel of peace, who bring glad tidings of good things."* I love that verse from Isaiah. It is one of my favorite Oldies but Goodies:

> *"How beautiful upon the mountains*
> *Are the feet of Him who brings good news,*
> *Who proclaims peace,*
> *Who brings glad tidings of good things,*
> *Who proclaims salvation,*
> *Who says to Zion,*
> *'Your God reigns!'"*
> (Isaiah 52:7)

Romans 11

Paul continues his very serious focus on the Jewish and Gentile issue, addressing both the current state of Israel as well as the future. Bringing in the story of Elijah after his contest with the 400 prophets of Baal is to remind any Jewish believer feeling alone that there are many others from amongst the Jewish people. We remember that Elijah thought he was the only one left amongst the prophets faithful to God; instead, God told him there were 7,000. Elijah was a trifle off. And so would be a Jew who thought no one else from his tribe had believed in the Messiah's advent.

Further, Paul takes heart that the broad acceptance of the Messiah on the part of Gentiles could bring a jealousy that would provoke many Jews to come over to the Lord. He predicts their return would bring great fullness – great blessing to all.

In verses Romans 11:16-18, Paul goes on to highlight by a wonderful analogy just how important his brother Israelites are. Truly, in the covenantal history of God, Abraham and Jacob's lineage is the ROOT. One translation of verse 17 renders the word *"fatness"* as a descriptor of the character of the root, i.e., the *"fat root."* I've always liked that translation. However, reading that verse in the Greek makes me realize that the emphasis is on those who have been grafted *ONTO* the olive tree and thus are able to partake *OF* the nourishment of the root *AND* the fatness of the olive tree itself. It really is a twofold emphasis, and it is all about receiving great richness, nourishment and fatness that no other type of tree speaks to as well as the olive tree. I think about how wonderful virgin olive oil is, how clear and golden, how fat in taste, how protective, how fluid. It is a beautiful reference to the Holy Spirit, a Biblical reference and a comparison made frequently in scripture along with water, fire, breath and wind. Yes, it is a wonder that we get to partake of the fatness of the olive tree *and* the nourishment of the root: the wonder and immeasurable supply of God's Spirit.

Paul makes a remarkable declaration in verse 29: *"For the gifts and the calling of God are irrevocable."* Paul undoubtedly is saying that the gifts that have been given and God's call to Israel is not revocable. This is a revelation of the nature of God. When God binds Himself, He is bound. The fact that many have resisted the Call does not mean that the children of Abraham and Jacob are no longer called. The Call still goes out to them; the gifts are still theirs for the receiving if they simply go further in God and receive what God has for them: the government of the Son and the guidance of the Holy Spirit.

Anyone who does not grasp the precious wonder of our Jewish friends is missing Paul's underlying message. They ARE beloved, still chosen, still desired, still sought after. Let no one disparage those our Father in heaven has called beloved!

Finally, one of the most beautiful sentences in the Bible sums up the chapter: *"For of Him and through Him and to Him are all things, to whom be the glory forever."* Another kernel of sorts. And all we can say is "Amen!"

Romans 12

Romans 12 starts out with two of my very favorite verses in the Bible: *"I beseech you therefore, brethren, by the mercies of God, that you present your bodies a living sacrifice - holy, acceptable to God, which is your reasonable service. And do not be conformed to this world, but be transformed by the renewing of your mind, that you may prove what is that good and acceptable and perfect will of God."*

Oh, I love these verses! *"By the mercies of God."* The word *"mercies"* here is *oiktermos* in the Greek. It means the *"deep recesses of God's heart which is filled with compassion, deep felt emotion and longings."* I read this two ways, and perhaps the verses imply both. Paul himself, moved by his heart for *oiktermos*, urges the believers to present their bodies as a living sacrifice. That's one way to read it. But it also may mean that it is BY the mercies of God that the Brothers present their bodies as living sacrifices. Either way, Paul is moving out of the deep recesses of God's heart, and we touch God's heart when we realize how much He wants us fully given over to Him. This is a relational thing – a powerful binding of the will. When we "give over," we turn over to God all that we are.

The verses also contain the heavy word, *"sacrifice."* This word speaks to how much God wants us to turn over ourselves: completely.

Finally, we see the outcome of being turned over fully to God: our minds get transformed. This is critical. We can then use our rational gifts to *PROVE* what is the good and perfect will of God.

Think about the roles the Spirit and the Word play in our lives, prompted by the previous chapters in particular. Jeremiah prophesies that we all will be able to know God's will in our inner person, i.e., through God's Spirit's work inside us. Jesus, as Isaiah says, will whisper in our ear *"this is the way"* through the Spirit. (Isaiah 30:21). 1st John says we have no need for any person to teach us as the anointing of the Holy Spirit will teach us. (1ˢᵗ John 2:27).

If these things be true, what are the roles of the rational mind and scripture? We get a glimpse here in the first two verses of the two-way partnership. The Spirit prompts us with direction or revelation while the renewed mind *proves* and bears witness that this is true through its knowledge of the scripture. In a sense, we need two tools for successful choices: the Spirit's prompting, the renewed mind's confirmation that scripture confirms (or permits) the prompting.

Let's say someone feels the Spirit prompting them with the revelation that Jesus is accursed. Paul takes this very situation up in 1ˢᵗ Corinthians 12:3: *"Therefore I make known to you that no one speaking by the Spirit of God says, 'Jesus is accursed;' and no one can say, "Jesus is Lord," except by the Holy Spirit."* We know from scripture that this is *NOT* from the Holy Spirit because scripture is entirely clear on this point. But it does take a renewed mind to properly use scripture as a proof of whether something be good or bad.

I am reminded of an instance where someone felt God telling them it was OK to have sexual relations with someone who was not their spouse because the spouse was to die soon. This was an entirely wrong thought. It clearly was prompted by the devil and not God because scripture completely stands against it. But the person who thought this knew scripture well. Their acceptance of the falsehood showed that their mind still needed renewing. Another way to say this is that they were not totally given over to God. If they had been, their renewed mind would have known better!

Paul shifts his emphasis away from the Jewish-Gentile question to normal Christian living issues. First, he deals with giftings from God, seeing the Christian community as one person, one body. Many members, many different gifts from God, many functions, but one body.

I like Paul's exhortation. Whatever God has given you as a gift is to be used and used fully. If you are a giver by God's gift and impartation, give liberally, in an overflowing manner, just as God gives. If one gifted to lead, lead diligently, and so forth. We need all the gifts working to have a healthy body. The Enemy's great ploy is to feed us the lie that it only takes a few to do a few functions, and the community is OK without our participation. We become seat warmers and not players on the field. This is so wrong! Communities cannot be truly healthy unless all the gifts are working. And EVERYONE has been given special gifts! *Everybody* is needed on the field and in the game.

"Let love be without hypocrisy. Abhor what is evil; cling to what is good. Be devoted to one another in brotherly love; give preference to one another in honor; not lagging behind in diligence, fervent in spirit, serving the Lord; rejoicing in hope, persevering in tribulation, devoted to prayer, contributing to the needs of the saints, practicing hospitality.

"Bless those who persecute you; bless and do not curse. Rejoice with those who rejoice, and weep with those who weep. Be of the same mind toward one another; do not be haughty in mind, but associate with the lowly. Do not be wise in your own estimation. Never pay back evil for evil to anyone. Respect what is right in the sight of all men. If possible, so far as it depends on you, be at peace with all men." (Romans 12:9-18).

"Do not be overcome by evil, but overcome evil with good." I can ponder the last verse for a long time on a personal level. It really encourages a very old practice in the history of the Church - overcoming temptation to one thing by giving oneself to something that is its very opposite. Our immersion in giving ourselves to a good thing (for example,

working our calling with great vigor or giving ourselves to a project that does true good) blocks much of the Enemy's assault – by God's grace.

A great chapter with much meat.

Romans 13

Paul continues general admonitions in Chapter 13. No discussion of Jew or Gentile! He is addressing common human issues that are applicable to all communities - not just those in Rome. Of course, Rome is the headquarters of the most powerful secular authority on earth, so perhaps it is not surprising that he spends a great deal of ink on the question of authority. As Watchman Nee said, authority is the greatest question in the universe. Who is in authority? How will you respond to that authority?

It has been 45 years since I read Nee's reflections. (Watchman Nee, *Spiritual Authority*). There is no question that his thoughts rested on the first five verses of Romans 13. Our old teacher, Bob Mumford, followed up with additional amplification. Ideally, the Christian becomes adept at spotting authority where it exists and responding to it. Bob's best example was the elevator.

In those days (the early 70s), high-rise buildings had elevator operators. My best memory of this was the elevator operator at the Sterrick Building in downtown Memphis. When you entered the elevator, there would be an elevator operator sitting on a stool. He or she would ask what floor you wanted. The door closed, and he took everyone to their destinations. Bob pointed out that even if the President of the United States got onto the elevator, the President had entered the realm where the elevator operator was in charge. It was the elevator operator who had the authority in the elevator, not the President.

Paul says that validly established authorities (and there are so many!) must be heeded or one will suffer the consequences. Heeding authority is one of the marks of the true Christian. Christians in Rome are even to pay their taxes to an entirely pagan state that is supporting pagan cults. We, no less, are to pay what is due in taxes, in both respect and deed. There are obvious limits (think of Peter's response before the Sanhedrin in Acts 5), but Paul choses not to address those problems in this section.

His relatively long discourse on authority is focused primarily on secular matters. But his observations are applicable in the Spiritual realm: in the Christian community as God's gifts operate and also on the higher plane of our overall orientation to the Universe. Who has the ultimate authority? God! All three of my brothers (Paul of Tarsus, Watchman Nee and Bob Mumford) recognized that the biggest issue was whether we would submit to the creator of the Universe or not.

Paul ends his discourse on authority with a wonderful sentence:

"Give to everyone what you owe them: if you owe taxes, pay taxes; if money, then money, if respect, then respect, if honor, then honor."

A man or woman who follows Paul's direction will move through their lives in an entirely different way than the nonbeliever. Paul reminds us in Philippians 2:6-7 that Jesus himself, *"existing in the form of God, did not consider equality with God something to grasp, but rather emptied Himself, taking the form of a servant, being made in human likeness.... He humbled Himself and became obedient even unto death...."*

At Romans 13:8, Paul shifts emphasis. Having addressed the most important question in the Universe, he takes up the most powerful thing in the Universe: Love. Love is the foundation of the Torah - its guiding force under every commandment and Jesus's core teaching. Even the way we relate to authority is a matter of love. Again, I recall Derek Prince's teaching: Love is the most powerful thing in the Universe, and God is love.

Paul finishes this chapter with verses that echo most Christian radio evangelists today: "The time is near. Things are about wrap up. Get ready. Put aside all deeds of darkness and put on Jesus Christ. Don't think for a second about how to gratify the desires of your flesh."

These pastoral encouragements that are *ALWAYS* timely no matter how you view TV evangelists. Paul shares these words of encouragement with the Romans not only because they needed them in a pagan culture, but because *WE* need them. I certainly do. May God help us.

Romans 14

Romans 14 is a chapter that might be entitled, "Let Your Conscience Be Your Guide but Keep It To Yourself." We have returned to the Jewish/Gentile earlier theme, though the chapter is more focused on behavior than theology.

Our Jewish forefathers were all about behavior. This is a characteristic of almost all fundamental religious expressions. In 2017, twenty people were killed in India because of how they treated cows. Orthodox Jews and Muslims can be very dangerous if you do many things contrary to what they think right. This is true of Buddhists as well. And the Inquisition proves it has been true of Christians as well. In Rome, Gentiles believers had bought non-kosher food at the market place where the meat had been offered up to pagan idols. This drove the Jewish brothers crazy. It is easy to be offended if you feel your righteousness comes from an identity that overlaps the behavior of your neighbor.

Paul outlines a great posture for the believer in Romans 14. It is one of quietness and peace with those whose practices differ.

"For the kingdom of God is not a matter of eating and drinking, but of righteousness, peace and joy in the Holy Spirit," (Romans 14:17).

Our posture is not that of a critic (God is in charge of judgment, not us) but of a man or woman of true peace and deep joy whose righteousness comes as a gift not based on personal effort.

It is tempting to think this chapter is about eating and drinking, but I don't think that it is the case. Most of all, it is about doing whatever we can to maintain peace with our brothers and sisters. If we took an honest evaluation of what sets us off - what drives us crazy in the beliefs or behaviors of other Christians, we would probably have a long list. Coming from a Protestant background, my list of what one should believe or do was VERY long and excluded beliefs like praying to Jesus's mother, religious paraphernalia (rosary beads), religious clothing (clerical collars and choir robes), holy water, non-observance of the Lord's Supper and so forth. Well, it was a long list.

Over the intervening years, God has been slowly demolishing my attention to "stumbling blocks." Why? Because the Kingdom of God is not about externals. The Kingdom of God is about our internal worlds. I am called to extend freedom to my brothers and sisters so long as their actions and beliefs are not truly hurtful to others. I am called to embrace and not punish. A heady call!

Romans 15

Paul continues his admonition for believers to accept each other even when there are differences, and to defer when it would cause another brother or sister to stumble:

"Each of us should please our neighbors for their good, to build them up. For even Christ did not please Himself but, as it is written: 'The insults of those who insult you have fallen on me.'" (Romans 15:2-3).

Then he wraps up one of the great values of Scripture:

"For everything that was written in the past was written to teach us, so that through the endurance taught in the Scriptures and the encouragement they provide, we might have hope." (Romans 15:4).

Why did God give us the scriptures? To encourage us that God will not forsake His people. Since we know that He will not forsake us, we should not give up when under trial. Clearly, being a Christian around 57 A.D. was not easy, particularly in Rome.

I am reminded of our brothers and sisters today in the Middle East who are under great persecution – even facing death. Paul is absolutely right; Christians have the scriptures which give them great hope no matter what is happening in the present. God will not forsake His people, and He will not forsake you!

"May the God who gives endurance and encouragement give you the same attitude of mind toward each other that Christ Jesus had, so that with one mind and one voice you may glorify the God and Father of our Lord Jesus Christ. Accept one another, then, just as Christ accepted you, in order to bring praise to God." (Romans 15:5-7).

Paul is nailing his point to the cross; we really must accept one another because of Jesus's own nature and action. Paul makes a related point in Philippians 2:

"Let this mind be in you, which was also in Christ Jesus: Who, being in the form of God, thought it not robbery to be equal with God, But made himself of no reputation, and took upon him the form of a servant, and was made in the likeness of men, And being found in fashion as a man,

he humbled himself, and became obedient unto death, even the death of the cross." (Philippians 2:5-8).

In a sense, our small fellowship, Servants of Christ, took its name from this passage and 2nd Corinthian 4:5: *"For we do not proclaim ourselves, but Jesus Christ as Lord, and ourselves as your servants for Jesus's sake."*

Since we run about with this affiliation, the name and these three verses are a triple encouragement to *ACCEPT* one another. Lord, have mercy! Let me not veer from your admonition!

"May the God of hope fill you with all joy and peace as you trust in him, so that you may overflow with hope by the power of the Holy Spirit." (Romans 15:13).

We saw that verse 4 spotlights scripture as a source of encouragement - God does not forsake His children! We saw that the result was hope. Now, in verse 13, we see that the power or effect of the Holy Spirit working within us brings *"abundant"* hope - overflowing hope, more hope than we even need. The work of the Holy Spirit in Paul's life obviously had led him to this conclusion as Paul has faced many trials, difficulties and opposition.

Paul sees the Romans through eyes of faith. *"I myself am convinced, my brothers and sisters, that you yourselves are full of goodness, filled with knowledge and competent to instruct one another."* (Romans 15:14). He is giving them a great vote of confidence, but he does not hesitate to tell them things they should already know. He has done this throughout his letter. And why has he done that?

Verses 15 and 16 answer the question. It is because of his specific gifting in God, given him not because he deserved the gifting, but entirely by grace. Given the gifting, Paul has to discharge his duty. This is true for each one of us. As Jesus admonished, we all are under obligation to not cover our individual gift with a bushel basket. Rather, we need to let it operate vigorously.

"Yet I have written you quite boldly on some points to remind you of them again, because of the grace God gave me to be a minister of Christ Jesus to the Gentiles." (Romans 15:15-16).

Paul restricts himself to the role God has assigned him:

"I will not venture to speak of anything except what Christ has accomplished through me in leading the Gentiles to obey God by what I have said and done — by the power of signs and wonders, through the power of the Spirit of God. So, from Jerusalem all the way around to Illyricum, I have fully proclaimed the gospel of Christ." (Romans 15:18-19).

Paul then shares something that has always interested me: the issue of who has laid the foundation. When we build a building, the foundation is truly the most important part. Nothing will hold up if the foundation is faulty. God's foundation is a foundation of Love, and the limits of any building are measured, oriented and set by the limits and nature of the foundation. For Paul, this meant that he wanted to avoid building on another man's foundation. He wanted to be sure of the foundation. I think of our own children. We wanted to give them a foundation that would work no matter where they lived and worked.

With brothers and sisters from different backgrounds, heritages and training, this can certainly be problematic. Often, I wonder why others do not see as I see. Part of the answer is that our foundations differ.

"It has always been my ambition to preach the gospel where Christ was not known, so that I would not be building on someone else's foundation." (Romans 15:20).

Finally, we reach verses 25-27, which allow us to date Paul's letter.

"Now, however, I am on my way to Jerusalem in the service of the Lord's people there. For Macedonia and Achaia were pleased to make a contribution for the poor among the Lord's people in Jerusalem. They were pleased to do it, and indeed they owe it to them. For if the Gentiles have shared in the Jews' spiritual blessings, they owe it to the Jews to share with them their material blessings." (Romans 15:25-27).

It is near the end of Paul's 3rd missionary journey, and we see that he is on his way to Jerusalem where he will be arrested and eventually sent to Rome itself. Remember, from our information in Acts, this allows us to place the date between 56 and 58 AD. Paul is no spring chicken. He is over 50 years old!

Romans 16

Chapter 16 is obviously a "post-script." Paul says hello to over 29 people in Rome. This is quite amazing. Many he mentions have house churches in their homes. Most are Roman names, but the distinctive thing is Paul's great affection for them. I have to assume he met them on his various voyages though some may have met Paul in Judea.

Over two-thirds of the chapter is devoted to these greetings. Paul ends by sending greetings from seven men with him: Timothy, Lucius, Jason, Sosipater, Tertius (his actual scribe), Gaius, and Quartus.

The chapter is a window into the practical functioning of the early Church. Several of those Paul addresses are "apostles:" (Andronicus and Junia). Since we often think of the "twelve" apostles, this may come as a surprise, but, of course, Paul is called an apostle. Since the word *"apostolos"* simply means *"ambassador"* or *"delegate,"* it should not be too surprising that the title describes a person's function. An apostle is one who goes forth representing someone (in this case, Jesus) or a nation (think Ambassador to Australia for example). Barnabas,

Timothy and Silvanus among other are called *"apostolos."* There are those with that function in Rome.

There also are "deaconesses" (Phoebe, at the start of the chapter). Some translations will shift the description of Phoebe to "servant" since that is the underlying meaning of the word we have in Greek *(diakonos)* from which we get the word "deacon." Deacons were early workers of a certain kind in the early church. We met them first in Acts when they were formally invested with authority to help with the distribution to the widows. You will remember that the key qualification was that they be "full of the Spirit." Paul often would address a church in his letter along with the *"bishops and deacons"* as he did in his letter to the Philippians: *"Paul and Timotheus, the servants of Jesus Christ, to all the saints in Christ Jesus which are at Philippi, with the bishops and deacons...."* (Philippians 1:1). Obviously, Phoebe is quite important. Paul spends more ink on her than anyone else.

The whole chapter is sprinkled with men *and* women beloved of God. It is worth reflecting just how beautifully mixed the early communities were. There is no select ethnic or gender group. Male, female, old, young, Gentile, Jew, black, white. A wonderful basket of diversity.

Paul ends with a thought that will be embellished a few years later as he writes the Ephesian church from Rome itself - God's mysterious secret:

"...the revelation of the mystery which has been kept secret for long ages past, but now is manifested, and by the Scriptures of the prophets, according to the commandment of the eternal God, has been made known to all the nations, leading to obedience of faith..." (Romans 16:25-26).

Paul devotes the entirety of Chapter 3 of Ephesians to this mystery. Compare the end of Romans with this section from the third chapter of Ephesians:

"by revelation He made known to me the mystery (as I have briefly writ-ten already, by which, when you read, you may understand my knowl-edge in the mystery of Christ), which in other ages was not made known to the sons of men, as it has now been revealed by the Spirit to His holy apostles and prophets: that the Gentiles should be fellow heirs, of the same body, and partakers of His promise in Christ through the gospel...." (Ephesians 3:3-6).

Paul ends his letter with a memorable and rousing flourish:

"to the only wise God, through Jesus Christ, be the glory forever!" Amen!

1st Corinthians

1st Corinthians 1

In many ways, 1st Corinthians is Paul's best-known letter. Like John 3:16, 1st Corinthians 13:13 has been spoken at innumerable wedding ceremonies to literally millions of people: *"the greatest of these is Love."* The letter also contains many controversial sections on a slew of topics.

Part of the reason for Paul's somewhat freewheeling breadth is the significant amount of time and contact he had with Corinth. A city of the southwestern edge of modern-day Greece, it had been totally destroyed by the Romans about 200 years before Paul's multiple visits. Rebuilt as a Roman colony by Julius Caesar in 44 BC, it must have been fresh and vibrant. Commercial activity was significant. But, because it served two shipping ports, it was like all great maritime cities – full of transients and sexual immorality. Think of Bordeaux, Marseilles and New Orleans as parallels.

When I was 17 years old, my summer college program, *Classrooms Abroad*, had a day and a night in Bordeaux, France. Three of the other fellows on the trip took me to what would formally be called a Bordello. The whole town seemed seedy, but the Bordello was like a spot on Tatooine in *Star Wars* with the giant bar and strange creatures, only the strange creatures were human. Though I sat immovable at a table, I got the picture. Corinth must have been a lot like Bordeaux. It had a terrible reputation.

From another point of view, however, there was immense diversity in the population, both ethnically and economically. And though it was in Greece, because it was a Roman colony, it would have been very Roman in character. Also, the city was heavily populated – around 200,000 freedmen and 400,000 slaves. Think of that.

As you will remember from Acts, Paul stayed there at least 18 months during his second missionary journey (see Acts 18:11,18) around 50 or 51 AD. He found a warm welcome with Aquila and Priscilla, with whom he collaborated in both ministry as well as tentmaking.

While away over the intervening years, Paul wrote the believers in Corinth several letters of which two have survived. 1st and 2nd Corinthians were probably written in the mid 50s. Scholars think 1st Corinthians may have been written within three or four years of Paul's first visit.

In spite of Paul's long stay and great connectedness to the Corinthian church and his basic founding of it, the community was full of serious issues. After a short introduction where he refers to them as those *"called to be saints,"* and after foregoing some of his normal introductory words (for example, he does not address the "bishops and deacons" as he does in his letter to the Philippians), Paul launches right into what may have been the biggest issue they faced: division.

Believers had apparently divided themselves into groups that followed various leaders. It certainly is not hard to imagine this today when people follow TV evangelists in a similar way (Jim Baker, Benny Hinn, Pat Robertson, and so forth), but at the level of true community, this was particularly hurtful to Paul – hurtful because he was being followed in a way that to some degree minimized Jesus's position as head. In body terms, the head rightly receives the glory. It is what most characterizes our identity, and in the "Body of Christ," only the head (Jesus) deserves the glory. We are to "honor" those who work amongst us (I think of brothers like my friend, Terry Smith), but we do not give them glory. True glory only emanates from God. There is a difference.

The Greek word, "timé," is our word for *honor*, and it means value. We value our brothers and sisters. *Doxa* is the Greek word for *glory* and it means splendor and majesty. "To God be the Glory," we sing. Glory *IS* God's, and I suspect it is only God who can give glory to us. We cannot. But we can and should honor and value each other immensely. There *is* a difference, and apparently some of the Corinthians had crossed the line.

Think of when the people of Lystra in Acts 14 saw Paul and Barnabas heal a man. They glorified the apostles, and Paul immediately stopped it:

"...when the people saw what Paul had done, they raised their voices, saying in the Lycaonian language, 'The gods have come down to us in the likeness of men!' And Barnabas they called Zeus, and Paul, Hermes, because he was the chief speaker. Then the priest of Zeus, whose temple was in front of their city, brought oxen and garlands to the gates, intending to sacrifice with the multitudes. But when the apostles Barnabas and Paul heard this, they tore their clothes and ran in among the multitude, crying out and saying, 'Men, why are you doing these things? We also are men with the same nature as you....'" (Acts 14:11-15).

To God be the Glory!

After decrying this tendency in Corinth to over-elevate, Paul shocks a baptism-thumping current day Christian when he says in verse 17:

"For Christ did not send me to baptize, but to preach the gospel, not with wisdom of words, lest the cross of Christ should be made of no effect."

Paul was a proclaimer first and foremost, though obviously he was a great Apostle (Ambassador) with many other giftings that he had other than just delivering messages. But Paul is crystal clear on the kernel of his message: The Cross - God's costly sacrifice that we might be united to Him intimately - Jesus's costly sacrifice that we might be united to God.

Beginning in verse 18, the next few verses are some of the most memorable in the letter:

"For the message of the cross is foolishness to those who are perishing, but to us who are being saved it is the power of God."

He wraps up the chapter with incredible language and a repeat of the admonition to glorify only God and not man:

"but God has chosen the foolish things of the world to put to shame the wise, and God has chosen the weak things of the world to put to shame the things which are mighty; and the base things of the world and the things which are despised God has chosen, and the things which are not, to bring to nothing the things that are, that no flesh should glory in His presence. But of Him you are in Christ Jesus, who became for us wisdom from God—and righteousness and sanctification and redemption— that, as it is written, "He who glories, let him glory in the Lord." (1st Corinthians 1:27-31, NKJV).

1ˢᵗ Corinthians 2

If we move from one chapter to another on a daily basis, we may miss a carryover from the day before. I think that could happen with the second chapter of 1ˢᵗ Corinthians. In the latter part of Chapter 1, Paul had focused on a remarkable tendency of God to focus on the weak of the world and not the strong. At the beginning of Chapter 2, he focuses on his own ministry and giftings (or lack thereof). He presents himself as weak in speech from a carnal and worldly point of view. This would be particularly evident to someone influenced by Greek culture, which prized fine oratory.

Apollos was a skilled orator, but Paul spoke the compelling truth directly – relying on the Spirit of God to enable his speech. Paul was simply doing exactly what Jesus directed. Remember Jesus's earlier admonition to his disciples:

"When you are brought before the synagogues, rulers, and authorities, do not worry about how to defend yourselves or what to say. For at that time the Holy Spirit will teach you what you should say." (Luke 12:11-12).

God said nearly the same thing to Moses in Exodus 4:12:

"Now then go, and I, even I, will be with your mouth, and teach you what you are to say."

This way of speaking had nothing to do with education or polished refined speaking. Often, we do not take God at His word and do not speak what God is speaking to those we are with. Usually fear holds us back – needlessly. If we have an upcoming encounter with someone, we simply should lift it up to God. One of the brothers with whom I walk recently had multiple important meetings, and we lifted those encounters up to God the day before and the day of the encounters. God was with him in the meetings; my brother responded with grace.

The Spirit of God was his Director that day. Otherwise, we suspect things could have gone terribly amiss.

In our own interpersonal encounters, on what do we really rely?

Paul had been taught to rely entirely on the Spirit of God. Bringing God's chosen words to the Corinthians meant that their faith was not based on rational thought but on the utterances of God Himself as He spoke through Paul in the Spirit.

It is easy to miss how enormous this is, but it is the very nature of the Promise articulated by the prophets Jeremiah and Joel.

The New Covenant Promise:

"This is the covenant I will make with the people of Israel
after that time," declares the Lord.
"I will put my law in their minds
and write it on their hearts.
I will be their God,
and they will be my people."
(Jeremiah 31:33).

"I will pour out my Spirit on all people.
Your sons and daughters will prophesy,
your old men will dream dreams,
your young men will see visions.
Even on my servants, both men and women,
I will pour out my Spirit in those days." (Joel 2:28-29).

This is *SO* important to recognize. All that Paul does is based on the immense shift that comes from the New Covenant promised by the prophets. It *has* come. Paul is just one on whom the Spirit rests, and he does his best to work entirely out of the Spirit. It is his internal and external Director. God's Spirit is not something we learn or innate human knowledge we gather; rather, it is a living force. Within Paul, it is a relationship and not a set of rules, a companion and counselor and not a bundle of good ideas.

The Spiritual revelation that Paul brings no man could have imagined, because it is a God thing and not a man thing. Look at verse 9 carefully.

> "...it is written,
> 'Things which eye has not seen, and ear has not heard,
> And which have not entered the heart of man,
> All that God has prepared for those who love Him.'"

No one could ascertain what actually God was doing based on mental gymnastics. It was not in the heart of man. But through the Spirit of God the message has been revealed, and, if received by men, it is only through the Spirit.

And what is this unworldly message? *"Jesus Christ and Him crucified"* (from verse 2 of Chapter 2). The *Kerygma*, the kernel. This may seem like foolishness to the erudite, but it is salvation for those who receive it. For God so loved the world and all mankind that He gave His only begotten Son that whosoever believes on Him should not perish but have everlasting life. Sacrifice, substitution, redemption, justification – all leading to Life in the Spirit of God. The message is one to receive in the heart that the mind might be flooded with the power of the Spirit.

1st Corinthians 3

Here is Paul's lead-in from the beginning of Chapter 1:

"I thank my God always concerning you for the grace of God which was given you in Christ Jesus, that in everything you were enriched in Him,

in all speech and all knowledge, even as the testimony concerning Christ was confirmed in you, so that you are not lacking in any gift, awaiting eagerly the revelation of our Lord Jesus Christ, who will also confirm you to the end, blameless in the day of our Lord Jesus Christ. God is faithful, through whom you were called into fellowship with His Son, Jesus Christ our Lord." (1st Corinthians 1:4-9).

And here is his surprising lead-in from Chapter 3:

"And I, brethren, could not speak to you as to spiritual men, but as to men of flesh, as to infants in Christ. I gave you milk to drink, not solid food; for you were not yet able to receive it. Indeed, even now you are not yet able, for you are still fleshly. For since there is jealousy and strife among you, are you not fleshly, and are you not walking like mere men?" (1st Corinthians 3:1-3). Quite a difference!

Paul is speaking plainly. He has returned to his earlier concern for division. There are many parts to the underlying problem. Some parts deal with the tendency to improperly relate to others. But underlying that emphasis lays an identity problem. When there is division, there is often an underlying identity problem. Rather than getting your identity from who you are in God, you get at least part of your essential identity from other things – in this case people you follow. *"I am of Paul; I am of Apollos."*

An honest look at "who" we think we are is sobering. We feel we need the right car, the right dress, the right church, the right friends, the right affiliations, the right children, the right job and so forth in order to be OK. These things are trappings of identity.

Identity is relational in character. I am reminded of Terry Smith's insight that under stress our unconscious solutions for happiness come forward, and we don't even realize it. Related to our identity, when we are under the spotlight and our identity trappings are touched, extreme discomfort typically occurs and we often act inappropriately.

It is revealing for me to think of when and where I can get very uncomfortable. If I am thrown into a business group where family heritage and prominence is longstanding in my birth city, I can feel inadequate. I find myself in that social situation occasionally, and I hate the feeling that emerges within me. It obviously comes from an internal calculation that I don't measure up. My "identity" is not sufficient.

That feeling arises from a lie, because its basis (that my generational "heritage" is somehow deficient) is a lie. My "heritage" is not what makes ME of value. My value is best shown by the crucifixion – not where my father went to school. Getting our identities straight is critical for a healthy and mature life.

Paul is straight about the source of his value. It comes from God's love, God's evaluation, God's action. Paul presents himself in Chapter 3 as a simple servant – doing only what God assigned him to do. He planted, Apollos watered, and God made the plant grow. Apollos and Paul are just co-workers; they are not to be part of a Corinthian's esteem bucket.

Any architects reading Chapter 3 will be happy with his building analogy in the second half of the chapter. There are two ways to take the building analogy. One is at an individual level, and one is at the corporate level. Regardless, the foundation is the most important part of a building. If the foundation is wrong, the whole building will eventually go wrong. The foundation MUST be properly constructed. I have often thought about the analogy that Jesus is the chief corner stone in the foundation. In the early days of our fellowship, I had a very clear vision of this. Visualize a foundation of large blocks of stone. The "chief" stone is the one that is laid first at one of the eventual four corners.

Its proper location and shape determine the exact location and form of the building. Jesus is the chief cornerstone, and all rests on Him as both a foundation and a determiner of the building.

Peter does an even more thorough use of the building analogy in 1st Peter 2:4-7:

"As you come to him, the living Stone—rejected by humans but chosen by God and precious to him, you also, like living stones, are being built into a spiritual house to be a holy priesthood, offering spiritual sacrifices acceptable to God through Jesus Christ. For in Scripture it says: 'See, I lay a stone in Zion, a chosen and precious cornerstone, and the one who trusts in him will never be put to shame.' Now to you who believe, this stone is precious. But to those who do not believe, 'The stone the builders rejected has become the cornerstone,'"

Paul, however, adds a thought Peter does not: it matters what materials are used. The foundation is CRITICAL, but even with a good foundation, bad materials will jeopardize at least parts of the future building. And those weaknesses may not be seen at first, but when a fire or earthquake comes, the deficiencies will be revealed.

I take this as one of the most sobering parts of the Bible for those who have even a slight involvement with the "work" of building a Christian fellowship or community. Goodness, it is critical that we be faithful to the "dimensions" Jesus sets, a spiritual house built on *HIS* sacrifice, built in love, with no prominence or splendor given to any man or woman - Godly principles throughout.

But the personal analogy is also sobering. I have on my mirror at home 1st Corinthians 3:16-17:

"Do you not know that you are the temple of God, and that the Spirit of God dwells in you? If anyone destroys God's temple, God will destroy that person; for the temple of God, which you are, is holy."

I take this as directed at sexual sin in particular, though we can think of many other actions that can destroy our lives in God. Pride, falsehood, the occult, envy, malice – there are many things with which we can build our lives that truly endanger God's work. The terrifying words, *"God will destroy that person,"* need to be my constant reminder. Goodness. Come, Lord Jesus.

1ˢᵗ Corinthians 4

Chapter 4 continues Paul's argument against division, and he addresses the danger of favorites. Who is better, Paul or Apollos? The question itself is a problem. The idea of ranking ministerial success or impact is hurtful to unity. This does not mean that rational evaluation does not have its place. What it means is that ranking to see who is best at something is, in a sense, no one's business but God's. Only the Lord is fit and capable of true judgment, because His judgment takes into account what a person has been called to do (only the Lord knows that for sure) *AND* what gifts the Lord has bestowed.

I am reminded of the sad result we would have if a child with a handicap was gauged "less than" someone else born with different skills. The question is not whose skills are better; the question rests on what that person was given intrinsically and whether that person is operating on all the cylinders given. Think about it. Only God can answer that question.

Jesus summed up Paul's thought in another way: *Judge not that you be not judged.* (Matthew 7:1-3). I cannot help but think of the normal Sunday danger of evaluating whether the worship or the Word or even the Scriptures were "good enough" in the assembly. Or, whether one person exceeds another in their work for the Body of Christ. It is good to give honor to servants; it is dangerous to place rank.

Paul adds another characteristic of the apostolic function in verse 1 of Chapter 4: *steward*. Apostolic ministry and call are about serving and stewarding. An apostolic steward is responsible for stewarding the mysteries of God while serving as envoy and representative. We have seen this way of categorizing the truths of God as mysteries before. These truths not easily seen about God, the Universe, mankind and Love. And, we have the remarkable mystery: Christ in you, the hope of glory. Both Paul and Apollos have the function of transmitting and taking care of these precious truths. Paul and Apollos are just stewards.

I think of the wine steward in Pharaoh's household. The steward was responsible for the wine and its delivery to all of Pharaoh's guests. The steward needed to be certain what he delivered was pure wine with no impurities. Paul and Apollos had to be diligent in their service and give great care to the purity of their teaching.

Paul turns to one of the apparent underlying problems in Corinth: Pride (arrogance). Pride has long been thought of as the worst of sins – the sin Satan carries in his bosom. Some of the Corinthians think very highly of themselves indeed. They put themselves before Paul. Paul relishes the opportunity to bring forth distinctions to make his point. Paul is sentenced to death, a spectacle, weak, foolish, often hungry, poorly dressed, without a permanent home, transient, a laborer, working with his own hands, frequently slandered. The Corinthians are none of those things. No, just the opposite. But as Paul draws the distinctions, he puts their arrogance in its place.

After a beautifully written rebuke, Paul shifts back to praise. He gives them the true reason behind his admonishment: Paul loves them as his true children. He is their father in the Faith, and as a father, hopes that they will imitate his healthy knowledge and understanding of himself. His fitness is not his own. Rather, it comes entirely from God's grace. As proof, Paul has sent Timothy, to remind them of the pattern Paul follows.

Paul ends with another key characteristic of the Apostle: power from God. When he sees them in person, he is quite willing to match what God has given him against all comers. Ideas are helpful, but ministers sent by God come not only with words but also with power. Witness what happened to many who challenged Paul (and therefore God) in Acts.

1st Corinthians 5

Immorality Rebuked

Chapter 5 introduces an abrupt shift that you might expect in a letter from someone you knew well. Paul is not trying to write a doctrinal theological dissertation. Instead, he is writing to a community he knows well and for which he cares deeply. He is moving topic by topic. Now, he hits another extremely serious issue: the church in Corinth is tolerating open and persistent sexual sin that not only is wrong but also deemed illegal in Corinthian society at large: *"a man is sleeping with his father's wife."* (1st Corinthians 5:1).

A good number of things are revealed in Paul's admonition.

1. We see how Paul wants the church to deal with the situation. The ideal response would have been mourning and separation from those involved if they would not stop.

2. Since the community did not do this, Paul, takes the reins as a trans-local apostle. He would have been glad to meet

with them earlier. Even though he is a long distance away, he assures them he is there in Spirit.

3. Paul is fully aware of the power and dimension of the Spirit itself, which is not bound by space.

4. He flexes his authority as apostle to cast judgment on the offenders.

5. When present, they will hand the man over to Satan for destruction of the flesh. Of course, this is both literal and figurative. Removing any Kingdom of God association leaves the man where he began, i.e., in the Kingdom of Darkness. But there is no physical punishment – only the punishment that comes to all who trespass in darkness.

6. Hopefully, the eventual outcome is that the man's spirit will be saved.

Thus, we learn about proper response, an apostle's authority that overrides the community, the power and nature of the Spirit in governmental and disciplinary action, authority to cast judgment, the frightening dimension of separation from a brother or sister and the hoped-for restoration. Quite a bit is wrapped up in Paul's response.

Clearly, Paul is upset because verse 9 tells us that he had written earlier about association with sexually immoral people *in the church*. Paul is very clear he is not prohibiting association with non-believers who have noxious practices. Otherwise, the Gospel would never reach them. Rather, he is entirely concerned with believers and their behavior. In verse 11, he calls all the believers in Corinth brothers and sisters, from which we are reminded of the intimate family nature of and community of believers. And he wants this strict rule to apply: don't associate with those who call themselves believers but are

a. sexually immoral

b. greedy

c. idol worshippers

d. drunkards

e. swindlers

And, why? To eventually see them restored (though Paul specifically does not say so in this passage).

In verse 12, Paul continues his spotlight on the apostle's function – particularly the function and responsibility of the founding father of a community. One like Paul has the responsibility to provide judgment when necessary to keep the believers safe from all sorts of danger. This is triply true in Corinth since we do not yet have a healthy functioning group of elders and bishops like we see in Philippi. At least, Paul's introduction in Chapter 1 is silent if there is one. Without a functional governing body of leaders, Paul must step up and help. Then Paul quotes the ancient authority for his demand from the Torah: *"Expel the wicked person from among you."* (Deut.13:5; 17:7, 19:19; 21:21; 22:21; 24:7). It is important to recognize that separation in the Torah was immediate and permanent, i.e., the person was to be put to death! Thank God for the New Covenant!

Even one immoral person can spoil a fellowship by his or her influence (see verse 6 concerning leaven). Paul is not tiptoeing or messing around. And neither should we.

As a footnote, we will see Paul's heart on this very issue revealed thoroughly in 2nd Corinthians, but I will wait until we reach those passages to dive in.

1st Corinthians 6

Paul introduced the issue of authority within the Church at the ministerial level in Chapter 5 when he pointed out that the Church had no authority over civil government but rather was responsible in the realm of the church (see verse 12 in Chapter 5). This was similar to the way Jewish communities were allowed to function in the Roman Empire. Their internal affairs were their own so long as they did not defy Roman law.

In Chapter 6, we find that the Corinthian believers are making the mistake of not coming to the church for judgment of difficulties between believers. Rather, they were going to the civil courts. Think divorce, property disputes, robbery, falsehood, economic or physical harm. Instead of going outside of the Kingdom of God for judgment on such matters, they should have been allowing members of the Body to settle their disputes. This is similar to the way Jews would have hoped to handle internal disagreements. Paul justifies his position by introducing a different revelation that surpasses that even of the Jews: the "saints" will judge the world. We don't judge civil cases beyond the church, but the church *"will judge the world!"* (1st Corinthians 6:2).

Paul asks the question: "If we are to judge the world, can we not also judge internal disputes?" Obviously, we can. But he ups the ante by revealing that our role also will include judging the angels! Goodness, we ought to be able to handle small matters between believers easily if we can do that.

Over the years, our community has been called to provide occasional judgment on such matters. I don't believe it is applicable when one party is a believer and the other is not. And, it even gets gray when both profess to be Christian but are from different streams of Christianity with very different attitudes toward church government. To be both practical and effective, both parties should be willing to adhere to the final judgment. My thinking suggests that a written document should be signed beforehand to that effect - a document that would be legal in civil proceedings if there were to be a dispute after the judgment.

By verse 7, Paul is clearly upset. The Corinthians have *"utterly failed"* to deal with internal disputes. Anger comes through as he writes. Verses 7 and 8 are red hot: *"Why do you not rather let yourselves be cheated? No, you yourselves do wrong and cheat, and you do these things to your brethren!"*

Paul hits a range of ungodly practices that cannot be tolerated and demands church intervention and judgment if any of the following involve two or more believers:

1. Fornication. Sex outside of marriage.

2. Idolaters.

3. Adulterers. Sex with a married person not your spouse.

4. Homosexual activity.

5. Sodomy. Middle English: from medieval Latin *sodomia*, from late Latin *peccatum Sodomiticum* 'sin of Sodom' (See Gen. 19:5, which implies that the men of Sodom practiced homosexual rape). Amazingly, this also could reference copulation with animals.

6. Thievery.

7. Covetous.

8. Drunkards.

9. Revilers. Slanderers whose action hurts another person.

10. Extortioners.

I follow Paul's logic and understand how dangerous and hurtful all of these actions are. The only one I can't quite understand from a legal point of view is "covetousness." How would that work? I don't know exactly what he means though he could be spotlighting a scheme to defraud or steal which has not yet come to final action (i.e., no theft has occurred but there is clear proof of action taken to steal). Perhaps this would include breaking into someone's home but being accosted before an actual robbery occurred.

The foregoing list outlines matters that should be dealt with internally. Obviously, they are bad ("wicked" would be Paul's word), but they are not a list of all bad behaviors or a list of all sin. Pride, for example, thought to be the worst foundational sin, is not included nor is gluttony. Those go on a different kind of list.

No surprise, we discover that the church at Corinth had people who had practiced all of these hurtful behaviors – behaviors that prohibit, if not dealt with, an inheritance in the Kingdom. But Paul affirms that for those who have been baptized, sanctified (set apart) through their faith in God by their submission to Jesus as Lord and justified by the name of the Lord Jesus (and His blood) through action of the Holy Spirit *WILL* inherit. It is the Gospel:

"But you were washed, you were sanctified, you were justified in the name of the Lord Jesus Christ and by the Spirit of our God." (1st Corinthians 6:11).

In verse 12, Paul dives into the deep theology of the believer's position in God. A believer is no longer bound by rules (that is, no longer made righteous by adherence to rules). Rather, he or she is free of rules and made righteous by God's saving action. Paul is concerned the Corinthians will be confused into thinking that since rules no longer "rule," righteous behavior is not necessary. Sexual immorality could rein, and there would be no worries in their minds. Paul won't let that way of thinking survive.

Brothels undoubtedly were all over the seaports and frequented by many. Totally wrong, for the body is not for sexual immorality but for the Lord. Once we become believers, we are body and soul His.

It would be wonderful if we could read these admonitions and be free from all temptation, but we remain in the flesh and subject to temptations. Paul's solution - one that we would hope every teenager could adopt, is to *"FLEE FROM SEXUAL IMMORALITY."* Flee! This means remove yourself from sources of temptation. That is easier said than done in our current technological world. But bars, lounges, movies and internet sites with a sexual overtone need to be totally avoided. Lord, have mercy!

1st Corinthians 7

In Chapter 7, Paul continues exploring the theme of sexual temptations while veering off into the relationship of marriage. The sexual drive in man is one difficult appetite, and Paul recognizes the problem without lingering over it. From his perspective, it would be better for all concerned if no one even touched. But, practically, Paul knows that total abstinence will be hard to maintain.

In one sense, sexual relations in marriage remind me of the simple and straightforward conversations between a husband and wife. Marriage expresses the mystery of God's own love for mankind and particularly the church. He wants to be in communion with us. For a man and a woman, this means being able to speak what is on your heart, to speak as well as listen. It does not mean shutting your spouse out – pouting in the corner so to speak, isolating or violently shouting. In its divine nature, marriage means "being with" in a fully committed and loving way.

Sexual relations are another form of "being with" with a practical outcome: children. Often, these relations involve even more sacrifice (of attention and time) than "being with" in conversation. But the sex drive takes the "being with" to a different level. One partner can get so carried away with the pleasure of contact that he (most likely he) gets lost in his own comfort and loses sight of his spouse and God's purpose. Paul seems to know all of this. He expresses the deep truth: marriage partners belong to each other. There is some "right" that a woman has over the man's body and vice versa. My only thought is that we must have a lot of grace in this zone – grounding ourselves in affection and esteem toward our spouses because this is one dangerous zone.

Paul uses the Greek word *apodidomi* in verse three. The word literally means, *"to give away for one's own profit what is one's own."* This describes in a remarkable way what each husband and each wife is called to do. It is better to give yourself to your spouse; you will get a reward if you do. You will "profit" in having both a true expression of unity as well as keeping your "house" on a solid foundation. You will not tempt your spouse to look for affection elsewhere.

Affection is the one of the singular "profits" of a marriage. Children are certainly a reward, but the wonder of affection is above most fleshly gifts. My wife, Fran, often stops as she passes me typing away at the computer and gives me a kiss on my bald head. This gesture of affection is a sweet reminder that affection is much more than some sexual activity. In fact, sexual activity in many forms is certainly *NOT* a gesture of affection. It can be simply an expression of carnal and perverted desire. May the Lord help us make many gestures of true affection in our marriages!

Paul outlines in verses 7 and 8 that an even better state, if one could maintain it, would be to remain unmarried. It is good for them if they remain even as Paul was at the time of his writing, though there is a hint in Chapter 9 that Paul may have been married at some point: *"Do we not have the right to take along a believing wife, as do the other apostles and the brothers of the Lord and Cephas [Peter]?"* (1 Corinthians

9:5). But I don't believe this is conclusive, since he may be referring to one of the other apostles traveling with him (Apollos for instance).

Clement of Alexandria is quoted by Eusebius as follows: *"'Or will they,' says he [Clement], 'reject even the apostles? For Peter and Philip begot children, and Philip also gave his daughters in marriage. And Paul does not hesitate, in one of his epistles, to greet his wife, whom he did not take about with him, that he might not be inconvenienced in his ministry.'"* Clement's reference may have been from the two Pauline letters we are missing.

But these questions to not take away from Paul's main thrust that singleness can be of great advantage if it can be maintained. From these verses and the observation that Jesus himself never married, one sees the eventual rise of the unmarried "religious:" monks, monasteries, nuns and convents. But one also sees that celibacy was not a universal rule even among the apostles.

In verse 10, Paul is very specific about divorce or separation. His language as translated in the Greek suggests he is "commanding" that there be no divorce just as Jesus commanded. The only difference is that Jesus made an exception for unchastity:

"Have you not read that he who made them from the beginning made them male and female, and said, 'For this reason a man shall leave his father and mother and be joined to his wife, and the two shall become one'? So, they are no longer two but one. What therefore God has joined together, let not man put asunder.... For your hardness of heart Moses allowed you to divorce your wives, but from the beginning it was not so. And I say to you: whoever divorces his wife, except for unchastity, and marries another, commits adultery; and he who marries a divorced woman, commits adultery." (Matthew 19:4-9).

Paul takes up an exception Jesus did not address, which concerned what should be the rule if one partner is a believer and the other not. We see in these verses (12-16) the power and potential impact of a believing spouse on a non-believer. *"An unbelieving husband is SANCTIFIED by the wife, and the unbelieving wife is SANCTIFIIED by the husband."* Remember, the Greek word *hagiazo* means, *"sanctified," "consecrated to God," "set aside,"* or *"purified."* This is a wonderful encouragement to remain married even when the spouses are unequally yoked. Additionally, we see the power of sanctification on the children. Just being the child of a believing parent puts the child in some position of sanctification.

Paul says that in the instances of a non-believing spouse, the believing spouse is *"free"* to leave, so Paul extends Jesus's one exception, or perhaps better clarifies His exception.

We see another Pauline principle enunciated in verse 17: *"As you were when the Lord called you, so remain."* Paul ordained this in all the churches. If circumcised, remain circumcised. If uncircumcised, remain uncircumcised. If a slave, don't worry about it.

Paul's point is that there is great freedom to use the state in which you find yourself to the glory of God, and no one should say otherwise. Then Paul gives a kernel of his teaching in verse 19:

"Circumcision is nothing and uncircumcision is nothing, but keeping the commandments of God is what matters."

This is a bit challenging. One has to hold the fact on one hand that external signs and external relationships (married, not married) mean nothing, while obeying the commands of God on the other hand means everything. But, the commandments in the Torah include circumcision. So, Paul is clearly meaning in the second clause something other than the 600 plus commandments that an Orthodox Jew tries to master.

I believe Paul is clearly talking about doing what God wants you to do, and what is that? The heart of God shows mercy, kindness, faithfulness, truth, gentleness and the like. From the inside out. From the heart.

Paul's thought of remaining in the condition in which one was found is carried on to the near end of Chapter 7. It is in verse 34 that Paul spotlights one of the great differences between the unmarried believer and the married.

"The unmarried woman cares about the things of the Lord, that she may be holy both in body and in spirit. But she who is married cares about the things of the world—how she may please her husband." (1 Corinthians 7:34)

A married person is not free to *totally* devote themselves to God or His church, because he or she has responsibilities to the spouse and to their children. For those in ministry, it is a juggling act.

Paul ends the chapter with further reflection on spousal freedom. If one is married and one's spouse dies, it is permissible to remarry, but ONLY to a believer.

We see Paul's amazing grasp of "best practices" in this chapter. Best outcomes often come from best practices. It is for the sake of best outcomes that God advises best practices!

My friend, Bob Philips, shared an interesting analogy that came to him as he studied Chapter 7:

"I know Chapter 7 is speaking of the principles that undergird marriage, but there are other reasons to guard against sexual sin. It can be thought of like leasing a house. Most landlords have things they don't allow to be

done to the house, e.g., no painting, no parking on the grass, no distur-bances in the neighborhood, etc. When I think this way, it's almost easier to be in alignment since I don't own this body - I'm not even leasing it - it was given to me, so I need to follow the rules! The scripture also applies to how we take care of this temple." I like Bob's analogy, and note it is not only addresses taking care of our own body but also that of our spouse.

1st Corinthians 8

Chapter 8 of Corinthians is a breather compared with the last few chapters because Paul moves to the subject of food offered to idols. In one sense, this chapter is about knowledge – what we know. Paul leads off with the reflection that knowing something is not a reason to be "puffed up." Rather, our focus should be that God knows us. That's what is important!

But what we think we know about the world and what is permissible and what is not can be a stumbling block for others. This comes in two ways.

First, we can believe that old prohibitions no longer are applicable under the New Covenant. Paul has done a pretty good job in his letter to the Romans of making it plain that obeying rules will not make you justified. Eating kosher will not make you righteous. Eating food offered to idols will not make you unrighteous. But, creating a scandal by breaking a rule in front of another brother who holds dearly to the rule is being needlessly un-thoughtful.

Second, even worse, doing something in full view of your brother may cause him or her to trespass the rule he or she holds to be important.

It is not hard to find plenty of examples of this in today's culturally divided world of Christianity. I am reminded of one of my friends who grew up in a Baptist church in Florence, Alabama. His father was a terrible alcoholic who went into fits of rage and often struck his mother. My friend is a complete teetotaler. He won't drink a sip of wine.

If I am having a dinner party and invite my friend, what might be the outcome? There are three possibilities.

The first: I serve wine and greatly offend my brother. He extends me freedom, but inside, his pain from his past would be drowning him.

The second possibility: I serve wine and he decides to go with the crowd and takes a drink. In the second case, I have caused him to stumble against his own conscience.

The third possibility: I don't serve wine at all. We have a delightful meal with chilled water in fine silver cups. Very elegant, and my friend is honored.

With this in mind, let me share with you a dream I had the morning of August 15th, 2017.

Dream of the Two Wine Glasses

I awoke at 3:34 a.m. from a dream about fellowship. Fran and I were at our house. There had been a Bible study earlier. About 14 people were present including Laurie and Bob Phillips as well as their daughter, Kayla. After the first part of the gathering, we had broken into two smaller groups. Bob and Laurie were in one group and Kayla was in the other. Each group gathered in a separate room for a meal and a reflection on the earlier study.

Fran and I were in the group with Bob and Laurie, and Kayla was in the other room. Our group gathered around a large rectangular table very similar to our old breakfast room table which daughter Elizabeth and her husband, Jay, now have in Birmingham. The table was made of weathered pine rubbed smooth with age.

I was at one end of the table, while Fran was seated on the right side and Bob and Laurie on the left. Additionally, there were two or three others at our table. It was a simple meal, but white wine earlier had been poured into tall, elegant wine glasses at each place setting.

Fran seems to have been picked to share her reflections from the earlier study. At first, she seemed hesitant, but then she shared smoothly for perhaps ten minutes.

I remember Bob saying how glad he was that we had put them at one table and his daughter at the other. This was not because they had not wanted to be with her, but because Bob felt it was good for her growth and development.

The Phillips stood to leave as they had an engagement. Bob had the two wine glasses in his hands to help clear some of the dishes, and I noticed the two glasses were still full of wine. Then, I remembered Bob's pledge to not drink any wine after he had taken his new job as Chairman of the local Christian CEO's program called C12. I reflected that Bob really was a man of his word and that such restraint would be surely helpful to be seen by children.

At that point, I awoke.

Reflection: The dream is broken into three simple phases. First, there is a Bible study at our home with a small number of people. The second phase is in our dining room having a fine fellowship meal. The third is the cleaning phase where I notice the two full wine glasses.

The emphasis of the dream is three-fold. First, there is an emphasis on home, fellowship and study in small groups. Next, there is a spotlight on the Phillips and their love for their daughter. Finally, there is a clear focus on the two wine glasses and Bob Phillips' steadfast character in his commitment to his C-12 organization. To be a C-12 local director, one must pledge to drink absolutely no alcohol of any kind.

1st Corinthians 9

Paul makes an abrupt shift as he discusses his rights. It seems likely that the chapter's content may have been provoked by a direct accusation that Paul was not a fully accredited apostle. From verse 2, it certainly appears that someone had arrived at Corinth questioning his authority: *"If to others I am not an apostle, at least I am to you, for you are the seal of my apostleship in the Lord."*

He immediately launches into a detailed defense of his position. The Corinthian church's very existence owes itself to Paul's apostolic efforts. He investigates "rights" that accrue to various ministry functions in the Body by focusing on those of an apostolic nature. "Rights" are an important question as they involve both behavior and money. Deuteronomy 25:4 probably underlies much of Paul's thought. It goes:

"You shall not muzzle the ox while he is threshing." (Deut. 25:4).

Additionally, we have Jesus's own direction to the disciples: *"Take no bag for the road, or second tunic, or sandals, or staff; for the worker is worthy of his provisions."* (Matthew 10:10). These two scriptures (plus the reality that 1/12 of all of Israel was fully supported by the tithe so that they would be able to perform full-time ministry) set the backdrop for Paul's focus. The laborer is worthy of his hire! And not only his hire, but also the support of his family (the entire Levitical household was to be supported, not just the priest). A current example was that Peter's wife was being supported as Paul reminds the Corinthians.

Paul brings in other obvious examples of how foolish it would be to expect full time workers not to be supported: the soldier in the trenches, the worker in the vineyard, the shepherd with the flock, the plowman in the field and the thresher.

By the time he gets to verse 12, he has established clear claim to support, but then points out the oddity that neither he nor Barnabas had made use of this right because they felt it could be an obstacle to winning the hearts and souls of the Corinthians. It is hard not to think of the TV evangelists as I read these verses. Some heap up thousands upon thousands of dollars daily with no apparent qualm. Not Paul!

"But I have made no use of any of these rights, nor am I writing these things to secure any such provision. For I would rather die than have anyone deprive me of my ground for boasting." (1 Corinthians 9:15).

I have no doubt that Paul asked for nothing because of his great zeal and love to win people to the Lord. He says that he did so in order that he would not lose his "reward," but it is unlikely his primary motivating force. I get his point beginning in verse 15:

"For I would rather die than have anyone deprive me of my ground for boasting. For if I preach the gospel, that gives me no ground for boasting. For necessity is laid upon me. Woe to me if I do not preach the gospel! For if I do this of my own will, I have a reward...." (1st Corinthians 9:15-17).

Like the effect of fire in Jeremiah's bones (Jeremiah 20:9), Paul preaches because he cannot help himself; a divine compulsion rests upon him, even if he wanted to quit.

Then we have what I think to be a marvelous reality of Paul's approach:

"To the Jews I became as a Jew, in order to win Jews. To those under the law I became as one under the law (though not being myself under

the law) that I might win those under the law. To those outside the law I became as one outside the law (not being outside the law of God but under the law of Christ) that I might win those outside the law. To the weak I became weak, that I might win the weak. I have become all things to all people, that by all means I might save some. I do it all for the sake of the gospel, that I may share with them in its blessings." (1st Corinthians 9:20-23).

Paul ends with a great example for all of us concerning the practical reality of our bodies: he is under FULL discipline:

"But I discipline my body and keep it under control, lest after preaching to others I myself should be disqualified." (1st Corinthians 9:27).

His thrust is more than exercise and watching what he eats; Paul is under a righteousness restriction in his body – not just for his own sake but that he might not lose anyone with his gospel message. The man is on fire!

I end with this reflection: we need to always be very careful to take care of those who work amongst us full or even part time for the Gospel. We are under obligation. We shouldn't have to be asked. There are many who serve us. And they are worthy of our hire.

1st Corinthians 10

Paul had focused on his person and his need to stay under strict discipline as Chapter 9 ended. In the 10th chapter, Paul expands his attention to the posture of the Corinthians, reminding them that it can be deadly to think one has arrived, setting aside their alertness to the danger of falling.

He compares the situation of the Corinthian believers to that of the Israelites in the time of Moses. Paul ticks off four privileges that both groups enjoyed and that could have made them feel they had "arrived."

1. The Israelites had been delivered from their oppression and the Kingdom of Egypt. The Corinthian believers had been delivered from oppression and the Kingdom of Darkness.

2. The Israelites had been baptized into Moses through the cloud and the sea. The Corinthian believers had been baptized into Jesus through the Holy Spirit and water.

3. The Israelites ate spiritual food (manna) and spiritual water: *"Take the rod, and you and your brother Aaron assemble the congregation and speak to the rock before their eyes, that it may yield its water. You shall thus bring forth water for them out of the rock and let the congregation and their beasts drink."* (Numbers 20:8). The Corinthian believers eat the Bread and drink the Cup of the Lord.

4. The Israelites drank from the Rock (Numbers 20); the Corinthian believers drink from the Rock (Jesus).

God's favor rested upon both groups in a similar fashion. Paul's point is straightforward: If the Israelites got into serious trouble in spite of their "favored" position, why should you Corinthian believers think you will not? You need to be on guard!

The actual text says Paul's response was, *"So, if you think you are standing firm, be careful lest you fall!"* (1st Corinthians 10:11).

Paul enumerates two examples of where they needed to be particularly careful. The first was sexual immorality. Given the way Paul frames his comments, he may have been thinking particularly about the Cultic Society Clubs that were plentiful in Corinth. These clubs held quasi-social affairs at the "Club House" of some idol, and they usually ended in drunkenness and debauchery. We have archeological examples of invitations to such feasts and banquets that give a sense of how alluring the opportunity could be to businessmen, etc. A parallel today might be a trip to a convention in Las Vegas or a hunting trip with buddies from High School, or a "Ladies Night Out."

The second was grumbling. In the first - your presence at a questionable event or setting - the easy answer is "don't go." Don't set yourself up for getting in trouble. Paul is saying firmly, "No matter how solid in God you feel, be very careful."

In the section beginning in verse 13, Paul reflects on the nature of temptation itself. No temptation (another meaning for the Greek is the English word, *"test"*) will overtake us that is not common to mankind. Paul includes in his thought *EVERY* possible sin in the word "temptation."

Paul spotlights a huge truth for all of us: Because God is faithful, He will not let us be tempted beyond what we can bear! But that is a two-edged bit of truth. On the one hand, Paul is saying we can handle every temptation that comes before us, that is, we have the internal strength to do so. On the other hand, we have no excuse if we don't handle the temptation properly because *THERE IS ALWAYS A WAY OUT!* We need this reality burned into our consciousness: There always is a way out!

Having said all of this about standing firm and recognizing that you are always in danger of falling, he inserts a *"therefore."* And of course, we always want to see what the "therefore" is there for. For all these reasons, *therefore*, flee idolatry. *FLEE!* With this background, Paul shifts to a particular problem in Corinth: meat sacrificed to idols. He uses the Christian communion sacrament as an example to show that one cannot take it physically without in some way participating in the Body and Blood of Jesus. We are all tied to it.

Likewise, the food that comes from animals that have been sacrificed to idols participates in cultic ritual – in the occult. The meat is perceived to be tainted by that participation since it had been offered to an idol. Behind the idol are demons, and Paul does not want the Corinthian believers to "participate" in any way with the demonic. When the meat is sold after the sacrifice, it still has participated with the demonic. The Christian wants *NOTHING* to do with the occult or the demonic.

Paul knows his admonition causes a question to arise since Paul is *par excellence* a preacher of the freedom enjoyed by the Christian believer. If the Corinthians are free to eat anything and if the Corinthians know that idols are nothing, then why should they worry about what has happened to the meat they buy in the market?

"'I have the right to do anything,' you say – but not everything is beneficial. 'I have the right to do anything,' but not everything is constructive. No one should seek their own good, but the good of others." (1ˢᵗ Corinthians 10:23).

The foregoing is a Pauline principle that has freedom in one hand and obligation to your brother or sister in the other. This allows Paul to end his discourse on food offered to idols with two directions. If an unbeliever invites you to their home and you are offered meat that had previously been sacrificed to an idol but makes no mention of its origin, *"eat whatever is put before you without raising questions of conscience."* But if someone says to you, *"this has been offered in sacrifice,"* then you should not eat it for two reasons: for the sake of the unbeliever and for the sake of that person's conscience.

I am fascinated with Paul's thinking. He will give honor (weight) to even an unbeliever's conscience. Paul is not worried about the meat; Paul is worried about the unbeliever's conscience. He does not want the unbeliever thinking he has caused you to err in some way, knowing that you are a Christian. I would have to say Paul is paying great attention to another person's internal world, and that is my take-away: Great sensitivity to all, believer and unbeliever alike.

Paul ends the chapter with another great Pauline principle, *"Whatever you do, do it all for the glory of God!"* Do not cause *ANYONE* to stumble, neither Jewish people, non-believers nor the church. Paul tries his best to *"please everyone in every way."* His posture is to seek the good of many that they may be saved!

1ˢᵗ Corinthians 11

Signs of Submissiveness

Chapter 11 provides yet another shift for Paul, and he finally praises the Corinthians for something: Paul states the Corinthians are holding firm to the *"traditions"* which he has given them. I cannot help but immediately think of the word "tradition" in the Catholic faith. Tradition for Catholics is a source of authority in addition to the written word. Tradition for my Catholic brothers encompasses the practices and teachings that have been handed down from Church Fathers who lived after the New Testament writings were completed. Tradition also includes those decisions which were codified in the rulings made by Church authority and Church Councils over the centuries.

The word in verse 1 that is translated *"traditions"* is the Greek word *paradosis*. This word literally means, *"giving up or giving over, i.e., the act of surrender."* Jesus's words in Aramaic were translated into Greek by Matthew and Mark several times using this word, *paradosis*. For example, *"Why do thy disciples transgress the **tradition** of the elders? For they wash not their hands when they eat bread."* (Matthew 15:2).

We can see the meaning here as contrasted with the Torah which was written. Jesus is focusing on what the elders in Judaism over a very long period of time taught regarding items not completely covered in the Torah. Likewise, Paul is focusing on what *he* has delivered over to the Corinthians. Paul uses the word again in his letter to the Thessalonians:

*"Therefore, brethren, stand fast, and hold the **traditions** which you have been taught, whether by word or our letter."* 2 Thessalonians 2:15).

The verse in Thessalonians underscores the meaning and validates in a sense that many things that are wise and helpful are delivered orally at the point that they most are needed. The Bible does not deal with every bit of life's minutia. But the Holy Spirit at all times and all places has the power to reveal through the Lord's servants truth that needs to be heeded. So, we get the long transmission of *"tradition"* alongside *"that which is written."*

And, in Chapter 11, we see hear that Paul is delighted that the Corinthians are following these teachings that he has given them, though one also can sense Paul is stretching. He already has mentioned a good number of things that he taught them previously that they are ignoring!

In the first half of Chapter 11, he focuses on patterns of behavior that are colored culturally. Paul says that if a man prays or prophesies with something on his head, *he disgraces his head*. If a woman doesn't have a headcovering while she prays or prophesies, *she disgraces her head*.

You can immediately see why Chapter 11 is a chapter that many would like to avoid. To an American man or woman brought up in a "Protestant" church, Paul's observations are nonsense. What in the world is he talking about? And what is this about women prophesying in church?

I don't know for sure how many millennia the practice of showing deference by headcovering has been in existence. We can tell it has been around at least 4,000 years. I read a fascinating behavioral scientist's book on authority years ago. He studied the habits of many animals to see how deference was expressed. Geese do so by lowering their head in front of the head goose. This puts their head in the vulnerable position of potentially being pecked. It also removes any chance that the deferring goose could cause the head goose trouble. Dogs, gorillas and many other forms of animal make these movements through their innate wiring and also through observation. As a baby, the goose watches older geese to see how things should go.

Headcovering, among other things, is a sign of deference and particularly a sign of being under authority. The earliest example in the Bible is Rebecca's first encounter with Isaac:

"And Rebekah lifted up her eyes, and when she saw Isaac, she lighted off the camel. For she had said unto the servant, 'What man is this that walks in the field to meet us?' And the servant had said, 'It is my master.' **Therefore, she took a veil, and covered herself.** *And the servant told Isaac all things that he had done."* (Genesis 24: 64-66).

Jewish people were sensitive to this issue, particularly that head covering expresses being under someone else's authority. Jewish married women would wear headcovering much as women today wear a wedding ring: both express they are married, and for the Jewish woman, it says she has her husband as her authority who himself stands under *Hashem* (God Himself).

Paul sees headcovering from two perspectives. A Christian man is only under the authority of God and not under the authority of man and thus does not need a sign. But the Christian woman, like the Jewish woman, is under the authority of her husband.

So where did Paul get this? I will suggest only that Paul's sensitivity is similar to that of the Centurion in Matthew 8:9:

*"For I am a man **under authority**, having soldiers under me: and I say to this man, 'Go,' and he goes; and to another, 'Come,' and he comes; and to my servant, 'Do this,' and he does it."*

This is a huge thing to grasp. One can be under authority and therefore have some measure of the power and authority of the one he serves. Jesus understood this implicitly as did the Centurion. There are two components: power and support. One has the delegated power he is given; one has the support of the higher authority.

We can reveal our "underness" in various ways. Bobby Sypole, a young friend and former officer in the U.S. Army, revealed his exact position to all military soldiers by a small symbol on his collar. As a Captain, he had two bars connected at top and bottom. Lieutenants and *all* enlisted men were below him in rank. His commission certificate said that he bore the authority of the President of the United States. In turn, the President and the government would give him full support if he was in need. This is a concept we grasped 40 years ago in our early days as a Christian community. It is good to be under Godly authority!

The Issue of Headcovering

In Paul's day, being under authority was revealed by headcovering, and he instructed the women of Corinth to reveal their submittedness to God and human authority by headcoverings. These headcoverings, however, had the added advantage of removing glamorous and enticing (aren't women funny!) hairdos from distracting their male counterparts. (This does not say much for the attractiveness of men, but hey, some were bald…).

It is interesting to me that, unlike their Jewish counterparts, Christian laymen did not wear a headcovering to reveal they too were under God's authority. I have no idea why they did not, but we see religious orders and officers in the Church as it evolved expressing their submissiveness through various head treatments.

The first time I even knew there could be an issue about what you wore to church (aside from looking your best - and that came from my mother), was when I lived in France the summer of 1962. All of the young women in the program were required to have a handkerchief on their heads to go into a cathedral; men could not enter in shorts. My, how times have changed!

But this only shows how my religious stream picked and chose what scriptures to respect. We were keen on water baptism, but anything that looked like Catholicism needed to be avoided. Instrumental music: out. Headcoverings: out.

Meanwhile, Christian headcovering had been unanimously practiced by the women from the Early Church all the way up to the late 1890s in both the Catholic and Orthodox streams. This is well attested by multiple writers throughout the first centuries of Christianity. Tertullian (150–220) explains that in his day, the Corinthian church was still practicing the headcovering that Paul had directed. Tertullian wrote, *"So, too, did the Corinthians themselves understand* [Paul]. *In fact, to this day the Corinthians do veil their virgins. What the apostles taught, their disciples approve."* Clement of Alexandria (150–215), another early theologian, wrote, *"A woman and a man are to go to church decently attired...for this is the wish of the Word, since it is becoming for her to pray veiled."* A few years later, Hippolytus of Rome (170–236), while giving instructions for church gatherings, said *"...let all the women have their heads covered with a solid cloth...."* At some point, it became normative for all of the churches, both East and West.

In the 4th century, the archbishop John Chrysostom (347–407) dealt with whether covering one's head was legislated by nature. *"But when I say Nature, I mean God. For He it is who created Nature. When therefore you overturn these boundaries, see how great injuries ensue."* (Chrysostom's Homily 26 on 1st Corinthians).

The great Latin translator, Jerome, before he died in 420 AD, noted that Christian women in Egypt and Syria do not *"go about with heads uncovered in defiance of the apostle's command, for they wear a close-fitting cap and a veil."* (To Sabinianus).

Augustine before 430 AD wrote, *"It is not becoming, even in married women, to uncover their hair, since the apostle commands women to keep their heads covered."*

So, what is my take on this? It is that we live in an age where we can set aside 2,000 years of practice, obedience and tradition with no real awareness that we are even doing so.

One could argue this is a small issue, though we can set aside very large issues like sexual orientation and behavior in the same exact way. Are we not free? Paul would have a heyday with the contentious sections of the church today because he would have over 2,000 different church streams with 2,000 ways of behaving and interpreting. But in Paul's day, he could say with assurance: *"We have no other practice, nor have the churches of God."* (1 Corinthians 11:16). Bottomline, the desire to express ones submissiveness is an issue of the heart.

Paul has been addressing the *expression* of submission to God in different forms. Now he tackles an extremely disturbing reality: the Corinthian time of communion was filled with disturbances.

Reading verses 17-22, I am struck with how much their communion experience mimicked that of the Cultic Social Clubs (note: I am making up this title, but I think it fits). Each god (idol) had priests and a temple. They would throw secret banquets during the day and night. There would be a feast with liquor and wine as enticing lures. Before the banquet had come to an end, many participants would be drunk. Perversions would occur at that point which do not need to be enumerated. If you read verses 17-22, you can see how concerned Paul would be with the pattern he saw. Also, the rich amongst the Corinthians could afford to come early. Laborers and slaves might not be able to arrive until very late, and the food already would have been exhausted by their rich brothers and sisters.

The verses that begin at verse 23 and go to the end of the chapter are some of the most important in Paul's entire letter. Paul reveals what he had *"received from the Lord,"* thus sharing a close retelling of the Last Supper that Jesus had with the Twelve. These verses have been repeated in portion almost verbatim at Christian gatherings for nearly two thousand years. It is for this reason that communion, like marriage, is not to be entered into lightly because it signifies and renews afresh the priceless covenantal action of God's part for mankind in the crucifixion and death of His Son. It is like celebrating our marriage vows on every anniversary, but with even more wonder and thankfulness.

It is so important that celebrating the Supper unworthily has caused many to be weak, sick and some dead. We don't judge ourselves, God does.

1st Corinthians 12

Gifts of the Spirit

In Chapter 11, Paul looked at headcoverings in the assembly and the Lord's Supper – both which occur in when the community assembles for worship. In Chapter 12, he shifts to examine the thorny problem of Spiritual Gifts. Paul's discourse is not exclusive to the assembly. Spiritual gifts are distributed through the Holy Spirit for many purposes and are not limited to the assembly, but often that is where they are deployed. When we get to Chapter 14, he will look particularly at how gifts are deployed in the assembly, but first he tackles the very nature of spiritual gifts.

Corinth, the urbanized seacoast of Greece and much of the ancient world were hotbeds of spiritualism. Writing in the third century, Porphyry described some of these non-Christian activities and manifestations: *"Some are agitated throughout the whole body; others, in some of their members; others, again, are entirely quiet. Sometimes there are pleasing harmonies, dances and according voices, and sometimes the reverse. Again the body either appears taller, or larger, or is borne aloft through the air, or is affected by the opposite of these.... The true cause is no other than illumination emanating from the very gods themselves, and spirits coming forth from them, and an obsession by which they hold us fully and absolutely, absorbing all our faculties even and exterminating all human motions and operations, even to consciousness itself."*

With a focus on gods, idols and the occult, it is not surprising that Corinth could be having trouble dealing with Spiritual Gifts from God and understanding the difference between what the believers may have experienced previously in pagan worship settings and what the Christian believer experiences.

First, Paul focuses on the *nature* of true Spiritual gifts. There are many differing gifts, and they all come from the Spirit of God, i.e., the Holy Spirit. Even though we all receive the One and same Spirit at our rebirth (*"For by one Spirit we were all baptized into one body...and have all been made to drink of One Spirit"*), the Holy Spirit has many dimensions and has chosen to give a special measure of various aspects of Himself to different individuals. The first thing to grasp is that the Holy Spirit of can manifest a specific dimension of Himself in each individual. For instance, all at one time or another may be able to prophesy, but only a few will receive the Gift of Prophecy in such a way that they normally will prophesy.

Fran and I are old enough that we now are giving to our children Christmas presents and birthday gifts that are **ours**! These are treasured objects that we currently own. They belong entirely to us. They manifest who we are. Some are generational: a silver platter from Fran's Grandmother, a silver pitcher from my Grandmother, and so on. Others may be an important book that was a gift to me from my father - my book on Uncle Remus comes to mind. The point is that they are entirely ours, and they reflect who we are.

Gifts from the Holy Spirit are like that. God gives to each son or daughter at least one specific dimension to manifest on a regular basis. We all have received the same Spirit, but each has a special gifting. Conceptually, it takes the entire Body to manifest all of the attributes God has chosen for mankind to reveal. One brother or sister can never do it all; it is only as the Body functions together that the full wonder of God comes forward.

Let me return to the Christmas analogy. Just because you get multiple gifts on Christmas does not mean you will unwrap all of them. You may overlook one. Your parent may set one aside for your birthday because you have received so many, and so forth. Getting a gift is not the same thing as unwrapping the gift, and many, many believers have several key presents under their tree waiting for unwrapping. Until unwrapped, they sit with phenomenal potential, but useless for the moment.

Thus, one key issue is how does one unwrap one's gift from the Holy Spirit. I will return to that in Chapter 14.

Ministries

Paul's next point is that Jesus (the *"Lord"* in verse 5) gives **ministries** to different believers (and communities) that need the Spiritual gifts that the Holy Spirit has distributed. I am not sure which comes first: Jesus's decision of what the ministry (service) should be and then the Holy Spirit giving the necessary gifts for that ministry or vice versa. In the order of Paul's discourse, it might be interpreted that the Spirit gives the gifts and the ministry forms around the gifts at Jesus's direction as Lord. Either way, gifts and ministries are directly linked.

Paul then says that God (I think he is referring to Father aspect of God in the Godhead) activates the activities of the ministries using the gifts.

"There are diversities of gifts, but the same Spirit. There are differences of ministries, but the same Lord. And there are diversities of activities, but it is the same God who works all in all." (1 Corinthians 12:4-6).

Gifts, ministries, activities. A three-fold chain from God to the Body of Christ on earth.

Every manifestation of a gift is given **to each one *symphero*!** The end of verse 7 is the Greek word, *symphero* which often is translated *"for the profit of all,"* but its actual meaning is *"to bring together in order to help."* A more literal translation of the verse would be, *"the manifestation of the Spirit is given to each one in order to help everyone together."*

The language is awkward, but the meaning is not. The Greek word *symphero* is the word from which we get the word symphony. Think of Paul's teaching this way: **The Spirit gives manifestations of various**

types to different brothers and sisters so that when they are brought together, people will be helped. I would like to underscore that. True profit comes when everyone is manifesting appropriately their divine gift at the perfect time and place.

That's the idea, but what are some of the manifestations? Paul provides a short list:

1. **A Word of Wisdom.** (God's wisdom which is beyond man's wisdom).

2. **A Word of Knowledge.** (What God knows beyond human knowledge).

3. **Faith.** (The ability to believe with a deep certainty that produces Godly action).

4. **Gifts of Healings.** (Ability to bring God's healing to a person).

5. **Working of Miracles.** (the Greek word is *dynamis* from which we get the word dynamite. It means Works of POWER. (More than just moving mountains; moves spirits).

6. **Prophecy.** (What God is speaking whether for the moment or the future).

7. **Discerning of Spirits.** (Knowing whether God or the Enemy is behind someone's action or position regardless of whether the person is a Christian or not).

8. **Tongues.** (Ability to pray or prophesy in a language not known to the believer).

9. **Interpretation of Tongues.** (Ability to interpret messages from Number 8).

I say this is a short list because we have seven gifts listed in Romans 12:6-8 which only overlap with one of the nine preceding gifts. Since

Paul wrote Romans, we can be sure the list was not meant to be exhaustive. In Romans, in addition to Prophecy, he lists:

10. **Serving.** (Special gifting for meaningful service).

11. **Teaching.** (Special God-given ability to teach the mind and reach the heart).

12. **Exhortation.** (Special God-given ability to stir up others to Godly action).

13. **Giving.** (The heart of God manifested in extra-ordinary giving).

14. **Leadership.** (God appointed gift of Leadership).

15. **Mercy.** (Extension of mercy even in the presence of judgment).

And I will make a bold statement: these 15 are not exhaustive. I say that because we are dealing with an infinite and glorious God, and it seems highly unlikely to me that His nature can be fully manifested with these 15 characteristics. Paul in Chapter 13 will add one more: **Love!** But first, let's test these fifteen against Exodus 34:6 *ff.* Five manifestations numbered above as 4, 5, 10, 13 and 15 (Healing, Miracles, Serving, Giving and Mercy) touch five of the Exodus 34 characteristics (Compassion, Kindness, Covenantal Love, Slowness to Anger and a Willingness to Forgive). Eight manifestations numbered above as 1, 2, 6, 7, 8, 9, 11 and 12 (Wisdom, Knowledge, Prophecy, Discerning, Tongues, Interpretation, Teaching, Exhortation) touch *Emeth* (Truth) in the Exodus 34 passage. I am not sure how to connect manifestations #3 (Faith) and #14 (Leadership) with the Exodus 34 revelation.

In Chapter 13, I believe Paul gives us the highest divine gift of all, Love, which is as direct translation of *Chesed* in the Exodus 34 passage as I know.

My point is simple: *ALL* of these are manifestations of God and reflect His glory. The authors of the Bible do not tie down their limit.

Having said that, it would be wise to look carefully at all of the 16 enumerated above and apprehend two things. First, each function is terribly important to the world, mankind and the Church. Each manifestation radiates the Glory of God on earth. It brings God near in a manifest way, and there is not much more important than that.

Second, none of these are natural to man. They are God-powered. They are dimensionally beyond our natural affinities and dispositions. So, to define them in detail is to go beyond any natural interpretation. Each Gift in the list goes **beyond** natural ability and inclination.

Some people have suggested that you can figure out your Spiritual Gifts by taking a test to see what your natural wiring might be. I have no idea that such a test could be helpful from a Spiritual standpoint. Such tests *are* very helpful from understanding the gifts that you received at conception, but remember, we are talking about a different dimension entirely - divine, supernatural giftings. Really, it is easier to spot Spiritual Gifting by discerning a man's weakness and where God shines forth in spite of that weakness.

From verse 12 to the end of the chapter, Paul is trying to correct a serious misunderstanding of what it means to belong to the Body of Christ. Some either felt excluded if they didn't have a certain role, or even worse, some felt unworthy (unpresentable!). Paul is all over this misunderstanding.

One Body; many members. All members are necessary for proper function; all parts should be honored. It is certainly "unchristian" to give special honor to the folks who may be "out front," (apostles, prophets, teachers, pastors, elders, bishops, etc.) when in fact we are called to give even greater honor to the parts that lack prominence.

Gifts of People

Summing up, Paul gives a list of *people* appointed to several important roles in the local church and *RANKS* them:

1. **Apostles**

2. **Prophets**

3. **Teachers**

4. **Workers of Miracles** (Power)

5. **Healers**

6. **Those gifted with the Serving Gift**

7. **Administrators**

8. **Tongues**

9. **Interpretation of Tongues** (mentioned in verse 30)

These are *people* given to the Church and the world. All of these appointments require certain supernatural Spiritual gifts. Several are easy to link since the functions (or offices) bear the same name as the Spiritual Gift. Apostle is not so easy. Based on Paul's other descriptions of his activity, we can see he has multiple Spiritual gifts (at a minimum the gift of Healing, Prophecy, Power, Teaching, Exhortation, Words of Wisdom, Knowledge, etc.). Being an effective apostle requires a good number of supernatural gifts in addition to just being appointed.

God is the one who appoints people. The normal way God effects the appointment is through the laying on of hands, fasting and prayer.

Again, this list of people gifts is not exhaustive, and Paul will include evangelists and pastors when he works a similar list in his letter to the Ephesians. These are people given to the church as opposed to Spiritual Gifts. They are People Gifts!

Paul ends with a VERY interesting observation: some gifts are better (more useful) than others, and you can pray to receive more gifting than you currently employ. How about that!

1st Corinthians 13

Possibly the best-known chapter of the entire Bible, Chapter 13 has been quoted in innumerable wedding ceremonies because of its subject matter: Love! I am thankful for this chapter for many reasons. One reason is that it gives us a good outline of 16 characteristics that tell us what true love is all about:

Patient

Kind

Not jealous

Doesn't brag

Not arrogant

Never acts in unbecoming manner

Doesn't seek its own way

Not provocable

Doesn't take into account a wrong suffered

Doesn't rejoice in unrighteousness

Rejoices in the truth

Bears all burdens

Believes all things (doesn't question)

Hopes all things

Endures all things

Never fails

Read the list and see the ones that cause you the most trouble. Eight of these cause me trouble in my close relations. At home, my number would be.... 7. Goodness, there are only 16, so I deserve an F. No wonder Paul thought it wise to pull out his list for the Corinthians. A lot of them were thinking highly of themselves and poorly of others. They were not manifesting the wondrous and divine Spiritual gift of Love.

Paul completely cut the legs out from under those who were puffed up because they had one gift or another. We can just guess which those were from his first paragraph:

The gifts of Tongues, Prophecy, Knowledge, Wisdom, Miracles, Power, Generosity and most remarkably, Faith (surrendering one's body to be burned). The Gift of Love trumps them all and is the most needed.

Almost all of these other gifts will fall away when we get to heaven (there will absolutely be no need), yet Love will remain. What a clear revelation Paul has of these wonders even though in comparison to Love, many seem downright childish. When all is said and done, Faith, Hope and Love will remain, and the greatest of these is Love!

This is a gift we all have received but perhaps not well unwrapped. Paul in Romans 5:5 pointed to the Love gift: *"And hope does not disappoint us, because God has poured out His love into our hearts through the Holy Spirit, whom He has given us."*

Think on that! Read this slowly: God has poured out His love into our hearts through the Gift of the Holy Spirit whom He has given us. Let's manifest His love in every place, in every setting.

"Come Holy Spirit, fill the hearts of your faithful and kindle in them the fire of your love. Send forth your Spirit and they shall be created. And You shall renew the face of the earth."

(From Psalm 104:30).

1ˢᵗ Corinthians 14

Pursuing the Gift of Prophecy

Once believers are straight that the most important thing is Love (remember, *"God* IS *Love!"* (1ˢᵗ John 4:8)), they can safely pursue other gifts, and especially the gift of Prophecy. In singling out Prophecy as the most helpful gift in the community aside from Love, Paul is automatically taking the attention away from some of the more flamboyant gifts – namely Tongues. That is not because Paul does not honor the gift of Tongues (he says in verse 5 that he wished that every believer in Corinth had the gift of Tongues), but Prophecy trumps Tongues any day because of its great usefulness.

The Gift of Tongues

In my early days, I knew nothing of these gifts on a personal basis. Nor did I have much understanding of them. I did not encounter the gift of Tongues until late 1973. Fran and I had recently married and found ourselves in a devotional setting in South Memphis - a home worship meeting. The small living room was overflowing with people. A few in chairs, some on the floor and almost everyone worshiping with great focus and fervor. Songs percolated up in a continuous stream.

After a while, the singing shifted one into what I can only call angelic singing. It sounded like choirs of heavenly angels singing in languages I didn't know. There were currents of words intermingled together and rising high into what seemed like the throne room of God. It was *VERY* beautiful and totally unorchestrated. Though I had been a professing Christian since childhood and was 28 years old at the time, I had never heard or experienced anything like it.

My reaction was very Berean. I went home and dug into my Bible. Chapter 14 of 1st Corinthians was one of the key places to which I turned. What I had experienced was others "singing in the Spirit."

"I will sing with the spirit and I will sing with the mind also." (1st Corinthians 14:15).

Paul's comments about his own practices reveal that one may share a message in a Tongue as well as sing in a Tongue. In verse 14, he says that he also prays in a Tongue, but when he prays, his spirit is praying but not his mind.

There are three manifestations of the gift of Tongues in Chapter 14: **speaking, praying and singing**. All are good if the time and place is right, but unhelpful if not. Further, none of those expressions is as helpful in an assembly of believers as the Gift of Prophecy.

My first personal experience with the Gift of Tongues was probably a year before I had an experience with the Gift of Prophecy. After reading through all of the sections in the Book of Acts where Tongues were mentioned, I was struck particularly with Acts 19:

"Paul passed through the upper country and came to Ephesus and found some disciples. He said to them, 'Did you receive the Holy Spirit when you believed?' And they said to him, 'No, we have not even heard whether there is a Holy Spirit.' And he said, 'Into what then were you baptized?' And they said, 'Into John's baptism.' Paul said, 'John baptized with the baptism of repentance, telling the people to believe in Him who was coming after him, that is, in Jesus.' When they heard this, they were baptized in the name of the Lord Jesus. And when Paul had laid his hands upon them, the Holy Spirit came on them, and they began speaking with tongues and prophesying." (Acts 19:1-6).

The Ephesians were somewhat like me. They had been baptized in water but had not experienced much, if anything, of the Holy Spirit. Unlike them, I had been baptized into Jesus's death, but not with the intention of receiving the Holy Spirit nor coming under Jesus's Lordship. I had given myself to baptism so that my sins would be forgiven. I pondered the problem for several weeks and then approached two or three men from the small house church we were attending with the problem. They basically said, "No problem. We just need to pray and lay hands on you that you would receive the Gift of the Holy Spirit." They asked me the simple question "Do you want to receive the Gift of the Holy Spirit?" I said I did, and they laid hands on me and prayed.

I expected fireworks, but there were none visible. My friend advised me not to worry or push things - that God in His own time would grant me the Gift of Tongues that was clearly a normal gift for those Paul taught. I was also cautioned that God would not force the gift's manifestation on me; I would need to step out in faith and begin to speak when the time was right. God would not "move my mouth," but He would take care of the rest if I did my part.

At the time, Fran and I were living in a small farmhouse on Hacks Cross Road. We had an outside hammock. One sunny Saturday, I was out in the hammock praying and worshipping. Looking back on it, my experience in some way must have mimicked Peter's on top of the house in Acts before he was called to Cornelius. I felt like Cornelius. I let my mind go and began to open my mouth in faith. Suddenly, I was praying out loud in a language I didn't know.

It was *VERY* wonderful and faith filling. It touched my spirit but not my mind. Though my mind was unfruitful while I was praying, I felt certain I was talking directly to God in my spirit. I learned a few days later while praying in the Spirit in my car that I could shift back and forth. Praying in the Spirit and then, seemingly, praying the same content in English. I was like a kid with a new scooter. I *LOVED* it.

Having a Prophetic Word was many months away. I was aware that on occasion a brother or sister might share during worship a clear and forceful message that seemed as if God Himself was speaking. It would only be a sentence, and often the message would be delivered in halting words, as if the messenger was having the words typed before his or her eyes. Of course, I focused on Chapter 14 of Corinthians to better understand what was happening.

Growing up, I had always associated the word Prophecy with knowing what was going to occur in the future. But, my experience in the South Memphis house was very different. It was a message for the moment, as if God was with us in the room and wanted to share something Himself. Very practical and it met the mark set by Paul in Chapter 14: it built up the small group in both faith and knowledge. It was just like your father at breakfast telling you something you needed to know before you left for school.

When the gift was first manifested in me publicly, I had felt prompted during worship for weeks to open my mouth and share one beginning word. Frankly, I was scared to take a chance as I didn't want to look a fool by saying one word and then having nothing else to say. Finally, I got my courage up and stepped out. I can't remember the word now. It may have been the word "the." If so, I began, "The…" and more words came, and I spoke a one sentence message that certainly seemed to be what God was saying for the moment, and I got a hardy "amen" as confirmation.

It was a bit terrifying, but if you look at 1st Corinthians with the heart of Paul and see how this can help build up your brothers and sisters, that knowledge helps spur you on.

In the late seventies, after hands had again be laid on me by Don Finto, a trusted minister from the Belmont Church in Nashville, I began to experience dreams and visions. The visions would sometimes occur during worship. I would see something and would share what I was seeing. Meantime, my brother, Steve Bowie, was experiencing something similar - both "message" Words and visions during prayer or worship. Others also were having dreams and an occasional vision. It was a heady time.

As the 1980s progressed, my understanding continued to shift. It was clearer that Word delivery (a teaching or message at a worship meeting) could be a form of Prophecy - nay, should be. Today, when we gather, we want what is spoken to be very much what God wants spoken and not what we think is a clever idea. There are three questions worth asking:

1. **Is this something God is prompting me to share?**
2. **Is this going to build up the community?**
3. **Is this the time?**

If the answer is yes to all three, you should be sharing.

Having said all of this, Chapter 14 is a treasure trove for the assembly. Paul gives very specific instructions that a meeting should be well ordered while still allowing gifts from God to flow. He restricts messages in Tongues to settings where known believers have the Gift of Interpretation. Otherwise, as he says, an unbelieving guest will think the Tongue speaker mad. Even when interpreters are present, he still restricts the number of messages to three.

The same is true of Prophecy. Three messages at most.

Paul ends with a practice that we have tried to use in our larger meetings and one that has great value. Wives are encouraged to not speak in the formal assembly (i.e., outside of the home) unless they are truly prompted to speak and permitted by their husbands. Obviously, there were cultural reasons for some of restrictions outlined in the Torah, but I have found that it is much safer, particularly when a wife may be confused about what has been said, to ask her husband in private rather than in the middle of the assembly. This has the added benefit of putting pressure on the husband to fulfill his role as head and removes the potentially awkward situation of having someone else have to answer, or worse, correct, someone else's wife if the question was out-of-order.

Over the years, I have seen clearly that random questioning regardless of spousal gender is most often disruptive and takes away from a message God really wants delivered. In the general freedom we have enjoyed as a small community, I have seen a good number of men introduce an unhelpful comment or question and thus bring confusion. Generally, it is better to talk privately apart from the meeting. The rule of the "Amen" is the best control. If someone does not receive at least one hardy "amen" after they have shared, watch out! What was shared was probably not what the Spirit is saying. The "amen" is not for making some feel good. It should exclusively be a bearing of witness to the activity of Holy Spirit. It is critical that the "amen" function.

Those comments do not mean women should not be allowed to speak when their husbands have given them permission or asked them to share. The rule we have employed seems a good one. If Fran thinks she may have something God wants spoken, she will lean over and quietly tell me in a condensed version what she wants to say. My permission covers her. The same thing would be true of all the gifts. Remember, that all of the Apostle Philip's daughters had the Gift of Prophecy. We don't want to shut our ears to what God is saying.

Paul sums up the whole chapter with a "therefore:

"Therefore, my brethren, desire earnestly to prophesy, and do not forbid to speak in tongues. But all things must be done properly and in an orderly manner." (1st Corinthians 14:39-40).

We should ask ourselves 2 things: "Am I experiencing a first century assembly experience, and what can I do to be helpful?"

1st Corinthians 15

Kerygma and Resurrection

Paul shifts from Gifts of the Spirit and corporate worship to the subject of what we are to believe about the Faith.

In the early 1970s, I found myself in graduate school in New Haven, Connecticut working on a Master's in Environmental Design. I could take one elective, and the elective I chose was a graduate course at the Yale School of Divinity taught by the Buckingham Professor of New Testament Studies, Abe Malherbe. As mentioned previously, Abe had a big impact on me outside of class, but it was his course that spotlighted 1st Corinthians 15.

Most scholars feel that this chapter contains one of the earliest creedal formations in the entire New Testament. What they are talking about is the *Kerygma*, the kernel of the gospel. Remember, we want to be *Kerygma* detectives, looking for the kernel of our Faith that grows into such a rich and amazing tree. Here are the key verses:

*"Now I make known to you, brethren, the gospel which I preached to you, which also you **received**, in which also you stand, by which also you are saved, if you hold fast the word which I preached to you, unless you believed in vain.*

*"For I **delivered** to you as of first importance what I also received, **that Christ died for our sins** according to the Scriptures, and **that He was buried**, and **that He was raised** on the third day according to the Scriptures, and **that He appeared** to Cephas, then to the twelve. After that He appeared to more than five hundred brethren at one time, most of whom remain until now, but some have fallen asleep; then He appeared to James, then to all the apostles; and last of all, as to one untimely born, He appeared to me also. For I am the least of the apostles, and not fit to be called an apostle, because I persecuted the church of God. But by the grace of God I am what I am, and His grace toward me did not prove vain; but I labored even more than all of them, yet not I, but the grace of God with me. Whether then it was I or they, so we preach and so you believed."* (1st Corinthians 15:1-11).

In the first 11 verses, we find what may be an earlier church formula for what one should believe at the core of his or her Faith. I could go on to explain in more depth why these verses have a special character, but I will mention a few reasons quickly (taking a few excerpts from Ryan Turner's excellent detective work at the Christian Apologetics & Research Ministry):

First, the words "received" (Greek *"parelabon")* and "delivered" (Greek *"paredoka")* "are the Greek equivalents of the technical rabbinic terms *"qibbel min"* and *"masar le,"* which are terms for the passing on of tradition. Paul **received** the facts that he is relating from Christians who preceded him, and in turn he **delivered** them to the people of his churches. Paul also used these words in Chapter 11 where we discussed the issue of tradition.

Second, the multiple use of *hoti* (translated *"that"* and bolded in the English translation above) indicates a streamlined formulaic pattern of creedal information. Scholars have noted that *hoti* (or *kai hoti*, translated *"and that"*) function as quotation marks to link all of the sections.

In fact, if one removed the *hoti* references, the material would still be grammatically and syntactically correct in the Greek. Without the *kai hoti* the text would read, "Christ died for our sins in accordance with the scriptures, he was buried, he was raised on the third day in accordance with the scriptures, he appeared to Cephas, then to the twelve." It is possible that Paul added the *kai* (English translated as *"and"*) for emphasis.

Third, there are non-Pauline words in the text such as *"for our sins," "according to the scriptures,"* the ordinal number after the noun in the third day reference, and *"the twelve."* These are words that Paul did not normally use.

Finally, the passage exhibits a four-fold pattern of death-burial-resurrection-appearance which many scholars believer to be *THE* kernel, the Kerygma. Let's outline the key statements:

1. **Christ died for our sins according to the Scriptures**
2. **He was buried**
3. **He was raised on the third day according to the Scriptures**
4. **He appeared**

Died, Buried, Raised, Appeared! This is what Paul received, and what he delivered to the Corinthians. The kernel. The fourth attribute, **appearance**, was critical. Men and women actually saw Jesus in physical form after His resurrection. Even Paul. It was that certainty that propelled Paul to take up the mantle Jesus gave him. His belief. It could not be shaken.

Creedal Development

Let's look quickly for how this initial kernel evolved into a clear state-ment of orthodox belief: Sometime before 250 AD, the Church was using what has come to be called the Apostle's Creed, even though we have no written example from a specific apostle for such a designation. It was what a believer *confessed*, no doubt at Baptism, and the wording had developed partially to counter Satan's strategy of sowing heresy amongst the believers. For this statement, many brothers and sisters met their death. To me, it is quite amazing that relatively unconnected church communities scattered throughout the Roman empire could be using similar statements in most all of their communities.

First in Latin:

"Credo in Deum Patrem omnipotentem,
Creatorem caeli et terrae,
et in Iesum Christum, Filium Eius unicum, Dominum nostrum, qui
conceptus est de Spiritu Sancto,
natus ex Maria Virgine,
passus sub Pontio Pilato,
crucifixus, mortuus, et sepultus,
descendit ad infernos,
tertia die resurrexit a mortuis,
ascendit ad caelos,
sedet ad dexteram Dei Patris omnipotentis,
inde venturus est iudicare vivos et mortuos.

"Credo in Spiritum Sanctum,
sanctam Ecclesiam catholicam,
sanctorum communionem,
remissionem peccatorum,
carnis resurrectionem,
vitam aeternam."

And now in English:

"I believe in God, the Father Almighty,
maker of heaven and earth;
And in Jesus Christ his only Son, our Lord;
who was conceived by the Holy Spirit,
born of the Virgin Mary,
suffered under Pontius Pilate,
was crucified, dead, and buried;
He descended into Hell
the third day he rose from the dead;
he ascended into heaven,
and sitteth at the right hand of God the Father Almighty;
from thence he shall come to judge the quick and the dead.

"I believe in the Holy Spirit,
the holy catholic church,
the communion of saints,
the forgiveness of sins,
the resurrection of the body,
and the life everlasting."

Look at each line. Can we confess this with all of our heart?

After letting down this anchor, Paul launches into belief issues in Corinth concerning the resurrection. In addition to being the *Kerygma* chapter, this is the Resurrection chapter. Some in Corinth say there is no resurrection. How can that possibly be since Number 3 above *("He was raised")* definitely shows that there is a resurrection? And if there were not a resurrection, their faith would be in vain.

Paul then expands his lens and draws further doctrinal conclusions: **First** Christ, **then** those who are Christ's when He returns, **then** the End, **then** *after* having abolished all rule and authority other than

His own, Jesus hands over the Kingdom to God the Father. Note that Death is included as a dominion that will be abolished at the end, *"the last enemy."* This is a tight statement of what is to come for all of us in these different phases of resurrection.

Next, we come upon the surprising practice of having one believer get baptized for a departed, unbaptized person. These could have been people in the midst of their catechism training who died prematurely. Perhaps others had in mind babies who died during childbirth (a frequent tragedy in the ancient world). I note that Paul does not comment on the practice, but uses the practice to emphasize the resurrection that believers look toward.

Paul addresses *"How are the dead raised?"* The seed of our bodies will spring up after our death as an imperishable body. Like a kernel of corn, that which springs up will contain all of the identity of the kernel but be manifest in an entirely new way. The natural body will be raised a spiritual body.

His closing addresses death straight on. We will all be changed, *"in a moment, in the twinkling of an eye, at the last trumpet… the dead will be raised imperishable and changed."* What great language ready for the funeral service!

"But when this perishable will have put on the imperishable, and this mortal will have put on immortality, then will come about the saying that is written, 'Death is swallowed up in victory. O death, where is your victory? O death, where is your sting?' The sting of death is sin, and the power of sin is the law; but thanks be to God, who gives us the victory through our Lord Jesus Christ!" (1st Corinthians 15:54-57).

But when? Augustine, in one of his sermons during the Easter season, advised:

"Where is death? Seek it in Christ, for it exists no longer. It did exist, and now death is dead. O Life, O Death of death! Be of good heart, death will die in us also. What has taken place in our Head will also take place in His members. Death will die in us also. But when? **At the end of the world, at the resurrection of the dead** *in which we believe and about which we have no doubt.... These are words given to those who triumph, that you may have something to think about, something to sing about in your heart, something to seek with faith and good works."* (Augustine, Sermon 233:3-4).

To me, scripture and the ancients attest that our true rising will be at the end of the world, that is, not immediately upon our death. From the point of view of our consciousness, it may be immediate, in spite of the fact that our souls will be held until the *"end of the world."* Surely, most funeral orations today are confused on God's timing.

1ˢᵗ Corinthians 16

We are back to practical matters in the first part of Chapter 16, as we leave Paul's views on the resurrection behind. "Practical" may not be the right word, because we see Paul's passion to help the church in Jerusalem.

Paul had already directed the churches in Galatia to raise money for the poor of Jerusalem's (see Galatians 2:10), and he directs the Corinthians to do likewise. I am willing to bet the Corinthians would have little idea where Galatia even was – given Corinth's location on the south-western side of Greece and Galatia's location on the other side of the Aegean Sea in the middle of what I grew up knowing as Asia Minor.

Now part of modern Turkey, we saw Paul spend many days there on several of his missionary journeys. You will remember Iconium, Lystra and Derbe, but as a refresher, look at the map in the reflections on Acts

17. See if you can find those three cities as well as Tarsus and Antioch (the latter to help orientation).

Regardless, every male Jew over the age of twenty years had to contribute toward the maintenance of the temple, the priests and its services. Paul's recall of his fundraising mentions the poor rather than the temple, and here in Corinthians, he identifies the recipients as the *"saints."* This is what our brothers and sisters in the Memphis Normal Station community call each other – a very Biblical term!

We catch in the opening paragraph another view of normal church practice: they apparently are meeting in Corinth on the first day of each week. Paul is directing (note, he is not asking) that they take up a special collection for the *"saints"* in Jerusalem so that they will not have to be stressed when Paul arrives in person.

We also can see from the first section early Christian attitudes toward stewardship - acting responsibly to support others in distress. Paul addresses the same issue in his letter to the Galatians, *"let us do good to all people, and especially to those who are of the household of the faith."* (Galatians 6:10).

Paul's suggestion for a special collection suggests that the Corinthians may have collected money for the poor on a regular basis. In a synagogue and in the temple, this was done by having a box where one could drop money for support at any time the facility was open, so it is unclear whether they passed a bag for donations or dropped money in a box stationed somewhere in the home in which they were meeting.

From the earliest days, communities of believers had been generous with their giving. Remember Acts 4:32-35:

"All the believers were one in heart and mind. No one claimed that any of his possessions was his own, but they shared everything they had. With

great power the apostles continued to testify to the resurrection of the Lord Jesus, and much grace was upon them all. There were no needy persons among them. For from time to time those who owned lands or houses sold them, brought the money from the sales and put it at the apostles' feet, and it was distributed to anyone as he had need."

When we get to Paul's letter which we call 2nd Corinthians, at the beginning of Chapter 8 we will see the heart of the churches in Macedonia who were under financial stress of their own:

"Now, brethren, we wish to make known to you the grace of God which has been given in the churches of Macedonia, that in a great ordeal of affliction their abundance of joy and their deep poverty overflowed in the wealth of their liberality. For I testify that according to their ability, and beyond their ability, they gave of their own accord, begging us with much urging for the favor of participation in the support of the saints, and this, not as we had expected, but they first gave themselves to the Lord and to us by the will of God. So we urged Titus that as he had previously made a beginning, so he would also complete in you this gracious work as well." (2nd Corinthians 8:1-6).

We can get a further practical glimpse into early Christian practice regarding giving from a letter written by Tertullian from Carthage in North Africa around 197 AD:

"Though we have our treasure-chest, it is not made up of purchase-money, as of a religion that has its price. On the monthly day, if he likes, each puts in a small donation; but only if it be his pleasure, and only if he be able: for there is no compulsion; all is voluntary. These gifts are... not spent on feasts, and drinking-bouts, and eating-houses, but to support and bury poor people, to supply the wants of boys and girls destitute of means and parents, and of old persons confined now to the house; such, too, as have suffered shipwreck; and if there happen to be any in the

mines or banished to the islands or shut up in the prisons, for nothing but their fidelity to the cause of God's Church, they become the nurslings of their confession." (Taken from Ante-Nicene Fathers, Vol. iii. Tertullian. Part 1, Chapter XXXIX).

Their giving was free, generous and periodic!

I note that Paul is writing his letter from Ephesus and will remain there until Pentecost. In Paul's closing verses of his letter, we get another glimpse behind the scenes of ministry – particularly of those called to trans-local work. Paul's assistant, Timothy, may be coming to minister in Corinth, but Paul is tentative about this. He also has encouraged Apollos to visit but reveals the time is not convenient.

Paul closes with an encouragement for the Corinthians to subject themselves (i.e., be under submission) to men like Stephanos who is in their midst. Stephanos, along with two other brothers, Fortunatus and Achaicus, have apparently visited Paul in Ephesus and *"brought what was lacking on their part."* His emphasis is on the refreshment Paul received in the Spirit, though they may have brought a monetary gift as well.

In the last two verses, Bible detectives see a few early church practices: there is a "church" (little "c") meeting in Aquila and Prisca's house, and Christians are greeting each other with a *"holy kiss,"* a practiced still followed in the ancient streams of Christianity. Whether hugs or kisses, it is important to embrace one another when we greet our brothers and sisters in the lord. They are due both honor and affection!

I end with Paul's rousing admonition in verse 13 – a verse I dearly love: *"Be on the alert, stand firm in the faith, act like men, be strong. Let all that you do be done in love."*

2nd Corinthians

2nd Corinthians 1

Paul probably wrote at least part of 2nd Corinthians from Northern Greece around AD 56, a year or so after he wrote what we call 1st Corinthians. As mentioned earlier, there appear to have been several Pauline letters to Corinth that are no longer in existence, and 2nd Corinthians also may be two letters stitched together into one scroll by early scribes for convenience sake. We will see there is a sharp division and change of tone that occurs in Chapter 10. In Chapters 1-9, Paul expresses his joy with the Corinthians response on several fronts in response to his earlier letter. He wrote in Chapter 7 that he had *"complete confidence"* in them. Chapter 10 shifts tone and content significantly.

Paul's greeting in Chapter 1 is a bit different from 1st Corinthians. In his earlier letter, he had written with Sosthenes as his collaborator. In 2nd Corinthians, he writes with Timothy. Again like the Normal Station folks, he calls those whom he writes *"the saints"* – those who are throughout Greece. Further, he writes the *"church"* (singular and lower case) in Corinth itself.

I pay attention to these small matters because it reflects how Paul sees jurisdictions as well as the theology of the Church. We already know that the church in Corinth is composed of a network of "house churches" from the text in 1st Corinthians. But from afar, Paul sees that they are one lump called forth to God. So we have the church in Corinth, the church in Rome and the big Church (capitalized) in the whole world. Since the word *"church"* is our word, *Ekklesia*, and means the *"called out,"* Paul expresses unity on different levels with a jurisdictional awareness.

We see the church in Corinth belongs to God. My Pentecostal brothers would be pleased with Paul's nomenclature in verse one: *"To the church of God which is at Corinth."* It's God's church, but we know from many other scriptures that the *"called out"* also belong to Jesus (see Romans 16:16).

In the New American Standard Bible translation of the New Testament, a group of believers is called:

- Church (Used 76 times)
- Saints (60 times)
- the Body or Body of Christ (over 40 times)
- Beloved (39 times)
- members of the Way or the Way of Righteousness (used approximately 11 times)
- Church of God (8 times)
- Flock (used 6 times)
- Friends (used 3 to 6 times)
- Servants of Christ (used 3 times)
- Household of God (2 times)
- Servants of God (2 times)
- Servants of a New Covenant (1 time)
- Churches of Christ (1 time)
- General Assembly (1 time)

- Royal Priesthood (1 time)
- Church of the living God (1 time)

Pretty interesting. As we see in verse one, normally the church is defined as those who are being addressed by the geographic extent of their dwellings. But then we have trans-local folks like Paul and Timothy who float all over the place. They are in the Big Church which was defined back then as all the people in the world that believed, but Paul also is part of the even bigger Church that includes all the believers that have ever lived. Perhaps the smallest unit is Jesus's *"two or more gathered together."*

Paul immediately launches into a eulogy of God, a "blessing." *"Blessed be the God and Father of our Lord Jesus Christ...."* A "blessing" in the Greek is the word from which we get the word eulogy. It is speaking well and highly of someone. In French, the word is *"beni,"* coming from the word for good from which we get the word Benefactor that simply means "good work" or "worker of good." My point is that Paul begins by exclaiming that God is good in absolutely marvelous language:

"Blessed be the God and Father of our Lord Jesus Christ, the Father of mercies and God of all comfort, who comforts us in all our affliction so that we will be able to comfort those who are in any affliction with the comfort with which we ourselves are comforted by God. For just as the sufferings of Christ are ours in abundance, so also our comfort is abundant through Christ. But if we are afflicted, it is for your comfort and salvation; or if we are comforted, it is for your comfort, which is effective in the patient enduring of the same sufferings which we also suffer; and our hope for you is firmly grounded, knowing that as you are sharers of our sufferings, so also you are sharers of our comfort." (2nd Corinthians 1:3-7).

Paul's focus is that God is Good when we are afflicted. Through the Holy Spirit that He has poured out on us, we are comforted when we suffer as Christ suffered. Through the Anointed One we are comforted, and our comfort is for others as well.

I think about the comfort in God we received when our grandson, Jack, battled cancer at age 11. That comfort, if manifest to others, comforts others whether they are in affliction at the moment or not. We are always comforted when we see others manifestly comforted by God. When we too are suffering, we remember the sweet comfort God brought to another in suffering. It is a beautiful and absolutely true reflection with which Paul begins.

Paul brings the believers up to date with Paul's situation in Asia beginning in verse 8 - things have not gone well.

Paul most likely is referring to what had been happening to him and the believers in Ephesus since we know Ephesus is in "Asia" and also where Paul was when he wrote them earlier. He nearly died and could not trust himself to survive the affliction he and the others were under, but could only trust God for deliverance. Again, great comforting language that also reminds me of our struggle for our grandson:

"God who raises the dead...will deliver us. He on whom we have set our hope. And He will yet deliver us. You also join in helping us through your prayers, so that thanks may be given by many persons on our behalf for the favor bestowed on us through the prayers of many." (2nd Corinthians 1:9-11).

It would appear that from verse 12 to the end of the chapter, Paul is answering a criticism that he may have heard from some in Corinth. We know the church in Corinth has cliques or divisions from our reading of 1st Corinthians. One group questions Paul's apostleship. One mark of an apostle must be one who lets his *"yes be yes and his no be no."* (Jesus speaking in Matthew 5:7). In other words, some would say that an apostle should know what is to take place and not promise anything that he would not be able to deliver.

Focused on Their Joy

Paul had indicated to the church in Corinth that he intended to visit them earlier but had not done so. Some must have accused him of vacillating – in their mind, that was not a sign of an apostle. Paul answers the accusation by saying he wasn't vacillating. Then he offers a passionate defense that brings in the very issue of how can one's "yes" be "no." In the Anointed One (Jesus), there is no "no," only "yes." *"For the Son of God, the Anointed Jesus, who was preached among you by us – by me and Silvanus and Timothy – was not yes and no, but yes in Him."* (2nd Corinthians 1:19).

It is an interesting defense, but he doesn't give the real reason until verses 23 and 24. Paul didn't come to spare them from judgment that surely would have been theirs if he had come before they had dealt with the man caught in incest. He decided that he would have been *"lording over their faith"* if he had done so – or at least might have appeared so. Instead, he was a worker with the Corinthians for their joy and felt restraint to be anything else.

My reflection of Paul's last section is twofold.

First, we need to be careful to not overstate what we going to do. James was very clear about this in the book of James. It is a good rule for all: *"Come now, you who say, 'Today or tomorrow we will go to such and such a city and spend a year there and engage in business and make a profit.' Yet you do not know what your life will be like tomorrow. You are just a vapor that appears for a little while and then vanishes away. Instead, you ought to say, 'If the Lord wills, we will live and also do this or that.'"* (James 4:13-15).

Second, we should be careful to give others caught in sin a chance to repent of it on their own after they are counseled as opposed to forcing them if their sin is not immediately life threatening. I love Paul's focus that he has delayed because he is focused on their joy. Our focus needs to be on how to help each other reach true joy! A great call.

2nd Corinthians 2

Chapter 2 begins with a few sentences tied to the end of the first chapter. Previously, Paul indicated his delay in coming to Corinth was caused by his desire to see the Corinthians full of joy when he came. Now, Paul reveals he had two more motives: he did not want to be sad upon arrival, but rather joyful – knowing that they had acted on his stern previous letter. Further, he wanted them to know the special love that he held for them.

We will find in Chapter 7 that Paul's earlier stern admonitions regarding the immoral man mentioned in 1st Corinthians 5 have been addressed fully. Jumping forward, we see the Corinthians had responded fully. The Godly sorrow that Paul's letter had produced in them led to righteous action.

Here is the text from 2nd Corinthians 7:8-13:

"For though I caused you sorrow by my letter, I do not regret it; though I did regret it — for I see that that letter caused you sorrow, though only for a while — I now rejoice, not that you were made sorrowful, but that you were made sorrowful to the point of repentance; for you were made sorrowful according to the will of God, so that you might not suffer loss in anything through us. For the sorrow that is according to the will of God produces a repentance without regret, leading to salvation, but the sorrow of the world produces death. For behold what earnestness this very thing, this godly sorrow, has produced in you: what vindication of yourselves,

what indignation, what fear, what longing, what zeal, what avenging of wrong! In everything you demonstrated yourselves to be innocent in the matter. So although I wrote to you, it was not for the sake of the offender nor for the sake of the one offended, but that your earnestness on our behalf might be made known to you in the sight of God. For this reason we have been comforted."

The Corinthians had responded by excommunicating the offending brother; he had responded in sorrow, and now it was time to extend forgiveness. Thus, Paul urges them to not only forgive but also comfort him, fearful that otherwise the man would be overwhelmed by excessive grief.

If they will forgive the man, Paul will forgive him as well.

Verse 11 is important. The difficulties we encounter in our fellowships often are the result of Satan's schemes, and Paul is very alert to what is going on behind the scenes, that is, what Satan is doing. Satan wanted to destroy the entire Corinthian church. The controversy and discredit brought about by the immoral man's behavior was just one tactic. There is no real fellowship of believers that Satan does not want to destroy. Including yours and mine.

Things could have gone otherwise.

Paul ends on another one of these extraordinary high notes that his passion, spirit and knowledge often produce. His words soar and testify to the Spirit of God's beautiful hand on him as he writes:

"But thanks be to God, who always leads us triumphantly in Christ, and manifests through us the sweet aroma of the knowledge of Him in every place. For we are a fragrance of Christ to God among those who are being saved and among those who are perishing; to the one an aroma from death to death, to the other an aroma from life to life. And who is

adequate for these things? For we are not like many, peddling the word of God, but as from sincerity, but as from God, we speak in Christ in the sight of God." (2nd Corinthians 2:14-17).

I would encourage you to read the end of Chapter 2 several times out loud. It excites me, and I believe you will be roused as well. God always is in the lead in our lives, leading us in triumph since we have been placed in the Anointed One, and through our presence manifests the sweet aroma of the Godhead everywhere we go. Goodness, may it be so!

2nd Corinthians 3

Paul leaves dangling his defense that he was *"peddling"* the Word of God at the end of the second chapter, but he will return to that matter in Chapter 4 as well as in Chapters 11 and 12. Meanwhile, he digresses in Chapter 3 to talk about the "New Covenant."

I am fascinated that we do not frequently meet these words in the New Testament. The Greek word we translate as "Covenant" is *diatheke*. This corresponds to the Hebrew word, *beriyth*. The word for "New" in Greek is *kainos*. So, *kainos diatheke* – New Covenant.

In the Old Testament, the phrase occurs only ONCE, in Jeremiah's pivotal verse in Jeremiah 31:31:

"Behold, days are coming," declares the Lord, when I will make a new covenant with the house of Israel and the house of Judah."

As we have reflected several times, Covenant in the Jeremiah passage is the Hebrew word *beriyth* that comes from the Hebrew word for "cutting." I always try to remember to translate the word "covenant" with its root meaning, *cutting*, because it gets across the life shedding aspect of making a compact that is cut in blood and will cause your life to hang in the balance between life and death, depending on whether you keep covenant or not.

Let me say that another way: The compact that God made with Abraham and extended to the Patriarchs, all of Israel and eventually to us, is a compact in blood.

We remember this "New Cutting," cut in the flesh of Jesus and His poured-out blood, when we take the cup at every communion service. Luke uses the phrase in Greek once in his gospel when he records Jesus's words about the cup at His last Passover meal: *"This cup which is poured out for you is the new* (kainos) *covenant* (diatheke) *in My blood."* (Luke 22:20).

It is a life or death matter to be in covenant.

This concept is so central to our belief as Christians that the books of the "New Testament" are called just that: the books of the New Covenant. "Testament" is just a word for compact, will or covenant. Yet the phrase New Covenant occurs only EIGHT times in the entire Bible: once in Jeremiah, once in Luke, once in 1st Corinthians, once in 2nd Corinthians and four times in Hebrews. I find that fairly incredible. It is in Chapter 3 of 2nd Corinthians that we find it.

The reason I am amazed is that the entire Gospel hinges on this covenantal reality. In fact, as we saw in Luke and Acts, the "Promise" that everyone was looking for in Jesus's day was the fulfillment of the Lord's promise spoken to Jeremiah in Chapter 31:31. The New Covenant or New Cutting would usher in an agreement with God where the law would be written on hearts of flesh and not tablets of stone, and the Spirit of God would rest upon His people. That fact makes the 3rd chapter of 2nd Corinthians particularly important.

Paul echoes Jeremiah and the original covenants made with Abraham and his descendants in verse 3 when he compares the Corinthians to a letter written on his heart, *"written not with ink but with the Spirit of the living God, not on tablets of stone but on tablets of human hearts,"* a direct reference to Jeremiah's passage.

What Paul shares with the Corinthians and with us is not from himself but from God who made Paul and his band of believers *"servants of a New Covenant."* (2nd Corinthians 3:6). That is what *WE* are, servants of a New Covenant. If someone asks who we are, we can respond, "We are servants of the New Covenant."

We are to serve the compact, the contract, the Will and Testament of Jesus. The writer of Hebrews will greatly expand this thought, but Paul is on the key effect: this covenant, made in Jesus's blood, is affected through the Spirit of God within us. As a servant, Paul serves the Spirit. As servants, we serve the Spirit. The law is written on our hearts.

In verses 7 through 11, Paul compares the Old Testament with the New. From Paul's point of view (we remember that he developed this thought fully in his letter to the Romans), the coming of the Old Testament, the Old Covenant, brought death since no one could meet the obligations it established for Israel. The New Covenant brings life by Jesus's substitutionary death and the inner nature of a Covenant whose laws are written on the heart and not on stone.

If the Old Covenant came with glory, how much more the New! Moses served Israel the Old; the Spirit serves us the New. When the two are compared, Paul says there is almost no comparison because the *glory* (translate *"weight"*) of the New Covenant has such incredible density.

When Jews turn to the Lord, a veil over their hearts is lifted as they move from the Old Covenant to the New. Likewise, when we turn to the Lord, a veil over our hearts is also lifted.

The last two soaring verses of the chapter, verses 17 and 18, are very important verses – both for understanding as well as for life.

"Now the Lord is the Spirit, and where the Spirit of the Lord is, there is liberty. But we all, with unveiled face, beholding as in a mirror the glory of the Lord, are being transformed into the same image from glory to glory, just as from the Lord, the Spirit."

We see in these verses one of the foundation stones of the doctrine of the Trinity. The LORD *is* the Spirit. The Spirit *is* the Lord. This is affirmed twice in these two verses. And where the wonder of the Spirit of God is, there is an exponentially different experience of freedom.

Paul reveals something each one of us needs to grasp deeply. We want God to write it on our hearts. What God is doing with us releases a freedom within, a freedom beyond compulsion, a freedom beyond corruption, a freedom beyond ethnicity, gender and culture, a freedom beyond the letter of the Law. This is an internal release, a dimensional change within us. May the Father, Son and Holy Spirit so reveal Himself to us that we are categorically changed from bondage and death to life in the Spirit. Come, Lord Jesus!

2nd Corinthians 4

Having *"this ministry,"* this *service* of the New Covenant, in proportion to the degree of mercy he had received, Paul does not lose heart. Our service is the same. In proportion to the degree of mercy each one of us has received, we can serve God and people, that is, be their servants and not lose heart.

Are we losing heart? What is the reason Paul does not lose heart in his ministry, his service to the New Covenant, to God and to people? It rests on the incredible mercy he had received in being **called, forgiven**

and empowered in the Spirit. From a practical point of view, it is also because he had renounced things that were ungodly in his life, *"things hidden because of shame,"* and is doing his work speaking only what is true.

The same must be true of us. I am struck with the word *"renounced"* in verse 2. Paul has renounced the things from his past. I am reminded of Terry Smith's admonition to renounce Satan's lie that was sown in our lives as youngsters.

"Renounce." It is a big word. It means to utterly reject something, and I think in this context it means to utterly reject an allegiance. The word in the Greek is *apeipon*, and this is the only time it occurs in the New Testament. It raises a good question for each of us: what did we renounce when we turned to the Lord. And do we renounce it today? Obviously, we need to!

Paul is writing to the Corinthians totally aware of his own personal afflictions and sufferings. He doesn't lose heart because he is on God's side, and God in His mercy has extended to him the greatest of treasures and power that comes only from God. Thus, Paul proclaims not himself but Jesus as both the Anointed One and Lord. Instead of proclaiming himself, he presents himself as a bondservant to the Corinthians.

Being a bondservant is about the lowest form of occupation one could choose. Paul is basically saying he belongs to the Corinthians. He is theirs, and his job is to serve them. On a platter, he brings to them the *"glory of Christ, the very image of God." "For God... is the One who has shown in our hearts to give the Light of the knowledge of the glory of God in the face of Christ!"* (2nd Corinthians 4:6).

People will NOT see the light and glory of God through our words unless our words reflect our hearts, and our hearts, in turn, reflect the heart of God. It is easy to get confused about this. People are moved by our hearts, not our cleverness, education or accolades. I hope I can express my heart more fully – that my heart would be God's heart. Yes, Lord!

We keep hitting in Corinthians these incredible soaring words that reveal Paul's true heart in the most exalted language. I love his wording that begins in verse 7:

"But we have this treasure in earthen vessels, so that the surpassing greatness of the power will be of God and not from ourselves; we are afflicted in every way, but not crushed; perplexed, but not despairing; persecuted, but not forsaken; struck down, but not destroyed; always carrying about in the body the dying of Jesus, so that the life of Jesus also may be manifested in our body." (2nd Corinthians 4:7-10).

Afflicted in every way, perplexed, persecuted, struck down, yet Paul is not crushed, despairing, forsaken or destroyed. Paul carried about in his body the dying of Jesus so that the life of Jesus could be manifest. He was constantly delivered over to death for Jesus's sake, so that the life of Jesus could be manifest.

This is not a "feel good, get rich" message that we might associate with some TV evangelists. Paul has grasped a deep thing: the more our lives are identified with Jesus's death and suffering through our own burdens and afflictions, the more his life can be manifest in us, and the manifestation of Jesus's life is as good as it gets here on earth.

"Afflictions" come, and truthfully, joy so often is not my immediate response. That is a confession, not a direction! But the second we turn our eyes to the mercy that has been shown to us through the *"cutting"* of Jesus and the New Covenant which his cutting initiated, things come quickly in perspective. Then, we see our witness to those about us shift to trust and peace rather than anxiety, worry and depression.

The afflictions are real – they hurt truly, but the hurt is transformed into glory when we allow the energy of Christ within us to rule.

Paul began the chapter saying he doesn't lose heart. He ends this chapter saying he doesn't lose heart. Day by day, his outer man was decaying. I think of not only the apostle Paul, but also our sick friends and loved ones. Yet Paul's inner man is being renewed day by day.

The last paragraph contains soaring words and the title of one of C.S. Lewis' most important works, *The Weight of Glory*:

"For momentary, light affliction is producing for us an eternal weight of glory far beyond all comparison, while we look not at the things which are seen, but at the things which are not seen; for the things which are seen are temporal, but the things which are not seen are eternal." (2nd Corinthians 4:17-18).

What a great reminder. We need to keep our eyes on what cannot be seen by the eye and not on the things that can be (earthquakes, car wrecks, decaying flesh, etc.). Light affliction produces an eternal weight of glory. Yes!

2nd Corinthians 5

I am writing my reflection on Chapter 5 alone, overlooking the Gulf of Mexico that appears endless, hearing the waves roar as they endlessly roll onto the long run of beach. It is hard here not to think about our future home in eternity. Our friend Paul is thinking much the same. And it is hard to not think of our friends who are near death as I read the opening verses:

"For we know that if the earthly tent which is our house is torn down, we have a building from God, a house not made with hands, eternal in the heavens. For indeed in this house we groan, longing to be clothed

with our dwelling from heaven, inasmuch as we, having put it on, will not be found naked. For indeed while we are in this tent, we groan, being burdened, because we do not want to be unclothed but to be clothed, so that what is mortal will be swallowed up by life. Now He who prepared us for this very purpose is God, who gave to us the Spirit as a pledge." (2nd Corinthians 5:1-5).

What strikes me are the words, *"earthly tent."* They recall a little vision I had as my friend, David Vaughan, prayed for Cathy Harding who was near death. I saw angels lifting almost a mantle of some kind over Cathy. I could not see her, but I thought of an image I had drawn 20 years ago.

Until this morning, I couldn't quite understand why it looked like a tent in my dream, but 2nd Corinthians Chapter 5 solves the puzzle. It was a tent I saw. The cords that held it in place have been removed, and the tent is being lifted up.

2nd Corinthians 5 is certainly a comforting and inspiring chapter. It contains several Gospel kernels:

"For the love of Christ controls us, having concluded this, that one died for all, therefore all died; and He died for all, so that they who live might no longer live for themselves, but for Him who died and rose again on their behalf. Therefore, from now on we recognize no one according to the

flesh; even though we have known Christ according to the flesh, yet now we know Him in this way no longer. Therefore, if anyone is in Christ, he is a new creature; the old things passed away; behold, new things have come." (2nd Corinthians 5:14-17).

This section succinctly restates the key Gospel message (*"Christ died for all"*) while at the same time pointing to some of the implications. Because Jesus died, all things have become new. *We* have become new, and now live for others and not ourselves, and the love of Christ that controls us comes from this reality. Before, we once saw people *"in the flesh,"* but we now see them in an entirely new way.

I certainly hope this is true for you and me. We want to see all things new, but being truthful, I often see through old glasses. I need your help, Lord!

The verses that follow contain another nugget: *"God was in Christ reconciling the world to Himself."*

Christ died for all; God was in Christ reconciling the world to Himself! *"Now all these things are from God, who reconciled us to Himself through Christ and gave us the ministry of reconciliation, namely, that God was in Christ reconciling the world to Himself, not counting their trespasses against them, and He has committed to us the word of reconciliation."* (2nd Corinthians 5:18-19).

To fulfill the ministry of reconciliation God has given each one of us, we have to see all things anew, and people in an entirely different way than we did before we received the Spirit. Otherwise, we simply will not fulfill our ministry.

Verse 21 contains the third kernel: *"He made Him who knew no sin to be sin on our behalf, so that we might become the righteousness of God in Him."*

It took a perfectly sinless sacrifice of inestimable value to redeem us so that we might be righteous IN HIM. Our imputed righteousness is for an entirely relational end. We are drawn close by the blood of Christ, the perfect sin offering. In a true sense, we rest on the "kernels" of the Gospel, and Paul's particular gift of understanding our foundations becomes our gift.

2nd Corinthians 6

After encouraging us in Chapter 5 that reconciling the Corinthians to Himself was God's aim, Paul moves on to a practical admonition: *"Do not let the grace that you have received from God be for nothing."* In other words, now that you can work *with* God toward reconciliation with others (having been reconciled yourself), work on reconciliation.

We can see Paul is struggling with some rift between himself and the Corinthians. Paul is doing all that he can to reconcile from his side. He launches into another defense of his team and himself:

"commending ourselves as servants of God, in much endurance, in afflictions, in hardships, in distresses, in beatings, in imprisonments, in tumults, in labors, in sleeplessness, in hunger, in purity, in knowledge, in patience, in kindness, in the Holy Spirit, in genuine love, in the word of truth, in the power of God; by the weapons of righteousness for the right hand and the left, by glory and dishonor, by evil report and good report; regarded as deceivers and yet true; as unknown yet well-known, as dying yet behold, we live; as punished yet not put to death, as sorrowful yet always rejoicing, as poor yet making many rich, as having nothing yet possessing all things." (2nd Corinthians 6:4-10)

Let's break this down in three nines. Paul gives a short review of all that he and his team have endured – *nine* things suffered followed by *nine* manifestations of God in their midst: purity, knowledge, patience, kindness, in the Holy Spirit, genuine love, the Word of Truth, power and the weapons of righteousness - followed by *nine* paradoxes: dying, yet alive, etc. What they have endured, what they have manifested and how they appear in one way but are another – all these speak to their position in God that should encourage the Corinthians to receive Paul and his team.

At this point, it is healthy to ask the question: Am I not receiving the ministry of another who may be a bit like Paul, that is, someone whom is easy to discount on the surface, but the evidence of God is visible in both the person's life and gifting?

Paul addresses part of the reason the Corinthians are having trouble receiving Paul's ministry in verse 12: *"you are restrained in your own affections."* In other words, the Corinthians are bound up in things they enjoy that keep them from fully opening their hearts to those God has given them that they might be built up.

It is not hard to see this on practical terms as we encounter the underlying issue frequently. For example, choosing to pursue our personal pleasures in conflict with assembling with the saints may reveal it. Or consistently missing our morning quiet time because things that interest us aside from God crowd our schedule. Or avoiding relationship building with those God has given us because of one thing or another. The list would be long indeed.

Paul specifically identifies the danger of too much association with unbelievers:

"Do not be bound together with unbelievers; for what partnership have righteousness and lawlessness, or what fellowship has light with darkness? Or what harmony has Christ with Belial, or what has a believer in common with an unbeliever?" (2nd Corinthians 6:14-15).

His focus is on a type of fellowship with unbelievers characterized by darkness, carousing, and even attendance at events honoring an idol.

Two personal remembrances unfortunately come to mind. Both occurred early in my walk. Amazingly, both involved idols in a certain way. In college, I was "tapped" into a rarified group at the University of Virginia called the IMP Society. This was a "ring" society at Virginia, signified by the wearing of a ring of gold emblazoned with the inscription "IMP." It was a pretty big deal to be tapped; there were only six tapped per class of 1,000, so I was surprised, honored and excited to be chosen. I dutifully bought the solid gold ring that would be a symbol to all of my IMPness. The organization had begun around 1900 and did philanthropic ministry at the University. It was respected by faculty and students alike.

I wore that ring proudly until 1974 when, under conviction, I removed it because the image reminded not only me but others of Satan. There was absolutely no Satanic activity, but it was NOT something I needed to promote or with which I needed to be associated.

A year later, Fran and I were asked to join Osiris, one of the "secret" Cotton Carnival societies. This was somewhat a big deal socially in Memphis. Many of my closest high school friends were joining. There were special parties during Cotton Carnival, a parade down Main Street, the barge arriving with the King and Queen and general hoopla. Fran and I went to the parade in our special Osiris outfits. My "affections" were running. I liked the idea of belonging to this social group made up of the rich and powerful in Memphis society. But the Spirit of God within me was relentless in bringing to mind that I was "wearing" an Egyptian cultic name. Though it caused some embarrassment to give up our membership within only a few months, neither Fran nor I felt comfortable in our spirits.

"I will dwell in them and walk among them;
And I will be their God, and they shall be My people.
Therefore, come out from their midst and be separate,"
says the Lord.
And do not touch what is unclean;
And I will welcome you.
"And I will be a father to you."
(2nd Corinthians 6:16-18)

Affections run deep. But God's promise to us as well as the Corinthians is completely true. Far better to walk as a child of the Father of the Universe than embrace any form of darkness or even the semblance of darkness. In our culture today, there is every opportunity to find yourself reading a questionable book, being at a questionable party or club, watching a questionable movie, TV program or computer game. Far better to walk as a child of God than be lured aside by momentary affections.

2nd Corinthians 7

Chapter 6 ended with a promise that is worth repeating:

"Therefore, come out from their midst and be separate,"
says the Lord.
"And do not touch what is unclean;
And I will welcome you.
And I will be a father to you,
And you shall be sons and daughters to Me,"
(1st Corinthians 6:17-18)

Here, Paul repeated promises that God had made in the Torah and in the Prophets (see Leviticus 26:12, Hosea 1:10 and Jeremiah 31:31 as examples). These promises form THE promise which the Jewish people had been looking toward. We saw this at the end of Luke, the beginning of Acts and in particular Acts 2:28*ff*. As we have seen, Jeremiah 31:31 is *THE* text for the promise of a New Covenant written in the Spirit on our hearts, and Paul is thinking of all of this as he starts Chapter 7 with his famous *"Therefore."*

"Therefore, having these promises (that God will welcome us and be a Father to us), beloved, let us cleanse ourselves from all defilement of flesh and spirit, perfecting holiness in the fear of God." (2nd Corinthians 7:1).

The promises he quoted are conditional: we must come out, be separate and touch nothing that is unclean. And, we know from Paul's writings that he is not talking primarily about the defilement that is from external touching but a defilement that is internal – the internal disposition of the heart that leads us to defile ourselves through all matter of affections. Paul is calling both the Corinthians and us to come out and be separate.

It partially was because of this high standard, both internal and their conduct, that Paul had written them earlier. They needed for a season to cut off contact with the immoral man. Having done so, Paul now is able to praise them on multiple fronts while reflecting on the difference between being sorry and having "Godly sorrow." He develops his thoughts carefully, because he sees a key point: being sorry is not the response God is after. He wants a sorrow that leads to repentance, to a turning away from an attitude or behavior that you are sorry about.

Wikipedia gives a detailed description of the meaning of our English word "repentance:" *"In Biblical Hebrew, the idea of repentance is represented by two verbs: שוב shuv (to return) and נחם nacham (to feel sorrow). In the New Testament, the word translated as 'repentance' is the Greek word μετάνοια (metanoia), meaning "after/behind one's mind", which is a compound word of the preposition 'meta' (after, with), and the verb 'noeo' (to perceive, to think, the result of perceiving or observing). In this compound word, the preposition combines the two meanings of time and change, which may be denoted by 'after' and 'different'; so that the whole compound means: 'to think differently after.' Therefore, Metanoia is primarily ... a change of mind and change of conduct, change of mind and heart, or a change of consciousness."*

Basically, Biblical repentance is a radical change in direction and behavior.

This is what God is after when we find ourselves "off track," or "missing the mark." He is not interested in us feeling bad or sorry for our misbehaving; He wants us to have a sorrow that leads to a radical change. Paul could praise the Corinthians for actually doing what no doubt was very difficult, removing fellowship from the immoral man for a time so that 1) they would not be infected with similar sin and 2) might win their brother back.

Paul also takes the occasion to praise them for Titus's visit. It may well be that it took Titus's presence to push them over the line, i.e., to get them to finally take action, because we note that Paul describes the manner in which the Corinthian church received Titus' arrival: *"in fear and trembling."* Further, Titus must have given them direct instruction that could be "obeyed," because Titus had reported to Paul that they had done so.

Would that we and God's people today could have sorrow that leads to repentance and could take direction when we get off track. Lord, help us!

2nd Corinthians 8

After bringing up Titus in the preceding chapter, and after praising the Corinthians for how well they received him, Paul shifts gears at the beginning of Chapter 8 to talk about giving monetarily to the needs of the saints, and the saints he has in mind are those in Jerusalem.

We know from the second chapter of Paul's letter to the Galatians that Paul had promised Peter, James and John in Jerusalem that he would surely *"remember the poor"* of Jerusalem as he went forward with his ministry to the Gentiles. This took place during the Jerusalem Council that occurred around 49 AD – a responsibility the Jerusalem "pillars" had placed on Paul's ministry. Some scholars think Paul's 2nd Corinthians letter was written around 56 AD. If so, nearly seven years may have passed since the Jerusalem Council recorded in Acts 15.

To prime the pump, Paul begins with a strategic news report on the churches in Macedonia and their response to the Jerusalem Collection:

"Now, brethren, we wish to make known to you the grace of God which has been given in the churches of Macedonia, that in a great ordeal of affliction their abundance of joy and their deep poverty overflowed in the wealth of their liberality. For I testify that according to their ability, and beyond their ability, they gave of their own accord, begging us with much urging for the favor of participation in the support of the saints, and this, not as we had expected, but they first gave themselves to the Lord and to us by the will of God. So, we urged Titus that as he had previously made a beginning, so he would also complete in you this gracious work as well." (2nd Corinthians 8:1-6).

This is a soaring paragraph and in particular, the first two sentences. Though in the midst of economic stress and deep poverty, the Macedonian churches (think Philippi, Thessalonica and Berea), have, out of an abundance of JOY, overflowed in liberality. Paul's second sentence calls to mind Jesus's love for the widow when give all that she had at the temple. Plus, the Macedonians had *begged* Paul and his missionary team to allow them to participate. They were eager givers!

Like Paul, I am quite amazed as I think of the liberality of the Macedonian churches. Mostly likely, none of the saints there had never even been to Judea or Jerusalem, but they were giving money for folks that were, in a sense, across the globe, in spite of having dire needs in their own community. No wonder Paul wants to give the Corinthians the news report.

We also see that Paul's praise of how the Corinthians earlier had welcomed Titus slides smoothly into the appeal that Paul is about to make. The Corinthians were first to raise money for the poor in Jerusalem. Their beginning had stimulated the Macedonians, and now Paul urges them to complete their efforts by more giving. With wonderful construction, he uses the powerful example of Jesus's own personal giving: Himself.

"For you know the grace of our Lord Jesus Christ, that though He was rich, yet for your sake He became poor, so that you through His poverty might become rich." (2nd Corinthians 8:9).

Jesus's whole life was an exchange for our sake; so too, the Corinthians may enter into the same exchange for others emulating Jesus.

"If the readiness is present, it is acceptable according to what a person has, not according to what he does not have. For this is not for the ease of others and for your affliction, but by way of equality— at this present time your abundance being a supply for their need, so that their abundance also may become a supply for your need, that there may be equality; as it is written, 'He who gathered much did not have too much, and he who gathered little had no lack.'" (2nd Corinthians 8:12-15)

I am reminded of my first exposure to what went on behind the scenes when I was a young man at the church my family attended. The elders there had appointed a shrewd businessman to be in charge of giving. His rule was worthiness - "Was the individual worthy to receive help from the church?" I knew in my spirit that this rule was not the issue, but I had not spent much time thinking about how and when to be helpful to brothers and sisters. The rule of equality that Paul outlines in the foregoing was certainly not the rule in my church growing up.

Paul ties that rule of equality to the rule of what one has. If one has *"gathered much,"* one can help the one *"who has gathered little."* It's a pretty simple rule and turns on one's capacity. I would rather err on the side of generosity than on the side of miserliness. May God help us to do so. The Macedonians are great examples to all.

"As for Titus, he is my partner and fellow worker among you; as for our brethren, they are messengers of the churches, a glory to Christ. Therefore openly before the churches, show them the proof of your love and of our reason for boasting about you." (2nd Corinthians 8:23-24).

Paul ends the chapter by outlining the safeguarding that will accompany any donations the Corinthians make to the poor of Jerusalem. Titus himself is Paul's *"partner"* and fellow worker and the rest of Paul's team are *"messengers of the churches, a glory to the Anointed One!"*

Confession: I have to remember how deeply true this is when we send out or receive a *"messenger to the churches"* ourselves. Those involved in full time ministry, the Birgungis, Happs and Smiths of the world, are true treasures. Sometimes, we can see their coming with a lack of enthusiasm – another appeal, another taking, another need, but truly we need to see them as a Glory to the Anointed One who sits on the throne at the right hand of the Father. Help us see, Lord Jesus!

The care Paul took of the funds received is also an admonition to the great care we should take of church funds. Only people of absolute integrity should safeguard the funds. And policies should see that there is not the slightest taint of corruption.

2nd Corinthians 9

Paul continues his thoughts on giving in Chapter 9, initially contrasting the churches in Macedonia to the church in Corinth. Paul had been bragging on the Corinthian church because of their initial intention to send funds for relief of the poor in Judea. But, having received nothing, Paul had dispatched some of his team back to Corinth to collect what was missing. Otherwise, he himself would have to come with brothers from Macedonia, much to his shame as well as theirs.

We encounter several key principles for giving in any church. First, in verse 6, we have the principle of sowing and reaping. He who sows (gives) abundantly will reap abundantly and vice versa. I have been walking now in the Lord for over fifty years and have had many occasions to observe the truth to Paul's statement. You can almost tell for certain that trouble is ahead when brothers or sisters are tight-fisted with their money with regard to participating in the work of the community.

Several times, we were able to see the course of eventual bankruptcy avoided by reproving someone who had ceased giving; once they began to give in their lack, their prospects changed. Unheeded, the reverse was true. From a pastoral position, the one thing you hope for is liberality on the part of everyone, and particularly on the part of the family head.

The second principle is in verse 7. In spite of the dire consequences of not giving, everyone must be free to give as they chose, not out of compulsion or grudgingly. So, Paul does not order people to give; doing so would remove the opportunity to please the God of the Universe. Further, Paul uses the word *"purpose,"* meaning a decision made in the will and one's innermost being – the heart.

On a personal basis, my normal approach for giving to the community is to seek God about an annual amount for the year though someone else might seek for clarity on a different period. I am conscious of probable monies to be earned during the time period, but I look for a number that comes to mind. Then I divide by twelve and set up automatic withdrawals. These withdrawals can be changed if clearly I have gotten off course.

For specific and unanticipated needs of the community or people with whom we walk, I use the same method. I look for a number to come to mind; I pray about it, seek consensus with my wife, and purpose to give the agreed amount. It seems to have worked well for nearly 50 years. And, I try very hard not to ask the "worthy" question we discussed in Chapter 8!

In verse 8, Paul affirms his pastoral view: the best possible outcome for people will be generosity because the flood gates of heaven will be more than open to that person. Who can forget Jesus's admonition: *"Give and it shall be given unto you, oppressed down, overflowing. For as you have given, so shall it be given unto you."* (Luke 6:38).

Paul ends his thoughts with the reflection that giving is really a form of investing that will produce fruit. He uses an agricultural example that is very fit. God gives us seed for the sowing. What we have in our hands comes from Him; we cannot manufacture seed. It is a gift to us that we, in turn, may sow to others. We invest in them. Their lack becomes our opportunity. The fruit is to God's glory, and He will get thanksgiving from the recipients. And in the case of the Corinthians, they will prompt similar thanks from those helped in Judea!

2nd Corinthians 10

Rather than reading a chapter at a time, if one reads 2nd Corinthians all the way through in one setting, the break at Chapter 10 stands out sharply. It is almost as if Paul himself had picked up pen and begun to write as opposed to dictating. Scholars are divided on why there is such a sharp change. Some suggest that the last four chapters of the letter are actually an entirely different letter, perhaps one of the "lost" letters that has simply been added to the end of the scroll of the preceding 9 chapters. Others suggest that Paul shifts to address the continuing anti-Paul faction lingering in Corinth. Either way, the shift brings us squarely into engagement with the anti-Paul faction.

From the start, Paul sets his goal to be meek and gentle when he comes again to Corinth, comparing his desire to Jesus's own character: meek and gentle. His reflection that all of our interactions hopefully will be meek and gentle is a good one – the norm for anyone involved in ministry. Through encouragement, Paul tries hard to avoid what sometimes is necessary for apostolic delegates: judgment and punishment. The offence against valid Spiritual Authority in Corinth is both serious and dangerous. In only 20 to 70 years (the date is indeterminate), an Elder in the Church named Clement from Rome will write a letter of appeal, rebuking the Corinthian church over the same issue. Serious heresy or the setting aside of valid authority doesn't go away if it is allowed to blossom. Paul needed to confront the problem head on and did.

Paul has been accused by those in the anti-Paul faction of being bold in his letters but meek in person. What an interesting charge. Would that all of God's servants conducted themselves with humility and meekness. Paul's weapons and our weapons do not rest on the power of the flesh but on the power of the Spirit of God. They need no theatrics, no "Big Man" posturing. I think of the difference between shouting and flamboyance that we sometimes see in deliverance ministries versus the still, quiet voice of God when He spoke to Elijah. (1st Kings 19:11-13). True Spiritual power does not need theatrics to be effective.

In the Elijah encounter with the false priests that preceded God's still, quiet voice, we read the following description: *"Elijah mocked them and said, 'Call out with a loud voice, for he is a god; either he is occupied or gone aside, or is on a journey, or perhaps he is asleep and needs to be awakened.' So, they cried with a loud voice and cut themselves according to their custom with swords and lances until the blood gushed out on them. When midday was past, they raved until the time of the offering of the evening sacrifice; but there was no voice, no one answered, and no one paid attention."* (1st Kings 18:27-29).

Our power rests simply on the Power of God Himself. Paul presents himself gentle and meek – which he is, but he wields weapons of the Spirit. Like modern day weapons, their effectiveness has nothing to do with the person who carries the weapon.

"For though we walk in the flesh, we do not war according to the flesh, for the weapons of our warfare are not of the flesh, but divinely powerful for the destruction of fortresses. We are destroying speculations and every lofty thing raised up against the knowledge of God, and we are taking every thought captive to the obedience of Christ, and we are ready to punish all disobedience, whenever your obedience is complete." (1st Corinthians 10:3-6).

Spiritual weapons are deployed to destroy "fortresses." A "fortress" is any Enemy position inside of a group or a person. These footholds have defenses; they are not easily dislodged, and since they are spiritual in nature, it takes Spiritual weapons to destroy them. Thankfully, the Body of Christ has many ways to deploy the weapons God wants to be used. In addition to prayer and the written Word of God, many of the Gifts of the Spirit are for this very confrontation.

In the foregoing "weapons" description, Paul includes a key verse for all believers: *"we are taking every thought captive to the obedience of Christ."* In my experience, this is key. If I fail on this front, the Enemy wreaks havoc. Lord, have mercy.

Paul is clear that the boasting of folks within the anti-Paul faction is wrong and that the only thing worth boasting about is God (*"he who boasts is to boast in the Lord"*), but Paul takes the opportunity to make very clear his God given role. He has authority and position because Corinth is very much within the sphere of influence God has given Paul. We already have seen Paul's attentiveness concerning spheres and missions. We know that Paul was called to minister to the Gentiles in Macedonia and beyond, whereas Peter's primary call was to the Jews (see Galatians 2:7). Staying in the track God has placed you is important. Paul's defense is that his own activities partially rest on that certainty.

"But we will not boast beyond our measure, but within the measure of the sphere which God apportioned to us as a measure, to reach even as far as you. For we are not overextending ourselves, as if we did not reach to you, for we were the first to come even as far as you in the gospel of Christ; not boasting beyond our measure, that is, in other men's labors, but with the hope that as your faith grows, we will be, within our sphere, enlarged even more by you, so as to preach the gospel even to the regions beyond you, and not to boast in what has been accomplished in the sphere of another." (2nd Corinthians 10:13-16).

2nd Corinthians 11

Paul continues his defense against the anti-Paul faction in Corinth. We learn more about his opponents, and the picture is not good. The situation is so serious that Paul resorts to a long litany of his accomplishments to verify his credentials that trump the Judaizers. In one sense, his credentials are the same as Jesus's: affliction, beatings and rejection. You feel the irony in his voice and the disdain that he has to make any boast whatsoever.

Paul loves the Corinthians and sees himself like a father to them, one who has betrothed them spotless to Christ. Yet now, he finds that people have come in from outside to sully the reputation of the bride by leading them astray. It is not perfectly clear what all the errors are, but the most serious errors involve presenting a false Jesus.

Paul compares Satan at the Garden with Eve to the Judaizers with the Corinthians. Satan presented a falsehood to Eve and the Judaizers have done the same: no doubt stressing dependence on circumcision and the minute regulations followed by practicing Jews. Paul says this repudiates the true gift of Christ.

My sad observation is that there is hardly a church community that does not have people *"preaching another Jesus."* It need not be from the pulpit; often it is espoused by people in leadership positions or those wanting to be in leadership positions.

There is a terrible tendency to go one of two ways in terms of bringing a message of a false Jesus. One way denies the gospel message of total justification in Jesus and rejects the intimate walk in the Spirit where moment-by-moment revelation comes to the believer about who God really is (Exodus 34:6*ff*). The Apostle John's following revelation is ignored:

"As for you, the anointing which you received from Him abides in you, and you have no need for anyone to teach you; but as His anointing teaches you about all things, and is true and is not a lie, and just as it has taught you, you abide in Him." (1st John 2:27).

Instead, it is replaced by focus on minute rules and regulations.

The second danger is the reverse. By over emphasizing personal freedom of conscience, the clear guidelines for life given to the community through the Bible are ignored and set aside. Satan used this deceit with Eve. Sinful action appears justified when it is not.

These observations are easy to write, but hurtful when actually active in a Christian community. Those God has placed in the community as shepherds or ministers find themselves besieged, threatened, maligned and put in the same position Paul found himself: wanting to be gentle but forced to deal with a problem which takes him away from the main thrust of imparting the Good News.

I am sad when I think about the undeserved hurt that Paul is experiencing, and unfortunately, I can think of hurt of a similar kind in our small community over the last forty years. Even sadder is the fact that the people so often sowing discord and *"another Jesus,"* have not the slightest idea they are doing so.

Paul describes in vivid detail the actions of the false apostles and messengers and how the Corinthians have tolerated them: *"For you, being so wise, tolerate the foolish gladly. For you tolerate it if anyone enslaves you, anyone devours you, anyone takes advantage of you, anyone exalts himself, anyone hits you in the face."* (2nd Corinthians 11:19-20).

It is the self-righteous attitude behind the slap that is most hurtful. Both Jesus and Paul faced the same attitude - an attitude fully clothed in righteous indignation. Toward Jesus, it was literal: *"Then they spat in His face and struck Him. Others slapped Him.*" (Matthew 26:67). And toward Paul: "*The high priest Ananias commanded those standing beside him to strike him on the mouth.*" (Acts 23:2).

For this type of attitude to be manifest amongst believers is unbelievable, but sadly, the attitude was abroad in Corinth.

Paul's great warning to us is summed up in verses 13-15: "*For such men are false apostles, deceitful workers, disguising themselves as apostles of Christ. No wonder, for even Satan disguises himself as an angel of light. Therefore, it is not surprising if his servants also disguise themselves as servants of righteousness, whose end will be according to their deeds.*" (2nd Corinthians 11:13-15).

We have to be very careful, both not to be deceived ourselves and to be on watch for those filled with deceit within the community of believers.

2nd Corinthians 12

Paul continues to bring forth answers to the accusations of the Judaizers in Corinth that he is not a valid apostle. In the process, we uncover his *"third heaven"* experience.

I can remember laboring with this revelation in graduate school. Third heaven? What could it mean? I think now that the language used in a Jewish context simply meant "in the realm of God" – where God was demonstratively present. The ancient view of the universe was like an onion, i.e., in layers. A Jew may well have seen only three layers: the earth, the area between earth and heaven and heaven itself. Using this way of seeing, Paul recalls being *"caught up"* to heaven as testimony of his special foundation for the work God gave him.

When Paul said *"fourteen years ago,"* it is hard to determine whether he was referring to his Damascus Road experience (which, in itself, validated his apostolic ministry) or not. Let's do the math. Assume it is 56 AD when he writes the letter to the Corinthians (scholars guess 56 or 57 AD). Take away 14 years and you get around 42 AD. Take away 5 for when Paul was born (most think around 5 AD), and Paul would have had to be around 37 years of age in the year 42 AD when the experience occurred. Many scholars place his actual Damascus Road experience during the year 34 AD, so *"fourteen years ago"* would be after his Damascus Road experience.

But, it doesn't matter greatly what his age or experience. Surely, Paul is describing an absolutely breathtaking encounter with God in the heavens, one that may have occurred during his early days in Antioch. The language he uses suggests a direct encounter with the God of the Universe. Few of his opponents in Corinth, though constantly boasting of their religious experiences, could boast of that.

Paul brings forward another accusation leveled against him: that he was afflicted. He talks at some length about his *"thorn in the flesh."* Today, we have no certainty of what this was. We know he had poor eyesight from what he wrote in his letters, but whether his *"thorn"* was something else, we do not know.

This brings me to St. John Chrysostom's homily on Corinthians. In ancient times, some of the most famous churchmen gave exhaustive commentaries on scripture from the pulpit. In the latter part of the 4th century AD, John Chrysostom was one of the most important. He expounded on nearly every verse in the New Testament in his Sunday homilies. No doubt, this was of immense help to the assembled believers because few scrolls were available to believers for study. There were no Kindles or books as we know them, just scrolls. Hearing a careful exposition of each letter Paul had written was a privilege indeed. Here is part of what John Chrysostom wrote on this section:

"'For I shall speak the truth; but I forbear, lest any man should account of me above that which he sees, or that he hears from me.' Here you have the acknowledged reason: for they even deemed them to be gods, on account of the greatness of their miracles. As then in the case of the elements, God has done both things, creating them at once weak and glorious; the one, to proclaim His own power; the other, to prevent the error of mankind: so truly here also were they both wonderful and weak," (St. John Chrysostom: Homily 26, written around 400 AD)

Chrysostom is saying that knowing that men would be tempted to exalt His messenger as Gods (we saw this multiple times in Acts) that He gave them evident weaknesses. *"Here also were they both wonderful and weak."* That's Paul.

We have seen over multiple chapters that Paul viewed his difficulties as one of the strongest proofs of his apostleship. He presents the very thing that his accusers bring forth (his weakness) as his strongest defense.

Paul's address also gives us a good "rule of thumb" when we too are suffering from an ailment or difficulty. As Watchman Nee once emphasized, "three times is enough!" After we have sought God on three different occasions about healing or a change in circumstances, we can follow Paul's example and simply assume God is using the difficulty for His glory and that it is ours to keep. More remarkable here is the reality that his *"thorn"* was from Satan. Would that we could really grasp the truth behind God's claim: *"My grace is sufficient for you, for power is perfected in weakness."* This is rarely something a young Christian will grasp, but hopefully by old age, we will be absolutely certain of His truth and intention.

Paul can say with absolute assurance *"I am well content with weaknesses, with insults, with distresses, with persecutions, with difficulties, for Christ's sake; for when I am weak, then I am strong."* (2nd Corinthians 12:10).

Today, we do not have to look far for people claiming they are modern day apostles in the Biblical meaning of the word. Paul is kind, therefore, to give a tight test of what an apostle, in addition to sufferings, should be able to manifest *"The signs of a true apostle* [that] *were performed among you with all perseverance, by signs and wonders and miracles."* Like the test for a Prophet (whether the prophecy comes true), it is good to have a test that can be verified.

Lastly, Paul declares his intention to come to Corinth yet a third time. This partially justifies a lot that he had written, for it was, *"all for your upbuilding, beloved. For I am afraid that perhaps when I come I may find you to be not what I wish and may be found by you to be not what you wish; that perhaps there will be strife, jealousy, angry tempers, disputes, slanders, gossip, arrogance, disturbances; I am afraid that when I come again my God may humiliate me before you, and I may mourn over many of those who have sinned in the past and not repented of the impurity, immorality and sensuality which they have practiced."* (2nd Corinthians 12:19-21).

This long list of attitudes and behaviors stands, like his list in 1st Corinthians on love, as a good "multiple choice" test. Let me list them:

Strife

Jealousy

Angry Tempers

Disputing

Slandering

Gossip

Arrogance

Disturbing

Impurity

Immorality

Sensuality

I wish I could say that I am free of every one of these, but I am not. May God help us as well!

It calls to mind, however, the extreme difficulty the Corinthians faced by living in a city dedicated to the Greek goodness, Aphrodite. Reading from an original source gives color to the context of how dangerous the city was (and what a magnet it was) for immorality amongst all the seacoast towns. This was written about the time of Paul by Strabo, a Greek geographer:

"And the temple of Aphrodité was so rich that it owned more than a thousand temple slaves, courtesans, whom both men and women had dedicated to the goddess. And therefore it was also on account of these women that the city was crowded with people and grew rich; for instance, the ship captains freely squandered their money, and hence the proverb, 'Not for every man is the voyage to Corinth.'" (Geography, Book VIII, Chapter 6, 392, Loeb Classical Library, 1927).

With the Internet and all sorts of perversions loose in the United States, I feel sure Paul would consider us a modern day, virtual Corinth!

2nd Corinthians 13

Paul is summing up his letter (or letters depending on your view of the last four chapters of 2nd Corinthians) in Chapter 13. His language does have the feel of being addressed to a hopefully small but definitive group within the Corinthian church. Compare 1st Corinthians

15:15-24 with Chapter 13 of 2nd Corinthians and you will see a marked difference. Only the last four verses of Chapter 13 are upbeat. It is not the warm closing Paul made to the Corinthians in his first letter. Aside from those last four verses, it is a tough chapter, in raised, almost strident tone. Paul's near desperation to win over the dissenters is clearly evident throughout most of the chapter.

We get a window into a very different type of trans-local relationship with a church community than one we have enjoyed with our trans-local brother, Terry Smith. Though we have had grave moral issues occasionally present within our community, Terry has consistently presented the gentle face of Christ, reproving much more than rebuking (that is, bringing light rather than harsh command). In Chapter 13, Paul ends his appeal with the prospect of serious judgment when he stands before them as Jesus's representative. It is a sober scene that he paints in verse 2:

"I say in advance to those who have sinned in the past and to all the rest as well, that if I come again I will not spare anyone...."

Whew, a tough prospect. Of course, what is at work here springs from Paul's love of the Corinthian church community, and his willingness to do whatever it takes to remove the leaven of unrighteousness. He is entirely too weak to do this in his flesh, but he is certain that God and God's power can have a radical and positive effect.

Built Up and Complete

Yet, he would much rather not have to deal with moral laxity when he is present, and therefore gives an antidote so to speak: personal examination, prayer and an unspoken result of personal examination: repentance. Paul is looking for a turn of direction for those he writes, that they may be *"complete."* This phrase occurs twice in Chapter 13 in verses 9 and 11 along with a phrase we meet in Peter's letters, *"building up,"* in verse 10. All the associated ideas we find elsewhere in the New Testament writings give color to Paul's desire for the Corinthians. He wants them complete, lacking in nothing, and he sees his personal role as one who helps builds them up.

I am reminded in particular of Paul's letter to the Ephesians where he explains the reason that certain men and ministries are given to the church - including of first rank the apostles: *"And He gave some as apostles, and some as prophets, and some as evangelists, and some as pastors and teachers, for the equipping of the saints for the work of service, to the building up of the body of Christ; until we all attain to the unity of the faith, and of the knowledge of the Son of God, to a mature man, to the measure of the stature which belongs to the fullness of Christ."* (Ephesians 4:11-13).

And also, *"So the church throughout all Judea and Galilee and Samaria enjoyed peace, being **built up**; and going on in the fear of the Lord and in the comfort of the Holy Spirit, it continued to increase."* (Acts 9:31).

This desire that people be **"complete"** was on Jesus's heart, and the completeness only comes with a radical following of the Lord:

*"Jesus said to him, "If you wish to be **complete**, go and sell your possessions and give to the poor, and you will have treasure in heaven; and come, follow Me."* (Matt 19:21).

So, Paul is not playing church; he is right on target as a Master Builder, working hard that the Corinthians be built up and made complete, lacking absolutely nothing. We see Paul and others express similar ideas in other places:

"Now I exhort you, brethren, by the name of our Lord Jesus Christ, that you all agree and that there be no divisions among you, but that you

*be made **complete** in the same mind and in the same judgment."* (1st Corinthians 1:10).

*"Now may the God of peace Himself sanctify you entirely; and may your spirit and soul and body be preserved **complete**, without blame at the coming of our Lord Jesus Christ."* (1st Thessalonians 5:23).

*"And let endurance have its perfect result, so that you may be perfect and **complete**, lacking in nothing."* (James 1:4).

*"You also, as living stones, are being **built up** as a spiritual house for a holy priesthood, to offer up spiritual sacrifices acceptable to God through Jesus Christ."* (1st Peter 2:5).

I find this personally inspiring as I consider my numerous shortcomings before my God. I want to be complete, lacking nothing, built up *"to a mature man, to the measure of the stature which belongs to the fullness of Christ."* (Ephesians 4:13). Brothers and sisters are given to help us grow into maturity. Don't push away those whom God has given to help you.

Paul ends his letter with hope for those he writes and for us as well:

"Finally, brethren, rejoice, be made complete, be comforted, be like-minded, live in peace; and the God of love and peace will be with you. Greet one another with a holy kiss. All the saints greet you. The grace of the Lord Jesus Christ, and the love of God, and the fellowship of the Holy Spirit, be with you all." (2 Corinthians 13:11-14).

Let's spotlight Paul's five directives in his closing words to this church on the Ionian Sea:

- **rejoice**
- **be made complete**
- **be comforted**
- **be like-minded**

- **live in peace**

As we allow these five directives to be expressed in our lives, we have the sure knowledge that the God of love and peace will be with us.

I cannot help but make two observations about verse 12, *"Greet one another with a Holy Kiss."* First, we have seen this before at the end of Romans and 1st Corinthians, and we will see it again at the end of his letter to the Thessalonians and Peter's first letter. This sign of brotherly love, unity and affection (read generally "on the cheek") has lasted for two thousand years in certain Christian cultures. In the United States it is almost entirely lost. Our local practice has been with a hug rather than a kiss. Either *IS* an important sign.

My second observation is that we find it placed at the end of these letters most likely because immediately after the letter was read to the assembled church, the Lord's Supper would be taken. In the early days of the Church, prior to taking communion, the congregants would give to each other a sign of *"peace"* and affection. We see this to this day in several old stream liturgies.

Augustine of Hippo, one of the Church's most scholarly churchmen, reflects on its spot during communion in one of his Passover messages around 400 AD:

"Then, after the consecration of the Holy Sacrifice of God, because He wished us also to be His sacrifice, a fact which was made clear when the Holy Sacrifice was first instituted, and because that Sacrifice is a sign of what we are, behold, when the Sacrifice is finished, we say the Lord's Prayer which you have received and recited. After this, the 'Peace be with you' is said, and Christians embrace one another with the holy kiss. This is a sign of peace; as the lips indicate, let peace be made in your conscience, that is, when your lips draw near to those of your brother, do not

let your heart withdraw from his. Hence, these are great and powerful sacraments." (Augustine's Sermon 227).

There is actually a lot in Augustine's reflection to think about, but my main point is that in the earliest of days, letters from people like Paul, Peter and James were read immediately prior to the Supper on Sundays. When Augustine speaks about the *"Holy Sacrifice,"* he is referencing the "words of institution" or "words of consecration" that are said during Communion: *"May these elements become for us the very body and blood of our savior, Jesus Christ,"* or words to that effect. That moment and God's corresponding action occurs before we individually take the loaf and the drink. In the practice at Hippo, after the words had been spoken, the entire congregation said together the Lord's Prayer and then *"Peace be unto you,"* and then embraced each other with a Holy Kiss. What a great sign of God's affection for His people!

Galatians

Galatians 1

Called by some "the Charter of Christian Liberty," Paul's letter to the churches in Galatia had a tremendous impact on the history of the church. Martin Luther said, *"The epistle to the Galatians is my epistle. To it I am as it were in wedlock,"* and Paul's emphasis on the importance and power of God's grace (as opposed to our works) will be quickly manifest as we go through the document.

In another sense, it is not a new subject. As we moved through Paul's missionary journeys in Acts, we found that time after time "Judaizers" came behind him to challenge his orthodoxy as a Jew. Later, Jewish believers came to refute Paul's practice of not requiring Gentiles to be circumcised or observe many aspects of the Torah regulations.

One could observe that the closer one gets to Jerusalem, the more strident the Jewish voice. Galatia, a Roman Province, is relatively close (much closer, for instance, than Ephesus, Philippi, Thessalonica, Corinth and Rome), and the problem seems more acute. Remember that Galatia is smack in the middle of modern day Turkey and the final destination of Paul's first missionary journey.

There has been a great deal of disagreement about to what area of Galatia Paul was actually writing. There are theories that it was to the northern region and theories that it was to the southern region where we find familiar town names from Paul's first missionary journey with Barnabas – Derbe, Iconium, Lystra, Antioch in Pisidia. I certainly don't know the answer, but suffice it to say, Jewish converts were demanding that Gentile converts keep most aspects of the Law, including circumcision.

There is also disagreement about when Paul wrote the letter. Some think it was written about the time he wrote Romans; others feel it was much earlier, just before or just after the Jerusalem Council in Acts 15. Regardless, Paul is deeply concerned about the attack on the revolutionary nature of God's intervention with mankind through the gift of

Himself in Jesus – His death, burial and resurrection, and the sweeping change this introduced to how followers of God related to God.

"Grace to you and peace from God our Father and the Lord Jesus Christ, who gave Himself for our sins so that He might rescue us from this present evil age, according to the will of our God and Father, to whom be the glory forevermore. Amen." (Galatians 1:3-5).

"Grace to you and peace" is Paul's normal way of addressing nearly everyone he writes, and because his letter will address grace with great emphasis, certainly appropriate. But his introductory greeting also is another kernel statement of the "Gospel," and that, too, will be the subject as well. They are part and parcel of the same cloth. Let's see if we can say that sentence in different words to emphasize what Paul is declaring to be the Good News:

"You are receiving grace (undeserved favor) *and peace from the God of the Universe who has become your very own Father as well as receiving undeserved favor and peace from the Lord* (the Sovereign, the One who has Authority) *Jesus, the One anointed with the Spirit of God and the One promised from of old because this Jesus gave Himself as substitution for ours sins in order that we might be rescued from this evil age in full accordance with the will of God. We are now God's children."*

That's it. The burial, the resurrection, the appearance to many after the resurrection, Jesus's exaltation to the right hand of the Father, and His coming again to judge the quick and the dead are not specifically mentioned, but implied.

Someone is preaching a different gospel to the Galatians, though Paul points out that a different "gospel" should not even have the Gospel descriptor since it is not "good news." Paul does something that is almost non-existent in his other writings, he utters a curse on anyone who would do such a thing, and to make it doubly clear, does it twice.

Double exclamation points. *"Let him be accursed!!"* Missing are Paul's extended greetings; he is right to the point.

Paul's justification is that the Gospel he preached when he was in the region was of divine origin. Paul hadn't received it from men or been taught by men, rather, he received it straight from God through a revelation of the resurrected Jesus. Paul's revelation trumps any contender's. The reference to his early encounter with Jesus causes Paul to retrace a good deal of his personal history. This makes sense because Paul was a Jew himself and particularly qualified to address the issue of the Law and the Gospel.

Paul picks carefully what he highlights in his personal history. Each fact is important to the subject at hand, but at the same time, we learn biographical pieces of information we didn't learn in the book of Acts. Paul was a Christian for three years before he returned to Jerusalem after leaving Syria and Damascus. It was only then that he met Peter *(Cephas),* staying with him for two weeks. The only other apostle he met at that time was James, Jesus's *"brother,"* who we learn from Acts at some point led the Jerusalem church. From Jerusalem, Paul went back to Syria (the Damascus area) and then home to Cilicia (the Tarsus area) where we know from Acts he stayed until Barnabas went to fetch him.

We can deduce that Paul's short two-week visit in Jerusalem was three years or so from the date that he was sent originally to Damascus to round up Christians for the Jewish leaders in Jerusalem. He held the cloaks while Stephen was stoned; he was remembered as a hater and a threat by the early Christian community, so news of his conversion and his stay with Peter brought great rejoicing to the believers in Jerusalem.

Paul will continue his autobiographical sketch in Chapter 2!

Galatians 2

Fourteen years have passed since Paul's first visit to Jerusalem after the Damascus Road experience. In the interim, we recall from Acts that Barnabas had fetched him from Tarsus to help the growing church that was established in Antioch. At the time. Antioch was a thriving Greek-Roman city that had been established on multiple trade routes by a general of Alexander the Great. About 300 miles north of Jerusalem, it would have taken over two weeks to walk the distance between Antioch and Jerusalem - plus one would have to ascend of over 2,500 feet. Paul opens the chapter with the simple words, *"I went up again to Jerusalem,"* but the journey would have been arduous.

In the opening sentences of Galatians 2, I believe we are reading about the famous Jerusalem Council of Acts 15 where the issue of Gentile believers initially was trashed out. If this is the case, instead of Luke's view that was only third hand, we get Paul's point of view as a key participant. We learn not only that he came up to Jerusalem with Barnabas, but that he brought Titus as well. Titus's presence was important since he was an uncircumcised Gentile believer. You can imagine the tension that caused amongst the Jewish believers who had been part of the Pharisee sect.

Let's read Luke's account afresh from Acts 15. His narrative begins in Antioch and moves to Jerusalem:

"Some men came down from Judea and began teaching the brethren, 'Unless you are circumcised according to the custom of Moses, you cannot be saved.' And when Paul and Barnabas had great dissension and debate with them, the brethren determined that Paul and Barnabas and some others of them should go up to Jerusalem to the apostles and elders concerning this issue. Therefore, being sent on their way by the church, they were passing through both Phoenicia and Samaria, describing in

detail the conversion of the Gentiles, and were bringing great joy to all the brethren. When they arrived at Jerusalem, they were received by the church and the apostles and the elders, and they reported all that God had done with them. But some of the sect of the Pharisees who had believed stood up, saying, 'It is necessary to circumcise them and to direct them to observe the Law of Moses.'

"The apostles and the elders came together to look into this matter. After there had been much debate, Peter stood up and said to them, 'Brethren, you know that in the early days God made a choice among you, that by my mouth the Gentiles would hear the word of the gospel and believe. And God, who knows the heart, testified to them giving them the Holy Spirit, just as He also did to us; and He made no distinction between us and them, cleansing their hearts by faith. Now therefore why do you put God to the test by placing upon the neck of the disciples a yoke which neither our fathers nor we have been able to bear? But we believe that we are saved through the grace of the Lord Jesus, in the same way as they also are.'" (Acts 15:1-11).

After Paul and Barnabas shared how God had manifested Himself in power and signs in Antioch, James arose with this judgment:

"'It is my judgment that we do not trouble those who are turning to God from among the Gentiles, but that we write to them that they abstain from things contaminated by idols and from fornication and from what is strangled and from blood. For Moses from ancient generations has in every city those who preach him, since he is read in the synagogues every Sabbath.'

"Then it seemed good to the apostles and the elders, with the whole church, to choose men from among them to send to Antioch with Paul and Barnabas—Judas called Barsabbas, and Silas, leading men among the brethren, and they sent this letter by them," (Acts 15: 19-23).

Paul's account in his Galatians letter of what happened in Jerusalem leaves out much of Luke's detail. Instead, Paul focuses on key points that relate to why he is writing the Galatians in the first place.

First, he went up to Jerusalem *"by revelation."* He can mean two things by that term. Remember when Paul and Barnabas were *"set apart"* by the Holy Spirit to go on their first missionary journey in Acts 13? He could mean that the Spirit had prophetically told them to go up to Jerusalem to share their understanding of Grace. But he also could mean that it was by revelation that Paul knew that the Gentiles would be free of the Law as interpreted by the Pharisees in much the same way that Peter came to learn through his housetop experience that Gentiles were "clean." Either way, no "man" sent him up to Jerusalem; he came by the Spirit. This gave initial weight to his message to the Galatians: what he had shared with them was by divine revelation.

Second, In Jerusalem, he had presented his understanding of the meaning of Christ's death, burial and resurrection to the leaders. Paul saw very clearly that the effect of the New Covenant created a whole new Kingdom based entirely on the saving work of God in Jesus and not on human performance. For Paul, this was part of the essential core of the Gospel. Paul presented his understanding to the Jerusalem leaders, and they *"contributed nothing to me,"* meaning that nothing was added to Paul's understanding of the Gospel message. If we look back at Acts 15, we see that there were four things that were laid on Gentile believers by the Jerusalem leadership, but clearly Paul did not feel this required a change in his personal understanding of the immensity of Christ's gift. In his Galatians letter, Paul reveals that the leaders had required that Paul not fail to remember the poor in Jerusalem, a charge that we know from his other letters that he took very seriously.

Third, Titus, an uncircumcised Gentile with Paul, did not have to be circumcised.

Fourth, he makes clear to the Galatians that his personal standing as an apostle is revealed by the fact that he personally took Peter, one of the key pillars of the church, to task concerning Peter's behavior in Antioch.

Finally, he ends Chapter 2 with theological support for his position against required circumcision. I feel certain that the first part of verse 16 is one of the thoughts that moved Martin Luther:

"a man is not justified by the works of the Law but through faith in Christ." (Galatians 2:16).

This verse is about as succinct a statement of fact as one could give. Paul is not giving his opinion; he is stating fact – speaking the truth.

The verse continues: *"we have believed in Christ Jesus, so that we may be justified by faith in Christ and not by the works of the Law; since by the works of the Law no flesh will be justified."* (Galatians 2:16).

Ceasing to depend on our actions, we are able to entirely depend on God. Paul ends the chapter with one of the most famous declarations in the Bible:

"I have been crucified with Christ; and it is no longer I who live, but Christ lives in me; and the life which I now live in the flesh I live by faith in the Son of God, who loved me and gave Himself up for me. I do not nullify the grace of God, for if righteousness comes through the Law, then Christ died needlessly." (Galatians 2:20-21).

The lurking question in my mind is "Am I really crucified? Have I fully allowed myself to be nailed to the cross?" Is my early action at Baptism - my death to sin, fully evident in my walk?" The life that I have, I surely have only in Jesus. But I long personally to be more conformed to His death that His life might be better revealed in me. Again, I can only cry, "Come Lord Jesus!"

Galatians 3

If I have died with Christ, why am I so troubled by my old self? Sometimes I feel like the not quite dead man being thrown on the "Dead Cart" in Monty Python: "Hold on, I'm not dead yet!" While paddle boarding out at sea one morning, I felt God speak clearly to me: *"You may not be fully dead, but Jesus absolutely and completely died. Dead. Entirely."* Perhaps Father was trying to tell me that the real issue was whether Jesus died or not. My faith is in that event, and my last fifty years rest there. His presence with me rests there and in His resurrection.

It is good to remember that we are not just archeologists rummaging through the annals of text and time. We are on the road of a true journey to the heavenlies, representatives of the King.

We certainly don't want to be bewitched! What an accusation against the Galatians Paul makes in his opening verse in Chapter 3, *"You foolish Galatians, who has bewitched you?"* Paul is down on the mat, struggling with every fiber in his body to move the Galatians back to the essential kernel of truth: they are saved by grace and not perfection in their every action. It is right to do the right thing, but doing the right thing will never save you. The only thing that is powerful enough to save you is Jesus's sacrificial death, and that has already occurred.

It is a simple argument. The Galatians obviously experienced an identifiable internal change when they first believed. Paul's language is clear:

"Did you receive the Spirit by the works of the Law, or by hearing with faith?" (Galatians 3:2). It is very hard for Paul to ask this key question without full assurance that the Galatians would understand exactly what he was referring to. The "receipt of the Spirit" has to be something that they could clearly remember.

If I give you a present and you open it, you know you have received it. You know what it is and how it affected and affects you. If I give you an air purifier entirely free for your asthma and you use it at home, you will be able to answer the question "Did you get the air purifier by paying for it or not?" Of course, the answer will be "no." Paul is clinching his argument on this simple question about the receipt of the Spirit, but it implies that the Galatians would have experienced something quite unique that would satisfy the proof. When the Spirit of God is poured out on flesh and received, there should be a quantum change, an identifiable change in the person.

I think it is clear from both Luke's record in Acts and Paul's use of language here in Galatians that he speaks to an experience of the Spirit that has to be in some way directly associated with the Gifts of the Spirit and most likely the experience of Tongues. If it is not the experience of Tongues, what could it be? Prophecy would qualify, ecstatic praise would qualify, deliverance from addiction would qualify, but in the examples from Acts, Tongues would have been the normal experiential sign. So, we have to ask the question, how, if asked by Paul, would I even interpret his question?

Paul brings forth Abraham's faith as final proof that it was from belief and not behavioral purity that they were imputed righteous before God and thus were able to receive the Spirit. Paul quotes a key verse from the Torah out of Genesis. He will quote it again a few years later when he writes the Roman church.

"Abraham believed God, and it was reckoned to him as righteousness." (Genesis 15:6).

Abraham's "belief" occurred immediately after God had taken him outside and said, *"'Now look toward the heavens, and count the stars, if you are able to count them.' And He said to him, 'So shall your descendants be.'"* Abraham simply believed, and God deemed him fit.

Paul tells us that is what we stand on, our faith. Then Paul quotes a back-up proof from the Prophet Habakkuk:

"The righteous man shall live by faith." (Habakkuk 2:4).

Paul continues to bring forward Old Testament scriptures as proof for his argument, both from the Torah (the first five books of the Bible) as well as the Prophets. His grasp and recall of the texts is nothing short of amazing.

Then we hit verses 13 and 14. Here we have another kernel of the Gospel in new language:

"Christ redeemed us from the curse of the Law, having become a curse for us—for it is written, "Cursed is everyone who hangs on a tree"— in order that in Christ Jesus the blessing of Abraham might come to the Gentiles, so that we would receive the promise of the Spirit through faith." (Galatians 3:13-14).

Let's unpack this together because it is a proof text for part of God's intent in sending Jesus in the first place. The Anointed One ("Christ") has redeemed us, bought us from the realm of the Law (the realm is basically a curse in the sense that we can never meet perfection in our behavior) by becoming *"a curse FOR US."* Paul quotes yet another Old Testament scripture *"Cursed is everyone who hangs on a tree"* as proof from Deuteronomy 21:23. *"IN ORDER THAT"* comes next, meaning that the perfect Lamb of God, Jesus the One Anointed with the Spirit, has been crucified on a cross *IN ORDER THAT* in this anointed Jesus, the blessing God first promised Abraham in Genesis 15 would come to *US*, so that by simply believing God in His action, we might **RECEIVE THE PROMISE OF THE SPIRIT!**

Paul is saying, "That's what this is all about." I hope you can forgive all of my capitalizations. I generally can't take reading a bunch of capitalized phrases, but I don't know a better way to emphasize what I think Paul is trying to pound into the Galatians and into us. Verses 13 and 14 are capsules of the core of our faith, but again they push us to **the heart of the New Covenant, the internal gift of the Spirit of God**. Please don't miss the emphasis.

At verse 15, Paul does a deep dive into the Abrahamic Covenant, the covenant that God made with Abraham and his seed after him, a covenant into which we have been added. That covenant was initially "cut" (remember the word covenant in Hebrew means "cutting" in reference to the shedding of blood) 430 years *before* Sinai and the written rules of the wilderness.

Like a good lawyer, Paul makes technical points that show that the original Covenant was not invalidated by later action on God's part. In fact, regarding covenants, we can see an unfolding over time of God's greater and greater willingness to bind Himself to mankind. In one sense, God increases the promised blessings as each codicil to the Will are added. With that view, we very much are still dealing with the Abrahamic Covenant in our time, as amended and expanded by God's unilateral binding of His will, firmly executed in the blood of Jesus.

So, *"now that faith has come, we are no longer under a tutor. For you are all sons of God through faith in Christ Jesus. For all of you who were baptized into Christ have clothed yourselves with Christ. There is neither Jew nor Greek, there is neither slave nor free man, there is neither male nor female; for you are all one in Christ Jesus. And if you belong to Christ, then you are Abraham's descendants, heirs according to promise."* (Galatians 3:25-29).

We will see Paul return to this theme gloriously in his letter to Ephesus. The writer of the letter to the Hebrews will do the same.

Galatians 4

The last verse of Chapter 3 ended with *"if you belong to Christ, then you are Abraham's descendants, heirs according to promise."* Paul builds on that thought in the first part of Chapter 4. If you think about it, Jesus's entire appearance can be seen as a direct response to God's initial covenant with Abraham. An example would be Genesis 18:18: *"all nations on earth will be blessed through him."* This revelation of what God would do through the seed of Abraham surely points directly to Jesus's appearance, life, death, resurrection and exaltation. How could the nations be any more blessed than by Jesus's appearing? Jesus's coming has made those who had given themselves over to Jesus *"heirs"* of Abraham, heirs according to the promise made to Abraham, heirs OF the promise.

"But when the fullness of the time came, God sent forth His Son, born of a woman, born under the Law, so that He might redeem those who were under the Law, that we might receive the adoption as sons. Because you are sons, God has sent forth the Spirit of His Son into our hearts, crying, 'Abba! Father!'" (Galatians 4:4-6).

This is another Gospel kernel, a restatement of the amazing Good News to mankind. Jesus was sent forth from God, a child of Abraham and in full accordance with the Law of Moses and yet a Son of God, that we might receive adoption as sons. This is a BIG thought. In Jesus, if you belong to Christ, the Anointed One of God, you are deemed as adopted sons of both Abraham and God. For a Gentile, that is amazing news indeed. For the Jew, it means a new stage in salvation history has been reached where they will no longer be under the tutelage of the

Law, but under the tutelage of the Spirit. And because you are sons, you are heirs, and if heirs, you receive *"the Spirit of His Son"* into your heart. You receive the Promise. Sons as heirs receive the Covenantal promise, and the promise for believers is receipt of the Spirit of Jesus – proof of sonship, proof of Jesus's effective work, proof of God's love for us as well as the Galatians.

And what is one of the experiential proofs that we are heirs and in receipt of the Promised Holy Spirit? Our hearts cry, "Abba! Father." This language is most important. *"Abba"* is straight Hebrew for *"Daddy"* and *"Papa"* in English. Paul could not convey the tenderness of the Hebrew in Greek and so he used the Hebrew, translated "Father" in Greek. When we receive the Spirit, our hearts cry out, *"Abba! Papa!"* In review of the last chapter, we talked about Tongues and other Spiritual Gifts as proof of the receipt of the Spirit. Here, Paul talks about an even more intimate and precious proof. Our hearts cry out *"Papa."*

Paul is immersed in Genesis 15-21 as he writes, because he is drawing from Abraham's experience with the promise of a son, the situation with Ishmael and Hagar, and the coming of Isaac. The heir is free in a household like Abraham's; a slave is not. Since the Galatians are heirs according to promise, why should they act like slaves again? Why be under the bondage of the Law when you are free? Paul has heard that some of the Galatians are observing "times and seasons," and he is no doubt referring to the Jewish religious calendar which is not just about holidays, but about religious actions on special days of remembrance like Yom Kippur when sacrifices must be made to be deemed righteous. Since the Galatians are now heirs, they are free and should not walk as slaves.

In the middle of the chapter, Paul inserts a very touching section about his love for the Galatians and how deeply moved he was by their love when he was amongst them. We learn that Paul was with them for a season because of a physical ailment that must have been serious. They had received him with great honor, *"as an angel, as Jesus Christ himself!"* Their drift away from what he had preached was made all the more grievous because of his memory of their affection.

Then Paul moves back to analogy of slave versus free. If they are going back to the Law, they should pay attention to the Genesis account of Abraham, Sarah and Hagar. In Genesis 21:10, Sarah directs Abraham, *"Wherefore she said unto Abraham, Cast out this bondwoman* [Hagar] *and her son* [Ishmael], *for the son of this bondwoman shall not be heir with my son, even with Isaac."*

Paul quotes a portion of this verse to the Galatians to make the point that there are two covenants represented in the story of Hagar and Sarah. Hagar, the slave, represents Mt. Sinai on which the Mosaic covenant was "cut." Sarah, the free, represents Jerusalem where the New Covenant was "cut" in Jesus's blood. The Galatians are under the new and not the old, the free and not the slave. Like Isaac, the Galatians are children of the promise as are we!

Galatians 5

Paul continues his reflections on the freedom of the Abrahamic seed versus the slave begun in Chapter 5. Why did Jesus die on a cross? To set us free. Paul's understanding hinges on God's intent: to redeem us from slavery, to adopt us, to set us free. Jesus did for us what we could not do ourselves. We stand on what He has done.

It is easy to forget this point in community. Without intending that we set up barriers or walls about behavior, we do. Often, it is about identity. We see a man or a woman who is not conforming in some way to our cultural or doctrinal standard and think them less a Christian than we are. But the reverse is also true; we feel we must fit within the cultural standard in which we find ourselves or meet the identity standard set for us unconsciously from childhood. If we don't, we feel less than acceptable in some important way.

I am still subject in various ways to unconscious, impossible to meet, goals of behavior or status. But Paul's red-hot focus rings out: I am free! I *will* be free from a practical point of view if I can rest simply on these facts that Paul hammers home. Free! Resting on eternal realities. When we come to Hebrews, the writer (no doubt a close follower of Paul's if not Paul himself) will hammer this point home even more.

Paul then virtually shouts, *"Mark my words! I, Paul, tell you that if you let yourselves be circumcised, Christ will be of no value to you at all!"* (Galatians 5:2). He is obviously talking to the Gentile male believers in Galatia. The Jewish men are already circumcised, though his admonition would affect a newborn Jewish male child.

At first glance, this rings a bit too loud for me, and I confess I don't fully understand his rigid position. Surely, Paul is addressing intent. If a Galatian believer's thought is that he will not be acceptable to God unless circumcised, I follow Paul's thought well enough and I both understand and affirm it. But, if one is circumcised for health reasons, the case is different. Like the prohibition against eating the flesh of pigs as well as many other proscriptions in Mosaic law, God appears to have been focused on health-related issues. There is a body of thought that circumcision was not only a perfect Covenantal sign (a "cutting" of the flesh of the household head to signify having entered into a lasting covenant), but also a practice that reduced disease and its transmission.

Thankfully, Paul seems to be on the "intent" trail from verse four onward: *"You who are trying to be justified by the law have been alienated from Christ; you have fallen away from grace."*

Paul seems to be using the Spirit as the new sign of the Covenant in verse 5: "*For through the Spirit we eagerly await by faith the righteousness for which we hope.*" But he may simply mean that through the assurance that the Spirit brings to our own spirit, we stand in faith believing righteousness is imputed to us by Jesus's death, burial and resurrection. Regardless, the next verse is clear as a bell and truly helpful:

"*For in Christ Jesus neither circumcision nor uncircumcision has any value. The only thing that counts is faith expressing itself through love.*" (Galatians 5:6).

Paul is saying a lot more than the few words he has written in the foregoing sentence. Our faith in God and God's love – our faith in Jesus's saving action, our faith that the New Covenant has been cut, our faith that Jesus now sits at the right hand of the Father and has poured forth His Spirit of love into our hearts naturally reveals itself by expressions of love to others. Another "proof."

"*and hope does not disappoint, because the love of God has been poured out within our hearts through the Holy Spirit who was given to us.*" (Romans 5:5)

Paul is basically saying, "Now, that is important!" Circumcision is not.

Part of Paul's great concern is that he knows "*A little yeast works through the whole batch of dough.*" He makes the same point in 1ˢᵗ Corinthians 5:6 and fully understood Jesus's parable where Matthew 16:12 states, "*Then they understood that He [Jesus] was not telling them to guard against the yeast used in bread, but against the teaching of the Pharisees and Sadducees.*" Paul knows that if they accommodate the practice of circumcision, other corruption will follow. More Jewish Old Law practices will creep into the New Covenant community in Galatia.

Mid-chapter, Paul returns to the glorious news that we are called to be *FREE.* Having said that now a good number of times, he then counters a danger that lurks from misinterpreting the Christian idea of freedom. Our freedom is *not* for indulging our flesh, rather it is to be free to help and serve others humbly in love. No one is excluded from the kindness of God, and no one should be excluded from our kindness regardless of his or her present state (male, female, Greek, Roman, Jew, pagan, etc.). Paul repeats half of Jesus's answer to the rich young ruler, *"the entire Law is fulfilled in one command: Love your neighbor as yourself."* (Galatians 5:14).

Paul ends the chapter with a terribly important section:

"But I say, walk by the Spirit, and you will not carry out the desire of the flesh. For the flesh sets its desire against the Spirit, and the Spirit against the flesh; for these are in opposition to one another, so that you may not do the things that you please. But if you are led by the Spirit, you are not under the Law...." (Galatians 5:16-18).

Acts of the Flesh

The Spirit of God has *NOTHING* to do with the flesh. Obviously, God's Spirit *IS* spirit. The mind, will and heart of God are expressed in and by the Spirit of God. So, if we are led by the Spirit, we will express only those things that come from the Spirit. They are not flesh connected. So, Paul lists a long outline of things directly expressive of the *"flesh"* that should no longer be expressed by those led by the Spirit. They are not rule inspired (i.e., like the Law), rather they are simply contrary to the Spirit of God. It is a long but non-exhaustive list:

"The acts of the flesh are obvious: sexual immorality, impurity and debauchery; idolatry and witchcraft; hatred, discord, jealousy, fits of rage, selfish ambition, dissensions, factions and envy; drunkenness,

orgies, and the like. I warn you, as I did before, that those who live like this will not inherit the kingdom of God." Fifteen in all. Again, note that the list is not exhaustive.

Fruits of the Spirit

Instead, Paul lists nine of the expressions (fruits) of the Spirit of God:

*"But the fruit of the Spirit is **love, joy, peace, forbearance, kindness, goodness, faithfulness, gentleness and self-control.** Against such things there is no law. Those who belong to Christ Jesus have crucified the flesh with its passions and desires. Since we live by the Spirit, let us keep in step with the Spirit. Let us not become conceited, provoking and envying each other."* (Galatians 5:22-26).

Take a quick look at Exodus 34:6-7 again and see how many are expressed there:

"The Lord, the Lord God, compassionate and gracious, slow to anger, and abounding in lovingkindness and truth; who keeps lovingkindness for thousands, who forgives iniquity, transgression and sin; yet He will by no means leave the guilty unpunished, visiting the iniquity of fathers on the children and on the grandchildren to the third and fourth genera-tions." (Exodus 34:6-7).

Obviously, there are some different English words, but they have their parallel in Paul's lists. Let me list the seven expressions of God included Exodus 34:6-7 to make it easier to compare:

Compassionate

Gracious

Slow to Anger

Abounding in Lovingkindness *(Faithfulness, Chesed)*

Truth

Forgiving of iniquity, transgressions and sin

Will Execute Necessary Judgment

We can see immediately that Paul's list is longer but does not include "truth" nor judgment. Rather, Paul includes self-control and his "goodness and faithfulness" correspond pretty well to *Chesed*, so one could say Paul's list has eight rather than nine and includes two aspects we don't find in Exodus 34 while excluding two found there. It is not a perfect parallel.

What is my point? That neither list is exhaustive. When I look at the extent of the ocean, I am struck with how little I see and how little I understand. The extent of who and what God is can hardly be encapsulated in human words. As Paul says in 1st Corinthians 13:12, we see through an unclear mirror. Yet, the descriptions in Exodus 34 and Galatians 5 stand true.

Galatians 6

Paul ended Chapter 5 with a focus on the moral and spiritual condition of the Galatians.

Paul turns to the "Spiritual" believers in Galatia to help those who may be in drowning in some moral morass. Those in trouble could be participating in one of the 15 moral lapses he had just mentioned in Chapter 5, or were manifesting the opposite of the nine fruits of the Spirit Paul also listed. If the Galatian church had been more advanced, Paul would likely have included the teachers, shepherds and elders, but it appears that not all "offices" of each individual congregation have been filled with men appointed for leadership in the area of counsel and guidance. Yet, some apparently were teaching on a near full-time basis, and as he admonishes these helpers to help, he also admonishes those helped to "*to share all good things*" with the helper. This likely means some kind of material support.

The thrust of the opening section is helping each other be freed from any hurtful entanglement, and Paul's direction is that such help must be gentle. This is such an important reminder. We are not judges or jailers; we are brothers and sisters walking along the way with each other, hopefully filled with the Grace of the Lord Jesus Christ, and to be of true help, we must manifest the Spirit of our Father in heaven who is gracious, kind and long suffering. As a parent for over forty years, I can attest that gentleness is a much greater help than harshness in dealing with children. It is as well with brothers and sisters.

Paul then gives an important Spiritual principle in the guise of agriculture:

"**whatever a man sows, this he will also reap**. *For the one who sows to his own flesh will from the flesh reap corruption, but the one who sows to the Spirit will from the Spirit reap eternal life. Let us not lose heart in doing good, for in due time we will reap if we do not grow weary. So then, while we have opportunity, let us do good to all people, and especially to those who are of the household of the faith.*" (Galatians 6:7-9).

If we "*sow*" to the flesh (do what the flesh wants), we will reap corruption. Goodness, this should be emblazoned on our foreheads and the foreheads of our children. No doubt, we do not talk about this truth enough. I want the principle front and center because it is so easy to ignore at the beginning of misbehaving. But amazingly, if we sow to the Spirit (do what the Spirit of God directs), we will reap eternal life. Seems like an easy choice! But, like the Galatians, we need to have this truth front and center.

Paul ends this letter with his own personal handwriting (he has dictated the rest to a scribe), pointing out that one of the reasons people are getting circumcised is to avoid persecution. Apparently, the Judaizers are causing judgment to fall on the uncircumcised, and yet they themselves do not really follow the Law – they just want to boast that they have gotten others to do so. This gives Paul the opportunity to end the letter with what *he* would boast about:

"May it never be that I would boast, except in the cross of our Lord Jesus Christ, *through which the world has been crucified to me, and I to the world. For neither is circumcision anything, nor uncircumcision, but a new creation."* (Galatians 6:14-15).

Paul boasts in what for the Jews is a stumbling block and for the Greeks is foolishness! (1ˢᵗ Corinthians 1:23). This is what Paul preached, and he is proud of it. His understanding has led him to write the entire letter. It his grasp of the immense change that Jesus's sacrifice brought that caused him to address the circumcision issue in the first place.

His last words echo his heart's desire for them, and please note, his focus is on their spirit:

"The grace of our Lord Jesus Christ be with your spirit, brethren. Amen." (Galatians 6:18).

Paul's valediction prays that the Grace (unmerited favor) of the Lord Jesus Christ be with each Galatian's spirit. He addresses them as family. We remember that he spent part of the letter pointing out they were the adopted sons and daughters of God, and heirs to the Kingdom. His *"Amen"* seals the letter, which means simply *"May it be so!"*

Ephesians

Ephesians 1

A lofty, glorious letter. Likely written by Paul from Rome in the early 60s AD, there is reason to believe that the letter was actually written to all of the churches over a broad region – perhaps even as large as all of the churches Paul had ever founded. Because three of the most early manuscripts do not mention Ephesus at the beginning, and because there is no real recognition of Paul's lengthy time in Ephesus (two years) in the text itself, some scholars believe there was a blank at the beginning where the church in receipt of the copy could inscribe its name or location. The practice of reading the letters of the apostles was wide spread. By 155 AD, Justin Martyr could write to the Roman Emperor in his First Apology that Christians,

"On the day called Sunday, all who live in cities or in the country gather together to one place, and the memoirs of the apostles or the writings of the prophets are read, as long as time permits; then, when the reader has ceased, the president verbally instructs, and exhorts to the imitation of these good things." (Chapter 67).

The letters of the apostles were read as a matter of course on Sundays. We actually find that "Lectionaries" (meaning lists of specific texts) were in use very early in Church history as a pastoral aid to assure that those who couldn't read or directly access the scrolls would hear key sections from the letters throughout the year. This was similar to the Jewish practice of having set texts from the Old Testament read on Sabbaths. Remember Jesus's participation in Nazareth when he read a providentially selected text from Isaiah 61:1-2, as recorded in Luke 4:16-21:

"He went to Nazareth, where he had been brought up, and on the Sabbath day he went into the synagogue, as was his custom. He stood up to read, and the scroll of the prophet Isaiah was handed to him. Unrolling it, he found the place where it is written...."

The letter certainly was sent to the church in Ephesus, but we also can be sure it was sent to many others as well. The larger point is that the letter is generic in character, that is, it works for all communities including our own!

The major theme of the letter is the unity and reconciliation of the whole of creation through and in Jesus Christ, and through and in His Body, the Church, according to the will of God the Father.

I don't want to have a favorite book in the Bible as the idea seems nonsensical to me. But, I have to confess that I have read the Book of Ephesians more times than I can count, in both French and English, over and over and many times out loud – many more times than any other book. The letter has always fascinated me. I love Ephesians, and Chapter 1 is as good as it gets.

Those of you who know me will know what is coming next: how many *"in Him"* can you count in the first chapter? *"In Jesus,"* *"in the Beloved,"* *"In Christ,"* – they all mean the same thing, so count them as well. It is an important quiz question, because you will immediately see that Paul either stutters a lot, or that he sees everything in and through the lens of the promised Anointed One of God.

How many did you count? But additionally, a careful read will reveal something else very important. With over 15 expressions about the importance of being in Christ, we have over 25 direct references to God or to the Father. It can be confusing reading this chapter if you can't keep straight which He is who. In other words, Paul sometime uses the pronoun *"His"* for God and sometimes *"His"* for Jesus.

Another immediate take-away is that Chapter 1 is very much about the Father of the Universe and His action as well as about His Son, Jesus. Paul could not have done more to emphasize the importance of both of their roles in the history of the Universe, and Paul tells us in Chapter 1 that *WE* are part of God the Father's great plan for the Universe.

My hearty recommendation is that you read out loud and slowly the entirety of the chapter. Unfortunately, when read in English, you will miss the beautiful rhythm and emphasis that one gets reading the text in French. If you don't read French, this comment may be hard to grasp, but you should be able to catch my point by just noticing the difference in the texts from verses 3 and 4 below.

Verse 3 generally has the same cadence in English and French, but we see a big difference in verse 4. The *"En Lui"* at the French version begins at the head of the sentence, and *"En Lui"* means *"In Him."* So, we have this beautiful pattern and cadence where *"En Lui"* begins many of the verses in French. The English version could have been simply reordered, and you would experience much of the same emphasis: "In Him, God has chosen us before the foundation of the world, so that we would be holy and not reprehensible before Him." When I read this out loud, I always put a strong emphasis on *"In Him"* or *"En Lui."*

Ephesians 1:3: *"Blessed be the God and Father of our Lord Jesus Christ, who hath blessed us with every spiritual blessing in the heavenly places in Christ."*

Ephesians 1:4: *"even as he chose us in Him before the foundation of the world, that we should be holy and without blemish before Him in love,"*

Ephésiens 1:3: *"Béni soit Dieu, le Père de notre Seigneur Jésus Christ, qui nous a bénis de toute sortes de bénédictions spirituelles dans les lieux célestes en Christ!"*

Ephésiens 1:4: *"En Lui, Dieu nous a élus avant la fondation du monde, pour que nous soyons saints et irrépréhensibles devant Lui,"*

To me, aside from its great beauty, Ephesians 1 is clear as a bell. We are unbelievably blessed *IN* Jesus Christ, our Lord and Savior. Let me just list the blessings Paul mentions:

1. Grace *in Him*
2. Peace *in Him*
3. Every Spiritual Blessing *in Him*
4. Chosen *in Him*
5. Holy and Blameless *in Him*
6. Adopted *in Him*
7. Redeemed through His Blood *in Him*
8. Forgiveness of Sins *in Him*
9. Wisdom and Insight *in Him*
10. Knowledge of the Mystery of His Will *in Him*
11. Summed Up with all Things *in Him*
12. An Inheritance *in Him*
13. We are the Praise to God's Glory *in Him*
14. Sealed with the Holy Spirit *in Him*

15. Power *in Him*

There are at least fifteen unbelievable blessings we receive because of our position in Him. I would say this whole chapter is a Gospel chapter. Good News indeed!

Ephesians 2

We were dead, but God the Father wanted us alive. How is it we were dead? In our sin, under the Prince of the power of the air, according to the spirit which works in the sons of disobedience.

Paul has virtually the same thought expressed in a different way in his letter to the Colossians:

"For it is because of these things that the wrath of God will come upon the sons of disobedience, and in them you also once walked, when you were living in them. But now you also, put them all aside: anger, wrath, malice, slander, and abusive speech from your mouth. Do not lie to one another, since you laid aside the old self with its evil practices, and have put on the new self who is being renewed to a true knowledge according to the image of the One who created him— a renewal in which there is no distinction between Greek and Jew, circumcised and uncircumcised, barbarian, Scythian, slave and freeman, but Christ is all, and in all." (Colossians 3:6-11).

Though two early manuscripts do not include the words, *"sons of disobedience,"* the thought is similar even if the words are not.

Paul's letter to the Ephesians is a universal letter, applicable no matter the town or place. Everyone is dead Spiritually apart from God, and Spiritual death is death indeed. Think about God's promise to Adam and Eve; *"If you eat of the tree of the knowledge of good and evil, you shall surely die."* Adam did not die in the flesh upon eating; he died in the Spirit. He was no longer intimately connected to the God of the Universe. There was a break, a gulf, a separation.

His Grand Amour

So, what did God do about it? I love the fourth, fifth and sixth verses. They are true Gospel kernel verses: *"But God, being rich in mercy, because of His great love with which He loved us, even when we were dead in our transgressions, made us alive together with Christ (by grace you have been saved), and raised us up with Him, and seated us with Him in the heavenly places in Christ Jesus, so that in the ages to come He might show the surpassing riches of His grace in kindness toward us in Christ Jesus."*

The beginning is also wonderful in the French translation: *"Mais Dieu, qui est riche en miséricorde, à cause du grand amour dont il nous a aimés…."* "But God, who is rich in mercy because of the *"grand amour"* with which He loves us!" Yes, I absolutely love this truth. Because of His great and passionate love for us, He has moved heaven and earth to make us alive. A massive cosmic reality.

Truthfully, I am absolutely overcome by the breadth of this chapter. Look at our position:

"But God, being rich in mercy, because of His great love with which He loved us, even when we were dead in our transgressions, made us alive together in Christ (by grace you have been saved), and raised us up with Him, and seated us with Him in the heavenly places in Christ Jesus, so that in the ages to come He might show the surpassing riches of His grace in kindness toward us in Christ Jesus." (Ephesians 2:4-7).

We are made alive by our union with the Anointed One, the one who saves us from our filthiness by offering Himself as a pure sacrifice, and having done so, our union with Him is so complete that we find ourselves raised up with Him by the Spirit and seated with Him at the right hand of the Father *IN* Christ Jesus! This wonder shows forth the surpassing riches of His Grace and His inestimable Kindness. All of these actions reveal who God really is, His very nature.

In verse 6 and verse 8, Paul repeats himself for heavy emphasis: none of this wonder is because of what we have done. Nothing whatsoever. It is all the unilateral gift of God – His own action, not ours, propelling the life-giving change wrought in our position and in our being. Of course, we have heard this refrain in all of Paul's letters, and we should have heard it - for it is a universal truth for all peoples. If we stand, we stand by Grace.

Ephesians is the book that reveals much of the mystery behind God's movements, even the mystery of the Universe. Why were we created anew in Christ Jesus? We have already seen it was because of Father's great love for us, His *"grand amour."* But now we see a further reason. Being made alive in Christ is for good works. *"For we are His workmanship, created in Christ Jesus for good works,"* (Ephesians 2:10). This is a big part of who we have become, i.e., for good works, and certainly this is worth thinking about seriously. It means any form of resistance to doing the right thing must be resisted.

Paul reveals even more about the mystery behind what God has done as he continues.

"But now in Christ Jesus you who formerly were far off have been brought near by the blood of Christ. For He Himself is our peace, who made both groups into one and broke down the barrier of the dividing wall, by abolishing in His flesh the enmity, which is the Law of commandments contained in ordinances, so that in Himself He might make the two into one new man, thus establishing peace, and might reconcile them both in one body to God through the cross, by it having put to death the enmity. And

He came and preached peace to you who were far away, and peace to those who were near; for through Him we both have our access in one Spirit to the Father." (Ephesians 2:13-18).

Both Gentile and Jew are brought together as one in Jesus. Enmity between the two has been put to death. Through His body, Jesus has reconciled both to God through the cross. And what does Jesus preach? Peace to those far off and peace to those who are near. And how do we both have access to the Father of the Universe? Through the one and same Spirit – the Spirit of Jesus which is the Spirit of God.

Many Christians have been raised with the view that Scripture is the really important thing for knowing God and even how one reaches God. Let me be very clear (I feel like Paul), scripture is a precious, precious gift from God, but it is not how we access Father. We access Father through the Spirit. We commune with God through the Spirit. Scripture leads us toward God and teaches about God. But our relationship is not with words; our relationship is with the Living God in and through the Spirit of God.

Think about a loved one. Your relationship with your spouse, your mother or your child is not with a letter about your loved one. If the two of you are apart, a letter can be precious as it lets you know things about your loved one. But your relationship is not with the words in your letter. Your relationship is with your loved one.

A Holy Temple in the Lord

Paul ends his reflection in Chapter 2 with an extremely important paragraph of revelation, particularly in reference to us as individuals as well as to the broader Church.

"So then you are no longer strangers and aliens, but you are fellow citizens with the saints, and are of God's household, having been built on

the foundation of the apostles and prophets, Christ Jesus Himself being the corner stone, in whom the whole building, being fitted together, is growing into a holy temple in the Lord, in whom you also are being built together into a dwelling of God in the Spirit." (Ephesians 2:19-22).

We will see this imagery amplified again in Paul's letter. It reflects in its own way the vision Ezekiel had of the Valley of Dry Bones in Ezekiel 37, particularly related to the words, *"fitting together."* It sees us as fellow citizens in a Kingdom but also as part of God's family and part of His house. The picture has been an important one for our small community from the beginning.

In the last part of Paul's language, he likens what God is doing to the building of a house – His house. God has laid the foundation with giant stones (that is, of course, what one did when building the temple in Jerusalem), and God choses human beings for His stones. Jesus is the chief cornerstone, i.e., the stone that sets the entire direction, placement and scope of what God is building. Alongside Jesus we find the Apostles and the Prophets. It is not clear whether Paul is talking about the Prophets of Israel (which would include, for instance, Moses), but personally, that would be my interpretation. So, you have on the bottom level these giant stones. Next, we have believers being placed on the first course above the foundation. Level upon level; generation upon generation. Eventually, you get to us!

Obviously, there are a lot of implications to be drawn. But the main thing as each stone is fitted together in place is the purpose: to be, *"a holy temple in the Lord, in whom you also are being built together into a dwelling of God in the Spirit."*

I have expressed this thought many times, but this is one of the key texts where we find the thought. *"Fitting together"* is a work of the Spirit. It is not our cleverness, and I also think the location God has for us relationally is not of our choosing; it is His. Here is a portion of Ezekiel's vision:

"So, I prophesied as I was commanded; and as I prophesied, there was a noise, and behold, a rattling; and the bones came together, bone to its bone. And I looked, and behold, sinews were on them, and flesh grew, and skin covered them; but there was no breath in them. Then He said to me, "Prophesy to the breath, prophesy, son of man, and say to the breath, 'Thus says the Lord God, Come from the four winds, O breath, and breathe on these slain, that they come to life.' So, I prophesied as He commanded me, and the breath came into them, and they came to life and stood on their feet, an exceedingly great army."" (Ezekiel 37:7-10).

The rattling was bone moving across bone to get to the proper bone with which it was to be joined. The picture is a great valley of dead and disconnected bones, like an elephant graveyard. Bones were strewn all over the place. When the Spirit begins to move the bones, they rattle because they are in movement. It is a great vision of what God is doing and hopefully will do amongst all His children in this day. Placement should not be based on your wants and desires - your neediness. True spiritual placement is based on where God wants you.

Ephesians 3

The Great Mystery

Chapter 3 sums up Paul's remarkable discourse on the mystery of God's heart, and in Chapter 4, we will move to the earthly manifestation of His heart in the Church.

We ended Chapter 2 with the remarkable temple vision of God building the Church on the foundation of Jesus and the Apostles and Prophets, and adding to it, generation by generation, people that reflect and transmit the very glory of God. This is the great Church vision, and Paul opens Chapter 3 with a "Therefore." In my New American Standard Bible, the words are *"For this reason,"* but they mean the same.

It is like Paul is saying, "Because God is doing this great building project, I have been chosen to present to you some of its great mystery. And the amazing thing is, God is building His Temple with ALL the different ethnic and racial groups of mankind - Jew and Gentile alike!" It is VERY hard to grasp how earthshattering this would have been for a Jew to recognize:

"... the mystery of Christ, which in other generations was not made known to the sons of men, as it has now been revealed to His holy apostles and prophets in the Spirit; to be specific, that the Gentiles are fellow heirs and fellow members of the body, and fellow partakers of the promise in Christ Jesus through the gospel," (Ephesians 3:4-6).

Stunning! Paul is sitting in a prison in Rome, totally amazed with God's great purpose, His great mystery, the working out of His *"grand amour."* Paul was chosen for proclaiming *"to the Gentiles the unfathomable riches of Christ,"* in order *"to bring to light what is the administration of the mystery which for ages has been hidden in God who created all things; so that the manifold wisdom of God might now be made known through the Church to the rulers and the authorities in the heavenly places. This was in accordance with the eternal purpose which He carried out in Christ Jesus our Lord."* (Ephesians 3:8-11).

God's Great Purpose

The unfathomable riches of the Anointed One, Jesus! Paul's job is to bring to light how this mystery of God's eternal will (He has intended this all along) is being worked out in Paul's day. The Church in its amazingly new and highly diversified character (think Jew, Gentile, male, female, black, white, every nationality) makes known to the rulers and authorities in the heavenlies **God's great purpose – to bring everything together in His Son, Jesus**.

Let's step back a moment and ponder what the heavenly "rulers and authorities" see as they gaze down on the earth today. It is painful to think what they see and how what they see does NOT show forth what God intended. A slight discursion from the World Christian Encyclopedia put together by Barrett, Kurian, and Johnson and published by the Oxford University Press in 2001:

"World Christianity consists of 6 major ecclesiastical-cultural blocs, divided into 300 major ecclesiastical traditions, composed of over 33,000 distinct denominations in 238 countries." (Vol. I, p. 16).

The WCE then goes on to break down "World Christianity" into the following broad categories:

Independents: 22,000 denominations

Protestants: 9000 denominations

Marginals: 1600 denominations

Orthodox: 781 denominations

Catholics: 242 denominations

Anglicans: 168 denominations

Personally, I have NO idea of the actual number of any of the apparent divisions, but you will grasp my point. One of the most important things to God was to show all of those angels in their different ranks the amazing unity of the people on earth in His Son, Jesus. This is God's eternal Will. But I fear those in the heavenlies only see division and strife as they look about.

We must do everything we can to contribute to unity within the Church, and the most important zones are our attitudes and our hearts.

Our attitudes flow out of our hearts. What to we show to the outsider and to the angelic host? Do we show a burning love for Christians of every stripe, or do we go about casting hurtful accusations about those different from us?

I grew up in a stream of Christianity that held a problematic world view, "We are right, and the rest of Christendom is wrong, and they are all going to Hell." This worldview was so pronounced that even sister churches often would have nothing to do with each other. This is not to say that what we believe is not important to our individual walk. But, to look down on others when we, like Paul, stand only by the Grace of God and not any merit of our own is a terrible mistake.

When we open our hearts toward God, God's Spirit will work a mighty work in our hearts. Judgment will be replaced with love. I pray it will be so!

Paul began Chapter 1 with a marvelous praise which began in verse 3 and didn't end until verse 15. The prayer is in the form of a Jewish "blessing," an acclamation of Paul's heart toward God. It took a form very similar to our Jewish prayer at Passover when we say *"Baruch atah, Adonai Eloheinu, Melech ha Olam," "Blessed are You, O God, ruler of the Universe..."* It is worth recording again:

"Blessed be the God and Father of our Lord Jesus Christ, who has blessed us with every spiritual blessing in the heavenly places in Christ, just as He chose us in Him before the foundation of the world, that we would be holy and blameless before in Him. In love He predestined us to adoption as sons through Jesus Christ to Himself, according to the kind intention of His will, to the praise of the glory of His grace, which He freely bestowed on us in the Beloved. In Him we have redemption through His blood, the forgiveness of our trespasses, according to the riches of His grace which He lavished on us. In all wisdom and insight, He made known to us

*the mystery of His will, according to His kind intention which He pur-
posed in Him with a view to an administration suitable to the fullness of
the times, that is, the summing up of all things in Christ, things in the
heavens and things on the earth. In Him also we have obtained an inheritance, having been predestined according to His purpose who works all
things after the counsel of His will, to the end that we who were the first
to hope in Christ would be to the praise of His glory. In Him, you also,
after listening to the message of truth, the gospel of your salvation—having also believed, you were sealed in Him with the Holy Spirit of promise,
who is given as a pledge of our inheritance, with a view to the redemption
of God's own possession, to the praise of His glory."*

As Paul ends Chapter 3 and his discourse on God's Purpose, which is
the theme of the first three chapters, he finishes with a prayer, a praise
and then the Amen. I can't help but think he might have intended
Chapters 1-3 to be read in the churches as a unit and then, on another
Lord's Day, Chapters 4-6.

Here is his prayer:

*"For this reason I bow my knees before the Father, from whom every
family in heaven and on earth derives its name, that He would grant
you, according to the riches of His glory, to be strengthened with power
through His Spirit in the inner man, so that Christ may dwell in your
hearts through faith; and that you, being rooted and grounded in love,
may be able to comprehend with all the saints what is the breadth and
length and height and depth, and to know the love of Christ which surpasses knowledge, that you may be filled up to all the fullness of God."*
(Ephesians 3:14-19).

Paul's prayer is that we would be strengthened with power through
His Spirit in our innermost being so that the Anointed One would live
in our hearts. This is Paul's great hope, squarely focused on internal

transformation through and by the Spirit of the living God. He didn't pray that the Ephesians would be able to remember verbatim every scripture then current, i.e., the Old Testament writings. That wouldn't be a bad thing, but it was not *THE* thing. Much more important would be the living reality of Jeremiah 31:31 and a full transformation of the heart brought about by the abiding presence of the Spirit of Jesus and the Father working inside each one of us. Yes! May it be so!

And then, finally, his praise and the Amen:

"Now to Him who is able to do far more abundantly beyond all that we ask or think, according to the power that works within us, to Him be the glory in the church and in Christ Jesus to all generations forever and ever. Amen." (Ephesians 3:20-21).

Ephesians 4

Since we begin what is clearly the second part of Paul's letter, I recall N.T. Wright's observation that the last three chapters might be titled *"Ephesians and the Church of God."* In the first three chapters, Paul has looked deeply into God's mystery of pulling all things together in heaven and on earth in His Son, Jesus. Now, he shifts to look at the practical implications for each one of us.

In the opening sentence of Chapter 4, Paul actually begs us and the Ephesians to *"lead a life worthy of the calling to which you have been called, with all humility and gentleness, with patience, bearing with one another in love, making every effort to maintain the unity of the Spirit in the bond of peace."* (Ephesians 4:1-3).

Aside from the overarching importance of the Spirit of God, four attributes will be critical to success:

- Humility

- Gentleness
- Patience
- Bearing with One Another

Another way of saying this is that these four will help us maintain the unity and peace that the Spirit brings us. Isn't this true in all of our relationships, particularly husband and wife relationships and those with whom we walk as yoke fellows?

Oneness, the Reality of Unity

Having given extremely practical direction, Paul underscores his thought with verses 4 and 5:

"There is one body and one Spirit, just as you were called to the one hope of your calling, one Lord, one faith, one baptism, one God and Father of all, who is above all and through all and in all."

The reason we lead a life of humility, gentleness, patience and peace is because it is the only kind of life that fits with the great spiritual realities: **one** Body of Christ, **one** Spirit, **one** Call, **one** Lord, **one** Faith, **one** Baptism, and **one** God and Father. One, one, one! Oneness, the reality of unity. The word "unity" itself comes to us from the Latin word *"unitas,"* and the root word *"unus"* which simply mean the number "one." Nothing added to it; there is just one thing.

Not two, but one. The only way we get "two" is division, and there is no division in unity. All is one, bound together. This is the true meaning of being in Covenant. Two wills are bounded together as one. It is the exact opposite of division where something is divided. Rather, that which is divided becomes fused together into one.

Oneness is the very property of the Godhead, and we are called into Oneness when we are called by God into Himself. God does an amazing thing. He creates multiplicity and then calls it into fusion - a great mystery and a great wonder. And each of us is called into this amazing Oneness with each other and with the Godhead.

Having struck the high note of Oneness, he shifts to the miracle of various graces. In spite of God's overarching movement to draw all things together, He simultaneously gives varying graces to each person for the very purpose of Oneness. How can this be so? Because by giving varying graces that are needed for the Body of Christ to function beautifully and well, each individual must pull together with his or her brother or sister. No one person gets all that is needed for the Body to fully express the wonder and the majesty of God. It takes all working together.

People Gifts

"The gifts he gave were that some would be apostles, some prophets, some evangelists, some pastors and teachers, to equip the saints for the work of ministry, for building up the body of Christ, until all of us come to the unity of the faith and of the knowledge of the Son of God, to maturity, to the measure of the full stature of Christ." (Ephesians 4:11-13)

And here we see an even greater example: God gives different PEOPLE as *"gifts."* Not just different graces of function, but different kinds of people themselves are given so that we call come to unity and to the knowledge of the Son – to maturity, to the full stature of the Anointed One. We saw the same revelation in 1st Corinthians 12.

So, we have this picture of diversity of giftings and diversity of people and diversity of function all combining to bring us to absolute Oneness. If this happens, we will manifest the full stature of the Son who, like God, exemplifies Oneness. This is the *Shema* of Israel: *"Shema Visrael, Adonai Eloheinu, Adonai Echad." "Hear, O' Israel, the Lord your God,* the Lord is One!" The *"echad"* in the *Shema* simply means ONE. I get literal goose bumps writing this and can hardly write another character. Goodness! I can see why our Jewish friends have to respond immediately after, *"Baruch shem kavod malchuto l'olam va-ed"* which means *"Blessed be His Name, Whose Glorious Kingdom is for ever and ever."* Blessed be He!

Yet, Chapter 4 is a practical chapter even though we are on a high plane. In the preceding verses 11-13, we get very practical information about five types of people in ministry. Verses 11-13 list several key ministries/people given to mankind to bring mankind into this deep unity. They vary; they are not all the same. They have different functions, but their overarching purpose is the same:

1. **To Equip the saints.**
2. **To Help Build Up the Body of Christ until it is Entirely Unified.**
3. **To Help Build Up the Body of Christ until we all have the full Knowledge of the Son.**
4. **To Help Build Up the Body of Christ until we all express His Full Stature.**

This is basically a job description for all Apostles, Prophets, Evangelists, Pastors/Teachers. Those are the goals. Today, Paul might have posted this on "Linked In," the website for connecting people to various jobs: *Equip and Build Up.* That's it.

A proper working of these gifted people will mean we will *"no longer be children, tossed to and fro and blown about by every wind of doctrine, by people's trickery, by their craftiness in deceitful scheming."* (Ephesians 4:14).

When they don't do their work properly, we will find ourselves tossed to and fro and blown about by every wind of doctrine. Note that there are two responsibilities in this zone. One is that those ministry people must be very careful to stick only to what is true, what was affirmed true by the original Apostles, Prophets, Evangelists, Pastor/Teachers, and not veer off into vain speculation, get off point and lead others astray. But on the receiving side, the people who receive ministry must guard their ears from listening to vain, off point, esoteric nonsense that brings only confusion and foolish focus on things that are not the true heart of the gospel.

The Body

In Ephesians, Paul gives us the true heart of the Gospel. It is a GREAT book to keep us from idle speculation. Verses 15 and 16 say this amazingly well:

"Speaking the truth in love, we must grow up in every way into him who is the head, into Christ, from whom the whole Body, joined and knit together by every ligament with which it is equipped, as each part is working properly, promotes the body's growth in building itself up in love." (Ephesians 4:15-16).

Please get the picture of the Body that Paul presents. It is made up of many members, but they are joined together. They are joined and knitted together by bands and ligaments of love and faithfulness, just as ligaments hold the bones of our own body together. This is in order that the entire Body may function properly: run, walk, jump, dance, love, sing – whatever God directs. There is a harmony necessary for the Body to function as it ought, and it takes a willingness to submit one to another in function and gifting for this glory to be manifest. Unfortunately, I feel today that we are plagued in Christendom with so many that suffer from "my way or the highway" and "not Your will, but my will be done." That attitude only leads to sadness and tragedy!

If we go God's way, it immediately follows that we can *"no longer live as the Gentiles live, in the futility of their minds. They are darkened in their understanding, alienated from the life of God because of their ignorance and hardness of heart. They have lost all sensitivity and have abandoned themselves to licentiousness, greedy to practice every kind of impurity."* (Ephesians 4:17-19). Lord, help us! May it not be so with us in even the slightest way.

Rather, we must *"put away"* our former way of life - our old self, corrupt and deluded by its lusts, and be renewed in the spirit of our minds, and clothe ourselves with the new self, created according to the likeness of God in true righteousness and holiness. (See Ephesians 4:22-24). *Put away* our former way of life.

As Paul finishes the chapter, he is waxing hot with practical focus on what else we must *"put away."* We must put away *"falsehood, speaking the truth to our neighbors, for we are members of one another."* (Ephesians 4:25).

We can *"be angry"* from time to time, but we can't *"let the sun go down"* on our anger, and we must not *"make any room for the devil.*

"Thieves must give up stealing; rather labor and work honestly with their own hands, so that they may have something to share with the needy." (Ephesians 4:27-28).

And, we must not let any *"evil talk come out of our mouths, but only what is useful for building up, as there is need, so that our words may give grace to those who hear. And we must not grieve the Holy Spirit of God, with which each of us was marked with a seal for the day of redemption. We've got to put away all bitterness and wrath and anger and wrangling and slander, together with all malice, and be kind to one another, tenderhearted, forgiving one another, as God in Christ has forgiven us."* (Ephesians 4:25-32 with slightly modified personal pronouns).

Put away, put away, put away. Put on the clothes of the newborn Christian! Amen!

Ephesians 5

A Prescription for Life

Paul begins Chapter 5 with a simple prescription for life – imitate God! But, what does Paul mean by this? If we ask how God actually operates, I think the answer is obvious: by the Spirit within Him. The Spirit of a being is its essence. God operates by expressing at all times and in all ways His essence. In the design of a building or the creation of a painting, the best goal is to express as deeply and clearly as possible the essence of an idea, the *logos*, the thing we are trying to express. God simply expresses that which coincides with who He is. This is both our mission and our challenge: To walk by the Spirit and express who God really is.

From scripture we know a great deal about who God is. Our texts over the last few chapters make clear that Exodus 34:6*ff* and 1ˢᵗ John 4:7 are good summations. In addition to His great Holiness, God is Love and all of those amazing characteristics revealed in Exodus 34: Compassionate, Kind, Slow to Anger, full of Loving Faithfulness and Truth and willing to Forgive even the greatest iniquity or sin. Yet, because of His Truth, He will punish disobedience and moral trespass.

Paul is asking the Ephesians to imitate the characteristics in their own walk. We could use the words "express," "manifest," or "reveal." We want to express, manifest and reveal the essence of God in our lives everywhere and all the time. Yes, may it be so.

But, Paul quickly clarifies that when he talks about imitating God's love, he is talking about reflecting the deep love evidenced in Jesus's love for each one of us – a love that caused Him to give *"Himself up for us, an offering and a sacrifice to God as a fragrant aroma."* (Ephesians 5:2). Paul is not calling us to a namby-pamby, robotic display of nice qualities, but to a life of sacrificial love on all fronts.

After setting the stage, Paul launches into some very specific aspects of behavior that are NOT OK for the believer. The first he mentions are related to what we say out loud and what we talk about – what comes off our tongues. Paul doesn't want folks talking about anything off-color whatsoever – neither things they may have done nor that others might have done. You don't have to think far back to realize such things DO happen in community, and we are to keep our mouths shut and not discuss them.

I can guess there are many reasons for this prohibition. One is that unbridled talking breeds judgment, and we can fall into the *"beam in our own eye while focusing on the speck in someone else's eye"* syndrome. But, more important is the danger of actually inspiring others by lurid talk into the same moral trespass; giving people an idea they weren't even thinking about.

Certainly, no *"filthy talk"* should be expressed, and this means an absolutely "clean mouth." No cursing, no "bad words," which are so prevelant in our current culture. Can you name a handful of current movies or TV shows that are not filled with inappropriate language? If we are not to speak of it, we shouldn't listen to it as well.

Paul includes in this group *"silly talk."* In Greek, this is the word *mōrología.* This is the only place in the Bible that the word occurs - speech flowing out of a dull, sluggish heart that has lost its grip on reality. I cannot help but think of the endless hours people spend on speculations about esoteric ideas associated with the Bible. Speculations about esoteric ideas bring to mind Jackie Chan singing

"What is it good for, ABSOLUTELY NOTHING!" Foolishness is giving time and attention to the unimportant, and God knows, the airwaves are full of foolishness. Lord, help us! Maybe one solution is to turn off all media! And, I am not kidding.

Paul antidote is simple: just be thankful. If your heart is thankful and your brain sees how good you have it, you will express your thankfulness frequently.

Having addressed what we talk about, he turns to what we listen. Both are important to the health of the believer and the believer's testimony to the unbeliever. Do not let anyone deceive you with EMPTY words. The radio talk show people have to talk all day long. Most of the time, many are talking foolishness to fill up the space. And we can spend our time listening to friends, even brother and sisters, talking about similar empty things. Satan will take empty words and deceive us, so we truly must be on guard.

"Let no one deceive you with empty words, for because of these things the wrath of God comes upon the sons of disobedience. Therefore, do not be partakers with them; for you were formerly darkness, but now you are Light in the Lord; walk as children of Light (for the fruit of the Light consists in all goodness and righteousness and truth), trying to learn what is pleasing to the Lord. Do not participate in the unfruitful deeds of darkness, but instead even expose them; for it is disgraceful even to speak of the things which are done by them in secret. But all things become visible when they are exposed by the light, for everything that becomes visible is light. For this reason, it says, 'Awake, sleeper, And arise from the dead,' And Christ will shine on you." (Ephesians 5:6-14).

The problem of getting caught up in foolishness is a big focus of Paul's in Chapter 5, and he associates getting drunk as a perfect example of extreme foolishness. Rather, spend your time in the Spirit: be *filled* with the Spirit of God. Paul's construction is willful, i.e., we can willfully be filled with the Spirit of God by turning to God and opening ourselves to His Spirit. We do this every time we worship. We can choose to give ourselves over to worship, and Paul lists three types of things that we might share together as we speak to one another in the Spirit: psalms, hymns and spiritual songs. Psalms we have out of the Bible, hymns are songs composed by men and women to bring out the truth of God and life, and spiritual songs (at least in my view) are songs given in the midst of worship that have never been sung before.

"speaking to one another in psalms and hymns and spiritual songs, singing and making melody with your heart to the Lord; always giving thanks for all things in the name of our Lord Jesus Christ to God, even the Father; and be subject to one another in the fear of Christ." (Ephesians 5:19-21).

Authority

Note that Paul ends his thought on being filled with the Spirit: If one is *in* the Spirit of Jesus, we will be *"subject to one another in the fear of Christ."* This shifts Paul's thought to an extremely important zone for every believer, the zone of Authority. Paul will talk about the zones or walls of authority for the rest of the chapter and into the next as he focuses first on marriage.

There are many authority walls around each one of us. Each of us is like an ancient castle with walls about us for protection. Only the walls are of a spiritual nature. Some of my Weber grandchildren were playing on the beach recently, building walls of sand around their sand castle. Each wall helped keep the tide at bay. God's walls of authority are real and not made of sand. But, they are of no use to us if we ignore them, breaching them in one way or another.

Our spouses are walls of protection around us as well as our children. A wife is meant to be a wall of protection for her children and, in various ways, for her husband. When she has Godly wisdom in her decisions and her counsel, she extends a wall of authority from God for the protection and freedom of her family. Likewise, a husband is meant to be a wall of protection and authority for his entire family.

This mimics Christ's wall of authority and protection around the Church. Thankfully, true Christian authority is full of Love. The world knows little of true Christian authority. Christian authority flows from Love.

It is key for us to be inside each circle of authority that God provides.

God's word in Holy Scripture also is a wall of protection, and to the degree that we know and honor it, we will be safeguarded and free of many adverse consequences that come from ignoring the wisdom found in the Bible. The Ten Commandments and Jesus's summation of them in Matthew, Chapter 22, are not to be trespassed, period. They especially stand as a wall of authority.

God has placed Spirit-inspired men and women in the Body of Christ, and some of these people are God's specific gifts to us. Their counsel also forms a wall of protection around us. If we don't heed their counsel, we put ourselves in danger.

But there are more walls of authority that God intends for protection. One is the wall of protection that comes from the government of the United States. God allows governments and their agents to be established to protect citizens, and each of us is inside the authority wall of the United States. Institutions, businesses, retail establishments and churches have walls of authority when we enter them or work for them.

Perhaps you will remember my reflection from the 13th Chapter of Romans about the elevator and the President of the United States in the old days when elevators had human operators. Even the President, when he stepped into the elevator cab, moved from a realm where he was in authority into a realm where the elevator operator had the authority. Think of that! Inside the elevator, you were inside the wall of the elevator operator's authority.

I repeat what Watchman Nee once said, *"Nothing is greater than authority in the universe; nothing can surpass it."* In particular, Christians should be entirely conscious of authority and desirous of being under all authority given by God for the proper working of mankind. We are meant to be a submissive people and not rebellious. It is just the nature of the Spirit.

"He who loves his own wife loves himself; for no one ever hated his own flesh, but nourishes and cherishes it, just as Christ also does the church, because we are members of His body." (Ephesians 5:28-29).

What does the Head (the one God has placed in authority) do? At every level - whether a person, a wife, a husband, a trustee, a chairman, or a president, the Head nourishes and cherishes those under the Head's area of responsibility. This is a far cry from domineering. Jesus sacrificially gave Himself for mankind, and we are called to give ourselves for those we serve. What a world this would be if this attitude were in every realm that claims to have authority.

Ephesians 6

"For You have girded me with strength for battle"
(Psalm 18:39)

Paul continues his concentrated thought on realms of authority as Chapter 6 opens. We remember from Chapter 5 that those in authority are called to both love and nourish those whom they both support and protect. He shifts now to children and the example they should set as ones being nourished, loved and protected by their parents. Not surprisingly, since children are in the same place with their parents that we are in relationship to God, children should take direction without complaint, thus honoring their father and mother.

Honor

As we discussed in Chapter 1 of 1ˢᵗ Corinthians, the word *"honor"* is important. Honor is an appropriate response for all those under someone's authority. For safety's sake, the one under authority does his or her best to please the one supporting and protecting, giving due honor.

The word *"honor"* is from the Greek *"timao"* which means to *"value."* Other words would include *"to revere"* and *"venerate."* *"Appreciate"* would be yet another word. Think of all the realms of support and protection in which we fall. Most of the time, we are not even conscious that we are being supported and protected. We certainly won't appreciate the support we receive if we are not even conscious of it. Let's be "honor" detectives!

Paul adds to his admonition by including the Fifth Commandment. This is the only Commandment which contains a specific and important promise: *"Honor your father and your mother, **that your days may be prolonged in the land which the LORD your God gives you."*** (Exodus 20:12). Deuteronomy adds some additional color to the promise portion when it repeats the Commandment: *"Honor your father and your mother, as the LORD your God has commanded you, that your days may be prolonged and **that it may go well with you on the land which the LORD your God gives you."*** (Deuteronomy 5:16).

This is a very clear promise, and every child would do well to grasp this truth. It is also true when we honor God given authority wherever we find it. Honor that we each appropriately bestow opens further God's window of Grace.

Paul includes one of the most difficult charges to fathers that he could make (and note, fathers are singled out): *"Fathers, do not provoke your children to anger, but bring them up in the discipline and instruction of the Lord."* (Ephesians 6:4). The Greek word translated *"provoke"* actually means *"irritate."* Goodness, this is difficult for men and reveals the incredibly high standard of shepherding and authority that God places on men. All of those God attributes (compassion, kindness, long-suffering and faithfulness) are called into play.

When addressing the lowest rung of society, Paul actually affirms the tie between truly honoring those over us and receiving a reward. He addresses slaves, the lowest of the low – the ones who must do everything they are called to do or face terrible consequences. But this shows how far reaching the very nature of God is, even to the one under the awful condition of slavery. Even the slave is called to honor his or her Master with sincerity of heart, and not just when the Master is looking at them, but also when the Master is not. In other words, never talking bad about the Master behind his back or doing one's work in sloppy fashion.

Finally, Paul addresses the slave's Master: *"...do the same things to them, and give up threatening, knowing that both their Master and yours is in heaven, and there is no partiality with Him."* (Ephesians 6:9). *"Do the same things to them"* in a true sense means to honor those under your direction and protection, even showing honor to a slave. This was a revolutionary concept, totally foreign to the existing culture.

Having completed his thoughts on relationships – on realms of authority and protection, Paul goes back to his earlier admonition to *"put off"* fleshly ways. Remember his opening sentence from Chapter 4 where Paul begs us and the Ephesians to *"lead a life worthy of the calling to which you have been called, with all humility and gentleness, with patience, bearing with one another in love, making every effort to maintain the unity of the Spirit in the bond of peace."* (Ephesians 4:1-3). Paul follows with his series of "putting off" various unrighteous garments.

Spiritual Warfare

Paul talked about how this could be done in Chapters 4 and 5, that is, by *"putting on"* the attributes of God – thus being like God. Now, as Paul completes his exhortation to the Ephesians, he addresses one of the greatest obstacles to success in *keeping on* the garments of God: Enemy activity. For the next ten verses, i.e., verses 10 thru 20, Paul addresses Spiritual Warfare.

What an important war plan Paul lays out. Again, it is about *"putting on."* Here we have a picture of a man or a woman clothed in the attributes of God but under constant attack from the Evil One and his henchmen. What is one to do? Put on the armor necessary for a Christian warrior. My brother, Terry Smith, is the first person who gave me the idea of doing this in a virtual way every morning. It is a practice Terry adopted to better prepare for the day ahead. So, as we inventory these pieces of armor, imagine God actually putting each article on your own body each morning.

Paul begins with the observation that we cannot in our own strength succeed – our war work must be allowing God's strength to do battle because we are not struggling with flesh and blood. Rather, we are up against *"rulers, against the powers, against the world forces of this darkness, against the spiritual forces of wickedness in the heavenly places."*

(Ephesians 6:12). Read that again. We are up against *"rulers, against the powers, against the world forces of this darkness, against the spiritual forces of wickedness in the heavenly places."* No wonder we suffer loss if we are not really armed with supernaturally powerful weapons.

"Take up the full armor of God, so that you will be able to resist in the evil day, and having done everything, to stand firm." (Ephesians 6:13).

Two important notes. First, we need every piece of armor – the full armor of God. Next, our goal is simply to *"stand."* This latter point is an important one. Note that Paul repeats it twice. My only conclusion is that Satan can only make a frontal assault. None of the armor protects the rear of the soldier pictured. His defense for attack from the rear is to never let the enemy get behind him. That is why the sword and the shield are so important. Those are offensive weapons meant to stop the enemy in his tracks.

So, let's look at the order of *"putting on."*

First is the **Belt of Truth**, which is buckled entirely around us. This means that being in any way "out of reality," out of truth, is extremely dangerous and we should every morning get our heads straight about who we actually are. Think of that: you are a child of the King, entirely justified by the Blood of Jesus, seated at the right hand of the Father in the person of Jesus, heir to the Kingdom.

Perhaps Paul mentions the Belt of Truth first because this is the very first spot the Enemy will attack on any given day, i.e., by accusing us of our unworthiness, our sin, our follies. Note that the Enemy never accuses us of something we would never believe; there is always a grain of truth, and surely each one of us would affirm there is some truth to our unworthiness, our sin and our follies. But the Truth of God trumps all accusations, and we must not allow Satan to get the drop on us.

Second comes the **Breastplate of Righteousness**. Truth includes in a certain sense the reality of our righteousness given to us in God, so it protects us from the Evil One's accusation about our righteousness. I also believe the Breastplate is an important piece of armor. Its solidity is strengthened by our own purity of conscience and behavior. If you want an entirely solid Breastplate, let it be made with the Righteousness of God which is entirely solid, and throw in a bit of your own as a humble contribution to the war effort!

Third, shod your feet with the *"preparation of the **Gospel of Peace**."* What an interesting piece of armor this is. Third in order of adornment, with your feet shod, you are ready to share with every Satanic encounter the Good News of God's saving love. What an intention for the day; this thought shoves aside Enemy tactics by its aggressive stance. Warring factions cease as we pledge allegiance to God's Kingdom and eternal purpose.

Peace also helps us *"stand firm."* Being at peace internally and toward others removes instability. It grounds us in God's nature. In fact, it is our feet that touch the ground. Think of this every morning as you press down into these special virtual shoes – you want with all your heart to be firmly grounded in peace.

Fourth, put on the **Shield of Faith**, *"with which you can extinguish all the flaming arrows of the evil one."* (Ephesians 6:16). This piece of armor - our belief in God and all that we know in God - deflects those flaming arrows of destruction that Satan sends our way. These are not bad events. Rather, they are bad thoughts. And we remember that we are to take every thought captive for healthy thinking, deflecting away entirely thoughts that are from Satan. Satanic thoughts are NOT hard to discern – they are flaming, for goodness sake! They often will be aimed at our identity, but they also may be aimed at the identity of our brother or sister. Deflect them with your shield of Faith! (Note that the shield is very much an offensive weapon as well as a defensive weapon.)

Fifth, let God place on your head the **Helmet of Salvation** that protects your thinking while in battle. Personally, when I get to this piece of armor, I picture myself with God placing a Greek looking silver helmet on my head, and every time I do this, I see blood dripping down from the helmet: Jesus's blood. Across the front is engraved "SALVATION." I *AM* saved! The question is not how I feel; the question is whether Jesus died for me or not. And the answer is, He did!

Sixth, another weapon is needed to be fully equipped, and that is *"the Sword of the Spirit, which is the Word of God."* (Ephesians 6:17). *"For the word of God is living and active and sharper than any two-edged sword and piercing as far as the division of soul and spirit, of both joints and marrow, and able to judge the thoughts and intentions of the heart."* (Hebrews 4:12).

What a picture this brings to mind of an ancient soldier wielding up and down, back and forth, in swirling motion, the Word of God as the Enemy attacks. Remember, it was scripture with which Jesus deflected the three attacks of Satan in the Wilderness temptations. If we don't pack our arsenal with a deep understanding and grasp of Scripture, we will incur many hurtful blows.

The Sword of the Spirit brings to mind a vision I had of my yoke-fellow, David Vaughan, during a Men's Meeting in 1996. David had declared his desire to have the fullness of God's Word, particularly with regard to how we as men might truly encourage our wives. I saw a two-edged sword in my mind's eye with David prostrate in the middle of the blade. Surely, God is calling all of us to prostrate ourselves before the Word of God, to be in the middle of the Word, fully submissive.

David V. — The Word of God

Steve Bowie spoke this prophetic word that evening: "Be strong and courageous. You will lead these people to My inheritance. Don't turn from my Word, neither to the right nor left. Be strong and courageous, not looking back at the wilderness to get your cues for the journey before you."

Seventh, I am going to suggest Paul includes one other weapon here because it immediately follows the Sword of the Spirit and could actually simply be another aspect of the Sword: **Prayer in the Spirit.** Look at the very next verse: *"With all prayer and petition pray at all times in the Spirit, and with this in view, be on the alert with all perseverance and petition for all the saints,"* (Ephesians 6:17-18). This is not something we should have at our side during the day; it is something we should *do* throughout the day. Pray in the Spirit! If you don't know what this means, learn what it means and do it!

Paul concludes with the confirmation that he has sent Tychicus to them with the letter and ends with this beautiful farewell prayer:

"Peace be to the brethren, and love with faith, from God the Father and the Lord Jesus Christ. Grace be with all those who love our Lord Jesus Christ with incorruptible love." Incorruptible means "unending!"

Philippians

Philippians 1

Paul was probably around 56 years old when he wrote the Philippian church while imprisoned in Rome. It was perhaps the spring of 62 AD. Paul had been under house arrest for several years awaiting trial. During this general timeframe, he had written at least three other letters – to the Ephesians, the Colossians, and one to Onesimus's master, Philemon. Now, he writes the Philippian church after receiving a financial gift through the hands of Epaphroditus.

It has been over ten years since Paul and his companions (including Silas, Timothy, and Luke) first arrived in Philippi after receiving a vision in Troas on the other side of the Aegean Sea. Philippi sat in the easternmost tip of Macedonia northwest of Troas.

"So, putting out to sea from Troas, we ran a straight course to Samothrace, and on the day following to Neapolis; and from there to Philippi, which is a leading city of the district of Macedonia, a Roman colony; and we were staying in this city for some days. And on the Sabbath day we went outside the gate to a riverside, where we were supposing that there would

be a place of prayer; and we sat down and began speaking to the women who had assembled." (Acts 16:11-13).

Philippi was an important Greek city. The Lord *"opened"* Lydia's heart there as she listened to Paul speak alongside the river. Back in town, Paul cast out a spirit of divination from a slave-girl; the slave owner was enraged; he and Silas were beaten and imprisoned; they sang songs at midnight; God sent an earthquake; the jailer became a convert and the Romans were terrified when they learned Paul was a Roman citizen – it was a memorable first visit.

Over ten years have elapsed, and community of believers in Philippi has grown and matured. We see this from Paul's first sentence,

"Paul and Timothy, bond-servants of Christ Jesus, to all the saints in Christ Jesus who are in Philippi, including the overseers and deacons: Grace to you and peace from God our Father and the Lord Jesus Christ." (Philippians 1:1-2).

At first glance, this may look like one of Paul's normal greetings. He always prays Grace and Peace on those he writes, but there are two specific things in the greeting to catch. First, Paul addresses those in Philippi as *"saints."* This was not his practice in his early letters. Rather, he addressed the *"called out,"* the *ekklesia*, the church, but from 1st Corinthians onward, he tended to address the *"holy ones,"* i.e., the *saints*. If we looked back at his greeting to the Roman community, we would see he was referring to the call of God. They were *"called to be saints."*

Paul's two most frequent ways of speaking about believers is to call them saints or brothers and sisters. That is, he calls them what they are called to be or who they are by reason of their adoption. I have been struck with our Normal Station friends; they call each other saints as a matter of course.

The Philippians had been called to be saints a long time back. In the meantime, elders and deacons had been appointed to serve the community. Paul addresses them in his salutation as well, and the Philippian salutation is the only one of Paul's letters to do so. Philippi by the time of Paul's writing is a mature community. Eventually, almost all communities will have these two helpful ministries.

We know from Paul's intimate letters to both Timothy and Titus that members of his traveling apostolic team normally appointed these ministerial positions in Paul's church plants. Paul had Timothy appoint elders and deacons in various churches under Paul's jurisdiction (1st Timothy 3:1-3) and also directed Titus to appoint elders (Titus 1:5) as well. All appointments occurred after seeking the will of the Spirit of God and prayer. Bottom line, Philippi was a mature church in many ways.

You can feel the love and affection Paul has for the Philippians in his opening sentences:

"For I am confident of this very thing, that He who began a good work in you will perfect it until the day of Christ Jesus. For it is only right for me to feel this way about you all, because I have you in my heart, since both in my imprisonment and in the defense and confirmation of the gospel, you all are partakers of grace with me. For God is my witness, how I long for you all with the affection of Christ Jesus." (Philippians 1:6-8).

This is a God thing. I love Paul's expression and his hope: *"He who began a good work in you will perfect it until the day of Christ Jesus."* It is something we hope for each other in a very real and specific way.

Paul's prayer for the Philippians also is noteworthy:

"I pray, that your love may abound still more and more in real knowledge and all discernment, so that you may approve the things that are

excellent," Think of that – Paul wants their love to be characterized by "real knowledge and discernment." This is another way of saying "wise." Wise love; it is worth considering that he means there can be unwise love amongst believers.

Paul then gives his friends in Philippi a sunny report on his imprisonment. He knows that the Philippians are walking God's path and enduring difficulty. It is the paradoxical lot of every Christian to exult in joy that comes from living a life of love and faithfulness to God while simultaneously suffering hardship. And Paul's assurance is that his imprisonment is bearing great fruit: *"Christ has become well known throughout the whole praetorian guard and to everyone else, and most of the brethren, trusting in the Lord because of* [his] *imprisonment, have far more courage to speak the word of God without fear."* (Philippians 1:13-14).

Unfortunately, some in Rome are talking about Jesus while bringing up accusations against Paul. I would expect Paul to have a negative view of these critics, but it is very interesting that he can rejoice in their accusations because he knows they must talk about Jesus even as they attack Paul, and for that he is delighted. That certainly is taking the broad view and is an interesting example for all of us struggling with denominational differences. Perhaps we should be rejoicing that Jesus is proclaimed even if the message is a bit distorted with regard to one practice or another!

Paul's earnest expectation and hope is that he would not waiver in any way as he nears his trial. He wants to boldly proclaim the Lord's saving grace even in the face of martyrdom. It is hard to grasp just how scary the thought of what might await him (and we know eventually does await him): an horrific, tortured death. He is not holding back from the Philippians his fears, but simultaneously sharing his hope that he will not waiver or flinch when the time comes.

"For to me, to live is Christ, and to die is gain." (Philippians 1:21). As we age in the Lord, this becomes clearer. I give it more and more thought as I age. Living in Christ in this world is such a privilege, and my affections run deep with much gratitude. But as my wife says, "There's a train a'comin," and we won't need any baggage. There is a clear tension between here and there. Frankly, right now, in reasonable health, I am not anxious to move on through the transition that must surely come. But the time is coming soon, and I hope I will not flinch or waiver, knowing that there is the most wondrous future ahead. Blessed in this life; blessed in the life to come. So often our hearts cry out, *"Come, Lord Jesus."* And He calls back, *"Come."*

The first chapter ends with a heartfelt plea that echoes his recent letter to the Ephesians: *"conduct yourselves in a manner worthy of the gospel of Christ, so that whether I come and see you or remain absent, I will hear of you that you are standing firm in one spirit, with one mind striving together for the faith of the gospel; in no way alarmed by your opponents—which is a sign of destruction for them, but of salvation for you, and that too, from God. For to you it has been granted for Christ's sake, not only to believe in Him, but also to suffer for His sake, experiencing the same conflict which you saw in me, and now hear to be in me."* (Philippians 1:27-30).

It is a special grace to be granted the opportunity to suffer for God's sake, and Paul knows the Philippians have been granted that special grace as well as he. There are two things Paul particularly hopes for the Philippians and hopes for us as well:

1. That they will **stand firm in the Spirit**. Think about Paul's last words to the Ephesians after telling them to put on the full armor of God: that they may stand firm. Firmly planted in the Spirit of God, unwavering, unflinching, even when attacked.

2. That they will **be one** – one mind and one spirit, in deep unity.

May it be so for all of us!

Philippians 2

Chapter 1 ended with Paul's prayer that the Philippians would stand firmly in the Spirit and be of one mind. Paul knew that one of the strongest defenses against the Enemy is our unity in God. As Chapter 2 is launched, Paul continues his plea. He wants them to be *"of the same mind, maintaining the same love, united in spirit, intent on one purpose."*

Perhaps this should be on church billboards:

> "Be of the Same Mind, Maintain the Same Love,
> Be United in Spirit, Intent on One Purpose!"

Goodness, this was so important to Paul. It is to me, and I hope to you, but it takes extreme diligence and understanding. One of the great helps is having a passion for unity and a willingness to forebear, but that to some degree only comes by grasping deeply that Unity is the very nature of God and the Godhead. Remember Paul's words in Chapter 1 of Ephesians:

"In all wisdom and insight, He made known to us the mystery of His will, according to His kind intention which He purposed in Him with a view to an administration suitable to the fullness of the times, that is, the summing up of all things in Christ, things in the heavens and things on the earth." (Ephesians 1:9).

How can one fail to honor God's deep intention to bring Unity to all things in Jesus and the extent to which He has gone to accomplish this?

On a practical level, this means a "closed mouth" regarding slighting comments concerning those who identify Jesus as Lord but have different histories and practices.

On a deeper level, it means admitting we individually have a serious need for deliverance from an underlying spirit of division. Division never arises because everyone is perfect. It always arises because everyone is NOT perfect, and we find ourselves getting stuck on that fact, taking offense, and simmering inside until a root of bitterness forms and by it many are defiled.

Unity can never be based on our perfection as humans. Our Unity cannot rest on us but only on the saving work of the Godhead - Father, Son and Spirit. So, confess it – we need an attitude overhaul!

In verse 1, Paul focuses on a huge help to overcoming the practical internal irritations we face in Christian relationships: our *fellowship in the Spirit, our affection and compassion.* It is extremely difficult to be divisive if you can understand and experience true fellowship in the Spirit. I remember the extraordinary healing effect toward Catholics that I experienced at the 1977 Charismatic Conference in Kansas City when I worshiped with 25,000 Catholic believers. Worshiping with them in that stadium was something I will never forget. It is entirely precious to me. Or my delight in coming along side and working with a Messianic Jew who has very different practices. Or being able to look back on my own personal denominational heritage and finally coming to appreciate the rich inheritance in the love of God's Word that I received. I have no stones to throw.

Verse 3 nails one of the key attitudes that helps maintain unity with people with whom we would otherwise be divided: *"with humility of mind regard one another as more important than yourselves."* This means consciously and willfully raising others to a higher stature in your mind than you held them previously - to a stature higher than you hold yourself! We are not necessarily called to think less highly of ourselves, but we must think more highly of them. This absolutely means we must "re-see" them in Jesus. If this wasn't the very heart of the Gospel, I wouldn't harp, but it is the heart of God, i.e., to bring all things together. It is God's nature.

Paul then writes one of the most important admonitions in the entire Bible:

"Have this attitude in yourselves which was also in Christ Jesus, who, although He existed in the form of God, did not regard equality with God a thing to be grasped, but emptied Himself (literally "laid aside His privileges"), taking the form of a bond-servant, and being made in the likeness of men. Being found in appearance as a man, He humbled Himself by becoming obedient to the point of death, even death on a cross." (Philippians 2:5-8).

If Jesus could humble Himself to become basically a slave in this life, under the physical domination of flesh, if he could give up His divine privileges and allow himself to be crucified, how can we not come down from our pinnacles? He does more than elevate us; he does in fact lower Himself.

Paul says that because Jesus was willing to take a much lower place, God has highly exalted Him. Remember that Jesus is not just God; He is also man - fully God and fully man at the same time.

I love this verse:

"God highly exalted Him and bestowed on Him the name which is above every name, so that at the name of Jesus every knee will bow, of those who are in heaven and on earth and under the earth, and that every tongue

will confess that Jesus Christ is Lord, to the glory of God the Father." (Philippians 2:9-11).

Jesus has already been exalted, and God has already bestowed on Him the name above every name, but there is coming a time when every knee will bow, both those in the heavens, on earth and under the earth, and confess that Jesus is Lord! It is worth pausing to see if you can catch a visual image of this. Three tiers: heaven, earth and under the earth with everyone kneeling. It is so interesting to me that I have not yet been able to find an historical painting of this key vision. There are literally hundreds of thousands of paintings of the resurrected Jesus on the Day of Judgment, but none that I have seen portray the vision in accordance with what Paul saw.

Verses 12 and 13 are important:

"Work out your salvation with fear and trembling; for it is God who is at work in you, both to will and to work for His good pleasure." (Philippians 2:12-13). This is a comforting verse because it affirms that God is always at work with us. Remember Paul's reminder to the Romans, *"And we know that all things work together for good to them that love God, to them who are the called according to* [His] *purpose."* (Romans 8:28). But why the *"fear and trembling?"* Because God is the one doing the work, and we are talking about the sovereign God, creator God, all-powerful God, and it is He who is doing the work. Oh my, no wonder there was fear and trembling. I suspect we simply don't realize with whom we have gotten involved.

Do you remember what Lucy said in C.S. Lewis's *The Lion, Witch, and the Wardrobe* when she encountered the great lion, Aslan, for the first time? She asked, *"Is He safe?"* And the answer, of course, is, *"No, He's not safe, but He's good!"* The God of the Universe is not safe, but, blessing upon blessing, He *IS* good.

Grumbling is what little children do. They have little hesitation. If they are not happy with something, they grumble. Paul knows adult believers too well; they also grumble, and it is a sign that they are still growing up into the Lord. It is the exact opposite of what Paul has already brought to mind – how Jesus behaved. So, get rid of the grumbling; Paul's picture is that God's children don't grumble. If you find yourself grumbling, ask God for an attitude adjustment. It is not just infantile and obnoxious; it is hurtful because it affects other "saints."

Frankly, the end of Chapter 2 saddens me. Paul has been hard at work for Jesus for several decades. He has suffered innumerable hardships, beatings, imprisonment, attacks, betrayals and slurs. He has, as he says, poured out his life as a drink offering before God for the sake of so many churches. Yet, as he writes from Rome, he openly confesses that he has *"no one else of kindred spirit who will genuinely be concerned"* for their welfare other than Timothy.

On the one hand, you would think men like Timothy would think twice about giving themselves to a life of hardship and suffering, yet God draws men and women by His supernatural Love, and they do give their lives to Him. We know from the numerous churches that Paul founded and the many individuals mentioned in his letters that God used him mightily. But, with the exclusion of Timothy, he seems very much alone as he writes this section.

Obviously, he has been well graced by Epaphroditus who was sent to Rome to bring Paul a love offering and to inquire about Paul's welfare. Either as he arrived or once in Rome, Epaphroditus had become seriously ill and barely survived. But Epaphroditus was not the kind of kindred spirit that Timothy was. Timothy had been with Paul for at least twelve years and suffered many of the same trials Paul had undergone. He started as a young disciple; he ended a mature worker in the Lord's vineyard. And Paul was about to send him with Epaphroditus to Philippi. Paul is sitting there in Rome a prisoner and feeling quite alone. It is just sad. Whether Timothy was able to leave immediately with Epaphroditus we do not know, but we do know Paul hoped to send him as soon as possible.

Paul ends with an encouragement to the Philippians to:

"Receive him [Epaphroditus] *then in the Lord with all joy, and hold men like him in high regard; because he came close to death for the work of Christ, risking his life to complete what was deficient in your service to me."* (Philippians 2:29-30).

Obviously, men and women like Epaphroditus that are on the front lines need to be incredibly well received. In a real way, they are risking their lives, particularly in a foreign country.

At first look, you may find the end of verse 30 perplexing. The Philippians had just sent Paul a love offering of some type and did so by sending it with Epaphroditus. One could read the last clause as a judgment against the Philippians for not having done more *("what was deficient in your service to me")*. I think it simply means that all of them were unable to come to him, and Epaphroditus supplied what they could not do themselves.

We are blessed to have representatives of our community go forth to represent our hands and our hearts. They face innumerable hardships in our stead, and certainly should be bettered honored and appreciated. Unfortunately, we take their efforts casually, and show little honor where honor is due. I suspect Paul was a bit worried about a casual reception of Epaphroditus when he returned to Philippi. I have been so impressed with the believers in Uganda. They sacrificially send off and welcome back those who go out from them with great fanfare. They are worth emulating.

Philippians 3

Sometimes I wonder why recent translators continue to use archaic religious words to describe something simple. An example is my beloved New American Standard Bible's translation of the underlying Greek word as *"brethren"* in the opening sentence.

I would not have paid much attention to the word *"brethren"* had it not been for reading my French version. In French, Paul says, *"mes frères,"* which immediately spoke to me that Paul was addressing the Philippians with a term of endearment. *"Brethren"* seems so much more detached. Often we gloss over words and don't catch their deeper meaning.

"Finally, my brothers, rejoice in the Lord." Paul's closing admonition is a true summation. Just rejoicing in the Lord does so much for us. For joy to come, three things are necessary. We have to know who God really is. We have to know who we really are. And, we have to respond.

I have good news: rejoicing is predominantly a matter of the will. If we can be told to rejoice, it means we are capable of willing a shift in our internal attitude coupled with a shift in our thinking. We can be in the midst of hardship, our emotions can be on the bottom, and we can choose to rejoice rather than despair.

What comes to your mind when Paul says *"To write the same things again is no trouble to me, and it is a safeguard for you?"* He is repeating himself for emphasis. Perhaps you will recall the lyric, *"Rejoice in the Lord always; again, I say rejoice!"* That lyric is from Chapter 4 of Philippians. If you do a quick scan of all four chapters, you will note that Paul mentions rejoicing in each chapter. Paul is in prison - rejoicing. We can rejoice anywhere.

Paul gives a short religious autobiography of his prior fleshly status in Chapter 3 to underscore what he gave up to follow Christ. All relate to identity and status. He emphasizes that he of all people had every reason to hold on to the value of the Jewish Law because of his exemplary status. If anyone had reason for confidence in the flesh, it was Paul. He brought a lot to the table. But it was nothing in comparison to what he received when he entered into the New Covenant cut in the blood of Jesus.

Paul counts all his status in the "flesh" as nothing, i.e., of no value whatsoever, when compared with the value of knowing the risen Lord, and he brings this point across with force by using a nasty word: *"I have suffered the loss of all things, and count them but rubbish so that I may gain Christ, and may be found in Him."* (Philippians 3:8-9). To make clear, Paul uses the Greek word *skybalon* to describe how he views all of his accomplishments in the flesh. This word, translated *"rubbish"* in the NASB, means animal excrement.... The only picture that comes to mind is how I feel when I have stepped in dog poo. Suffice it to say, when compared to the glories when one's status comes from the Son of God, everything else is dog poo.

Being connected to the Godhead through Jesus Christ is beyond comparison – not only in connection to Jesus's resurrection power but also in the fellowship of knowing His sufferings. Paul knows a lot about the latter. And he clearly rejoices in his hardships because he sees them as conforming him to Jesus's crucifixion so that Paul might attain to the resurrection from the dead as well.

It is worth saying this another way. Knowing hardship of any form draws us closer to the cross, which in turn draws us closer to experiencing death, which in turn draws us closer to our final resurrection! In a true sense, this too is the Gospel message, the kernel, but one not often proclaimed.

When my wife was preparing for her hip replacement, she had an early appointment to give a blood sample. Fran HATES giving blood samples. She turned her key in the ignition and had no power. I had to come home from the office to jump the battery. No success. Pressure was building. I drove her to the doctor's office. The doctor's practitioner made three valiant but unsuccessful attempts to draw a blood sample. No success. Pressure was building. She had to go to another office to get a lung X-ray. Then to the hospital to have another practitioner make an attempt for blood.

At this point, Fran was emotionally frazzled, but Jesus and Job came to her mind, and she realized how insignificant her morning difficulties had been. She thought of Jesus on the cross. She was being conformed in a small measure into His death. A slow rejoicing was able to emerge. This makes me take heart!

I love Paul's conclusion to this whole line of thought:

"Not that I have already obtained it or have already become perfect, but I press on so that I may lay hold of that for which also I was laid hold of by Christ Jesus. My brothers, I do not regard myself as having laid hold of it yet; but one thing I do: forgetting what lies behind and reaching forward to what lies ahead, I press on toward the goal for the prize of the upward call of God in Christ Jesus." (Philippians 3:12-14). Oh, I love this verse! Yes!

This is a clear expression of the attitude we hope to have within us. Let's imitate Paul. Let's forget about what is in the past, what lies behind, and *"reach forward to what lies ahead."* Let's press on to the goal. Let's head for the prize that awaits us as we respond to the call of God in Christ Jesus. I remember the sweet refrain of my boyhood, *"Jesus is tenderly calling you home, calling today, calling today."* The call of God in Christ Jesus.

"Jesus is calling the weary to rest—
Calling today, calling today,
Bring Him your burden and you shall be blest;
He will not turn you away.

"Calling today, calling today,
Jesus is calling, is tenderly calling today."
By Fannie Crosby

"Our citizenship is in heaven, from which also we eagerly wait for a Savior, the Lord Jesus Christ; who will transform the body of our humble state into conformity with the body of His glory, by the exertion of the power that He has even to subject all things to Himself." (Philippians 3:20-21).

For those getting old in the tooth, Paul gives a glimpse here of the new body we will have in the resurrection: a body transformed into conformity with the Body of His Glory. Wow. Come, Lord, Jesus!

Philippians 4

What a delightful letter Paul has written! Imprisoned, facing possible execution, Paul spends most of the letter rejoicing. Philippians is the rejoicing letter for those in dire straits. *"Rejoice in the Lord always,"* And he says it twice: *"Rejoice!"*

And, like the Ephesians and the Corinthians, he wants the Philippians to *"stand firm."* Paul expressed the same thing in Chapter 1. He wants them to stand firm in one spirit. So, rejoice, stand firm, be of one mind, be like Jesus – Paul's message to the Philippians as well as us.

Paul often finishes his letters with a bit of housekeeping before he signs off, and he does a modest amount of this at the start of the chapter. Two important women in the church apparently are not thriving relationally. Paul directs them to be in harmony like the strings of an instrument. Different strings, but a harmonious melody should come when the Lord plays them. We then see that Euodia and Syntyche are doing some kind of ministry because Paul urges that they be supported in some way along with Clement and his other *"fellow workers."*

Speaking about Euodia and Syntyche, Paul uses terms he had applied previously to Timothy and Epaphroditus. When Paul writes that Euodia and Syntyche had worked together with him *"in the Gospel."* Earlier in his letter, Paul described Timothy as someone who had served with him *"in the Gospel."* (Philippians 2:22). Furthermore, He refers to Euodia and Syntyche as his *"co-workers."* Earlier, Paul had referred to Epaphroditus as his *"co-worker."* (Philippians 2:25). These ladies appear to be part of his apostolic team or at least deployed directly in ministry, and thus eligible and worthy of support. Their position in the text also reveals that when Paul uses the term *"brothers"* or *"Brethren,"* he includes both sexes.

This bit of housekeeping tells me three things, none of which are surprising. First, the ministry of women is key. Second, when there is disagreement amongst leaders, it needs to get resolved quickly and thoroughly. Third, Paul does not take sides; he leaves the two ladies the responsibility of coming into *"harmony."*

Then we have two of the most memorable texts Paul ever wrote and certainly among the most useful.

"Rejoice in the Lord always; again I will say, rejoice! Let your gentle spirit be known to all men. The Lord is near. Be anxious for nothing, but in everything by prayer and supplication with thanksgiving let your requests be made known to God. And the peace of God, which surpasses all comprehension, will guard your hearts and your minds in Christ Jesus." (Philippians 4:4-7).

Rejoice all the time! Be anxious for nothing, but *in everything*, by prayer and supplication *with thanksgiving* let your requests be known… and the *peace* of God… *will guard your hearts and minds* in Christ Jesus. This is a GREAT promise!

The next paragraph is just as terrific, practical and - when employed in our thinking, will assure that the great God of all Peace will be with us:

"Finally, brothers, whatever is true, whatever is honorable, whatever is right, whatever is pure, whatever is lovely, whatever is of good repute, if there is any excellence and if anything worthy of praise, dwell on these things. The things you have learned and received and heard and seen in me, practice these things, and the God of peace will be with you." (Philippians 4:8-9).

For me, this is one of the most practical and helpful verses in the whole Bible because it addresses both my heart and my mind – my innermost being as well as how I think. It is *SO* easy and so dangerous to dwell on the news of the day (which almost always is bad) or on what is wrong in every situation. There is always something wrong if you are looking for it. Do you see how counter-productive this is? Instead, Paul calls us (and we need to seriously listen) to focus on what is lovely, what is honorable, what is true, what is pure, those things about which people are giving a good report – those things worthy of praise. What a game changer for your mind. But obedience and discipline are required.

I woke this morning thinking about this verse, and mulling over where my mind normally goes. For people like me that tend toward perfectionism, the challenge can be daunting. But I truly want to major in being a Blessing Detective instead of a Fault Detective.

Robert McGee years ago wrote a book called *"Search for Significance."* His book identified thought tendencies that plague people. One obsession was playing what he called the Blame Game. You are looking for people to blame so you don't have to blame yourself. And you will find plenty! Or your default is the reverse: you spot every reason to believe YOU are to blame, i.e., you are a failure and there is plenty of proof laying about to prove that is the case. Both of these thought patterns are highly toxic to a Godly life. Better to be a Blessing Detective than a Fault Detective!

Paul ends with the recognition that our giving sends up a sweet aroma to God and then shares a tidbit about how the Gospel is spreading in Rome – it even has entered Caesar's household!

Like Paul, I end our excursion into Philippi with this prayer: *"May the grace of the Lord Jesus, the Anointed One of God, be with your spirit! Amen!"*

Colossians

Colossians 1

As we begin Paul's letter to the Colossians, let's step back and look at where Paul and his brother apostles are. Jesus has been gone from the earthly realm in a physical sense for almost thirty years. It is about 61 or 62 AD. Paul is imprisoned in Rome and has just written a letter to the Ephesians and the broader *Ekklesia*. He has been working nearly three decades delivering the message that Jesus was sent from God to radically change mankind.

The change Paul proclaims requires that his message be received, believed and incorporated into life. Otherwise, transformation will not occur. God Himself, in the form and presence of His Holy Spirit and the Spirit of Jesus, must come and dwell in your heart. We know the Gospel message was not a "get rich" message. Instead, it presented a life that included persecution and suffering for those that entered into Jesus's reality.

Paul is writing to a town he perhaps never visited, addressing men and women who may have received that message from someone else and responded positively to it.

Paul, a Jew, had gone forth nearly thirty years earlier into the sea of mankind with a message he had not received in person – sent to an earthly population at the time estimated to exceed 150 MILLION people - a people who did not like Jews. He was from a very unpopular ethnic group sent to everyone who was not Jewish. So, it is really hard to imagine exactly how Paul thought about the impossible task before him, much less the chance of impacting mankind in any material way.

That brings me square to the first verse of his letter: *"Paul, an apostle of Jesus Christ by the will of God, and Timothy our brother."* We can trace a great deal of Paul's faithfulness to the mission to the fact that he was a true apostle of Jesus. *"Apostolos"* is the Greek word we translate into *"apostle,"* and it is a partial key to understanding Paul's remarkable follow-through. Remember that in Greek, it means, *"one sent forth with orders."* We have to go back to Paul's amazing encounter with the risen Lord in Acts 9. Paul's mission is summed up in the vision that Ananias received. You will recall that Ananias ended up baptizing Paul. In the vision, Jesus told Ananias that Paul was *"a chosen vessel unto me, to bear my name before the Gentiles, and kings, and the children of Israel."*

To bear Jesus's name before the Gentiles, Kings and the Children of Israel! That's it – that was Paul's job description from that day forward - and Paul was faithful to that concise mission no matter what. It did not matter how much he was persecuted, rejected, or beaten. It did not matter how far he had to travel, and it did not matter how many received the message he carried. He was called to do one thing, and he did it. As it turns out, there are now over 2 BILLION people who have heard the message of Jesus's saving grace and have actually responded to it.

What an encouragement to simply trust the call of God on one's life and be faithful to it.

At a human level, the task was absolutely impossible. The success that came from Paul's efforts couldn't be because the message was easy to receive mentally. It was not. A crucified Jew, now God, and guess what, persecution and suffering await His followers. Yet men and women not only followed; many gave their very lives for the message of Jesus. Only the amazing drawing power of God's Spirit possibly could have achieved the results that we see. All Paul did was to be faithful to *his* call. The rest was up to God, and God delivered.

Apostolos is Paul's descriptor to every church that he wrote. It was his job assignment, and it was, along with others, a unique call. His wonderful assistant, Timothy, did not wear it in the way that Paul wore it. Timothy was PAUL's *apostolos*, i.e., the one Paul sent out. But Jesus had directly commissioned Paul, and Paul knew the difference and tried all his life to be faithful to it.

Paul is writing to believers in Colossae, a relatively small town in Asia Minor (now Turkey) in the region of Phrygia. It always is worth looking thoughtfully at Colossae's location.

From this blowup we can make several important observations. First, Paul was very near to Colossae on several of his journeys, but apparently didn't begin a church in it. You will recognize Antioch in Pisidia to the northeast and Laodicea about six miles to the west. Colossae lies near the River Lycus that runs westward over toward Ephesus and Miletus. We remember that Paul taught and labored in Ephesus for over two years. Many important centers for early Christianity in the next century are close - including all of the famous seven churches of the Book of Revelation: Ephesus, Smyrna, Pergamum, Thyatira, Sardis, Philadelphia and Laodicea.

None of these church communities could have existed much longer than fifteen years! Paul's first excursion into Asia Minor dates from around 47 AD and it is approximately 61 AD as he writes to the Colossians. Perhaps 14 years have passed since his first journey. But his stay in Ephesus was around 52-55 AD, and it is most likely that he met Epaphras there during his sojourn. We see in verse 7 that it was Epaphras who first shared the gospel in Colossae. So, with the Ephesus dating, the church that Paul writes is likely only ten years old from its initial formation. It is a YOUNG Christian community.

My take is that Epaphras must have done his job very well, because we see little of the problems that plagued the Corinthians. As Paul writes, Epaphras is actually imprisoned with him in Rome, so Paul is using a particularly accurate adjective when he calls Epaphras, a *"beloved fellow bond-servant."* Perhaps Epaphras shared with Paul some of the specific issues that the Colossians were facing in terms of dangerous teaching. Note that Paul addresses what appears to be a slightly different problem in Colossae than he addressed elsewhere.

Paul has been praying for them specifically, even though he had not ever visited them. I am reminded that often the Spirit of God will put brothers on sisters on our heart that we have never met.

Paul's prayer for the Colossians is not dissimilar to the one he prayed for the Ephesians. He prays they will:

- Be filled with the knowledge of God's will (what God wants).
- Walk in a manner worthy of the Lord.
- Please Jesus in all respects.
- Bear fruit in every good work.
- Increase in the knowledge of God (who God is).
- Be steadfast, patient, joyful, and thankful to the Father.

When we basically get to a list of important things, it is well to list them, review them, and ponder how we each line up with God's desire for us. Paul has a good prayer list. And note Paul's deep understanding that it is the heart of the Father that caused Him to rescue us from the domain of darkness and transfer us into the Kingdom of His beloved Son. I frequently notice how amazingly balanced Paul's understanding is of the varying roles in the Godhead.

In verse fifteen, Paul launches into one of those grand flights of acclamation about the Son of God, as Paul's passion and understanding meet. This helps us better appreciate who Jesus truly is:

"He is the image of the invisible God, the firstborn of all creation. For by Him all things were created, both in the heavens and on earth, visible and invisible, whether thrones or dominions or rulers or authorities— all things have been created through Him and for Him. He is before all things, and in Him all things hold together. He is also head of the body, the church; and He is the beginning, the firstborn from the dead, so that He Himself will come to have first place in everything. For it was the Father's good pleasure for all the fullness to dwell in Him, and through Him to reconcile all things to Himself, having made peace through the blood of His cross; through Him, I say, whether things on earth or things in heaven." (Colossians 1:15-20).

This reminds me so much of the Apostle John's opening discourse in the Gospel of John. These verses are not casual. They are carefully constructed, and part of the reason for their importance is that they refute various misconceptions with which the Colossians were struggling. Colossae was a New Age community if there was one in Asia Minor - though the issue ran through the entire known world. They were focused on angels, their nature and their being. Could it be that Jesus was an angel of some type? Who exactly was this Jesus? Paul answers these questions clearly in verses 15-20. These verses are almost a creedal statement, and they affected future creedal statements ever since they were pinned. It is a treat to read these verses several times.

"He is the image of the invisible God, the firstborn of all creation. For by Him all things were created, both in the heavens and on earth, visible and invisible, whether thrones or dominions or rulers or authorities— all things have been created through Him and for Him. He is before all things, and in Him all things hold together. He is also head of the body, the church; and He is the beginning, the firstborn from the dead, so that He Himself will come to have first place in everything. For it was the Father's good pleasure for all the fullness to dwell in Him, and through Him to reconcile all things to Himself, having made peace through the blood of His cross; through Him, I say, whether things on earth or things in heaven." (Colossians 1:15-20).

Paul ends Chapter 1 with a reflection on his participation with Jesus's sufferings and his call as a minister. What drove Paul to endure hardship and suffering? *"I was made a minister according to the stewardship from God bestowed on me for your benefit, so that I might fully carry out the preaching of the word of God...."* (Colossians 1:25) *"Fully carry out the preaching of the word of God!"* is God's order to Paul, *his* assignment. Can we fully carry out what God has entrusted us individually to do? It is worth pondering.

"Christ in you, the hope of Glory." (Colossians 1:27). This is another facet of the mystery Paul unveiled in his earlier letter to the Ephesians (which Paul probably wrote a few months earlier). There, the mystery was the Father drawing all things together in Jesus. This is the other side of the coin. It is Christ in us that allows us to be drawn together in Him.

I love the last two sentences: *"We proclaim Him, admonishing every man and teaching every man with all wisdom, so that we may present every man complete in Christ. For this purpose also I labor, striving according to His power, which mightily works within me."* (Colossians 1:28-29). Paul strives according to God's power and not his own. Let's do the same!

Colossians 2

Paul continues to address facets of the great mystery of God as Chapter 2 opens. The knowledge of the mystery is actually revealed in the Father and the Anointed One. All the treasures of wisdom and knowledge are hidden in them and personified in Jesus Himself. If we truly understand Jesus, the gift from Father out of the Father's love, we, once far off, are brought close. Through a focus on Jesus, we see the amazing nature of the Godhead. By knowing the Father and the Son as fully as possible, we are protected from getting off track by the delusions that the forces of evil deploy.

This is an extremely practical admonition. Instead of focusing on lesser issues (and I can think of a great many), we let our attention and focus squarely on seeing God and His Son more clearly – learning who God really is throughout the entirety of our earthly life.

When I was growing up, my focus was on an amazing number of lesser issues. Perhaps you will remember some of your own.

In our house, we were focused on the exact way that many religious actions were to occur - for example, how we took communion and the exact mode of baptism, how we worshipped, what clothes we wore and didn't wear, and so forth. What should our buildings look like; how could we possibly marry anyone who wore a denominational name.

It is not that such questions could not be asked, but our gaze was so far below the heavenly nature of God that life was only about getting a long series of getting less important questions right – regardless of our thoughts about God's radical nature. Certainly, I picked up some important things about God – He did love us, He did give His son for us, but the meaty things of His very nature that were hidden from my attention by an emphasis on lesser things.

Paul, instead, was focused like a laser on the Big Picture – the full knowledge of who God is and how God's nature moves all of His actions. Paul will call the Colossians to this focus just as he did the other churches. Peter will do the same in his late letters.

Paul wants to fortify the Colossians, assuring them of the truth about who God is. He doesn't want anyone to take them *"captive through philosophy and empty deception, according to the tradition of men, according to the elementary principles of the world, rather than according to Christ."* (Colossians 2:8). He had started his acclamation of truth about God in verse 15 of the preceding chapter, and now he picks up his theme again beginning in verse 9 of Chapter 2:

"For in Him all the fullness of Deity dwells in bodily form, and in Him you have been made complete, and He is the head over all rule and authority; and in Him you were also circumcised with a circumcision made without hands, in the removal of the body of the flesh by the circumcision of Christ; having been buried with Him in baptism, in which you were also raised up with Him through faith in the working of God, who raised

Him from the dead. When you were dead in your transgressions and the uncircumcision of your flesh, He made you alive together with Him, having forgiven us all our transgressions, having canceled out the certificate of debt consisting of decrees against us, which was hostile to us; and He has taken it out of the way, having nailed it to the cross. When He had disarmed the rulers and authorities, He made a public display of them, having triumphed over them through Him." (Colossians 2:9-15).

What do we learn here? Nine major facts related to how God has moved:

- The fullness of God dwells in Jesus's flesh.
- In Jesus we are made complete.
- Jesus is head over all rule and authority, period.
- Jesus is our circumcision, i.e., our sign of the New Covenant [Cutting].
- We have been buried with Him through the act of baptism.
- We have been raised with him through our faith in the working of God.
- We were dead in our transgressions and our distance from the original covenant; now we are made alive in Him.
- Our transgressions and our debts have been forgiven, canceled by the payment of His life.
- The certificate that affirms our debts has been paid and is nailed to the cross.

This, too, is the Gospel message, and many of these points clarified and worked their way into creedal statements over the centuries.

Given these nine realties, Paul asserts that no one should judge any of the Colossians (or us) over food, drink, the days we honor or don't honor – things that are shadows of true reality. The truest reality is simply Jesus Himself. We know some of the accusations are from the Judaizers, but some are undoubtedly from the hands of the Gentiles wrapped up in the worship of angelic beings.

When we come to verse 18, we come straight to a verse that deals with trouble emanating from Christian communities, but even more so from activity on the airwaves. A man can take *"his stand on visions he has seen, inflated without cause by his fleshly mind, and not holding fast to the head, from whom the entire body, being supplied and held together by the joints and ligaments, grows with a growth which is from God."* (Colossians 2:18-19).

This describes accurately believers who are puffed up with pride because of some spiritual encounter, dream or vision. They are sure that what they think God told them gives them authority to no matter what witness the rest of the Body gives to the revelation. It is sad to recognize that we still face this Enemy tactic. Like the early church in Colossae, we are not immune to Satan's tricks. The problem is an unwillingness to *"hold fast to the Head, from whom the entire Body being supplied and held together by the joints and ligaments, grows with a growth is from God."*

We ran into similar language in Ephesians 4:14-16: *"As a result, we are no longer to be children, tossed here and there by waves and carried about by every wind of doctrine, by the trickery of men, by craftiness in deceitful scheming; but speaking the truth in love, we are to grow up in all aspects into Him who is the head, even Christ, from whom the whole body, being fitted and held together by what every joint supplies, according to the proper working of each individual part, causes the growth of the body for the building up of itself in love."*

The description here is of a Body where every joint supplies what the Body needs to be healthy. The bones (members) are held together by the ligaments (Steadfast Love) and directed by the Head (Jesus through the Spirit), and when the members truly are submissive to the various ministries in the Body, the Body is protected as well as the individual member.

This is Normal Christian Life in the Church, but we find thousands going the line of individual revelation no matter what the Body thinks. Out of touch with the Body – even rejecting the Body. No longer truly a part, they have little to no protection from such deceit.

My final take-away from Paul's closing word is that when we are dealing with *"fleshly indulgence,"* self-abasement and severe treatment of the body will not help one be delivered. It is the Church working together in the Spirit, with true confession, prayer, fasting and repentance that will have the most effect. That is another way of saying that it is only by the grace of God and not by human effort that the flesh successfully can be disciplined.

Colossians 3

Since self-abasement and severe treatment of the body will not help deliver us from *"fleshly indulgence,"* Paul begins Chapter 3 by admonishing the Colossians to stay on track by *"seeking the things above, where Christ is, seated at the right hand of God."* (Colossians 3:1).

Over the long race of life, it is the direction that we are going that is one of the key determinants of where we finish. My brother, Terry Smith, continually reminds me that the direction we are going is key.

We can stumble, fall, slow down, but if the direction is right, hopefully, we stay on track. Of course, the Enemy tries to get us to take our eyes off the goal and wander. But Paul's admonition is to keep our direction solidly toward God.

If we set our mind on heavenly realities day by day – if we set our focus on the wonder of the Godhead and our position in it, we will keep our direction straight.

I learned an interesting thing about toasting from our friends, Don and Karen Young. Most people in the United States, if about to clink glasses with the person across the table, keep their eyes on the glasses. But Europeans keep their eyes on the eyes of the person across from them. This means they may "clink" a bit off, but their gaze is where is should be, that is, on the person whom they wish well. Americans lose sight of the relationship in this sign of fellowship.

We need to keep our eyes on the One who birthed us, saved us and calls us.

The other spiritual reality is that *"we have died, and our life is hidden in Christ in God."* (Colossians 3:3). Our true spiritual home is heaven, and we are headed home. As an old man reflecting on this truth, I like it. I like the sound of it; I like the truth of it. We are in a sense simply heading home. Whether you are thirty or sixty, you are headed home. And we don't want to get off track.

If we are, in truth, dead to our old life force and alive in Jesus, we must reckon that the *"members of our earthly bodies are dead"* to a great number of bad things. (See Colossians 3:5-9). Paul lists eleven:

- Immorality
- Impurity
- Passion
- Evil Desire
- Greed
- Anger
- Wrath
- Malice
- Slander
- Abusive Speech
- Lies

Let's look at these, think about ourselves, and see those that we need to confess and *"put off."* Again, Paul is using the language of clothing: taking off and putting on.

How many of these could involve sexual sin? I would suggest four. How many do you count?

How many of these involve our tongues – what we say to others? I would suggest six. How many would you say?

How many of these involve anger in one form or another? I would suggest five. What do you think?

How many involve our desires? I would suggest five. How many would you say?

Sexual sin, what comes out of our mouths, anger and what we desire are four broad categories to consider. Let us soberly look at our situation, confess our issues, and "take off the improper clothing."

If we look back at Chapters 4 & 5 of Paul's Ephesians letter, he addresses most of the same issues in different language. His approach to the Colossians is also similar to his message in Chapter 5 of Galatians - but with a few differences. There, Paul includes idolatry, witchcraft, hatred, discord, jealousy, dissensions, factions, and drunkenness. One conclusion from looking at Paul's various lists is that Paul hits the key issues in each community. The key issues appear to differ depending on the locale. Obviously, the Galatians had trouble being of the same mind. Paul's 2nd Corinthians' 12th Chapter contains another list of wrong behaviors as well as 1st Corinthians, Chapter 6.

It may be useful for you to list Paul's categories from six of his letters to compare them. Look not only at specifics but also at the broad groups that most afflict our individual walks. Underneath such behaviors lies the Core Wound that Terry so vigorously tries to identify. Below that is the Core Lie that Satan employs to bring us darkness and destruction.

Colossians 4

There is one sentence at the start of Chapter 4 that concludes Paul's admonitions to people in various positions of submission or authority, a thought he began in Chapter 3. It is interesting to think how the original scrolls got divided up into these chapters. Often, chapters were broken along clear thought lines where possible. If that were the case, the sentence on Masters at the beginning of Chapter 4 would have been the last sentence of Chapter 3. Masters are to treat their slaves with justice and fairness. Remember, chapter divisions are not divine….

As is his norm, the end of one of Paul's letters is a "summing up." Two paragraphs on key behavior follow. He wants the Colossians to *"devote themselves to prayer, keeping alert in it with an attitude of thanksgiving."* (Colossians 4:2).

He doesn't mean pray occasionally or at random. When you devote yourself to something (think of a nurse with a sick child) you are on point – alert, on duty. The Greek word in verse 2, *proskartereō*, means to be *"steadfastly attentive,"* to give unremitting care to a thing or a person. So, we are called to give continuous and unremitting care to prayer. Over ten years earlier, Paul wrote the Thessalonians a very similar admonition: *"pray without ceasing, giving thanks in all circumstances."* (1 Thessalonians 5:17-18).

Think about it. Prayer is meant to be the behavioral foundation of our thought life and clothed in thanksgiving. We are not to use our prayer time just for our own comfort, our needs, our opportunities and obstacles. Think of the Lord's Prayer stretched out over a day as we focus on the God of the Universe. Think of our Father and His glory - His Will coupled with our immediate needs, our continuous need for forgiveness and our need to continually forbear with one another, our sharp cries for deliverance from Satanic schemes as they arise during each day. Think of entreaties for others far off. We want to be walking so tightly with God in the Spirit that we have a running conversation with God in our minds. Be alert. Learn to pray continuously.

Verse 6 calls to mind the amazing kind of speech that Christians are to deploy with unbelievers and strangers: "steadfast love" speech. *"Let your speech always be with grace, **as though seasoned with salt**, so that you will know how you should respond to each person."* (a culinary observation from Colossians 4:6)! Salt is a sign of faithfulness. We remember Jesus's teaching about salt recorded in the Sermon on the Mount:

"You are the salt of the earth, but if the salt has lost its flavor, with what will it be salted? It is then good for nothing, but to be cast out and trodden under the feet of men." (Matthew 5: 13).

Salt in ancient times as well as today was used to keep livestock healthy. Perhaps the blocks of salt from the Dead Sea were used, cut into cubes and placed in pens. The chemical attributes of salt caused it to stick together and not dissolve quickly under the onslaught of the elements. It was sticky - it stuck together. This is one of the best pictures for relational faithfulness (think *Chesed*). It has always inspired me.

Paul's admonishes us to let our speech be seasoned with *Chesed*, with faithfulness and steadfast love even when dealing with unbelievers. Practically, this means we never lie nor speak harshly, always evidencing the humility of Christ in our dealings - with airline agents, shopkeepers, business associates and anyone else with whom we come into contact.

Turning to his farewell, Paul mentions a good number of yoke-fellows. Onesimus, the slave who ran away from Philemon, will return to them accompanied by Tychicus, an important fellow worker of Paul's. We suspect they were to carry with them not only Paul's letter to the Colossians but also his letter to Philemon.

Others with Paul in Rome sends their greetings. Some are prisoners along with Paul - perhaps converts not unlike the results of Paul's ministry to other prisoners. Only two are Jews. We learn that Mark, the cousin of Barnabas, is in Rome as well as Epaphras. Paul had mentioned Epaphras earlier. It was he who probably founded the church in Colossae and exhibited such a devotion to them as well as those in Laodicea who were only six miles away. Luke also sent his greetings.

Paul asks the church in Colossae to share his letter with those in Laodicea, and this confirms what we have come to know, i.e., Paul's letters would be circulated to other churches, read orally and eventually be bound with other letters and hand copied to become part of our "New Testament."

Paul asks the church to greet *"Nympha and the church that is in her house."* (Colossians 4:15). I love those words. Churches in our houses. Yes! Come, Lord Jesus!

1st Thessalonians

1st Thessalonians 1

There are multiple reasons I am excited to arrive at Paul's letters to the Thessalonians. These two letters are amongst the earliest of our New Testament, written only a few months after Paul left Thessalonica while on his Second Missionary Journey. They are *very* early letters, perhaps the earliest in our Bible.

The other reason for my enthusiasm is that my friend, mentor and professor, Abraham (Abe) Malherbe, wrote his great 500 page treatise on these two letters while serving as the Buckingham Professor Emeritus of New Testament Criticism and Interpretation at Yale University. I found Abe entirely trustworthy. He served me well, and I am excited to journey afresh with him through Paul's writings.

We remember that Paul was sent into Macedonia by a vision from the Holy Spirit, and initially established a church in Philippi after a sojourn of several months. He ended up getting thrown in prison but was quickly released. Leaving Luke in Philippi, he walked with Silas and possibly Timothy a hundred miles westward along the Egnatian Way to Thessalonica. They may have been in route to Rome but were soon to learn that the emperor Claudius had expelled all Jews from Rome. This news may have shifted Paul's focus over to Athens and Corinth.

It was probably in the summer of 49 AD that Paul arrived in Thessalonica. He stayed there two or three months and then fled for Berea. Jews from Thessalonica soon arrived behind him stirring up trouble, and Paul made his way to Athens and then Corinth. Abe believed that Paul wrote his first letter from Corinth approximately four months after departing Thessalonica, which would place his first letter at the beginning of 50 AD. Paul had been a follower of Christ at that point approximately 16 years and was in his mid 40s.

Everything Paul writes takes on a special character because this is likely Paul's first extant letter, and even his terminology deserves careful attention. His salutation is to the *"called out,"* the *ekklesia*, the church of the Thessalonians, those who are *"in God the Father and the Lord Jesus Christ."* Paul's other early letters (Galatians and Corinthians) also address the *"ekklesia."* But after 2nd Corinthians, he shifts to more frequently addressing the *"saints"* in the places he writes instead of those *"called out."*

The subtle shift in salutation spotlights Paul's increasing awareness that even though he is often addressing squabbling, fractious Christians, his key ministry focus has turned to fighting the accusation that men and women are not made holy by the work of Christ but rather by the work of men (circumcision, the Law, etc.). That observation makes sense to me.

Further, Paul's entire letter takes on a special character since he has only been apart from the Thessalonians four months. That is like writing home before the end of a semester in college. His language becomes more emphatic when we realize he had just been with them.

"We give thanks to God always for all of you, making mention of you in our prayers, constantly bearing in mind your work of faith and labor of love and steadfastness of hope in our Lord Jesus Christ in the presence of our God and Father, knowing, brethren beloved of God, His choice of you." (1st Thessalonians 1:2-3)

I believe Paul's words. He had a deep love and affection for this fresh band of believers, barely six months old at the max. The whole idea of Paul and the Holy Spirit's impact on the Jews and Gentiles in Thessalonica as well as on the other communities Paul visits amazes me. Those accepting the message are walking in a new freedom in Christ as well as experiencing the immediate power of God in their midst. It is breathtaking to consider.

God chose them; He chooses us. Paul came *"in power and in the Holy Spirit and with full conviction."* So what made these Jewish and pagan Thessalonians shift from darkness into light? Aside from Jesus's saving action, it was:

- A message delivered with complete conviction.
- The supernatural power demonstrated before them (healings, deliverance, words of knowledge, etc.).
- The impact of the Spirit of God in their midst.

No wonder Paul saw impact. Today, as much as then, we must not water down our message nor hesitate to move out as the Spirit of God directs, knowing that it is only the full presentation of God's saving Grace and His power and presence that pierces through the darkness.

But there is one other aspect of Paul's presentation that was also key: his personal example. I am inspired and convicted when I think of this. Others see everything we do. They may learn good things from us by observation, but they may also discredit our message because of the way we walk. People sort us quickly into "can be trusted" or "cannot be trusted." Part of that sorting is by what we say, but there are so many other cues to our reliability and the nature of the life within us: our facial expressions, our interests, how we spend our time, etc. It is the whole package.

Paul could say with confidence that he and those with him were good examples for the Thessalonians, and they in turn were good examples for all in Macedonia and Greece. In the space of less than a year, their robust response to the Word of God had become a wonderful testimony to God as other natives of Greece and Macedonia heard of their reception of the Gospel and Paul's little band of servant messengers.

They had *"turned to God from idols to serve a living and true God, and to wait for His Son from heaven, whom he raised from the dead, Jesus, who rescues us from the wrath to come."* (1ˢᵗ Thessalonians 1:9-10).

These closing verses of Chapter 1 are another kernel of Paul's early Gospel message, a call to leave the worship of vain idols and come to the living and true God, rescued by Jesus who was crucified and raised from the dead and coming again. Yes, come Lord Jesus!

1ˢᵗ Thessalonians 2

Paul's remembrance of his time in Thessalonica was sweet in spite of severe opposition. He had been run out of Philippi after being stripped, beaten and thrown into prison.

In Thessalonica, some of the Jews became jealous of the inroads Paul was making in the synagogue and no doubt disliked the message that Gentiles were included in God's mercy. They stirred up a mob and went to the home in which Paul, Silas and Timothy had been meeting. Paul and his brothers were not there, so the mob took the householder (Jason) and some of the other believers before the Roman court and accused them of defying the emperor by calling Jesus King. Jason and the others had to post bond, and were set free to await trial. That night, Paul and Silas left for Berea.

As Chapter 2 opens, Paul reflects on how he and his brothers had behaved amongst the Thessalonians. They proclaimed the Good News of what God had done in Jesus boldly in spite of opposition from some of the Jews. They did this free of charge, not looking for a handout, but rather giving themselves freely. They had not minced words, speaking the truth plainly with no hint of flattery.

The most endearing part of Paul's band's behavior had been its gentleness: *"as a nursing mother tenderly cares for her own children."* (1ˢᵗ Thessalonians 2:7). They felt such a *"strong affection"* toward the Thessalonians that they imparted their very lives to them. As Paul recalls, the Thessalonians *"had become very dear"* to the missionary band.

What an important reflection. They had been sent by God and they had come, seeking nothing but the benefit of those God let them encounter. But they weren't just people doing a job. Their very hearts were intertwined with those God gave them.

Backing away a distance, we can see the Holy Spirit at work, binding hearts and lives together. This God-thing, this binding of hearts and souls is just that – a God thing. He binds individuals, groups, peoples, nations, the even angelic hosts together. We know from Paul's letter to the Ephesians that this is one of the great expressions of the mystery of God's purpose, to bind all things together in Christ.

When we see the Holy Spirit at work in a community, this binding force will be on display, working into hearts and souls oneness. When we see division, we know that it is, in one way or another, almost always the work of the Evil One.

The "proofs" that Paul brings forth of his authenticity and position in God are simply his heart and his behavior. For this reason, those working missions for God must be without blemish, because any taint of ungodliness reduces the proof that God is working through the various ministers and ministries. Obviously, Satan loves to discredit by shedding light on moral failures amongst God's people. When Satan does so, both the ministry and God are discredited – one of Satan's ultimate aims.

As Paul ends the chapter, he tells the Thessalonians he had been trying to return, but Satan had in some way hindered him. Paul doesn't disclose the hindrance, but it must have occurred some time before he departed from Athens. It may have been sickness or the sickness of another. It may have been opposition to Paul's work in Athens that caused him to be unable to return. But it was his heart to return.

Finally, he likens the Thessalonian believers to his hope, his joy and his crown of exultation that will be brought forth when Jesus returns. For the believers there in Thessalonica are Paul's *"glory and joy!"*

We may rarely think along those lines when we think of our brothers and sisters, those whom we serve, our children and our grandchildren. There is coming a day when Jesus will return and all things will be wrapped up on that day. May all we have served and supported be our glory and crown. That thought should spur us on in faith and passion to treat all with that gentleness Paul so well describes.

1st Thessalonians 3

Paul, hindered from returning to his beloved Thessalonians, sent his yoke-brother and assistant, Timothy, back to Thessalonica to check on them. This provided Timothy an opportunity to strengthen and encourage them in their faith. One of Timothy's messages was that the *"afflictions"* Paul and his group had been suffering were not unexpected. In fact, they were anticipated and predicted. Apparently, Paul had included this tidbit of reality in his teaching to the new converts: affliction will come (we are not immune to it) and especially affliction would come to Paul and Silas' little band of workers.

We have spotlighted this reality before. Paul's message includes the disheartening news that affliction will come to those who follow Christ. Jesus Himself had predicted it. That piece of Paul's message helps underscore the wonder of the Holy Spirit's draw on our hearts, because in spite of that message, men and women turned toward God in the face of His Son Jesus – the "Suffering Servant" Isaiah predicted in Isaiah 53. Jesus Himself said to His disciples, *"If anyone wishes to come after Me, he must deny himself, and take up his cross and follow Me."* (Matthew 16:24).

This prediction of suffering, which likely was in Paul's case, a specific word of prophecy, produces *"an eternal weight of glory"* in the believer. (2nd Corinthians 4:17). But as we have said before, this is not the spiel of the TV evangelist. It underscores the powerful draw of the Holy Spirit.

Timothy had returned and brought Paul the good news that their new brothers and sisters in Thessalonians were growing in faith and love. Additionally, they missed the little missionary band and longed to see them. Because of this encouragement, Paul and his band were thanking God for the joy they had received from Timothy's report, night and day *"praying most earnestly"* that they might see them once again and minister anything that might be lacking.

Paul's heart was that they would *"increase and abound in love for one another."* (1st Thessalonians 3:12). We often say we love someone, but it is something else altogether to say, "I will love you the more

– I will increase in the love I have." Yet, that is Paul's prayer for the Thessalonians – not only amongst themselves, but with all people. Note that! Paul wants God to *establish their hearts without blame in holiness.* (1st Thessalonians 3:13). Yes, Lord, establish OUR hearts in holiness. May they be established! And may OUR love increase!

1st Thessalonians 4

Increasing in Love is a good thing, and we see in Chapter 4 that Paul wants them to excel even further in how they walk out their daily lives. He testifies that they are walking well, but he wants them to walk in an even more excellent way. It is an interesting encouragement. I am reminded of the child who made an A on an exam. The parent says, "that's great, but what about an A+?"

If an A is good enough, why encourage the A+? I think Paul is really saying, "You are doing great expressing who God really is, but He is beyond all comprehension, and we always have room to express even more the Glory of God and His nature."

You might ask, "Well, isn't revealing as much as I have revealed enough? After all, my righteousness is not based on how well I do. It's based on how well Jesus did. Paul, that's what you taught me!"

Paul might respond, "Good point, but it's not about you. It's about revealing the Glory of God in the earth. If we bear his nature, it is only natural that we want it to shine through as much as possible. Not for our sakes, but for the sake of others. So go for the A+ and by the way, when you get there, go for the double plus and keep going." I like Paul; he is after it!

God's Will is that we be entirely Holy - fully set apart for Him and entirely reflecting His Spirit, His nature, His power, His love. FULL of the Spirit.

So what are some clear markers that we aren't getting off track? First, NO sexual immorality. Let me be more specific. This means not meeting your God given desires outside of God given channels. Men are not made for men, and women are not made for women. Men and women were made for each other, but only in the bonds of matrimony. Jesus was explicit on this. Also applicable under this general line of thought is having your desires met virtually. Computers and robots were not made by God to meet needs any more than same sex encounters are.

Sexual immorality is a big, dark zone, and Paul had already warned the Thessalonians to be very careful, particularly because the Gentile culture had few boundaries. In fact, Greek civilization accepted a degree of homosexual and lesbian liaisons. It is such a danger zone that Paul had warned them that the Lord would avenge anyone wronged.

Obviously, if one was married, and did anything sexual outside of marriage, the spouse was defrauded. Who would bring vengeance? The Lord. *"Vengeance is Mine, and recompense. Their foot shall slip in due time, for the day of their calamity is at hand, and the things to come hasten upon them."* (Deuteronomy 32:35). That is a BIG warning.

Paul puts an exclamation point at the end of this thought: *"He who rejects this is not rejecting man but the God who gives His Holy Spirit to you."* (1st Thessalonians 4: 8). It is a big NO!

Having put a nail in the coffin of sexual immorality, Paul moves to a question that the Thessalonians must have asked Timothy during his visit. Someone asked about what happens to those that die before Jesus returns. We need to remember that most every believer had no idea that Jesus would tarry. They thought *"come quickly"* meant right away. So, what does happen to a believer who dies before the end?

I think this is a verse either ignored or not understood very well by many. It is more comforting to think that the dead in Jesus are walking about heaven, but that is not the picture here. Rather, the dead are *"asleep."* They are alive, but asleep. They will only rise to meet Jesus when He returns.

Does this mean they are miserable? Not at all. They exist, in some way they are alive, but not awake. I have pondered this for many years. I believe Paul describes an arrested state in the spirit. Dead in the flesh but not yet in the spiritual body that will eventually clothe them when they *"rise."* There is no time in God's domain, so one way to think about this is that those who have died in the flesh will be raised almost simultaneous to their death.

I have no thought that those who *"sleep in the Lord"* are conscious whatsoever of the passing of time that we experience on this earth. In the twinkling of an eye, they will arise to meet Jesus as He comes, and then the rest of us will be caught up together with them. The end result will be that we *"shall always be with the Lord."* Judgment will come, but he or she who is in Christ will rise to eternal life in a spiritual body. Read verses 13 through 18. See if you have a different thought.

"But we do not want you to be uninformed, brethren, about those who are asleep, so that you will not grieve as do the rest who have no hope. For if we believe that Jesus died and rose again, even so God will bring with Him those who have fallen asleep in Jesus. For this we say to you by the word of the Lord, that we who are alive and remain until the coming of the Lord, will not precede those who have fallen asleep. For the Lord Himself will descend from heaven with a shout, with the voice of the archangel and with the trumpet of God, and the dead in Christ will rise

first. Then we who are alive and remain will be caught up together with them in the clouds to meet the Lord in the air, and so we shall always be with the Lord. Therefore comfort one another with these words." (1st Thessalonians 4:13-18).

I must confess that there are other scriptures to ponder that show other nuances to life after death. This is particularly true of the martyrs who are seen under the altar in heaven. (See Revelation 6:9).

Some of these scriptures lead to an understanding of a holding place - a paradise (see Jesus's words to the criminal beside him at the crucifixion in Luke 23:43: *"Jesus answered him, 'Truly I tell you, today you will be with me in paradise.'")* *"Today,"* Jesus was dead. He didn't rise until the third day. So that place that he and the criminal went after death was a place Jesus called paradise. This is NOT heaven. He had not yet ascended.

This idea of a holding place is probably the origin of the evolving thought on *purgatory,* a word that means *"purifying."* It is not at all clear in scripture exactly what Jesus means, but it surely is a type of holding place.

For me, it is experienced in the twinkling of an eye because there is no time in God. *Paradeisos* comes from a word used amongst the Persians that describes *"a grand enclosure or preserve, a hunting ground, a park, shady and well watered, in which wild animals, were kept for the hunt. This area was enclosed by walls and furnished with towers for the hunters."* Jesus obviously is referring to a place that was not unpleasant where he would be with the man being crucified beside him - not heaven, not hell.

Our focus is not to be on the holding place, but on our final destination. We want to rise to meet Christ no matter what!

1ˢᵗ Thessalonians 5

Paul continues his response to the question about life after death in Chapter 5. He says the Thessalonians already know about *"times and epochs,"* but Paul is quick to repeat his previous teaching. First, the *"Day of the Lord"* will come like a thief in the night. He is saying people will not expect it, and Jesus will come. People will be thinking *"peace and safety,"* and suddenly destruction will descend upon them.

When Jesus comes, those in darkness will not escape reaping what they have sown. Believers also will have no immediate warning, but they already are in the light and are sons of the day, i.e., they do not fear what happens in darkness.

Without doubt, Paul's understanding of future events has been influenced by what the apostles shared with him at different points in his maturing ministry. You may recall that both Matthew and Mark record at some length Jesus's response to his disciples' question on the Mount of Olives two days before Passover about the *"end of the age"* and Jesus's return. The disciples had come to him *"privately."*

Jesus sits with them as they overlook Jerusalem. It is a sweet picture. Fran and I were on that exact spot with Terry and Charlotte Smith and our Jerusalem friends, Norma and Martin Sarvis. The view of the Temple Mount and the wall around Jerusalem is breathtaking, enhanced by the twisted and gnarled ancient olive trees. His disciples asked Him, *"Tell us, when will these things happen, and what will be the sign of Your coming, and of the end of the age?"* (Matthew 24:3).

As recorded, Jesus gave a lengthy reply – a reply that runs two chapters in Matthew. His first response was that He wanted them to not be mislead by those who would come saying one thing or another. Rather, *"be on the alert, for you do not know which day your Lord is coming. But be sure of this, that if the head of the house had known at what time of the night the thief was coming, he would have been on the alert and would not have allowed his house to be broken into. For this reason you also must be ready; for the Son of Man is coming at an hour when you do not think He will."* (Matthew 24:42-44).

Jesus told them a great deal of difficulty would precede His return: wars, famines, earthquakes – and those would just be the beginning of tribulation. This would be followed by hatred of Christians and martyrdom. Lawlessness would be rampant.

In the meantime, many will arise in Jesus's name and say, *"Here is the Anointed One,"* but Jesus told his disciples not to believe them. When Jesus does return after that tribulation, He said the world would grow dark as both the sun and moon cease to shine: *"the sun will be darkened, and the moon will not give its light, and the stars will fall from the sky, and the powers of the heavens will be shaken."* (Matthew 24:29). Scientifically, without a change in God's laws, these cosmic changes suggest the end of the Universe as we know it. Another interpretation is that our ability to see heavenly light is blocked by dark clouds and an eclipse of the Sun, but the words *"the stars will fall from the sky"* is hard to interpret without anticipating a major collapse of all that we know.

Regardless of how the darkening occurs, the *"sign of the Son of Man will appear in the sky* (perhaps the cross), *and then all the tribes of the earth will mourn, and they will see the Son of Man coming on the clouds of the sky with power and great glory. And He will send forth His angels with a great trumpet and they will gather together His elect from the four winds, from one end of the sky to the other."* (Matthew 24:30-31). I see a cosmic cross coming toward the earth from on high - blazing in the darkness with looming clouds behind and the Son of Man (Jesus) coming accompanied by the angelic host which will gather men and women (the elect) from all parts of the earth.

Then, Jesus shifts to the scene of Judgment, *"But when the Son of Man comes in His glory, and all the angels with Him, then He will sit on His glorious throne. All the nations will be gathered before Him; and He will separate them from one another, as the shepherd separates the sheep from the goats; and He will put the sheep on His right, and the goats on the left."* (Matthew 25:31-33).

I repeat all of the Master's words here because they are the His. Paul had shared with the Thessalonians basic pieces of this prophetic unfolding that began when Jesus privately answered some of the disciples' questions a few days before his crucifixion. Don't lose sight of the fact that all the apostles were sharing on the foundation of what Jesus Himself taught, and not vice-versa.

After answering the question raised in Thessalonians, Paul somewhat abruptly shifts at verse 12 to relational questions amongst the Thessalonians.

"But we request of you, brethren, that you appreciate those who diligently labor among you, and have charge over you in the Lord and give you instruction, and that you esteem them very highly in love because of their work." (1st Thessalonians 5:12).

Verse 12 is interesting to me for two reasons. Normally, when we encounter language like this in Paul's letters, I believe he is talking about monetary compensation as well as relational honor and simple appreciation. It is hard to imagine that this is the case in such a young community, because it normally references brothers who have given up their secular occupations in order to minister fulltime spiritually. But perhaps that has occurred.

We know from other letters that Paul thought the *presbuteros* (Greek for *elder* and the word from which we eventually get the English word priest) who *"ruled well"* as elders in churches were to be supported.

"The elders who rule well are to be considered worthy of double honor, especially those who work hard at preaching and teaching." (1st Timothy 5:17).

Or, perhaps Paul was referencing some of his band of missionaries who had been left behind in Thessalonica.

Another interpretation is a simple one: Paul's language just means what he says on a relational level, that is, be sure you really appreciate those brothers and sisters who labor hard watching over and teaching you. But again, we note the young age of the church in Thessalonica, and must wonder what Paul means by *"have charge over you."* Perhaps Paul had chosen a few to shepherd the flock he left behind. We just do not know.

The Greek word *eido* translated in the NASB as *"appreciate"* in verse 12 is not easy to translate in English. *Eido* really means *"know them well,"* – a call to the Thessalonians to know the worth of their leaders working with them and not take those leaders for granted.

I am reminded of early teachings we received on honoring those who labor amongst us. Unfortunately, honoring is NOT common in our American culture, and I recognized in the early 70s that I would have to lean into this concept of HONOR since it affected not only my relation to God but also my brothers and sisters – really all of my dealings with men and women. I immediately caught the lack of honor I had bestowed on my earthly father and also my tendency to ignore those who gave themselves to me in the church community.

Terry Smith was the one brother who stood out most clearly when I thought about support in those days. Even though he had had moved to Searcy, I began to drive over at least once a month to see how he and Charlotte were doing, and I felt prompted to look for practical and demonstrative ways to demonstrate my appreciation of his labor for me and others.

There was a monetary component, though Terry never sought it. I felt responsible because I received rather continuously spiritual support from him! As I look back, it has been a fifty-year run!

In verse 12, the NASB translates the Greek word *kopiao* as *"diligently labor."* The root of *kopiao* means *"toil, sweat,"* and describes pretty well the passionate giving of oneself that marks those God has given to us to be brought to maturity. It certainly describes my yoke-fellow, Terry.

As Jesus said, the *"laborer is worthy of his hire."* (Luke 10:7). We have many brothers and sisters who labor faithfully without monetary reward and basically receive no recognition, and they deserve *HIGH* accolades from my point of view. I don't do enough in this regard, and I am not alone. Paul's admonition is "Open your eyes to those around you; so many are laboring diligently and in various ways for the Kingdom." They need and deserve our appreciation.

Paul uses present tense Greek participles to describe the nature of oversight and the kind of teaching effort the Thessalonians were receiving. Using participles instead of nouns of office emphasizes the act of ministry.

"Diligently labor" (*kopiao* from *kopos* = labor, fatigue) is one of the key words. The root word *kopos* is used in secular Greek to designate *"a beating," "weariness"* (as though one had been beaten) and *"exertion."* It was the proper word for physical tiredness induced by work, exertion or heat. *"Kopiao"* means to exhibit great effort and exertion, to the point of sweat and exhaustion.

Paul ends the chapter with a laundry list of behavioral admonishments: Live in peace, admonish the unruly (those lacking discipline in their lives), encourage the fainthearted, help the weak and be patient with everyone. Good advice for any church community or a family with a particular focus on the importance of patience. Paul's emphasis is to help the weak in every way possible.

Then we come to his repetition of *"Rejoice always, pray without ceasing."* Paul told every nearly every church that he wrote to rejoice. In Romans, four times. To Corinth, five times. To the Galatians, once. To Philippi, TEN times. To the Colossians, once. To the Thessalonians, once. You can see why I call the letter to the Philippians, the Letter of Rejoicing. But rejoicing in the Holy Spirit was a major need in every community. That requires a focus on our amazing situation in God. Yes! Praying fervently and rejoicing in the Holy Spirit!

His last admonition to not *"quench the spirit; do not despise prophetic utterances. But examine everything carefully, holding fast to that which is good."* (1st Thessalonians 5:19-21). Paul's words reveal two things in early church development. First, even though the church in Thessalonica probably was less than a year old, spiritual gifts were active. Actually, this should not surprise us as the "Promise" from Joel 2:28 predicts Holy Spirit activity. What is the first gift mentioned after God pours out His Spirit? That *"your sons and daughters shall prophesy."* So, things were going as predicted by the Prophet Joel.

The second observation is that the phenomenon was not easy to handle in a youthful community with many inexperienced in spiritual matters. There was a critical need for discernment and knowledge of the scriptures (at that point they only had Old Testament texts and oversight was needed). Timothy may have reported back to Paul that some had discouraged the delivery of a prophetic word during assemblies. Regardless, Paul basically says "Don't despise prophetic utterances, but be sure they are they are from God."

One could argue this is not nearly as important today as it would have been in Thessalonica because we have the entire New Testament writings in hand, and prophecy should be easier to evaluate. But remember, Jesus taught that, *"false prophets would arise and perform great signs."* (Matthew 24:24). Further, He predicted they will come in sheep's clothing (Matthew 7:15). That means they will say things that sound right like, "Praise Jesus" and "Jesus is Lord" while leading others astray.

So, how do we judge? Obviously, the Bible is one major testing ground in itself. Jesus said another important key is the fruit that comes from their activity. This is impossible to judge if you actually do not walk with them (today, many come through the airwaves). Fom my point of view, being unable to actually judge the fruit of one speaking as a prophet means I simply will not listen. A third testing is our own spirit which may detect that *"inwardly, they are ravenous wolves;"* i.e., we discern that they are driven from their own internal, ravenous need for attention and/or control.

Finally, if they predict an event, it needs to come to pass. There are plenty on the radio predicting all sorts of things that are date specific and that do not meet this test, and yet people continue unreservedly to follow them. Big mistake.

On a practical and historical level, our little community has run into this problem before, and I will end with this reflection: it is hard to handle without someone taking offense. But it must be handled.

2nd Thessalonians

2nd Thessalonians 1

Paul's second letter forms a perfect couplet with 1st Thessalonians. It was written only a few months after the Thessalonians received his first letter, and a good part of it focuses on the same subject he addressed earlier. Most probably, Paul wrote it in the early days of AD 51. By that time, he was in Corinth along with Silas (Silvanus) and Timothy.

Paul had received news from Thessalonica that the situation in Thessalonica had deteriorated – or at least there was more confusion with regard to Jesus's return. Some believed His return was so imminent that they had ceased working. This inaccurate focus may have come from faulty teaching, but it also could have come from a misguided prophetic utterance or even a letter reputed to be from Paul himself. (See 2nd Thessalonians 2:2). Whatever the reason, some of the Thessalonians were off track in their thinking, and Paul was keen to get them back on track.

Paul's opening salutation is nearly identical to that of his first letter. He writes *"the called out,"* the *ekklesia* of the Thessalonians who find themselves *"in God our Father and the Lord Jesus Christ."* There is a slight difference as the word *"our"* appears instead of simply the word *"Father."* This tiny change emphasizes that Paul and the Thessalonians together are connected in the most amazing way: they are all members of the Family of God.

Paul praises God for their continued growth in faith and love. Similar to his first letter, we see a dynamic that only the Spirit of God can bring: faith and love both enlarging, brought about by the supernatural work of the Spirit within each believer. Imagine the energy within each believer who has received the Spirit of God and the energy God has placed within you. Left free to do God's mighty work, over time, both our faith and our love increases. If it does not, then something is shackling the power of the Spirit within us.

It seems clear from his opening that the Thessalonians are under persecution – no doubt from other religious factions. Paul emphasizes their perseverance and faith at the same time, because perseverance doesn't last if faith fails. Perseverance stands upon the foundation of our faith. As persecution increased and the Thessalonians continued to persevere and not waiver, Paul knew with certainty that their faith had to increase as well. And we can know with certainty that when affliction and rejection come our way, God's Spirit within us wants to increase our faith all the more.

Faith builds over time. As we look back over longer and longer stretches of time, we can see more of God's faithfulness to us - His steadfast love revealed in new ways. Our faith grows both naturally and supernaturally.

In the middle of Chapter 1, Paul begins to bring in the subject of the End of the Age by noting that those afflicting the Thessalonians will receive retribution at the Lord's "revealing" while the steadfast believers will receive incredible comfort. Paul's language describes a somewhat terrifying picture, and the word translated as *"revealed"* is the word *apokalypsis* from which we get the word Apocalypse. The Bible book of "Revelation" is entitled *Apokalypsis* from the first Greek word in John's writing. When Jesus is *"revealed,"* words can hardly describe it:

"... the Lord Jesus will be revealed from heaven with His mighty angels in flaming fire, dealing out retribution to those who do not know God and to those who do not obey the gospel of our Lord Jesus. These will pay the penalty of eternal destruction, away from the presence of the Lord and from the glory of His power, when He comes to be glorified in His saints on that day, and to be marveled at among all who have believed—for our testimony to you was believed." (2ⁿᵈ Thessalonians 1:7-10).

You will recall that Paul had referenced the End of the Age in the last chapter of 1ˢᵗ Thessalonians. Included in my reflections was a long section from Jesus's Mount of Olive teachings that occurred a few days before his crucifixion. The *"sign of the Son of Man will appear in the sky, and then all the tribes of the earth will mourn, and they will see the Son of Man coming on the clouds of the sky with power and great glory. And He will send forth His angels with a great trumpet and they will gather together His elect from the four winds, from one end of the sky to the other."* (Matthew 24:30-31).

Paul describes Jesus and His mighty angels coming *"in flaming fire,"* whereas Jesus had referenced *"power and great glory,"* but regardless, it will be beyond human description. And like Jesus, Paul connects His coming to judgment. The angels will gather together His elect, and we know from Jesus's words that they will also gather those who are not among the elect into a different group.

I would encourage you to read Paul's description of the Jesus's revealing in verses 7 through 10 a second time with a focus on what happens to the *"elect."* It is a compelling and comforting vision of the last days for those who remain faithful. The elect will be in the presence of the Lord and the glory of His power and on that day, He will be glorified in His saints and the elect will truly marvel. I would say that is an understatement!

Paul wants the Thessalonians in that marveling group at the end of the age. He is praying to that end. His focus is that they *"fulfill every desire for goodness and the work of faith with power."* (2nd Thessalonians 1:11).

"Fulfill every desire for goodness and the work of faith with power." Is that how you would describe your hope for yourself, your spouse or your children? That they would fulfill every Godly desire and thus display goodness? And what does Paul mean when he says *"the work of faith with power?"*

A work of faith is something we are called to accomplish that will not happen unless we are full of a deep confidence in God's presence with us. God's intention is to do good things beyond our natural desire and ability. Just being kind to someone who has lied to us or disparaged us is nearly impossible in our own strength. But it is a work of faith to be kind in those circumstances and it reveals God's power within us. We thus reveal His nature.

When we work goodness for others through our faith, we reveal God's power and thus glorify God. As Paul ends the chapter, we do it only through and according to the amazing *"grace of our God and the Lord Jesus Christ!"*

2nd Thessalonians 2

This is a bear of a chapter. The first 12 verses in Chapter 2 are not easy to understand. Abe Malherbe's exhaustive commentary helps us get our bearings.

As the chapter opens, Paul returns to his eschatological discussion, which he began in the middle of the preceding chapter and in Chapter 5 of his preceding letter. *"Eschatological"* comes from the Greek word that means *"last."* We use it to describe what comes at the End of the Age.

Chapter 2 hits the real reason for Paul's follow-up letter – a concern that falsehood concerning the End of the Age has disturbed a lot of the Thessalonian believers. Many are *"shaken"* and *"emotionally wrought."* Paul's aim (aside from walking in what is true) is that the community live calmly, faithfully and undisturbed regardless of the season in which they find themselves.

Paul underscores what likely caused the confusion and misinterpretation of what he had already taught. Verse 2 tells us that the trouble may have come from a prophetic message or even a letter reported to be from Paul himself. And it very likely could have come from a misinterpretation of his first letter where he told the Thessalonians that they were already *"sons of light and sons of the day."* (1 Thessalonians 5:4). Since darkness comes immediately prior to Jesus's appearing, *"the sun will be darkened, and the moon will not give its light, and the stars will fall from the sky, and the powers of the heavens will be shaken."* (Matthew 24:29), and Paul had stressed that they were *"sons of light and sons of the day,"* then some may have believed that Jesus had already come.

Regardless of the exact reason, many of the Thessalonians were disturbed, some believing *"that the Day of the Lord had come."* (2nd Thessalonians 2:2). Verses 3-12 are written forcefully to get everyone back on track. It helps to divide these 10 verses into four parts for clarity. In these ten verses, Paul shifts back and forth from one point to another.

What Has to Happen (Verses 3-5).

The *"Day of the Lord"* has not come because two things have to occur before Jesus returns. Apostasy must come in full force and *"the Son of Lawlessness"* must be revealed. Paul identifies this Son of Lawlessness as one who will oppose God and exalt himself above God and take his seat in the Temple (literally, the "shrine") of God. This Son of Lawlessness has NOT yet been revealed because he has been restrained since it is not yet God's time.

What Is Happening Now (Verses 6-7).

There IS lawlessness already at work in the earth, though restrained. The restraining force is not clearly identified though Paul says in verse 6 that the Thessalonians know what that force is. My only thought is that the force is the amazing news of God's intervention in the earth through the gift of His Son. Others have attributed the retraining force to the Church itself or the Bible. Regardless, Paul is saying that sin is all about us but not in the degree that will come prior to Jesus's return. (It is hard to imagine that things will get substantially worse in our own day as society breaks down most moral boundaries, though when I think about the horrors of Nazi Germany, obviously things could get worse).

What Will Happen at the End (Verses 8-10).

Once the restraint is removed, the Man of Lawlessness will be revealed, and only then will the Lord come. Jesus will slay the Man of Lawlessness *"with the breath of His mouth"* and bring to an end the one tied to Satan, in spite of his deceptive signs, power and miracles. Those *"who did not receive the love of truth"* shall perish.

What Is Happening Now (Verses 11-12).

God sends upon those who do not *"love the truth,"* i.e., those who reject the truth, and *"take pleasure in wickedness"* a deluding influence that they may be clearly marked for judgment.

A focus on the "End Times" often brings anxiety and emotional disturbance, and this was the case in Thessalonica. We *DO* need to have a clear grasp of where we were going, and be ready. Jesus's emphasis was much more on being ready (he gave three great parables about being ready in Matthew, Chapters 24 and 25: the Faithful Servant who is ready when his Master returns, the parable of the 10 virgins with their oil lamps, and the parable of the talents).

As my sweet wife says, *"Get ready. There's a train a'comin."* But we don't know when, and I think back on the innumerable incorrect interpretations of the Man of Lawlessness (the Anti-God or Anti-Christ) and the countless predictions that Jesus is about to return. Nero, Antiochus Epiphanes IV, the Renaissance Popes, Hitler, Obama, Trump. The list goes on. Fran's focus is right. Just be ready because you do not know the hour. No matter what, He is coming.

Personally, I am thankful Paul shifts to thanksgiving in verse 13:

"But we should always give thanks to God for you, brethren beloved by the Lord, because God has chosen you from the beginning for salvation through sanctification by the Spirit and faith in the truth. It was for this He called you through our gospel, that you may gain the glory of our Lord Jesus Christ. So then, brethren, stand firm and hold to the traditions

which you were taught, whether by word of mouth or by letter from us." (2nd Thessalonians 2:13-15).

Paul's thanksgiving is much easier to reflect upon! God loves the believers in Thessalonica; they are His beloved. They were chosen to be saved in some mysterious way at the very beginning of time.

Paul brings forward two important components of how that salvation became theirs. He doesn't mention the most important reason because Paul knows it is understood, that is, that Jesus died that they might be saved *("For God so loved the world that He gave....").* But Paul does emphasize the importance of the sanctifying (making holy) work of the Holy Spirit as well as their initial belief in Paul's message. Martin Luther would have noticed that Paul did not reference their good works as activators of their salvation. We need to stand firm in our faith and also let the Holy Spirit work continuously on our hearts.

Both we and the Thessalonians are called *"that we may gain the glory of our Lord Jesus Christ!"* Paul's deduction (which we note is frequent) is that because of this call, we must *"stand firm and hold to the traditions which we were taught, whether by word of mouth or by letter."* (2nd Thessalonians 2:15). "Standing firm" is amazingly important, and I would have to add, not easy. Of course, that is why Paul keeps saying, *"stand firm."* We don't want the enemy getting past us; we don't want to waiver.

Paul clearly felt the traditions he taught both by "word and by letter" needed to be followed. Trace this line of thought through the centuries and you see what the Church universal has held binding from the point of view of initial apostolic teaching. Not everything was written; some directions were simply handed down verbally. The early church soon began to codify these instructions and pass them down in writing. The *"traditions"* of the apostles as well as what they wrote were binding. Both were binding. People often get confused on this subject. Paul wasn't.

2nd Thessalonians 3

"Finally, brethren, pray for us that the word of the Lord will spread rapidly and be glorified, just as it did also with you; and that we will be rescued from perverse and evil men; for not all have faith. But the Lord is faithful, and He will strengthen and protect you from the evil one. We have confidence in the Lord concerning you, that you are doing and will continue to do what we command. May the Lord direct your hearts into the love of God and into the steadfastness of Christ." (2nd Thessalonians 3:1-5).

Paul beseeches the Thessalonians to pray for Paul's team that they would be successful in delivering the Good News of God's great gift. His passion is evident; his hope solid. He also prays that the little apostolic band might be *"rescued"* from evil and perverse men who attack it almost continuously.

In turn, Paul prays for the Thessalonians. He wants the Lord to direct their hearts into the love of God and into the steadfastness of Christ. The triune God *IS* love. Directing their hearts into the love of God directs their hearts into God. Jesus as the Anointed One stands as the steadfast one, 'sticky" in spite of affliction and persecution. Paul hopes the same quality will be evident in the *"brethren"* in Thessalonica. It is worth reflecting that God's intention is to communicate His marvelous nature to every person on earth. But with evil and lawlessness abroad, the steadfast Spirit of Jesus is a special prize.

Paul also comforts the Thessalonians with the certainty that God *WILL* strengthen them as well as protect them from the Evil One. We remember that Jesus's last line in His prayer training for disciples was to implore God to deliver them from evil. Like putting on the armor of God every morning, our petitions to the Father for daily deliverance do not go unheeded.

In verse 6, Paul sharply changes tone as he addresses a problem in the Thessalonian church: some individuals are not working. Instead, they are meddling in other people's affairs, being busybodies. Paul had addressed this issue in his first letter:

"Now about your love for one another we do not need to write to you, for you yourselves have been taught by God to love each other. And in fact, you do love all of God's family throughout Macedonia. Yet we urge you, brothers and sisters, to do so more and more, and to make it your ambition to lead a quiet life: You should mind your own business and work with your hands, just as we told you, so that your daily life may win the respect of outsiders and so that you will not be dependent on anybody." (1st Thessalonians 4:9-12).

This is the Golden Rule of work. Out of our love for each other, we lead a quiet life, minding our own business while earning our own subsistence so that we are not dependent on others. This has the salutary result that outsiders will view us with respect.

Both Greek and Jew had a high view of work. Jewish tradition regarding work traced back to God's command to Adam.

"Cursed is the ground because of you;
In toil you will eat of it
All the days of your life.
"Both thorns and thistles it shall grow for you;
And you will eat the plants of the field;
By the sweat of your face
You will eat bread…"
(Genesis 3:17-19).

Work was a responsibility, and Paul viewed it as a reflection of love for others as well as a duty. One who labored did not need monetary help. It also meant one could help others. Paul would later write the brethren in Ephesus, *"Let the thief no longer steal, but rather let him labor, doing honest work with his own hands, so that he may have something to share with anyone in need."* (Ephesians 4:28).

Paul had gotten a report that instead of getting better, the work issue in Thessalonica had deteriorated. Paul was quite concerned about the effect on the congregation in Thessalonica, and urged them to take the serious step of not *"associating"* with the idlers and busybodies.

Paul refers them not only to his verbal and written teaching on work but also to his behavior amongst them. Though deserving of support *("the laborer is worthy of his hire")*, Paul had worked the entire time that he had been in Thessalonica so that he would not be a burden to them and prove to be a good example. These are two important reasons for every man to seriously consider their behavior regarding work – particularly those involved in ministry.

In verse 10, we learn that Paul had given them a clear rule when he had been present in Thessalonica: *"If anyone is not willing to work, then he is not to eat either."* Taken at face value, this would mean people would die, but Paul is referencing the common practice amongst Christian communities of having a common meal (think pot luck). Paul had taught that new believers were not to mooch off the community, but rather work so they could buy their own bread. He withheld freebies to those who were idle.

In most third world countries, begging is an art form, and you could say the same in Memphis. I love the interim solution that some students at Rhodes University developed called "The Bridge" where homeless folk can sell newspapers for one dollar. They buy the newspapers for 25 cents and make 75 cents per transaction. Overnight, they own a small business! It is meant to be a small step to more productive employment.

"Not associating" with the unruly spotlights Paul's thoughts on withdrawal, i.e., it is not total. Verses 14 and 15 makes this clear:

"If anyone does not obey our instruction in this letter, take special note of that person and do not associate with him, so that he will be put to shame. Yet do not regard him as an enemy, but admonish him as a brother." You can't admonish if you don't have some form of contact. Perhaps it was through notes ("Missing you," "Thinking of you," "Praying for you"). Regardless, Paul wanted the unruly to still be seen as family.

Paul ends his second letter with a blessing and his personal signature. The latter points out not only a personal touch, but also served as authentication. We have letters from the first few centuries that said they were from various apostles, but many were forgeries. Paul draws attention to his signature as a "distinguishing mark." "This is the way I write." As our study continues, be thoughtful about the problems of transmission of the ancient texts, from copying issues to glosses added by well meaning grammarians.

1st Timothy

1st Timothy 1

I wish I knew more about Timothy. He is a useful example of a long serving disciple, and we find him scattered throughout Paul's life of nearly 60 years. No doubt, Timothy met Paul during Paul's First Missionary Journey in the 40s (AD) when Paul visited Lystra where Timothy lived with his Jewish mother, Eunice, his Jewish grandmother, Lois, and his Greek father. Timothy perhaps was born around 17 AD, and that would have made Timothy a young man in his late twenties or early thirties when he first met Paul. I am guessing he was about 12 years younger than Paul.

If my deductions are correct, Timothy was about the age I was when I got married (28 years old) during Paul's first visit to Lystra. That math helps me think about his level of maturity at the beginning of their contact because that was the time I first was introduced to the Holy Spirit.

Paul took Timothy with him when he returned to Lystra on Paul's Second Missionary Journey. Because Paul wanted Timothy to join his missionary band as they continued further west, Timothy had to be circumcised in spite of Paul's firm view that circumcision was not needed for salvation. Paul knew that having a Jewish mother, Timothy's lack of circumcision would cause Jewish audiences to reject Timothy out of hand. The practical solution is painful to ponder.

Timothy ended up as one of Paul's key assistants and protégés. His prominence is heightened in our minds by the fact that Paul wrote two important letters to him that are included in our Bible. These letters were written most likely sometime between 60 and 65 AD. At that point, Paul and Timothy had been working together for nearly twenty years. Timothy would have been have been about 45 years of age when Paul's letters arrived in Ephesus.

Dr. Daniel B. Wallace wrote a short summary in 2004 of the context of the first letter that may be helpful in setting the stage:

"Timothy... had been with Paul toward the end of the apostle's first Roman imprisonment (cf. Phil 2:19-24). When Paul was released, he took Timothy and Titus with him back to Asia Minor after they had left Titus on Crete. They went by way of Ephesus en route to Macedonia. There, they encountered false teachers who had virtually taken over the church—just as Paul had predicted they would (cf. Acts 20:29-30). Two of them, Hymenaeus and Alexander, were excommunicated by Paul (1st Tim 1:19-20). Paul had to press on to Macedonia (cf. Phil 2:24), but the situation at Ephesus needed help. He left Timothy in charge of the church, giving him instructions to deal with the heretics who had become leaders in the church (cf. 1st Tim 1:3-4)." (Dr. Daniel B. Wallace, 2004).

There has been some question historically regarding the authenticity of the letters to both Timothy and Titus. My position is simple; I accept them as "received texts of the Church." I trust God's complete ability to guide the Church through the power and activity of the Holy Spirit. As the issues of language differences and emphasis rage, I take my stand on my faith in God's ability to safeguard what is truly important. In other words, I want to heed the messages in the four letters, regardless of linguistic differences with Paul's other letters to the churches.

Having said that, note that we meet a new way that Paul expresses his view of God and Jesus. In his opening sentence, Paul describes God as the Savior and Jesus as our hope. Obviously, God *IS* our savior, but we are so accustomed to calling Jesus our savior that one has to pause and consider that Paul's own understanding of the connection between Jesus and Father may be tightening. We see this continue as the first century closes and Ignatius of Antioch writes numerous letters on his way to martyrdom in Rome. Writing in around 110 AD, Ignatius refers to *"our Savior and God, Jesus Christ,"* a frequent phrase in his writings.

I also note a change from Paul's normal salutation to the churches. He adds *"mercy"* to his normal wish for *"grace and peace."* That makes total sense to me. Timothy was a man like Paul, working in the vineyard of the Lord, and no doubt as much in need of mercy as anything else! Old men know the fragility of their walk.

A Vibrant, Living Relationship

Timothy is one of the Bible's great examples of a disciple, and the reverse is also true: Paul is the great example of a discipler. Timothy and Paul have a vibrant, familial relationship. Paul relates to Timothy as his child in the faith, i.e., his son. To me, this is the highest form of discipleship – not a program, but a relationship. A vibrant, living relationship. That observation is important.

Paul gets down to the key purpose of his letter in verse 3: Paul wants Timothy to remain in Ephesus to counter the *"strange teachings"* that have infiltrated the Ephesian church. His description of what is happening because of these teachings sounds familiar to my ears. People are wrapped up in giving attention to *"myths and endless genealogies."* Today, I find church people wrapped up in prophecies and speculations about all matter of off-topic doctrines like angelic intercourse with early humans creating giants, etc. When our focus gets off of our relationship with the Godhead and our fellowman, Paul would be quick to intervene.

"The goal of our instruction is love from a pure heart and a good conscience and a sincere faith. For some men, straying from these things, have turned aside to fruitless discussion...." (1st Timothy 1:5-6).

Verses 5 and 6 sum up the issue: focus on an irrelevancy compared to having a pure heart and a good conscience (read: a focus on one's behavior). We have to be on guard to stay on track with our hearts open to those around us. Otherwise, we can find ourselves entrapped in the all-too-present media of today, listening to endless non-consequential theories that keep us from visiting the sick, helping those in trouble and lending a helping hand in true friendship. Paul knew the problem.

These people who are drawing others astray want *"to be teachers of the Law, even though they do not understand either what they are saying or the matters about which they make confident assertions."* This is so true; I think most have no idea that they are off track and getting their listeners off track.

Paul has another highly personal Gospel kernel imbedded in the second half of the first chapter:

"I thank Christ Jesus our Lord, who has strengthened me, because He considered me faithful, putting me into service, even though I was formerly a blasphemer and a persecutor and a violent aggressor. Yet I was shown mercy because I acted ignorantly in unbelief; and the grace of our

Lord was more than abundant, with the faith and love which are found in Christ Jesus. It is a trustworthy statement, deserving full acceptance, that Christ Jesus came into the world to save sinners, among whom I am foremost of all. Yet for this reason I found mercy, so that in me as the foremost, Jesus Christ might demonstrate His perfect patience as an example for those who would believe in Him for eternal life." (1ˢᵗ Timothy 1:12-16).

What was God's purpose in sending Jesus into the world? To save sinners. Paul focuses in this autobiographical recap on God's mercy, grace, love and patience - characteristics of God that are intimately intertwined with Paul's personal story.

He ends this flight of insight with what has become the lyrics of one of my favorite songs: *"Now unto the King eternal, immortal, invisible, the only* [wise] *God, be honor and glory forever and ever!"* Amen!

Paul recalls earlier prophesies that concerned Timothy's life and work. In light of those prophesies, Paul wants Timothy to keep *"fighting the good fight, keeping faith and a good conscience"* (think good behavior). Paul reveals that others not unlike Timothy have gotten seriously off track. Daily, we should remind ourselves that we could get off track as well.

Paul gives as examples two men that he has *"handed over to Satan."* He means that he withdrew fellowship and support, effectively putting them in the hands of the evil one. Apparently, they in some way spoke words diminishing who God is. They had blasphemed. This is something none of us want to ever do, i.e., diminish in any way who God is.

1st Timothy 2

Reading the entire letter through does spotlight a sharp change from Paul's normal language. The warmth so evident in some of his other letters is clearly missing. There is no mention of Timothy's surely deceased grandmother, Lois, nor his mother, Eunice. No highly personal reflection that might have come to mind as Paul wrote his 20-year yoke-fellow. This gives some credence to the thought that Paul's secretary may have written most of the letter very much in freehand – that is, only working off of general items Paul wanted to address in the secretary's own language. Yet it is still a bit odd.

Chapter 2 opens with Paul urging Timothy to be sure that a great many types of prayers and petitions be offered up to God in all the churches. Obviously, Timothy would have known Paul's thoughts on this matter already, so one could guess most of Paul's letter is written to others beyond Timothy. In other words, he knows other yoke-fellows and entire churches will read the letter. Paul may be using the opportunity to provide broad instruction on matters affecting all church communities.

Paul identifies four types of prayers in verse 1: entreaties, prayers, petitions and thanksgivings. His choice of these four may have been partially rhetorical. Paul wanted to emphasize how many things and in how many ways we can bring our innermost thoughts to the Father of the Universe.

But, he is right. There are many ways to converse with God, and Paul sees the wonder of prayer being critical to our time on this earth. Why? Because we need both the personal communion time with God as well as God's personal hand intervening in the world.

To entreat God means basically to plead with our heart and soul a passionate and important request. The type of request that a father or mother might raise to God concerning cancer in a child.

To pray covers almost all of the other forms listed. In other words, "to pray" is to bring wishes one has before God. Entreaties, petitions and thanksgivings all are included.

The Greek word translated *"petition"* is also a broad verb meaning to go meet with or converse with someone. It also brings to mind a more legal aspect - simply making something known. "Father, I am having a wonderful day. The sun is shining; the sky bright." In other words, the word emphasizes the conversational aspect of going before God.

And finally, thanksgiving is another aspect of conversing. The Bible is chock full of *"thanksgivings."* Psalms is weighted down with thanksgivings. "Lord, You *are* good! Your mercies never come to an end," and so forth.

In verse 8, he clarifies where he wants all of these prayers to God lifted up: *"in every place."* This is broader than a church building. It includes all the churches, all the homes, all the dinner tables, all the offices, all the hospitals and all the closets - everywhere.

Paul even specifies how he wants each person to be positioned: *"with hands lifted up."* The latter is quite clear, but I recall how very difficult I found this posture of supplication to be when I first began my walk in the Spirit. It is an interesting question to ask: how could we have ignored Paul's encouragement so long that my problem would be lifting up my hands? Rather, you would think it would have been just the reverse if I had been part of a culture of worship that took Paul's lead.

We have to conclude that posture and position are importance. Derek Prince was quick to teach that the word we translate as *"worship"* from the Hebrew *shachah* actually means *"to bow down, to prostrate one's self."* Worship strikes a slightly different note from much of our praying because is has within it the very sense of what one does when coming into the presence of God. One's whole body is involved. Notice that sitting is NOT a posture of worship from a linguistic point of view.

Personally, I want to be as expressive as possible with my body during *"worship."* I want my heart to direct my body and not vice versa. Kneeling and lying prostrate are unbelievably appropriate (goodness, it is the meaning of the word), but we also find those serving in the Temple standing during the night as they praised God. *"Bless ye the Lord, all you servants of the Lord, who by night stand in the House of the Lord...."* (Psalm 134:1). *"Lift up your hands in the sanctuary and bless the Lord."* (Psalm 134:2). All are body responses to the presence of God.

Sequentially in worship, we have been helped by catching the order of our thoughts and actions from Psalm 100:4: *"Enter His gates with thanksgiving and His courts with praise."* The author of Psalm 100 is giving a command, and we can give ourselves a command. At the beginning of a time of worship, we can direct our mind first to those things for which we are thankful and then to the praise that God is due because of those gifts we have received. Personally, that "rule" has been practically helpful.

"Without wrath or dissension" in verse 8 is also a call to the same condition of our hearts and mind that we are called to when taking the Lord's Supper. Like inappropriate baggage, we should not go into God's presence harboring enmity with anyone. So everyday, we must shed any *"wrath or dissension."*

The second half of Chapter 1 is devoted to the ladies and what they should wear. Dior would not have been pleased with Paul's take on appropriate adornment, but assembling together to worship does put obligations on all who assemble. We don't want in any way to distract others from the real focus of gathering together. What's the focus? To be with God all together, and to learn from Him. So, anything that distracts, whether on a man or on a woman, is just that, a distraction. Paul's emphasis on modesty and discreetly is well taken.

Men are men; Satan is Satan. Our airwaves and our newspapers are full every day with news of yet another Christian leader brought down by sexual misconduct. Satan is after everyone but particularly Christian leaders. Satan plays the sex card at every opportunity. The most inappropriate thing imaginable is to get off track when gathering about the God of the Universe. Jesus promised to be in our very midst when only two are gathered in His name. Paul's admonitions come from that line of thought.

Frankly, I think part of Paul's concern about women teaching in a congregational meeting is partially the spotlight that such an event would put on the woman. I assume Paul knew how vulnerable males are to enticement since he was a male. Unfortunately, it is not necessary that a woman entice a man willfully. Her simple presence can do so, and to put a woman in the spotlight during a long teaching with somewhat unruly men present, does create potential problems.

1st Timothy 3

Church Leadership

Chapter 3 of Paul's letter to Timothy deals with church leadership. It is important to look at the underlying Greek when we try to grasp early church functioning. From a practical church structure point of view, this is one of the most important chapters in the entire Bible. Paul's first focus is on those who shepherd the overall flock of believers.

Our English translations often can be misleading. The first verse of Chapter 3 is a good example. In the King James, the translation is, *"This is a true saying, 'If a man desire the office of a bishop, he desireth a good work.'"*

In the NASB, the translation is *"It is a trustworthy statement: if any man aspires to the office of overseer, it is a fine work he desires to do."*

The NIV renders this, *"Here is a trustworthy saying: Whoever aspires to be an overseer desires a noble task."*

Which is the better translation? Take a careful look at each translation. What do you notice?

In two of the translations, we have the term *"office"* showing up. Just a tip: the word is not there in the Greek. There probably is a latent meaning of office or position in the word that it modifies (i.e., bishop or overseer), but there is no separate word. It is more the function that is being addressed in the Greek. Otherwise, it sounds a bit like an institutional employee.

Another thing to notice and ponder is that one translation focuses on the work of a bishop; the other two focus on the work of an overseer. Which is more correct?

There is no way of deciding which is more correct without looking at the Greek words in the text. Even that does not solve matters, because we then need to look from the Greek back to the Hebrew. In fact, we have to journey in Latin as well to really understand such an important word in church history. Please hold on to the sides of your roller-coaster car.

In Greek, the word translated *bishop* and *overseer* is *episkope*. This Greek word has roots that are combined to form the total thought: the words *epi* which means *"on"* or *"over"* and the Greek word *skopos* which means *"watcher."* So, the function that Paul is talking about in each church community is the function of being *"on watch"* or *"watching over."*

In my early days, I always interpreted the core meaning of this word as related to the shepherd who "watches over" his flock. But my view has changed somewhat. The reason is how the word was used in translating the Hebrew Old Testament scriptures into Greek. In translating the Hebrew Bible into what was called the Septuagint, the Jewish translators translated the Hebrew word, *pĕquddah*, with the Greek word, *episkopos*. Let's step back one more step and look at when the word was used in the Old Testament.

The first time *pĕquddah* was used is in the book of Numbers:

"And Eleazar the son of Aaron the priest shall be chief over the chief of the Levites, and have the oversight of them that keep the charge of the sanctuary." (Numbers 3:32).

We see here that the term is used for one who oversees other ministers - or staff related to the ministers. So there is a double sense of the function - both the shepherding function and providing spiritual oversight to other ministers. This double insight helps understand how the function evolved within the first 80 years of Jesus's resurrection.

But how did we get the King James using the word *bishop* rather than *overseer*? Hang on a little more tightly.

The Old English word *bisceop*, from which we get our English word *bishop*, comes from the Latin word *episcopus*. Like many other Latin words, this was borrowed from our Greek word. *episkopos*. So, you could say that the King James was using the English word *"bishop"* directly derived from the original Greek word. But by that time, it was very much associated with the structure and function within the English church of the 17th century. This perhaps clouded for many its original functional meaning and its tie to the *"servant of the servants of God."*

The reason I am spending so much time on this is that the evolution of the function and the office in the historical Church is important to fully grasp, and some of that history revolves around the difference between the Greek word Paul used and the different Greek word he used writing Titus – the word *presbyteros*. In verses 5 and 7 in the first chapter of the letter he wrote Titus, Paul uses the two words interchangeably, but they have different meanings.

We see that *bishop* actually means *"overseer"* whereas *presbyteros* means *elder* or *ancient one*. The latter Greek word referred initially to those who had a leadership function in the synagogue as well as the village gate. In the most early days of the Church, we see them functioning in the communities of believers along with another class of ministers, the deacons. Ignatius, *Bishop* of Antioch only about forty years after Paul's death in or around 65 AD, showed how the difference between the two words had evolved in church structure:

"See that you all follow the bishop, even as Jesus Christ does the Father, and the presbytery as you would the apostles; and reverence the deacons, as being the institution of God. Let no man do anything connected with the Church without the bishop. Let that be deemed a proper Eucharist, which is [administered] either by the bishop, or by one to whom he has entrusted it. Wherever the bishop shall appear, there let the multitude [of the people] also be; even as, wherever Jesus Christ is, there is the Catholic Church. It is not lawful without the bishop either to baptize or to celebrate a love-feast; but whatsoever he shall approve of, that is also

pleasing to God, so that everything that is done may be secure and valid."
(Ignatius to the Smyrnaeans, circa 107 AD).

As the churches grew in number and full time leaders increased (particularly those who both *"labored in the word and in doctrine"* – 1st Timothy 5:17), there was a need for someone to oversee the elders. Paul will use the term *presbyteros* in Chapter 5 of 1st Timothy to describe those worthy of double honor (read "more support"), but soon a "president" would be chosen from amongst the *presbyteros* to provide overall oversight. At some point, he would be called the *episkopos*.

This is a long way to say that Paul may have wanted Timothy to pick bishops to manage the elders in Ephesus in Chapter 3. It is hard to know for sure! What we do know is that Ignatius, Bishop of Antioch, while on his way to martyrdom in Rome around 107 AD, wrote a letter to these same Ephesians and identified the former slave, Onesimus, as the Bishop then presiding over the church of the Ephesians. James, the *"brother of the Lord,"* may have provided the same function in the early Jerusalem church.

I've taken several pages to get to verse 2 of Chapter 3, and I hope you will bear with me as we will move more quickly now that the previous thoughts are expressed. Paul simply lists the minimum criteria for an *episkopos*. I think without question *"full of the Holy Spirit"* is understood without being in the outline (see Acts 6). Because of the early interchangeability with the word *presbyteros*, many would also assume these are minimum qualifications for an "elder." I will simply list them:

- Above reproach
- Husband of one wife
- Temperate
- Prudent
- Respectable

- Hospitable
- Able to teach
- Not addicted to wine
- Gentle
- Peaceable
- Free from the love of money
- Not pugnacious (quick to argue or fight)
- One who manages his household well
- Keeps his children under control with dignity
- Not a new convert
- Has a good reputation in the community abroad

Whew. Quite a filter. I am reminded of how seriously the Church at one time took this list. On of our early mentors, E.H. Ijams, refused the position of Elder when it was offered him because one of his children appeared to have fallen away. My reflection after fifty years of walking along God's path is that it is a serious mistake to ignore one word of scripture. E.H. Ijams would not take a chance, and he stands as a great reminder of how serious we all should take appointed leadership.

Deacons and Deaconesses

Paul next moves to the earliest known appointed ministries in the church aside from the apostles: the deacons and deaconesses. You will remember the first deacons were appointed in Jerusalem when the apostles could no longer both teach and take care of the daily distribution of food to those in need. (see Acts 6:1-6). We see in verse 6 how they were installed. First, the community chose seven men, prayed, and then *"laid hands on them"* (a formal investiture of Holy Spirit empowerment). The word *"deacon"* comes almost directly from the Greek word *"diakonos"* which simply means one who executes the commands of another - a servant, a messenger, one who serves food and drink. By the time Paul writes to Timothy in the early 60s AD, the role had become important to the functioning of the church communities. Paul outlines some key criteria for deacons and deaconesses (who probably received monetary support for their labor when full time):

- Men and women of dignity
- Not double-tongued (they needed to be straight shooters)
- Not addicted to much wine
- Not fond of sordid gain (unrighteous behavior regarding money)
- Faithful believers who had a clear conscience
- Tested
- Beyond reproach in their service
- Not malicious gossips
- Temperate
- Faithful in all things
- Deacons could have had only one wife and be good managers of their households

Having been blessed by the ministry of several deacons and deaconesses who function in deed if not in title, I can personally affirm how sweet is their service, particularly at the table of the Lord.

Paul ends with a very interesting reflection on the mystery of godliness, which undoubtedly is to reflect on the criteria he has outlined. It really is a praise of Jesus, the real source of godliness for every servant. It may have been an early Christian hymn, but undoubtedly it is an Ode to Jesus and another way of expressing the kernel of the Gospel:

"He who was revealed in the flesh,
Was vindicated in the Spirit,
Seen by angels,
Proclaimed among the nations,
Believed on in the world,
Taken up in glory."
(1 Timothy 3:16).

Imagine a red-hot branding iron pressed into your conscience, searing and destroying it. This was Paul's picture of people who had *"fallen away from the faith,"* and in process were leading others astray. Paul reminds Timothy that this had been prophesied. Paul himself had told the small emerging church in Thessalonica twenty years earlier that apostasy would surely come before Jesus's return. "Apostasy" comes from the Greek word for *"falling away."*

Paul gives several examples of the problems that Timothy could encounter in Ephesus. In each case, emphasis is placed on the false belief that some form of religious behavior can assure salvation. This is in direct opposition to Paul's often-stated belief that only the death, burial and resurrection of Jesus saves us. There is no human behavior that can accomplish salvation. No cutting of the flesh, celibacy or abstaining from certain foods can save us. Only the Father's great love and Jesus's atoning sacrifice truly saves us.

Thinking about the issue of one food versus another, Paul makes a very interesting observation. Everything God created is good. When presented food of one type or another, our prayer and thanksgiving *"sanctifies"* it all. The power of true thankfulness for everything that comes our way when coupled with prayer has the power to make holy the mundane. My thought is that this is true of things the world may see as very bad indeed - things like cancer, war and other forms of loss. A heart of thanksgiving coupled with prayer makes holy things the world considers bad. Only a Christian can take that position!

Mid-chapter, Paul focuses on what a *"good servant of Christ Jesus"* does. A good servant is *"constantly nourished on the Words of faith and of sound doctrine."* (1st Timothy 4:6). That reminds me of a wonderful mosaic in the thousand-year-old Church of St. Mark in Venice, Italy.

The mosaic depicts a disciple of Jesus named Athanasius who lived in the late 300s. I am fascinated with the picture. It reminds me of was the practical problem Timothy faced when presented with Paul's admonition to *"constantly be nourished on the Words of faith and of sound doctrine."*

St. Athanasius is holding a scroll. Scrolls were the only way a believer could immerse themselves in scripture aside from memorization. And that was no easy task when you think about the 39 or 46 "books" of the Old Testament. Plus, Timothy might well have carried with him hand copied scrolls of various letters from Paul, Peter and John. I constantly remind myself how easy we have it with our Kindles and beautifully readable books.

Timothy, on the other hand, had to carry with him scrolls or visit depositories of such treasures to be *"constantly nourished on the words."*(1ˢᵗ Timothy 4:6). You can catch the practical implications by looking at this photo of clay pots made for preserving a scroll found at the Qumran caves:

Photo by Abraham Meir Habermann taken 1958.12.31, Public Domain

Imagine the practical difficulty of reading much less checking on a verse. Below is an image of the Great Isaiah Scroll from Qumran opened and stretched out for documentation:

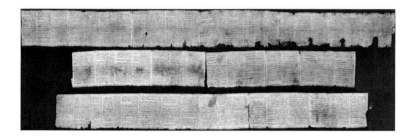

The Great Isaiah Scroll, Qumran, Photos by
Ardon Bar Hama in the Public Domain

Paul also warned Timothy to have nothing to do with worldly fables *"fit only for old women."* I am not sure what Paul meant by his description of the old women, but as I have said before, the airways are full of falsehood, and many then and today are enthralled with esoteric minutia. Esoteric minutia focuses on "secret knowledge" held by only a few select people. This focus can be on an obscure point of doctrine (you can pick any: female leadership, instrumental music, speaking in tongues, angels, eating fish on Friday, prophecy, politics, culture – the list is exhaustive) – you name it. But in every case, the focus will pull you away from a simple devotion to God and attentiveness to your neighbor's well being. Paul wanted Timothy to have none of that.

Paul stressed to Timothy the true value of discipline, both morally and physically. Compared to moral discipline, physical discipline is only of small reward (but it *does* bring a small reward). Godliness, however, is profitable for all things, both now and in the life to come. Paul is absolutely clear on that.

The last third of the chapter contains more specific personal admonitions to Timothy. I must confess that all my life I have misinterpreted verse 12: "*Let no one look down on your youthfulness....*" Because of that verse, I have always seen Timothy as a young man when Paul was writing the letter. I visualized a 25 year old trying to teach a 60-year-old getting pushback because of his youthful age. But by 60 AD, Timothy is probably 43 years old, i.e., no spring chicken. Still, Paul may have been addressing a tendency in the culture of his day where only the truly old were granted real honor and weight. I saw that in Uganda where the elderly are given true deference and honor, and a 43 year old might be looked down on because of "youthfulness." Regardless, Paul noted a shyness and lack of confidence in Timothy that made Timothy shrink back.

Paul had the advantage of knowing that Timothy had already received a spiritual gift for ministry when "*hands* [were] *laid on him*" by a body of elders (*presbyterion*, i.e., "*body of elders*"). This commissioning and appointing function in the church with entreaties to God for "*filling up the hands*" of the one commissioned through the power and agency of the Holy Spirit brings true and needed spiritual gifts.

Paul is quick to remind Timothy of his commissioning which also was accompanied by "*prophetic utterance.*" I am thankful we live in a time when prophetic utterance is not entirely in disdain. On a personal level, I have experienced several moments when hands were laid on me and I received a type of commissioning. Probably the most memorable was by Don Finto in the late seventies or early eighties. Twenty years ago, Jim Goll spoke important prophetic words over Steve Bowie and me, for which we are still accountable and that still inspire us to be very diligent in our work. These special points of clarification are highly useful in keeping us on track, knowing that God has called us to specific tasks for which we must be faithful.

Paul ends his encouragement to Timothy with a well-crafted and deep admonition: *"Take pains with these things; be absorbed in them, so that your progress will be evident to all. Pay close attention to yourself and to your teaching; persevere in these things, for as you do this you will ensure salvation both for yourself and for those who hear you."* May each of us do the same!

1st Timothy 5

Paul continues giving practical instructions in Chapter 5. The big picture is that all Christians are part of God's family and therefore share an important familial relationship.

Again, I think of many of the believers in Uganda who relate as Paul hopes. A younger man in Uganda not only treats an older man as a father but also sees him as a father. Older men see the younger men as true sons and relate to them as such. Young men deem the older women as their mothers. The same is true between the women. Younger men see each other as brothers, and younger women see each other as sisters. Honor (weight) is given to each relationship in a special way because of age.

I don't believe this has been the general experience in most American churches, particularly in Protestant communities. Part of the reason may be Jesus's admonition:

"Do not call anyone on earth your father, for you have one Father, who is in heaven. Nor are you to be called instructors, for you have one Instructor, the Christ." (Matthew 23:9-10).

Growing up, I called E. H. Ijams "Brother Ijams," in spite of the fact that he was at least 50 years my senior and the most respected man in our church congregation. We were particularly careful about Jesus's admonition to call no man father, as least regarding appellation. But Paul in Chapter 5 is not addressing the name we have for each other; he is addressing the way we relate.

Paul's focus is particularly on how Timothy relates to men who are clearly older and more mature. In spite of the fact that Timothy is working under the direction of an apostle and in spite of the fact that hands have been laid on Timothy and prophetic charges given, he still must give honor to the *presbyteros*, the elder man, and treat him as a true father.

For a man soaked in the Ten Commandments and particularly the Fifth as recorded in Deuteronomy 5:16, *"Honor your father and your mother, as the Lord your God has commanded you, that your days may be prolonged and that it may go well with you on the land,"* this means true deference and deep respect. Thus, giving a *"sharp rebuke"* is entirely out of the question, and basically impossible if one heeds the commandment.

The Greek word rendered *"sharp rebuke"* is the word *epiplēssō*. It is a word that means *"strike upon or beat upon or chastise with words."* Had Paul spoken in the positive rather than the negative, I believe Paul would have told Timothy to *"elegchō"* an older man, meaning to reprove him. Paul uses the word in the preceding chapter when he outlines several things that Timothy should be doing. One is to rebuke when appropriate and the other is to reprove when appropriate.

Over the years, I have found Paul's instruction of great value. The word *elegchō* has the sense of *"bring light to."* Hopefully, it is our normal mode of relating with anyone when some instruction is needed. We bring light to an issue rather than rebuke. Rebuke is appropriate when a brother or sister is clearly out of order and walking in some form of darkness. A rebuke carries with it the sense of "command" as opposed to instruction. "Stop doing that!" we say when the issue is dangerous and the situation clear. But otherwise, we *"bring light to."*

The difference between the two actions is useful to ponder when dealing with children. There is a great temptation to continually rebuke a child when only reproof is needed.

Paul then shifts to how widows should be treated within every Christian community, and we look back to the very beginning of the Church when dissension arose in Jerusalem over the food being distributed to the *"widows." "The number of followers was growing. But during this same time, the Greek-speaking followers had an argument with the other followers. The Greek-speaking widows were not getting their share of the food that was given out every day."* (Acts 6:1).

From the earliest time, the church community supported widows who had no one to care for them. With government programs like social security, the plight of the unsupported widow has become less clear, but when believers truly see each other as family, care comes forth. But it remains a sticky question how unsupported is enough for care to be extended.

I must confess that I don't even like the question. It reminds me of my surprise when I first encountered the concept of "worthy" growing up. My congregation had one man (a deacon) charged with giving aid to those in need. The test was "worthiness." Were they worthy of support? It wasn't just a question of need but also some test of whether they were "worth" helping. I internally recoiled at this. We have always thought it better to err on the side of compassion than on the side of tight handedness.

But Paul does give Timothy some clear rules for determining whether aid is appropriate, and this surely is because the open handed posture of the early church brought abuse by many. I would point out that these are general rules. For example, Paul says widows should not receive aid unless they are sixty years of age or older. But suppose a fifty-year-old widow has fallen from her roof and is paralyzed. Is she to be ignored? I think not.

Paul clearly is trying to help the church in Ephesus work through the task of determining whom normally should receive help.

In the ancient church, the decision of need was a matter of discernment. Goods were given to the church by putting them at the feet of the "presiding elder," who treated those funds as "Trust Funds of Piety" in a similar fashion as to how goods were laid at the Apostles' feet and given *"unto each according as any had need."* (Acts 4:35).

Eighty years or so after Paul wrote Timothy concerning the widows, we have this commentary concerning how the church functioned in Samaria:

"Those who were prosperous and wished to do so, gave each as he determined beforehand what he would, and that the collection was laid up with the presiding [elder], who personally relieved orphans and widows and those who were in distress from sickness or any other cause...and in a word took care of all who were in any necessity." (Justin Martyr, c. 140 AD).

One solution is always available when the situation is not clear. A brother or sister may extend their own support without using church funds. We have used that approach in our community with some success.

Concerning *"presbyteros who rule well,"* Paul advises Timothy that they should receive *"double weight"* (honor). It appears Paul has shifted from a discussion of how Timothy should relate to older people to how the church should relate to their appointed *"Elders."* I must say, the wording is not totally clear to me because it could be that Paul is thinking about the daily distribution to those in need, and simply saying that older men who also have served the church well should receive more distribution than simple members on the basis of the rule, *"the laborer is worthy of his wages."*

Paul quotes Jesus in verse 18 as recorded in Luke 10:7 when He was sending out the Seventy: *"And in the same house remain, eating and drinking such things as they give: for the labourer is worthy of his hire."* But Paul seems to be talking about those who are appointed to serve as full-time Elders in the congregations.

Paul goes on to address the important situation that frequently arises in church communities: someone will always have a problem with those appointed to provide oversight and make determinations about the distribution of funds. We can be sure tension will come because people are human, ministers are human, and the Enemy targets every minister for destruction.

The worse accusation is when there has been actual moral failure. But because false accusations can arise, Paul wants two or three people to agree about a charge. If there is a sin being committed and it continues after the charge has been laid, then the Elder is to be brought before the entire community and rebuked. Paul doesn't hesitate with delivering a sharp rebuke *(epiplēssō)* because this is a most serious matter, endangering the entire flock.

Paul solemnly charges Timothy in the presence of God and of the Anointed Jesus and in front of His chosen angels to maintain these principles without any bias. Paul couldn't have made his command more emphatic! The problem with errant *"Elders"* is particularly grave, and therefore Paul counsels Timothy to not *"lay hands upon anyone too hastily."* And also, Timothy has to keep himself free from sin as well. He, too, is subject to serious discipline.

1ˢᵗ Timothy 6

As he has done in several of his letters, Paul is wrapping up issues that are on his mind. Like his letter to the Ephesians, he addresses first those who are slaves and then those who are slave owners. (see Ephesians 6:5-9). In Ephesus, some believing slaves have Christian masters, and Paul emphasizes that they must serve their masters all the more because they are both believers and *"beloved."* Paul exhorts Timothy to affirm these principles because the social harmony that arises is a clear proof of the Gospel to the outsider. Paul anticipates (and perhaps knows) that his principle concerning the relationship between a slave and a slave owner may be difficult to stomach.

Anyone who advocates a way of thinking that does not jive with the teachings of Jesus (who is both Lord and the Messiah) is in great spiritual danger. Such a person becomes a danger to the church.

Paul specifically identifies teachings about what it means to live a Godly life. The Ephesian church was no different from our churches today in one respect: there are always people who focus on making a big deal out of a small thing. It is not that small things do not matter; rather it is that small things are small.

Even well meaning people get stuck on their view of something that is of little consequence, blowing it up until it takes on a perverted focus. When this occurs, the things that are very important become obscured, and people begin to argue and take sides about an idea that may be blown out of proportion or is even false.

Dissension and strife arise, and before you know it, people are speaking critically of one another. When *"constant friction"* is the outcome, it is highly likely that this phenomenon is at work.

Sadly, those who focus on their special knowledge about something that actually is wrong (either in content or emphasis) can become quite conceited in their knowledge. It becomes nearly impossible to discuss things with them pertaining to true Godliness because they quickly get off track.

It appears that some believers in Ephesus were peddling their faulty ideas for gain. Many Radio and TV celebrities today, purported to be Christian, peddle screwball ideas about an abundance gospel or sideline items like vitamins, prayer cloths and bumper stickers. One fellow was selling the "Greatest Vitamin in the World" to treat diabetes and cancer for $35 a pop until the FDA caught up with him.

Once people have a following, it is always a temptation to monetize their audience, and teachers in Ephesus were no exception.

In verse 6, Paul morphs from his observation that false teachers end up motivated to make money to his view on riches. Rather than crazy teaching ideas about how to get rich, only true Godliness is the source of true riches. The Greek word Paul uses here that is translated *"Godliness"* is the word *eusebeia*. This is a word you may be able to remember because it calls to mind the great Christian historian of the late fourth century, Eusebius of Caesarea. His name meant *"respect"* or *"Godliness."* What a great name.

"Eusebeia," Paul tells us, *"is a means of great gain when accompanied by contentment."* The gain Paul is referencing is spiritual gain, which is truly valuable. All believers, from the recently baptized to full time ministers, may store up true riches by their Godliness. In contrast to making a big deal out of a small thing, focusing on *eusebeia* (Godliness) makes a big deal out of something that is a big deal.

But what is Godliness? Let's first think what it is not. It is not worrying about disputes over words and or knowledge of esoteric things that

Paul mentioned earlier in the chapter. Rather, it is mirroring who God is; it is being like God through and through. I always go back to the touchtone of Exodus 34:6-7: *"the Lord God, compassionate and gracious, slow to anger, and abounding in lovingkindness and truth; who keeps lovingkindness for thousands, who forgives iniquity, transgression and sin...."*

These are the things worth focusing on, i.e., who we are in our innermost nature. Thus we pray God will continually transform us. We don't need earthly riches; we need spiritual riches laid up in heaven just as Jesus Himself taught. We want to keep the big thing the big thing!

Paul ends his meditation on money with the well known observation that the *"love of money is a root of all sorts of evil."* The NASB correctly employs the article "a" as opposed to "the" because the love of money certainly is not the only root of evil. But it *is a* root of evil.

In verse 11, Paul uses emphatic language in the Greek to describe Timothy. Following the Greek construction, he says *"O man of God."* I often have wondered exactly what to call Timothy. He was certainly Paul's assistant. Certainly, he was a *"minister"* – a word Paul calls himself in Colossians 1:25 (*diakonos* in the Greek from which we get our word *"deacon"* and which means *"servant"*). But in verse 11, we come to the most striking description: a *"man of God!"* This same term is used to describe Moses, David, Elijah, and Elisha.

Since Timothy is a man of God, he is certainly a target of Satan, and could be tempted by Satan to monetize in someway his ministry. Paul warns him to flee all dangers and simply pursue six virtues:

- Righteousness
- Godliness
- Faith
- Love (*chesed*, steadfast love – which embodies perseverance)

- Perseverance (not giving up in a relationship when the going gets tough)
- Gentleness

You will note immediately that three of these are directly brought over from Exodus 34:6-7, but three are broader terms. Godliness in a sense is all of Exodus 34:6-7. Righteousness is always doing the right thing - what God wants done for the moment. And Faith simply believes the things that are true. Thus, Faith sounds the *emeth (truth)* bell from Exodus 34.

These six qualities are important for every minister. They are not the only virtues, but they are the virtues Paul particularly believes are critical for Timothy's work and the call of God on his life.

In verse 13, we come to another serious command that Paul issues with serious words behind it:

"I charge you in the presence of God, who gives life to all things, and of Christ Jesus, who testified the good confession before Pontius Pilate, that you keep the commandment without stain or reproach until the appearing of our Lord Jesus Christ, which He will bring about at the proper time—He who is the blessed and only Sovereign, the King of kings and Lord of lords, who alone possesses immortality and dwells in unapproachable light, whom no man has seen or can see. To Him be honor and eternal dominion! Amen." (1st Timothy 6:13-16).

Goodness, ponder that Paul would issue the very same charge to each of us! And consider that we have the same authority to charge our own children to do the same, before the gaze of God and the Lord Jesus Christ who is seated on the throne of Heaven beside the Father! What a great and terrible (in the ancient sense of the word) charge.

Paul ends his letter with further admonitions to Timothy to avoid *"worldly and empty chatter"* as well as getting pulled into arguments about *"knowledge"* that is *"no knowledge."* Instead, Paul wants Timothy to guard the deposit he has been given. Paul uses a Greek word that means *"treasure given to a trustee to keep safe,"* i.e., the Gospel of Christ! May we do the same.

2nd Timothy

2nd Timothy 1

I am glad and I am sad. I am glad to get to read the last (from a chronological point of view) recorded letter of the New Testament written by Paul, and I am sad because Paul is writing from Rome, shackled in chains in a dank and dark prison cell. He eventually will be beheaded.

It is likely 67 AD. By this point, the Emperor Nero is seriously deranged. A great fire nearly destroyed Rome three years earlier, and Nero chose the Christians to blame. Paul is at least sixty years of age; his life and work on earth are coming to an end.

Unlike my reading of 1st Timothy, this "second" letter rings with Paul's heart and voice. Timothy is his *"beloved son"* in the faith, and Paul looks back over their many years of collaborative work. He remembers fondly Timothy's tears when they last separated, Timothy's grandmother Lois and his mother Eunice, both of whom Paul met in Lystra during his missionary journeys. (Acts 16:1-3).

Timothy is in a difficult situation in Ephesus where he has been stationed for perhaps four years. You also will recall he and Paul were there in the early days of Paul's ministry for nearly three years. To some degree, Timothy is responsible for keeping the Ephesian church on track. Nero's persecution of the Christians through the empire and Paul's second imprisonment in Rome lie heavily on the hearts of the Ephesian believers. Paul knows his life is about to an end. Undoubtedly, Paul would be concerned that his passing could destabilize the church in Ephesus. Further, he would have concern for Timothy's own safety.

Verses 6 and 7 take us to the heart of Paul's admonition:

"I remind you to kindle afresh the gift of God which is in you through the laying on of my hands. For God has not given us a spirit of timidity, but of power and love and discipline." (2nd Timothy 1:6-7).

This gentle reminder is the crux for all of our lives as believers. It takes us back to our beginnings in the Lord – the time of our baptism in the Spirit which normally accompanies the laying on of hands of a faithful believer and our baptism in water. Paul may have been with Timothy when Timothy was originally baptized in Lystra and could actually be the one who baptized him. But it is also possible that Paul *"laid hands on"* Timothy at Timothy's commissioning as a delegate for the Lord. If that is Paul's reference, Paul would have prayed that God grant Timothy all of the spiritual gifts Timothy would need for the work ahead.

The main point, of course, is that Timothy did receive powerful spiritual gifts through the laying on of Paul's hands, and he needed to *"stir them up!"* Let's again look back briefly at the importance of this action. The *"laying on of hands"* is one of the six *"elementary teachings"* in which every believer should be grounded:

"Therefore leaving the elementary teaching about the Christ, let us press on to maturity, not laying again a foundation of repentance from dead works and of faith toward God, of instruction about washings and laying

on of hands, and the resurrection of the dead and eternal judgment." (Hebrews 6:1-2).

I recall running into this passage in Hebrews as a young man and thinking how deficient my understanding was. In those early days, I dove into the Bible looking for content on all six. The laying on of hands appears from the earliest of times in the Bible.

We find it mentioned throughout Leviticus - in both the sacrificial and ordination ceremonies.

We find it the conveyance of blessings when Jacob lays hands on the two children of Joseph:

"Joseph took them both, Ephraim with his right hand toward Israel's left, and Manasseh with his left hand toward Israel's right, and brought them close to him. But Israel stretched out his right hand and laid it on the head of Ephraim.... He blessed them that day, saying, "By you Israel will pronounce blessing, saying, 'May God make you like Ephraim and Manasseh!'" (Genesis 48:13-14, 20).

We find it in the New Testament when Jesus healed: *"And He laid His hands on her; and immediately she was made erect again and began glorifying God."* (Luke 13:13).

And we find it when spiritual gifts were given for ministry: *"Now Joshua the son of Nun was filled with the spirit of wisdom, for Moses had laid his hands on him;"* (Deuteronomy 34:9).

"While they were worshiping the Lord and fasting, the Holy Spirit said, 'Set apart for Me Barnabas and Saul for the work to which I have called them.' So after they had fasted and prayed, they laid their hands on them and sent them off." (Acts 13:2-3).

"Do not neglect the spiritual gift within you, which was bestowed on you through prophetic utterance with the laying on of hands by the presbytery." (1ˢᵗ Timothy 4:14).

The foregoing verses are only the tip of the iceberg. We should never neglect the gift or the act. It is precious for God's children. It is identification, representation and transmission.

When we have hands laid on us by a brother or a sister, it is as if Jesus Himself is touching us. The brother or sister represents Jesus, and the Holy Spirit transmits special Grace as needed. It may be for discernment, wisdom, healing, commissioning, empowerment – a great many things. It is God's doing; not ours. And it is a GREAT blessing!

The Spirit that God gives, continues Paul, is not a spirit of timidity. Rather, it is a spirit of power and love and discipline. Power, love and discipline. Think of that, for you too have been given the Spirit if the love of God is within you. I believe that is the normative gift. But I believe Timothy was given a special spiritual gift for the work to which he was called.

With the Spirit of God working within Timothy, he can rejoice in Paul's sufferings because of the power of God. This is a miracle in itself. On the outside, Paul is wasting away, but on the inside, Paul is going from strength to strength. Paul is fully confident of the message for which he is in chains. He is not worried about his death for he knows Jesus has "abolished death." With Jesus's advent, life and immortality burst forth.

I love Paul's reflection on his circumstance, a reflection that takes great faith: *"I am not ashamed; for I know whom I have believed and I am convinced that He is able to guard what I have entrusted to Him until that day."* (2ⁿᵈ Timothy 1:12).

Paul's reflection allows him to admonish Timothy to *"retain the standard of sound words"* which he had received from Paul. This is a call on each one of us. We always need to be careful with what we say, what we allege, what impact our words have. They need to jive with the revelation we have received from God.

Words are powerful for both good and evil. It is easy to lecture someone with a forcefulness that maims rather than enlightens. When our childhood solutions for protection "kick in," God help us and particularly those we address! Instead, we want our speech to be full of salt in the ancient sense of the word, i.e., full of faithfulness and truth.

As Paul recounts, we need the Holy Spirit within to guard the truth that has been entrusted to each one of us. Truly, Truth is a treasure – one that must be safeguarded. Satan never tires in his attempt to destroy that treasure.

As we end the chapter, Paul shifts to his own personal situation. You can feel the sadness he carries as he uses the language of rejection and shame:

"All who are in Asia turned away from me, among whom are Phygelus and Hermogenes." (2nd Timothy 1:15). Thankfully, we know Paul is using hyperbole because Timothy is in Asia, and he has not turned against Paul. But Paul's sense of being forsaken by many because of the stain of his captivity hurts. Some of his most beloved communities are in Asia. Many of these communities will grow in numbers and strength as the first century comes to a close. But, from Paul's dark cell, things look dark indeed.

2nd Timothy 2

We must pass on the treasure of truth to other faithful men and women. What we have received from others has been handed down to us. Some people see the transmission of the truth of God generationally to have begun with the apostles, continued for less than a century, and then skipped to the 16th century when people like Luther came along at which time the "passing on" began afresh. I certainly held that view firmly during my teenage years. That view weakened a bit in my 20s, and began to morph into a much different view by my 30s.

The truth is that in every age and every generation faithful men and women have done their best to pass down the kernel of truth that they have received, and the Holy Spirit is quite able to guard the truth's transmission. If it were not so, we would not be Christians today.

And this is not just a matter of the early texts being preserved through the centuries. In fact, the early texts have had a checkered transmission. The Bible as "Protestants" know it was not finally affirmed until Luther removed seven books within the Septuagint version of the Old Testament into a separate group which he called the Apocrypha. They had been included for 1,500 years up to that point. The first two books of Esdras he removed entirely. Luther also questioned Hebrews, James, Jude and Revelation and placed them at the end of his New Testament.

The King James version of 1611 generally followed Luther's lead as did the Calvinist Geneva version of the Bible of 1560.

Eighteen years earlier, Pope Clement VIII had published a revised Catholic edition of the Bible by moving three books not found in the canon of the Council of Trent from the Old Testament collection into an appendix *"lest they utterly perish."* Those three were the Prayer of Manasses and 3rd and 4th Esdras. Otherwise, the Vulgate collection of books prepared by Jerome in 384 AD, which was consistent with the

Synod of Carthage's determination in 397 AD, remained authoritative for over 1,700 years.

Meanwhile, the Eastern Orthodox stream of Christianity took a less rigid approach, valuing the collection of spiritual books that had been passed from generation to generation according to their helpfulness. In other words, they put more emphasis on some books, and included useful spiritual works within their gaze that were not found in the strict canons of the West.

I have a simple point. It is difficult to put your *ultimate* trust in a specific collection of texts. I find it easier to put my trust in the Holy Spirit to keep alive the transmission of truth from brother to brother and sister to sister. But, for that to be effective, one has to do exactly what Paul says in the first chapter, i.e., *"Retain the standard of sound words."* (2nd Timothy 1:13). *"Retain"* means *"keep it!"* To keep it, you have to have it. It has been the responsibility of every generation to diligently keep the truth of God embedded in our lives, understood in our minds and enlivened in our spirits by the Holy Spirit. I am entirely certain that this has been done. Why do I say that? Because I trust the Lord and the Spirit of the Lord a great deal more than I trust mankind.

Paul admonishes Timothy to not get entangled in the things of this world. Timothy is like a soldier in the army of the Lord or an athlete in competition. He has to stay on point, and we have to stay on point. There is no such thing as a true "vacation." We can never vacate our relationship with the Lord and our spiritual connection to those God has put in our paths. No matter what the day, not matter what the season, we are engaged with God and the work God has for us. It is a harmful thing to think otherwise.

Just writing that makes me wince, but I believe it is true and the point that Paul is making to Timothy. We have to be careful not to be *"entangled"* with lesser things than the things of God. But how do we recognize entanglements? Entanglements are those things that we cannot get out of - that we will not stop – those things that take precedence over the responsibilities to God and those brothers and sisters that He has given us. I suppose every age has this danger, but in today's culture, it seems particularly easy for people to choose some form of pleasure regardless of the cost to their responsibilities in God.

"The word of God is not imprisoned." (2nd Timothy 2:9). I love that! Paul is imprisoned, but the word of God is not. This is deeply true. Both the spoken and written word of truth is fully alive and able to ignite life and joy. Jesus, the Word of God, is not imprisoned. No, He is seated at the Father's right hand in the heavenlies, fully able to direct this or that.

Paul then shares with Timothy four sharp truths:

- If we died with Him, we will also live with Him;
- If we endure, we will also reign with Him;
- If we deny Him, He also will deny us;
- If we are faithless, He remains faithful…
  (2nd Timothy 2:11-13).

Paul is speaking truth not only to Timothy but to himself and to us as well. Each of the four truths is applicable to Paul, to Timothy and to us. What I love is the surprise in the fourth couplet: *"If we are faithless, He remains faithful!"* This is the true nature of God, true *chesed*. God remains faithful in a relationship no matter the cost. May His name be praised!

Paul wants everyone reminded of these 4-fold truths. Paul then uses that forceful language that we encountered from time to time in Paul: the solemn charge. As a reminder, I will recall three examples including this one:

- *"I charge* [you] *in the presence of God."* (paraphrased from 2nd Timothy 2:14).
- *"I charge you in the presence of God…and of Christ Jesus…."* (1st Timothy 6:13).
- *"I solemnly charge you in the presence of God and of Christ Jesus and of His chosen angels…."* (1st Timothy 5:21).

Remember Paul's encounter with Elymas on the island of Cyprus? Luke doesn't use the word *"charge,"* but the effect of Paul's authority in God is clearly evident. Here is what happened:

"Saul, also known as Paul, was filled with the Holy Spirit, and he looked the sorcerer in the eye. Then he said, 'You son of the devil, full of every sort of deceit and fraud, and enemy of all that is good! Will you never stop perverting the true ways of the Lord? Watch now, for the Lord has laid his hand of punishment upon you, and you will be struck blind. You will not see the sunlight for some time.' Instantly mist and darkness came over the man's eyes, and he began groping around begging for someone to take his hand and lead him." (Acts 13:9-11).

When Paul gets emphatic, watch out! In 2nd Timothy, he is emphatic about not *"wrangling about words."* For him to use his *"charge"* language was a big deal. I am not sure exactly what he is referencing, but we know Paul battles at every hand dangerous false doctrines that hinge on the interpretation of one word or another. I remember (shamefully) wrangling as a boy with my first Baptist believer encounter while on retreat in Arkansas. We were sitting on a rock above the river hotly arguing over *"once saved, always saved"* and the meaning of baptism. Lord, deliver me!

Paul knows that Timothy will have to *"accurately handle the word of truth"* to be helpful. Remember that the New Testament did NOT exist. A few letters existed from Paul, but the collection of the New Testament was not extant. The word of truth Paul is referencing would include the Old Testament writings in the Septuagint, the oral transmission of truth from mentors like Paul and the revelation of the Holy Spirit to spirit-filled believers. Having the truth at hand is one thing; rightly handling it is another.

It seems to me that the crux rests on the Holy Spirit, because the last 2000 years indicate only too well that people using their reasoning faculty reach very different conclusions about how to apply and utilize received truth. We do need insight and reliable second party confirmation in how we deploy what we believe to be true.

In Ephesus, Paul had heard that two brothers, Hymenaeus and Philetus, believed that the resurrection had already taken place. They apparently taught that the new birth of a Christian at baptism was the resurrection from the dead that Jesus had promised. They may have even denied a resurrection after physical death. It is hard to know for certain. Regardless, their beliefs had negatively impacted some of the Ephesian believers. Appropriately dealing with such problems requires the ability to rightly handle the word of truth.

This is not an abstract problem, and we have faced it every three or four years in our little community. It is SO easy to get off track, enticed by esoteric nonsense, tickled by what truly is of no value whatsoever to living the Christian life. It also is easy, when enticed by Satan to lust in one form or another, to justify outright disobedience, twisting the Word of God to fit one's pleasure.

"Now in a large house there are not only gold and silver vessels, but also vessels of wood and of earthenware, and some to honor and some to dishonor. Therefore, if anyone cleanses himself from these things, he will be a vessel for honor, sanctified, useful to the Master, prepared for every good work. Now flee from youthful lusts and pursue righteousness, faith, love and peace, with those who call on the Lord from a pure heart." (2ⁿᵈ Timothy 2:20-22).

This section can be read at least two ways. One is that any large church community will have weeds as well as wheat as Jesus somewhat predicted. (Matthew 13:24-30). But it can also be taken on a personal basis, and that seems more to the point. It certainly is my experience in *my "large house,"* meaning ME. Paul's observation leads to a direct admonition to Timothy and us to cleanse ourselves from anything slightly dirty, from *"youthful lusts."* I suspect his focus is on sexual conduct. Men (I can't speak for women) are ALWAYS Satan's targets in this zone no matter their age. We don't have to look far today to see this.

Paul's focus on what could distract Timothy lets Paul spotlight four virtues that he wants Timothy to pursue: *righteousness, faith, love and peace.* A *"man of God"* has these goals before him and he needs to go after them with gusto while pushing aside rabbit trails like foolish and ignorant speculations. A focus outside of God's goals only lead to arguments.

Paul is saying that a man or woman of God is called to speak the truth simply and in a straightforward manner, not getting caught in the trap of arguing points. We speak the truth in love with authority. But we don't argue. This is an important point.

"The Lord's bond-servant must not be quarrelsome, but be kind to all, able to teach, patient when wronged, with gentleness correcting those who are in opposition, if perhaps God may grant them repentance leading to the knowledge of the truth, and they may come to their senses and escape from the snare of the devil, having been held captive by him to do his will." (2ⁿᵈ Timothy 2:24-26). *"The Lord's bond-servant"* - Paul's reference to Timothy's identity - that of a slave who, when freedom is presented, instead chooses to bind himself to his master.

This is another way I can refer to Timothy. He is a *"man of God,"* a *yoke-fellow* **and** a *bond-servant*. All of these designations refer to someone who must not be quarrelsome. Instead, he should fully express the character of God that is always kind to all, a great teacher, patient when wronged, and gentle when opposed. I am not at all enamored with tattoos (just the opposite), but having these attitudes emblazoned on my hand might be good! Kind, patient when wronged, gentle when opposed; they are nearly three of a kind. And then, able to teach. A great combination for all of us, and a combination that will help bring others in opposition to us *"to their senses."* Again, it is not hard to find relationships where this instruction applies!

2nd Timothy 3

The middle of Paul's letter is really addressed to the entire church in Ephesus, because it describes what already may have been happening there. With Nero as emperor and fully deranged, undoubtedly difficult times had come or were coming. Paul knows that they are in that season between the ascension of Christ after the resurrection and the time of His return. Only Paul does not know *when* Jesus will return, and Jesus had made it clear that no one would know the exact time of His return. Paul could see things were getting worse on multiple fronts - plus he was in prison near death. It was difficult for Paul; it would be difficult for Timothy and the Ephesians.

His opening is a warning that evil will increase in the *"last days"* before Jesus's return. His description of the evil has made nearly every generation since Paul think the *End* was at hand. Let's take a look and see if these signs are evident today:

lovers of self   lovers of money
boastful   arrogant

revilers	disobedient to parents
ungrateful	unholy
unloving	irreconcilable
malicious gossips	without self-control
brutal	haters of good
treacherous	reckless
conceited	lovers of pleasure rather than God

Finally, holding to a form of godliness, although denying its power.

I suppose it is a matter of degree, because in all ages we find sinful man to be just that – sinful. But there have been times when things were so amuck that evil took almost complete control over various world populations. The Roman Empire itself was a good example. Many of the emperors were demonstratively and horribly evil. As Christianity began to spread, probably the worst was Caligula who reigned during Paul's own lifetime (from 37-41 AD). His practices I cannot reference, as they are too gruesome and disgusting. Nero was a close second. Paul and the Ephesians were living at a time when evil was rampant in high places.

Obviously, it was not the end as here we are 2000 years later. In the interim, we have seen the rise of Islam beginning in the 7th century. Christianity was basically stamped out by the Muslims throughout Judea and Asia Minor. The greatest ancient church edifice in the world, the Hagia Sophia (built in 537 AD), was transformed by the Muslims into a mosque in 1453 AD. A mosque sits atop the ancient temple to God in Jerusalem.

During the Renaissance, there was wide spread licentiousness in different parts of Christendom, particularly concentrated in Rome and Venice. Pope Alexander VI, a Borgia, had such a checkered history that a Dominican monk publicly opposed him, ending up both hanged and burned.

In the last century, we experienced two amazingly corrupt and evil eras, i.e., the reign of godless communism and Nazi Germany. The governments of Stalin and Hitler brought horror to the Church and corruption to the doorway of every home under their control. When I visited the Holocaust Museum in Jerusalem, I was overwhelmed with the horror of rampant evil that oozed from every crack of the Nazi apparatus.

All of that is to say that the degree of evil present prior to Jesus's return must be nearly beyond imagination. Yes, I see disturbing signs in our American society. Things that are clearly wrong are considered right. Homosexuality is embraced even inside of some Christian communities. Sexual relations before marriage is actually recommended by a majority of young people. "Living together" outside of marriage has increase by 900 % in the past 50 years. But we are a long way from Nazi Germany and Communist Russia. Things can get worse!

Regardless, what Paul has done by listing the 19 evils is give us a pretty good outline of sins that we each should passionately avoid. I note that it is easy to criticize our society while engaging in many behaviors on the list. It is easy to revile society, even churches and political leaders. It is easy to gossip. It is easy to be overly focused on yourself. It is easy to carry a view that you are better than others in one test or another, but isn't that simply arrogance and conceit? It is easy to love pleasure; to some degree we are wired for it.

My most important take-away is that a list like this can be helpful if you are a "End Times" detective, but few have that call on their lives. More importantly, it is always good when reviewing Paul's list of virtues and vices to turn the spotlight on yourself and not others. Otherwise, you may find that you are a sign of the End Times yourself, i.e., a reviler!

In light of his list, Paul issues a warning to ladies. Even in the church assembly, they always need to be on guard when men are concerned. This is both timely and true in all eras and all places. Men are wired differently and subject to massive attacks from the evil one in the zone of sexual conduct. Plus, women generally are wired as comforters, and most men today want comfort. When we put the two together, no matter how Godly the man or woman may be, both are vulnerable to get off track and fall into sin, whether married or not.

This means we should be particularly careful about our encounters, having as many safeguards in place as possible, and avoid too much physical contact. I say this from experience as well as observation. We must be *very* careful. It is for this reason that I have never encouraged solo counseling or ministry where a man or woman is involved with the opposite sex unless it is *absolutely* certain that there is no latent danger.

Timothy had seen Paul endure much suffering for the cause of Christ. Paul had nearly been killed in Timothy's hometown of Lystra. He had been rebuked, persecuted and punished by imprisonment. Paul was an excellent example of how to handle the difficulties that were increasing in Ephesus. Paul warned that *"evil men and impostors will proceed from bad to worse, deceiving and being deceived."* (2nd Timothy 3:13). In other words, things would get worse, and deception would be one of the key carriers of evil. By it, many would be deceived.

Deception is perhaps the greatest threat that we face in small and large communities of believers. It has certainly taken an emotional toll on Servants of Christ. Ask yourself the question, "Who is the greatest deceiver?" We know it is Satan. He is the great liar, the great con man, the great accuser of the believers who sows lies, lies, and more lies. I remember a drawing I drew in my journal in 1999. It showed Satan's henchmen going through God's fields showing lies, fear and perversion.

Falsehood is His nature; deception his primary tool.

It is SO easy to be deceived. Can you tell how you are being deceived even right now? We are all deceived to the same degree that we believe a lie that Satan has sown in the unconscious part of our mind. For many, the lie is that we are not "good enough," that we are not smart enough, that we are not attractive enough, that we are not loved enough, that we are alone and that we don't measure up. This lie rests as a seedbed for sin. You can see that sexual sin lies at the door when our internal world is believing the lie. We want love and acceptance. All sorts of sin crop up.

Paul is quick to point out that even though Satan is hard at work sowing deception at every turn, we are amazingly blessed to have Scripture as our ally. When Paul wrote, he was specifically referring to the Old Testament scriptures because the New Testament did not exist as we know it. Paul's comment today is applicable to the entire Bible. It is "God inspired." The chapter ends with one of Paul's most quoted sentences illustrating how valuable the Word of God is for the believer:

"All Scripture is inspired by God and profitable for teaching, for reproof, for correction, for training in righteousness; so that the man of God may be adequate, equipped for every good work." (2nd Timothy 3:16-17).

A bit like a miracle drug, it can do so many things. It can teach us how to live and conduct ourselves in the world. It can shine light on areas clouded by misunderstanding and darkness. It can correct us, and it can train us how to do the right thing so that we are truly competent as a man or woman of God. May God bless the reading of His Word today!

2nd Timothy 4

"I solemnly charge you in the presence of God and of Christ Jesus, who is to judge the living and the dead, and by His appearing and His kingdom..." (1st Timothy 4:1). This time, Paul charges Timothy in front of God and Jesus, His appearing AND His Kingdom. It is another solemn charge, and it is a simple but challenging one - preach the "Word" and be ready at all times to do three things: *"reprove, rebuke and exhort."*

In the previous chapter, Paul addressed the importance of using Scripture to *reprove* (bring light to an issue or subject) and to train (see 2nd Timothy 3:16). Paul now adds a new word: *rebuke.* What is the difference between reproving and rebuking? We reflected on these very same words in Chapter 5 of 1st Timothy and our general thoughts are worth repeating with a slightly different emphasis.

Epitimaō is the Greek word for *rebuke*, and it is used in the sense of issuing a command or charge to someone who is doing something wrong. We bring *reproof* to a brother or sister when we shed more light on an issue, trusting God to help the person see a more accurate picture of something. But when it is clear a brother or sister is doing something wrong, we tell them simply that they must stop. We could even *"solemnly charge them in the presence of God and Jesus Christ."* A *rebuke* is reserved for serious and usually willful misbehaving.

Paul also admonishes Timothy to *exhort* (NASB translation). In the Greek, this is the word *parakaleō* which immediately brings to mind the promised *"Paraclete,"* i.e., the *Comforter* Jesus promised, the Holy Spirit. It is often used in the New Testament when the sick entreat Jesus to heal them, but Jesus really shows its meaning in the story of the Prodigal Son.

Remember that the Elder Brother was angry about how well his younger brother was being treated by his father, and refused to come into the house. We've all seen such behavior in children. What did the father do? He went out to his son and *parakaleō*'d him. He *entreated* him. He did not command him; instead, he spoke to the elder boy's heart. (Luke 15:28).

When the situation demands it, out of love we are called to bring light, to rebuke and to entreat our brothers and sisters in Christ. Paul has already admonished Timothy to be gentle and kind to everyone with whom he works. Remember his words from the second chapter:

"The Lord's bond-servant must not be quarrelsome, but be kind to all, able to teach, patient when wronged, with gentleness correcting those who are in opposition, if perhaps God may grant them repentance leading to the knowledge of the truth, and they may come to their senses and escape from the snare of the devil, having been held captive by him to do his will." (2nd Timothy 2:24-26).

Early in the chapter, we see another descriptor for Timothy –*evangelist.* The evangelist is the one who brings "good news" to those who need to hear it. It is almost the original Greek word, *euaggelistēs.* When the Greek word is spoken, it sounds like yü-än-ge-lē'-zō. You will note that our English word for *angel* is hidden inside that pronunciation.

In Greek, the word derives from two roots, one of which sounds like "angel", meaning *"messenger of God"* and the other word is the preface, an adverb meaning *"good."* So we have the meaning: *Godly Messenger of Good Tidings*, or in more familiar terms, Messenger of the Gospel. That was Timothy's role, his job, his office, and his responsibility on earth, i.e., to be God's messenger.

Messengers have different responsibilities and therefore different spiritual gifts from an apostle, a shepherd or a bishop (overseer). It is always good to know your job!

Paul sums up his life for Timothy, and another famous quote comes from verses 7 and 8:

"I have fought the good fight, I have finished the course, I have kept the faith. Henceforth there is laid up for me a crown of righteousness, which the Lord, the righteous judge, shall give me at that day: and not to me only, but unto all them also that love His appearing."

That would be the result for Paul, for Timothy and hopefully for each of us who look forward to His appearing.

Paul wants Timothy to come to him as quickly as possible. Many have left him. In Rome, only Luke is there with him. We notice in Paul's updates a lot of movement amongst the apostolic team: Titus to Dalmatia, Tychicus to Ephesus, Crescens to Galatia. Paul hopes Timothy will bring Mark when he comes.

As Paul's letter ends, it seems clear he is not giving up nor retiring. He wants his cloak for the winter and his scrolls as well. To get Paul his coat, Timothy will have to go to Troas where Paul left it. Paul warns Timothy to be on guard there for Alexander the coppersmith who did Paul much harm when Paul was in Troas. Alexander had vigorously opposed Paul's teaching, and Paul knew he would oppose Timothy's messages as well.

Paul is amazingly confident as he nears the end. He trusts the Lord and knows He will deliver him from every evil deed and bring him safely to the heavenly Kingdom. We should have the same trust and certainty as well.

Titus

Titus 1

In Paul's opening salutation to his *"true child in the faith,"* Titus, Paul calls himself a *doulos*, a *bond-slave* of God, as well as an apostle of Jesus Christ. Paul calls himself a bond-slave only once in letters written to individuals (at least those that are extant), and it is here in his letter to Titus.

Paul refers to himself in the same way in his letter to the Romans and to the Philippians. Recall that Paul also referred to Timothy as a bond-servant when he wrote their joint letter to the Philippians. And remember that a bond-servant freely became the slave of another – he was one who devoted himself entirely to another person's interest in total disregard of his own. In the case of Paul, Titus and Timothy, that other person was Jesus. We individually should ask ourselves the obvious question, "Do I qualify as a true bond-servant?"

Like Timothy, Titus is one of Paul's "children" in the faith. Titus had worked alongside Paul from around 47 AD. We find him first mentioned in relationship to Paul and Barnabas's visit to Jerusalem from the church community in Antioch. as recorded in Acts which I quote below in its entirety:

"Now those who had been scattered by the persecution that broke out when Stephen was killed traveled as far as Phoenicia, Cyprus and Antioch, spreading the word only among Jews. Some of them, however, men from Cyprus and Cyrene, went to Antioch and began to speak to Greeks also, telling them the good news about the Lord Jesus. The Lord's hand was with them, and a great number of people believed and turned to the Lord.

"News of this reached the church in Jerusalem, and they sent Barnabas to Antioch. When he arrived and saw what the grace of God had done, he was glad and encouraged them all to remain true to the Lord with all their hearts. He was a good man, full of the Holy Spirit and faith, and a great number of people were brought to the Lord.

"Then Barnabas went to Tarsus to look for Saul, and when he found him, he brought him to Antioch. So for a whole year Barnabas and Saul met with the church and taught great numbers of people. The disciples were called Christians first at Antioch.

"During this time some prophets came down from Jerusalem to Antioch. One of them, named Agabus, stood up and through the Spirit predicted that a severe famine would spread over the entire Roman world. (This happened during the reign of Claudius.) The disciples, as each one was able, decided to provide help for the brothers and sisters living in Judea. This they did, sending their gift to the elders by Barnabas and Saul." (Acts 11:19-29).

Luke makes no mention of Titus accompanying Paul and Barnabas, but Paul recalls that Titus came with him when the three went up to Jerusalem in Paul's letter to the Galatians:

"I went up again to Jerusalem, this time with Barnabas. I took Titus along also. I went in response to a revelation and, meeting privately with those esteemed as leaders, I presented to them the gospel that I preach among the Gentiles. I wanted to be sure I was not running and had not been running my race in vain. Yet not even Titus, who was with me, was compelled to be circumcised, even though he was a Greek. This matter arose because some false believers had infiltrated our ranks to spy on the freedom we have in Christ Jesus and to make us slaves. We did not give in to them for a moment, so that the truth of the gospel might be preserved for you." (Galatians 2:1-5).

From this short excursion into two other New Testament books, we learn that Titus was Greek and not Jewish, and met Paul in Antioch. We also see that very early disciples of Jesus had escaped from Jerusalem at the time of the persecution that occurred when Stephen was stoned. Some of those disciples went to the islands of Cyprus and Cyrene, and from there on to Antioch.

In Antioch, these disciples shared the good news of God's love and Jesus's ascension to Greeks as well as Jews. Titus was perhaps one of those that responded in faith. He may have even become a follower in Cyrene (northern Africa), Cyprus or even Crete (the large island due north of Cyrene in the Mediterranean).

The Orthodox Church believes that Titus was born on Crete, had moved to Jerusalem and became a member of Jesus's Seventy, and later left during the persecution of Christians around the time that Stephen was stoned. This, I find hard to imagine since clearly Titus was an uncircumcised Jew. Regardless, when Barnabas brought Paul to Antioch from Tarsus, Paul became Titus's mentor.

We see that Titus was not circumcised when he accompanied Paul and Barnabas to Jerusalem. Two years later, Timothy had to be circumcised in Lystra, Asia Minor, at Paul's direction. This had to be done because Paul wanted Timothy, who was half Greek and half Jewish, to accompany him further into Asia Minor. Paul already had encountered severe opposition to his teaching about non-Jews being allowed to convert to Jesus without circumcision, and he didn't want to stir things up further, particularly because Timothy had a Jewish mother. Apparently, Titus was able to avoid circumcision and be received in Jerusalem without great controversy.

Titus is mentioned in Paul's second letter to the Corinthians in relationship to Paul's work in Troas. The passage is a bit hard to interpret.

"Now when I went to Troas to preach the gospel of Christ and found that the Lord had opened a door for me, I still had no peace of mind, because I did not find my brother Titus there. So I said goodbye to them and went on to Macedonia." (2nd Corinthians 2:12-13).

Apparently, Paul had anticipated that Titus would be there. We don't know exactly what occurred, but we do note that Paul was worried about his *"brother"* not being there.

"For when we came into Macedonia, we had no rest, but we were harassed at every turn—conflicts on the outside, fears within. But God, who comforts the downcast, comforted us by the coming of Titus, and not only by his coming but also by the comfort you had given him. He told us about your longing for me, your deep sorrow, your ardent concern for me, so that my joy was greater than ever." (2nd Corinthians 7:5-7).

Titus must have rejoined Paul by the time Paul first ministered in Corinth. When the famine in Jerusalem arose, Titus went back to Corinth *"on his own accord"* to raise funds. Paul speaks highly of Titus's work in Corinth throughout Chapter 8 of Paul's second letter to the Corinthians. Paul called him his *"partner and fellow worker,"* and also an apostle (the word for a special messenger).

"As for Titus, he is my partner and fellow worker among you; as for our brethren, they are messengers (apostolos) *of the churches, a glory to Christ."* (2ⁿᵈ Corinthians 8:23).

All of this is to introduce Titus, a key yoke-fellow of our brother Paul. My guess is that he is somewhat younger than Paul, but not by much – perhaps in his early fifties, a mature man. He and Paul have worked together for at least 20 years. He is rock-solid and a bond-slave of Jesus Christ, deeply appreciated by Paul.

The Mission

Paul likely writes to Titus just before he writes his last letter to Timothy. Remember, we are in the mid 60s (AD) and at the end of Paul's career. Paul and Titus had visited the large island of Crete after Paul's first imprisonment in Rome, and Paul left Titus there to *"set in order what remains and appoint elders* (presbyteros) *in every city."* (Titus 1:5).

You will recall that Paul wrote a very similar letter to Timothy (see 1ˢᵗ Timothy 3) about the same time regarding the region in and around Ephesus concerning the same issue: setting in place clear oversight responsibilities in the different church communities.

Crete is a large island in the middle of the Mediterranean, about 250 miles due south of Athens. It is a long island that stretches nearly 250 miles in an east/west direction and contained in the first century over a hundred towns. In very ancient times (around 1700 BC), Crete was the center of the Minoan civilization. I had to study its architecture in some detail while at the University of Virginia. It was advanced in many ways, and created the precursor of the great Greek architecture that developed over the next thousand years. The palace of Knossos was a true marvel. It was also from Crete that we got the famous legend of the Minotaur, King Minos and the labyrinth.

Paul wanted to strengthen all the congregations on the island. Think of what an enormous task that would be if the island had seen a good number of house churches emerge in different cities spread out over 250 miles. That is further than the distance between Memphis and Nashville. Plus, no automobiles! Add the difficulty of developing trusting relationships with each congregation - a necessary step before Titus could actually appoint elders successfully. And then, Titus must find men that could pass through Paul's filter.

Similar to what Paul wrote Timothy, Paul has a list of the qualifications that must be met.

- Above reproach. *
- The husband of one wife. *
- Having children who believe.
- Not accused of dissipation.
- Not accused of rebellion.
- Not self-willed.
- Not quick-tempered (temperate).*
- Not addicted to wine (not an alcoholic). *
- Not pugnacious (one who tends to fight and argue). *
- Not interested in sordid gain (free from the love of money).*
- Hospitable (one who opens his house). *
- Loving what is good.
- Sensible.
- Just.
- Devout.
- Self-controlled.
- Holding fast to the faithful word of God (in accord with both scripture and what has been passed down).
- Able both to exhort to sound doctrine and refute the opposition (able to teach).*

This is at least an 18-point filter. I have included an asterisk * in the list above if I felt it was mentioned in Paul's list to Timothy. But the following six qualities that Paul enumerated for Timothy were not directly included in Titus' list:

- Respectable.
- Gentle.
- Peaceable.
- One who manages his household well (keeping his children under control with dignity).
- Not a new convert.
- One who has a good reputation with outsiders.

That makes 24 hurdles that must be cleared if the two lists are combined.

Two of those not in Timothy's list relate to accusations from others, and the only way this could be ascertained is by asking the congregations for any issues they might have concerning people Titus might be thinking of appointing: accusations of dissipation and a rebellious spirit.

Other points not covered in Timothy's list include *"not self willed...loving what is good...sensible...just...devout...self-controlled...holding fast to the faith as received."* Of course, Paul did not mean to exclude any of the qualifications; he was not trying to make a perfect and exhaustive list in either letter. Rather, Paul was addressing the need for Godly men and using words he thought would be helpful to each man.

This observation is true of almost all lists in the Bible. It is wise to remember that the Holy Spirit is quickening words and meanings as each writer writes to a specific audience. We have to catch the thrust of what the writer is saying, recognizing it is to a specific audience at a specific time. But, we also must realize the words are useful for us in perhaps a somewhat different way.

I could use different words than Paul and be looking for similar men. We want men as leaders of our communities who passionately love God, who are not in the least dangerous, who have been tested over time in both their families and the household of God so that their fruit clearly can been seen, who are not afraid to confront evil but gentle to all and fully able to teach. They should not be addicted to anything unwholesome, but rather devoted to God. Men who truly care about the welfare of others.

We could go further describing good qualities of faithful men, but hopefully you see my point. We want God's choices – men full of the Holy Spirit. A tall order, but not a tall order for God.

Paul is being extremely careful to be sure that Titus does not get fooled and appoint the wrong people. I again note that in many American churches today, many of these qualifications are totally ignored. When we were in our twenties and in a fellowship of young people, brothers were appointed as shepherds at a very young age and called to function as elders. This proved foolhardy, and many later shipwrecked. It is always better to be safe than sorry.

Men Off Track

Paul immediately follows his qualification list by reminding Titus of the kind of people he will encounter that would be a disaster for the churches. These men will be vocal but deceivers, saying things that are not true but not so obvious, and also they are basically rebellious in nature. So often, this kind of person will rise to prominence in a community, but that does not mean that the person would be a good pick. Instead, Titus needs to be searching for this very type of man to be sure not to pick him.

Apparently, Paul expected a good number of this type of person on Crete amongst those pushing circumcision. They were upsetting families, causing strife, and most amazingly, asking for monetary support from the congregations. Such men *"profess to know God, but by their deeds they deny Him, being detestable and disobedient and worthless for any good deed."* (Titus 1:16). Paul wants Titus to soundly *"reprove them"* so that those on the wrong track might be righted.

The Question of Elders and Bishops

In Paul's letter to Titus, we see each fully vested community having their key leadership either appointed or confirmed by *outside* trustworthy Servants of God. Once these communities are fully equipped with oversight, it is not entirely clear what Paul expected to happen about new appointments. Would the existing leadership appoint them, or would some form of trans-local authority be involved?

Additionally, Paul uses the word we discussed at some length in his letter to Timothy, the word *episkopos*. We recall this is the Greek word that means overseer and that the two words, *presbyteros* (elder) and *episkopos* (overseer or bishop), appear interchangeable in these early church communities.

It is interesting to also reflect that Titus is considered by both the Orthodox Church and the Roman Catholic Church to be the first Bishop over the entire island of Crete, serving basically as an "archbishop" if you assume he had been appointing bishops all over the island. Paul's letter to Titus brings us front and center in the middle of the 3rd decade of the church (i.e., around 65 AD) to an early church structure that would eventually be forcefully disputed 1,700 years later by Protestants.

As we pointed out previously, in another sixty years, many of the church communities would be organized with one bishop *(episkopos)* and a plurality of elders *(presbyteros)*. We are not there yet. The question remains, "Can we trust the Holy Spirit or not to guide the fledgling churches as they mature or not?"

Titus 2

As Chapter 2 begins, Paul shifts to address the way other groups of believers in Crete are to behave. Older men are to be temperate, dignified, sensible, sound in faith, loving and willing to endure difficulty and hardship.

Paul wants the older women to be reverent and not malicious gossips, not addicted to wine, and directs them to teach the younger women good things. Paul particularly has in mind that older women will encourage the younger women to love their husbands and their children.

Though Paul goes on with his list of good behaviors, let's pause and consider the differences between his description of Godly older men and Godly older women. A spotlight shines on the responsibility of the older women to teach the younger women. No doubt, there are many reasons for Paul's emphasis. But most important is the fact that older women are simply more appropriate to teach younger women than men – particularly as it comes to loving their husbands.

Paul uses the Greek word *philandros* which simply means *"loving her husband."* One of the roots is *philos* which means *friend.* To be the true friend of one's spouse is a great goal for every wife. Paul used *agapē* for the type of love he felt older men should exhibit which emphasizes *sacrificial love.* Older men and women would do well to ponder Paul's emphasis.

Paul wants the younger women to be sensible, chaste, workers at home, kind and subject to their husband's authority. When this is not the case, outsiders will revile the faith because of the poor example set in wise and harmonious living.

Many years ago, Fran and I were in New York at an Urban Land Institute meeting. She was at the table with a high-powered female executive who turned and asked her in a condescending fashion, "So, what is your area of expertise?"

Fran was taken aback, but replied, "Homemaking." I was very proud of her because once children are in the roost, it is best for moms to do that very thing: make the home a true home for both spouse and children. That doesn't mean a woman cannot work from home base, but a wife's top priority should be her home.

I like Paul's admonition to young men that follows. He wants them to be sensible as well. On the whole, young men today exhibit delayed adolescence and appear easily distracted by empty pursuits. This often has been the case, but American society and parents today unintentionally support dependence and frivolousness in many ways. *"Failure to Launch"* was a movie that caught the drift well.

Young men desperately need the example of hard working older Christian men given to service in the community as well as earning a living. In particular, men need to learn to take care of their equipment and live in a thoughtful way. Paul stresses the importance of majoring in *"good deeds"* as well as the importance of learning – particularly with regard to Scripture and how to best order one's life. He knows how important it is not to get caught up in worldly desires and frivolous pursuits.

Paul makes a great emphasis on what young men spend their time talking about; they need to be *"sound in speech which is beyond reproach."* (Titus 2:8). Honestly, this is an amazing challenge for most young men. If you ever get a chance to listen to "locker room talk," you would be exactly what Paul feared, i.e., "ashamed."

Like his letters to the Ephesians, Colossians and to Timothy, Paul addresses the situation of slaves who have become believers on the island. There must have been many. Paul calls for the type of behavior that is the exact opposite of what one would expect from a worldly perspective: being totally subject to their masters *"in everything,"* pleasing, not argumentative, not stealing, and showing great faithfulness. A bold goal. I am reminded of how well this should describe the Christian worker in any job position.

Paul closes the chapter with a great summary statement of how we all should be postured before God and the world:

"For the grace of God has appeared, bringing salvation to all men, instructing us to deny ungodliness and worldly desires and to live sensibly, righteously and godly in the present age, looking for the blessed hope and the appearing of the glory of our great God and Savior, Christ Jesus, who gave Himself for us to redeem us from every lawless deed, and to purify for Himself a people for His own possession, zealous for good deeds." (Titus 2:11-14).

Sensible, righteous and expressing the character and nature of God in our settings. This is our hope and our earthly goal.

Note particularly how Paul describes Jesus's appearing: *"and the appearing of the glory of our great God and Savior, Christ Jesus, who gave Himself for us to redeem us from every lawless deed, and to purify for Himself a people for His own possession, zealous for good deeds."*

Words such as these help clarify our understanding of the nature of the Godhead. The Anointed Jesus is both God and Savior!

Titus 3

Paul ends with another list of good and bad behaviors. Is he right to focus on these lists?

There is a clear tension between focusing on *how* we act versus *why* we act. Jesus was quick to point out that our external behavior was not a sign of our internal condition. He called the Pharisees *"white washed tombs,"* because they looked good on the outside, did the right things and yet were corrupt on the inside. The Prophet Jeremiah said, *"The heart is deceitful above all things and beyond cure."* (Jeremiah 17:9).

The importance of the heart was not lost of Paul. His lists of behavior served as yardsticks to gage how believers were actually doing. *"Watch over your heart with all diligence, for from it flow the springs of life."* (Proverbs 4:23).

"With all diligence" means we must know the condition of our heart, and yet Jeremiah has reminded us that the heart is deceitful. That means it is hard to truly know the condition of one's heart. Thus, Paul provides these lists as a reminder; when we read each behavior, our minds can scan our true reality.

Of course, our minds also are subject to deceit. In fact, one of the negative behaviors Paul mentions is deceitfulness. God knew all of this. It was for this reason that God intervened.

Paul says it well: Out of His kindness and love, *"He saved us, not on the basis of deeds which we have done in righteousness, but according to His mercy, by the washing of regeneration and renewing by the Holy Spirit, whom He poured out upon us richly through Jesus Christ our Savior."* (Titus 3:5-6).

The Importance of Baptisms

Paul focuses on two aspects of God's mercy shown to us through Jesus's death – the washing of regeneration and the renewing of the Holy Spirit, which has been poured out upon us. These are the baptisms that the writer of Hebrews will mention as elementary to the Christian's walk – baptism in water and baptism in the Holy Spirit.

Once, during a time of worship, I saw the feet of Jesus nailed to the cross and the blood and water flowing down from His wounded side. His blood and water was dripping down his legs and feet onto the earthen ground. I was conscious that His blood continues to drip, cleansing yet another generation of sin and allowing His Spirit to be *"poured out upon us."* *"Yadah Yehovah towb chesed olwam."* Thanks be to God for his goodness; His steadfast love never comes to an end! (Psalm 118: 1).

Detail of Fresco by Fra Angelico at San Marco, Florence

Our challenge is to be immersed in His Spirit every day and every moment. We must always give ourselves to God, rejecting our old way of life while allowing the newness that His Spirit brings to renew our hearts.

Paul list six positives and seven negatives that everyone, old and young, male and female, can use as touchstones. As we look at each behavior, let your mind search your heart and your actual behavior and use Titus 3 as the help it was meant to be.

Let's ask ourselves the question, "Are we truly submissive to those God has put over us, doing their bidding and abiding by their direction?" Are we on the alert for every opportunity to extend help to others even when we know it will be difficult? Are we speaking poorly of someone? Are we gentle, peaceful and thoughtful with those closest to us?

On the negative front, Paul asks whether we are acting foolishly in one way or another way? This is a broad question. He also asks whether we are disobeying God-given authority in some zone, and whether we are deceived about our condition. Are we enslaved to various lusts and pleasures? Is there someone who has wronged us and we continue to hold a grudge, speaking ill of him or her? Is someone doing better than we are, and envy and jealously have welled up in our hearts leading us to hate and be hateful?

Good Deeds

Paul wants the Cretans and all of us to be focused on doing good for others. Look at his language: "*be careful to engage in good deeds.*" (Titus 3:8), and "*Our people must learn to engage in good deeds to meet the pressing needs so that they will not be unfruitful.*" (Titus 3:14). It is easy to fill our time with religious focus on building ourselves up while many with true needs go unaided. The Spirit of God, left to itself, often prompts us to action and thus produces fruit!

Paul advises Titus to avoid endless strife and disputing about foolish controversies and to not associate with fractious men or women after they have been warned twice to stop such behavior. This is an important rule for communities. Satan sows discord through a spirit of discord.

Personal Instructions

Paul ends his letter with apostolic team business. After his imprisonment, his team has grown. He intends to send either Artemas or Tychicus to Titus in the hope that Titus can meet Paul in the seaside town of Nicopolis on the Adriatic where he hopes to winter. Nicopolis is about 120 miles northwest of Corinth. The lawyer Zenas and Apollos must either be on Crete or about to arrive there as Paul hopes they will be well received by Titus.

Philemon

Paul's shortest letter in the New Testament is a simple note he had written to his Christian brother, Philemon, who lived in the town of Colossae. We gather Philemon lived in Colossae because of the letter Paul wrote to the church in Colossae where he mentioned Philemon's escaped slave, Onesimus. Likely a non-believer when he ran away, I suspect Onesimus became a believer under Paul's ministry in Rome.

Paul is writing Philemon around the year 61 or 62 AD, likely at the same time that he wrote the church in Colossae and perhaps a year before he wrote 1st Timothy. Timothy is in Rome with Paul as he writes and is included in the salutation to Philemon. The context of Paul's letter sheds light on the true and radical nature of the Gospel.

Slavery was rampant throughout the Roman Empire. The Roman scholar, Mark Cartwright, estimates that thirty percent of Rome's population was composed of slaves and that one in five were in the rest of the empire. He gives a good description of the normal citizen's viewpoint in his article on *"Slavery in the Roman World:"*

"Slavery, that is complete mastery (dominium) of one individual over another, was so imbedded in Roman culture that slaves became almost invisible, and there was certainly no feeling of injustice in this situation

on the part of the rulers. Inequality in power, freedom and the control of resources was an accepted part of life and went right back to the mythology of Jupiter overthrowing Saturn.... Freedom...was not a general right but a select privilege."

Regardless of how embedded slavery was in Colossae, Onesimus wanted his freedom and chose escape as the solution. Yet, after meeting Paul and hearing the good news of Jesus's remarkable sacrifice and elevation to Heaven, he gave his life to the Lord and found true freedom.

Paul taught that living in Christ under the direction of the Holy Spirit meant that regardless of one's circumstance, a person could be content – in a sense, truly free. Practically, this meant that one could be in very tough circumstances, even living as a slave, and be content.

"I am not saying this because I am in need, for I have learned to be content in any circumstance." (Philippians 4:11).

Coupled with Paul's teaching about circumstances was his teaching of the importance of being submissive under authority. Jesus's eventual sacrifice set the bar high for obedience:

"although He existed in the form of God, [He] did not regard equality with God a thing to be grasped, but emptied Himself, taking the form of a bond-servant, and being made in the likeness of men. Being found in appearance as a man, He humbled Himself by becoming obedient to the point of death, even death on a cross. For this reason also, God highly exalted Him...." (Philippians 2:6-9).

Being an obedient bondservant was a high calling because it exemplified Jesus. I feel sure the culture throughout the Roman Empire was stunned by the shift in attitude exhibited by slaves to their owners when slaves gave their lives to Jesus.

In Onesimus's case, the impact was even clearer as he knew that his former rebellion was beneath the wonder of a life in the Messiah. His change of heart must have been profound, and in spite of being of great service to Paul during Paul's house arrest in Rome, he was willing to return to his master in Colossae.

Thus, Paul's letter has a simple purpose. He wanted Philemon, a well-to-do man in Colossae who also had given his life to the Lord, to receive Onesimus with kindness.

Apparently, Paul had not planted the church in Colossae. Rather, his fellow worker, Epaphas, had done so. (Colossians 1:7-9). But Paul probably went through the town on his third missionary journey while going from Antioch in Pisidia to Ephesus. I assume he met Philemon on the way and brought him to the Lord.

Paul addresses Philemon and other members of his household. Philemon is Paul's *"beloved brother and fellow worker,"* and it is clear Paul thinks well of Philemon and has heard good reports of his love and faith toward the Lord and all the believers there in Colossae.

Then Paul says something that interests me; Paul wants the *"fellowship of Philemon's faith"* to become *"effective"* by Philemon knowing every good thing that has been placed within him because of Jesus.

Two things strike me. First is the idea of your faith in God being something with which you can fellowship. Think of that. Your trust in God is like a companion to you. You can have a relationship with that trust – finding it a comfort and as well as an inspiration.

Second, God puts *"good things"* in you that we likely don't grasp at first. Paul prays that Philemon will come to know those special gifts. This reminds me of a teaching we received early in our walk with the Lord: you must unwrap the gifts under the tree. It is a mistake to not realize that you have been given gifts that need to be both unwrapped and deployed. Every believer should be encouraged to have faith and unwrap giftings they haven't unwrapped.

Philemon has been generous in the support of others, and this has delighted Paul. *"The hearts of the saints have been refreshed through you."* (Philemon 7). For this reason, Paul is quite confident that Philemon will receive Onesimus in love, and also knows that he will respect Paul's request if for no other reason than deference for Paul's advanced age and circumstance. Remember that Paul is still in prison.

But to be sure of Philemon's reception, Paul makes an earnest plea, backing it up with a promise to personally right any wrong that Onesimus might have caused. He ends his plea with a hope that I would turn around, i.e., I hope *we* might *"benefit"* our brothers and sisters in concrete ways, that *we* might *"refresh"* each other's hearts in Christ. Yes, may we refresh each other as we walk in love and the Holy Spirit! That is a great and practical goal for all of our relationships.

Paul ends his short appeal hoping that he will soon be released and able to visit Philemon. *"Prepare me a lodging."* I think of our brothers Medad and Terry Smith who often surprise us with their coming.

In closing, Paul sends Philemon greetings from Rome, and we get some idea who is there in Rome with Paul: Epaphras (also a prisoner), Mark, Aristarchus, Demas and Luke.

Hebrews

Hebrews 1

Better Than Angels

I've realized we would eventually come to Hebrews, and I have been excited but also intimidated. Excited because my old missionary mentor, Bob Frahm, who worked tirelessly with me in Sweden during the late 60s while I was completing an American Scandinavian Foundation Thord-Gray Fellowship, thought that the key to understanding God's great work was explained clearly in Hebrews – if you had ears to hear it. Intimidated, because Hebrews is a dense book. Some think it second only to Romans in terms of theological impact, though I am not inclined to rank such things. Hebrews *is* an important book – a book that has certainly directly influenced my life in important ways.

Growing up, along with most people in my church community, I assumed Paul wrote Hebrews. As a young man at Yale, I realized that others were not so sure. The first known alleged reference to Paul as the possible author was Clement of Alexandria around 210 AD. But Tertullian, writing from Carthage around the same time, thought

Barnabas had written Hebrews, and used the fact that Barnabas was a Levite to prove it. Martin Luther 1300 years later argued for Apollos. Bottom-line, no one can be absolutely sure.

Scholars, however, generally agree the book was written in the late 60s AD prior to the destruction of the Temple. Clearly, it was written to a knowledgeable Jewish audience. There are 29 direct quotations from the Old Testament (interesting, not a one references the books of the Apocrypha), plus 53 allusions to the Old Testament. That makes 82 references total. Keep your Old Testament scriptures handy!

The book easily could have been a well-structured early church sermon. There is no salutation. Rather, the writer (or speaker) begins with a series of truths. He speaks as Jesus advised. He is not worrying about what to say; he is speaking straight out and he is speaking with authority. *"When Jesus had finished saying these things, the crowds were amazed at His teaching, because He taught as one who had authority, and not as their scribes."* (Matthew 7:28-29).

How God Speaks

When I was a young man back from graduate school, I was deeply impacted by a book written by Francis Schaeffer, *"He is There and He is not Silent."* His book became a milestone in my life. I tightened my direction after I read that book. His thesis was that God is and He is not silent. In other words, God speaks to mankind. The writer of Hebrews affirms the same, but he couches the affirmation in two distinct epochs: *"long ago"* (before Jesus) and in *"the last days"* (Jesus and beyond).

Before Jesus, God spoke using many ways: by revelation, by dream, by vision, by angel, by circumstance, by encounter (burning bush, pillar of fire), by prophet and by the written word. But when Jesus came, God spoke Jesus. Jesus Himself was the message of God's love and grand intention. All is summed up in Jesus.

Who is Jesus?

And who is God's son? He is the heir of all things (this will be key later as we move through the book), and through Him all things were made (remember, Jesus is the Word of God, the *Logos* (John 1:1).

But He is also the radiance of God's glory and the *"exact representation of His nature."* Let's stop here and think. We remember that God's nature is outlined in shorthand in Exodus 34:6 and following: Compassionate, Kind, Slow to Anger, Steadfast in Love and entirely True, inclined to show Steadfast Love to many and One who tends to Forgive serious sin. The Anointed One, Jesus of Nazareth, the Only Begotten Son of the Father, fully man and fully God, is the *"exact representation of God's nature."* When you see Jesus, you see God.

All things are upheld by Jesus's power. After the crucifixion, when the sacrifice of His life purified us from sins, this same Jesus sat down at the right hand of the *"Majesty"* in the heavenlies, being at a much higher rank than the angels, not only because of His obedience, His life and His sacrifice but also because Jesus has inherited a name above all names.

I think of the many names that Jesus has *"inherited."* *"Inherited"* means that a death has occurred, and because of the will (think Covenant or Testament depending on your preference), the will has been effected. This Jesus *IS* SAVIOR. He *IS* KING. He *IS* LORD. He IS The Holy One. The Lamb of Judah, The Lion of Judah. The Unblemished One. The Prince of Peace. Frankly, all of these names are above the angels, so I am not sure which one the writer of Hebrews addresses, but bottom-line,

Jesus is above mankind and above the Angels. He is the *"exact representation of God's nature"* and full of the radiant glory of God!

The writer gives five key Hebrew texts and quotes them to drive home his points: Psalm 2:7, 2nd Samuel 7:14, Psalm 45:6-7, Psalm 102:26 and Psalm 110:1. Let there be no mistake. Jesus is high above the angels. *"Are they not just "ministering spirits, sent out to render service for the sake of those who will inherit salvation?"* (Hebrews 1:14). They are, and this Jesus is above all. Salvation has broken in!

Hebrews 2

Lest We Drift Away

Why was the book of Hebrews written in the first place? Lest we *"drift away"* from what we have heard. It was written with the Jewish believers primarily in mind, but obviously, it is written to us as well.

Drifting away is always a danger. It is a subtle danger, a danger that barely shows itself. Little by little, we drop our attention to what we originally heard, felt and believed. Drifting away doesn't happen in an afternoon; it happens slowly, normally years pass and the slow drip of acedia erodes our certainty and our love for God, Jesus and the Holy Spirit.

The writer's answer? To *"pay much closer attention to what we have heard, so that we do not drift away from it."* (Hebrews 2:1). How in the world, he asks, can we escape the consequences if we neglect so great a salvation? If anything deserves our attention, it is the great fact of our salvation.

We were trapped in our sinful nature, unable to draw near to the creator of the Universe, imprisoned and under the power of the darkness.

But by Jesus's sacrificial death, we have been set free – we have been saved! But not only saved. We are saved *"in Jesus."* We are being elevated above even the angelic host. *"For He did not subject the world to come to angels...."* (Hebrews 2:5); instead, He subjects it to His Son Jesus, who is both God and man.

How amazing this is! The writer remembers by heart something from the scrolls of the ancient scripture, but he cannot remember exactly where it is found. I like that! It encourages me that the content is more important than the reference. He copies down what he remembers, and consistent with the Septuagint (the ancient Greek translation of the Hebrew), he includes the tiny word τι in the Greek that means *"for a little while"* so that Psalm 8:4-6 reads *"What is man, that You remember him? Or the son of man, that You are concerned about him? You have made him for a little while lower than the angels...."* (Hebrews 2:7).

The meaning is clear. The writer sees that man was originally in rank below the angelic host, but God intended that the *"son of man"* would eventually be elevated above the angels, and for those hidden in Christ, us as well. Amazing.

We are in an "in between" time. I think of the Wood between the Worlds from C. S. Lewis's *The Magician's Nephew*, one of my favorite Lewis books.

The writer of Hebrews says that all things are being subjected to Jesus:

"You have crowned him with glory and honor,
And have appointed him over the works of Your hands;
You have put all things in subjection under his feet." (Hebrews 2:7-8).

"But now we do not yet see all things subjected to Him." (Hebrews 2:8). The writer knows that Jesus has been given all authority, but he also

knows that it does not mean that all of us or Satan and his hosts are willing to be subject to His authority.

This is a personal issue we all face. Are we actually willing to subject ourselves to God's authority? The Jewish writer knew the history of his people. And, no doubt, he understood that the tendency for rebellion was not an ethnic thing; it came with the creature.

Rebellion in no way diminishes Jesus's authority. He *IS* over all – regardless of our personal actions. But like all God appointed authority, those in rebellion have serious consequences to face, even eternal consequences.

Better than Angels. Made Perfect through Sufferings

"For it was fitting for Him, for whom are all things, and through whom are all things, in bringing many sons to glory, to perfect the author of their salvation through sufferings. For both He who sanctifies and those who are sanctified are all from one Father; for which reason He is not ashamed to call them brethren...." (Hebrews 2:10-11).

To be an adequate sacrifice for the sins of mankind, at least four things were necessary. First, the sacrifice had to be more valuable than all of mankind put together because it was a sacrifice for the evil that man had done and the evil that man would do. The sacrifice had to be equal or greater worth than all mankind - past, present and future. An angel was not of sufficient worth. It took the sacrifice of the only creature worthy – that is, God Himself.

Second, to be truly representative of Mankind, it had to be an actual man. The blood of bulls and goats or angels and seraphim were not sufficient. Only one of the flesh of Adam would do. Thus, we see God's challenging solution – a child from the race of Adam and Eve combined with God Himself, i.e., the child of a virgin quickened by the Holy Spirit.

Third, this "God-Man" had to be perfect. To be perfect, He had to be without sin, but for that actually to count, He had to be vulnerable to temptation and able to sin, i.e., a true man in every sense of the word but perfect. At the same time, He had to be God in every sense of the word.

Fourth, the perfect life had to be sacrificed. Blood had to be shed be shed. Suffering must occur.

When we get to Chapter 8, we will see that an entirely *NEW* covenant would have to be made with mankind, a covenant *"cut"* (remember that covenant is the English word for the Hebrew word, *beriyth*, which means cutting) in the precious flesh of Jesus. Jesus would have to die and His blood be shed for the sacrifice to have its full effect.

The writer of Hebrews knew all of the foregoing and spent the first two chapters of his book reminding his audience that Jesus was able. There was no other.

For this reason, David could say:

> *"I will proclaim Your name* [Jesus] *to My brethren,*
> *In the midst of the congregation I will sing Your praise."*
> (Psalm 22:22),

> and *"I will put My trust in Him* [Jesus]."
> (A paraphrase of Psalm 9:10).

We note again that the author of Hebrews uses ancient scripture to speak to his audience. The early Church worked almost entirely out of the ancient texts. When addressing the Jewish people, God spoke through the ancient texts.

Chapter 2 ends with a "mini-kernel" of the Gospel proclamation:

"Therefore, since the children share in flesh and blood, He Himself likewise also partook of the same, that through death He might render powerless him who had the power of death, that is, the devil, and might free those who through fear of death were subject to slavery all their lives. For assuredly He does not give help to angels, but He gives help to the descendant of Abraham. Therefore, He had to be made like His brethren in all things, so that He might become a merciful and faithful high priest in things pertaining to God, to make propitiation for the sins of the people. For since He Himself was tempted in that which He has suffered, He is able to come to the aid of those who are tempted." (Hebrews 2:14-18).

"He is able to come to the aid of those who are tempted." This is a wonderful encouragement to every man and every woman. Jesus, seated at the right hand of Father, is able to come to our individual aid through the gift of the Holy Spirit – at any time, day or night. My heart cries out, *"Come, Lord Jesus."*

Hebrews 3

Jesus, Apostle and High Priest

"Lest You Drift Away....Pay Attention.....Consider Jesus!" Interestingly enough, the author of Hebrews calls Jesus both Apostle and High Priest. As far as I can tell, this is the only time in the New Testament that Jesus is directly called an Apostle, but Jesus Himself probably did refer to Himself when He addressed the Jewish Law experts:

"Therefore also said the wisdom of God, I will send them prophets and apostles, and some of them they shall slay and persecute." (Luke 11:49).

Regardless, it is an apt title for Him. He is both the divine messenger (Apostle) *and* the divine message to mankind.

Jesus also has been given to the world as the eternal High Priest in the full Jewish meaning of the title. The High Priest in Mosaic Law had multiple functions, but the most important was dealing with the sins of the people. Annually on the day called *Yom Kippur*, (actually, *Yom Ha-kippurim* in Hebrew, that is, the Day of Cleansing), the High Priest would offer sacrifices for the for the sins of the people, then enter the Holy of Holies before the Mercy Seat of God and sprinkle upon it the blood of the sacrifices, change his clothes, exit the tabernacle, and taking a goat for the final ritual cleansing outside of the camp, lay his hands on its head to transfer from himself all of the contamination of the sins of the people onto the goat. The goat would then be sent off into the desert.

This ceremony is literally overflowing with deep meaning, and I encourage everyone reading these reflections to patiently take the time to read slowly the Chapter 16 of Leviticus. In the early days of our community, we spent many weeks learning about the function and nature of both the High Priest and the key sacrifices. I pray that God will speak to you as He did to me. I hope that you will slowly allow yourself to be immersed in the ceremony.

While the author of Hebrews will bring forward one of the most important understandings of Jesus's mission as High Priest in Chapters 4 through 7, in Chapter 3 he focuses primarily on Jesus's pre-eminent worthiness as builder of a spiritual house and the danger of not being part of that house.

Moses was acclaimed by the Jewish people as the great deliver and served God while God added spiritual bricks and mortar to the spiritual house He was building in the Wilderness. Jesus, however, is more worthy than Moses as a builder. Unlike Moses, Jesus is God's true and obedient Son, and as such, head over God's house. Moses was a servant to God's family, but Jesus is the Son himself. It is *His* house – *"whose house we are!"* (Hebrews 3:5).

But the author worries that we will not remain as part of Jesus's house, fearful that we might not be faithful to the end.

The author had every reason to be concerned because of the horrific example of the children of Israel in the Wilderness. The parallel is easy to make. Moses came as a savior to deliver the Children of Israel out of bondage. With God's supernatural help, he did so. But before they had journeyed far from Egypt, (remember, they were delivered), their trust in God dried up and their hearts hardened toward God.

Because of their hardness of heart and their lack of trust, God was provoked as He noted that they *"always go astray in their heart."* (Hebrews 3:10). God promised that He would not allow those in the Wilderness to reach the Promised Land, saying *"They shall not enter My rest."* (Hebrews 3:11).

The Peril of Unbelief and the Deceitfulness of Sin

"Take care, brethren, that there not be in any one of you an evil, unbelieving heart that falls away from the living God. But encourage one another day after day, as long as it is still called "Today," so that none of you will be hardened by the deceitfulness of sin. For we have become partakers of Christ, if we hold fast the beginning of our assurance firm until the end," (Hebrews 3:12-14).

"Lest you drift away....Pay attention....Consider Jesus....Take care.... Hold fast!"

God's concern is that we will have our hearts hardened by *"the deceit-fulness of sin"* and *"fall away."* My early Baptist friends should take note. The entire book of Hebrews is concerned with just that: falling away. And none of us are any more immune than the Israelites were who perished in the Wilderness. We are all subject to the deceitfulness of sin that eventually hardens the heart. May we pay attention, truly consider Jesus, take care that we not fall into the rut of sin, holding fast to God.

Here is the entire description of the High Priest's function on *Yom Kippur*, the Day of Cleansing from Chapter 16 of Leviticus. This will be helpful to read prior to Hebrews, Chapter 5.

"The Lord said to Moses: 'Tell your brother Aaron that he shall not enter at any time into the holy place inside the veil, before the mercy seat which is on the ark, or he will die; for I will appear in the cloud over the mercy seat. Aaron shall enter the holy place with this: with a bull for a sin offering and a ram for a burnt offering. He shall put on the holy linen tunic, and the linen undergarments shall be next to his body, and he shall be girded with the linen sash and attired with the linen turban (these are holy garments). Then he shall bathe his body in water and put them on. He shall take from the congregation of the sons of Israel two male goats for a sin offering and one ram for a burnt offering. Then Aaron shall offer the bull for the sin offering which is for himself, that he may make atonement for himself and for his household. He shall take the two goats and present them before the Lord at the doorway of the tent of meeting. Aaron shall cast lots for the two goats, one lot for the Lord and the other lot for the scapegoat [literally, goat of removal]. Then Aaron shall offer the goat on which the lot for the Lord fell, and make it a sin offering. But the goat on which the lot for the scapegoat fell shall be presented alive before the Lord, to make atonement upon it, to send it into the wilderness as the scapegoat.

"Then Aaron shall offer the bull of the sin offering which is for himself and make atonement for himself and for his household, and he shall slaughter the bull of the sin offering which is for himself. He shall take a firepan full of coals of fire from upon the altar before the Lord and two handfuls of finely ground sweet incense, and bring it inside the veil. He shall put the incense on the fire before the Lord, that the cloud of incense may cover the mercy seat that is on the ark of the testimony, otherwise he will die. Moreover, he shall take some of the blood of the bull and sprinkle it with his finger on the mercy seat on the east side; also in front of the mercy seat he shall sprinkle some of the blood with his finger seven times.

"Then he shall slaughter the goat of the sin offering which is for the people, and bring its blood inside the veil and do with its blood as he did with the blood of the bull, and sprinkle it on the mercy seat and in front of the mercy seat. He shall make atonement for the holy place, because of the impurities of the sons of Israel and because of their transgressions in regard to all their sins; and thus he shall do for the tent of meeting which abides with them in the midst of their impurities. When he goes in to make atonement in the holy place, no one shall be in the tent of meeting until he comes out, that he may make atonement for himself and for his household and for all the assembly of Israel. Then he shall go out to the altar that is before the Lord and make atonement for it, and shall take some of the blood of the bull and of the blood of the goat and put it on the horns of the altar on all sides. With his finger he shall sprinkle some of the blood on it seven times and cleanse it, and from the impurities of the sons of Israel consecrate it.

"When he finishes atoning for the holy place and the tent of meeting and the altar, he shall offer the live goat. Then Aaron shall lay both of his hands on the head of the live goat, and confess over it all the iniquities of the sons of Israel and all their transgressions in regard to all their sins; and he shall lay them on the head of the goat and send it away into the wilderness by the hand of a man who stands in readiness. The goat shall bear on itself all their iniquities to a solitary land; and he shall release the goat in the wilderness.

"Then Aaron shall come into the tent of meeting and take off the linen garments which he put on when he went into the holy place, and shall leave them there. He shall bathe his body with water in a holy place and put on his clothes, and come forth and offer his burnt offering and the burnt offering of the people and make atonement for himself and for the people. Then he shall offer up in smoke the fat of the sin offering on the altar. The one who released the goat as the scapegoat shall wash his clothes and bathe his body with water; then afterward he shall come into the camp. But the bull of the sin offering and the goat of the sin offering, whose blood was brought in to make atonement in the holy place, shall be taken outside the camp, and they shall burn their hides, their flesh, and their refuse in the fire. Then the one who burns them shall wash his clothes and bathe his body with water, then afterward he shall come into the camp."

An Annual Atonement

"This shall be a permanent statute for you: in the seventh month, on the tenth day of the month, you shall humble your souls and not do any work, whether the native, or the alien who sojourns among you; for it is on this day that atonement shall be made for you to cleanse you; you will be clean from all your sins before the Lord. It is to be a sabbath of solemn rest for you, that you may humble your souls; it is a permanent statute. So the priest who is anointed and ordained to serve as priest in his father's place shall make atonement: he shall thus put on the linen garments, the holy garments, and make atonement for the holy sanctuary, and he shall make atonement for the tent of meeting and for the altar. He shall also make atonement for the priests and for all the people of the assembly. Now you shall have this as a permanent statute, to make *atonement for the sons of Israel for all their sins once every year.' And just as the Lord had commanded Moses, so he did."* (Leviticus 16:2-34).

Hebrews 4

Hold Fast...Hear His Voice...Draw Near

If any one of you seem to have fallen short of being able to enter God's rest, *"be terrified."* The word translated *"be terrified"* is the Greek word *phobeō* from which we get the English word, phobia. The author of Hebrews is not letting up on getting us to God's rest as he begins Chapter 4.

There remains a *"Sabbath"* rest for the people of God. Already, Jesus has entered that rest since His assignment was completed, just as God rested after completing His work in creating the Universe.

The ancient Israelites did not enter God's rest (the Promised Land) because of disobedience. Disobedience, what the author in Chapter 3 called *"going astray in their hearts"* and being *"hardened by the deceitfulness of sin,"* keeps us from entering God's promised rest. This is an important personal issue for us.

What is God's rest like, anyway? It is when our job is done, and one can sit back and relax? With regard to our salvation, what was needed has been done. And who has done that which most needed to be done? You? Nay, the Lord Jesus Himself!

The writer of Hebrews is keen to make clear that it is our trust in God's work that allows us to enter His rest. Without that confidence, we worry about this behavior and that, always trying to get things right. But only God can truly get things right, and He has done already so through His Son, Jesus.

I feel trumpets should sound because we come in verse 12 to one of my all time favorites verses in the Bible. I love this verse:

"For the word of God is living and active and sharper than any two-edged sword, piercing as far as the division of soul and spirit, of both joints and marrow, and able to judge the thoughts and intentions of the heart." (Hebrews 4:12).

Oh, I love this verse. It reminds me of the phenomenal gift of the Word of God on two levels. There is the Word, the Logos - Jesus Himself. Jesus is fully able to judge the thoughts and intentions of our hearts. He is living and active.

But on a different level, it is the written or spoken word, always well timed, always fully "alive," always active - a living Word. This means that a message from God has vital power in itself and can exert that power within us. The Word of God is not passive; it stirs us and invigorates us when we allow it to come into our being.

But is also is sharp – sharper than a two-edged sword, and thus able to cut between soul and spirit, that which is of man and that which is of God, between falsehood and truth. The Word of God reveals what is passing away and what is eternal.

The normal transmission of the Word of God's presence is through the Holy Spirit. God sees all. He sees our deepest internal world, our needs and our desires. He also sees the lies we carry within us, our hurts, both ancient and present. And God *ALWAYS* wants to help us. Because of His deep love, He sends for His Word which pierces us, cutting down into the depth of our soul. It is like a Photon Beam, cutting with great precision so that something we could not see is revealed. In the end, it brings both revelation and conviction.

Because of the incredible power of God's word to pierce, reveal and convict, those who are prompted by the Spirit of God to speak a word to us must do so. Like the text of God's written word, it needs no embellishment, no forcefulness. God's Word, once released before us, has the ability and power to do its work because it is alive, active and sharp.

I can't tell you how many times God has spoken to me and convicted me through the slightest comment. Sometimes, I even hear something that deeply pieces me while listening to a side conversation. Sometimes, God speaks through the medium of a dream. Sometimes it is through an occurrence. But make no mistake, when the God of the Universe speaks, His Word can unravel the tightest web Satan can weave. But, of course, we have to listen for His Word to do its work.

We have a precious opportunity every day to hear God speak to us through His written word. We don't have to travel to some great religious shrine to hear God's word or go on retreat. We can open our Bibles and read with a listening ear and an open heart. Lord, help us to do so every day!

In the context of the writer's carefully crafted thought, his observations about the nature of the Word of God is that we must give it heed if we are to truly enter the Sabbath rest God has for us. He has done what was necessary. Let His Word confirm this; let it pierce you so that you will trust Him entirely and enter His rest.

The writer now returns to the cosmic revelation of Jesus, the Son of God who has passed through the heavens to perform in a better way what only a High Priest could perform. The next few chapters will focus on Jesus's unique role as High Priest. We are greatly advantaged because He can entirely sympathize with our weaknesses (please hear this). I say it again, *"He can entirely sympathize with our weaknesses."*

He was tempted in everything that tempts us, yet, unlike us, He did not sin.

Read the last sentence of Chapter 4 with the image of the earthly tabernacle in mind for that is exactly the writer's purpose. This is an important sentence.

"Therefore let us draw near with confidence to the throne of grace, so that we may receive mercy and find grace to help in time of need." (Hebrews 4:16).

The imagery described shows each one of us able to enter into the Holy of Holies where no one before Jesus's cruxifiction was ever allowed to go except the High Priest.

The language takes us to the *"throne of grace,"* that is, the Mercy Seat which sits atop the Ark of the Covenant - to God Himself. We are able to do this unimaginable thing because of what God has done through the sacrifice of His Son, and His Son is now seated with Him in the Heavenly sanctuary.

And the preceding sentence in verse 15 gives us confidence when we are conscious of our weaknesses, because He who sits on the throne can fully sympathize with our struggle with temptations. He has a compassionate ear, and can extend yet again *"mercy and grace to help in time of need."*

Who does not know weakness? Who does not know failure and pressure in this life? No one. That the Throne Room of God in the heavens has One at the helm who had experienced temptation and knows its pull is a huge Word of encouragement!

"Hold Fast…Hear His Voice…Draw Near!"

Hebrews 5

Jesus: High Priest Forever

Why should it matter that Jesus is a High Priest forever? He is unlike the High Priests who served by their generation in those things pertaining to man's interaction with God. The earthly High Priests served until their service ended at death or removal. Jesus now serves *forever*. He is, as the writer of Hebrews clearly points out, not of the order of Aaron. Rather, He is of the order of Melchizedek, the priest to whom Abraham offered tithes. Melchizedek was not an Israelite, but a man representing all mankind in their dealings with God.

So it is with Jesus. He represents all, and His term of service is eternal. The writer's comparison of Jesus's High Priestly function is directly related to the issue of sin and its contamination.

Before the Jewish High Priest could minister in front of the Mercy Seat (within the Holy of Holies), he first had to offer the sacrifice of a large bull for his own sins and then the goat that was chosen by lot to be sacrificed for the sins of his fellow Israelites. The High Priest would tip his fingers into the blood of both and sprinkle them on the Mercy Seat before sending the scapegoat (the goat that was not chosen for sacrifice) into the wilderness.

Note that the High Priest did not run for office; he was chosen by God. By the Father's choice, Jesus was born for this high spiritual service. And He was appointed because He had learned true obedience though difficulty and suffering, in the same way that we also learn obedience. Only Jesus was entirely faithful in every test that had been set before Him.

Having proved perfect and unblemished, He became both the perfect sacrifice (more perfect than the bull or the goat, no matter how unblemished they were) and the perfect High Priest – a dual role.

Obviously, there is so much to say when considering the wonder of what God did and is doing that the writer of Hebrews warns his audience that some of what needs to be explained will be difficult. One reason it would be hard to explain was because of their lack of knowledge and their dullness of hearing.

The writer is about to introduce an outline of the most fundamental principles for beginning a walk with God. If his audience had grasped thoroughly what they already had been taught, he would not have had to consider laying again those foundational teachings. They should by now be teachers themselves. Instead of solid food, they needed milk like infants.

Real maturity is the ability to discern what is good and the willingness to live accordingly. Real maturity is learned by hearing and by application. We have to practice what we think we have learned. In time, we become better at discerning the Will of God as well as good and evil. But we must wait until Chapter 6 to learn the outline of the fundamental principles that were taught to the early church. Then we may ask ourselves whether or not we are ready for solid food!

Hebrews 6

Even though it appears the writer's target audience was *not* ready for meaty teaching, he decides to forego laying again the six fundamental teachings *"about the Christ"* that he calls *"elementary."* For "Emerging Ekklesia" sleuths, his outline of those six elementary teachings gives us a glimpse of what foundational teachings were taught to new believers in that era - at least in the writer's church community:

- **Repentance from Dead Works.** (His reference suggests real repentance from both evil as well as righteous acts by which we think we can be acceptable).
- **Faith toward God.** (Trusting the goodness of God and His nature plus believing Jesus's sacrifice saves us and not our works).
- **Instruction about Baptisms.** (Note: *baptismos* in the Greek means baptisms, i.e., plural).
- **The Laying on of Hands.** (The distribution of spiritual gifts including the Baptism in the Holy Spirit).
- **Resurrection from the Dead.** (Jesus's and ours).
- **Eternal Judgment.** (All mankind including us).

We see these teachings in many of Jesus's interactions. After His resurrection, He shared a good number of revelations with his disciples. Luke records a few of Jesus's last sentences in Chapter 24 of the book of Luke:

"Now He said to them, 'These are My words which I spoke to you while I was still with you, that all things which are written about Me in the Law of Moses and the Prophets and the Psalms must be fulfilled.' Then He opened their minds to understand the Scriptures, and He said to them, 'Thus it is written, that the Christ would suffer and rise again from the dead the third day, and that repentance for forgiveness of sins would be proclaimed in His name to all the nations, beginning from Jerusalem.'" (Luke 24:44-47).

There are five things Jesus emphasized in this passage, and three are part of the foundational teaching Hebrews mentioned. Here are the five:

- The Torah, the Prophets and the Psalms (note: all three) foretell Jesus's coming, His mission and what He has yet to do. They predicted the following:
- Christ had to suffer (be crucified).

- He would be resurrected.
- Repentance for forgiveness of sins would be granted.
- And Salvation proclaimed throughout the earth.

It seems to me that three of the six "elementary teachings" are included in these farewell words. Of course, Luke was not present. If we add Matthew's report, we pick up several more:

"Then the eleven disciples went to Galilee, to the mountain where Jesus had told them to go. When they saw him, they worshiped him; but some doubted. Then Jesus came to them and said, "All authority in heaven and on earth has been given to me. Therefore go and make disciples of all nations, baptizing them in the name of the Father and of the Son and of the Holy Spirit, and teaching them to obey everything I have commanded you. And surely I am with you always, to the very end of the age." (Matthew 28:16-20).

Matthew records three additional points, one of which is clearly in the Hebrews 6 list, i.e., Baptism.

- ALL authority has now been given to Jesus.
- The disciples are sent to the nations where they are to baptize in the name of the Father and of the Son and of the Holy Spirit.
- The disciples are to teach that everyone should do what Jesus commanded. (Love God with all their heart and their neighbor as themselves, etc.).

In a sense, the last instruction He gave also picks up the sixth in Hebrews, that is, *Eternal Judgment*, because Jesus spoke of it often.

In any event, the six zones of teaching were obviously foundational. Let's look at them one more time and ask, "Which, if any, did I not receive detailed instructions about after I became a believer?" Here they are again:

- **Repentance from Dead Works.** (His reference suggests real repentance from both evil as well as righteous acts by which we think we can be acceptable).
- **Faith toward God.** (Trusting the goodness of God and His nature plus believing Jesus's sacrifice saves us and not our works).
- **Instruction about Baptisms.** (Note: *baptismos* in the Greek means baptisms, i.e., plural).
- **The Laying on of Hands.** (The distribution of spiritual gifts including the Baptism in the Holy Spirit).
- **Resurrection from the Dead.** (Jesus's and ours).
- **Eternal Judgment.** (All mankind including us).

It seems to me that most folks are clear about *Repentance, Faith toward God, and Eternal Judgment.* The three that often need more elaboration are *Baptisms, the Laying on of Hands,* and what really happens when we die, i.e., *the Resurrection from the Dead.* If you were vague about any of these, I would encourage you to do a sidebar study on those.

There are many good books that focus on each of the six topics from reliable saints, but figuring out which saints are reliable is not easy. With web services like Blue Letter Bible, one can simply search for every verse in the Bible with the words baptism, baptisms, laying on of hands, eternal judgment, etc. Just carefully reading all the applicable verses will help supply what may be lacking.

Since we have encountered these terms *many* times in Acts and Paul's letters, our previous reflections also might be revisited.

The writer's concern thus far is very clear. He is worried about people drifting away. In verse 4 we see why:

"For in the case of those who have once been enlightened and have tasted of the heavenly gift and have been made partakers of the Holy Spirit, and have tasted the good word of God and the powers of the age to come, and

then have fallen away, it is impossible to renew them again to repentance, since they again crucify to themselves the Son of God and put Him to open shame." (Hebrews 6:4-6).

I cannot think of a worse crime in the Universe than to *"crucify the Son of God and shame Him."* Of course, one cannot literally do so, but the writer is speaking of the horror that comes when one has actually *"tasted the heavenly gift of the Spirit"* (he is surely speaking of the Baptism in the Holy Spirit that Jesus himself brings to us) and then turned away. The problem is that if we truly fall away, no one can get us back. The warning is stark and scary.

A counter might be the reminder of Peter's address on Pentecost:

"'You, with the help of wicked men, put him to death by nailing him to the cross....' When the people heard this, they were cut to the heart and said to Peter and the other apostles, 'Brothers, what shall we do?' Peter replied, 'Repent and be baptized, every one of you, in the name of Jesus Christ for the forgiveness of your sins. And you will receive the gift of the Holy Spirit. The promise is for you and your children and for all who are far off—for all whom the Lord our God will call.'" (Acts 2:23, 37-39).

Peter's words are remarkable because those to whom he speaks *HAVE* crucified the Lord, yet Peter calls them to repentance in spite of their hideous crime. I wish that would be the opportunity (repentance and re-gifting) for those who fully fall away, but it does not appear that is possible from our Hebrews passage. One reason may be that Jesus's crucifixion was actually in God's plan for mankind. It had an eternal purpose. A later crucifixion (figuratively) would accomplish nothing.

In spite of the danger, the writer is confident that few would actually fully fall away. He remembers that God remembers every act of kindness that we extend to others – particularly to the saints. Those count in some measure. His hope is that we will have full assurance of our salvation to the very end.

The writer's mind begins to shift to the thought that working out our salvation is a bit like being a race. He will come back to this thought as we progress in later chapters. He doesn't want the believers to become "sluggish," but rather imitate the great heroes of faith – people like Abraham.

His focus is on the very positive promise that God made to Abraham. *"I WILL surely bless you and I WILL SURELY multiply you."* What God promises, He performs; we can be sure of that!

Adding an oath to something God says is surely redundant, but the Hebrews writer doesn't hesitate to drive home his point by reminding them that God, when dealing with Abraham on the mount with his son Isaac, affirmed His promise by saying *"I have sworn."* (Genesis 22:16). Normally, the meaning of "swear" is that one backs up his or her word by the commitment of a higher authority, a higher power. But for God to swear, there was none higher; He had to swear in reference to Himself. He did this because of our weakness of faith. He, like the Hebrews writer, knew we needed perfect assurance and wanted to make sure Abraham had it.

And what more assurance could we have than Jesus in the throne room of God, seated at the right hand of the Father who Himself is seated on the throne called "Mercy." This Jesus can sympathize fully with our temptations, but also functions as our Great Advocate, our Great Defender, and the One who is ready to come to our aid in every weakness. To Him be the glory!

Hebrews 7

The Power to Bless

Melchizedek was the forerunner of Jesus by type. Abraham recognized him as the priest of the Most High God as well as a king. In fact his name is composed of two root words: *Melek* (King) and *tsedeq* (Righteousness) – King of Righteousness. We also learn that he was King of the town of Salem (*Shalem)* which means King of Peace and likely refers to Jeru*salem*. A great forerunner by type, and the writer of Hebrews will use this chapter to underscore how the two are similar.

First, we recognize Jesus in the same way that our Father in heaven does. Jesus is King of Righteousness as well as King of Peace. Jesus is the only one who is both human and divine and He also is the only one who has lived an unblemished life. He became King of Peace because He removed the enmity between man and God, between man and woman, between ethnic groups and nations. In Him, God is wrapping up and pulling together the entirety of the Universe. Peace is pulling together, not drawing apart.

Melchizedek had the ***power to bless*** Abraham. Likewise, Jesus has the power to bless. He had the power to bless while on earth; how much more does He have that power at the right hand of God!

Note that in verse 7 the nature of blessing is highlighted: only the greater blesses the lesser and not vice versa. Melchizedek was greater than Abraham and could therefore bless him. Jesus is greater than mankind and all earthly priests. He can therefore bless us. It is important to remember that Abraham honored the greater, and in turn the greater blessed him.

Honoring is a great spiritual principle that shines light on our human relations as well as our relationship to God. Our current generation is short on honoring; we want to be long on honoring!

Melchizedek was not out of the loins of Levi (the son of Jacob whom God chose to begin a family of priests through Aaron, his great grandson), yet Melchizedek was chosen to be priest of the Most High God, and this was affirmed by Abraham's giving a tenth of his spoils. Jesus came not from the loins of a man, but from God Himself.

Further, Levi actually paid homage to Melchizedek through Abraham because Levi (who would be born through the lineage of Abraham some 70 years after Abraham's death), was Abraham's great grandson. To the Jewish mind, Levi was very much in the loins of Abraham and of course so was Aaron, Levi's grandson. When Abraham offered homage to Melchizedek and thus to God, Levi and Aaron were there in Abraham's loins.

This is most remarkable to consider. The impact of the older generation's actions affects later generations - both the good as well as the bad. When we act, it would be wisdom to see that our children and our grandchildren yet unborn are acting in a sense through us and with us. And in our actions, they act. A most remarkable thought that should give us pause!

Because Jesus has been chosen as High Priest after the Order of Melchizedek, there is no need for the Levitical priesthood to continue. For it to cease, the Law governing the priesthood had to change. What we call "the Law" are the Covenantal documents developed at God's direction during the time of Moses that gave direction for life as well as detailed ordinances for the priesthood.

The Need to Change

This brings us to God's need to cancel or modify the older Covenant while substituting a better one. For those of us who are involved in real estate, the language is easy to follow because it is normal for us to put covenants on property when we agree to sell.

All of the developments with which I have been involved over the years have covenants on them that I have written. When someone buys property in one of our developments, they take title SUBJECT to the covenants we have established. In a true sense, they enter into the covenant, becoming both subject to the restrictions as well as in receipt of the benefits the covenants assure (certainty of what will be built on the lot next door and the like).

Sometimes, for the betterment of the development, we decide to change the covenants, substituting better controls and restrictions. We just did this at Schilling Farms earlier this year. As the original developer, we had retained the unilateral right to make changes in the covenants whenever we chose. This is basically what God knew He would do several centuries before Jesus was born. He knew that there would come a time when he would need to change the covenant He made with the children of Israel. Several of the prophets foretold that a "new" Covenant was coming.

And with a contract, we must back it up. When you make a covenant or contract with a bank to borrow money on your house, you have to put up security to assure the bank that you will do what you say you will do. In the case of God, He figuratively put up the life of His new High Priest, Jesus, as surety. Surety is a guarantee that the New Covenant will not be broken on God's part. The writer of Hebrews shines light on yet another way of seeing the wonder of what God did through Jesus.

Because Jesus has been raised from the dead and has been given the role of eternal High Priest, *"He is able also to save forever those who draw near to God through Him, since He always lives to make intercession for them."* (Hebrews 7:25). He is forever able!

Psalm 110 was written by King David and is basically a prophecy of what would come to pass when the Father of the Universe received back His Son into heaven. Let's read the first 5 verses with Jesus in mind:

"The Lord says to my lord:
'Sit at my right hand,
while I make your enemies your footstool.'
The scepter of your might:
the Lord extends your strong scepter from Zion.
Have dominion over your enemies!
Yours is princely power from the day of your birth.
In holy splendor before the daystar,
like dew I begot you.
The Lord has sworn and will not waver:
'You are a priest forever in the manner of Melchizedek.'"

At your right hand is the Lord…. And the Lord has sworn and will not change His mind; Jesus will be High Priest forever.

"For it was fitting for us to have such a high priest, holy, innocent, undefiled, separated from sinners and exalted above the heavens; who does not need daily, like those high priests, to offer up sacrifices, first for His own sins and then for the sins of the people, because this He did once for all when He offered up Himself. For the Law appoints men as high priests who are weak, but the word of the oath, which came after the Law, appoints a Son, made perfect forever." (Hebrews 7:26-28).

This is a terrific truth and ends Chapter 7 with a figurative shout. What sort of High Priest did God chose for His New Covenant? One who is…

- Holy
- Innocent
- Undefiled
- Separated from sinners
- Exalted above the heavens
- Who offered up Himself once and for all
- God's own Son, appointed by God Himself
- Perfect forever

YES!

Hebrews 8

Let's do a quick review of some of the highpoints from the first 7 chapters before we plunge into the 8th:

Jesus – He is better than an angel, made perfect through suffering, the perfect representative for mankind. He was appointed as High Priest over all creation, having presented Himself as the perfect sacrifice and having allowed Himself to be sacrificed one time for all of our sins. He is fully able to come to the aid of those who are tempted since He too was tempted.

Watch out, be on your guard, lest you fall away. If it happened to the Israelites in the Wilderness; it can happen to any of us - if we lack confidence in God and what God has done.

Don't harden your hearts toward God; rather, enter His rest. Hold fast your confession even if you are weak, since Jesus as High Priest can sympathize with your weakness. His Priesthood is eternal; His sacrifice entirely acceptable and functioning at all times.

If you do fall way after having tasted the heavenly gift of the Spirit of God, no one can fix your fall. But God is faithful, and you have a perfect High Priest, an anchor for the soul. Jesus saves all those who draw near to God since He lives forever.

God has made a new and better Covenant with mankind and with you. It is better than the one He had with the Children of Israel, and Jesus stands as surety to back up what God has proclaimed.

Now, in Chapter 8, let's dive deeply into the nature of Jesus's *"mediation"* of the New Covenant which has been enacted on better promises than the old. What does it mean to mediate a covenant? The word for mediate in the Greek is *mesitēs* (which one pronounces me-se-tas). It means one who intervenes between two opposing sides to restore peace and freedom. It can also mean one who ratifies an agreement.

Which did Jesus do? Did he intervene between God and mankind to restore peace and freedom? Or did He ratify the new agreement God was making? There is another word we might think about - the word *"ratify."* In the Greek, the word is *epikyró.* So what does *"ratify"* mean? It means, *"to make valid."*

I think Jesus mediated the New Covenant between God and Man by making it valid! The author of Hebrews has taken seven chapters to underscore just how valid Jesus's ratification would be! He is the *surety*, the *perfect sacrifice* AND the *ratifier* of this change in covenants.

While Jesus does His High Priestly service, it is not on earth but in heaven, where the true temple of God exists. The temple on earth and its pattern simply reflect the real temple in heaven.

Plus, the New Covenant has better promises than the old. This is important to ponder. What are the major differences between the promises of the Old and the New? In the Old, God promised that the Children of Israel would be *"His"* people.

"Now then, if you will indeed obey My voice and keep My covenant, then you shall be My own possession among all the peoples, for all the earth is Mine; and you shall be to Me a kingdom of priests and a holy nation." (Exodus 19:5-6).

On God's side under the old covenant, He would care for the Children of Israel as if they were His own offspring and let them serve as a Kingdom (think government) of priests and a Holy nation. On their side, they would simply obey God's commands that He gave them through Moses and the Priests.

But in the New Covenant, there would be several huge differences. Let's look carefully at Jeremiah's prophesy of the New Covenant again.

> *"Behold, days are coming, says the Lord,*
> *When I will effect a new covenant*
> *With the house of Israel and with the house of Judah;*
> *Not like the covenant which I made with their fathers*
> *On the day when I took them by the hand*
> *To lead them out of the land of Egypt;*
> *For they did not continue in My covenant,*
> *And I did not care for them, says the Lord.*
> *"For this is the covenant that I will make with the house of Israel*
> *After those days, says the Lord:*
> *I will put My laws into their minds,*
> *And I will write them on their hearts.*
> *And I will be their God,*
> *And they shall be My people.*

"And they shall not teach everyone his fellow citizen,
And everyone his brother, saying, 'Know the Lord,'
For all will know Me,
From the least to the greatest of them.
"For I will be merciful to their iniquities,
And I will remember their sins no more." (Jeremiah 31:31-34).

Wow, what an agreement! God promises in the New Covenant to...

- Put His laws into their minds (not their scrolls).
- Write His laws on their hearts (not their scrolls).
- Be their God.
- Take them for His people.
- No one need teach for all shall know God internally.
- Be merciful to their iniquities.
- Remember their sins no more.

Several of these promises are contained in the first covenant. *"Be their God and take them for His people"* is part and parcel of the Old Covenant. And God *was* merciful to their iniquities in the Old as He provided a way to deal with horrible actions by either punishment or through the annual removal of corruption at *Yom Kippur.*

The quantum change is internal. In the New Covenant, God promises to write His laws in their minds and on their hearts so deeply that they will have no need for others to teach them. Something so deep will happen that the scrolls will hardly be needed. Plus, amazingly, He will remember their sins no more.

Again, we have to turn to the 2nd chapter of Joel to finish the picture:

"And it shall come to pass afterward
That I will pour out My Spirit on all flesh;
Your sons and your daughters shall prophesy,
Your old men shall dream dreams,

Your young men shall see visions.
And also on My menservants and on My maidservants."
I will pour out My Spirit in those days."
(Joel 2:28-29).

So, we have tremendous internal change brought about by the pouring out and indwelling of the Spirit of God AND complete forgiveness.

God's plan is marvelous and totally undeserved were it not for Jesus's sacrifice.

Chapter 8 ends with the thought:

"When He said, "A new covenant,"
He has made the first obsolete. But whatever is becom-
ing obsolete and growing old is ready to disappear."
(Hebrews 8:13).

The truth is that the Aaronic priesthood was passing away – disappearing. There was no need for that form of the priesthood in the New!

Hebrews 9

The Making of a Better Covenant

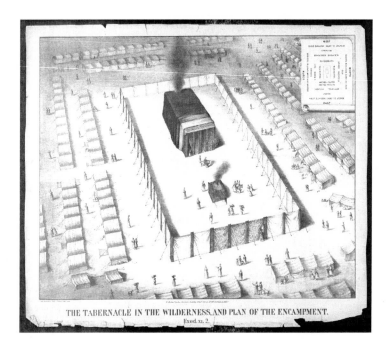

THE TABERNACLE IN THE WILDERNESS, AND PLAN OF THE ENCAMPMENT.
Exod. xl. 2.

Let us imagine that it is *Yom Kippur* - the Day of Atonement. You are the High Priest and have come to do service at the Tent of Meeting - the ancient tabernacle in the Wilderness. All of the tribes of Israel are camped outside in their own tents.

As High Priest, you are in your full regalia. On your forehead is a golden plate with the words HOLY TO THE LORD engraved in Hebrew characters held in place by a blue cord. You have on several layers of linen garments overlaid with a square breastplate made of gold, blue, purple and scarlet linen on the front with twelve stones fastened upon it. The breastplate is attached to a blue robe arranged a bit like an apron with golden bells at the hem. Every piece of your garment has meaning.

You come to the gates at the end of a long double-square rectangular enclosure 75 feet by 150 feet in width and depth. You bring a large bull and two goats. At the gates you pause, and cast lots to determine which goat will accompany you and the bull inside the enclosure. You leave the unchosen goat with a priest outside. Entering through the gates, you offer up thanksgiving and praise.

A large brazen altar is situated in the middle of a 75-foot square before you. Beyond is a narrow 15-foot high structure. You leave the bull and the goat beside the altar and go over to the basin filled with water standing beside the entry into the 15-foot high structure. There, you remove your garments, wash yourself and put on linen breeches and a linen tunic.

You return to where the bull is standing and place your hands on the bull. You ask God to see the bull instead of you - that the sin imputed to you may be transferred to the bull and extinguished. Then, you step beside the bull, put your arm over its neck and carefully cut its throat. As the blood comes forth from the bull, you catch some of it in a bowl.

With the bowl and a censer of burning coals from the brazen altar and two handfuls of finely ground incense, you enter through the first veil into the Holy Place. There, you see three different objects. A seven-branched golden candelabrum is ablaze; there is a small golden table to the side with unleavened bread upon it, and by the veil to the Holy of Holies, there is a small golden altar for the burning of incense immediately in front of the second curtain.

Cutaway of Tabernacle

You place the burning coals on the small golden altar in front of the curtain and sprinkled incense upon it. Smoke from the censer is rising; its fragrance fills the tent and the smoke obscures the Ark of the Covenant before you. The bowl of blood in hand, you enter cautiously into the Holy of Holies through the curtain. Above the Ark is the golden Mercy Seat of God flanked by golden wings representing the angelic cherubim.

The Mercy Seat and the Ark

You dip your fingers into the bowl full of blood and sprinkle it 14 times - seven times on the front of the cover and then seven times over it. (*see Leviticus 16:1-14*).

Having sprinkled the blood of the bull, you return to the goat outside the curtains. Again, you place your hands on the head of the goat and ask God to see you as representative of all the Children of Israel and transfer the sins of the People to the goat symbolically. You carefully cut the goat's throat. Some of the gushing blood is caught in the bowl.

You retrace your steps into the Holy Place and then enter between the curtains barring access to the Holy of Holies. Standing there in the presence of God above the Seat of Mercy, you repeat the earlier sprinkling, only this time with the blood of the goat.

Turning toward the walls and the other objects in the Holy Place, you sprinkle them with blood for they are in the midst of the People, to cleanse the contamination of their sin, the sin of your household and the whole community of Israel.

You then exit and do the same to the brazen altar and the horns at its four corners. Having completed your series of cleansings, you return to the living goat. For the third time you lay your hands on an animal's head and confess over it all of the sins of the People and send it away into the Wilderness.

Almost complete with your duties on Yom Kippur, you return to the tent, take off your linen garments, and leave them in the Holy Place. Then you bath with water in the court and put on your normal garments. There in the courtyard you sacrifice the bull and goat as burnt offerings atop of the brazen altar. Your work is complete. (*Leviticus 16:15-25*).

Hopefully, you have now a great sense of the ancient process of cleansing and atonement that our Jewish ancestors used in the Wilderness. Close your eyes and take a moment to retrace your steps. The author of Hebrews runs through the highpoints. Unfortunately, both gifts and sacrifices have been offered *"which **cannot make the worshipers perfect in conscience**, since they relate only to food and drink and various washings, regulations for the body imposed until a time of reformation."* (Hebrews 9:10-11).

The Good News is that the time of reformation has come! It came when Jesus entered into God's actual dwelling place. We know the earthly sanctuary is only a figure of the true dwelling place. Let's think about what happened after the crucifixion, again in shorthand.

First, Jesus ascends to heaven and comes before God, His very own Father. He brings with Him His blood, the blood of a New Covenant *"cut"* in His flesh, His blood sprinkled over all mankind.

It is critical that we remember the Hebrew word *"beriyth"* which is translated "covenant" or "testament" in our Hebrew Bibles. I feel as though I have repeated this a thousand times in these reflections, but it is because I want to be sure it sticks with every reader. This is the word whose true meaning is *"cutting."* A cutting signified the shedding of blood to enforce any important agreement. Remember among other things; if the covenant promises are broken, death will occur. Lives are on the line. The God of the Universe chose to make just such a promise with Abraham, and you will remember the heifer, goat and ram plus a dove and a pigeon that were split in two during Abraham's night vision. A smoking firepot and a blazing torch passed between the pieces ratifying God's presence and His personal covenantal action.

Jesus entered the Holy Place once for all, both to cleanse mankind and to ratify a New Covenant, *"cut"* in His blood. His sacrifice obtained eternal redemption.

"if the blood of goats and bulls and the ashes of a heifer sprinkling those who have been defiled sanctify for the cleansing of the flesh, how much more will the blood of Christ, who through the eternal Spirit offered Himself without blemish to God, cleanse your conscience from dead works to serve the living God?" (Hebrews 9:13-14).

Because Jesus's body was broken and His blood shed, His sacrifice occurs once and once only. It requires no repetition. It is for all humanity.

We end the chapter with an interesting observation, a parallel between men who die and come to judgment. There is an inevitable action (death) and an inevitable result (judgment). In the same way, Jesus has been offered an action once and for all. His one sacrifice and its inevitable result (forgiveness) creates certainty that His next appearing will be for our salvation without any reference to our sin. How amazing is that!

"Inasmuch as it is appointed for men to die once and after this comes judgment, so Christ also, having been offered once to bear the sins of many, will appear a second time for salvation without reference to sin, to those who eagerly await Him." (Hebrews 9:27-28).

One Important Closing Observation to Chapter 9

This amazing "seeing" in Hebrews, this remarkable revelation of both the wonder of the Old Testament practices of the priesthood and the actual New Testament heavenly acts of Jesus, can easily catapult us into the heavenlies during our times of worship. In fact, a deeper dive than we have just made can yield immense results as we enter into worship, understanding what has been done before us when we *"come into His gates with thanksgiving and into His courts with praise."* (Psalm 100:4). During any time of worship, whether at home or with others, let your mind consider the actions in the tabernacle – on earth and in heaven. Likely, you will be transported into the heavens yourself!

Hebrews 10

The Shadow

The Law is only a shadow. But what *is* a shadow? A shadow is cast by the form of something real when light shines upon it. The shadow speaks to the form and existence of a real thing, but the shadow is not the real thing. Only that which casts the shadow is real.

So it is with the Law and the earthly Tabernacle. They show the form and the existence of that which is truly real, but they are not the reality; they only speak to the reality. They have great value, but they cannot effect the change that God felt was needed in His relationship with mankind.

We can surmise that God wanted to introduce something greater than a shadow, something that would not require repetition year after year, and even if repeated, would only be a shadow of what was real.

God was interested in deep cleansing - a cleansing that goes beyond the surface, a cleansing that would only need to occur once. Let's think of a simple example. Take my house. Every week, Fran has a young lady come to our house for four hours to clean. She has to do that because the house, though clean immediately after the lady leaves, gets dirty again. To be able to tell her, "All is well. You need not come back because nothing will get dirty again" requires a complete change in the nature of the house (and to those that live in it)! Based on observation,

I would say it would take a complete miracle for our house not to get dirty again!

The complete change God was looking for required major intervention. First, He had to deal once and for all with the consequences of sin. Then He had to change the nature of those who live in the House.

> "Sacrifice and offering You have not desired,
> But a body You have prepared for Me;
> In whole burnt offerings and sacrifices for sin
> You have taken no pleasure.
> "Then I said, 'Behold, I have come
> (In the scroll of the book it is written of Me)
> To do Your will, O God.'"
> (Hebrews 10:5-7).

I quote above the NASB version. Surprisingly, in the footnotes, there is no reference to the word *"body"* in the second line. The author has quoted in its entirety Psalm 40:6-8. But the verse contains one of the few questionable translations of the Septuagint, the Greek version of the Hebrew Bible translated by Jewish scholars some time before Jesus's birth. Bear with me for a moment.

As far as we can tell from the Hebrew text, the clause translated *"But a body you prepared for me,"* was actually *"My ears you have pierced."* (Psalm 40:6). The word the NASB translates as *"body"* is the word for *ears* in the Hebrew, and the word translated *"prepared"* is the word *"karah"* in Hebrew. *Karah* means "digged" or *"pierced."* One of the most famous verses in the Old Testament predicting Jesus's crucifixion is Psalm 22:16 which uses *"karah:"*

"For dogs have compassed me: the assembly of the wicked has enclosed me: they pierced (karah) *my hands and my feet."*

If we substitute *"pierced"* for *"prepared"* and *"ears"* for *body* in Hebrews 10:5, we get *"My ears you have pierced."* That makes more sense to me because it speaks to the process of becoming a bond-slave:

"But if the slave plainly says, 'I love my master, my wife, and my children; I will not go out free,' then his master shall bring him to God, and he shall bring him to the door or the doorpost. And his master shall pierce his ear with a needle, and he shall be his slave forever." (Exodus 21:5).

It is impossible for me to be sure exactly what happened to the Septuagint manuscript and whether the original author of Hebrews actually used the words *"body"* and *"prepared."* It doesn't make a lot of difference, for both approaches would be true for the Son of God. God did prepare a *"body"* for Him, and His Son did voluntarily and willfully become Father's bond slave.

The larger emphasis of verses 5 through 7 is on animal sacrifices and burnt offerings. These were a key part of the Mosaic Law. *"You did not desire"* simply means God really allowed the use of animal sacrifices to encourage the Children of Israel that there could be some lifting of the natural guilt they felt for their own misbehaving – their own sin.

God has so fashioned us that, so to speak, we have an internal clock that goes off when we sin. We experience an internal *dis*-ease, and the weight of guilt begins to build.

The sacrifice of animals for the sins of the Children of Israel was a blessing when looked at from this point of view – a true blessing; it lifted the guilt. But it doesn't take a rocket scientist to see that animal sacrifices were not desired by God. Can you really imagine that the God of the Universe would have any need for some dead, burnt-up animals? I think not. It was the truth that they communicated that mattered.

That is the point of the quote from Psalms 40; the sacrifices and burnt offerings were a blessing for the Children of Israel, but God clearly wanted a deeper relationship with His people.

Jesus came to "set aside" the first covenant and ratify a second. Then we have a one-sentence kernel of the Gospel message:

"by [His] will, we have been made holy through the sacrifice of the body of Jesus Christ once for all." (Hebrews 10:10).

And again,

"by one sacrifice He has made perfect forever those who are being made holy." (Hebrews 10:14).

This IS the gospel message. Of course, "For God so loved the world, that He gave His only begotten Son, that whoever believes in Him shall not perish, but have eternal life. For God did not send the Son into the world to judge the world, but that the world might be saved through Him." is an even fuller rendition, because it references WHY we have been made holy through God's Son (John 3:16-17).

We ARE being made holy. The Holy Spirit continues the transforming work within us. The author references the early prediction by the Holy Spirit through the prophet Jeremiah: an amazing change was coming and had now come. Once again (I never tire of repeating this), we remember:

> "This is the covenant I will make with them
> after that time, says the Lord.
> I will put my laws in their hearts,
> and I will write them on their minds.
> Their sins and lawless acts
> I will remember no more."
> (Jeremiah 31: 33-34).

Then, the author wraps up the result of all of the aspects of ancient Law, the shadow of what was to come, and the temple service:

"Therefore, brothers and sisters, since we have confidence to enter the Most Holy Place by the blood of Jesus, by a new and living way opened for us through the curtain, that is, his body, and since we have a great priest over the house of God, let us draw near to God with a sincere heart and with the full assurance that faith brings, having our hearts sprinkled to cleanse us from a guilty conscience and having our bodies washed with pure water." (Hebrews 10:19-23).

Goodness, I love these verses! If there ever was a reason to see what the *"therefore"* was there for, this is it! Not only Jesus, but now us. We are able to actually enter with Him and in Him as we proceed into the Holy of Holies. My, my. This is amazing and very wonderful. There are no words to express how wondrous it really is.

It is no wonder that the author immediately calls everyone hearing his message to *"hold fast unswervingly to the hope we profess, for He who promised is faithful."* (Hebrews 10:23).

Next comes a warning that is most applicable to us today. If we don't spur each other onward toward love, good deeds, and meeting together, if we don't encourage each other, there is a chance that we will fall away after having tasted the heavenly gift he spoke of in Chapter 6, verse 4.

There is a cancer abroad today that is being accelerated by the technological advances of the airwaves. People can sit alone in their homes and listen to varying qualities of Christian proclamations. They can listen to fine singing and some not so fine. But they are not gathering with flesh and blood brothers and sisters with whom they can have continuity and vibrant relationships. Sadly, they gather with a TV, a radio, an Alexa. But, there is NO substitute for flesh and blood. Plus, as I have noted with force, it is impossible to gage fruit through the medium of electronics. You have to walk together to grasp to what degree a man or woman is trustworthy.

If we become discouraged, if we lose touch with true brothers and sisters, we risk falling. And be assured, if we fully fall, there is only the terrifying expectation of judgment.

We don't hear a lot about God's judgment today. It certainly is more comforting to focus on His great love. But the peculiar thing about judgment in general is that "judgment" is another way of saying "consequence." When we throw a ball into a plate glass window, the window shatters. We don't see the shattering as a judgment, but it is a judgment. It is the outcome. It is the consequence of having thrown the ball into the window.

God's judgment is the outcome of people's behavior. He so much wants a different outcome and through Jesus has done an amazing work to prevent a sad outcome for each human being. But "hell" can be the outcome of our choices, plain and simple. My friend, Terry Smith, is fond of quoting a sentence from the very next chapter: "*...anyone who approaches Him must believe that He is and that He rewards those who earnestly seek Him.*" (Hebrews 11:6).

What we don't want to do is *"trample underfoot the Son of God."* You might ask, "How could I possibly trample underfoot the Son of God?" The truth is that it is rather easy. All one must do is not recognize and honor the preciousness and effectiveness of the blood of the Son. I think the writer particularly had in mind returning to reliance on ritual to save oneself – circumcision, burnt offerings and the blood of bulls and goats. But, in a real sense, we dishonor the Son whenever we go a different way than His. Any action that honors Satan's perverted wishes for us rather than God's dishonors our Head, that is, Jesus.

If I don't have your attention, consider the next point:

"It is a terrifying thing to fall into the hands of the living God." Jonathan Edwards preached one of the most famous sermons on this very subject over 260 years ago. Of course, I would prefer to fall into God's hands rather than those of any human I have ever known. Edwards' sermon was entitled "Sinners in the Hands of an Angry God," not a "living" God. Let me fall into God's hands, but it still is terrifying to consider if we have in anyway trampled underfoot the Son of God.

Chapter 10 ends with a hearty call to remember the sufferings you have endured for God's sake. Truthfully, we have endured basically nothing. I have only known God's goodness my many years. But our early Christian forbearers endured terrible sufferings - economically, socially and politically. Those the writer wrote had truly suffered and held firm. He just doesn't want them to waiver under continued pressure. It is a heartfelt appeal.

"Hold on.... Don't shrink back!"

Hebrews 11

Faith, Confidence and Trust

"Without faith it is impossible to be well-pleasing; for he that cometh to God must believe that He is, and [that] He is a rewarder of them that seek after Him." (Hebrews 11:6).

Chapter 11 is the great Faith chapter and famous for it. In one sense, Faith is about confidence in something that cannot be tangibly seen, even though it can be tested. Every time we sit down, we exhibit a form of confidence that our willful movement (beginning to descend with our backside without seeing whether the chair will support us or not) will produce rest and our intended result. We turn the keys of our car anticipating that the car will start even though we have not seen the internal wiring nor understood the science behind electricity and mechanics.

Faith fills our everyday walk. It is a confidence that what we have learned to trust will most likely happen. Almost every action we take is based on confidence that things will work out as we anticipate in spite of the fact that we have not seen the unseen forces that lay behind most everything.

Let me give you an easy example. Last year, we purchased an Alexa from the internet merchant, Amazon. Alexa sits on our kitchen counter. We ask "her" every morning for the time. She tells us 5:30 AM, and we believe her. Yet we have no idea how "she" works. Her voice comes to us through electrical and electronic impulses which are carried through airwaves we can neither see nor touch. Yet, we fully anticipate that her answer will be correct to the second. Yes, she can be a bit frustrating if our Wifi is acting up, but we base our schedule for the day on the time she gives us or on her weather report.

When we first took "her" out of the box, we had to get used to her. We bought with confidence from Amazon; we grew more impressed with her prowess through our interactions.

We are like that with God. When I was young, I heard that God existed and loved me. Since the source of this information was my mother whom I trusted, I "believed her," that is, I trusted her and extended belief toward God. But then I began to test what she had told me. I prayed to this Creator of the Universe, I sang songs to Him, I tried to do what He wanted me to do. Slowly, He and I developed an invisible relationship. As the years passed, my trust in His existence increased. My faith has become a tangible confidence that He is as He says He is.

So, there are three words for me: faith, confidence and trust. All three wrap up my side of my relationship with Him. I suspect it was the same for each of us and all those on the great list of spiritual heroes in Chapter 11.

Hebrews 11:6 is a simple deduction. If you don't think God exists, you have no relationship with Him from your point of view. This is like a child who can neither hear, see nor touch his parent. The child has no idea that the parent exists. There is no functional relationship. This would be a very sad situation for the parent if the parent *did* exist. And, of course, it would be a sad situation for the child though the child would not know it. Belief and trust do usher in all of the rewards of being in a relationship.

"By faith Abraham, when he was called, obeyed to go out unto a place which he was to receive for an inheritance; and he went out, not knowing whither he went." (Hebrews 11:8)

Faith, confidence and trust allow us and cause us to respond. Like Abraham, if we have faith, confidence and trust in God, when we hear God calling us to one thing or another, we do it not fully knowing what the outcome will be. We know He who calls us.

Our actions are based on who He is, not our exact knowledge of the outcome. What we do know is that the outcome will be much better than it would be if we did not do what we were called to do. We have this confidence increasing as we grow older in the Lord because we have tested it time after time. Without question, looking back over 73 years, this is a certainty for me. I know this: that whatever God wants will yield a better outcome than any alternative choice of mine, *without question*. I know this with greater certainty than whether the chair will support me when I descend.

A City With Foundations

"for he looked for the city which hath the foundations, whose builder and maker is God." (Hebrews 11:10).

When we started out 50 years ago on our journey in God, we were a bit like Abraham. This verse from Hebrews inspired us. We were looking for the place that God had built, a City with foundations, a place where we would not be shaken when the storms and tremors of life arose. This is a spiritual habitation, but we had to extend trust to God to find it. So it was with Abraham, and so it is with us.

> *"And these all, having had witness borne to them*
> *through their faith, received not the promise,"*
> (Hebrews 11:39).

Faith is always in front of the outcome, and for most of the heroes mentioned in Chapter 11, they endured, hoping for a promise they did not personally receive. Some received only the vision and hope of what would come. Some received the promise but only decades later. Yet, as we found when thinking about the loins of a man or a woman, those who did not receive in their own generation looked forward to a later generation receiving the promise, so in one sense they did receive it through their offspring. Yet, they endured because of the strength of their internal faith, confidence and trust.

When old people plant a tree, they do so for the generations that follow and not themselves. Remaining faithful under great duress is not only an exhibition of the very nature of God (*Chesed*), but also a love for those who come after. It is an expression of faith.

Hebrews 12

One of my favorite chapters in the Bible with a great opening, a ringing "Therefore," and packed with helpful content, Chapter 12 is a must read. THEREFORE,

"since we have so great a cloud of witnesses surrounding us, let us also lay aside every encumbrance and the sin which so easily entangles us, and let us run with endurance the race that is set before us, fixing our eyes on Jesus, the author and perfector of faith, who for the joy set before Him endured the cross, despising the shame, and has sat down at the right hand of the throne of God." (Hebrews 12:1-2).

The Race!

This vision of the race always brings me back to the end of my officer training days in the Marine Corp. Toward the end, we had several things we needed to accomplish, and one was running in our fatigues and our big leather boots 9 miles. All I can remember now is the constant internal voice that said, "pace yourself."

The captain who had originally chosen me had given me an important tip, "If you ever think you can't run another step, just tilt your body a bit forward." He was right; the tilt let gravity work for you.

But the race wasn't easy that day. I was running with a pack of about fifty men, and it was blazing hot. We were running in the hills of Quantico.

There is no question that running with others is a help. Their presence encouraged me; my pacing worked, and occasionally I tilted forward. I think of all three of these helps (pacing, tilting, others) when I read Chapter 12's opening.

I would have been helped that day even more if I had been able to visualize the race Jesus had already run. The greatest danger I faced was growing wearing *AND* losing heart. Losing heart is a horror, a black hole, a terrible danger, and the author of Hebrews knew all of us are susceptible to losing heart.

Weariness is a great danger. I have a friend who went into a black hole for almost an entire year. It was not pretty, and it impacted a huge number of people. Though many tried to extend encouragement, deliverance ended up being a God thing. Regardless, what a blessing it is to have brothers and sisters who love you and give themselves to encourage you.

One of Satan's most effective tools is telling us that we are alone. In fact, I have shared before that I think at the base of the unconscious lie that I carry from early childhood is the lie that I am alone. People that know me might be surprised at that confession, but I must always remember that it is a lie and the truth is that I am NOT alone. I have true flesh and blood brothers and sisters, a very attached wife and a great number of offspring. But even more important to my walk, I have the continuous presence of God.

"People in Zion, inhabitant in Jerusalem, you will weep no longer. He will surely be gracious to you at the sound of your cry; when He hears it, He will answer you. Although the Lord has given you bread of privation

and water of oppression, He, your Teacher, will no longer hide Himself,
but your eyes will behold your Teacher. Your ears will hear a word behind
you, 'This is the way, walk in it,' whenever you turn to the right or to
the left. And you will defile your graven images overlaid with silver, and
your molten images plated with gold. You will scatter them as an impure
thing, and say to them, 'Be gone!'" (Isaiah 30:19-22).

Isaiah 30 is an important chapter for me because it speaks to the New Covenant era when "your Teacher" will not be hidden from you. In a true sense, you will be able to see Him and hear His voice as you walk the adventurous course of life. You are NEVER alone.

Difficulty also is dangerous, especially when it continues for a long period of time. But the author points out that difficulty is of great use when building character and integrity. Fathers use difficulty as a tool. I suspect my children got very tired of me saying time after time that every difficult situation they encountered "builds character." I tried to say it somewhat in jest, but I meant it. Persistence in spite of grave difficulty over time builds character. *"It yields the peaceful fruit of righteousness."* (Hebrews 12:11).

Midway in the chapter, we come to another *"Therefore."* I am impressed with the great number of "therefores" in Hebrews. One reason there are so many is that the writer makes a point and consistently follows it with a deduction. It is the way the writer both thinks and writes – a very helpful approach. Since we know the race is going to be long and difficult, there *are* some things we need to do.

"Strengthen the hands that are weak and the knees that are feeble, and
make straight paths for your feet is that the limb that is lame may not be
put out of joint, but rather be healed." Hebrews 12:12).

Unfortunately, I have weak knees. On one occasion, I was walking across a street in Franklin, Tennessee and had to step a bit too quickly in the middle of the road to avoid an oncoming car. As soon as I did so, I felt my legs buckling and intense pain in one of my knees. I had to walk with a cane for several weeks until my knee recovered.

When I took son Christopher hiking in Ireland, an orthopedic doctor stuck what appeared to be a four-inch-long needle in my knee and injected cortisone to give me some relief for the trial ahead.

The writer of Hebrews is well aware that we all have spiritual weaknesses of one sort or another. And he knows that the trail before us will have difficult twists and turns. He gives us two prescriptions. The first is to *strengthen* the areas of weakness by exercise. Since we are dealing with spiritual weaknesses, the actual instructions will vary with the ailment.

Fran has just had a hip replaced – a perfect physical example. The Physical Therapist gave her specific instructions of what exercises would be helpful and those that would be off limits. Depending on our weakness, we need God's direction. Likely, that will come best through a trusted brother or sister. If your weakness is hiding your failures from others, this is a hard one, and takes courage to employ. But many will attest it is best to get counsel for strengthening weak joints! If you don't share your weaknesses, no one can help you get better!

The second solution is *"make straight paths for your feet."* This one is not hard to visualize. If you have an addiction to something, it is incredibly stupid to put yourself in settings and locations where you are going to be tempted. I remember the good habit one of my brothers has when he has to travel solo. He never turns the TV on in the hotel room. This is making a straight path for his feet, because if he does turn it on, he may drift to filthy channels. It is a practical outworking of Hebrews 12's instruction.

Another practical help is staying in tight relationship with those the Lord has placed you. And, *"Pursue peace with all men."* (Hebrews 12:14).

In verse 15, we come to one of the most practical tips for running the race of life that I know. This verse is so important:

"See to it that no one comes short of the grace of God; that no root of bitterness springing up causes trouble, and by it many be defiled." (Hebrews 12:15).

Goodness, this is important. Bitterness is a killer. It hurts the person both spiritually and physically. The Mayo Clinic has found that holding grudges and bitterness negatively impacts mental health, increases blood pressure and the danger of clinical depression, and hurts the immune system and cardiovascular function.

Worse, it is one of Satan's great traps. It *defiles* many. It is not a solo attack. It is like putting a poisonous chemical in the drinking water. Many may lose their way because of one person's harbored bitterness. Pride often holds back healing, and pride is difficult to touch. Pride is a defense of sorts that people with severe hurts employ to keep anyone from getting too close and seeing their real situation.

I say all of this with great certainty. We have walked closely with others who were trapped in bitterness. Unfortunately, great suffering resulted, not only to them but many others. Each one of us has to *"see to it."* We have a responsibility to maintain peace with everyone, and we also have responsibility to stay clean of bitterness and not let the sun go down on our anger. (Ephesians 4:26).

"For you have not come to a mountain that can be touched and to a blazing fire, and to darkness and gloom and whirlwind, and to the blast of a trumpet and the sound of words which sound was such that those

who heard begged that no further word be spoken to them. For they could not bear the command, 'If even a beast touches the mountain, it will be stoned.' And so terrible was the sight, that Moses said, 'I am full of fear and trembling.' But you have come to Mount Zion and to the city of the living God, the heavenly Jerusalem, and to myriads of angels, to the general assembly and church of the firstborn who are enrolled in heaven, and to God, the Judge of all, and to the spirits of the righteous made perfect, and to Jesus, the mediator of a new covenant, and to the sprinkled blood, which speaks better than the blood of Abel." (Hebrews 12:18-24).

Rhetorically, Chapter 12 is a masterpiece from beginning to end, but the content is precious as well. I am taken up and away with the preceding section. Read it again and as you read each piece, close your eyes and visualize what he is describing. If you think the scene at Sinai was terrifying, think of the true wonder of the heavenly scene – not the shadow but the reality. I can hardly stay in my seat as I touch this. Goosebumps are all over me!

So, what is the result of this chapter; what is the "therefore?" **See to it that you do not refuse Him who is speaking!** Rather, since we have received a kingdom which cannot be shaken, let gratefulness spring up from our hearts toward God. *"Let us show gratitude to God, by which we may offer to Him an acceptable service with reverence and awe!"* (Hebrews 12:28). Gratitude is better than an opioid!

Amen! FOR OUR GOD *IS* A CONSUMING FIRE, worthy of all praise, glory, reverence and awe!

Hebrews 13

I love this chapter. *"Let the love of the brethren continue!"* After Hebrews' rousing review of God's intervention in the world and a focus on some of its most striking implications, the author wraps up his letter with sweet reminders of what each community should embrace. *"Love of the brethren"* is first on the list.

Though the NASB translates this sentence as shown above, in the Greek there are only three words: *menō philadelphia menō. Menō* means *"continue"* or *"to abide continually." Philadelphia* means brotherly or sisterly love. In a sense, the short sentence could be rendered "Continue love continually" or "Continue to abide in love as you would with your closest family member."

Christians, by the remarkable sacrifice of their great High Priest, Jesus Christ, have become family. In the most vivid way, they are "blood" brothers and sisters. This thought is a great revelation.

I think how different this is from what many experience. When I think of my brothers and sisters, it is hard to see them without the blood of Christ running down their faces. We are together in a most mysterious way, purchased and sprinkled clean by the great High Priest of the heavens. In Him, in His body, we have intimate access to the God of the Universe whom we discover is Father to us. This seeing is very precious.

Maybe His revelation has meant more to me than most people because I grew up an "only child;" I can be quite overcome when looking around the table with some of my brothers and sisters and *SEE* them for who they are. It happens often on Sunday mornings as we gather for worship. It is a marvelous thing, and *philadelphia* springs forth in my heart.

Certainly, *"Church"* is not a delicatessen where one simply goes to pick up tidbits of knowledge. The *Ekklesia* is the living Family of God in all of its glory, a true wonder – the House of God. We are *"called out"* of the world into Jesus, and in Jesus, we are brothers and sisters – not only of Him but also of each other. A "God blessing" is to be able to touch this in reality, in flesh and blood. We are certainly not alone; each one of us is part of the Body of Christ, the Family of God, the Household of Faith.

"Hospitality to strangers" in the second sentence of the chapter brings us front and center to our attitude and actions toward the alien and the immigrant - those not of our own ethnic or geographic band of brothers and sisters. The writer says that some are angelic beings in disguise. It is an inspiring thought that pushes us past our comfort zone.

My friend, Clay Wilson, comes to mind when I think about angelic visitation. In spite of Clay's many serious challenges with addiction and the fact that he lost both of his legs to a train, he is a sweet gift in a rough package. I suspect he would smile at that thought.

I am thankful for the many displays of hospitality amongst us to those who are immigrants or the disenfranchised, incarcerated or alone. The phrase reminds me of the command at the Passover meal to accommodate at table those who are not a part of the blood family. I feel conviction as I read this call to hospitality for I have barely opened my home to those in need of care and attention. Lord, help me!

"Remember the prisoners as though in prison with them...." May God bless those who have made a dent in piercing through the prison walls with God's love. The reference is particularly meant for those brothers and sisters incarcerated for being Christians. The writer says *"since you yourselves also are in the body,"* but obviously, anyone in prison is in extremely difficult straits and worthy of comfort.

"And those who are ill-treated." This primarily refers to Christians in persecution, but the whole thrust of the Bible and Jesus's teachings in particular are to those who are outcasts and the mistreated ones. If you live in the South, you know that a huge percentage of people continue to suffer from the vestiges of slavery. Everywhere, all over the earth, we

find prejudice and maltreatment. The heart of God is on display whenever brothers and sisters extend gentle care to the disenfranchised.

It may seem a bit odd to find in this list of people to target with kindness a comment about *"the marriage bed,"* but the writer shifts gears to warn against two particular dangers that face the Body of Christ. The first is sexual immorality. Sex outside of marriage is fornication; a word I grew up with that to me described the vilest of actions.

Today in America, we live in a society where fornication is practiced openly and without qualms. Young men and women sleep together for long seasons as they enjoy the enticements of sexual union that is meant only for those who have entered into the covenant of marriage. This would have astounded C.S. Lewis who wrote many years ago that those in love could not stop professing their love. He would have been surprised that love had not led to covenant.

Today, we find a hesitancy gripping young people - a fear of making a lifelong commitment. The frequency of divorce, another practice nearly unknown in the Body of Christ two generations ago, is part of the reason for the fear. Unchecked, this undoubtedly will lead to a total breakdown of our society.

The second warning is about riches. *"Make sure that your character is free from the love of money."* (Hebrews 13:5). *"Be content with what you have."* The attitude of contentment would relieve a lot of internal stress that plagues most of us. Being content with what we have *IS* a sign of trust in God's promise *"I will never desert you, nor will I ever forsake you."* (Hebrews 13:5).

"I will never desert you, nor will I ever forsake you," is a direct quote from the Torah scrolls in the book of Deuteronomy 31, verse 6. The writer's grasp of the Hebrew Scriptures is remarkable; no doubt prompted by God at every reference. Many brothers and sisters need to hear God's

voice as He binds His will to each of us and declares, *"I will never desert you, nor will I ever forsake you."*

The second verse he quotes is from Psalm 118: *"The Lord is my helper, I will not be afraid. What can man do to me?"* Of course, man can do a great many terrible things, but with a solid foundation in God, a Christian believer is able to stand when others fall. I am reminded of the horrible litany of atrocities against the People of God since the beginning of time. But the great sign of a deep relation with God is the lack of fear. I am reminded of Polycarp and Ignatius of Antioch as I write, but of course we have nearly every apostle meeting horrid deaths as well as Jesus Himself.

The writer of Hebrews shifts away from warnings back to those who deserve special attention. These are those who faithfully delivered the Word of God to us. In the first century, the Word was delivered at great personal cost. Thankfully, we live in a time where there is still cost, but normally not the cost of lives – at least not now in the United States. As I write, the State of California is in the midst of enacting a law that would prohibit the publication and sale of Bibles along with any other documents that openly affirm that homosexuality is wrong. So, perhaps we will pay a greater price for the delivery of the Word of God in the next generation.

Paul said ingratitude is a sign that the Age is wrapping up. (see 2nd Timothy 3:1-2). I find that the longer I live, the more that gratitude wells up in me, particularly for the brothers and sisters who have so faithfully, in season and out of season, brought the Word of God to me.

I suspect each of us has a long list. Certainly, I do. My mother, Leon Sanders, E.H. Ijams, Landon Saunders, Terry Smith, Jim Woodruff, Watchman Nee, Bob Mumford, Derek Prince, Dr. Carroll Stone, Bob

Frahm, Pope John XXIII, Pope John Paul II, Thomas à Kempis, Henri Nouwen – goodness, my list would go on for many pages. It contains the brothers and sisters with whom I have walked these many years and all the saints who brought us the Word of God from days of old, including Abraham, Moses, David, Daniel, Isaiah, Jeremiah, Ezekiel and Micah.

The author of Hebrews is focused on contemporary flesh and blood, that is, those who are still in our presence. What an honor to honor those who have labored with us. We have been truly blessed, and we are wise to imitate their faith and conduct,

"Jesus IS the same yesterday, today and forever." By the grace of God, He is eternal in the Godhead, and we are foolish to think there is new information about Him. The prophetic ministries in the world today are replete with danger. One would think an esoteric understanding about silly things would be easy to avoid, but amazingly, many are enticed to such foolishness. We need to be on guard and stick to the tried and true.

"It is good for the heart to be strengthened by grace." (Hebrews 13:9). How can our hearts be strengthened by grace? Grace is favor extended to us by God; a favor that we didn't deserve but receive because of God's own action through Jesus. There is no way for our hearts to be touched and strengthened if we don't catch the magnitude of the favor that God has poured out on us. It is multifaceted. It is extensive - actually, it is immeasurable. And when awareness of that favor touches our hearts, our hearts are strengthened in God.

Verses 10-13 portray a reflection about Jesus's crucifixion *"outside the gate."* Jesus *did* die outside the walls of Jerusalem. This reminds us of the animals brought on various days to the temple as sin offerings for individual people. After the blood had been sprinkled and portions of the body of the sacrificed animal had been offered as a burnt offering on the brazen altar, the remainder of the body – the hide, the head, the legs, and most of the internal organs along with the intestines - were taken outside the camp and burned until they became only ashes.

"But the hide of the bull and all its flesh, as well as the head and legs, the internal organs and the intestines— that is, all the rest of the bull— he must take outside the camp to a place ceremonially clean, where the ashes are thrown, and burn it there in a wood fire on the ash heap." (Leviticus 4:11).

Obviously, those who served in the tabernacle could not "eat" that which was burned outside the camp. Likewise, the Jewish priests were having a similar aversion to Jesus. But we, finding true food in the Lord Jesus, must be willing to be *"outside the camp,"* to bear His reproach as well.

"So, let us go out to Him outside the camp, bearing His reproach. For here we do not have a lasting city, but we are seeking the city which is to come." (Hebrews 13:13-14).

Like Abraham, followers of Jesus are looking for a city whose foundations are designed and built by God. (See Hebrews 11:10). The only eternal City is in heaven, and we are headed toward it.

I am reminded of a sterling truth: *"Except the Lord build the house, they labour in vain that build it: except the Lord keep the city, the watchman waketh but in vain."* (Psalms 127:1). We don't want to get enamored with things here on the earth. Particularly, we don't want to try to design and build a spiritual community of God's people. That is God's work – not ours!

Through Jesus, let each one of us serve in his tabernacle, His Body, His Church, and continually offer up sacrifices of praise and thanksgivings to God, doing good and sharing with others. This is the kind of "temple service" that God really enjoys. The once and for all true sacrifice has been made 2000 years ago. That frees us to be able to express the true nature and kindness of God to the earth and to all mankind.

The writer entreats those he writes to pray for him and those with him that they would be honorable in all things. A good prayer for all of us as well.

Our fine author ends his letter with a priestly prayer of "benediction, a "good saying:"

"Now the God of peace, who brought up from the dead the great Shepherd of the sheep through the blood of the eternal covenant, even Jesus our Lord, equip you in every good thing to do His will, working in us that which is pleasing in His sight, through Jesus Christ, to whom be the glory forever and ever. Amen." (Hebrews 13:20-21).

Amen!

James

James 1

Old Camel Knees

I've had a special view of James since graduate school. It was there that I read Eusebius of Caesarea's section on James in Eusebius's *History of the Church*. As far as we know, this was the first full-length narrative of Church history until Eusebius's day. Written around 323 AD, he wrote at some length concerning James. What caught my heart was his report that James was nicknamed "Camel Knees" because of callouses on his knees caused by long prayers in the temple at Jerusalem.

Hegesippus, an even earlier historian, wrote:

"And he was in the habit of entering alone into the temple and was frequently found upon his knees begging forgiveness for the people ... in consequence of constantly bending them in his worship of God."

There is a good bit of controversy over the Book of James and the identity of James himself. There is almost universal agreement that James is the one who concludes the Jerusalem Council in Acts 15 when a decision is made by the brethren in Jerusalem about how to receive the Gentile converts in Antioch. It also appears that this James is the same James that Paul visited when Paul went up to Jerusalem to meet with Peter.

"Then three years later I went up to Jerusalem to become acquainted with Cephas (Peter) *and stayed with him fifteen days. But I did not see any other of the apostles except James, the Lord's brother."* (Galatians 1:18-19).

Fourteen years passed, and again Paul went up to Jerusalem:

"recognizing the grace that had been given to me, James and Cephas (Peter) *and John, who were reputed to be pillars, gave to me and Barnabas the right hand of fellowship, so that we might go to the Gentiles and they to the circumcised. They only asked us to remember the poor—the very thing I also was eager to do. But when Cephas came to Antioch, I opposed him to his face, because he stood condemned. For prior to the coming of certain men from James, he used to eat with the Gentiles; but when they came, he began to withdraw and hold himself aloof, fearing the party of the circumcision."* (Galatians 2:9-12).

We learn several key facts about James from these references. First, he was surely a devout Jew and probably a member of the "circumcision" party within the church in Jerusalem. Second, he was closely related by blood to Jesus – either a first cousin or a half-brother. Third, he was a "Pillar" in the church in Jerusalem. And finally, James prayed a lot.

Because of his attention to what each man or woman *does*, Martin Luther cared little for him. Luther certainly was not hesitant to ignore things that didn't agree with his personal views. Luther called James's letter a *"strawy epistle."*

Early Book

James may be one of the earliest books of the New Testament - if not the earliest. Regardless of its date, there was disagreement amongst early church fathers as to whether it should be received into the canon of Scripture. Eusebius listed it amongst the *"disputed"* books as late as 323 AD, but it was championed by Origen, Jerome and Augustine and received into the canon at the Councils of Hippo and Carthage at the very end of the 4th century.

Digging In

James begins with a greeting reminiscent of Paul. He refers to himself as *"a bond-servant of God and of the Lord Jesus Christ."* You will recall that Paul began his letters to the churches in Rome and Philippi by referring to himself as a "slave" of Christ Jesus. But there is no mention of James as an apostle, which further suggests that he was not amongst the Twelve and rather a *"brother of Jesus."*

James is writing the *"the twelve tribes."* Certainly, James is writing the Jewish believers, and we will find that the five chapters of James contain a great number of dos and don'ts. In many ways, his admonitions are extremely similar to those Jesus made. For your reference, here is a "parallel" of points James makes and points Jesus made in the Sermon on the Mount:

JAMES	SERMON ON THE MOUNT
1:2	Matt. 5:1-2
1:4	Matt. 5:48
1:5	Matt. 7:7 (21:26)

1:12	Matt. 5:3-11
1:20	Matt. 5:22
1:22-25	Matt. 7:24-27
2:5	Matt. 5:3 (25:34)
2:8	Matt. 5:43; 7:12
2:13	Matt. 5:7 (6:14-15; 18:32-35)
3:6	Matt. 5:22,29,30
3:12	Matt. 7:16
3:18	Matt. 5:9; 7:16-17
4:4	Matt. 6:24
4:11-12	Matt. 7:1
4:13	Matt. 6:34
5:2	Matt. 6:19-20
5:10-11	Matt. 5:12

James's letter is a collection of truths and certainties, and the letter bears a resemblance to wisdom books like Proverbs as well as Jesus's extended teaching sessions. Since these truths come rapid-fire, I will just comment on a few.

The early Christian community was well acquainted with trials, and James starts by pointing out that difficulty will surely come and that we should be delighted with it because it tests our faith. Faith then produces endurance and endurance produces a perfect result - a faithful, steadfast life.

James addresses the practical side of faith. If you are uncertain about something, you will not get the result you want. If you want wisdom and ask for it with a solid confidence in God's ability to give it, you can rest easy. It will be given to you.

Verses 9-11 are interesting because James points out that each man and each woman should *"glory"* in their circumstances regardless of what they are. Rich or poor, free or in prison, persecuted or exalted – in every state we can glory. Importantly, it is not that poverty is wonderful, but that we know God looks at the poor with great compassion. And it is not a glory that we are rich, for we know God only receives the humble. If we are Christian, we glory in following the rejected and crucified. All things are upside down for the Christian.

Temptation

James's commentary on temptation and lust is important and full of insight from a man who has undoubtedly battled with both temptation and lust:

"Let no one say when he is tempted, 'I am being tempted by God;' for God cannot be tempted by evil, and He Himself does not tempt anyone. But each one is tempted when he is carried away and enticed by his own lust. Then when lust has conceived, it gives birth to sin; and when sin is accomplished, it brings forth death." (James 1:13-15).

God surely does not tempt us to do anything bad, and Paul promises us that *"No temptation has overtaken you but such as is common to man; and God is faithful, who will not allow you to be tempted beyond what you are able, but with the temptation will provide the way of escape also, so that you will be able to endure it."* (1 Corinthians 10:13).

God always supplies a way out. The Evil One tempts us, but God always provides a way out. We pray, *"lead us not into temptation, but deliver us from evil."*

James's point is that we better gird up our loins and look for a way out if we see temptation emerging because the sequence is clear: desire rises within us (for revenge, relief or for getting something another has) and the desire gives birth to the intention to sin, and once the sin is accomplished we receive… death! James is a no-nonsense guy.

Verse 17 is a very beautiful revelation of God: *"Every good thing given and every perfect gift is from above, coming down from the Father of lights, with whom there is no variation or shifting shadow."*

The picture here is one of utter brilliance, entirely steady and pure. Let's engrave on our hearts and minds the internal affirmation that everything good that we receive did not come from our doing, but came instead from God's doing. Pound this into your being, *"Every good thing given and every perfect gift is from above, coming down from the Father of lights."*

James ends the chapter with five certainties.

He begins by focusing on a piece of God's eternal character: God is slow to anger. God is not a hot-head. James describes the proper sequence of being with each other:

"Everyone must be quick to hear, slow to speak and slow to anger; for the anger of man does not achieve the righteousness of God." (James 1:19-20). Quick to hear (a patient listener), then slow to speak, and then very slow to anger if anger is appropriate.

I think James modeled this beautifully in the Jerusalem Council. So far as I can tell, he never got to the point of anger. But that is the beauty of the sequence. Listen ever so carefully to others – their thoughts and their positions - consider what you have heard, and then speak.

"The apostles and the elders came together to look into this matter. After there had been much debate, Peter stood up and spoke…. All the people kept silent, and they listened to Barnabas and Paul as they were relating what signs and wonders God had done through them…. After they had stopped speaking, James answered…." (Acts 15:6,7,12,13).

That critical day in Jerusalem, James spoke last. God had given him the gift of listening, considering and summing up. What James spoke, the church adopted.

"In humility, receive the Word implanted, which is able to save your souls. But prove yourselves doers of the word, and not merely hearers who delude themselves." (James 1:21-22).

This is a terrific "word" itself. To actually receive a Word from God, it needs to be planted in our minds and our hearts. But within us, our unconscious beliefs push back any truth that threatens our established beliefs, both conscious and unconscious. From a practical point of view, that is why humility and the Word of God are directly connected. You may be able to "talk the talk," but you won't be able to "walk the walk" unless you have been willing to receive the Word of God in your heart, you mind and your will. Our pride wars against God's intervention in our belief systems. We have to acknowledge this and pray that God will help us receive with a humble heart.

The next to last point is that a man or woman may think they are on God's path, but if their tongue is not under control, they delude themselves and their "religion" is worthless. James will return later to the issue of the tongue. There is no question that we need to listen more carefully, consider and then speak only what we feel Father is speaking.

Pure Religion

James sums up with what pure religion really is: care for orphans and widows in distress and *"keeping oneself"* unstained by the world. This is a somewhat odd couplet. We know from Scripture that God does look with remarkable compassion on the widow and the orphan, and so should we. *"Keeping oneself"* unstained from the world focuses on our action of not touching anything that could pollute or contaminate. Since James was a Jew's Jew, he may have been thinking as much about eating and drinking as he was about his internal world. We know from Acts and Galatians that his own understanding was in flux about "the Law." He had sent brothers to Antioch to dissociate from the Gentiles. Yet, after listening to Paul and Barnabas, he shifted.

For us, *"keeping oneself"* unstained means staying far from the perverted flood of sexually charged media, events, books and those who hype division, discord, racism, materialism and the like.

James 2

Partiality

As Chapter 2 opens, James returns to a theme he has already touched in Chapter 1: not showing favoritism to the rich. This is an amplification of Jesus's teaching about the poor receiving the kingdom, and it reminds me a lot of Jesus's parables about what chair to take at a Wedding Feast and whom to invite to a party. Here is James's opening:

"Do not hold your faith in our glorious Lord Jesus Christ with an attitude of personal favoritism. For if a man comes into your assembly with a gold ring and dressed in fine clothes, and there also comes in a poor man in dirty clothes, and you pay special attention to the one who is wearing the fine clothes, and say, "You sit here in a good place," and you say to the poor man, "You stand over there, or sit down by my footstool," have you not made distinctions among yourselves, and become judges with evil motives? Listen, my beloved brethren: did not God choose the poor of this world to be rich in faith and heirs of the kingdom which He promised to those who love Him?" (James 2:1-5).

The word *"assembly"* in verse 2 in the NASB is actually the word for synagogue. James's use of this word reminds us that James is not only writing a Jewish audience, but that we are early in the evolution of Church history. His thinking is in flux. Some people date James's letter to around 50 AD. This is basically the same time that the issue of Gentiles in the Church is coming to a head – the time that Paul and Barnabas go up to Jerusalem and meet before the Church council, which James appears to lead, in Acts 15.

James is totally against showing favoritism within the community. It occurs to me that he has not quite worked through the issue of showing favoritism to the children of Israel over Gentiles, but more on that in a minute. Basically, James says "Make no economic distinctions." I think he definitely calls Jesus's teachings about not only the rich, but also how Jesus honored the poor of Israel.

One Sabbath day, Jesus had been eating at the home of an important Pharisee and told three stories to illustrate a related point after noticing that the Pharisee's invited guests picked the best seats at the table:

"When he noticed how the guests picked the places of honor at the table, he told them this parable: "When someone invites you to a wedding feast, do not take the place of honor, for a person more distinguished than you may have been invited. If so, the host who invited both of you will come and say to you, 'Give this person your seat.' Then, humiliated, you will have to take the least important place. But when you are invited, take the lowest place, so that when your host comes, he will say to you, 'Friend, move up to a better place.' Then you will be honored in the presence of all the other guests. For all those who exalt themselves will be humbled, and those who humble themselves will be exalted."

"Then Jesus said to his host, 'When you give a luncheon or dinner, do not invite your friends, your brothers or sisters, your relatives, or your rich

neighbors; if you do, they may invite you back and so you will be repaid. But when you give a banquet, invite the poor, the crippled, the lame, the blind, and you will be blessed. Although they cannot repay you, you will be repaid at the resurrection of the righteous.'" (Luke 14:7-14).

And finally, Jesus told the story of the great banquet:

"A certain man was preparing a great banquet and invited many guests. At the time of the banquet he sent his servant to tell those who had been invited, 'Come, for everything is now ready.'

"But they all alike began to make excuses. The first said, 'I have just bought a field, and I must go and see it. Please excuse me.'

"Another said, 'I have just bought five yoke of oxen, and I'm on my way to try them out. Please excuse me.'

"Still another said, 'I just got married, so I can't come.'

"The servant came back and reported this to his master. Then the owner of the house became angry and ordered his servant, 'Go out quickly into the streets and alleys of the town and bring in the poor, the crippled, the blind and the lame.'

"'Sir,' the servant said, 'what you ordered has been done, but there is still room.'

"Then the master told his servant, 'Go out to the roads and country lanes and compel them to come in, so that my house will be full. I tell you, not one of those who were invited will get a taste of my banquet.'" (Luke 14:16-24).

It is easy to see that Jesus understood deeply that God loved everyone, and that God was in the process of giving great honor to those who had not originally been chosen for His special affection. As my brother Terry Smith says, "We are all God's favorites." I don't believe James had fully grasped at this point in his walk the depths of God's love for the Gentiles. But as we saw in Acts 15, he will.

James's thoughts about partiality also tie to the underlying concept of Peter's address to Cornelius where he says, *"I perceive that God is no respecter of persons."* (Acts 10:34-35). But see the difference: James is focused on not showing any partiality between Jews because of economic differences, whereas Peter is focused on the fact that God shows no partiality with respect to ethnic differences. The day Peter spoke, he too was very much in transition. He was discovering that God's kindness in sending Jesus broke down the wall of division between Gentile and Jew.

The Law

Chapter 2 divides into three overlapping parts. We have the focus on partiality in verses 1 through 13. In verses 8 through 13, James focuses on the Law. Then, in verses 14-26, he focuses on the issue of works versus faith.

As he writes, the Apostle Paul is working hard to change a Jew's understanding of the Law of Moses with regard to "justification." Paul is completely clear that there is nothing a man or woman can do to be fully righteous before God. James in this section is also focused on the Law, and in one sense says almost the same thing that Paul says, but without the light-bell going off.

"For whoever keeps the whole law and yet stumbles in one point, he has become guilty of all." (James 2:10).

If you read the context of James's observation, you will see that for James, this means each believer must be ever diligent to not have the slightest touch sin in their life, including the sin of partiality. The

Jewish believer must follow every prescription of the Law or he or she will be guilty of breaking the entire Law.

Paul and the writer of Hebrews come at this issue from a different direction. Paul would agree fully that we don't want the slightest sin in our lives, but he would be quick to point out that no one, aside from Jesus, has ever been able to pull this off. He would turn the believer's focus (and particularly the Jewish believer's focus) to the amazing kindness of God that Jesus had become our justification.

James is tough as nails on sin, but we do notice that the hope of mercy creeping into verses 12 and 13:

"So speak and so act as those who are to be judged by the law of liberty. For judgment will be merciless to one who has shown no mercy; mercy triumphs over judgment." (James 2:12-13).

James grasps Jesus's teaching on the importance of having God's heart of mercy resident in our hearts. You will remember that Jesus said,

"But if you do not forgive others their sins, your Father will not forgive your sins." (Matthew 6:25).

James calls this the Law of Liberty. In the Law of Liberty, mercy trumps judgment.

Faith and Works

Beginning at verse 14, James is thinking hard about the issue of faith versus works. Undoubtedly, his thoughts are provoked by what he hears of Paul and Barnabas's teaching in Antioch.

Paul is teaching that faith in Jesus's atoning death is what saves us. James is fearful that too much emphasis on faith without some emphasis on works will lead believers to stop doing the right thing.

This whole issue of the Law and what each man or woman should do is a bit confusing. I think it a terrible mistake to think that the Scriptures written before the New Testament have been set aside. The contract or covenant *has* been modified and amplified; we are right to call it a New Testament (Covenant, Will), but the thousands of "truth tips" in what we call the Old Testament are still truth. When the Psalmist says, *"Bless the Lord, O my soul,"* he gives himself a good command. When we are told not to defraud our neighbor in Leviticus 19:13, we are told something good and true; it is wrong to defraud our neighbor.

You can see that James understands that all of the good truth tips contained in Scripture have not been set aside. They should be heeded if we truly have faith in God. So, James can conclude, faith without works is no faith indeed. For James, the two are tied at the hip.

I think this section is meant to correct what could have been an unintended consequence of Paul's teaching where some believers were setting aside ancient Scriptures' great encouragement to do good things. In my faith community, we are continually asking the question, "What would the Lord have me to do – what is The Holy Spirit prompting me to do today?" The result of our faith and our belief that the Holy Spirit is very much present within us leads us to ask, "What shall we *do* today."

James 3

Chapter 3 deals extensively with one of our most dangerous gifts, the tongue. James also contrasts the nature of Godly wisdom against earthly and demonic wisdom toward the end of the chapter.

The Tongue

You will remember James's earlier admonition in Chapter 1: be quick to hear and slow to speak. You will also remember the reverse stepping stones:

> Poor listening leads to…
> Being too quick to speak…
> leads to Anger bursting forth.

James connects the tongue with one of its most important occupations, that is, teaching.

"Let not many of you become teachers, my brethren, knowing that as such we will incur a stricter judgment." (James 3:1).

Like prophets, those who teach deserve special scrutiny because they can draw people into error. But because of the nature of teaching, the teacher must talk a lot, and much speech brings much danger.

From a practical point of view, a teacher should be following James's admonition in Chapter 1, i.e., being slow to speak. This means thoughtful preparation (checking his or her sources, being steeped in the Scriptures and careful about accuracy) and doing their best to speak in such a way as to reveal the true nature of God.

The airwaves are full of "teachers" screaming their way through rapid-fire admonitions as opposed to thoughtful, gentle, kind and compassionate speech untinged with anger. Such talk rarely produces Godly results. More likely, it wounds in one way or another.

James's point about the tongue is not only for teachers. Everyone has a tongue, and Chapter 3 has some of the most dramatic references to its power and danger ever written.

"For we all stumble in many ways. If anyone does not stumble in what he says, he is a perfect man, able to bridle the whole body as well." (James 3:2).

There are two important points to verse 2. First, James recognizes that we all stumble. Christians stumble, you stumble, and I stumble. We all stumble. Personally, I resist admitting that reality, but the fact is, I stumble. Hearing James is an encouragement. We don't wallow or glory in our stumbling. Instead, we recognize it and set our will to align with God's will that we stumble no longer.

Second, *"bridling the whole body"* yields perfect results. James's focus is using the restrained tongue as a bridle, since once the tongue gets going, the whole body follows – emotions as well as actions.

Jesus specifically talked about the tongue and connected it to a precursor – the heart.

"...But the things that come out of a person's mouth come from the heart, and these defile them. For out of the heart come evil thoughts—murder, adultery, sexual immorality, theft, false testimony, slander. These are what defile a person; but eating with unwashed hands does not defile them." (Matthew 15:18-20).

"Bridling the tongue" means deploying the reins of our heart. Watching carefully what we say is truly an act of love. We become more and more careful with what we say out of love. Spouses must be so careful in this area because their close contact gives many opportunities for the tongue to inflict all sorts of damage. The ears hear it, the brain records it, and the heart reflects it.

I am afraid James is a little pessimistic about ever getting this organ under control.

"For every species of beasts and birds, of reptiles and creatures of the sea, is tamed and has been tamed by the human race. But no one can tame the tongue; it is a restless evil and full of deadly poison." (James 3:7-8).

I have an older friend whose tongue brings my friend great harm. He can talk non-stop for two hours. In bitterness, he repeats a litany of hurts. Nearly any thought can begin the process. Once engaged with the thought of a slight from the past, his head and heart take over and out spews forth a recital of hurts, the same litany, over and over.

The tongue is a danger to us as well as others. This poor person hears his own words. And every time he speaks in this way, a groove deepens within his heart and within his brain - making ready for the next thought to get in the groove and trigger the long litany.

Let's pay close attention to this unruly part of our being!

Godly Wisdom Versus Dark Wisdom

James's admonition is to check yourself: are you really operating out of the wisdom and the nature of God? Look at what you do. Like your faith, your acts should reveal the underlying nature of God.

Exodus 34 reminds us that the God of the Universe is gentle, kind, compassionate, slow to anger, focused on steadfast love and what is true, plus willing to forgive. In particular, I believe I can say God also is content with Himself. If our "wisdom" does not reflect these qualities, it is darkened by the taint of Satan.

James focuses on two specific qualities of the dark nature: bitter jealousy and selfish ambition in the heart. Let's read the passage again.

*"Who among you is wise and understanding? Let him show by his good behavior his deeds in the gentleness of wisdom. But if you have **bitter jealousy and selfish ambition in your heart**, do not be arrogant and*

*so lie against the truth. This wisdom is not that which comes down from above, but is earthly, natural, demonic. For where **jealousy and selfish ambition** exist, there is disorder and every evil thing. But the wisdom from above is first pure, then peaceable, gentle, reasonable, full of mercy and good fruits, unwavering, without hypocrisy."* (James 3:13-17).

Dark wisdom springs forth from bitter jealousy and selfish ambition. Take a moment and think about the fall of Satan. What caused him to fall? Think further about what the fall produced in him. Jealousy and selfish ambition are likely the source of Satan's fall, and James rightly connects them to Satan. We have to be ever so careful about the sources that drive what we do. If our hearts are jealous and selfishly ambitious, many will end up being defiled. Satan defiled himself; his nature grew more and more perverted until there came a point that there was no evil he would not do. He was corrupted.

In dealing with our teachers in particular, look for the signs of Godly wisdom. Do they sow peace or not?

James 4

Lust and Envy

"What is the source of quarrels and conflicts among you? Is not the source your pleasures that wage war in your members? You lust and do not have; so you commit murder. You are envious and cannot obtain; so you fight and quarrel. You do not have because you do not ask. You ask and do not receive, because you ask with wrong motives, so that you may spend it on your pleasures." (James 4:1-3).

There is a war going in our members. Chapter 4 is chock-full of rapid-fire admonitions about that war – factoids for those filled with lust and envy that reveal the war.

The whole chapter could be read as a diatribe against lust and envy. James speaks to the hidden drives that spawn quarrels, conflicts, malicious slander, adultery and even murder.

First, James identifies the underlying sources to the war: lust and envy. We know from the work of our friend, Terry Smith, that these desires spring from our innate human condition and are accelerated by our unconscious childhood solutions to life. An example would be the procreative function within every human being. Hormones and emotions naturally activate this function, but it is accelerated or diminished depending on our conscious and unconscious worlds.

In other words, we may find that the desire for sex is accelerated or diminished by how we unconsciously solved our childhood difficulties and traumas. We may find ourselves more susceptible to adultery if we missed demonstrative love from our parents, and so forth.

Often, we unconsciously seek relief from internal, unhealed wounds that happened long ago, and we seek relief in all the wrong places instead of the healing we need. For example, wanting what others have in a covetous way may spring from an unconscious need for status or a fear of not surviving.

The safest thing to desire is the Spirit of God. God's Spirit - His nature and indwelling - is something really worth bending toward, as opposed to riches, sexual embrace and revenge for received hurts.

""God is opposed to the proud but gives grace to the humble." Submit therefore to God. Resist the devil and he will flee from you. Draw near to God and He will draw near to you. Cleanse your hands, you sinners; and purify your hearts, you double-minded. Be miserable and mourn and weep; let your laughter be turned into mourning and your joy to gloom. Humble yourselves in the presence of the Lord, and He will exalt you." (James 4:6-10).

There are many practical guidelines in James, and James 4:6-10 outlines two of the most important. First, the question is whether or not you are going to lead or follow, be unsubmitted or submitted. Will *you* lead, or will you let God lead? Count yourself amongst the proud if you lead; count yourself amongst the humble if you let God lead. This is terribly important because God gives a special grace to the humble, and we all desperately need His special grace.

Unfortunately, it is easy to deceive yourself by saying "I just do what God is telling me to do," while being absolutely unwilling to go anyway but your own. The trail of tears is filled with many who have been deceived in this way – outwardly saying one thing (and believing it) while inwardly staying fully in control.

This problem of spiritual pride is easy to see when one is confronted with a clear scriptural injunction that is ignored. *"Forsake not the assembling of the saints,"* is one example because many feel quite spiritual in spite of the fact that they are practically disconnected from any real fellowship or church community. *"Fornicators will not inherit the Kingdom of God,"* (see 1st Corinthians 6:9) is an admonition ignored by scores of young people who feel entirely justified before God while ignoring this truth by "living together" for months and even years outside of marriage.

Resist the Devil

"Resist the devil and he will flee from you." This is such an important truth imbedded in Chapter 4. I don't say it is easy to resist the enemy's tricks because he is smart enough to hit us in our most vulnerable places. But James is entirely right. Strong and immediate resistance causes the enemy to stop and go elsewhere to sow his destructive perversions.

Who Are You to Judge Your Brother?

Criticalness of others often has an underlying root in the lust for personal status or the envy of others. The perverted desire within us makes us masters of putting others down while unconsciously thinking that we are lifting ourselves up. I remember an insight that came to a young brother 45 years ago. He had gone on a long fast. He wanted to humble himself before God. During his fast, he felt God saying to him, "If you truly want to humble yourself, lift others up." In other words, rather than seeing yourself as a dog, learn to see others in a much more approving light.

Lord Willing

Another one of James's very practical admonitions is to not be presumptuous in your mind or your speech. *"Lord willing"* long ago enter my vocabulary, and I like having it displayed in my conversation because it signals that I am (or at least desire) to be subject to circumstances that God may orchestrate or that are beyond my own control. *"Lord willing,"* I will do this or that.

People close to me know that I have to be particularly hesitant in my speech when it comes to predicting my arrival time on any trip! Who in the world other than God knows when I will arrive because I learned long ago that I am an expert at getting travel dates and even airplane carriers confused on the day of possible departure. Truly, it is *"Lord willing,"* and me functional – which I am not 100 percent of the time.

James 5

Weep and Howl

James 5 is very bad news for rich believers. Miseries are coming. Since I feel particularly blessed with so many things, it is a troublesome chapter. On the one hand, everything we have of true value is a blessing from God. Yet this recognition is in great tension with Jesus's admonition to not store up riches on the earth.

James's focus flows along with his preceding renunciation of jealousy and envy producing covetousness.

Jesus gave multiple parables on this subject. Probably the most famous is the story of the rich farmer.

"Someone in the crowd said to Him, 'Teacher, tell my brother to divide the family inheritance with me.' But He said to him, 'Man, who appointed Me a judge or arbitrator over you?' Then He said to them, 'Beware, and be on your guard against every form of greed; for not even when one has an abundance does his life consist of his possessions.' And He told them a parable, saying, 'The land of a rich man was very productive. And he began reasoning to himself, saying, 'What shall I do, since I have no place to store my crops?' Then he said, 'This is what I will do: I will tear down my barns and build larger ones, and there I will store all my grain and my goods. And I will say to my soul, 'Soul, you have many goods laid up for many years to come; take your ease, eat, drink and be merry.' But God said to him, 'You fool! This very night your soul is required of you; and now who will own what you have prepared?' So is the man who stores up treasure for himself and is not rich toward God." (Luke 12:13-21).

The context immediately draws me in; much that we have enjoyed as a family came from the work of earlier generations. The man that approached Jesus was in the middle of settling the family's estate. How to get the man's share was the question.

But Jesus ignored that question and presented a much more important one: "What will you do with what God gives you?" And more importantly, will you be *"rich toward God?"*

I think James points out one way that those who employ others can be rich toward God – they can pay really good wages to those that work for them. I suppose there might be two ways to get rich: pay other less than they deserve or pay others even more than they deserve and have your business prosper even more.

From one point of view (not God's), it would be wise to be tight-fisted with your money, but just the reverse is actually true. Again, Jesus focused on this like a laser as Luke records:

"Give, and it will be given to you. They will pour into your lap a good measure—pressed down, shaken together, and running over. For with the measure you use, it will be measured to you in return." (Luke 6:38). This is very similar to Jesus's observation in His model prayer, *"for as you forgive others, so shall you be forgiven."* (Matthew 6:14). Truly, they are tied together.

All of this spotlights the nature of God. What "Person" is truly the richest? God wins hands down. But, He is the God of generosity. We see that clearly in Exodus 34, and we see that in Jesus's parables. God is not tight-fisted. Far from it, He is generous beyond belief. Both in pure giving (to people who do not deserve a gift), in reward (He rewards those who seek Him), and He is very generous with those who reflect His nature as the passage in Luke 16:38 assures.

The Lord's Return

James fully expects the Lord to come soon. But like the farmer who waits for the seed to produce fruit, you need to be:

"patient; strengthen your hearts, for the coming of the Lord is near. Do not complain, brethren, against one another, so that you yourselves may not be judged; behold, the Judge is standing right at the door." (James 5:8-9).

Almost two thousand years have passed, and we wait patiently for the Lord, reflecting that He has been very patient with us. Many close to the Lord may feel certain things are about to happen, and James perhaps should have included his admonition from Chapter 4, *"Lord willing!"* We know Jesus will return, but we just don't know when!

Oaths

James puts great emphasis on Jesus's teaching about oaths. Compare what James says to what Jesus said:

"But above all, my brethren, do not swear, either by heaven or by earth or with any other oath; but your yes is to be yes, and your no, no, so that you may not fall under judgment." (James 5:12).

"Again you have heard that it was said to those of old, 'You shall not swear falsely, but shall perform your oaths to the Lord.' But I say to you, do not swear at all: neither by heaven, for it is God's throne; nor by the earth, for it is His footstool; nor by Jerusalem, for it is the city of the great King. Nor shall you swear by your head, because you cannot make one hair white or black. But let your 'Yes' be 'Yes,' and your 'No,' 'No.' For whatever is more than these is from the evil one." (Matthew 5:33-37).

These passages are very similar. James perhaps puts even more emphasis on oaths than Jesus did because he says, *"Above all..."* But Jesus makes the underlying reason for His restrictions clearer: All of the things that Jesus lists not to be used to bind an oath are not under the control of the person making the oath. You can't swear by heaven; it belongs to God. You cannot swear by the earth; it also is the Lord's. The same is true for Jerusalem (it belongs to the King - either David or Jesus Himself!). And you cannot swear by your head, because again, you have no power over it. That leaves possessions which you do own and could put up as security on a contract, but Paul said, *"Owe no man anything."* (Romans 13:8). That only leaves your word.

Jesus's trust is that God does exactly what He says He will do, and we, if we are led by the Spirit, will always do what we say we will do. A Christian is bound by his word, and I think it incredibly important to be very careful to always do what we say we are going to do. And not do what we say we are not going to do. Both Jesus and James were focused in on the connection between our hearts, our words and our integrity. They are bound at the hip.

Before James lays aside his pen, he enumerates several practices that have fallen aside in almost every community of God's people, but need restoration:

"Is anyone among you suffering? Then he must pray. Is anyone cheerful? He is to sing praises. Is anyone among you sick? Then he must call for the elders of the church and they are to pray over him, anointing him with oil in the name of the Lord; and the prayer offered in faith will restore the one who is sick, and the Lord will raise him up, and if he has committed sins, they will be forgiven him. Therefore, confess your sins to one another, and pray for one another so that you may be healed. The effective prayer of a righteous man can accomplish much." (James 5:13-16).

These four verses sum up perhaps 20% of the operating manual that should be well worn in every church community.

- If there is anyone suffering…? Goodness, what community does not have someone suffering? Prayer should be going up to God.
- Is anyone cheerful? I certainly hope so. What is the appropriate response? Singing praises!
- Is anyone sick? Certainly, every month several will suffer sickness in our communities. The Early Church solution is quite clear. First, you call the elders of the community and ask them to pray OVER him (i.e., not on the phone, in a text, in a letter, etc.). Over him!

The elders need to be with the person partially because they need to *anoint him with oil in the name of the Lord Jesus."* This is very important, and about 98% of the time ignored in our community and our culture. Neither are the elders called nor is the person anointed with oil. Why in the world not?

I will tell you a three-fold answer: we are afraid of bothering people, we have too much pride and we lack trust in God's word. I pray that whoever reads this will be under conviction and not hesitate the next time he or she is sick, sinful or in need of following carefully James' admonition.

I would make one additional observation. What James describes is a "sacrament" in the technical meaning of the word just like baptism. Both events include a physical action that mimics a spiritual grace being bestowed on the believer. Augustine called it a *"visible form of an invisible grace."* The process involves anointing with oil while simultaneously the Holy Spirit anoints the needy believer with special healing grace.

- *"if he has committed sins, they will be forgiven him. Therefore, confess your sins to one another, and pray for one another so that you may be healed."*

The emphasis is on confession. If we do a specific thing, we can expect God to do a specific thing. In this case, if we confess to another, we can expect God to forgive us. All of this is Good News… but only if we do it!

1st Peter

1st Peter 1

We come to our fifth New Testament writer (after Luke, Paul, the author of Hebrews and James, excluding the Gospels). Peter, like Paul, served as an apostle and so designates himself at the beginning of his letter, but he also was leader of the Twelve, that initial core group of men who bore a special responsibility after Jesus's ascension.

After Jesus's ascension, Peter threw himself into the proclamation of the Good News, both in Jerusalem and beyond. He was a man who had been severely humbled before Jesus's crucifixion, but also had been received with immense grace afterwards.

At least thirty years have passed, and we find him writing from Rome (he calls it Babylon, a code word for Rome) to Christians in Bithynia and Asia Minor. The actual Greek language in which the letter was written may have been composed by Peter's colleague, Silvanus (Silas), who was in charge of bringing the letter to each church community. The letter itself is extremely well composed and contains some of the most important insights that have guided me and those I have been with for over forty years.

Peter's opening salutation is reminiscent of many of those that Paul wrote. Peter is writing those *"chosen by the foreknowledge of God the Father by the sanctifying work of the Holy Spirit that they might obey Jesus the Anointed One and be sprinkled with His blood."* (1st Peter 1:1-2).

This is actually a beautiful and tight reference to the Godhead, the Trinity, and the threefold Personhood of God. Peter shows how intimately God works with each of us: we are chosen, His Spirit works in us to make us Holy, and we are able to obey the leadership of the anointed Jesus and receive His cleansing blood.

Like Paul, Peter's opening prayer is the petition that those he writes receive both grace and peace, but he adds a modifier: *"May grace and peace be yours **in the fullest measure.**"* Yes, the people of God delight in His grace and peace. We also have the responsibility to evidence them fully. Plus, the underlying Hebrew word, *shalom*, carries with it the sense of completeness. Fully complete is a great wish for ourselves and others.

Peter, an apostle from the beginning, affirms in his own words the Good News he heralds:

"Blessed be the God and Father of our Lord Jesus Christ, who according to His great mercy has caused us to be born again to a living hope through the resurrection of Jesus Christ from the dead, to obtain an inheritance which is imperishable and undefiled and will not fade away, reserved in heaven for you, who are protected by the power of God through faith for a salvation ready to be revealed in the last time." (1st Peter 1:3-5).

This is another one of those special Gospel kernels we look for; it is truly "good news." You might want to read it again. There is another kernel coming up before the end of the chapter.

We have a living hope that an inheritance will be obtained that is imperishable, undefiled and that remains forever – an eternal inheritance. This inheritance becomes ours by way of Jesus's death and resurrection. Nearly the entire book of Hebrews makes it clear that where a death has occurred, an inheritance will follow in accord with one's Will and Testament. Jesus is both the required death and the surety that the Will shall be enforced.

By now (the early sixties), the saints are experiencing various forms of suffering and persecution. It helps them to look forward toward their long-term goal, i.e., eternal life and an eternal inheritance:

"you have been distressed by various trials, so that the proof of your faith, being more precious than gold which is perishable, even though tested by fire, may be found to result in praise and glory and honor at the revelation of Jesus Christ; and though you have not seen Him, you love Him, and though you do not see Him now, but believe in Him, you greatly rejoice with joy inexpressible and full of glory, obtaining as the outcome of your faith the salvation of your souls." (1st Peter 1:6-9).

We are included in Peter's observation because we too have not *"seen"* Him in the flesh. This is a great scripture to remember when we are faced by any trial, whether we suffer for our faith or are just suffering what all mankind suffers: sickness, death, hunger, financial deprivation and sometimes the ravages of war. One of the most riveting outcomes of having and exhibiting bold faith under trial is the praise and glory and honor that we receive when the Son of God is revealed.

You can take verses 6 and 7 two ways. They can point us to the return of Jesus or they can reference the revelation of Jesus that outsiders see when saints undergo severe trial. My hope is that the world will see a person filled with *"grace and peace"* and not a "whiny baby." Unfortunately, the latter negates our testimony; the former puts the spotlight on God – thus giving Him glory.

We owe a lot to the prophets and teachers who searched the Scriptures for predictions of the "Promise" centuries before Jesus's birth and the outpouring of the Holy Spirit. They served those who came afterwards (including those in Asia Minor and us), in spite of the fact that the prophets did not live to see the Promise fulfilled.

"they were not serving themselves, but you, in these things which now have been announced to you through those who preached the gospel to you by the Holy Spirit sent from heaven—things into which angels long to look." (1st Peter 1:12).

"Therefore, prepare your minds for action, keep sober in spirit, fix your hope completely on the grace to be brought to you at the revelation of Jesus Christ. As obedient children, do not be conformed to the former lusts which were yours in your ignorance, but like the Holy One who called you, be holy yourselves also in all your behavior; because it is written, "You shall be holy, for I am holy." (1st Peter 1:13-16).

Yes, we are called to be like Him – holy in all of our ways. The Godhead is entirely Holy – Father, Son and Holy Spirit. John the Revelator says the four living creatures aside God's throne cry out continually, *"Holy, Holy, Holy,"* – thrice fold Holy.

"And each of the four living creatures had six wings and was covered with eyes all around and within. Day and night, they never stop saying: 'Holy, Holy, Holy, is the Lord God Almighty, who was and is and is to come!" (Revelation 4:8).

More "good news" follows - another Gospel kernel from Peter. And yes, you were...

"not redeemed with perishable things like silver or gold from your futile way of life inherited from your forefathers, but with precious blood, as of a lamb unblemished and spotless, the blood of Christ. For He was foreknown before the foundation of the world but has appeared in these last times for the sake of you who through Him are believers in God, who raised Him from the dead and gave Him glory, so that your faith and hope are in God." (1st Peter 1:18-21).

Our faith and hope are in God! We must fully trust God who chose not only the sacrifice, but also the place and time. What was needed has been done. We connect ourselves with the sacrifice by our willful identification in our individual baptisms and thus stand purified. This allows a sincere love to build for our newly found brothers and sisters, leading us to fervently love one another from the heart. All of this has come to us through the living and enduring word of God which is Jesus Himself but also includes the message of salvation and our Scriptures.

Peter ends Chapter 1 with a stanza from the prophet Isaiah to make his point about the eternal word of God:

"All flesh is like grass,
And all its glory like the flower of grass.
The grass withers,
And the flower falls off,
But the word of the Lord endures forever."
And this is the word which was preached to you.
(1st Peter 1:24-25; see also Isaiah 40:7-8).

1st Peter 2

As Newborn Babes

"Therefore, putting aside all malice and all deceit and hypocrisy and envy and all slander, like newborn babies, long for the pure milk of the word, so that by it you may grow in respect to salvation, if you have tasted the kindness of the Lord." (1st Peter 2:2-3).

Peter had finished Chapter 1 with the reflection that the Word of the Lord endures forever. Since Jesus Himself is the Word - the *Logos* and remains forever in His position as both Lord and Savior, and since His Spirit resides within us who have tasted His kindness, we find within us a longing to draw close as a suckling child draws close to its mother. We want to nourish ourselves from the Word. If we draw close and receive the Word as pure milk, what we receive makes us grow spiritually in the Lord – just as a baby grows physically from mother's milk.

The awareness that immersing ourselves in the Word of God brings true spiritual growth, transforming us just as a child grows day by day, is certainly an encouragement to *"draw near,"* – to plunge ourselves into the Word. But, I feel the primary meaning is relational, that is, we are drawing near to the Godhead. Certainly, Scripture is a vehicle, but it is a person that we embrace beyond the written word. This is helpful to remember.

As Living Stones

"And coming to Him as to a living stone which has been rejected by men but is choice and precious in the sight of God, you also, as living stones, are being built up as a spiritual house for a holy priesthood, to offer up spiritual sacrifices acceptable to God through Jesus Christ." For this is contained in Scripture:

"Behold, I lay in Zion a choice stone, a precious corner stone,
And he who believes in Him will not be disappointed." (1st Peter 2:4-6).

I am not certain that words anywhere else in the Bible (aside from Ezekiel's vision of the Valley of Dry Bones) have given me more understanding of the nature of Christian relationships than 1st Peter 2, verses 4 through 6. This is a great seeing. I have little doubt that Peter was visualizing the massive stones of the actual temple in Jerusalem. Seeing Jesus as the *"corner stone"* spoke volumes to Peter. Like the corner stone of the Temple, it supported all that was laid upon it and it set the direction for all that would be built alongside.

An example of a Foundation Stone in Israel

As important, Peter saw each one of us like stones fully alive being placed in the temple that God was building in the Spirit. This was a great seeing and had many implications for me.

My biggest take-away was seeing the wall made of golden glass rather than opaque stone, and that God's presence inside the temple (the place of His habitation) would shine through gloriously. When we sing praises together, it is as if the wall is truly singing and shining forth the glory of God.

But my second take-away was the relational character of what God was doing with people. They were meant to be placed in such a way that their lives were entirely stable, supported both from below, alongside and from those that would in turn press down on them. Stability in the Body of Christ can be seen in this way.

Stone upon Stone

Depending upon how much we press in to relationships (including with Jesus) affects our stability in God. As we "press" into relationships, particularly our support relationships, we become more secure. We also are more secure by our horizontal relationships and how tightly we allow ourselves to be fitted together. And we are made even more stable by those who press into us for support and encouragement. The architect in me revels in this "seeing."

A Royal Priesthood – The People of God

"But you are a chosen race, a royal priesthood, a holy nation, a people for God's own possession, so that you may proclaim the excellencies of Him who has called you out of darkness into His marvelous light; for you once were not a people, but now you are the people of God; you had not received mercy, but now you have received mercy." (1ˢᵗ Peter 2:9-10).

Another marvelously expressed revelation of who **we** are – who we are called to be - a royal Priesthood. The word "royal" in the Greek is the word *basíleios* which means *"related to the King,"* priests of a Kingly rank. This, too, is an amazing seeing.

Hieráteuma is the Greek word for *priesthood*. The Kingly priests are exalted to a moral rank and freedom which exempts them from the control of everyone but the King, which means Christ as King and the Godhead. A priest is a special servant to the people of God, to mankind and of course to God Himself. Since we are a holy (set apart) nation of Kingly priests, born again into a totally new identity, this priestly function becomes a core part of who we are. It is a high calling and a serious calling. And a calling that I fear few Christians fully comprehend.

A Holy Nation

*"But you are a chosen race, a royal priesthood, **a holy nation**…"* We also become part of a nation – a nation made up of priests. Those who have been born of water and the Spirit have their passports changed. Unlike immigrants that hope for eventual acceptance, we are marked "citizen" as soon as we are born again. This means we not only share a filial

relationship with other believers, but together we make up a nation. This, too, is a matter of identity.

"Beloved, I urge you as aliens and strangers to abstain from fleshly lusts which wage war against the soul. Keep your behavior excellent among the Gentiles, so that in the thing in which they slander you as evildoers, they may because of your good deeds, as they observe them, glorify God in the day of visitation." (1ˢᵗ Peter 2:11-12).

Obviously, as both priests and part of God's household, we must absolutely abstain from fleshly lusts which are part of our old identity but now wage war against our soul. Clearly, we cannot serve as holy people if we are not walking in Holiness. It appears the early Christians were being severely maligned by the non-Christian populace. But, seeing beautiful behavior amazed the non-believers, particularly when those behaving well were under serious stress and mistreatment.

Honor Authority

"Submit yourselves for the Lord's sake to every human institution, whether to a king as the one in authority, or to governors as sent by him for the punishment of evildoers and the praise of those who do right. For such is the will of God that by doing right you may silence the ignorance of foolish men. Act as free men, and do not use your freedom as a covering for evil but use it as bond-slaves of God. Honor all people, love the brotherhood, fear God, honor the king." (1ˢᵗ Peter 2:13-17).

Peter is quite sensitive to authority – showing honor even to the king or emperor who undoubtedly were not even slightly Christian. He wants every believer to submit to legal authority, and as our old teacher, Bob Mumford, was fond of saying, authority is everywhere.

Whether a "free" man or a slave, there are realms of authority under which we function, and each should be honored by our submissiveness as well as by giving those in authority weight and value. This is even when the person who is in a position of authority is unreasonable.

We can see that the resulting behavior of this kind of teaching yields a very different people from the general population.

"Honor all people." This is beyond recognizing authority. ALL people are worthy of honor. In one sense, grasping this truth broke the shackles of Communism. John Paul II's proclamation of the great dignity of every human, no matter their station, flowed from understanding the inestimable worth God places on each person.

Christ Is Our Example

Peter ends the chapter with another short Gospel outline:

"For you have been called for this purpose, since Christ also suffered for you, leaving you an example for you to follow in His steps, who committed no sin, nor was any deceit found in His mouth; and while being reviled, He did not revile in return; while suffering, He uttered no threats, but kept entrusting Himself to Him who judges righteously; and He Himself bore our sins in His body on the cross, so that we might die to sin and live to righteousness; for by His wounds you were healed. For you were continually straying like sheep, but now you have returned to the Shepherd and Guardian of your souls." (1st Peter 2:21-25).

We are reminded that Jesus did not commit one sin nor was deceit found in His mouth, even when He was reviled. He entrusted Himself to God, bearing our sins in His body on the cross so that we might die to sin and live for righteousness. We had been wounded before; now we are healed. And Jesus is watching out for us just like a shepherd does with his sheep!

1st Peter 3

Wives and Husbands

"In the same way, you wives, be submissive to your own husbands so that even if any of them are disobedient to the Word, they may be won without a word by the behavior of their wives, as they observe your chaste and respectful behavior. Your adornment must not be merely external—braiding the hair, and wearing gold jewelry, or putting on dresses; but let it be the hidden person of the heart, with the imperishable quality of a gentle and quiet spirit, which is precious in the sight of God. For in this way in former times the holy women also, who hoped in God, used to adorn themselves, being submissive to their own husbands; just as Sarah obeyed Abraham, calling him lord, and you have become her children if you do what is right without being frightened by any fear." (1st Peter 3:1-6).

The foregoing section has both encouraged and perplexed me. I am encouraged with the thought that even when the one in authority over us is not a believer, having a *"gentle and quiet spirit"* (the "hidden person of the heart") can transform that person into a believer by simply having him or her encounter God's nature through the one being submissive.

It only takes a second to realize that this is NOT the usual strategy deployed by many believers with unbelievers, particularly those in spousal relationships. Nagging and lecturing is more common! But this first section gives all of us a clear tip: a gentle and quiet spirit is precious to God and can have a terrific effect with others – particularly those who clamor after control and prominence.

The perplexing part concerns the clothing of women. Not being a woman, I am not immediately impacted by this verse as translated in the NASB. I really like the way the NASB reads, but I note that the King James Version is more emphatic:

"Whose adorning let it not be that outward adorning of plaiting the hair, and of wearing of gold, or of putting on of apparel..."

I like the NASB; I have no idea about the King James though I know the Greek can probably be translated either way. Depending on how you translate this passage, it could be good news for jewelry and cosmetic stores - or very bad news. What I *AM* sure about is the primary emphasis: *internal* adornment, that is, a gentle and quiet spirit.

This is not about behavioral modification, and it is not really a man versus woman adornment question; it is about an internal change of the heart. Submissiveness is a key Jesus quality as well as a matter of the heart. It is a God thing. If the Son of God can be submissive in the manner that Jesus was submissive, both men and women can be submissive as well!

Then we come to verse 7:

"You husbands in the same way, live with your wives in an understanding way, as with someone weaker, since she is a woman; and show her honor as a fellow heir of the grace of life, so that your prayers will not be hindered." (1st Peter 3:7).

"In the same way." I think Peter encourages submissiveness to a husband's head, i.e., the Lord Jesus Christ, as well as pointing out what those of us married already know: women are different from men and vice versa. Very different.

I had a dream back in March of 1996 about a Guatemalan tribe. The dream pointed to the fact that males are assigned a protective role by their specific giftings. Women are assigned a nurturing role in a similar way. Since Peter spotlights men and their lack of understanding, one could observe that Peter has noticed that men are generally clueless about many things. Men *DO* need to gain understanding. The best understanding comes from giving full attention to both the heart of God and His nature. Men, let's love and protect our wives, and women, let's love our husbands in spite of their cluelessness.

"To sum up, all of you be harmonious, sympathetic, brotherly, kindhearted, and humble in spirit; not returning evil for evil or insult for insult but giving a blessing instead; for you were called for the very purpose that you might inherit a blessing." (1ˢᵗ Peter 3:8-9).

This admonition is for "everyone" – husbands and wives, men and women, slave and free, Jew and Gentile, but it is particularly good teaching for those who are married. If you are, let me ask you a question: Is the Spirit of Christ fully evidencing itself in the sympathy, harmony, humbleness and kindness you extend? Are you responding when slighted by returning a slight, or are you able to be kind in your response, not endangered by the attack? And are you really speaking well of your spouse when he or she is not around? When I see the word *"bless,"* I always do a mental translation to *"speak well of."* This is basically the meaning of the New Testament word, *"bless."*

"The one who desires life, to love and see good days,
Must keep his tongue from evil and his lips from speaking deceit.
"He must turn away from evil and do good;
He must seek peace and pursue it.
"For the eyes of the Lord are toward the righteous,
And His ears attend to their prayer,
But the face of the Lord is against those who do evil."
(1ˢᵗ Peter 3:10-12; see also Psalm 34:12-16).

If we really want God to respond to our petitions, our tongues need to major in blessing and *NOT* criticizing. Lord, help each one of us!

Suffering for Right and not Wrong

Christians are easily maligned, and this was particularly true in the second half of the First Century. They were often in trouble with "the authorities" for not exalting the Emperor or being charged with sedition (following another Ruler). Under attack, you would need to *"sanctify Christ as Lord in your hearts, always being ready to make a defense to everyone who asks you to give an account for the hope that is in you, yet with gentleness and reverence; while keeping a good conscience so that in the thing in which you are slandered, those who revile your good behavior in Christ will be put to shame. For it is better, if God should will it so, that you suffer for doing what is right rather than for doing what is wrong."* (1st Peter 3:17-19).

Two precious things stand out to me in this passage. One is that holiness in our own lives springs forth when we make Jesus truly Lord. The second is that our "testimony" springs from the internal hope that we have in God. Testimonies need to be delivered in gentleness and reverence. A lot of Christian "witnessing" does not happen this way. Peter is describing the exact opposite of argument and hostile force.

"Quiet and gentle spirit, sympathy, harmony, humbleness, kindness, gentleness and reverence" – all of these are the qualities spotlighted in Chapter 3, and those qualities we hope to fully internalize. Truly, these should mark our walk in every venue, which means we need to petition God for help!

The Good News of the Gospel

Peter ends the chapter with another carefully worded Gospel proclamation, using slightly different words but almost the same meaning. In the process, he reflects on the nature of water baptism.

"Baptism now saves you—not the removal of dirt from the flesh, but an appeal to God for a good conscience—through the resurrection of Jesus Christ...."

Baptism is an outward sign of your full embrace of Jesus's death, burial and resurrection, which you mimic, for the entire world to see. It occurs in water signifying both the cleansing of the sins of the flesh by the blood of Jesus as well as your immersion into the Holy Spirit.

Note how well Peter again summarizes the Good News:

"For Christ also died for sins once for all, the just for the unjust, so that He might bring us to God, having been put to death in the flesh, but made alive in the spirit; in which also He went and made proclamation to the spirits now in prison, who once were disobedient, when the patience of God kept waiting in the days of Noah, during the construction of the ark, in which a few, that is, eight persons, were brought safely through the water. Corresponding to that, baptism now saves you—not the removal of dirt from the flesh, but an appeal to God for a good conscience—through the resurrection of Jesus Christ, who is at the right hand of God, having gone into heaven, after angels and authorities and powers had been subjected to Him." (1ˢᵗ Peter 3:18-22).

1ˢᵗ Peter 4

"For Christ also died for sins once for all, the just for the unjust, so that He might bring us to God, having been put to death in the flesh.... Jesus Christ, who is at the right hand of God, having gone into heaven, after angels and authorities and powers had been subjected to Him." (1ˢᵗ Peter 3:18,22).

Therefore

After speaking of Jesus's death in the flesh in the preceding chapter and ending with the rousing reality that He who died is now seated at the right hand of the Father with all realms under His authority, Peter begins Chapter 4 with another *"Therefore."* Therefore, let's do the same, that is, let's also suffer in the flesh by ceasing from all sin.

This is an interesting observation: dying to lusts *DOES* cause a type of suffering at the level of our desires. It can be a suffering by simply ceasing from eating sugar because you know the outcome will be hurtful for your body, but your natural enjoyment of sugar must be put aside to help your body. In the same way, putting aside desires that lead to much more serious consequences does cause us a small amount of physical and emotional hurt. If it doesn't cause hurt, then why would Peter call it suffering?

So, let's be clear: setting aside our lusts will cause a small amount of suffering, but be assured that this small amount of suffering is nothing compared to the alternative consequence of not following God's path.

I am old enough to have an opinion about measurement. On the one hand, we have the amount of suffering involved in not doing something that everyone around you is doing that is clearly not God's will - things like bodily cravings, *"drunkenness, carousing, drinking parties and abominable idolatries."* (1st Peter 4:3). Refraining from such things in a social situation may cause you an internal feeling of not being in the club, not being included, but that angst is modest when compared to the other hand, i.e., doing the will of God. Modest suffering yields eternal reward. Really, there is hardly a comparison.

God is focused on the outcome of our actions as much as the action itself. I would suggest that He is primarily focused on the outcome of our actions. Think of all of the seemingly small sins: a glance at something improper, an extra glass of wine at table, a fudge on one's tax filing and the like. The actual action *IS* in and of itself small, but the outcome is often horrific: adultery, divorce, drunkenness, a car wreck, jail, loss of one's testimony, etc. When we break covenant, the ancient consequence would have been death.

Peter is also focused on the fact that our restraint and unwillingness to participate in different forms of darkness bring slights from those with whom we associate: "goody two shoes," "Mama's boy," "too good for us." Yes, that hurts a bit, and to an adolescent it hurts a lot. But setting aside our lusts for acceptance, status and inclusion saves us and our children from a multitude of bad consequences - the most serious of which is separation from God.

The Time for Fervent Love

God's purpose is straightforward: He wants everyone to live in the Spirit according to His will. And God is wrapping up the Age and us with it. So, what is Peter's recommendation? He recommends that we love each other fervently. This is a suggestion that takes my breath away. No "do this and do that." Rather, love each other with great passion – not the passion of the flesh but the passion of the Spirit. And one of his reasons is that *"love covers a multitude of sins."* (1st Peter 4:8).

Peter may have in mind that love trumps sin, and he knows that even though we don't want to, we all sin. So, God will pay less attention to our sin if He sees great love in our life toward mankind. Peter is looking forward to the Day of Judgment. But, he may also be thinking about the interesting power of love, which causes us to do right actions for each other as opposed to wrong actions.

Fervent love dampens down and even eliminates wrong actions because we are looking for what would be helpful to those God has placed us with - from our spouses and children to the waiter at the lunch table. Loving others fervently reduces our selfish, lustful behavior, which is always focused on us and our needs - not the needs of others. So, stir up a fervent love in your heart for others and deploy it!

Your Special Gift

*"**As each one has received a special gift, employ it** in serving one another as good stewards of the manifold grace of God. Whoever speaks, is to do so as one who is speaking the utterances of God; whoever serves is to do so as one who is serving by the strength which God supplies; so that in all things God may be glorified through Jesus Christ, to whom belongs the glory and dominion forever and ever."* (1st Peter 4:10-11).

EVERY believer has received a special gift from God! What an important declaration. The sad fact is that few in the Body of Christ have any idea what their "special gift" might be or that they even have one. Trust me, you have one, and I truly believe that the God of great generosity gives out a lot of gifts. You have, at minimum, one of these awesome gifts: the gift of hospitality, helping, healing, exhortation, faith, prophecy, teaching, leadership, mercy, words of knowledge or words of wisdom, tongues and/or the interpretation of tongues. (See Romans 12:6-8 and 1st Corinthians 12:8-10). Or even a special gift not identified. Just being a faithful friend mimics God and is a special gift.

Gifts are given to be **deployed**. I told a friend the other day that I am more quickly identifying when I can do something. Perhaps it is simply meeting someone arriving at the airport. I take a quick look at me and say to myself, "I can do that." Or perhaps writing a short note of appreciation or encouragement. I say to myself, "I can do that." Or perhaps a bigger thing like writing a book: "Yes, I can do that." There are a lot of "I can do that" in my life today. Not everything we can do is helpful, but there are many things we can do with what God has given us.

Jesus said don't put your light under a bushel. (Matthew 5:15). When I was a child, I sang,

> "This little light of mine,
> I'm going to let it shine....
> Hide it under a bushel? No!
> I'm going to let it shine.
> Let it shine, all the time, let it shine."

This is another way of saying "I can do that." Peter says we stewards of the manifold grace of God. What are you doing with what God has given you to steward? Whatever you do, do it through the strength that God supplies!

Tough Times Coming

Tough times are coming! Peter is certain of this, no matter whether an individual is a believer or not. Tough times come to the non-believer. Murderers, thieves, evildoers and even troublesome meddlers end up in trouble, but so do Christians. Doing the right thing in an evil generation often brings difficulty, but *"you are blessed, because the Spirit of God's glory rests on you."* (1st Peter 4:14).

Peter saw that God was wrapping up the Age, and He still is. Remember, time with God is not gaged as we measure time. He *IS* wrapping things up in Jesus! Your current suffering in the flesh for His sake yields an eternal reward. Set aside those lusts of the flesh, and don't lose heart!

1ˢᵗ Peter 5

Elders

Peter ends his letter with an exhortation to his "fellow" elders who reside in the towns and regions he is writing.

"Shepherd the flock of God among you, exercising oversight not under compulsion, but voluntarily, according to the will of God; and not for sordid gain, but with eagerness; nor yet as lording it over those allotted to your charge, but proving to be examples to the flock."
(1ˢᵗ Peter 5:2-3).

There is a great deal in this exhortation. Peter and these *presbyteros* ("old men") share a common function in the Body of Christ. Peter personally has witnessed Jesus's sufferings; his fellow elders in Asia Minor likely have not. But both they and Peter have the same charge, i.e., to *"shepherd the flock among you."* For Peter, it is a large flock stretching over many regions. For the men he writes, it is likely over believers in a town or a neighborhood.

Peter's exhortation informs us how communities of believers are governed. They are not inspired through these men; that is the job of the Spirit of God. But the communities are led by them from a practical point of view. Of course, *the Holy Spirit leads everything in the New Covenant world*, but attending to the flock in a human way is primarily the job of these old men, these *presbyteros*.

It has been nearly fifty years since I noticed the second key Greek word, the word *"poimainō."* This is a verb meaning *"shepherd"* in English. Shepherding is a key function that the appointed elders are called to perform. The language in 1ˢᵗ Peter 5 is almost entirely from a pastoral point of view - a view of sheep and their caretakers. Members of a Christian community are called by Peter *"poimnion,"* a *"flock"* in Greek.

Shepherds have four primary functions:

- to guard sheep from attack by predators,
- to retrieve lost sheep,
- to feed the sheep by keeping them in "green pastures,"
- To care for those sick or lame.

The ones who *"look over them,"* *"episkopeō"* them in the Greek. From this word we get "Episcopal" and the word "Bishop." It is worth an observation that Presbyterians draw their name from the emphasis they place on *"presbyteros"* (elders) and the Episcopalians derive their name from the emphasis they place on "Bishops." But here in Peter, we meet both forms of leadership – the plurality of Elders and the function of Bishops applied to the same people.

As we have pointed out, this practice by 110 AD in many communities had morphed into a President (or Bishop) of the Elders; in other words, there was a singular head to many communities supported by a council of Elders. (See Ignatius of Antioch's letters to the churches on his way to martyrdom in Rome).

But there is much more to see. Elders/Bishops are not to "Lord it over" their flock; rather, they are to care for it – voluntarily (i.e., not for pay though they may receive some form of compensation if full-time *(see 1ˢᵗ Timothy 5:17))*, being great examples of Christ - long suffering, gentle, kind, and full of steadfast love toward their flock. This vision of the "Good Shepherd" should certainly be the standard held before elders/bishops of our own day.

And who is the "Chief Shepherd" *(Archipoimen)* in our day? The same "Chief Shepherd" in Peter's day: Jesus Christ, the Great Shepherd of the Sheep!

Humility

Peter called the younger men to be "subject" to the older men, but he also was thoughtful to commend an attitude of humility toward everyone, regardless of age, rank or job title. This was totally revolutionary. I suspect there was absolutely no place under the sun where all men and women were called to humility.

"Therefore humble yourselves under the mighty hand of God, that He may exalt you at the proper time, casting all your anxiety on Him, because He cares for you." (1st Peter 5:6-7).

Peter can commend humility to every believer, because he knows it is God's way and that in the end, God will exalt the humble. We can cast all of our anxiety on God. But why? Because He cares for each one of us. Each one! This is such an antidote to the lie of Satan that no one cares for us.

I believe most people suffer from the lie that no one cares for us. The lie is sown at a deep level, but years of thoughtful work by Terry Smith makes this abundantly clear: it is one of Satan's Master Strategies. And Peter stands firmly against it as do all of Jesus's early servants.

Satan Tricks

"Your adversary, the devil, prowls around like a roaring lion, seeking someone to devour. But resist him, firm in your faith, knowing that the same experiences of suffering are being accomplished by your brethren who are in the world." (1st Peter 5:8-9).

We have to be on the alert for Satan's tricks. He DOES prowl around like a lion seeking to devour us. In Uganda, I was stunned with the experience of seeing a female lion in a grain field, hardly visible, waiting for prey. A lion can be hard to detect. When the lion starts to move, there is almost no time to respond. Yet, we have the power of the risen Lord in us and can resist if we stand firm in our faith.

Remember James' admonition: *"Submit yourselves, then to God. Resist the devil and he will flee from you."* (James 4:7). These two verses (one in James and one in Peter) are so helpful in dealing with the lies that Satan sows. Stand against them in Jesus's name. Whatever is the lie, God's truth is almost always the opposite.

Perfect, Confirm, Strength and Establish

Listen to the Apostle Peter's closing words: *"After you have suffered for a little while, the God of all grace, who called you to His eternal glory in Christ, will Himself perfect, confirm, strengthen and establish you. To Him be dominion forever and ever."* (1st Peter 5:10-11). Amen! The God of all grace, the Father of mankind, will *"perfect, confirm, strengthen and establish you."* This is a four-fold promise that God is granting you even as I write.

Stand Firm

"Stand firm in the true grace of God. Stand firm in it!" (1st Peter 5:12). Yes, stand firm! *"Greet one another with a loving kiss."* See what affection the early church displayed! May we show affection to each other from the heart!

2nd Peter

2nd Peter 1

Everything Pertaining to Life and Godliness

This is the "Step Ladder" letter. I always think of a stepladder when I think of the first chapter of 2nd Peter because he immediately dives into how we become more like God using the image of a stepladder.

But first, a quick overview. This letter has been questioned with regard to authorship. Though there are many clear references to Peter's life, it was not formally acknowledged as a letter from the Apostle Peter until the 3rd and 4th centuries when Methodius, Jerome, Athanasius, Augustine and Ambrose all testified to Peter's authorship as well as did the Church Councils of Laodicea (372 AD) and Carthage (397 AD).

Regardless of disagreements between modern day scholars, I find the content extremely useful and full of insight. Assuming Peter wrote it, the letter was written late in Peter's life - probably from Rome and likely after 1st Peter was written.

Peter begins by affirming that God's divine power has given us everything we need for true life and godliness:

*"Simon Peter, a bond-servant and apostle of Jesus Christ, To those who have received a faith of the same kind as ours, by the righteousness of our God and Savior, Jesus Christ: Grace and peace be multiplied to you in the knowledge of God and of Jesus our Lord; seeing that **His divine power has granted to us everything pertaining to life and godliness**, through the true knowledge of Him who called us by His own glory and excellence. For by these He has granted to us His precious and magnificent promises, so that by them you may become partakers of the divine nature, having escaped the corruption that is in the world by lust."* (2nd Peter 1:1-4).

You and I are well equipped, having received the true knowledge of both God and Jesus. We were called by the excellence of God's nature and granted precious and magnificent promises for one key reason: that we might become partakers of the divine nature of God. Immersed in Early Church letters, we find the nature of God to be our destination and God's goal for us. I posit this because we are brought front and center before God's deep love for us – for those He has created in His own image, and we see God's own nature which always moves toward deep communion.

Think of that for a second. If God's nature is our designation and goal, that is another way of saying that God wants a close bond with each one of us. Think of how much closer our communion with God can be if we become more and more like Him, having His nature entirely within us.

Last night I was putting to bed my grandson, Jack Mitchell. Jack is eleven years old and visiting with us for three weeks while he undergoes Hodgkin's Lymphoma treatment at St. Jude. Jack is "all boy." Yet as

I sat on the small couch in the guest bedroom, Jack got out of the bed and curled up in my arms. I was a bit overwhelmed with the wonder of this strapping boy curled up as I prayed. There was a likeness between us, and we were drawn closely to each other as we entered God's throne room. I thought it a great God thing and was reminded of the wonder of truly close and pure communion with each other and the Father of the Universe.

A Step Ladder to the Nature of God

God's nature is the exact opposite of the corrupt nature that is in the world because of lust. That corrupt nature cannot cuddle up with God. It is impossible. Peter saw that it is for this very reason that we need to diligently ascend the stair steps of progressive change that we will be more and more like God. Truly, *"deep calls unto deep."* (Psalm 42:7).

"Now for this very reason also, applying all diligence, in your faith supply moral excellence, and in your moral excellence, knowledge, and in your knowledge, self-control, and in your self-control, perseverance, and in your perseverance, godliness, and in your godliness, brotherly kindness, and in your brotherly kindness, love. For if these qualities are yours and are increasing, they render you neither useless nor unfruitful in the true knowledge of our Lord Jesus Christ." (2nd Peter 1:5-8).

Peter outlines almost every element of God's appearance to Moses in the Sinai, which I will repeat below to make inspection easier. Note that these characteristics are also Jesus's characteristics. The true knowledge of Jesus is the true knowledge of God and the true knowledge of God is knowing God in His essence - His very nature. Like a telescope probing deep into the elements of the Universe, we are probing the very nature of the Godhead.

"The Lord descended in the cloud and stood there with him [Moses] as he called upon the name of the Lord. Then the Lord passed by in front of him and proclaimed, 'The Lord, the Lord God, compassionate and gracious, slow to anger, and abounding in lovingkindness and truth; who keeps lovingkindness for thousands, who forgives iniquity, transgression and sin; yet He will by no means leave the guilty unpunished, visiting the iniquity of fathers on the children and on the grandchildren to the third and fourth generations.'" (Exodus 34:5-7).

The steps from bottom to top:

- Moral excellence.
- Knowledge
- Self-control
- Perseverance
- Godliness
- Brotherly Kindness
- Love

Trying to stitch these together properly is beyond my human ability, but both lists are true of God's nature and most of the connections are quite obvious. Lovingkindness (*Chesed* in the Hebrew) is a direct parallel of the top rung of the ladder in the Greek for Sacrificial Love, the Greek word *Agapē*. Knowledge (*Gnosis* in the Greek) corresponds to Truth (*Emeth* in the Hebrew), and so forth.

What Peter does is suggest a sequence of focus for the believer. Ceasing from overt sin, in other words, having Moral Excellence, is the first thing to get straight.

The second is deep Knowledge which likely meant spending effective communion time in prayer with God in the Spirit and plunging deeply into Scripture. A foundation for wise self-control is having a better knowledge of God and the true nature of holiness.

Has it ever occurred to you that self-control is not always helpful? We can restrain ourselves from taking risks, going to the aid of someone in trouble, and so forth. Remember the self-control that the priest exhibited when he walked around the injured man in the parable of the Good Samaritan. To have Godly self-control, we have to let the Spirit of God lead us and not our false belief systems.

With knowledgeable and Godly self-control active in our lives, we will immediately encounter difficulty, trials and suffering. Though we probably would experience trouble the minute we tried to exert righteous self-control, Peter is outlining a steadfastness that to some degree mimics part of the quality of *Chesed*, but perseverance in my book is another word for dependability under duress. Who better exemplified dependability under duress than Jesus, but actually, there are tens of thousands Saints who have done so since Jesus's death. Perseverance is a necessary quality to be developed deep in our nature if we are to get to our goal.

At this point, we are exhibiting a great deal of the character and nature of the Godhead, but Godliness is deeper than what is personal behavior. Godliness relates to the heart, and Brotherly Kindness is almost a combo of the Compassion and Graciousness that we find in the Hebrew words, *Rachuwm* and *Channuwn*.

The summit (think of stepping off into Heaven from your step ladder) is Love in all the fullness of the word – a fullness I barely grasp, but I know it is more full than we can imagine. "Onward and upward" as my friend, Steve Bowie, likes to say. Onward and upward.

Lest we be discouraged with this high vision, Peter is quick to observe that we may only be exhibiting in our hearts and in our lives a small measure of each rung, but his encouragement is to keep growing, increasing at every level. Peter assures us that so long as we are making progress day by day, we can be useful and fruitful to both ourselves and to those about us.

If we lack these emerging qualities, we truly are blind. That would mean, for instance, that we are back walking in ungodly patterns, having forgotten our purification from sins. On the other hand, if we embed these qualities in our hearts and minds, *"we will never stumble."* (2nd Peter 1:10). That is a BIG promise and makes one want to read the list every day of the year.

Peter knows that those he writes understand these things, but he doesn't hesitate to remind them. He wants to stir them. These important qualities must have been present to a degree in every new believer, but Peter feels his days are truly numbered, and he wants to stir his audience to the highest of pursuits.

Eyewitness and the Prophetic

In Chapter 2, Peter will shift his focus to the problem of false prophets amongst the saints. He lays down his own credentials, both with regard to authenticity as well as a kernel from the voice of God Himself heard on the Mount of Olives.

"For we did not follow cleverly devised tales when we made known to you the power and coming of our Lord Jesus Christ, but we were eyewitnesses of His majesty. For when He received honor and glory from God the Father, such an utterance as this was made to Him by the Majestic Glory, 'This is My beloved Son with whom I am well-pleased' — and we ourselves heard this utterance made from heaven when we were with Him on the holy mountain." (2nd Peter 1:16-18).

Peter is the real deal. He actually heard with his own ears what would be God's key testimony to mankind, **"This is My beloved Son with whom I am well-pleased."** If prophecy is hearing what God is saying through someone, what could be more prophetic than hearing God Himself speak!

"So, we have the prophetic word made more sure, to which you do well to pay attention as to a lamp shining in a dark place, until the day dawns and the morning star arises in your hearts. But know this first of all, that no prophecy of Scripture is a matter of one's own interpretation, for no prophecy was ever made by an act of human will, but men moved by the Holy Spirit spoke from God." (2 Peter 1:19-21).

We learn three more things about prophecy from Peter's reflection. Prophetic words are like lights shining in the dark. To mankind, they are amazingly important, revealing things that cannot be seen otherwise. Second, no prophecy of Scripture can be properly understood unless interpreted, and most important, it must be affirmed by the community, i.e., not one's own private interpretation. Third, no prophecy is true prophecy if it is just the good thinking of a well-meaning soul. Instead, it must be from the movement of the Holy Spirit of God working on the prophet.

All three of these points are foundational for dealing with the prophetic, and I can assure you that we hear on the airwaves numerous "prophecies" that bear the stamp of human invention and cannot even be placed alongside an utterance like the one Peter uses as his example.

2nd Peter 2

The Rise of False Prophets

"But false prophets also arose among the people, just as there will also be false teachers among you, who will secretly introduce destructive heresies, even denying the Master who bought them, bringing swift destruction upon themselves. Many will follow their sensuality, and because of

them the way of the truth will be maligned; and in their greed they will exploit you with false words; their judgment from long ago is not idle, and their destruction is not asleep." (2nd Peter 2:1-3).

As Chapter 2 begins, Peter remembers the days that the Children of Israel spent in the Wilderness after their deliverance from Egypt. Moses, a true prophet, had appeared before them earlier and had spoken the words that God was speaking – the true meaning of the word, "prophet."

"God, furthermore, said to Moses, 'Thus you shall say to the sons of Israel, "The Lord, the God of your fathers, the God of Abraham, the God of Isaac, and the God of Jacob, has sent me to you."'" (Exodus 3:15).

"Thus you shall say," God directed, and Moses took up his mantle and went to the Israelites. But Peter recalls that once the Israelites had been delivered from Egypt, false prophets arose to challenge Moses and to speak what God was *not* speaking. Korah particularly comes to mind. He and two other men stirred up 250 community leaders against Moses and challenged the words that Moses had spoken that had been from God. A great earthquake occurred, swallowing up the entire group.

In the case of Korah, a careful reading of Numbers Chapter 16 reveals an underlying jealousy and bitterness against Moses. The false prophecy arose from *within* the community, not from without. As the writer of Hebrews pointed out, bitterness unaddressed defiles many, and many can be led astray.

We have seen that the Early Church frequently struggled against the false teaching that ritual actions were necessary for salvation. This belief came pre-imbedded in the mindset of every Jew that came to Jesus. Paul spent a great deal of his time confronting this "false teaching" that outward actions made us acceptable before God.

But Peter is addressing a slightly different problem. Men soon would arise again from *within* the community challenging the very nature of God, Jesus's sonship and how Christians should behave.

Heresy

The word heresy comes straight to us from the Greek. Its root is from the Greek word *haireō* which means *"to choose."* In other words, rather than accept what has been passed down through trusted teachers, a man or woman may choose to believe whatever they wish. When this tendency to self define truth is presented as being a Word from God, we have false prophecy.

Underlying Motivations

Peter points out that in addition to jealousy and bitterness, an underlying motivation for seeing things in a different way is caused by a desire that springs from covetousness. The Greek word is *pleonexia*, which means *"a greedy desire to have more."* Truth and even Scripture can be turned inside out to prove a position that creates the reverse of what God intended.

It is not hard to think of specific situations we have encountered in community where that which is wrong is presented as right. Even Adultery can be justified by "messages" one has received supposedly from God.

My observation is that it is highly probable that the conscious mind of the false prophet often has no idea how the unconscious mind with its false belief systems and carnal needs is producing heretical doctrines – doctrines that are made up out of the unconscious to fit personal desires.

We remember that Peter affirmed in last verse of Chapter 1 that *"no [true] prophecy was ever made by an act of human will, but men moved by the Holy Spirit spoke from God."* (2nd Peter 1:21).

It is a terrible thing that false doctrines arise from *within* the community.

Expulsion

"And that prophet, or that dreamer of dreams, shall be put to death; because he hath spoken to turn you away from the LORD your God, which brought you out of the land of Egypt, and redeemed you out of the house of bondage, to thrust thee out of the way which the LORD thy God commanded thee to walk in. So shalt thou put the evil away from the midst of thee." Deut.13:5).

As I mentioned in my reflections on Chapter 1, God cannot cuddle up with the corrupt nature, and He puts aside those who corrupt the Body of Christ by teaching false doctrine. Actually, he who veers away from the truth removes himself from God.

Peter goes to some length to make the consequence of separation clear by recounting several examples of expulsion: angels cast into hell, those living in the time of Noah, and Sodom and Gomorrah.

Verses 9 and 10 are particularly important. God will *"keep the unrighteous under punishment for the day of judgment, especially those who indulge the flesh in its corrupt desires and despise authority."* (2nd Peter 2:9-10). In a certain way, those who follow the lust of the flesh while despising authority reap their own punishment prior to the inevitable judgment that is to come.

God's spotlight is *"especially* [on] *those who indulge the flesh in its corrupt desires and despise authority."*

"Daring, self-willed, they do not tremble when they revile angelic majesties, whereas angels who are greater in might and power do not bring a reviling judgment against them before the Lord. But these, like unreasoning animals, born as creatures of instinct to be captured and killed, reviling where they have no knowledge, will in the destruction of those creatures also be destroyed, suffering wrong as the wages of doing wrong. They count it a pleasure to revel in the daytime. They are stains and blemishes, reveling in their deceptions, as they carouse with you, having eyes full of adultery that never cease from sin, enticing unstable souls, having a heart trained in greed, accursed children; forsaking the right way, they have gone astray, having followed the way of Balaam, the son of Beor, who loved the wages of unrighteousness; but he received a rebuke for his own transgression, for a mute donkey, speaking with a voice of a man, restrained the madness of the prophet." (2nd Peter 2:10-16).

"Daring, self-willed," false prophets tell us what they want us to hear and what they themselves want to hear – not what God is speaking. We have to be ever so careful today to put aside listening to modern day prophets who tell us what we subconsciously want to hear just as the Israelites had to put aside listening to ancient soothsayers and diviners:

"You shall be blameless before the LORD your God. For these nations which you will dispossess listened to soothsayers and diviners; but as for you, the LORD your God has not appointed such for you." (Deut. 18:13-14).

To Whom Do You Listen?

One important question is "whom has God appointed for you to listen?" We know Scripture is appointed and we know that God ordained leadership is appointed. We don't want to fall unknowingly into a trap of deceit listening to a source God has not appointed.

"These are springs without water and mists driven by a storm, for whom the black darkness has been reserved. For speaking out arrogant words of vanity they entice by fleshly desires, by sensuality, those who barely escape from the ones who live in error, promising them freedom while they themselves are slaves of corruption; for by what a man is overcome, by this he is enslaved. For if, after they have escaped the defilements of the world by the knowledge of the Lord and Savior Jesus Christ, they are again entangled in them and are overcome, the last state has become worse for them than the first. For it would be better for them not to have known the way of righteousness, than having known it, to turn away from the holy commandment handed on to them. It has happened to them according to the true proverb, 'A dog returns to its own vomit,' and, 'A sow, after washing, returns to wallowing in the mire.'" (2nd Peter 2:17-22).

Peter's words make me tremble. They are terrifying. They are written to believers who had been set free but have become enslaved afresh by addiction and corruption. Truly, we all need to be on guard for deceit and not kid ourselves.

2nd Peter 3

End of the Age

Peter shifts as Chapter 3 opens to a topic related to false prophecy: the End of the Age. Peter had mentioned this important issue in his first letter:

"The end of all things is near; therefore, be of sound judgment and sober spirit for the purpose of prayer. Above all, keep fervent in your love for one another, because love covers a multitude of sins. Be hospitable to one another without complaint." (1st Peter 4:7-9).

"This is now, beloved, the second letter I am writing to you in which I am stirring up your sincere mind by way of reminder, that you should remember the words spoken beforehand by the holy prophets and the commandment of the Lord and Savior spoken by your apostles." (2ⁿᵈ Peter 3:1-2).

Peter references three authorities for what he is about to share: Prophetic Scripture from the Old Testament, Jesus's own words, and what the apostles (including Peter himself) were sharing.

Without question, early believers fully expected Jesus to return during their lifetime. We have already read a good deal about the Day of the Lord (1ˢᵗ Thessalonians 4 and 5) from the apostle Paul, plus we have Jesus's extensive reflections on the End of the Age when He was on the Mount of Olives two days before His last Passover meal. (See particularly Matthew 24).

Though most of the churches that have sprung up over the Roman world after Jesus's resurrection are less than thirty years old, eyewitnesses are dying off. A whole new internal question has arisen, "Why has Jesus not returned?"

Jesus fully anticipated that such questions would arise since *"about that day or hour no one knows, not even the angels in heaven, nor the Son, but only the Father."* (Matthew 24:36). Peter says that one of the signs that Jesus will return soon is the ridicule thrown at believers who *have* been expecting the immediate arrival of Jesus for several decades and Jesus has not appeared.

Peter draws out of the Psalms with the observation that trying to judge "God time" is nearly impossible. A day to God is like 1,000 years for mankind. On that timetable, even now in 2018, Jesus has only delayed His return less than 2 "God Days" past the ascension!

"For a thousand years in Your sight
Are like yesterday when it passes by,
Or as a watch in the night."
(Psalm 90:4).

The point is not that "God time" is measurable. There is a very good chance that in God's domain, there is *NO* time. I don't even know how to think about time from God's point of view. But one thing Jesus was quite clear about: it is the Father's decision. His time is the right time. He delays that many will be saved.

Then, Peter shares an observation:

"But the day of the Lord will come like a thief, in which the heavens will pass away with a roar and the elements will be destroyed with intense heat, and the earth and its works will be burned up." (2nd Peter 3:10).

Compare this with Paul's prediction in his first letter to the Thessalonians: *"For you yourselves know full well that the day of the Lord will come just like a thief in the night. While they are saying, 'Peace and safety!' then destruction will come upon them suddenly like labor pains upon a woman with child, and they will not escape. But you, brethren, are not in darkness, that the day would overtake you like a thief."* (1st Thessalonians 5:2).

Peter's prediction that, *"the heavens will pass away with a roar, and the elements will be destroyed with intense heat, and the earth and its works will be burned up,"* is terrifying, but as Christians we look to an entirely new world *"in which righteousness dwells."* (2nd Peter 3:13). Because of this, we want to be absolutely sure we may be found in the Lord – peaceful, *"spotless and blameless."*

Paul's letter to the Thessalonians has already been written, and it seems likely that Peter has read it and other letters from Paul. Peter makes an interesting observation about his *"beloved brother, Paul."* (2nd Peter 3:13). Peter says that in Paul's letters, there are some things that are difficult to understand, and ignorant and unstable men are abroad distorting what Paul wrote. I can well believe it. Today, there are so many teachings on the "End Times" available: countless books, podcasts, broadcasts, videos and movies – an astounding deluge of material dwelling on the End of the Age. And with the deluge, comes much distortion. If our attention rests on the contemplation of End Times and not on an internal and external change in our hearts and action, it is worse than a distraction.

Peter ends Chapter 3 with a clear admonition to those who might be led astray by these teachers:

"You therefore, beloved, knowing this beforehand, be on your guard so that you are not carried away by the error of unprincipled men and fall from your own steadfastness...." (2nd Peter 3:17). We want to be steadfast in love and devotion to God and our neighbor, at peace with those about us, spotless and blameless in our walk, *"growing in the grace and knowledge of our Lord and Savior, Jesus the Anointed One, both now and to the day of eternity!"* (2nd Peter 3:18).

Remember, *"The end of all things is near; therefore, be of sound judgment and sober spirit for the purpose of prayer. Above all, keep fervent in your love for one another, because love covers a multitude of sins. Be hospitable to one another without complaint."* (1st Peter 4:7-9).

Peter's advice is consistent: we don't want to get tied up in endless speculation and false teaching. Rather, we want to be fervent on our love for one another in a very practical way and continue to grow in the grace and knowledge of Jesus. The Lord is coming. There is still time to amend our ways. Yes!

1ˢᵗ John

1ˢᵗ John 1

The "little Johns" are a great treat. They remind me of both the wonder of God's love and the noteworthy difference between each man and woman who follows Jesus. How different is John's apprehension from Peter's, James's or Paul's! Each retains his or her distinct personality and character. Importantly, each relates to God in a slightly different way and catches different aspects. Yet all carry the same wonder of God's love. When you think about these rough characters: fishermen and tent makers, that *is* pretty remarkable.

Over fifty years may have elapsed before 1ˢᵗ John was written. The Apostle John was now an old man and had lived longer than most of the other apostles. He had become a great disciple of younger men – men like the famous martyr, Polycarp, Bishop of Smyrna, about whom Ignatius of Antioch wrote so glowingly, as well as Papias, Bishop of Hierapolis, a town close to Colossae. John spent much of his latter years in Ephesus and then Patmos, ministering to those in "Asia," modern day Turkey.

The way John began this first letter is very similar to the way he began his gospel, only shorter. Remember that John's gospel begins, *"In the beginning was the Word, and the Word was with God and the Word was God...."* 1st John begins, *"What was from the beginning, what we have heard, what we have seen with our eyes, what we have looked at and touched with our hands...."*

The beginnings are basically the same, though in 1st John we have a significant emphasis on John's personal witness. John *knew* that Jesus was the eternal Word. Jesus was not imaginary. John had *seen* Him here on the earth, had *heard* Him, had *touched* Him and therefore was able to testify to Jesus's authenticity as God's great Message.

John says that he *proclaims* Jesus so that those who read his short letter may be part of God's household, in fellowship not only with John and all the saints but also in fellowship with *"Father and His Son."* That fellowship will make John's joy complete.

Think of receiving this letter one day in your mailbox. You open it up and see that it is from an old man far away, a man whose name you have heard perhaps, but a man you don't actually know. You are not a believer in Jesus Christ; in fact, you are leading a rather normal and secular life in some small town. Your experiences are quite normal. You have friends and acquaintances. You struggle to earn a living. You struggle with the lusts that beset every human being. Darkness tinges everything around you. You know nothing of true joy nor anyone who wants you to be full of joy. And you open this letter.

It will be undoubtedly the most amazing letter you have ever received. Immediately, your heart is captured. The letter is about deep things, eternal things. It is about a message from God whom the writer calls Father, and the message is condensed into a living person who brings joy and fellowship. The darkness, aloneness and nagging guilt that you experience daily fades a bit, and you read on.

"This is the message we have heard from Him and announce to you, that God is Light, and in Him there is no darkness at all. If we say that we have fellowship with Him and yet walk in the darkness, we lie and do not practice the truth; but if we walk in the Light as He Himself is in the Light, we have fellowship with one another, and the blood of Jesus His Son cleanses us from all sin. If we say that we have no sin, we are deceiving ourselves and the truth is not in us. If we confess our sins, He is faithful and righteous to forgive us our sins and to cleanse us from all unrighteousness. If we say that we have not sinned, we make Him a liar and His word is not in us." (1st John 1:5-10).

The eternal God is pure light. In Him is absolutely no darkness. If you are in the presence of God, darkness dissipates. He is Father God whose Son forgives sin by His shed blood. John has seen Him, heard Him, touched Him and now proclaims Him as the sweetest message you will ever hear. If you can respond to that message, you may have true fellowship and joy with the Creator, with the Son and with each other.

And what is the nature of the response *each* of us must make? We must recognize our condition. What does John mean by his certainty that we all sin: *"If we say that we have no sin, we are deceiving ourselves,"?* It would appear that John is not just referencing the condition of the unbeliever but the believer as well. And God knows, we all sin. Even after our initial baptism.

If the Word of Christ is within us, we will need to confess that we sin. Why? Because the Son of God, like the Father, is Truth and Truth cannot lie. I suspect that John is battling in his letter a deception that has crept into the church, a deception that if one has been baptized and filled with the Spirit, no one can sin thereafter. But that is a falsehood that doesn't come from God since God is Truth (*Emeth* in Hebrew) – the very nature of God. As John attests, we *all* sin. Confessing our sin allows the blood of Jesus to continue its amazing work. By His blood we are continually cleansed if, in fact, we confess our sins.

To confess our sins requires both humility (understanding our true condition) and personal awareness. I don't believe there is any other answer to those two problems than praying earnestly everyday, "Lord, show me where I really am. Show me where I have fallen short that I may confess and be cleansed by the precious blood of Jesus. And may I forgive those who have wronged me."

Remember Jesus's clear words:

"But you, when you pray, go into your inner room, close your door and pray to your Father who is in secret, and your Father who sees what is done in secret will reward you. And when you are praying, do not use meaningless repetition as the Gentiles do, for they suppose that they will be heard for their many words. So, do not be like them; for your Father knows what you need before you ask Him. Pray, then, in this way:

> *'Our Father who is in heaven,*
> *Hallowed be Your name.*
> *Your kingdom come.*
> *Your will be done,*
> *On earth as it is in heaven.*
> *Give us this day our daily bread.*
> *And forgive us our debts, as we also have forgiven our debtors.*
> *And do not lead us into temptation, but deliver us from evil.*
> *For Yours is the kingdom and the power and the glory forever. Amen.'*

"For if you forgive others for their transgressions, your heavenly Father will also forgive you. But if you do not forgive others, then your Father will not forgive your transgressions."
(Matthew 6:6-15).

1ˢᵗ John 2

"My little children, I am writing these things to you so that you may not sin. And if anyone sins, we have an Advocate (Paraklētos) *with the Father, Jesus Christ the righteous and He Himself is the propitiation for our sins; and not for ours only, but also for those of the whole world."* (1ˢᵗ John 2:1-2).

"But I tell you the truth, it is to your advantage that I go away; for if I do not go away, the Helper (Paraklētos) *will not come to you; but if I go, I will send Him to you."* (John 16:7).

Paraklētos

Right off the bat, we see that John is writing his letter with a purpose: that those who receive his letter not sin. But at the same time, we learn a great deal about God, Jesus, The Holy Spirit and true Truth. For one, John affirms that Jesus *is* with the Father; in fact, we learn that just like the third person of the Godhead, the Holy Spirit, Jesus is the *Paraklētos,* our Advocate and Helper. The Spirit of God is the Spirit both of the Father and the Son, and Jesus stands before the Father as our Advocate, just as a great lawyer would stand beside us before the judge in court. In fact, he is the *"propitiation"* for our sins as well as our Advocate.

Propitiation

"Propitiation" in Greek is the word *hilasmos* and only occurs two times in the New Testament. Both of these are in 1ˢᵗ John. It is not a common English word and it could be translated as *atonement* or *appeasement*. A gift to a King may appease a hurt that has been inflicted. Jesus is God's gift – in a sense both to us and to Himself. Jesus's great and self-less obedience appeases the hurts we have afflicted on God.

Truth Man

John is Truth biased. This is not hard to believe because through his writings, he is continuously focused on truth and lies.

John is interested in the true Truth, the deep Truth - that which is both seen and that which lies below the surface. He is not interested in a snapshot; he wants to know the whole truth, the entire truth - the great enchilada of truth. John is Truth Man.

Truth is so much more than words. Words speak to the reality of something, but they are not normally the reality. I say the automobile is "red," but red is only a word that speaks to what the car looks like, but it is an approximation. What shade of red? If I look closely at the red under a spectroscope - an instrument used to measure properties of light, wavelengths and intensities - I can determine some of the nature of red. But neither the spectroscope nor the description is the "red" – it simply tells us *about* red as it is perceived through the rays it emits.

If I scrape off samples of the red automobile paint and send them out for chemical analysis, I get a report on the paint's chemical composition, but the report is not red. John wants to know "red;" he wants to know all about it - both its composition, history, nature and its "isness." It is a gift from God to think like John, and when he wants Truth, he wants the whole shebang. John is a Truth Detector, and a Truth Detector by default is also a Lie Detector!

"By this we know that we have come to know Him, if we keep His commandments. The one who says, "I have come to know Him," and does not keep His commandments, is a liar, and the truth is not in him; but whoever keeps His word, in him the love of God has truly been perfected. By this we know that we are in Him: the one who says he abides in Him ought himself to walk in the same manner as He walked." (1st John 2:3-6).

Now, if we say that we know God yet do not keep God's tips for life and joy, we don't speak the Truth, because one of the only ways to get to know God is to experience being like Him. Think of that challenge. He gave His own Son for our sake; can we suffer as He did? God is absolutely steadfast in His love; does our love waver from time to time? But to the degree that we are as He is, we know Him. We cannot know Him in truth unless we walk His walk.

Enmity and Darkness

"I am writing a new commandment to you, which is true in Him and in you, because the darkness is passing away and the true Light is already shining. The one who says he is in the Light and yet hates his brother is in the darkness until now. The one who loves his brother abides in the Light and there is no cause for stumbling in him. But the one who hates his brother is in the darkness and walks in the darkness and does not know where he is going because the darkness has blinded his eyes." (1st John 2:8-11).

John spotlights a truth about enmity in the covenant community. If a brother or sister says they are walking in the Light, yet struggle with enmity and bitterness against another, to the degree that they harbor enmity, to the same degree he or she is in darkness. If you walk in darkness, you cannot truly know where you are walking because you cannot see. Enmity has a terrible debilitating effect on our walk in God. In fact, we may not be walking in God at all!

Lust, Lust, Pride

*"Do not love the world nor the things in the world. If anyone loves the world, the love of the Father is not in him. For all that is in the world, **the lust of the flesh and the lust of the eyes and the boastful pride of life**, is not from the Father, but is from the world. The world is passing away,*

and also its lusts; but the one who does the will of God lives forever." (1st John 2:15-17).

This is one of the most insightful verses from my point of view in the New Testament. It sums up three pervasive dangers. They have endangered me most of my life. My recent book, *Visions, Dreams & Encounters*, records two "God-dreams" that I believe God sent me as a warning regarding these great dangers.

One danger springs from my natural gifting: my eyes are gifted with seeing visually. Unlike my ears that certainly are *not* gifted at hearing (no aptitude for pitch discrimination or rhythm memory), my eyesight and mental three-dimensional processing is acute. I can distinguish color discrimination and harmonies when others cannot. But I can struggle with too much attraction to the visual. I always think of my struggle when I read John's insight.

Of course, we also are subject to the lure of the flesh and the pride of life. So, we have three major zones of sin entrapment:

- Lust of the Flesh
- Lust of the Eyes
- The Pride of Life

Luster in God's Will

Can we find the luster in God's will and be so "captivated" by it that we become slaves to what God wants rather than what we are naturally drawn to? The lust of the flesh, the lust of the eyes and the pride of life only lead to destruction. They are passing away. But the one who focuses on and delights in the will of God will last forever. I think that unless we catch the true wonder and beauty of God - His very nature - it will be hard to be captured by the wonder and beauty of His will.

Antichrists

John feels the End of the Age must be very near because he is sickened with the false prophets and false "Christs" who have gone out *"from"* the Body of Christ. They were not really "from" the Body of Christ because they would not have gone out if they had been. Rather, they were deceived and went out deceiving, and appeared to be believers when in fact they were following a lie. I wish this did not ring so true to me, but my experience confirms the same pattern continues in our day and is accelerating because of technological changes.

The Anointing

Thankfully, *"you have an anointing from the Holy One, and you all know. I have not written to you because you do not know the truth, but because you do know it, and because no lie is of the truth. Who is the liar but the one who denies that Jesus is the Christ? This is the antichrist, the one who denies the Father and the Son. Whoever denies the Son does not have the Father; the one who confesses the Son has the Father also. As for you, let that abide in you, which you heard from the beginning. If what you heard from the beginning abides in you, you also will abide in the Son and in the Father."* (1st John 2:20-24).

John points to two safeguards. One is practical and rational: if people claiming to be God's people bring a message that denies the deity and sacrificial function of Jesus, they are false. Another way to say this is that Scripture is an excellent yardstick.

The other is the safeguard of the Holy Spirit. By nature, the Spirit of God is not rational; it is spiritual. The Spirit is alive, all Truth, entirely God. I remember with fondness the Wednesday night that Professor Malherbe went through perhaps fifty key scriptures on the Holy Spirit.

The Spirit is quite beyond our ability to rationalize. Can you rationalize yourself? Or me? We are living entities, fully alive, as is the Spirit.

Through the Spirit, we should be able to *"know all."* (1st John 2:20). I think what John means is that the Spirit prompts us to what is true and what is false, to what is good and what is bad. God's Spirit is like a magnetic compass. It *always* points due North, i.e., toward the truth. All other points are off base, i.e., false.

But please, do not miss this point. If we do not walk *IN* the Spirit, we have no way of knowing God's gentle nudge and prompting. Be filled, therefore, with the Spirit of God. This requires being open to His presence and leading. If you have not been baptized in water, be so. If you have not received the precious gift of the Holy Spirit through the Laying on of Hands and Jesus's heavenly pouring out, humble yourself before the One who promised to pour out His Spirit upon all flesh.

If we want to spot the antichrists, they will be the ones that overtly or subtly deny the Father or the Son. There are many ways to deny either. We can say they do not exist. Or we can live as if they do not exist. Either way, we are "anti" God and "anti" Jesus.

Jesus promised us an amazing gift: eternal life. Many will try to convince us otherwise. But the same Spirit that allows us to "know all," that same Spirit means that we no longer need teachers:

"These things I have written to you concerning those who are trying to deceive you. As for you, the anointing which you received from Him abides in you, and you have no need for anyone to teach you; but as His anointing teaches you about all things, and is true and is not a lie, and just as it has taught you, you abide in Him." (1st John 2:26-27).

Before all the teachers quake in their boots, the Spirit gives the Gift of Teaching just as the Spirit gives the Gift of Prophecy. Both are from the *"anointing"* of the Spirit on one believer or another. But John's emphasis is true. If we can give ourselves to be trained in the Spirit, if we can learn to walk in and by the Spirit, if we can allow the Spirit of God to lead us, in one sense we do not need human teachers. Remember all of the letters we have read together by men very much trying to help us stay on track, in the Truth, in the Way, on the road. It may take (and likely will take) a lifetime to get adept at a balanced Spiritual walk. Be thankful for the Spirit and be thankful for the gifts given to the Church while we learn how to walk fully in the Spirit. From a practical point of view, we actually need both in the Body of Christ: the Spirit and the Gift of Teaching given by the Spirit.

1ˢᵗ John 3

John calls the God of the Universe "Father." In the Greek, he does not say "the" Father; he just says, "Father" because God is *his* father. He is *our* Father; He is *my* Father. Jesus, as Matthew records Him when He was teaching what we call the Lord's Prayer, said to pray *ego pater*, that is *"my* Father."

Understanding that the God of the Universe is *our* Father is one of the most astounding things about becoming a follower of God in Jesus. Truly, it is astounding and a stretch to imagine, but it is true. If God is our Father in the truest since of the word (we are made by Him and, so to speak, have His DNA in our nature), then we will be Holy as He is Holy and will not sin.

To the degree that this quality of likeness is in us, the people around us who have not had His nature released within them will hardly know us. Our actions and reactions will be so different from theirs that we will appear to be from a foreign planet.

This is a work that only God can do - making us like He is. As John says, we are growing up into the very nature of God. *"And everyone who has this hope fixed on Him purifies himself, just as He is pure."* (1st John 3:3). Fixing our hope on God causes our continual purification that begins at baptism. We will become more and more like Him if our gaze is focused on Father.

"Everyone who practices sin also practices lawlessness; and sin is lawlessness. You know that He appeared in order to take away sins; and in Him there is no sin. No one who abides in Him sins; no one who sins has seen Him or knows Him." (1st John 3:4-6).

It is impossible to abide in God – *live* in Him – and sin. Impossible. But we know from 1st John 1:8 that *"if we say we have no sin, we deceive ourselves."* At first glance, it would appear that the two chapters are in conflict.

The NASB translation makes some of the conflict dissipate by using the word *"practice."* I believe this translation uses the word to indicate the underlying verb tense, which indicates a continuing action.

*"No one who is born of God **practices** sin, because His seed abides in him; and he cannot sin, because he is born of God. By this the children of God and the children of the devil are obvious: anyone who does not **practice** righteousness is not of God, nor the one who does not love his brother."* (1st John 3:9-10).

Still, John's thrust is unmistakable. If we truly abide in God, we will not be sinning. "Lord, help us to rest fully in You. Help us to abide in You, live in You and be a shining light in Your household."

The Evil One is always trying to lure us outside of God's house – outside of His presence – that we might sin. In one way, the answer is simple: stay in the house! But we would be foolish to not recognize the pull of our own lusts and desires that make us want to "jump the fence." All I can pray is "Lord, help us and have mercy on us. The truth is that we do not want to leave Your house!"

The children of the devil are obvious. One sign is that they will have enmity with one another. Do you remember being on the playground as a young child? Do you remember the teeter-totter? I knew it as the seesaw. I loved the seesaw as a young child, but it reminds me of the danger of enmity. Just a push up or down can push us over into enmity as opposed to love for a brother or sister. So much depends on whether our heart and mind are working together in harmony or in discord. We can see many things wrong with our brother if we look for things that are wrong, and resentment will spring up. Or, we can see many things right with our brother, and gratitude will spring up. May the Spirit of God give us a royal push to gratitude and love!

Cain looked over at his brother Abel and jealousy arose from his heart. John says Cain was *"of the Evil One."* Cain was not looking with God glasses at his brother. He was wearing the glasses of the Evil One.

A good test for our true spiritual condition is whether we love the *"brethren,"* whether we love our brothers and sisters. If we do not have a heart for each one, we have not fully passed out of death into life. "Father, do a work in us that we would love those with whom you have placed us!"

John says that if love does not spring forth from our hearts, we *"abide in death."* (1st John 3:14). "Lord, help us. This is not a place we want to abide!" Rather, we want to abide in love, and the only way to do so is to abide in God. If we hate someone, we are nothing but a murderer, and no life abides in us. We are basically dead.

Conversely, the love that springs forth from God is immeasurable. *"We know love by this, that He laid down His life for us; and we ought to lay down our lives for the brethren."* (1ˢᵗ John 3:16). So surely, we will help those around us who are in need and not close our hearts to them.

I've always thought that John's emphasis on loving action versus loving talk hits a high note. There is a danger of talking the talk, but not walking the walk. True love gets us out of our seat and on the move to help, to embrace and to encourage. False love doesn't move us into action. 1ˢᵗ John allows us to take inventory of our condition as we read it. No one wants to admit that they tend to fall on the wrong side of the seesaw. But we need to be honest with our condition and cry out for both help and mercy from the Father of Lights.

"We will know by this that we are of the truth, and will assure our heart before Him in whatever our heart condemns us; for God is greater than our heart and knows all things. Beloved, if our heart does not condemn us, we have confidence before God; and whatever we ask we receive from Him, because we keep His commandments and do the things that are pleasing in His sight." (1ˢᵗ John 3:19-22).

"...assure our heart before Him in whatever our heart condemns us; for God is greater than our heart and knows all things." I am thankful for John's reminder that one of the key things that God knows is that Jesus's sacrifice is precious beyond calculation, and stands for us even when our hearts condemn us. Yet, when our heart does not condemn us, we have even greater confidence before God and great access to His throne room. If we want to see our petitions answered, then we will do what is pleasing to Him.

Verses 19 – 22 are important, and the promise of receiving what we ask God for should be a real motivator to *"do the things that are pleasing in His sight."* This emphasis puts a spotlight on what particularly pleases Him:

"...that we believe in the name of His Son Jesus Christ, and love one another, just as He commanded us. The one who keeps His commandments abides in Him, and He in him. We know by this that He abides in us, by the Spirit whom He has given us." (1st John 3:23-24).

Believe in Jesus and love one another. This reminds me of Jesus's summation of the Law and the Prophets: Love God and love our neighbor. The Son's heart is toward the Father; the Father's heart is toward the Son. If we can keep love flowing for God and our brothers and sisters, we truly do abide in God and He abides in us. The Spirit of God dwelling in us and directing our path is proof certain!

1st John 4

"Greater is He who is in you than he who is in the world."
(1st John 4:4).

Testing the Spirits

The Spirit of God Himself is within you, if you are His and have received God's Spirit. Though the evil one is active in the world, God is greater, and the Spirit of God is greater. As the Apostle Paul reminds us, *"our struggle is not against flesh and blood, but against the rulers, against the authorities, against the powers of this dark world and against the spiritual forces of evil in the heavenly realms."* (Ephesians 6:12). But *"greater is He who is in you that he who is in the world!"*

Unfortunately, we are faced with the same forces of darkness that John and Paul faced. One of their manifestations is through false prophets. Sometimes we encounter those who say they speak for God overtly. They may be TV evangelists, radio commentators or podcast pros. And they may even be in our pulpits. Unfortunately, it is often difficult to distinguish the falsehood and spirit behind their message.

Satan is the great deceiver. The Spirit of Darkness is a pro; he is quite adept at spinning a lie that has just enough truth to capture those whose spiritual armor is tarnished or non-existent. We need to be like John – a pro Lie Detector – looking for that tinge of darkness in what is being said and who is saying it.

The most difficult problem I have faced in the Christian community is detecting and dealing with those spinning lies who are not out front (the TV evangelists, radio commentators, podcast pros and pulpit pumpers). It is with everyday lay people. Satan attempts to weave his webs diligently in us and those with whom we walk on a daily basis. We can be as damaging as the more overt message bearers of falsehood.

Particularly, I think of advice that is given to those struggling with genuine problems. One of the danger zones is casual relationship counseling. A wife goes out with some friends to lunch and shares the struggle she is experiencing in her marriage. One of her friends is quite certain that she should "get out of the marriage." "God wouldn't want you to be miserable," she says. "Divorce that jerk."

Or a young 20-year-old is in his third year at college. He is living in a one-bedroom apartment off campus and has been dating a girl in his class for several months. At lunch, a friend advises, "Get her to move in with you and cut your rent in half."

Worse are those who are moving outside of God's will but protesting that they are, in fact, doing what God would want them to do. The spouse that decides to divorce for non-biblical reasons, or the student living with someone he or she is only dating may justify their behavior by citing an obscure scripture, a dream or "God told me it was OK."

"And pray in the Spirit on all occasions with all kinds of prayers and requests. With this in mind, be alert and always keep on praying for all the Lord's people." (Ephesians 6:18).

Paul's comments to the Ephesians are a good companion for Chapter 4 of 1st John. Paul gave this admonition immediately after his discussion of the daily "putting on" of armor for spiritual battle. We are on the fields of war every day. Read Paul's admonition in Ephesians 6:18 one more time. Constantly praying when we are with others – being constantly on the alert for danger but also for how God might lead us – is an important practice.

John says we can spot the spirit of truth and the spirit of error when we are prompted by God to share with another person and what we share is not received. If we truly are moving by God's promptings and are aligned with the truth of Scripture, *"he who knows God listens to us; he who is not from God does not listen to us. By this we know the spirit of truth and the spirit of error."* (1 John 4:6).

Every born-again and Spirit-filled Christian has a certain amount of spiritual discernment that is meant to increase over time. The writer of Hebrews reminds us that those who are mature in Christ are able to discern both good and evil. (Hebrews 5:13-14). But one of the gifts of the Spirit is the *"discerning of spirits"* which Paul mentioned in his first letter to the Corinthian church:

"to each one is given the manifestation of the Spirit for the common good. For to one is given the word of wisdom through the Spirit, and to another the word of knowledge according to the same Spirit; to another faith by the same Spirit, and to another gifts of healing by the one Spirit, and to another the effecting of miracles, and to another prophecy, and to another ***the distinguishing of spirits****...."* (1 Corinthians 12:7-10).

The gift of discerning spirits, or *"distinguishing"* spirits, is given by the Holy Spirit to build up and protect the Body of Christ on earth. It is a very useful gift to the Body, and like prophecy, one to both desire and heed. A gift this important most likely will be given through the Laying on of Hands and be clearly attested.

All of this focus on "truth detecting" in the Body of Christ leads John to follow up his concern for false prophets with the admonition to *"love one another."* God *is* love, and everyone who springs from God's own nature loves. We "know" God when we touch love, because God *is* love. Loving is another sign that we know God. But if this is so, we will deal lovingly with those who have gotten off tract; we will exhibit the other attributes of God: gentleness, kindness, patience and quickness to forgive and slowness to anger.

When we find ourselves dealing with deep falsehood, it is good to remember that our anger (when appropriate) should be focused on the originator of the falsehood, i.e., Satan, and not on the poor victim of his darkness. Victims need all the gentleness, kindness and patience that we can muster.

Clearly, John and the early Church were dealing with a heresy directly focused on Jesus's nature. As the only begotten Son of God, God's nature abides fully within Him and vice-versa – Jesus abides fully within God. To say otherwise is dead wrong. But in a similar way, God wants to abide fully in us and vice-versa; He wants us to abide fully in Him.

This is a great wonder. It reminds me of Jesus's "High Priestly" prayer in "big" John 17:

"I do not ask on behalf of these alone, but for those also who believe in Me through their word; that they may all be one; even as You, Father, are in Me and I in You, that they also may be in Us, so that the world may believe that You sent Me. The glory which You have given Me I have given to them, that they may be one, just as We are one; I in them and You in Me, that they may be perfected in unity, so that the world may

know that You sent Me, and loved them, even as You have loved Me." (John 17:20-23).

The word *"perfected"* occurs in Chapter 17 of John and Chapter 4 of 1st John: Perfected in unity and perfected in love. This is God's great intention for each one of us. Being perfected in love means being delivered from our fears that limit our love. *"There is no fear in love; but perfect love casts out fear."* (1st John 4:18).

Come, Lord Jesus, and deliver us from all fear!

1 John 5

What Does It Mean to Believe?

It is worth asking, is it enough to believe that Jesus is the Messiah and born of God? Many will say yes to this question and give it lip service. They will believe it at some level of consciousness – an intellectual level. "Yes, I believe there is a God and that His Son is Jesus Christ." This certainly seems enough, but God is actually wanting something much greater than intellectual assent. He wants our hearts.

You could posit that grasping the relational move of God toward us, that is, His giving of Himself in the most humiliating way through Jesus's sacrificial death, when truly believed, will move our hearts out of love. We will be moved in our heart toward God. The movement toward God is like a magnetic force once it is unleashed in our hearts.

But, as we saw in the preceding chapter, when we truly respond to His love, we will find our hearts also moving to others. So, we have a threefold movement when our hearts are engaged. First, our hearts move in the beginning of a lasting love toward God. Then, our hearts move outward to our brothers and sisters. And then, our hearts move beyond - to all mankind.

This deepening love of God propels us and allows us to do what Father wants us to do. For this reason, God's commands are not burdensome. Even His commands are propelled by love; in fact, "commands" may be the wrong word. What He wants is the very best for us; His directions are a guidebook for righteousness. And righteousness makes manifest the Will of God, which brings into our path spiritual riches and great joy.

Three Stamps

We overcome the world by the love that comes from our initial encounter with God's love that has been so amply demonstrated by Jesus's sacrificial death. Leaving aside the Virgin Birth, John tells us that Jesus came to us as Messiah (the Anointed One who was sought for centuries) with three authenticating stamps. First, there is the Spirit, second, the Water and third, the Blood. Two of these occurred at Jesus's baptism when the Holy Spirit fell upon Him as He rose from the water, and God's voice rang out from Heaven, *"This is my Beloved Son; in whom I am well pleased."* (Matthew 3:17). The third stamp was at His crucifixion when His blood was shed for mankind. All three of these testifying stamps are from God and not from men.

Life Bubbling Up

"The one who believes in the Son of God has the testimony in himself; the one who does not believe God has made Him a liar, because he has not believed in the testimony that God has given concerning His Son. And the testimony is this, that God has given us eternal life, and this life is in His Son. He who has the Son has the life; he who does not have the Son of God does not have the life." (1st John 5:10-12).

Believing in the Son means trusting in the Son. If we can put our trust in Jesus and that internal trust is activated, we find that the reality of the Son of God supports us and goes with us in our daily walk. Fully trusting in Jesus is a high place – not always reached. But, by His enablement, we stretch our faith and walk with Him in an intimate manner, and our testimony is that God's testimony is true: God has given us eternal life and that life is in Jesus's presence within us. If you have received Him and His Spirit, true life bubbles up – streams of living water flow.

John wrote about Jesus's experience with the Samaritan woman at the well in John 4:13-14: *"Jesus answered, "Everyone who drinks this water will be thirsty again, but whoever drinks the water I give them will never thirst. Indeed, the water I give them will become in them a spring of water welling up to eternal life."* Jesus gives each of us living water springing and welling up to eternal life in and through His Spirit.

Conclusion

John ends his letter with a series of truth statements. He has written his letter that those who believe in the *"name"* of the Son will know that they have eternal life. Believing in the name means *trusting* in Jesus as the Beloved, the Son of God, the Messiah who was prophesied, the Lord who sits on the throne, the Sacrificed One. The titles speak to who He is. And it means trusting in your place in Him. This should give us great confidence to be able to approach both the Beloved and the Father.

John says that anything we ask according to God's will, He hears and will grant. Undoubtedly, there are two stipulations to this wonder. First, we have to ask. Second, what we ask for must be a good thing in truth, that is, something that is pleasing to God and in alignment with His will. Most of the time, that will be the case. If we could see as God sees, we would see this is always the operative rule. When we are concerned about something, it is always good to begin with asking God a question, "What is Your will in this matter?" God may show you at the very beginning how to pray in alignment with His will.

John follows this connection between our prayers and God's will with something John is certain about. If we see our brother committing a sin that is *"not leading to death,"* and we pray to God for mercy for our brother, God will grant that brother mercy. Blasphemy against the Holy Spirit is one sin that comes to mind that we know will not be forgiven because Jesus said so. *"I say to you, all sins and all blasphemies that people utter will be forgiven them. But whoever blasphemes against the Holy Spirit will never have forgiveness, but is guilty of an everlasting sin."* (Mark 3:28-29). Blasphemy against the Holy Spirit is attributing to God what is of Satan and to Satan what is of God.

The idea of the Seven Deadly Sins developed into the Middle Ages and lays out sins which lead eventually to death. The Seven so identified were thought to be pride, greed, lust, envy, gluttony, wrath and sloth. Unchecked, they end up killing the life of sanctifying grace. But for me at this point in my walk, except for the issue of Blasphemy against the Spirit of God, I would encourage everyone to pray for their brothers and sisters when they see them tied up in sin. Why take a chance that your prayer might not be effective? Remember Jesus on the cross. My observation is that most people do not know they are even sinning. *"Therefore, confess your sins to one another, and pray for one another so that you may be healed. The effective prayer of a righteous man can accomplish much!"* (James 5:16).

John finishes with four certainties:

- *"We know that we are of God, and that the whole world lies in the power of the evil one.*

- *"And we know that the Son of God has come, and has given us understanding so that we may know Him who is true;*
- *"and we are in Him who is true, in His Son Jesus Christ.*
- *"This is the true God and eternal life."*

(1st John 5:19-20).

2ⁿᵈ John

We read the following concerning the Apostle John in Eusebius of Caesarea's famous history of the Church which was written sometime between 310 and 325 AD:

"In Asia [modern-day Turkey], moreover, there still remained alive the one whom Jesus loved, apostle and evangelist alike, John, who had directed the churches there since his return from exile on the island, following Domitian's death. That he survived so long is proved by the evidence of two witnesses who could hardly be doubted - ambassadors as they were of the orthodoxy of the Church - Irenaeus and Clement of Alexandria. In Book II of his Against Heresies, Irenaeus writes:

"'All the clergy who are in Asia came in contact with John, the Lord's disciple, testify that John taught the truth to them; for he remained with them till Trajan's time.' In Book III of the same work he says the same thing: 'The church at Ephesus was founded by Paul, and John remained there till Trajan's time; so, she is a true witness of what the apostles taught.'" (Church History of Eusebius, Book III, Chapter 23).

Since Trajan began to reign in 98 AD, we can postulate that John was in his 90s when he died. John is thought to be the only Apostle who died a natural death of old age. Certainly, by the time he wrote 2ⁿᵈ John, he was an old man. John begins his short letter to the Church with that very word in the Greek, *Presbyteros,* in reference to himself.

Presbyteros is the word we encounter in both Peter and Paul's writings regarding those who are selected to help shepherd the earthly flock of God on the earth. But, of course, it also means *"Old Man."* In Peter's letter, he refers to himself as a fellow elder when addressing the elders he was writing. (1ˢᵗ Peter 5:1). It is both a word that signifies function as well as age, and the word, when traced back in the corresponding word in Hebrew, has a rich history amongst God's people. It means both leader and servant at the same time.

Whether John withheld his name to avoid trouble with the Roman authorities we do not know. What we do know is that the end of the first century was a time of intense persecution. John was jailed on the Isle of Patmos for some period of time. Aside from John's 3ʳᵈ short letter, it is the only letter in the Bible with such a salutation.

"The Elder to the chosen lady and her children, whom I love in truth; and not only I, but also all who know the truth, for the sake of the truth which abides in us and will be with us forever: Grace, mercy and peace will be with us, from God the Father and from Jesus Christ, the Son of the Father, in truth and love." (2ⁿᵈ John:1-3).

It may be that John is actually writing a lady with children. His third letter is to an individual named Gaius, so it could be a short encouragement to an actual person. But the apostle's language works well as an epistle to the Church in the region near Ephesus where John lived for many years and we see from Eusebius's account that he *"directed the churches there since his return from exile on the island, following Domitian's death."*

In Ecclesiastical terms, John was functioning as the "archbishop" of the churches in the region around Ephesus, so it is entirely possible that his letter is a very short admonition to all the communities under his charge.

John's opening words focus on both love and truth. Remember, John is "Truth Man." If there ever was a writer in Scripture enamored with "truth," it was John. He loves the lady *"in truth,"* and all believers *"who know the truth,"* and it is for the *"sake of truth"* that he writes.

So, we are not surprised to find that John is glad to hear that *some* of the "chosen lady's" children are *"walking in the truth."* Not all of the lady's children, but some of her children are walking in the truth. This may be true in our own households, and John's immediate admonition, to *"love one another,"* applies both to those that believe and those that do not.

Love to John means that we follow God's way, because what could be more loving than treating each other as God would have us treat our brothers, sisters and all mankind. We don't love others when we treat them in opposition to God's clear instruction regarding a host of matters, all of which are addressed in Scripture. Left to our own devices, we can do many things that might seem helpful on the surface but end up producing long-term harm.

I immediately think of co-signing on a loan. This was one of my early mistakes: I co-signed on a brother's loan to build a house. The loan was a balloon note for $10,000 back in the mid-seventies – a great deal of money back then. I knew at the time that Proverbs 22:26-27 was quite emphatic that co-signing was not to be done *("Don't agree to guarantee another person's debt or put up security for someone else. If you can't pay it, even your bed will be snatched from under you."),* but I wanted to do it for three reasons. First, I thought my brother would not default.

Second, I wanted to show solidarity with my brother. Third, I wanted him to have the house.

The recession that began in 1974 hit, and the loan came due a few years later and my brother could not pay the balance due. There was nothing to do but for me to pay the $10,000. You will not be surprised to learn that I did not have $10,000 sitting in a drawer, and so I had to scramble to make the pay-off.

This is a good example, because there were other options available to me at the time I so unwisely co-signed. I could have *given* the brother $10,000. Or I could have personally loaned the brother $10,000 at no interest. Both would have required that I sell something in order to get the $10,000. I ended up having to do the same thing anyway to pay off the eventual default. The difference was that I could have weighed the real implications at the time I made the action. By co-signing, I had no way to know what my circumstances might be when the loan came due. Bottom-line, the loving thing to do would have been not to co-sign. Further, looking back 42 years, it is not at all clear that the timing was right for the brother to build the house in the first place.

John then addresses a common theme from this era: many are denying that Jesus came in the flesh. John knows the lady and her children must be on guard. Those abroad are deceivers, false prophets and people who say they believe but actually are working against Christ (anti-Christ's).

Theories of how Jesus could be God's "Son" were rampant. Some said he was not even a real human. Docetics and Gnostics believed that Jesus's physical body was an illusion, that is, Jesus only seemed to have a physical body and to physically die, but in reality, he was incorporeal, a pure spirit, and hence could not physically die.

"Anyone who goes too far and does not abide in the teaching of Christ, does not have God; the one who abides in the teaching, he has both the Father and the Son. If anyone comes to you and does not bring this teaching, do not receive him into your house, and do not give him a greeting; for the one who gives him a greeting participates in his evil deeds." (2nd John:9-11).

"Anyone who goes too far." Even in our midst, there is always the danger of embellishment. It is tempting when reporting an event to make it a bit more exciting by adding something that is simply not true. I think this is a common error that those who deal with Scripture must discern. It is tempting to go beyond the truth.

Another temptation is to say something is such-and-such in the Bible without actually checking. I cannot tell you how many times I go to *blueletterbible.com* to check my initial interpretation of a verse. I see a word translated one way and my brain or a prompting from God kicks in and says, "Check that out." An easy example is the translation of the first word in the first verse of 2nd John. In the NASB translation, the text begins *"The elder to the chosen lady...."* The word *"The"* is not in the Greek. In the Greek, the verse begins *"Presbyteros eklektos kyria"* which literally means *"Elder chosen lady."* There is no *"The"* and the exclusion of the word makes a slight difference in the way I interpret the word "elder."

My point is that we must always be Truth Detectors if we are to follow in the footsteps of the apostle John and Jesus. We must be ever so careful handling the Word of God. If we do not know for sure about this or that, we should say so. The Early Church did so when they sent the Jerusalem Council's conclusion to those in Antioch: *"For it **seemed good** to the Holy Spirit and to us to lay upon you no greater burden than these essentials...."* (Acts 15:28). Because of the danger of actually blaspheming the Holy Spirit, I suspect that the brothers in Jerusalem did not want to overstate their certainty of what God was saying. Let each one of us be diligent to not overstate what we know!

3rd John

Gaius

The first word (*Presbyteros* which means Elder) in 3rd John is identical to the beginning of John's second letter to the *"chosen lady,"* but further comparison of the openings of both letters will reveal immediately that 3rd John is written without a doubt to a specific person, one Gaius.

There appear to be at least three men with that name in the New Testament records: the Gaius who traveled with Paul (identified as a man of Macedonia in Acts 19:29), the Gaius of Derbe in Galatia (Asia Minor) and the Gaius Paul baptized in Corinth (1st Corinthians 1:14). It is possible and perhaps likely that the Gaius John addresses is one of John's own disciples and therefore a fourth Gaius. Or, he may be the Gaius of Derbe whom, after Paul's death, John could have shepherded as one of his "children."

The Child Walking in the Truth

Regardless, John's letter is quite personal. John has received news through *"brethren"* who visited John and reported that Gaius continued *"walking in the truth."* John was delighted with this positive news and confesses that he experiences *"no greater joy than this, to hear of my children walking in the truth."* (3rd John:4).

John expresses a great truth here for both himself and every one of us. And the truth has a deeper truth: God and Jesus likely experience no deeper joy than seeing any of their spiritual family *"walking in the truth."* It is a parent thing and a God thing.

There is no greater joy than seeing one of your own blood and flesh children walking in the truth of God. Goodness, what a joy. Walking in the truth does not require pleasant circumstances. While I write, my grandson, Jack Mitchell, has been under severe physical distress, but I rejoice in the transparency and faith that Jack's mom and dad have exhibited during the crisis. Joy can be in the midst of great sorrow.

We also rejoice when we see our children helping the church community as well as the outsider, and as John testifies, especially the alien brother, that is, one from an entirely different geographic neighborhood or ethnic group. Clearly, Gaius's community and Gaius himself have been receiving saints traveling through their region and have extended hospitality. As John says, *"we ought to support such men, so that we may be fellow workers with the truth"* that they minister. (3rd John:8).

Loving to be First is a No

John mentions to Gaius that he had written something to the church where perhaps Gaius was a member or at least to a church near Gaius, but what John had written had not be received well by a man named Diotrephes. Wouldn't you hate to get into the Gospel record as the one who didn't accept John's admonitions?

John's spotlight reveals the challenge of any church composed of human beings. Diotrephes *"loves to be first."* (3rd John:9). Of course, this is the exact opposite of what Jesus emphasized in His teaching. Those who love to be first are down-right dangerous in the church, and particularly if they can get into a leadership position. Apparently, Diotrephes has unjustly accused John, *"with wicked words, and not satisfied with this, he himself does not receive the brethren either, and he forbids those who desire to do so and put them out of the church."* (3rd John:10).

John is using the Greek word *ekklesia* to describe the community of God's people and the one where Diotrephes is a member. This was the word over time that people began to consistently use to describe the local, regional and universal communities of the Body of Christ on earth. We remember that the word simply means *"a gathering of citizens called out to an assembly."* The word was used in the Greek Septuagint version of the Scriptures to describe the assembly of the Israelites - especially when gathered for sacred purposes. It is the same word that morphs into English as *ecclesial* or *ecclesiastic* or in French into the word *eglise*.

Diotrephes is clearly at serious odds with other parts of the professing Body and appears to be functioning in the role of a Bishop who has singular authority over the Presbyters and flock.

I call this very serious business and very unfortunate business. But Paul, Peter, James and John have predicted that people will fall away from the church and that *"false teachers"* will arise. The disturbing thing here is that Diotrephes is actually an appointed leader *in* the Church. Goodness, this emphasizes how careful we all need to be about spiritual leadership requirements. It has been the practice in many churches of our day to elevate men to the position of Elder on the basis of their proven success as a secular business leader. This has nothing to do with the qualifications of which we read in Paul's letters. Let us all beware!

Do Not Imitate What is Evil

John has the solution for Gaius, which in a sense commends peace rather than conflict between the communities. *"Beloved, do not imitate what is evil, but what is good."* (3rd John:11). Just do the right thing. Those in Diotrephes' congregation need to the right thing (which appears to be the eventual removal of Diotrephes from office).

John ends his short letter with the confession that he has a lot on his mind, but he hopes to see Gaius very soon and will wait until they are together. That is often best.

His sign off is sweet and to the point. Plus, it may have inspired the Quakers who have the habit of calling each other "friends."

"Peace be to you. The friends greet you. Greet the friends by name." (3rd John:15).

Jude

You are going to like the little letter of Jude if you don't already. It is a hum-dinger and a fitting end to the series of letters of early church fathers that we have been reading.

It is helpful to know that Jude was blood-related to Jesus in some way. He is called the brother of Jesus along with James, the author of the book of James in the New Testament. Whether he was the actual brother of Jesus as we commonly know the term is debatable. What we do know is that Hegesippus, a believer and author of the 2nd century related the following words which then were recorded in Chapter 20 of Eusebius's *Church History* in the third century:

"Still surviving of the Lord 's family were the grandsons of Jude, who was said to be his brother according to the flesh...." (Book III, section 20 of Eusebius's Church History).

Jude for sure was the brother of James who appears as president of the assembly of believers in Jerusalem (see Acts 15). This is not James the Apostle, the son of Zebedee and the brother of John, but a cousin or actual brother of Jesus. Because the universal church still struggles with which, there remains great controversy about the kinship of both

James and Jude to Jesus. My solution to such matters is to not be definitive because I do not know the answer. Regardless of your position, we still should pay attention to Jude's letter!

Jude declares his position straight away. He makes no claim to be Jesus's brother, but he does position himself as brother of James and a bond-servant of Jesus Christ. Remember, a bond-servant means a servant for life – a slave who, when given the opportunity for freedom, rejects it and chooses instead lifelong servant-hood. May we all be bondservants (bond-slaves) of Jesus Christ for life!

Kept

He is writing those whom have been called by God and have responded with "Yes!" He identifies them as *"sanctified in God the Father and kept for Jesus Christ."* (Jude:1). *"Kept"* is a unique salutation in the New Testament. *Tēréō* in the Greek means *"to safeguard from loss or injury."* Jude's opening identification of those he writes includes us, and Jude affirms that we are *safeguarded from loss or injury* in and for the Son of God. This reminds me of the 17th Chapter of John beginning in verse 6 where Jesus prays that those who have safeguarded from loss or injury the Word of God are *"kept"* by God for Him. John uses the same Greek word, *tēréō*, in different tenses:

*"I have manifested Your name to the men whom You gave Me out of the world; they were Yours and You gave them to Me, and they have **kept** Your word.... I am no longer in the world; and yet they themselves are in the world, and I come to You. Holy Father, keep them in Your name, the name which You have given Me, that they may be one even as We are. While I was with them, I was **keeping** them in Your name which You have given Me; and I **guarded** them and not one of them perished but the son of perdition, so that the Scripture would be fulfilled.... I do not ask*

*You to take them out of the world, but to **keep** them from the evil one."* (John 17:6,11,12,15).

Another sense of the word *tēréō* is to preserve. This is extremely heartening to me. Think of it. Those Father gives to Jesus are those who keep His word, and Father in turn *"keeps"* them in Jesus. This means God safeguards them from loss or injury. He *"keeps"* them preserved until the end. Jesus does not ask the Father to take them out of the world but to preserve them intact from the evil one.

In this simple salutation, Jude reveals three essential comforts for the believer. First, they are *"called."* Then they are *"sanctified"* - rendered sacred and holy by the blood of Jesus. And third, they are *"safeguarded and preserved from loss or injury until the end."* This is very good news indeed. If we add in the first word from verse three, *"beloved,"* we have even more good news.

Since I know this is God's will, and I recall from 1st John 5 that

"if we ask anything according to His will, He hears us," (1st John 5:14), and I know that if we pray for one who is born again but caught up in a non-mortal sin, we may ask God to forgive that person and God promises to give that person's *"life."* What an encouragement this is to both pray and confess to each other. This is a *terrific* promise.

Contend for the Faith

Jude had started out with the purpose of writing the *"beloved"* about our common salvation, but it is clear that the Holy Spirit intervened. Jude uses a special Greek word to describe the pressure he felt – the word *anagkē*. It describes a situation imposed by either an external condition or an internal pressure.

Rather than write about our common salvation, Jude felt compelled to write about the pressing need to contend for the faith *"which was once for all handed down to the saints."* Note the *"once for all"* character of the revelation that had been handed down for perhaps sixty years. It was enough when it was first handed down, and it is enough sixty years later – and it is enough today. But people had come into the Body of Christ over the intervening years and were perverting the original message and turning the grace of God into licentiousness - even denying the Lord Himself – a two-fold problem.

Paul had made it abundantly clear in his writings that we were not saved by works, but rather by our faith which then causes us to walk in God's ways. He had to almost over emphasized Grace to counter the engrained view of the Jewish people who were focused on the command more than the grace of the Commander. Plus, many of the Jewish people of Paul's day refused to grasp the implications of a crucified Messiah who literally came to die for our sins.

Paul countered the reaction that came from those hearing that actions like circumcision and the like were not necessary. Apparently, men began to morph Paul's teaching into, "What we do doesn't matter. It is Jesus's death that is key. So live as you like."

In our day this becomes, "Move in with your girlfriend before marriage. Do as you like. God loves you all the same. Jesus's blood stands for you." It doesn't take a magician to get men and women on the wrong track when grace becomes so dominant that we lose sight of the holiness to which we have been called.

Jude wrestles with the consequences. Jacob's children escaped from the bondage of Egypt, but Jude remembers that the first generation of those delivered ended up being destroyed before their own children could enter the Promised Land. Over one million people left Egypt. But only two of those were able to eventually live in Canaan. Along that journey, Korah, Datham and Abiram (all important princes of the tribe of Levi) challenged God's leadership choices and were swallowed up in an earthquake along with all their goods and their extended households. An additional 14,700 died by plague and 250 of their chief men by fire. (See Numbers 26). The remainder of the people grumbled their way through the desert, and what should have been a two-week journey to Kadesh-Barnea took nearly forty years. Only Joshua and Caleb entered Canaan with what was basically the second generation.

Jude is saying the same thing was happening in his day. Those delivered from the kingdom of darkness will not necessarily end up at their hoped-for destination.

The Red Sea Israelites were not the only ones to suffer such a fate. Many even amongst the angelic beings did not get to stay where they had dwelt because of their rebellion. They live in darkness until the eventual Judgment arrives.

Similarly, the inhabitants of Sodom and Gomorrah were destroyed for gross immorality by fire that mimics the final punishment for the wicked.

A quick aside: In our current drift where we call things that are wrong, right, I have to wonder how some clergymen deal with the section I highlight below:

*"He has kept in eternal bonds under darkness for the judgment of the great day, just as Sodom and Gomorrah and the cities around them, since they in the same way as these indulged in gross immorality and **went after strange flesh**, are exhibited as an example in undergoing the punishment of eternal fire."* Jude: 6-7). The worst thing they did was go *"after strange flesh."* From the Genesis 19 account, we know that the men of the city, both old and young, encompassed the house of Lot and

demanded the men that were within that they might "know" them. The Hebrew is the same word for Adam "knowing" Eve and causing her pregnancy. It seems to me abundantly clear that the men of Sodom were intent on unnatural relations with the males in Lot's household. This was, as Jude recalls, "gross immorality." How then can we defend in any manner such behavior in the Church of God? It is impossible to defend. My focus is on the behavior and not the person. We do people a great disservice if we are not clear about the nature of the behavior.

But back to the text! All of these instances recall the Church's problem in Jude's day. It was an awful problem then and still is.

"Yet in the same way these men, also by dreaming, defile the flesh, and reject authority, and revile angelic majesties. But Michael the archangel, when he disputed with the devil and argued about the body of Moses, did not dare pronounce against him a railing judgment, but said, "The Lord rebuke you!" But these men revile the things which they do not understand; and the things which they know by instinct, like unreasoning animals, by these things they are destroyed." (Jude:8-10).

Jude points out three extremely serious sins. On appears to be related to perverted sexual activity (*"defiling the flesh"*), but two are closely related. Rejecting authority and reviling angelic majesties spring from the same source: pride. Rejecting authority at its foundational level is a rejection of God Himself. It is an extremely serious sin. Even more, it is a *presumptuous* sin, that is, to criticize or reject God appointed authority presumes the critic is above or better than those whom he criticizes. This springs from an underlying drive to be preeminent – or as Terry Smith has long pointed out, from seeking power and control. It is the sin of Satan.

Jude had likely heard the story of the archangel Michael and Satan from oral transmission, though Zechariah 3:1-5 does provide color as well as the actual phrase, *"the Lord rebuke you."* Origen writing sometime between 210 and 250 AD referenced Jude's story from a tract available in the First Century called the *Assumption of Moses* (see Book III, chapter 2 of *De Principles* by Origin).

The alternative section from Zechariah's remarkable and prophetic night vision is worth comparing with Jude, verse 9. God predicted Jesus's coming in the vision as the Branch, but in the immediately preceding section, he showed Zechariah a scene with the high priest, Joshua, standing before the *"angel of the Lord"* with Satan standing at his right side ready to sling accusations against Joshua. Instead, the Lord (or the angel of the Lord) said to Satan, *"The Lord rebuke YOU!"* Here is the full text:

"Then he showed me Joshua the high priest standing before the angel of the Lord, and Satan standing at his right hand to accuse him. The Lord said to Satan, "The Lord rebuke you, Satan! Indeed, the Lord who has chosen Jerusalem rebuke you! Is this not a brand plucked from the fire?" Now Joshua was clothed with filthy garments and standing before the angel. He spoke and said to those who were standing before him, saying, "Remove the filthy garments from him." Again he said to him, "See, I have taken your iniquity away from you and will clothe you with festal robes." Then I said, "Let them put a clean turban on his head." So they put a clean turban on his head and clothed him with garments, while the angel of the Lord was standing by. And the angel of the Lord admonished Joshua, saying, "Thus says the Lord of hosts, 'If you will walk in My ways and if you will perform My service, then you will also govern My house and also have charge of My courts, and I will grant you free access among these who are standing here.'" (Zechariah 3: 17).

The import of Jude's remembrance is that the *"angel of the Lord"* was the archangel Michael, and that rather than rebuking Satan himself, the archangel called on God to rebuke Satan. Great care is necessary when dealing even with ungodly authority, and in particular Satanic authority.

It was forty-five years ago that Jude's spotlight drove home to me the seriousness of railing against authorities of any kind. I am certain I have erred many times over the intervening years, but my heart remains pointed toward not railing against those who are set in authority, even when they may be grossly deficient. I think of past and current presidents of the United States, religious groups and heads of religious groups as potential targets of our ire. We need to be very careful! God help us!

Jude gives other examples of those who grasp for affection, esteem and even sordid gain in the examples of Cain, Balaam and Korah. They were precursors of those Jude saw coming boldly into fellowship meals with toxic intentions, *"caring for themselves; clouds without water, carried along by winds; autumn trees without fruit, doubly dead, uprooted wild waves of the sea, casting up their own shame like foam; wandering stars, for whom the black darkness has been reserved forever."* (Jude:12-13).

Describing bad intentions, Jude writes beautifully. "Uprooted wild waves of the sea, casting up their own shame like foam."

Then, he continues, *"It was also about these men that Enoch, in the seventh generation from Adam, prophesied, saying, 'Behold, the Lord came with many thousands of His holy ones, to execute judgment upon all, and to convict all the ungodly of all their ungodly deeds which they have done in an ungodly way, and of all the harsh things which ungodly sinners have spoken against Him.' These are grumblers, finding fault, following after their own lusts; they speak arrogantly, flattering people for the sake of gaining an advantage."* (Jude:14-16).

Jude describes attitudes and behaviors that each of us should avoid at all costs. We need to set aside our pride and let the Holy Spirit search our hearts that He might pinpoint zones where we are guilty of the very same. Here are five behavior types we want to studiously avoid and have removed from our hearts:

- Grumblers
- Fault Finders
- Lust Followers
- Arrogant
- Flatterers

We certainly don't want to be amongst those the Apostles predicted would arise in the last days: *"mockers who follow after their own ungodly lusts."* It is interesting to me that Jude connects mockers who go after their own hidden desires in the midst of a community (or family) end up causing division. I have certainly seen this; it is sad and hurtful.

In verses 20 and 21, we come to Jude's prescription for spiritual health:

"But you, beloved, building yourselves up on your most holy faith, praying in the Holy Spirit, keep yourselves in the love of God, waiting anxiously for the mercy of our Lord Jesus Christ to eternal life."

This is a key verse for understanding a most important dimension of the Baptism in the Spirit prophesied by the ancients and brought to pass by the Lord Jesus Christ for every believer. I connect the admonition to pray *"in the Holy Spirit"* to Paul's teaching on the gifts of the Spirit in 1st Corinthians 14. Praying in the Spirit is not for the assembly of the saints. Rather, it is for our times of personal prayer, because, as Paul says, *"For one who speaks in a tongue does not speak to men but to God; for no one understands, but in his spirit, he speaks mysteries."*

What is the effect of praying in the Spirit? It builds up our most holy faith, that is, our trust in God; our trust strengthens the relationship we share with the Godhead. It is *our* spirit speaking to God who *is* Spirit. I find this so practical – a key defense against the evil one and a source of experiential blessing. If you remember nothing other than this from Jude's letter, remember to Pray in the Spirit! Pray in your car, pray as you walk, pray all the time!

Praying in the Spirit is praying in tongues as Paul so accurately describes. The mind is unfruitful, but we make a connection with and through the Holy Spirit that is like two electrical wires meeting. The effect is deep, electric and desirable. Pray in the Spirit!

But also show mercy to all. Be patient with the doubting; encourage everyone to draw close to God and leave toxic ways. "Snatch" away those who are falling into the fire if you can.

What a great little letter is the letter of Jude. And what a great benediction with which Jude ends. I love both the sentiment and the rhetoric. Remember, if you ask God to keep you from stumbling today, He is entirely able. In fact, He can make you stand *BLAMELESS WITH GREAT JOY*. Unbelievable! I get goose bumps writing this. We are so blessed, so loved. May God be praised forever and ever!

This ends our excursion into *The Emerging Ekklesia!* May the Lord bless and keep you, make His face to shine upon you and give you peace!

"Now to Him who is able to keep you from stumbling, and to make you stand in the presence of His glory blameless with great joy, to the only God our Savior, through Jesus Christ our Lord, be glory, majesty, dominion and authority, before all time and now and forever. Amen!" (Jude:24-25).

BIBLIOGRAPHY

Ambrose of Milan. *The Letters of S. Ambrose*, Letter XLIII, to Horontianus, revised by Rev. H. Walford, Oxford, James Parker & Co., 1881, Print.

Apostolic. *Ante-Nicene Fathers*, Vol. 7, Apostolic Constitutions, translated by James Donaldson, Buffalo, Christian Literature Publishing Co., 1886, Print.

Aristides. *Ante-Nicene Fathers*, Vol. 9, The Apology of Aristides, translated by D.M. Kay, Buffalo, Christian Literature Publishing Co., 1896, Print.

Athanasius. *Life of Antony and the Letter to Marcellinus*, edited by Robert Gregg, Mahwah, Paulist Press, 1980, Print.

Augustine of Hippo. *Confessions,* translated by Pine-Coffin, London, Penguin Books, 1970, Print.

Augustine of Hippo. *Nicene and Post-Nicene Fathers*, 1st Series, Vol. 1, To Possidius, Letter 245 translated by J.G. Cunningham, Buffalo, Christian Literature Publishing Co., 1887, Print.

Augustine of Hippo, *The Works of Saint Augustine, Sermons* , Vol. III/7, translation by Edmund Hill, Hyde Park, New City Press of the Focolare, 1993, Print.

Bloodworth, Russell. *Visions, Dreams & Encounters*, Pennsauken, BookBaby, 2018, Print.

Cartwright, Mark. *Slavery in the Roman World*, Ancient History Encyclopedia, 11-01-2013, Web.

Chrysostom, John. *Nicene and Post-Nicene Fathers*, First Series, Vol. 11, Homilies on the Acts of the Apostles, translated by Walker, Sheppard & Browne, Buffalo,

Christian Literature Publishing Co., 1889, Print.

Chrysostom, John. Homily 26 on First Corinthians, translated by Talbot Chambers, New Advent, 26 Nov. 2018, Web.

Clement of Alexandria. *Nicene and Post-Nicene Fathers*, 12nd Series, Vol. 1, Eusebius' Church History, translated by Arthur McGiffert, Buffalo,

Christian Literature Publishing Co., 1890, Print.

Clement of Rome. *The Ante-Nicene Fathers*, Vol. 1, 1st Epistle to the Corinthians, translated by John Keith, Grand Rapids, Eerdmans Publishing, 1973, Print.

Congar, Yves. The Spirit of God, Short Writings on the Holy Spirit, translated by Brown, Ginter, Mueller and Clifford, Washington, Catholic University of America Press, 2018, Print.

Congar, Yves. *Mystery of the Temple*, translated by Reginald Trevett, Westminster, The Newman Press, 1961, Print.

Congar, Yves. *I Believe in the Holy Spirit*, Volumes 1-3, translated by David Smith, New York, Seabury Press, 1983, Print.

Council of Carthage. *Nicene and Post-Nicene Fathers*, Second Series, Vol. 14, Translated by Henry Percival, Edited by Philip Schaff and Henry Wace, Buffalo, Christian Literature Publishing Co., 1900, Print.

Cullman, Oscar. *The Early Church*, translated by Dr. A. J. Higgins, Philadelphia, Westminster Press, 1956, Print.

Cyril of Jerusalem. *The Catechetical Lectures of St. Cyril of Jerusalem*, edited by Paul Boer, Sr., Veritatis Splendor, 2014, Print.

Dunn, James D. G. *Jesus and the Spirit*, Philadelphia, Westminster Press, 1975, Print.

Dunn, James D. G. *The Baptism in the Holy Spirit*, Philadelphia, Westminster Press, 1970, Print.

Edersheim, Alfred. *The Temple*, London, The Religious Tract Society, 1885, Print.

Eusebius of Caesarea. *Eusebius, the Church History*, Commentary by Paul l. Maier, Grand Rapids, Kregel Publications, 1999, Print.

Eusebius of Caesarea. The Ecclesiastical History of Eusebius Pamphilus, translated by Christian Cruse, Grand Rapids, Baker Book House, 1973, Print.

Frend, W.H.C. *The Early Church*, Philadelphia, Fortress Press, 1982, Print.

Hilary of Poitiers. *The Fathers of the Church,* Commentary on Matthew, translated by D. H. Williams, Washington, Catholic University of America Press, 2012, Print.

Institute of Classical Studies. *Ancient Christian Commentary on Scripture*, N.T. Vol. V-XI, edited by Oden and Hall, Downers Grove, Inter Varsity Press, 1998, Print.

Irenaeus. *The Ante-Nicene Fathers*, Vol. 1, Against Heresies, translated by Roberts and Rambaut, Buffalo, The Christian Literature Company, 1885, Print.

Jerome. *Nicene and Post-Nicene Fathers*, 2nd Series, Vol. VI, translated by Schaff and Wace, New York, The Christian Literature Company, 1893, 2017, Print.

Jerome. *The Sacred Writings of St. Jerome*, translated by Fremantle & Schaff, Altenmunster, Jazzybee Verlag Publisher, Print.

Josephus, Flavius. *The Works of Josephus in Four Volumes*, translated by William Whiston, Grand Rapids, Baker Book House, 1974, Print.

Justin Martyr. *The Ante-Nicene Fathers*, Vol. 1, First Apology of Justin Martyr, translated by Dods and Reith, Buffalo, Christian Literature Publishing Co., 1885, Print.

Lewis, C. S. *The Magician's Nephew*, New York, Collier (Macmillan), 1973, Print.

Lewis, C. S. *The Lion, the Witch and the Wardrobe*, New York, Collier (Macmillan), 1973, Print.

Lewis, C. S. *The Weight of Glory*, New York, HarperCollins, 2001, Print.

Luther, Martin. *Preface to the Letter of St. Paul to the Romans*, Amazon, 2010, Kindle edition.

Malherbe, Abraham. *The Letters To The Thessalonians*, New Haven, Yale University Press, 2000, Print.

Martin, Ralph. *Worship in the Early Church*, Grand Rapids, Eerdmans Publishing, 1981, Print.

McGee, Robert. *Search for Significance*, Nashville, Thomas Nelson, 2003, Print.

McDonald, Kilian & Montague, George. *Christian Initiation and Baptism in the Holy Spirit*, Collegeville, The Liturgical Press, 1994, Print.

Nee, Watchman. Spiritual Authority, New York, Christian Fellowship, 1972, Print.

Nee, Watchman. *Spiritual Reality or Obsession*, New York, Christian
Fellowship, 1970, Print.

Nee, Watchman. *Assembling Together*, New York, Christian Fellowship,
1973, Print.

New American Standard Bible, La Habra, Lockman Foundation, 1995, Print
& Web.

Nicander of Collophon. *The Poems and Poetical Fragments*, edited by
Scholfield and Gow, London, Bristol Classical Press, 1998, Print.

Origen of Alexandria. *The Fathers of the Church*, Commentary on Romans,
Washington, The Catholic University of America Press, 2009, Print.

Origin. *The Ante-Nicene Fathers*, Vol. IV, Against Celsus, Book VI, translated by Frederick Crombie, Grand Rapids, Eerdmans Publishing,
1982, Print.

Origin. *The Ante-Nicene Fathers*, Vol. IV. De Principiis, translated by
Frederick Crombie, Edited by Roberts, Donaldson & Coxe. Buffalo,
Christian Literature Publishing Co., 1885. Print.

Pierce, Larry. *Outline of Biblical Usage*, Powder Springs, Creation.com,
2018, Web.

Prince, Derek. *The Roman Pilgrimage*, Vol. 1, Charlotte, Derek Prince
Ministries – International 1988, Print.

Prince, Derek. *Foundational Truths for Christian Living*, Lake Mary,
Charisma House, 2006, Print.

Richardson, Cyril. *Early Christian Fathers*, New York, Collier Books,
1970, Print.

Rohr, Richard. *Things Hidden – Scripture as Spirituality*, Cincinnati, St.
Anthony Messenger Press, 2008, Print.

Saunders, John. *The House of God*, Guardian Books, 1988, Print.

Snaith, Norman. *The Distinctive Ideas of the Old Testament*, New York,
Schocken Books, 1975, Print.

Sparks, T. Austin. *God's Spiritual House*, Shippensburg, MercyPlace
Ministries, 2001, Print.

Strabo, *The Geography of Strabo*, Vol. IV, Loeb Classical Library, Boston, Harvard, 1927, Print.

St. Serpahim. On the Acquisition of the Holy Spirit, Waxkeep Publishing,

St. Symeon. The Book of Mystical Chapters: Meditations on the Soul's Ascent from the Desert *Fathers and Other Early Christian Contemplatives*, translated by John Anthony Guckin, Boston, Shambhala, 2003, Print.

Stevens, Gerald. *Acts: A New Vision of the People of God*, Eugene, Pickwick Publications, 2016, Print.

Strong, James. *Strong's Exhaustive Concordance of the Bible*, Nashville, Crusade Bible Publishers, 1960, Print.

Synod of Laodicea. *Nicene and Post-Nicene Fathers*, Second Series, Vol. 14, Translated by Henry Percival, Edited by Philip Schaff and Henry Wace, Buffalo, Christian Literature Publishing Co., 1900, Print.

The "Twelve Apostles." *Didache*, translated by Charles H. Hoole, Acheron Press; Charles River Editors, 2014, Print.

Thayer, Joseph. Thayer's Greek-English Lexicon of the New Testament, Peabody, Hendrickson Publishers, 1995, Print.

Tertullian. *Ante-Nicene Fathers*, Vol. III: Tertullian: Parts 1-3, edited by Roberts & Donaldson, Grand Rapids, Eerdmans Publishing, 1980, Print.

Vonier, Anscar. *The Spirit and the Bride*, Assumption Press, 2013, Print.

Wallace, Daniel B. *1 Timothy: Introduction, Argument, Outline*, archive.org, http://archive.li/oUp5l, 2018, Web.

INDEX

A

Aaron   36, 70, 206, 412, 481, 482, 483, 488, 496

Abba! Father   14, 15, 158, 295, 296

Abraham   xviii, 8, 9, 12, 44, 46, 48, 62, 139, 142, 145, 146, 147, 148, 159, 160, 162, 163, 249, 250, 292, 293, 294, 295, 296, 297, 372, 418, 478, 488, 494, 495, 496, 508, 518, 519, 530, 531, 570, 590, 643

affliction   239, 243, 244, 254, 263, 264, 271, 378, 391, 398

Agabus   79, 117, 452

Ambrose   583, 641

Ananias   55, 71, 74, 75, 273, 357

Anointed   36, 37, 39, 57, 59, 66, 112, 127, 138, 144, 159, 244, 245, 248, 252, 265, 293, 295, 307, 310, 315, 318, 321, 355, 362, 384, 398, 425, 462, 473, 560, 597, 617

Apocalypse   392

Apocrypha   436, 472

Apollos   105, 106, 181, 184, 185, 187, 188, 197, 240, 466, 472

Aquila and Priscilla   102, 104, 178

Aristides   54, 641

Athanasius   418, 583, 641

Augustine   137, 214, 236, 237, 281, 282, 535, 557, 583, 641

authority   7, 17, 29, 46, 49, 54, 66, 67, 68, 69, 71, 88, 97, 151, 154, 167, 168, 175, 190, 191, 203, 209, 211, 212, 213, 235, 268, 270, 328, 329, 330, 331, 332, 333, 363, 364, 365, 369, 429, 439, 441, 459, 461, 465, 468, 472, 475, 476, 491, 494, 568, 569, 570, 575, 592, 629, 636, 638, 640

B

baptism   9, 25, 39, 67, 68, 72, 75, 76, 77, 80, 87, 97, 107, 108, 109, 180, 213, 226, 227, 320, 363, 364, 432, 439, 440, 464, 492, 557, 573, 574, 600, 609, 617

Baptisms   464, 490, 492

Barnabas   78, 79, 81, 83, 85, 87, 88, 89, 90, 91, 92, 99, 174, 179, 204, 284, 286, 287, 288, 289, 371, 433, 451, 452, 453, 472, 534, 538, 540, 541, 544

beriyth   7, 248, 477, 508

Birungi   105

bishop   87, 89, 90, 108, 117, 411, 412, 413, 449, 459, 460

blood of Christ   311

Bob Frahm   xix, 471, 530

Body of Christ   606

Bowie   xviii, 6, 150, 151, 229, 337, 420, 587

C

Carroll Stone   xix, 529

Cartwright   467, 641

Charlotte Smith   383

Chesed   10, 220, 301, 302, 370, 519, 586, 587

Christ   xvii, 5, 6, 13, 15, 16, 17, 24, 36, 37, 38, 39, 43, 45, 46, 47, 49, 51, 53, 59, 66, 73, 76,
    77, 78, 79, 89, 97, 110, 127, 128, 129, 135, 137, 139, 141, 142, 143, 144, 145, 150, 153,
    155, 156, 158, 169, 171, 172, 173, 175, 176, 179, 180, 183, 184, 186, 188, 194, 205, 218,
    221, 232, 233, 235, 236, 237, 242, 243, 244, 247, 252, 254, 255, 256, 257, 258, 264, 265,
    269, 270, 271, 273, 276, 278, 279, 280, 282, 285, 289, 290, 291, 293, 294, 295, 297, 298,
    299, 301, 303, 304, 306, 307, 308, 309, 310, 311, 313, 315, 317, 318, 319, 320, 321, 322,
    323, 324, 327, 328, 329, 330, 337, 339, 340, 341, 342, 343, 345, 346, 348, 350, 351, 352,
    353, 354, 357, 362, 363, 365, 366, 367, 370, 373, 374, 376, 378, 381, 382, 391, 393, 396,
    397, 398, 404, 405, 413, 417, 421, 429, 430, 432, 439, 442, 445, 447, 448, 451, 453, 454,
    455, 462, 463, 468, 470, 475, 480, 489, 490, 493, 509, 513, 526, 527, 528, 532, 535, 540,
    560, 561, 562, 563, 564, 566, 567, 569, 571, 572, 573, 574, 577, 579, 580, 582, 584, 585,
    588, 592, 594, 599, 600, 602, 606, 608, 612, 614, 615, 616, 620, 622, 624, 625, 629, 632,
    634, 639, 640

Christopher   v, xviii, 523

Chrysostom   24, 214, 274, 275, 641

Cicero   102

Clay Wilson   527

Clement of Alexandria   90, 197, 213, 471, 621, 641

Clement of Rome   125, 642

Congar   xviii, 1, 642

Cornelius   75, 76, 77, 78, 89, 96, 97, 227, 543

Council of Carthage   642

Council of Trent   436

Covenant   xviii, 3, 5, 7, 9, 10, 12, 15, 17, 23, 26, 28, 37, 55, 119, 160, 182, 191, 200, 242,
    248, 249, 250, 251, 253, 261, 289, 294, 297, 299, 320, 350, 364, 473, 487, 497, 499, 500,
    501, 502, 504, 506, 508, 509, 522, 545, 579

Cullman   642

Cyril of Jerusalem   642

D

Daniel   403, 530, 645
David   xviii, 32, 52, 55, 255, 336, 428, 477, 498, 530, 556, 642
Day of the Lord   383, 394, 395, 595
deacon   175, 415, 423, 428
Didache   81, 82, 83, 645
Dunn   642

E

Edersheim   642
E.H. Ijams   415, 529
ekklesia   3, 56, 64, 85, 339, 373, 390, 629
Ekklesia   xvii, 3, 14, 29, 54, 55, 59, 72, 242, 356, 489, 526, 640
Elders   62, 64, 69, 424, 425, 459, 579, 580
Elizabeth   xviii, 202
End of the Age   391, 392, 394, 594, 595, 597, 606
Epaphras   359, 371, 470
Epaphroditus   338, 347, 348, 353
Eternal Judgment   490, 491, 492
Euodia and Syntyche   353
Eusebius   19, 20, 197, 427, 533, 535, 621, 622, 631, 641, 642

F

Faith   xviii, 110, 129, 144, 189, 219, 220, 224, 231, 232, 320, 335, 391, 428, 429, 490, 492, 516, 517, 518, 519, 536, 544, 633
Family of God   14, 15, 391, 526
Finto   229, 420
foundation   xvii, xviii, 13, 51, 108, 168, 173, 185, 186, 196, 251, 273, 307, 308, 313, 314, 317, 369, 385, 391, 432, 529, 563, 586
Fra Angelico   464

G

Gallio   102, 104

H

Happ   xviii, 105, 129

Hart   xviii

Hebrews   4, 14, 108, 249, 250, 295, 298, 336, 433, 436, 464, 471, 472, 473, 474, 475, 476, 477, 478, 479, 480, 481, 484, 485, 487, 488, 489, 490, 491, 493, 494, 495, 497, 498, 499, 500, 503, 504, 508, 509, 510, 511, 512, 513, 514, 515, 516, 518, 519, 520, 521, 522, 523, 524, 525, 528, 529, 530, 531, 532, 544, 561, 590, 614

Henri Nouwen   xviii, 530

High Priest   478, 479, 481, 486, 487, 488, 489, 496, 497, 498, 499, 500, 504, 526

Hilary of Poitiers   108, 642

holiness   261, 324, 379, 573, 586, 634

Holy of Holies   479, 487, 488, 505, 506, 507, 514

Holy Place   507

Honor   331, 421, 422, 568, 569

Horontianus   641

house   11, 15, 30, 32, 36, 41, 51, 59, 63, 64, 76, 96, 110, 135, 136, 147, 174, 186, 196, 199, 201, 227, 228, 239, 240, 242, 248, 254, 280, 313, 338, 363, 371, 383, 425, 440, 441, 448, 456, 469, 479, 480, 497, 501, 510, 514, 531, 542, 564, 592, 609, 623, 624, 625, 635, 637

Household of Faith   527

I

Ignatius, Bishop of Antioch   413, 414

Ignatius of Antioch   404, 529, 580, 598

Irenaeus   19, 55, 621, 643

Isaiah   51, 71, 72, 110, 134, 135, 162, 164, 306, 378, 419, 522, 530, 563

J

Jacob   44, 70, 160, 162, 163, 433, 496, 590, 634

James   3, 4, 22, 29, 43, 89, 90, 117, 118, 128, 133, 232, 245, 263, 280, 282, 286, 288, 411, 412, 413, 414, 436, 533, 534, 535, 536, 537, 538, 539, 540, 541, 542, 543, 544, 545, 546, 547, 548, 549, 550, 551, 552, 553, 554, 555, 556, 557, 559, 571, 582, 598, 619, 629, 631, 632, 641, 642, 645

Jassu   xix

Jeremiah   11, 12, 117, 156, 157, 164, 182, 204, 248, 249, 250, 260, 319, 463, 501, 502, 513, 530

Jerome   214, 436, 535, 583, 643

Jerusalem Council   88, 94, 105, 114, 117, 263, 284, 287, 534, 538, 625

Jesus   xvii, xviii, 1, 2, 3, 5, 6, 7, 9, 10, 11, 12, 13, 14, 15, 16, 17, 18, 20, 21, 22, 23, 24, 25,
        26, 27, 28, 29, 31, 32, 34, 35, 36, 37, 38, 39, 42, 43, 44, 45, 46, 47, 48, 49, 50, 51, 52, 53,
        56, 57, 58, 59, 60, 61, 63, 64, 65, 66, 67, 68, 69, 72, 73, 74, 75, 76, 77, 78, 79, 81, 86,
        87, 89, 90, 92, 97, 98, 102, 105, 106, 107, 108, 110, 111, 112, 113, 115, 117, 121, 123,
        125, 126, 129, 134, 135, 137, 138, 141, 143, 144, 145, 146, 148, 149, 150, 151, 154, 155,
        156, 157, 161, 164, 165, 168, 169, 170, 171, 172, 173, 174, 175, 176, 179, 180, 181, 183,
        185, 186, 187, 194, 197, 198, 203, 206, 207, 209, 210, 212, 215, 218, 226, 227, 233, 235,
        236, 239, 242, 243, 244, 245, 249, 250, 251, 252, 253, 256, 264, 265, 267, 268, 271, 272,
        278, 279, 280, 282, 285, 286, 288, 289, 290, 291, 293, 294, 295, 297, 299, 300, 301, 303,
        304, 306, 307, 308, 310, 311, 312, 313, 314, 315, 316, 317, 319, 325, 328, 329, 330, 334,
        336, 337, 339, 340, 341, 342, 343, 345, 346, 347, 350, 351, 352, 353, 354, 355, 356, 357,
        358, 360, 361, 362, 364, 365, 367, 370, 371, 373, 374, 375, 376, 377, 378, 379, 380, 381,
        382, 383, 384, 385, 387, 389, 390, 391, 392, 393, 394, 395, 396, 397, 398, 404, 405, 406,
        410, 412, 413, 416, 417, 421, 425, 426, 428, 429, 433, 434, 438, 439, 440, 441, 442, 444,
        447, 448, 451, 452, 453, 454, 455, 462, 463, 464, 468, 469, 472, 473, 474, 475, 476, 477,
        478, 479, 480, 481, 484, 485, 486, 487, 488, 490, 491, 492, 493, 494, 495, 496, 497, 498,
        499, 500, 503, 508, 509, 511, 513, 514, 515, 520, 521, 525, 526, 527, 529, 530, 531, 532,
        534, 535, 536, 540, 541, 542, 543, 544, 547, 553, 554, 555, 556, 557, 559, 560, 561, 562,
        563, 564, 565, 566, 569, 571, 573, 574, 575, 577, 578, 579, 580, 581, 582, 584, 585, 587,
        588, 590, 591, 594, 595, 596, 597, 598, 599, 600, 601, 602, 606, 607, 608, 611, 612, 615,
        616, 617, 618, 619, 620, 621, 622, 624, 625, 628, 629, 631, 632, 633, 634, 637, 639, 640,
        642

Jim Woodruff   529

Joel   xix, 11, 33, 34, 157, 161, 182, 388, 502, 503

John   xviii, 2, 4, 5, 10, 12, 13, 18, 22, 24, 25, 26, 31, 42, 43, 48, 49, 52, 67, 68, 71, 76, 77,
        78, 79, 86, 87, 90, 92, 106, 108, 115, 128, 138, 154, 157, 164, 177, 214, 225, 226, 227,
        263, 271, 272, 274, 275, 325, 361, 392, 418, 473, 513, 530, 534, 562, 569, 598, 599, 600,
        602, 603, 604, 605, 606, 607, 608, 609, 610, 611, 612, 613, 614, 615, 616, 617, 618, 619,
        620, 621, 622, 623, 624, 625, 627, 628, 629, 630, 631, 632, 633, 641, 642, 644, 645

John Paul II   xviii, 530, 569

Joseph   433, 645

Josephus   48, 95, 643

Joshua   56, 70, 71, 104, 433, 635, 637

Justin Martyr   54, 305, 424, 643

K

Kingdom   5, 6, 7, 10, 15, 17, 23, 24, 26, 42, 50, 55, 66, 67, 68, 77, 113, 127, 141, 144,
        150, 151, 152, 153, 154, 157, 170, 190, 192, 194, 206, 236, 289, 304, 313, 322, 334, 335,
        360, 387, 447, 450, 501, 551

L

Laying on of Hands   70, 490, 492, 607, 615

Leon Sanders   529

Lewis   55, 254, 346, 475, 528, 643

Lewises   xix

Love   2, 153, 154, 156, 168, 173, 177, 188, 220, 223, 224, 225, 300, 325, 329, 343, 347, 365, 379, 428, 473, 491, 526, 576, 586, 587, 612, 623

Luke   4, 7, 12, 18, 19, 20, 21, 24, 26, 28, 31, 38, 40, 41, 42, 45, 48, 49, 52, 55, 56, 58, 62, 63, 64, 65, 66, 67, 73, 74, 75, 78, 83, 85, 90, 91, 92, 94, 96, 98, 99, 100, 101, 108, 109, 110, 114, 115, 122, 123, 124, 126, 128, 129, 130, 131, 132, 134, 138, 181, 249, 261, 267, 287, 289, 292, 306, 338, 371, 372, 382, 387, 425, 433, 439, 448, 449, 452, 470, 478, 490, 491, 542, 553, 554, 559

Luther   89, 138, 283, 290, 397, 436, 472, 534, 643

M

Malherbe   xviii, 231, 372, 394, 606, 643

Martin   138, 283, 290, 383, 397, 472, 534, 643

Matthew   4, 7, 21, 25, 27, 29, 47, 49, 50, 55, 108, 128, 187, 197, 203, 209, 212, 244, 273, 299, 329, 370, 378, 383, 384, 385, 389, 392, 394, 396, 421, 441, 472, 491, 544, 547, 554, 555, 578, 595, 601, 608, 617, 642

maturity   280, 321, 387, 402, 432, 489

Mays   xix, 72

McGee   354, 643

McGraw   xix

Melchizedek   488, 495, 496, 498

Mercy Seat   479, 487, 488, 506

Mitchell   584, 628

Moses   32, 35, 36, 46, 56, 61, 62, 69, 70, 71, 73, 127, 134, 153, 181, 197, 205, 206, 250, 287, 288, 295, 313, 428, 433, 479, 480, 481, 484, 490, 496, 501, 525, 530, 543, 585, 586, 590, 636, 637

Mullins   xviii, xix

Mumford   xviii, 148, 167, 168, 529, 568

mystery   13, 47, 70, 82, 120, 128, 155, 175, 176, 188, 195, 311, 314, 315, 318, 319, 321, 343, 362, 376, 416

N

Nee   xviii, 151, 167, 168, 275, 330, 529, 643, 644

Nicander   25, 26, 644

Nixes   xix

Normal Station   238, 241, 339

O

Onesimus   338, 371, 414, 467, 468, 469, 470

Origen   47, 140, 535, 637, 644

Oster   xix

P

Paul   xviii, 2, 3, 6, 13, 14, 15, 16, 19, 20, 47, 51, 53, 73, 74, 75, 81, 84, 85, 86, 87, 88, 89, 90, 91, 92, 93, 94, 95, 96, 97, 98, 99, 100, 101, 102, 103, 104, 105, 106, 107, 108, 109, 111, 112, 113, 114, 115, 116, 117, 118, 119, 120, 121, 122, 123, 124, 125, 126, 127, 128, 129, 130, 131, 132, 133, 134, 135, 137, 138, 139, 140, 141, 142, 143, 144, 145, 146, 147, 148, 150, 154, 155, 156, 158, 159, 160, 161, 162, 163, 164, 165, 166, 167, 168, 169, 170, 171, 172, 173, 174, 175, 176, 177, 178, 179, 180, 181, 182, 183, 184, 185, 186, 187, 188, 189, 190, 191, 192, 193, 194, 195, 196, 197, 198, 199, 200, 203, 204, 205, 206, 207, 208, 209, 210, 211, 212, 213, 214, 215, 216, 218, 219, 220, 221, 222, 223, 224, 225, 226, 227, 228, 229, 230, 231, 232, 233, 235, 236, 237, 238, 239, 240, 241, 242, 243, 244, 245, 246, 247, 248, 250, 251, 252, 253, 254, 257, 258, 260, 261, 262, 263, 264, 265, 266, 267, 268, 269, 270, 271, 272, 273, 274, 275, 276, 277, 278, 279, 280, 282, 283, 284, 285, 286, 287, 288, 289, 290, 291, 292, 293, 294, 295, 296, 297, 298, 299, 300, 301, 302, 303, 304, 305, 307, 308, 309, 311, 312, 313, 314, 315, 317, 318, 319, 320, 322, 323, 324, 325, 326, 327, 328, 331, 332, 333, 334, 337, 338, 339, 340, 341, 342, 343, 344, 345, 346, 347, 348, 349, 350, 351, 352, 353, 354, 355, 356, 357, 358, 359, 360, 361, 362, 363, 364, 366, 367, 368, 369, 370, 371, 372, 373, 374, 375, 376, 377, 378, 379, 380, 381, 383, 385, 386, 387, 388, 390, 391, 392, 393, 394, 395, 396, 397, 398, 399, 400, 401, 402, 403, 404, 405, 406, 407, 408, 409, 410, 412, 413, 414, 415, 416, 417, 418, 419, 420, 421, 422, 423, 424, 425, 426, 427, 428, 429, 431, 432, 434, 435, 437, 438, 439, 440, 441, 442, 443, 444, 445, 446, 447, 448, 449, 450, 451, 452, 453, 454, 455, 456, 457, 458, 459, 460, 461, 462, 463, 464, 465, 466, 467, 468, 469, 470, 471, 492, 529, 530, 534, 535, 537, 538, 540, 541, 543, 544, 545, 556, 559, 560, 569, 590, 595, 596, 598, 612, 614, 621, 622, 627, 629, 634, 639, 640, 642, 643

Peter   xviii, 2, 4, 15, 16, 17, 21, 22, 23, 28, 33, 35, 37, 38, 39, 40, 42, 43, 44, 45, 46, 47, 48, 49, 50, 51, 52, 55, 56, 57, 58, 59, 67, 68, 71, 74, 75, 76, 77, 78, 79, 88, 89, 90, 97, 115, 118, 157, 168, 186, 196, 197, 203, 227, 263, 270, 279, 280, 281, 282, 286, 288, 289, 290, 363, 418, 493, 534, 538, 543, 559, 560, 561, 562, 563, 564, 565, 567, 568, 569, 570, 571, 572, 573, 574, 575, 576, 577, 578, 579, 580, 581, 582, 583, 584, 585, 586, 587, 588, 589, 590, 591, 592, 593, 594, 595, 596, 597, 598, 622, 629

Philemon   4, 125, 338, 371, 467, 469, 470

Philip   5, 60, 65, 66, 67, 68, 71, 72, 73, 95, 117, 197, 230, 642, 645

Phillips   xviii, 201, 202, 203

Pierce   644

Polycarp   529, 598

Pope Clement VIII   436

Prayer in the Spirit   337

presbyteros   85, 86, 88, 113, 114, 115, 413, 414, 422, 424, 455, 459, 460, 579, 580

Prince   xviii, 45, 58, 141, 148, 153, 169, 309, 408, 473, 529, 644

Promise   5, 9, 10, 11, 17, 23, 24, 26, 28, 34, 35, 39, 40, 50, 106, 182, 249, 296, 388, 562

prophecy   25, 33, 36, 51, 79, 83, 91, 112, 276, 378, 389, 419, 498, 577, 588, 589, 590, 591, 592, 594, 614

R

Repentance   112, 490, 491, 492

Resurrection   231, 235, 490, 492

Richardson   644

Righteousness   7, 151, 242, 335, 428, 429, 495

Ritmeyer   44

Rohr   118, 119, 644

S

saints   xvii, 51, 127, 139, 156, 166, 175, 178, 192, 235, 238, 239, 241, 258, 263, 264, 279, 280, 308, 312, 318, 321, 322, 337, 339, 340, 347, 373, 392, 393, 470, 492, 493, 530, 551, 561, 562, 588, 599, 628, 634, 639

salvation   13, 40, 49, 134, 138, 144, 162, 183, 243, 246, 295, 318, 342, 346, 396, 397, 403, 417, 421, 462, 474, 476, 484, 494, 509, 560, 561, 563, 564, 590, 633, 634

Sarvis   383

Saunders   529, 644

Schaeffer   472

Septuagint   412, 436, 440, 475, 511, 512, 629

shepherd   69, 87, 111, 113, 114, 204, 385, 386, 411, 412, 449, 569, 579, 622

Silas   90, 91, 92, 93, 94, 95, 97, 98, 99, 100, 103, 288, 338, 339, 372, 375, 378, 390, 559

Sparks   644

Spirit   xvii, xviii, 1, 2, 5, 7, 9, 10, 11, 12, 13, 14, 15, 16, 17, 18, 22, 24, 25, 26, 28, 29, 30, 31, 32, 33, 34, 35, 36, 37, 38, 39, 40, 41, 42, 45, 46, 48, 49, 51, 52, 53, 54, 55, 56, 57, 58, 60, 61, 63, 65, 66, 67, 68, 69, 70, 71, 73, 74, 75, 76, 77, 78, 79, 83, 86, 87, 88, 89, 90, 91,

92, 94, 97, 98, 103, 104, 105, 106, 107, 108, 109, 110, 111, 112, 113, 114, 116, 117, 130, 133, 149, 153, 154, 156, 157, 158, 163, 164, 165, 170, 172, 173, 175, 176, 181, 182, 183, 187, 190, 194, 206, 210, 215, 216, 217, 218, 224, 226, 227, 230, 231, 235, 240, 243, 247, 249, 250, 251, 252, 255, 256, 257, 258, 259, 261, 269, 270, 271, 279, 280, 285, 288, 289, 291, 292, 293, 294, 295, 296, 299, 300, 301, 302, 303, 308, 310, 311, 312, 313, 314, 315, 317, 318, 319, 320, 324, 325, 327, 328, 329, 330, 333, 336, 337, 340, 342, 343, 344, 356, 358, 359, 365, 366, 370, 372, 374, 376, 378, 380, 388, 391, 396, 397, 398, 402, 403, 408, 414, 415, 416, 420, 432, 433, 434, 435, 436, 437, 439, 440, 448, 452, 457, 458, 460, 463, 464, 465, 468, 470, 474, 477, 478, 485, 486, 490, 491, 492, 493, 500, 502, 503, 509, 513, 545, 550, 556, 557, 560, 562, 564, 565, 567, 572, 574, 576, 578, 579, 586, 587, 589, 592, 600, 602, 606, 607, 610, 612, 613, 614, 617, 618, 619, 625, 633, 638, 639, 640, 642, 643, 645

spiritual gifts   216, 388, 420, 432, 433, 449, 490, 492

Spiritual Warfare   333

Stephen   60, 61, 62, 63, 64, 65, 286, 452, 453

Stevens   18, 92, 93, 112, 116, 645

Strabo   277, 645

Strong   140, 551, 645

St. Serpahim   645

St. Symeon   119, 645

synagogue   96, 98, 99, 104, 122, 238, 306, 375, 413, 541

Synod of Carthage   437

Synod of Laodicea   645

Sypole   212

T

Terry Smith   xviii, 179, 184, 252, 278, 333, 366, 386, 470, 515, 529, 542, 550, 581, 636

Tertullian   19, 213, 239, 240, 471, 645

Thomas à Kempis   530

Timothy   4, 29, 84, 85, 88, 92, 93, 100, 103, 118, 174, 175, 189, 240, 241, 243, 245, 338, 339, 340, 347, 353, 357, 358, 372, 375, 377, 378, 380, 386, 388, 390, 402, 403, 404, 405, 406, 407, 410, 414, 415, 416, 417, 418, 419, 420, 421, 422, 423, 424, 425, 426, 428, 429, 431, 432, 434, 435, 436, 437, 438, 439, 441, 442, 445, 447, 448, 449, 451, 453, 455, 456, 457, 459, 462, 467, 529, 580, 645

Titus   4, 86, 128, 239, 262, 263, 264, 265, 287, 289, 340, 403, 413, 449, 451, 452, 453, 454, 455, 456, 457, 458, 459, 460, 462, 463, 465, 466

Toms   xix

Torah   87, 144, 153, 154, 156, 157, 168, 191, 198, 210, 230, 260, 283, 292, 293, 490, 528

truth   xvii, xviii, 12, 13, 16, 35, 63, 82, 87, 138, 181, 196, 199, 207, 210, 223, 257, 266, 275, 290, 291, 301, 302, 303, 310, 311, 318, 323, 324, 327, 328, 332, 334, 363, 365, 367, 376, 396, 428, 429, 435, 436, 437, 438, 439, 440, 441, 448, 453, 485, 499, 503, 512, 515, 521, 531, 539, 545, 549, 551, 569, 582, 586, 590, 591, 592, 600, 602, 603, 604, 606, 607, 610, 611, 613, 614, 615, 618, 621, 622, 623, 625, 627, 628

U

unity   52, 53, 187, 196, 242, 279, 281, 306, 316, 319, 320, 321, 322, 333, 343, 344, 615, 616

V

Vaughan   xviii, 255, 336
Vonier   645

W

Walker   xviii, 641
Wallace   403, 645
Watson   xix
Wilson   527

Y

Yom Kippur   96, 296, 479, 481, 502, 504, 507